Mastering
AutoCAD® 2018 and
AutoCAD LT® 2018

George Omura

with Brian C. Benton

AUTODESK.
Authorized Publisher

Acquisitions Editor: Jody Lefevere
Development Editor: Gary Schwartz
Technical Editor: Richard Hawley
Production Editor: Rebecca Anderson
Copy Editor: Judy Flynn
Editorial Manager: Mary Beth Wakefield
Production Manager: Kathleen Wisor
Executive Editor: Jim Minatel
Book Designers: Maureen Forys, Happenstance Type-O-Rama; Judy Fung
Proofreader: Kim Wimpsett
Indexer: Ted Laux
Project Coordinator, Cover: Brent Savage
Cover Designer: Wiley
Cover Image: ©Wilfried Krecichwost/Getty Images

To my friend and colleague David Fawcett, who is retiring soon: fair winds and following seas...

Acknowledgments

Many talented and hardworking people gave their best effort to produce *Mastering AutoCAD 2018 and AutoCAD LT 2018*. I offer my sincerest gratitude to those individuals who helped bring this book to you.

Heartfelt thanks go out to the editorial and production teams at Sybex for their efforts. Mary Beth Wakefield managed the project and helped us make all the right connections. Jody Lefevere made sure things got off to a great start and provided support from beginning to end. Gary Schwartz skillfully managed the development process. Richard Hawley did an excellent technical editing job and offered many great suggestions. On the production side, Rebecca Anderson kept the production end of things running smoothly, and Judy Flynn made sure that I wasn't trying out new uses of the English language.

Thanks also go to Denis Cadu, who has always given his support to our efforts over many projects. Jim Quanci always gives his generous and thoughtful assistance to us author types. Thanks to Elinor Actipis for providing help with general Autodesk matters. Finally, thanks go to Alison Keller, Daniel Kuhman, and KB Lee of the AutoCAD Customer Counsel and the AutoCAD team for generously allowing us to have a look at the prerelease software.

And a great big thank you to my family and friends, who have been there for me through thick and thin.

About the Authors

 **George Omura** is a licensed architect, Autodesk Authorized Author, and CAD specialist with more than 28 years of experience in AutoCAD and over 35 years of experience in architecture. He has worked on design projects ranging from resort hotels to metropolitan transit systems. George has written numerous other AutoCAD books for Sybex, including *Mastering AutoCAD 2017 and AutoCAD LT 2017*.

 **Brian C. Benton** is a CAD manager, CAD service provider, technical writer, and blogger. He has over 20 years of experience in various design fields (mechanical, structural, civil, survey, marine, environmental) and is well versed in many design software packages (CAD, GIS, and graphics). He has been *Cadalyst* magazine's Tip Patroller, AUGI HotNews production manager, and Infinite Skills' AutoCAD training video author.

Contents at a Glance

Introduction . . . . *xxv*

Part 1 • The Basics **1**

    Chapter 1 • Exploring the Interface 3

    Chapter 2 • Creating Your First Drawing 31

    Chapter 3 • Setting Up and Using the Drafting Tools 79

    Chapter 4 • Organizing Objects with Blocks and Groups 119

    Chapter 5 • Keeping Track of Layers and Blocks 149

Part 2 • Mastering Intermediate Skills **181**

    Chapter 6 • Editing and Reusing Data to Work Efficiently 183

    Chapter 7 • Mastering Viewing Tools, Hatches, and External References 225

    Chapter 8 • Introducing Printing, Plotting, and Layouts 273

    Chapter 9 • Adding Text to Drawings 305

    Chapter 10 • Using Fields and Tables 341

    Chapter 11 • Using Dimensions 363

Part 3 • Mastering Advanced Skills **415**

    Chapter 12 • Using Attributes 417

    Chapter 13 • Copying Existing Drawings from Other Sources 445

    Chapter 14 • Advanced Editing and Organizing 473

    Chapter 15 • Laying Out Your Printer Output 517

    Chapter 16 • Making "Smart" Drawings with Parametric Tools 543

    Chapter 17 • Using Dynamic Blocks 563

    Chapter 18 • Drawing Curves 595

    Chapter 19 • Getting and Exchanging Data from Drawings 627

Part 4 • 3D Modeling and Imaging **659**

    Chapter 20 • Creating 3D Drawings 661

    Chapter 21 • Using Advanced 3D Features 703

    Chapter 22 • Editing and Visualizing 3D Solids 759

    Chapter 23 • Exploring 3D Mesh and Surface Modeling 805

Part 5 • Customization and Integration **853**

    Chapter 24 • Customizing Toolbars, Menus, Linetypes, and Hatch Patterns 855

    Chapter 25 • Managing and Sharing Your Drawings 897

Part 6 • Appendixes **947**

    Appendix A • The Bottom Line 949

    Appendix B • Installing and Setting Up AutoCAD 973

    Appendix C • The Autodesk AutoCAD 2018 Certification 1003

Index *1007*

Contents

Introduction xxv

Part 1 • The Basics 1

Chapter 1 • Exploring the Interface 3
Taking a Guided Tour 3
   Launching AutoCAD 4
   The AutoCAD Window 5
   Using the Application Menu 8
   Using the Ribbon 9
   Picking Points in the Drawing Area 14
   Using the UCS Icon 15
   Working in the Command Window 15
Working with AutoCAD 16
   Opening an Existing File 16
   Getting a Closer Look 18
   Saving a File as You Work 21
   Making Changes 22
   Working with Multiple Files 23
   Adding a Predrawn Symbol with the Tool Palettes 26
The Bottom Line 28

Chapter 2 • Creating Your First Drawing 31
Getting to Know the Home Tab's Draw and Modify Panels 31
Starting Your First Drawing 34
Specifying Exact Distances with Coordinates 38
   Specifying Polar Coordinates 40
   Specifying Relative Cartesian Coordinates 41
Interpreting the Cursor Modes and Understanding Prompts 43
   Understanding Cursor Modes 43
   Choosing Command Options 45
Selecting Objects 50
   Selecting Objects in AutoCAD 50
   Providing Base Points 53
   Using Noun/Verb Selection 56
Editing with Grips 61
   Stretching Lines by Using Grips 62
   Moving and Rotating with Grips 64
Understanding Dynamic Input 66
Displaying Data in a Text Window 71
Displaying the Properties of an Object 72

Getting Help 75
   Using the InfoCenter 75
   Finding Additional Sources of Help 76
The Bottom Line 77

Chapter 3 • Setting Up and Using the Drafting Tools **79**
Setting Up a Work Area 79
   Specifying Units 80
   Fine-Tuning the Measurement System 82
   Setting Up the Drawing Limits 83
   Looking at an Alternative to Limits 85
   Understanding Scale Factors 85
   Using Polar Tracking 87
   Setting the Polar Tracking Angle 88
Exploring the Drawing Process 90
   Locating an Object in Reference to Others 90
   Getting a Closer Look 91
   Modifying an Object 91
Planning and Laying Out a Drawing 95
   Making a Preliminary Sketch 97
   Using the Layout 98
   Erasing the Layout Lines 103
   Putting on the Finishing Touches 106
   Aligning Objects by Using Object Snap Tracking 107
Using the AutoCAD Modes as Drafting Tools 113
   Using Grid Mode as a Background Grid 113
   Using Snap Modes 116
The Bottom Line 117

Chapter 4 • Organizing Objects with Blocks and Groups **119**
Creating and Using a Symbol 119
   Understanding the Block Definition Dialog Box 121
   Inserting a Symbol 123
   Scaling and Rotating Blocks 126
   Using an Existing Drawing as a Symbol 128
Modifying a Block 130
   Unblocking and Redefining a Block 130
   Saving a Block as a Drawing File 132
   Replacing Existing Files with Blocks 133
   Understanding the Write Block Dialog Box Options 134
   Other Uses for Blocks 134
Understanding the Annotation Scale 135
Grouping Objects 138
   Modifying Members of a Group 140
   Ungrouping, Adding, and Subtracting from a Group 143
   Working with the Object Grouping Dialog Box 144
   Working with the AutoCAD LT Group Manager 146
The Bottom Line 147

Chapter 5 • Keeping Track of Layers and Blocks **149**

Organizing Information with Layers 149
    Creating and Assigning Layers 150
    Working on Layers 158
    Controlling Layer Visibility 161
    Finding the Layers You Want 163
    Taming an Unwieldy List of Layers 164
    Assigning Linetypes to Layers 171
    Adding a Linetype to a Drawing 172
    Controlling Lineweights 177
Keeping Track of Blocks and Layers 177
    Getting a Text File List of Layers or Blocks 178
The Bottom Line 179

Part 2 • Mastering Intermediate Skills **181**

Chapter 6 • Editing and Reusing Data to Work Efficiently **183**

Creating and Using Templates 184
    Creating a Template 184
    Using a Template 185
Copying an Object Multiple Times 186
    Making Circular Copies 186
    Making Row and Column Copies 188
    Fine-Tuning Your View 190
    Finishing the Kitchenette 192
    Array Along a Path 193
    Making Changes to an Associative Array 194
Developing Your Drawing 198
    Importing Settings 198
    Using Osnap Tracking to Place Objects 201
Finding an Exact Distance Along a Curve 218
Changing the Length of Objects 220
Creating a New Drawing by Using Parts
  from Another Drawing 221
    Eliminating Unused Blocks, Layers, Linetypes, Shapes, Styles, and More 222
The Bottom Line 224

**Chapter 7 • Mastering Viewing Tools, Hatches, and
External References** **225**

Assembling the Parts 225
Taking Control of the AutoCAD Display 229
    Understanding Regeneration and Redrawing 229
    Saving Views 230
    Understanding the Frozen Layer Option 233
Using Hatch Patterns in Your Drawings 235
    Placing a Hatch Pattern in a Specific Area 235
    Adding Predefined Hatch Patterns 237

Positioning Hatch Patterns Accurately 239
Updating a Block from an External File 240
Changing the Hatch Area 242
Modifying a Hatch Pattern 243
Understanding the Boundary Hatch Options 245
Controlling Boundaries with the Boundaries Panel 245
Fine-Tuning the Boundary Behavior 245
Controlling Hatch Behavior with the Options Panel 246
Controlling Hatch Default Layer, Layout Scale, and ISO Line Weight 247
Using Additional Hatch Features 248
Using Gradient Shading 249
Tips for Using Hatch 250
Space Planning and Hatch Patterns 251
Using External References 254
Attaching a Drawing as an External Reference 255
Other Differences Between External References and Blocks 259
Other External Reference Options 260
Clipping Xref Views and Improving Performance 262
Editing Xrefs in Place 265
Using the External Reference Tab 268
Adding and Removing Objects from Blocks and Xrefs 268
Understanding the Reference Edit Dialog Box Options 270
The Bottom Line 272

Chapter 8 • Introducing Printing, Plotting, and Layouts **273**
Plotting the Plan 273
Understanding the Plotter Settings 277
Paper Size 278
Drawing Orientation 278
Plot Area 278
Plot Scale 280
Shaded Viewport Options 283
Plot Offset 284
Plot Options 285
Exit Options 286
Plotting Using Layout Views 286
Setting Plot Scale in the Layout Viewports 289
Adding an Output Device 291
Editing a Plotter Configuration 293
Storing a Page Setup 295
Using Electronic Plots 299
Exporting to PDF Through the Plot Dialog Box 299
Exporting to PDF Through the Export To DWF/PDF Ribbon Panel 301
Exporting Autodesk DWF and DWFx Files 302
The Bottom Line 302

Chapter 9 • Adding Text to Drawings **305**

Preparing a Drawing for Text 305
    Organizing Text by Styles 306
    Getting Familiar with the Text and Annotation Scale Control Panels 308
Setting the Annotation Scale and Adding Text 308
    Inserting Text 309
    Exploring Text and Scale 310
Understanding the Text Style Dialog Box Options 313
    Styles 313
    Set Current/New/Delete 313
    Font 313
    Size 314
    Effects 314
Exploring Text Formatting in AutoCAD 315
    Adjusting the Text Height and Font 315
    Understanding the Text Editor Tab 317
    Adding Symbols and Special Characters 319
    Setting Indents and Tabs 321
What Do the Fonts Look Like? 324
Adding Simple Single-Line Text Objects 326
    Justifying Single-Line Text Objects 328
    Using Special Characters with Single-Line Text Objects 330
Using the Check Spelling Feature 331
    How Check Spelling Works 331
    Choosing a Dictionary 332
Substituting Fonts 334
Finding and Replacing Text 335
The Bottom Line 339

Chapter 10 • Using Fields and Tables **341**

Using Fields to Associate Text with Drawing Properties 341
Adding Tables to Your Drawing 345
    Creating a Table 345
    Adding Cell Text 346
    Adjusting Table Text Orientation and Location 348
Editing the Table Line Work 351
Adding Formulas to Cells 354
    Using Formulas Directly in Cells 354
    Using Other Math Operations 355
Importing and Exporting Tables 356
    Importing a Table 356
    Exporting Tables 358
Creating Table Styles 359
    Adding or Modifying a Table Style 359
    The Table Style Options 361
The Bottom Line 361

Chapter 11 • Using Dimensions **363**

Understanding the Components of a Dimension 363
Creating a Dimension Style 364
    Setting Up the Primary Unit Style 367
    Setting the Height for Dimension Text 368
    Setting the Location and Orientation of Dimension Text 369
    Choosing an Arrow Style and Setting the Dimension Scale 370
    Setting Up Alternate Units 374
    Setting the Current Dimension Style 375
    Modifying a Dimension Style 375
Drawing Linear Dimensions 376
    Understanding the Dimensions Panel 376
    Placing Horizontal and Vertical Dimensions 377
    Continuing a Dimension 378
    Drawing Dimensions from a Common Base Extension Line 380
    Adjusting the Distance Between Dimensions 382
Editing Dimensions 383
    Appending Data to Dimension Text 383
    Using Grips to Make Minor Adjustments to Dimensions 385
    Changing Style Settings of Individual Dimensions 387
    Editing Dimensions and Other Objects Together 388
    Associating Dimensions with Objects 391
    Adding a String of Dimensions with a Single Operation 392
    Adding or Removing the Alternate Dimensions 393
Dimensioning Nonorthogonal Objects 394
    Dimensioning Nonorthogonal Linear Distances 394
    Dimensioning Radii, Diameters, and Arcs 396
    Skewing Dimension Lines 400
Using the Dimension Tool 401
Adding a Note with a Leader Arrow 404
    Creating Multileader Styles 406
    Editing Multileader Notes 409
    Breaking a Dimension Line for a Leader 409
Applying Ordinate Dimensions 410
Adding Tolerance Notation 411
    Inserting Tolerance and Datum Values 411
    Adding Inspection Dimensions 413
The Bottom Line 414

Part 3 • Mastering Advanced Skills **415**

Chapter 12 • Using Attributes **417**

Creating Attributes 418
    Adding Attributes to Blocks 418
    Copying and Editing Attribute Definitions 421
    Turning the Attribute Definitions into a Block 423
    Inserting Blocks Containing Attributes 424

Editing Attributes 428
   Editing Attribute Values One at a Time 428
   Editing Attribute Text Formats and Properties 429
   Making Global Changes to Attribute Values 431
   Making Invisible Attributes Visible 432
   Making Global Format and Property Changes to Attributes 433
   Other Block Attribute Manager Options 434
   Redefining Blocks Containing Attributes 435
Extracting and Exporting Attribute Information 436
   Performing the Extraction 436
   Extracting Attribute Data to an AutoCAD Table 441
The Bottom Line 443

Chapter 13 • Copying Existing Drawings from Other Sources 445
Methods for Converting Paper Drawings to AutoCAD Files 445
Importing a Raster Image 446
Working with a Raster Image 449
   Scaling a Raster Image 449
   Controlling Object Visibility and Overlap with Raster Images 450
   Adjusting Brightness, Contrast, and Fade 452
   Clipping a Raster Image 454
   Turning Off the Frame, Adjusting Overall Quality, and
      Controlling Transparency 456
Working with PDF Files 458
   Importing a PDF 458
   Scaling and Osnaps with PDFs 460
   Controlling the PDF Display 461
   Importing a PDF as an AutoCAD Drawing 463
   Reconstructing Imported AutoCAD SHX Fonts 465
Coordinating Geographic Locations 466
   Making Adjustments to the Map 470
   Finding Measurements and Distances 471
The Bottom Line 472

Chapter 14 • Advanced Editing and Organizing 473
Using External References 473
   Preparing Existing Drawings for External Referencing 474
   Assembling Xrefs to Build a Drawing 476
   Updating Blocks in Xrefs 480
   Importing Named Elements from Xrefs 482
   Controlling the Xref Search Path 485
Managing Layers 486
   Saving and Recalling Layer Settings 486
   Other Tools for Managing Layers 490
Using Advanced Tools: Filter and Quick Select 492
   Filtering Selections 493
   Using Quick Select 496

Using the QuickCalc Calculator 499
    Adding Foot and Inch Lengths and Finding the Sum of Angles 501
    Converting Units with QuickCalc 503
    Using QuickCalc to Find Points 505
    Finding Fractional Distances between Two Points 508
    Using QuickCalc While in the Middle of a Command 510
    Storing Expressions and Values 511
    Guidelines for Working with QuickCalc 513
The Bottom Line 515

Chapter 15 • Laying Out Your Printer Output **517**
Understanding Model Space and Paper Space 517
    Switching from Model Space to Paper Space 518
    Setting the Size of a Paper Space Layout 520
    Creating New Paper Space Viewports 521
    Reaching Inside Viewports 523
Working with Paper Space Viewports 524
    Scaling Views in Paper Space 526
    Setting Layers in Individual Viewports 528
    Creating and Using Multiple Paper Space Layouts 531
Creating Odd-Shaped Viewports 532
Understanding Lineweights, Linetypes, and Dimensions in Paper Space 535
    Controlling and Viewing Lineweights in Paper Space 535
    The Lineweight Settings Dialog Box 537
    Linetype Scales and Paper Space 537
    Dimensioning in Paper Space Layouts 538
    Other Uses for Paper Space 541
The Bottom Line 541

Chapter 16 • Making "Smart" Drawings with Parametric Tools **543**
Why Use Parametric Drawing Tools? 543
Connecting Objects with Geometric Constraints 544
    Using AutoConstrain to Add Constraints Automatically 545
    Editing a Drawing Containing Constraints 546
    Using Other Geometric Constraints 549
    Using Constraints in the Drawing Process 550
Controlling Sizes with Dimensional Constraints 550
    Adding a Dimensional Constraint 551
    Editing a Dimensional Constraint 553
Using Formulas to Control and Link Dimensions 554
    Adding a Formula Parameter 555
    Testing the Formula 557
    Using Other Formulas 557
Editing the Constraint Options 559
Putting Constraints to Use 561
The Bottom Line 562

Chapter 17 • Using Dynamic Blocks **563**

Exploring the Block Editor 563
   Opening the Block Editor 563
   Editing a Block and Creating New Blocks 565
Creating a Dynamic Block 566
   Adding a Parameter 567
   Adding an Action 568
   Adding an Increment Value 570
   Editing Parameters and Actions 572
   Keeping an Object Centered 572
Using Constraints in Dynamic Blocks 574
Adding a List of Predefined Options 578
Creating Multiple Shapes in One Block 582
Rotating Objects in Unison 586
Filling in a Space Automatically with Objects 590
Including Block Information with Data Extraction 591
The Bottom Line 594

Chapter 18 • Drawing Curves **595**

Introducing Polylines 595
   Drawing a Polyline 595
   Setting Polyline Options 597
Editing Polylines 598
   Setting Pedit Options 602
   Smoothing Polylines 602
   Editing Vertices 604
Creating a Polyline Spline Curve 613
Using True Spline Curves 615
   Drawing a True Spline 616
   Understanding the Spline Options 617
   Fine-Tuning Spline Curves 619
Marking Divisions on Curves 621
   Dividing Objects into Segments of Equal Length 622
   Dividing Objects into Specified Lengths 624
The Bottom Line 625

Chapter 19 • Getting and Exchanging Data from Drawings **627**

Finding the Area of Closed Boundaries 627
   Finding the Area of an Object 628
   Using Hatch Patterns to Find Areas 629
   Adding and Subtracting Areas with the Area Command 631
Getting General Information 634
   Determining the Drawing's Status 635
   Keeping Track of Time 636
   Getting Information from System Variables 637
   Keeping a Log of Your Activity 638

Capturing and Saving Text Data from the AutoCAD Text Window 639
Understanding the Command Window Context Menu 639
Storing Searchable Information in AutoCAD Files 640
Searching for AutoCAD Files 641
Recovering Corrupted Files 642
Using the DXF File Format to Exchange CAD Data
with Other Programs 642
Exporting DXF Files 643
Opening or Importing DXF Files 644
Using AutoCAD Drawings in Page Layout Programs 646
Exporting Raster Files 646
Exporting Vector Files 650
Using OLE to Import Data 652
Editing OLE Links 654
Importing Worksheets as AutoCAD Tables 655
Understanding Options for Embedding Data 657
Using the Clipboard to Export AutoCAD Drawings 657
The Bottom Line 658

Part 4 • 3D Modeling and Imaging **659**

Chapter 20 • Creating 3D Drawings **661**
Getting to Know the 3D Modeling Workspace 661
Drawing in 3D Using Solids 663
Adjusting Appearances 664
Creating a 3D Box 665
Editing 3D Solids with Grips 666
Constraining Motion with the Gizmo 667
Rotating Objects in 3D Using Dynamic UCS 668
Drawing on a 3D Object's Surface 670
Pushing and Pulling Shapes from a Solid 672
Making Changes to Your Solid 674
Creating 3D Forms from 2D Shapes 676
Isolating Coordinates with Point Filters 681
Moving Around Your Model 684
Finding Isometric and Orthogonal Views 684
Rotating Freely Around Your Model 685
Changing Your View Direction 686
Using SteeringWheels 688
Changing Where You Are Looking 690
Flying through Your View 690
Changing from Perspective to Parallel Projection 691
Getting a Visual Effect 692
Using Visual Styles 692
Creating a Sketched Look with Visual Styles 693
In-Canvas Viewport Controls 696

Turning a 3D View into a 2D AutoCAD Drawing 696
Using the Point Cloud Feature 699
The Bottom Line 700

Chapter 21 • Using Advanced 3D Features **703**
Setting Up AutoCAD for this Chapter 703
Mastering the User Coordinate System 704
    Defining a UCS 705
    Saving a UCS 707
    Working in a UCS 708
    Building 3D Parts in Separate Files 709
Understanding the UCS Options 712
    UCS Based on Object Orientation 712
    UCS Based on Offset Orientation 714
    UCS Rotated Around an Axis 715
    Orienting a UCS in the View Plane 717
    Manipulating the UCS Icon 717
    Saving a UCS with a View 718
Using Viewports to Aid in 3D Drawing 719
Using the Array Tools 723
    Making Changes to an Associative Array 724
Creating Complex 3D Surfaces 724
    Laying Out a 3D Form 725
    Spherical and Cylindrical Coordinate Formats 726
    Using a 3D Polyline 727
    Creating a Curved 3D Surface 729
    Converting the Surface into a Solid 733
    Shaping the Solid 733
    Finding the Interference between Two Solids 735
    Creating Tubes with the Sweep Tool 738
    Using Sweep to Create Complex Forms 740
Creating Spiral Forms 742
Creating Surface Models 745
    Slicing a Solid with a Surface 747
    Finding the Volume of a Cut 748
    Understanding the Loft Command 750
Moving Objects in 3D Space 754
    Aligning Objects in 3D Space 754
    Moving an Object in 3D 756
    Rotating an Object in 3D 757
The Bottom Line 758

Chapter 22 • Editing and Visualizing 3D Solids **759**
Understanding Solid Modeling 759
Creating Solid Forms 762
    Joining Primitives 762
    Cutting Portions Out of a Solid 763

Creating Complex Solids 766
   Tapering an Extrusion 766
   Sweeping a Shape on a Curved Path 767
   Revolving a Polyline 768
Editing Solids 771
   Splitting a Solid into Two Pieces 771
   Rounding Corners with the Fillet Tool 772
   Chamfering Corners with the Chamfer Tool 773
   Using the Solid-Editing Tools 775
Streamlining the 2D Drawing Process 784
   Drawing Standard Top, Front, and Right-Side Views 784
   Creating 2D Drawings with the Base View Command 787
   Adding Dimensions and Notes in a Layout 792
   Using Visual Styles with a Viewport 793
Visualizing Solids 794
The Bottom Line 804

Chapter 23 • Exploring 3D Mesh and Surface Modeling **805**
Creating a Simple 3D Mesh 805
   Creating a Mesh Primitive 806
   Understanding the Parts of a Mesh 807
   Smoothing a Mesh 808
Editing Faces and Edges 809
   Stretching Faces 810
   Moving an Edge 813
   Adding More Faces 816
   Rotating an Edge 818
   Adding a Crease 820
   Splitting and Extruding a Mesh Face 822
Creating Mesh Surfaces 825
   Revolved Surface 825
   Edge Surface 826
   Ruled Surface 827
   Tabulated Surface 828
Converting Meshes to Solids 829
Understanding 3D Surfaces 830
Editing Surfaces 832
   Using Extrude, Surface Trim, and Surface Fillet 834
   Using Surface Blend, Patch, and Offset 836
   Understanding Associativity 840
   Editing with Control Vertices 843
   Editing with the CV Edit Bar 846
   Making Holes in a Surface with the Project Geometry Panel 849
   Visualizing Curvature: Understanding the Analysis Panel 849
The Bottom Line 852

Part 5 • Customization and Integration **853**

Chapter 24 • Customizing Toolbars, Menus, Linetypes, and
Hatch Patterns **855**
Using Workspaces 855
Customizing the User Interface 857
   Taking a Quick Customization Tour 857
   Understanding the Customizations In All Files Panel 861
   Getting the Overall View 864
   Finding Commands in the Command List 866
   Opening Preview, Button Image, and Shortcuts 866
   Getting to the Core of Customization in the Properties Group 867
   Creating Your Own Ribbon Panels and Menus 868
   Customizing Ribbon Panel Tools 869
Creating Macros in Tools and Menus 873
   Pausing for User Input 874
   Opening an Expanded Text Box for the Macro Option 875
Editing Keyboard Shortcuts 876
Saving, Loading, and Unloading Your Customizations 878
Understanding the DIESEL Macro Language 881
   Using DIESEL at the Command Line 881
   Using DIESEL in a Custom Menu Macro 882
   Using DIESEL as a Menu Bar Option Label 883
   Using DIESEL and Fields to Generate Text 886
Creating Custom Linetypes 887
   Viewing Available Linetypes 887
   Creating a New Linetype 888
   Understanding the Linetype Code 889
   Creating Complex Linetypes 890
Creating Hatch Patterns 892
The Bottom Line 894

Chapter 25 • Managing and Sharing Your Drawings **897**
Sharing Drawings Online 897
   Sharing Project Files with eTransmit 898
   Protecting AutoCAD Drawing Files 902
Publishing Your Drawings 906
   Exchanging Drawing Sets 906
   Exploring Other Publish Options 908
   Creating a PDF or DWF File by Using the Plot Dialog Box 910
Sharing Files with A360 Drive 912
   Getting Started with A360 Drive 912
   Viewing Files and Adding Comments 914
   Sharing Files 915
   Opening and Saving Files Directly to A360 Drive 916
   Collaborating with Others Using Design Feed 917

Adding Hyperlinks to Drawings 920
   Creating Hyperlinks 920
   Editing and Deleting Hyperlinks 922
   Taking a Closer Look at the Hyperlink Options 922
Managing Your Drawings with DesignCenter and the Tool Palettes 923
   Getting Familiar with DesignCenter 924
   Opening and Inserting Files with DesignCenter 927
   Finding and Extracting the Contents of a Drawing 928
   Exchanging Data between Open Files 931
   Loading Specific Files into DesignCenter 932
   Customizing the Tool Palettes with DesignCenter 932
Establishing Office Standards 936
   Establishing Layering and Text Conventions 936
   Checking Office Standards 937
Converting Multiple Layer Settings 942
   Exploring Other Layer Translator Options 944
The Bottom Line 945

Part 6 • Appendixes **947**

Appendix A • The Bottom Line **949**
Chapter 1: Exploring the Interface 949
Chapter 2: Creating Your First Drawing 950
Chapter 3: Setting Up and Using the Drafting Tools 951
Chapter 4: Organizing Objects with Blocks and Groups 951
Chapter 5: Keeping Track of Layers and Blocks 952
Chapter 6: Editing and Reusing Data to Work Efficiently 953
Chapter 7: Mastering Viewing Tools, Hatches, and External References 954
Chapter 8: Introducing Printing, Plotting, and Layouts 954
Chapter 9: Adding Text to Drawings 955
Chapter 10: Using Fields and Tables 956
Chapter 11: Using Dimensions 957
Chapter 12: Using Attributes 958
Chapter 13: Copying Existing Drawings from
   Other Sources 959
Chapter 14: Advanced Editing and Organizing 960
Chapter 15: Laying Out Your Printer Output 960
Chapter 16: Making "Smart" Drawings with
   Parametric Tools 961
Chapter 17: Using Dynamic Blocks 962
Chapter 18: Drawing Curves 963
Chapter 19: Getting and Exchanging Data
   from Drawings 965
Chapter 20: Creating 3D Drawings 965
Chapter 21: Using Advanced 3D Features 966
Chapter 22: Editing and Visualizing 3D Solids 968

Chapter 23: Exploring 3D Mesh and Surface Modeling 969
Chapter 24: Customizing Toolbars, Menus, Linetypes, and Hatch Patterns 969
Chapter 25: Managing and Sharing Your Drawings 971

Appendix B • Installing and Setting Up AutoCAD **973**
Before Installing AutoCAD 973
Proceeding with the Installation 973
Configuring AutoCAD 974
    The Files Tab 974
    The Display Tab 978
    The Open And Save Tab 980
    The Plot and Publish Tab 983
    The System Tab 983
    The User Preferences Tab 985
    The Drafting Tab 988
    The 3D Modeling Tab 989
    The Selection Tab 993
    The Profiles Tab 996
    The Online Tab 997
Configuring the Tablet Menu Area 998
Turning On the Noun/Verb Selection Method 999
Turning on the Grips Feature 999
Setting Up the Tracking Vector Feature 999
Adjusting the AutoCAD 3D Graphics System 1000
Finding Folders That Contain AutoCAD Files 1001
Setting Up AutoCAD with a White Background 1001

Appendix C • The Autodesk AutoCAD 2018 Certification **1003**

Index *1007*

Introduction

Welcome to *Mastering AutoCAD 2018 and AutoCAD LT 2018*. As many readers have already discovered, this book is a unique blend of tutorial and reference, which includes everything that you need to get started and stay ahead with Autodesk® AutoCAD® software. With this edition, you get coverage of the latest features of both AutoCAD 2018 and AutoCAD LT® 2018 software along with detailed information on existing features.

How to Use This Book

Rather than just showing you how each command works, this book shows you AutoCAD 2018 in the context of a meaningful activity. You'll learn how to use commands while working on an actual project and progressing toward a goal. This book also provides a foundation on which you can build your own methods for using AutoCAD and become an AutoCAD expert. For this reason, we haven't covered every single command or every permutation of a command response. You should think of this book as a way to get a detailed look at AutoCAD as it's used on a real project. As you follow the exercises, we also encourage you to explore AutoCAD on your own, applying the techniques that you learn to your own work.

Both experienced and beginning AutoCAD users will find this book useful. If you aren't an experienced user, the way to get the most out of this book is to approach it as a tutorial—chapter by chapter—at least for the first two parts of the book. You'll find that each chapter builds on the skills and information that you learned in the previous one. To help you navigate, the exercises are shown in numbered steps. To address the needs of all readers worldwide, the exercises provide both Imperial (feet/inches) and metric measurements. Some exercises use generic units of measurement, and if the focus of the exercise is not dependent on the measurement system, Imperial is used.

After you've mastered the material in Part 1 and Part 2, you can follow your interests and explore other parts of the book in whatever order you choose. Part 3 takes you to a more advanced skill level. There you'll learn more about storing and sharing drawing data and how to create more complex drawings. If you're interested in 3D, check out Part 4. If you want to start customizing right away, go to Part 5. You can check out Chapter 25 at any time because it gives you general information about sharing AutoCAD files with your co-workers and consultants. You can also use this book as a ready reference for your day-to-day problems and questions about commands. "The Bottom Line" section at the end of each chapter will help you review and look at different ways to apply the information that you've learned. Experienced users will also find this book a handy reference tool.

Finally, you can learn more about AutoCAD through the author-supplied bonus chapters found at www.omura.com/chapters. For example, if you run into problems using AutoCAD, see the section "When Things Go Wrong" in Bonus Chapter 3, "Hardware and Software Tips." To delve into the details of printers and plotting, check out Bonus Chapter 5, "Understanding Plot Styles."

AutoCAD and AutoCAD LT 2018

Autodesk has released AutoCAD 2018 and AutoCAD LT 2018 simultaneously. Not surprisingly, they're nearly identical in the way they look and work. You can share files between the two programs with complete confidence that you won't lose data or corrupt files. The main differences are that AutoCAD LT doesn't support all of the 3D functions of AutoCAD 2018, nor does it support the customization tools of AutoLISP® or the .NET Framework. But AutoCAD LT still has plenty to offer in both the productivity and customization areas. Because they're so similar, we can present material for both programs with only minor adjustments.

When a feature is discussed that is available only in AutoCAD 2018, you'll see the AutoCAD Only icon. For the purposes of this publication, the "ACAD only" icon means that the relevant (or adjacent) content applies only to AutoCAD software and not to AutoCAD LT software.

You'll also see warning messages when tutorials vary between AutoCAD 2018 and AutoCAD LT. If only minor differences occur, you'll see either a warning message or directions embedded in the exercise indicating the differences between the two programs.

We've also provided workaround instructions wherever possible when AutoCAD LT doesn't offer a feature found in AutoCAD 2018.

Getting Information Fast

In each chapter, you'll find extensive tips and discussions in the form of sidebars set off from the main text. These provide a wealth of information that we have gathered over years of using AutoCAD on a variety of projects in different office environments. You may want to browse through the book and read these boxes just to get an idea of how they might be useful to you.

Another available quick reference is Bonus Chapter 4, "System Variables and Dimension Styles." It contains descriptions of all the dimension settings with comments on their uses. If you experience any problems, you can consult the section "When Things Go Wrong" in Bonus Chapter 3, "Hardware and Software Tips."

The Mastering Series

The *Mastering* series from Sybex provides outstanding instruction for readers with intermediate and advanced skills in the form of top-notch training and development for those already working in their field, and clear, serious education for those aspiring to become pros. Every *Mastering* book includes the following:

- Skill-based instruction with chapters organized around real tasks rather than abstract concepts or subjects

- Self-review test questions so that you can be certain you're equipped to do the job right

What to Expect

Mastering AutoCAD 2018 and AutoCAD LT 2018 is divided into five parts, each representing a milestone in your progress toward becoming an expert AutoCAD user. Here is a description of those parts and what they will show you.

Part 1: The Basics

As with any major endeavor, you must begin by tackling small, manageable tasks. In this first part, you'll become familiar with the way that AutoCAD looks and feels.

- Chapter 1, "Exploring the Interface," shows you how to get around in AutoCAD.

- Chapter 2, "Creating Your First Drawing," details how to start and exit the program and how to respond to AutoCAD commands.

- Chapter 3, "Setting Up and Using the Drafting Tools," tells you how to set up a work area, edit objects, and lay out a drawing.

- Chapter 4, "Organizing Objects with Blocks and Groups," explores some tools unique to CAD: symbols, blocks, and layers. As you're introduced to AutoCAD, you'll also get a chance to make some drawings that you can use later in the book and perhaps even in your future projects.

- Chapter 5, "Keeping Track of Layers and Blocks," shows you how to use layers to keep similar information together and object properties such as linetypes to organize things visually.

Part 2: Mastering Intermediate Skills

After you have the basics down, you'll begin to explore some of the subtler qualities of AutoCAD.

- Chapter 6, "Editing and Reusing Data to Work Efficiently," tells you how to reuse drawing setup information and parts of an existing drawing.

- Chapter 7, "Mastering Viewing Tools, Hatches, and External References," details how to use viewing tools and hatches and how to assemble and edit a large drawing file.

- Chapter 8, "Introducing Printing, Plotting, and Layouts," shows you how to get your drawing onto hard copy.

- Chapter 9, "Adding Text to Drawings," tells you how to annotate your drawing and edit your notes.

- Chapter 10, "Using Fields and Tables," shows you how to add spreadsheet functionality to your drawings.

- Chapter 11, "Using Dimensions," gives you practice in using automatic dimensioning (another unique CAD capability).

Part 3: Mastering Advanced Skills

At this point, you'll be on the verge of becoming a real AutoCAD expert. Part 3 is designed to help you polish your existing skills and give you a few new ones.

- Chapter 12, "Using Attributes," tells you how to attach information to drawing objects and how to export that information to database and spreadsheet files.

- Chapter 13, "Copying Existing Drawings from Other Sources," details techniques for transferring paper drawings to AutoCAD. You'll also learn how to include aerial and map views in your drawings.

◆ Chapter 14, "Advanced Editing and Organizing," is where you'll complete the apartment building tutorial. During this process, you'll learn how to integrate what you've learned so far and gain some tips on working in groups.

◆ Chapter 15, "Laying Out Your Printer Output," shows you the tools that let you display your drawing in an organized fashion.

◆ Chapter 16, "Making 'Smart' Drawings with Parametric Tools," introduces you to parametric drawing. This feature lets you quickly modify a drawing by changing a few parameters.

◆ Chapter 17, "Using Dynamic Blocks," shows you how you can create blocks that can be edited with grips without having to redefine them.

◆ Chapter 18, "Drawing Curves," gives you an in-depth look at some special drawing objects, such as splines and fitted curves.

◆ Chapter 19, "Getting and Exchanging Data from Drawings," is where you'll practice getting information about a drawing and learn how AutoCAD can interact with other applications, such as spreadsheets and page layout programs. You'll also learn how to copy and paste data.

Part 4: 3D Modeling and Imaging

Although 2D drafting is the workhorse application in AutoCAD, its 3D capabilities give you a chance to expand your ideas and look at them in a new light.

◆ Chapter 20, "Creating 3D Drawings," covers basic features for creating three-dimensional drawings.

◆ Chapter 21, "Using Advanced 3D Features," introduces you to some of the program's more powerful 3D capabilities.

◆ Chapter 22, "Editing and Visualizing 3D Solids," takes a closer look at 3D solids and how they can be created, edited, and displayed in AutoCAD 2018.

◆ Chapter 23, "Exploring 3D Mesh and Surface Modeling," introduces you to free-form 3D modeling using mesh and surface objects. With the latest additions to the 3D feature set in AutoCAD, there isn't anything you can't model in 3D.

Part 5: Customization and Integration

One of the greatest strengths of AutoCAD is its openness to customization, which you'll explore in this section.

◆ Chapter 24, "Customizing Toolbars, Menus, Linetypes, and Hatch Patterns," shows you how to use workspaces, customize the user interface, and create custom linetypes and hatch patterns. You'll also be introduced to the DIESEL macro language.

◆ Chapter 25, "Managing and Sharing Your Drawings," shows you how to adapt AutoCAD to your own work style. You'll learn about the tools that help you exchange drawings with others and how to secure your drawings to prevent tampering.

Part 6: Appendixes

Finally, this book has several appendixes.

- ◆ Appendix A, "The Bottom Line," contains the solutions to the book's "Master It" review questions.

- ◆ Appendix B, "Installing and Setting Up AutoCAD," contains an installation and configuration tutorial. If AutoCAD isn't already installed on your system, follow the steps in this tutorial before starting Chapter 1.

**Certification
Objective**

- ◆ Appendix C, "The Autodesk AutoCAD 2018 Certification," shows you where in the book the learning objectives are covered for the Certified User and Certified Professional Exams. If you want to get certified, this information will be very useful.

Where to Get the Exercise Files and Bonus Chapters

Many of the exercises in this book make use of sample files that you can download from the following website: www.sybex.com/go/masteringautocad2018. With these files, you can pick up an exercise anywhere you like without having to work through the book from front to back. You can also use these sample files to repeat exercises or to just explore how files are organized and put together. You can also download additional bonus chapters that cover other AutoCAD features from www.omura.com/chapters. The bonus chapters are as follows:

- ◆ Bonus Chapter 1, "Using the Express Tools," gives you a gentle introduction to the world of AutoCAD customization. You'll learn how to load and use existing Express tools that expand the software's functionality, and you'll be introduced to AutoLISP as a tool to create macros.

- ◆ Bonus Chapter 2, "Exploring AutoLISP," is a primer to this popular macro language found in AutoCAD. You'll learn how you can create custom commands built on existing ones and how you can retrieve and store locations and other data.

- ◆ Bonus Chapter 3, "Hardware and Software Tips," provides information about hardware related to AutoCAD. It also offers tips on improving the performance of AutoCAD and troubleshooting and provides more detailed information on setting up the plotting feature.

- ◆ Bonus Chapter 4, "System Variables and Dimension Styles," provides a reference to dimension style settings.

- ◆ Bonus Chapter 5, "Understanding Plot Styles," discusses methods for controlling lineweights and shading in your printer output.

- ◆ Bonus Chapter 6, "Rendering 3D Drawings," shows how you can use AutoCAD to produce lifelike views of your 3D drawings.

- ◆ Bonus Chapter 7, "Keeping a Project Organized with Sheet Sets," shows you how to use the Sheet Set Manager to simplify your file management. By using the Sheet Set Manager, you can automate some of the tedious drawing coordination tasks.

THE AUTOCAD FREE TRIAL

If you don't have AutoCAD, you can download and install a trial version from the Autodesk website (www.autodesk.com). Be aware that the trial is good for only 30 days and cannot be reinstalled to add time to the trial period—don't start to use it until you're certain you'll have plenty of free time to practice using AutoCAD.

FREE AUTODESK SOFTWARE FOR STUDENTS AND EDUCATORS

The Autodesk Education Community is an online resource with more than five million members that enables educators and students to download—for free (see the website for terms and conditions)— the same software used by professionals worldwide. You can also access additional tools and materials to help you design, visualize, and simulate ideas. Connect with other learners to stay current with the latest industry trends and get the most out of your designs. Get started today at www.autodesk.com/joinedu.

The Minimum System Requirements

This book assumes that you have a Windows-based PC with at least a dual-core processor or equivalent CPU. Your computer should have at least one DVD drive and a hard disk with 4 GB or more of free space for the AutoCAD program files and about 200 MB of additional space for sample files and the workspace. In addition to these requirements, you should have enough free disk space to allow for a Windows virtual memory page file that is about 1.5 times the amount of installed RAM. Consult your Windows manual or Bonus Chapter 3, "Hardware and Software Tips," available at www.omura.com/chapters, for more on virtual memory.

AutoCAD 2018 runs best on systems with at least 4 GB or more of RAM. Your computer should also have a high-resolution monitor and an up-to-date display card. An HD/VGA display with a resolution of 1366×768 or greater will work fine with AutoCAD, but if you want to take full advantage of the 3D features, you should have a 128 MB or greater, OpenGL-capable, workstation-class graphics card. We also assume that you're using a mouse and have the use of a printer or a plotter. Finally, you'll need an Internet connection to take full advantage of the support offerings from Autodesk.

If you want a more detailed explanation of hardware options with AutoCAD, see Bonus Chapter 3. You'll find a general description of the available hardware options and their significance to AutoCAD.

Doing Things in Style

Much care has been taken to see that the stylistic conventions in this book—the use of uppercase or lowercase letters, italic or boldface type, and so on—are the ones most likely to help you learn AutoCAD. On the whole, their effect should be subliminal. However, you may find it useful to be conscious of the following rules:

◆ Menu selections are shown by a series of options separated by the ➤ symbol (for example, choose File ➤ New). These are typically used to show selections from a context menu or the Application menu, which you will learn about in Chapter 1.

- Keyboard entries are shown in boldface (for example, enter **Rotate↵**).

- Command-line prompts are shown in a monospaced font (for example, `Select objects:`).

For most functions, this book describes how to select options from Ribbon panels and the Application menu. In addition, where applicable, we include related keyboard shortcuts and command names in parentheses. These command names provide continuity for readers who are accustomed to working at the Command prompt.

New Features of AutoCAD 2018

AutoCAD 2018 has a long list of new features, many of which are aimed at making your work easier and faster. Some features, like Autodesk 360® and Autodesk Exchange, are web tools that help you share your work, keep up with the latest on AutoCAD, and discuss issues you may be having. Here are some of the new features that we cover in this book:

- Resizable dialog boxes

- Improved 2D and 3D display quality and performance

- Improved Move and Copy tools

- PDF vector import

- Center mark dimensioning tool

- 3D printing support

Contact the Authors

We hope that *Mastering AutoCAD 2018 and AutoCAD LT 2018* will be of benefit to you and that, after you've completed the exercises, you'll continue to use the book as a reference. If you have comments, criticism, or ideas about how the book can be improved, you can email us at the following addresses:

George Omura: `george.omura@gmail.com`

Brian C. Benton: `bbenton@cad-a-blog.com`

If you find errors, please let our publisher know. Visit the book's web page, `www.sybex.com/go/masteringautocad2018`, and click the Errata link to find a form to use to identify the problem.

And thanks for choosing *Mastering AutoCAD 2018 and AutoCAD LT 2018*.

Part 1

The Basics

◆ **Chapter 1: Exploring the Interface**
◆ **Chapter 2: Creating Your First Drawing**
◆ **Chapter 3: Setting Up and Using the Drafting Tools**
◆ **Chapter 4: Organizing Objects with Blocks and Groups**
◆ **Chapter 5: Keeping Track of Layers and Blocks**

Chapter 1

Exploring the Interface

Before you can start to use the new capabilities of the AutoCAD® 2018 software, you must become familiar with the basics. If you're completely new to AutoCAD, you'll want to read this first chapter carefully. It introduces you to many basic operations of AutoCAD, such as opening and closing files, getting a close-up look at part of a drawing, and changing a drawing. If you're familiar with earlier versions of AutoCAD, you should review this chapter anyway to get acquainted with the features that you haven't already used.

Autodesk releases new versions of AutoCAD every year. Part of this strategy is to introduce improvements that focus on a particular category of features. AutoCAD 2018 offers updates that cover a wide range of features. The user interface is easier to customize. There are more ways to access drafting and layer settings. External references have been revamped to allow easy modification to file paths. Font recognition in PDFs has been improved, and display performance has been enhanced. Finally, a new 2018 file format has been updated to accommodate these new features. Before you begin the exercises in this chapter, make sure that you have loaded the sample files from this book's web page at www.sybex.com/go/masteringautocad2018. See the introduction for details. If you have purchased the e-book version, please see the introduction for instructions on how to download the sample files.

In this chapter, you will learn to

- Use the AutoCAD window
- Get a closer look with the Zoom command
- Save a file as you work
- Make changes and open multiple files

Taking a Guided Tour

First, you'll get a chance to familiarize yourself with the AutoCAD screen and how you communicate with AutoCAD. As you do the exercises in this chapter, you'll also get a feel for how to work with this book. Don't worry about understanding or remembering everything you see in this chapter. You'll get plenty of opportunities to probe the finer details of the program as you work through the later chapters. To help you remember the material, we have included a brief set of questions at the end of each chapter. For now, just enjoy your first excursion into AutoCAD.

AUTOCAD REFERENCES IN THIS BOOK

In this chapter and throughout the rest of the book, when we say AutoCAD, we mean both AutoCAD and AutoCAD LT®. Some topics apply only to AutoCAD. In those situations, you'll see an icon indicating that the topic applies only to AutoCAD and not to AutoCAD LT. If you're using AutoCAD LT 2018, these icons can help you focus on the topics that are more relevant to your work by letting you skim over items that do not apply.

AutoCAD 2018 is designed to run on Windows 7, Windows 8, Windows 8.1, and Windows 10. This book was written using AutoCAD 2018 running on Windows 7 Professional.

Launching AutoCAD

If you've already installed AutoCAD (see Appendix B, "Installing and Setting Up AutoCAD") and are ready to jump in and take a look, proceed with the following steps to launch the program:

1. Choose Start ➤ All Programs ➤ Autodesk ➤ AutoCAD 2018 ➤ AutoCAD 2018. You can also double-click the AutoCAD 2018 icon on your Windows Desktop. AutoCAD LT users will use AutoCAD LT 2018 in place of AutoCAD 2018.

2. The AutoCAD Start tab appears, offering options to open existing drawings or to create a new drawing. You may also see the Design Feed panel, which allows you to use a cloud-based collaboration feature. Click the Start Drawing thumbnail in the left side of the view under "Get Started" (see Figure 1.1).

FIGURE 1.1
The Start tab offers easy access to previous work.

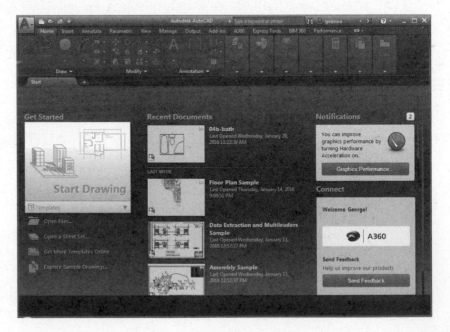

3. The AutoCAD window displays a blank default document named Drawing1.dwg. Users may see the Sheet Set Manager palette to the left of the AutoCAD window. In brand-new installations, you will see the Design Feed panel. Close the Design Feed panel for now. AutoCAD LT users may see the Info palette to the left of the AutoCAD window.

If you're using the trial version, you'll see the Product License Activation window before step 2. This window shows you the number of days you have left in the trial version. You can also activate the product here if you purchase a license. Click the Try button to continue opening the program. Now let's look at the AutoCAD window in detail. Don't worry if it seems like a lot of information. You don't have to memorize it, but by looking at all of the parts, you'll be aware of what is available in a general way.

The AutoCAD Window

Certification Objective

The AutoCAD program window is divided into several parts:

◆ Application menu

◆ Quick Access toolbar

◆ InfoCenter

◆ Ribbon

◆ Drawing tabs

◆ Drawing area

◆ UCS icon (User Coordinate System icon)

◆ Viewport controls

◆ ViewCube®

◆ Navigation bar

◆ Command window

◆ Status bar

Figure 1.2 shows a typical layout of the AutoCAD program window. You can organize the AutoCAD window into any arrangement you want and save it as a *workspace*. You can save and recall a workspace at any time using the Workspace Switching tool in the Quick Access toolbar. (You'll learn more about this tool in the next chapter.) The default workspace in Figure 1.2 is called the Drafting & Annotation workspace, and it is one of several workspaces built into AutoCAD.

FIGURE 1.2

A typical arrangement of the elements in the AutoCAD window

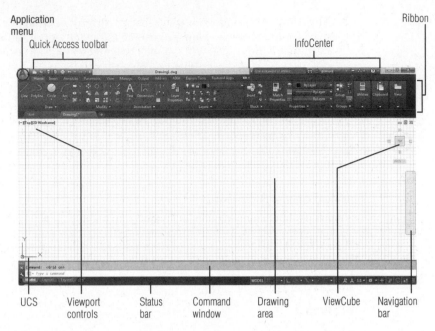

AUTOCAD FOR 3D

For 3D modeling work, AutoCAD offers the 3D Modeling workspace and 3D drawing templates. The combination of these two features can make AutoCAD look like a very different program, but beneath the different appearance, the underlying program is the same. You'll learn more about workspaces and templates later in this chapter and in Chapter 24, "Customizing Toolbars, Menus, Linetypes, and Hatch Patterns." Part 4 of this book shows you the 3D features and tools of AutoCAD in more detail.

In the upper-left corner of the AutoCAD program window, the red AutoCAD icon displays the Application menu, which offers a set of options not directly related to drawing; we'll elaborate on this menu in the next section. The Quick Access toolbar at the top of the drawing area (shown in Figure 1.3) includes the basic file-handling functions, which you find in nearly all Windows programs. The InfoCenter is the AutoCAD online help facility; you'll learn more about it in Chapter 2, "Creating Your First Drawing." The Ribbon uses icons to provide nearly all of the commands that you'll need; you'll learn more about it in the section "Using the Ribbon" later in this chapter.

FIGURE 1.3

The Quick Access toolbar, featuring basic Windows file-handling functions, appears above the Ribbon.

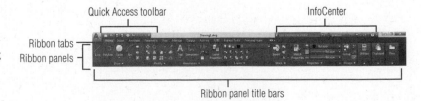

The drawing area occupies most of the screen. Everything you draw appears in this area. As you move your mouse around, crosshairs appear to move within the drawing area. This is the drawing cursor that lets you point to locations in the drawing area. You'll get your first chance to work with the drawing area later in the section "Picking Points in the Drawing Area."

Just above the drawing area are the Drawing tabs that let you create new drawings or switch between open drawings in a way similar to popular web browsers. Notice the X in the current tab, which lets you close the current drawing, and the plus icon just to the right of the tab, which lets you create a new drawing or open an existing one. When you click the plus icon, a new drawing tab appears that you can save as a new file. Right-click the plus icon and a context menu opens that offers you the option to open an existing drawing or to create a new one in the form of an additional tab by using a template.

If you hover over the Drawing tab, you'll see preview images of the model and layouts of the drawing. You'll learn more about model and layout spaces later in this chapter.

Within the drawing area, you see several items along the side and in the corners. The UCS icon appears in the lower-left corner. You'll learn more about the UCS icon in a moment. In the upper-right corner, you see the ViewCube. The ViewCube is primarily for 3D modeling, and we look at those techniques in Chapter 20, "Creating 3D Drawings." You'll also see a Navigation bar along the right edge of the AutoCAD window. This bar offers tools that you can use to get around in your drawing. Basic tools like Zoom and Pan can be found here as well as some advanced tools for viewing 3D models.

The Viewport controls in the upper-left corner of the drawing area offer menu options to control 3D and 2D views and visual styles, and they duplicate some of the functions of the ViewCube. You'll explore the Viewport controls when you delve into 3D modeling in Chapter 23, "Exploring 3D Mesh and Surface Modeling."

Just below the drawing area in the lower-left corner are the Model and Layout tabs. These tabs enable you to switch quickly between different types of views called the *model* and *layout* views. You'll get to see firsthand how these views work in a section called "Working with AutoCAD" later in this chapter.

The Command window, located just below the drawing area, gives you feedback about the AutoCAD commands as you use them. You can move and resize this window just as you move and resize other display components. The Command window can be placed in a docked position as shown in Figure 1.4 by dragging it into the status bar. We'll elaborate on the Command window in the section "Working in the Command Window" later in this chapter.

FIGURE 1.4
The Command window and the status bar

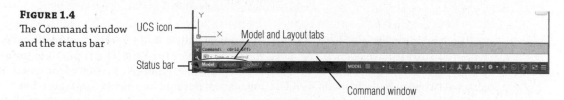

Below the Command window is the status bar (also shown in Figure 1.4). The status bar gives you information at a glance about the state of the drawing. The tools in the status bar offer aids to the drafting process.

Using the Application Menu

The Application menu offers tools to help you manage your AutoCAD files. It is basically the File pull-down menu from earlier versions of AutoCAD. Try it out to see how it works:

1. Click the Application menu icon in the upper-left corner of the AutoCAD window. A list of options appears.

2. Move the cursor slowly down the list of options in the left column. As you highlight the options, additional options appear in a column to the right.

3. Highlight the Export option to see the various formats available for export (see Figure 1.5).

FIGURE 1.5
The Export option in the Application menu showing the list of export options

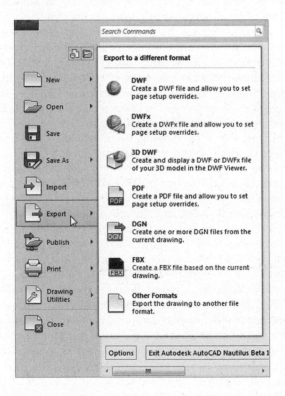

The Application menu also gives you a convenient way to find recently used files or to get to a file you already have open. If you move your cursor away from the list of options to the left in the Application menu, you'll see Recent Documents in the upper-left portion of the menu. You'll also see two icon tools, named Open Documents and Recent Documents (see Figure 1.6).

The Open Documents option lets you quickly change from one open file to another when you are viewing your files full-screen. The Recent Documents option displays a list of documents on which you've recently worked.

FIGURE 1.6
The Open Documents
and Recent Documents
tools

FIGURE 1.6
The Open Documents
and Recent Documents
tools

Open Documents
Recent Documents

List of recent documents

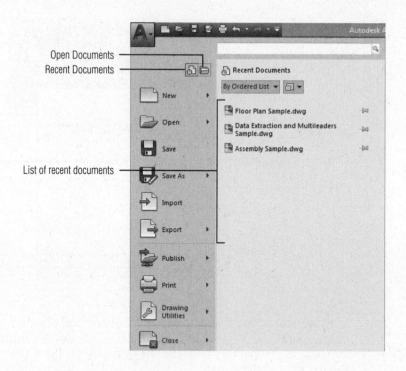

You can use the View tool in the upper-right portion of the Application menu to select the
way the list of files is displayed in a manner similar to the way you would use the Windows
Explorer View option. You can click this icon and select Small Images to have the list display the
files with thumbnail images of their content. Hover over a filename and you will see a tool tip
that displays a larger thumbnail of the drawing.

Using the Ribbon

Certification
Objective

The most prominent feature in the AutoCAD window, besides the drawing area, is the Ribbon
(see Figure 1.7). This is where you'll be selecting tools to draw, edit, or perform other functions.
The Ribbon contains a set of panels representing groups of tools and features. The name of
each Ribbon panel is found in its title bar at the bottom of the panel. Tabs that appear above the
Ribbon panels further organize them. Each tool in the Ribbon offers a tool tip and cue card that
provides a short description to help you understand what the tool icon represents.

If you see only the Ribbon tabs, click the arrowhead button in the Ribbon Control tool. If you
don't even see the tabs, type **Ribbon**↵.

Move the arrow cursor onto one of the Ribbon panel tools and leave it there for a moment;
you'll see a tool tip appear just below the cursor. Hold the cursor there a bit longer and the tool
tip changes to give you even more information about the tool.

FIGURE 1.7
A typical cue card from
a Ribbon panel tool

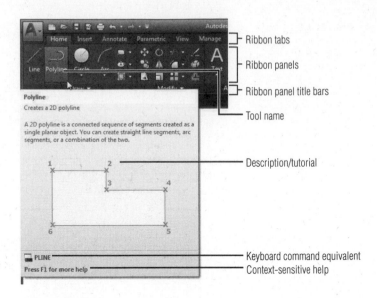

In most cases, you'll be able to guess what each tool does by looking at its icon. The icon with an arc in the Draw Ribbon panel, for instance, indicates that the tool draws arcs; the one with the circle shows that the tool draws circles; and so on. For further clarification, the tool tip gives you the name of the tool.

COMMUNICATING WITH THE COMMAND WINDOW AND DYNAMIC INPUT DISPLAY

AutoCAD is the perfect servant: It does everything you tell it to do and no more. You communicate with AutoCAD by using tools and menu options, which invoke AutoCAD commands. A *command* is a single-word instruction you give to AutoCAD telling it to do something, such as draw a line (the Line tool in the Draw Ribbon panel) or erase an object (the Erase tool in the Modify Ribbon panel). Whenever you invoke a command, either by typing it or by selecting an option or tool, AutoCAD responds by presenting messages to you in the Command window and the Dynamic Input display or by displaying a dialog box. The Dynamic Input display is the display of information that appears at the cursor and consists of messages, dimensions, and coordinates.

The messages in the Command window, or in the Dynamic Input display, often tell you what to do next, or they may display a list of available options. A single command often presents a series of messages that you answer to complete the command. These messages serve as an aid to new users who need a little help. If you ever get lost while using a command or forget what you're supposed to do, look at the Command window for clues. As you become more comfortable with AutoCAD, you'll find that you won't need to refer to these messages as frequently.

You can also right-click to display a set of options that relate directly to your current activity. For example, if you right-click before picking the first point for the Rectangle command, a set of options appears displaying the same options that are listed in the Command prompt along with some additional options.

Finally, the Dynamic Input display allows you to enter dimensional data of objects as you draw them. Besides echoing the command-line messages, the Dynamic Input display shows temporary dimensions, coordinates, and angles of objects that you're drawing and editing. As you enter coordinate or angle values through the keyboard, they appear in the Dynamic Input display. You can easily turn the Dynamic Input display on or off by clicking the Dynamic Input tool when it is visible in the status bar or by setting the Dynmode command to 0 for off or 3 for on. When the Dynamic Input display is turned off, your keyboard input appears only in the Command window.

As a new user, you'll find these tool tips helpful because they show you the name of the tool and a brief description of how to use it. Typically, when we ask you to select a tool, we'll use the name shown in the tool tip to help you identify the tool. In the case of a tool with flyouts, the tool name changes under different conditions. For those tools, we'll use a general description to identify the tool. You'll learn more about flyouts a bit later in this chapter (see the section "Understanding Flyouts").

As you work through this book, we'll ask you to select tools from the Ribbon panels. You'll often be asked to switch between different tabs to select tools from other sets of panels. To make the process simpler to read, we'll use a somewhat abbreviated description of a tool's location. For example, for the Line tool we'll say, "Click the Line tool in the Home tab's Draw panel." For the Move tool, we'll say, "Click the Move tool in the Home tab's Modify panel."

EXPANDING HIDDEN PANELS

Certification
Objective

In addition to the visible tools, some buttons are hidden from view. You can expand many of the Ribbon panels to select more of them. If you see an arrowhead to the right of a panel's title bar, you can click the title bar to expand the panel (see Figure 1.8). The panel expands to reveal additional tools. If you move the cursor to the drawing area, the expanded panel shrinks to its original size. You can also click the pushpin icon in the expanded panel title bar to lock the panel in its open position.

FIGURE 1.8
The arrowhead in the panel title bar tells you that additional tools are available.

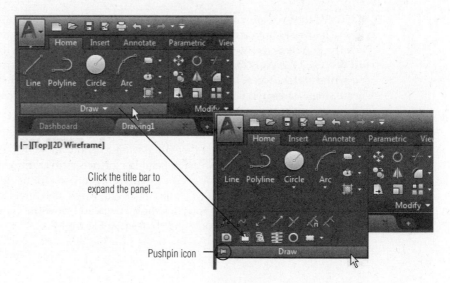

Click the title bar to expand the panel.

Pushpin icon

From now on, we'll refer to the location of additional tools as the expanded panel. For example, we'll say, "Click the Ray tool in the expanded Draw panel" when we want you to select the Ray tool.

If you are working on a smaller screen with low resolution, some of the Ribbon panels to the far right may look different from what you are shown in this book. On a low-resolution screen, AutoCAD will automatically reduce the size of the panels to the right of the Ribbon so that they show only their title (see Figure 1.9).

FIGURE 1.9
The Layers, Block, Properties, Groups, Utilities, and View panels are reduced to single icons with a smaller AutoCAD window.

To see the tools, hover over the panel (see Figure 1.10).

FIGURE 1.10
Hover over the panel to see the tools.

Finally, the Workspace drop-down menu in the Quick Access toolbar may be hidden from view in a low-resolution display. If you don't see these options in your AutoCAD window, click the double arrowhead icon to the far right of the Quick Access toolbar to reveal it. If you still don't see the Workspace menu, click the downward-pointing arrow icon at the far-right end of the Quick Access toolbar and select Workspace. See "Can't Find the Tool or Panel We're Discussing?" later in this chapter for more on "missing" interface items.

UNDERSTANDING FLYOUTS

The *flyouts* are one more feature that you'll want to know about. Flyouts are similar to expanded panels because you can click an arrowhead to gain access to additional tools. Unlike a whole panel, however, flyouts give you access to different methods for using a particular tool. For example, AutoCAD lets you draw circles in several ways, so it offers a flyout for the Circle tool in the Home tab's Draw panel. If you click the arrowhead below the Circle icon in the Draw panel, you'll see additional tools for drawing circles (see Figure 1.11).

FIGURE 1.11
Flyouts

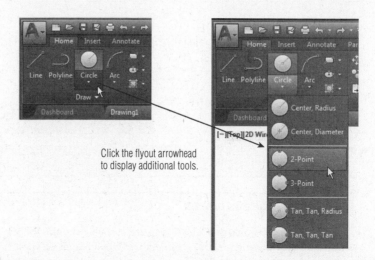

Click the flyout arrowhead
to display additional tools.

If you select a tool option from a flyout, that option becomes the default tool for the icon you chose. For example, when you hover your cursor over the Circle icon in the Draw panel, the tool tip shows "Center, Radius" for the tool's name. If you click the arrowhead below the Center, Radius tool and select 2-Point, then 2-Point becomes the default tool and you'll see "2-Point" for the name of the tool in the tool tip (see Figure 1.12).

FIGURE 1.12
The tool with a flyout will change to the last tool used.

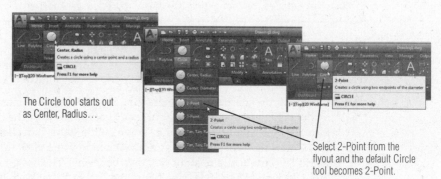

The Circle tool starts out
as Center, Radius…

Select 2-Point from the
flyout and the default Circle
tool becomes 2-Point.

GENERAL TOOL NAMES VS. TOOL TIP NAMES

Because the tool tip for tools with flyouts can change, describing them by name can be a bit problematic. The name may have changed based on the last tool you used from a flyout. For this reason, if a tool has a flyout, we'll refer to it by a general name that is related to the set of tools contained

continues

continued

within it rather than by the tool tip name. For example, we'll call the circle icon tool the Circle tool rather than the Center, Radius tool.

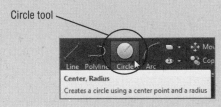

TOOLS VS. THE KEYBOARD

Throughout this book, you'll be told to select tools from the Ribbon panels to invoke commands. For new and experienced users alike, the Ribbon panels offer an easy-to-remember method for accessing commands. If you're an experienced AutoCAD user, you can type commands directly from the keyboard. Most of the keyboard commands you know and love still work as they did before.

Many tools and commands have *aliases*. Aliases are one-, two-, or three-letter abbreviations of a command name. As you become more proficient with AutoCAD, you may find these aliases helpful. As you work through this book, the shortcuts will be identified for your reference.

Finally, if you're feeling adventurous, you can create your own aliases and keyboard shortcuts for executing commands by adding them to the AutoCAD support files. Chapter 24 discusses how to customize menus, Ribbon panels, toolbars, and keyboard shortcuts.

Picking Points in the Drawing Area

Now that you've seen the general layout of AutoCAD, take a look at the coordinate readout and the drawing cursor to get a sense of how the parts of the AutoCAD screen work together:

1. Move the cursor around in the drawing area. As you move it, notice how the coordinate readout changes to tell you the cursor's location. It shows the coordinates in an X, Y, Z format. If the coordinates are not shown on the status bar, click the customization tool at the bottom-right corner of the AutoCAD window and click the Coordinates option check mark. The coordinate readout will then be visible. The Customization tool looks like three horizontal bars. See "Can't Find the Tool or Panel We're Discussing?" later in this chapter for more information.

2. Place the cursor in the middle of the drawing area and click the left mouse button. Move the cursor and a rectangle follows. This is a *window selection*; you'll learn more about this window in Chapter 2. You also see a coordinate readout following the cursor and the message Specify opposite corner or. This display at the cursor is called the *Dynamic Input display*. You'll learn more about it a little later in this chapter (see Figure 1.13).

FIGURE 1.13
The Dynamic Input
display cursor

3. Move the cursor a bit in any direction, and then click the left mouse button again. Notice that the window selection disappears, as does the Dynamic Input display.

4. Try picking several more points in the drawing area. Notice that, as you click, you alternately start and end a window selection. If you happen to click and drag, you will see a lasso selection (see "Click and Drag to Lasso Objects" in Chapter 2 for more on the lasso selection method).

If you happen to click the right mouse button, a context menu appears. A right-click frequently opens a menu containing options that are *context sensitive*. This means the contents of the menu depend on the location where you right-click as well as the command that is active at the time. If there are no appropriate options at the time of the right-click, AutoCAD treats the right-click as an Enter (↵) keystroke. You'll learn more about these options as you progress through the book. For now, if you happen to open this menu by accident, press the Esc key to close it.

Using the UCS Icon

In the lower-left corner of the drawing area, you see an L-shaped line. This is the *User Coordinate System (UCS)* icon, which tells you your orientation in the drawing. This icon becomes helpful as you start to work with complex 2D drawings and 3D models. The X and Y indicate the x- and y-axes of your drawing. Chapter 21, "Using Advanced 3D Features," discusses this icon in detail. For now, you can use it as a reference to tell you the direction of the axes.

IF YOU CAN'T FIND THE UCS ICON

The UCS icon can be turned on and off, so if you're on someone else's system and you don't see the icon or it doesn't look like it does in this chapter, don't panic. See Chapter 21 for more information.

Working in the Command Window

As mentioned earlier, at the bottom of the screen, just above the status bar, is a small horizontal window called the *Command window*. Here AutoCAD displays responses to your input while you're using a command. By default, it shows one line of text. This line shows the current responses to your command input as well as command options. As you work through a command, you'll see more responses, with earlier responses scrolling upward in faded text. You can view text that has scrolled out of sight by clicking the up-pointing arrowhead at the far right of the Command window. Right now, the command line displays the words "Type a command" in a box (see Figure 1.4, earlier in this chapter). This tells you that AutoCAD is waiting for a command. When you click a point in the drawing area, you see the message `Specify opposite corner or [Fence/WPolygon/CPolygon]:`. At the same time, the cursor starts to draw a window selection that disappears when you click another point. The same message appears in the Dynamic Input display at the cursor.

As a new user, pay special attention to messages displayed in the Command window and the Dynamic Input display because this is how AutoCAD communicates with you. Besides giving you messages, the Command window records your activity within AutoCAD. You can use the scroll bar to the right of the Command window to review previous messages. You can also enlarge the window for a better view. (Chapter 2 discusses these components in more detail.)

Now let's look at the AutoCAD window components in detail.

THE COMMAND WINDOW AND DYNAMIC INPUT DISPLAY

The Command window and the Dynamic Input display allow AutoCAD to provide text feedback on your actions. You can think of these features as a chat window for communicating with AutoCAD—as you enter commands, AutoCAD responds with messages. As you become more familiar with AutoCAD, you may find that you don't need to rely on the Command window and Dynamic Input display as much. For new and casual users, however, the Command window and Dynamic Input display can be helpful in understanding what steps to take as you work.

Working with AutoCAD

Now that you've been introduced to the AutoCAD window, you're ready to try using a few AutoCAD commands. First you'll open a sample file and make a few modifications to it. In the process, you'll become familiar with common methods of operation in AutoCAD.

Opening an Existing File

In this exercise, you'll get a chance to see and use a typical Select File dialog box.

Before you start, make sure that you have installed the sample files for this book from the book's web page. See the introduction for instructions on how to find the sample files.

To start, you'll open an existing file:

1. In the Drawing tab at the top left of the drawing area, click the Close icon to the far right of the tab.

   A message appears, asking whether you want to save the changes you've made to the current drawing. Click No.

2. In the Start tab, click the Open Files option just below the Start Drawing icon in the left column. The Select File dialog box opens. This is a typical Windows file dialog box with an added twist: In the large Preview box on the right, you can preview a drawing before you open it, thereby saving time while searching for files. To the left is a panel known as the Places list, in which you can find frequently used locations on your computer or the Internet (see Figure 1.14).

   If you don't see a Preview box in the Select File dialog box, click the word *Views* in the upper-right corner and select Preview from the list that appears. Note that the Select File dialog box can be resized if you need to view more of your drawing list.

3. In the Select File dialog box, open the Look In drop-down list and locate the Chapter 1 folder of the Mastering AutoCAD 2018 sample files. (You may need to scroll through the list to find it.)

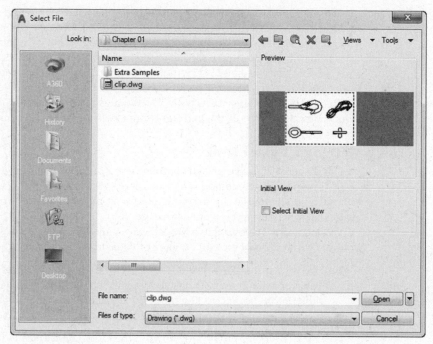

4. Move the arrow cursor to the clip.dwg file and click it. Notice that the clip.dwg file-name now appears in the File Name text box below the file list. The Preview box also now shows a thumbnail image of the file. Be aware that a thumbnail may not show for files from older versions of AutoCAD.

5. Click the Open button at the bottom of the Select File dialog box. AutoCAD opens the clip.dwg file, as shown in Figure 1.15.

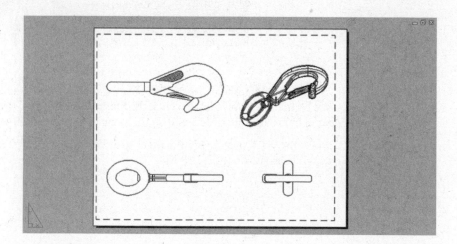

The clip.dwg file opens to display a *layout* view of the drawing. A layout is a type of view in which you lay out different views of your drawing in preparation for printing. You can tell you are in a layout view by the white area over the gray background. This white area represents your drawing on a printed page. This view is like a print preview.

Also note that the AutoCAD window's title bar displays the name of the drawing. The name is also displayed in the Drawing tab. This offers easy identification of the file.

This particular file contains both 2D drawings and a 3D model of a typical locking clip. The layout view shows top, front, and right-side views as well as an isometric view.

Getting a Closer Look

One of the most frequently used commands is Zoom, which gives you a closer look at part of your drawing. This command offers a variety of ways to control your view. In this section, you'll enlarge a portion of the clip drawing to get a more detailed look. You use a *zoom window* to tell AutoCAD which area you want to enlarge.

 Certification Objective

You'll start by switching to a Model Space view of the drawing. The Model Space view places you in a workspace where you do most of your drawing creation and editing. Follow these steps:

1. Hover over the Clip tab at the top left of the drawing area (see the left panel in Figure 1.16). You'll see two preview icons showing the Model Space on the left and the layout on the right. If you hover over the Model Space image, the drawing area will temporarily change to show you the full view of the Model Space.

2. Click the image on the left showing the Model Space (see Figure 1.16).

FIGURE 1.16
Hover over the Drawing tab, and click the Model Space image (left) or click the Model tab in the lower-left corner of the drawing area (right).

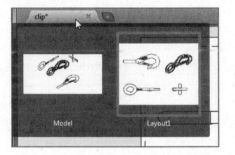 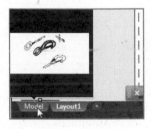

Your view changes to show the full 3D model with the 2D representations of the model (see Figure 1.17). You can also click the Model tab below the drawing area (see the right panel in Figure 1.16) to accomplish the same change from the layout to Model Space.

3. Type **PLAN**↵↵. Your display changes to a two-dimensional view looking down on the drawing, as shown in Figure 1.18.

Figure 1.17
3D model with 2D
representations of
the model

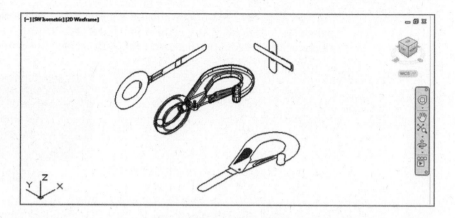

Figure 1.18
Placing the zoom
window around
the clip

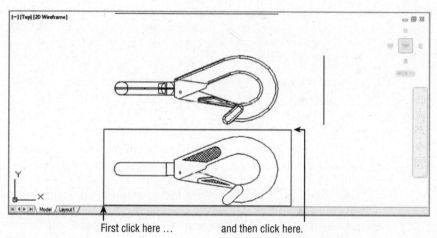

First click here …   and then click here.

4. Click the Zoom Window tool from the Zoom flyout in the Navigation bar (see Figure 1.19).
   Remember that to open the flyout, you need to click the arrowhead next to or below the tool.

Figure 1.19
Choosing the Zoom
Window tool from the
Zoom flyout in the
Navigation bar

Flyout arrowhead

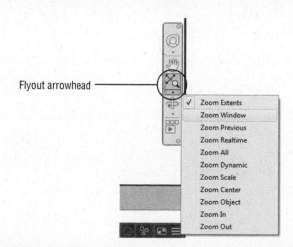

You can also click the Window tool from the Zoom flyout in the View tab's Navigate panel (see Figure 1.20) or type the command **Z↵W↵**. If you don't see the Navigate panel, right-click in the Ribbon and choose Show Panels ➤ Navigate.

FIGURE 1.20
The Zoom flyout and
Window tool in the
View tab's Navigate
panel

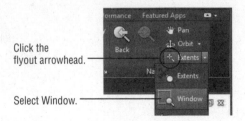

Click the
flyout arrowhead.

Select Window.

5. The Dynamic Input display shows the `Specify first corner:` prompt. Look at the image in Figure 1.18. Move the crosshair cursor to a location similar to the one shown in the figure labeled "First click here," and then left-click. Move the cursor, and the rectangle appears with one corner fixed on the point you just picked; the other corner follows the cursor.

6. The Dynamic Input display now shows the `Specify opposite corner:` prompt. Position the other corner of the zoom window so that it encloses the lower image of the clip, as shown in Figure 1.18, and left-click the mouse again. The clip enlarges to fill the screen.

In this exercise, you used the Window option of the Zoom command to define an area to enlarge for your close-up view. You saw how AutoCAD prompts you to indicate first one corner of the window selection and then the other. These messages are helpful for first-time users of AutoCAD. You'll use the Window option frequently—not just to define views but also to select objects for editing.

Getting a close-up view of your drawing is crucial to working accurately, but you'll often want to return to a previous view to get the overall picture. To do so, choose Zoom Previous from the Zoom flyout in the Navigation bar (see Figure 1.21). You may also type **Z↵P↵**.

FIGURE 1.21
The Zoom Previous
option

Do this now and the previous view appears. Click Zoom Previous again, and the view showing the entire clip returns to the screen.

You can quickly enlarge or reduce your view by using the Zoom Realtime option of the Zoom command. Follow these steps to change your view with Zoom Realtime:

<table>
<tr><td>Zoom Realtime</td><td>

1. Click the Zoom Realtime option from the Navigation bar's Zoom flyout. You can also type Z↵.

</td></tr>
<tr><td>🔍</td><td>

2. Place the Zoom Realtime cursor slightly above the center of the drawing area, and then click and drag downward. Your view zooms out to show more of the drawing.

</td></tr>
</table>

3. While still holding the left mouse button, move the cursor upward. Your view zooms in and enlarges. When you have a view similar to the one shown in Figure 1.22, release the mouse button. (Don't worry if you don't get *exactly* the same view as the figure. This is just for practice.)

FIGURE 1.22
The final view you want to achieve in step 3 of the exercise

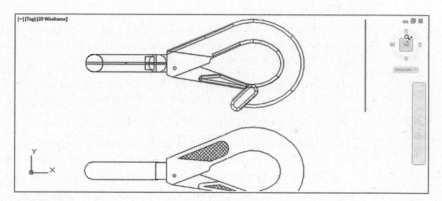

4. You're still in Zoom Realtime mode. Click and drag the mouse again to see how you can further adjust your view. To exit, you can select another command besides Zoom or Pan, or press the Esc key twice.

If you prefer, you can use the wheel on your mouse to zoom and pan over your view. Roll the wheel to zoom in and out, or click and drag the wheel to pan. Be aware that Zoom Realtime offers finer control over the amount of magnification than does the mouse wheel.

As you can see from this exercise, you have a wide range of options for viewing your drawings just by using a few tools. These tools are all you need to control the display of 2D drawings.

Saving a File as You Work

It's a good idea to save your file periodically as you work on it. As with any Windows program, you can save it under its original name (click the Save tool on the Quick Access toolbar) or under a different name (choose Save As from the Application menu or the Quick Access toolbar), thereby creating a new file.

By default, AutoCAD automatically saves your work at 10-minute intervals under a name that is a combination of the current filename plus a number and that ends with the .sv$ filename extension. This is known as the *Automatic Save* feature. Using settings in the Options dialog box or system variables, you can change the name of the autosaved file and control the time between autosaves. See "The Open and Save Tab" in Appendix B for details.

"I Can't Find My Automatic Saves!"

As an IT manager at ELS Architecture and Urban Planning, this author (George) is often asked, "Where does AutoCAD put the Automatic Save files?" By default, in Windows 7, Windows 8, and Windows 10 the Automatic Save file is stored in `C:\Users\`*User Name*`\appdata\local\temp\`. You can find the exact location for your system by typing **Savefilepath**↵ at the Command prompt. This file location is often set as a hidden folder, so you may need to set up File Explorer to display hidden folders before you can get to the Automatic Save file. You can also specify a different location for the Automatic Save files. See Appendix B for information on how to locate hidden files and specify a location for your files.

Making Changes

You'll frequently make changes to your drawings. One of the primary advantages of AutoCAD is the ease with which you can make modifications. The following exercise shows you a typical sequence of operations involved in changing a drawing:

1. Use the Save As option in the Application menu to save the current `clip.dwg` file under the name **MyFirst**. For convenience, you can save your files in the `My Documents` folder.

2. From the Home tab's Modify panel, click the Erase tool.

3. Notice that the cursor has turned into a small square. This square is called the *pickbox*. You also see `Select objects:` in the Command window and the Dynamic Input display. This message helps remind new users what to do.

4. Move the pickbox over the drawing, placing it on various parts of the clip. Don't click anything yet. Notice that as you hover your cursor over objects with the pickbox, they're dimmed and a red X appears by the cursor. This helps you see the objects that the pickbox is likely to select and erase should you click the left mouse button.

5. Place the pickbox on the crosshatch pattern of the clip (see Figure 1.23), and click. The crosshatch dims. The pickbox and the `Select objects:` prompt remain, indicating that you can continue to select objects.

FIGURE 1.23
Erasing a portion of the clip

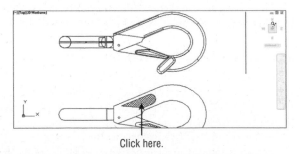

Click here.

6. Press ↵. The crosshatch disappears. You've just erased a part of the drawing.

In this exercise, first you issued the Erase command, and then you selected an object by using a pickbox to click it. The pickbox tells you that you must select items on the screen, and it shows you what you're about to select by highlighting objects as you hover the cursor over them. Once you've clicked an object or a set of objects, press ↵ to move on to the next step. This sequence of steps is common to many of the commands you'll work with in AutoCAD.

You can also click an object or a set of objects and then press the Delete key.

Working with Multiple Files

You can have multiple documents open at the same time in AutoCAD. This feature can be especially helpful if you want to exchange parts of drawings between files or if you want another file open for reference. Try the following exercise to see how multiple documents work in AutoCAD:

1. In the Start tab, locate the Templates option at the bottom of the Start Drawing icon and click it (see Figure 1.24).

FIGURE 1.24
Click the Templates option below the Start Drawing icon.

2. Select acad.dwt from the drop-down list.

3. Go to the Ribbon and, in the View tab's Interface panel, click Tile Vertically to get a view of both drawing files and the Start tab.

4. Click the minimize button in the upper-right corner of the Start tab window, and then click Tile Vertically in the Interface panel again to get a better view of the two drawings.

When you create a new file in AutoCAD, you're actually opening a copy of a *template file*, as you saw in step 1. A template file is a blank file that is set up for specific drawing types. The acad.dwt file is a generic template set up for Imperial measurements. Another template file, called acadiso.dwt, is a generic template useful for metric measurements. Other templates are set up for specific drawing-sheet sizes and measurement systems. You'll learn more about templates in Chapter 6, "Editing and Reusing Data to Work Efficiently."

Next let's try drawing a rectangle to see how AutoCAD behaves while drawing objects:

1. Making sure that you have the newly created drawing as the active window, click the Rectangle tool in the Home tab's Draw panel, as shown in Figure 1.25.

FIGURE 1.25
Click the Rectangle tool in the Draw panel.

Notice that the Command window now shows the following prompt:

```
Specify first corner point or
[Chamfer/Elevation/Fillet/Thickness/Width]:
```

AutoCAD is asking you to select the first corner for the rectangle, and in brackets, it's offering a few options of which you can take advantage at this point in the command. Don't worry about those options right now. You'll have an opportunity to learn about command options in Chapter 2. You also see the same prompt, minus the bracketed options, in the Dynamic Input display at the cursor. You can view the command options at the cursor by pressing the down arrow key on your keyboard.

2. Click a point roughly in the lower-left corner of the drawing area, as shown in Figure 1.26. Now as you move your mouse, a rectangle follows the cursor, with one corner fixed at the position you just selected. You also see the following prompt in the Command window, with a similar prompt in the Dynamic Input display:

```
Specify other corner point or [Area/Dimensions/Rotation]:
```

FIGURE 1.26

Selecting the first point of a rectangle

Click here to start the rectangle.

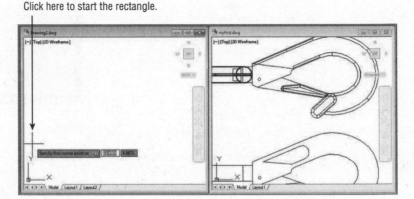

3. Click another point anywhere in the upper-right region of the drawing area, but avoid getting too close to the ViewCube (see Figure 1.27). A rectangle appears. If you happen to accidentally open the ViewCube context menu, press Escape once and you will be able to position the corner. You'll learn more about the different cursor shapes and what they mean in Chapter 2.

FIGURE 1.27

After you've selected the first point of the rectangle, you'll see a rectangle follow the motion of your mouse.

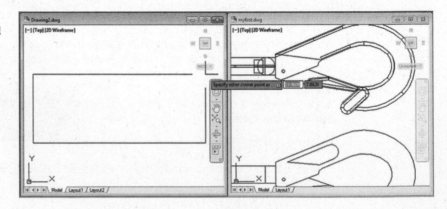

4. Let's try copying objects between these two files. Click in the window with the clip drawing to make it active.

5. Click Zoom All from the Zoom flyout of the Navigation bar to get an overall view of the drawing (see Figure 1.28). You can also type **Z↵A↵**.

FIGURE 1.28
The Zoom All option gives you an overall view of your drawing.

6. Click the 2D version of the clip at the bottom of the drawing to select it. A dot appears at the center of the clip, and a rectangle encloses it. You may find that some parts of the drawing within the rectangle have not been highlighted. If this happens, just click them in addition to the main clip drawing. The dot is called a *grip*; you'll learn more about grips in the next chapter (see Figure 1.29).

FIGURE 1.29
Grip shown in the 2D drawing

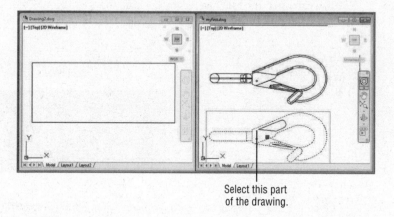

Select this part of the drawing.

7. Right-click, select Clipboard, and then select Copy. You can also press Ctrl+C to invoke the Windows Copy To Clipboard shortcut.

8. Click inside the other drawing window to make it active.

9. Right-click, select Clipboard, and then select Paste. You can also press Ctrl+V to invoke the Windows Paste From Clipboard shortcut. The Specify Insertion Point prompt appears.

10. Click inside the rectangle. The clip appears at the cursor in the new drawing.

11. This ends the exercises for this chapter. Save your `myfirst.dwg` file for future reference. You can close the new drawing without saving it. You may have to maximize the Start tab, which will still be minimized at the bottom of the screen.

LOSE THE NAVIGATION BAR?

If for some reason the Navigation bar is not visible, you can find it on the View tab's Viewport Tools panel. Click the Navigation Bar tool. The tool will highlight in blue and the Navigation bar will appear. You can also type **Navbar.⏎** at the command line and choose one of the two options (On/Off). This panel also shows the tool to display the UCS icon and ViewCube if they also get misplaced.

Note that you've had two files open at once. You can have as many files open as you want as long as your computer has adequate memory to accommodate them. You can control the individual document windows as you would any window, using the window control buttons in the upper-right corner of the drawing area.

Adding a Predrawn Symbol with the Tool Palettes

In the preceding exercise, you saw how you could easily copy an object from one file to another by using the standard Windows Cut and Paste feature. AutoCAD offers several tool palettes that enable you to click and drag predrawn objects into your drawing.

You can open the tool palettes by clicking the Tool Palettes tool in the View tab's Palettes panel, as shown in Figure 1.30.

FIGURE 1.30
Open the Tool Palettes tool from the View tab.

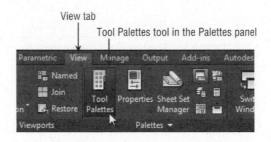

Once the tool palettes are open, you can select a tab containing the predrawn objects you want to use and then click the specific object you want to add. The object appears at the cursor, ready for you to select a location (see Figure 1.31).

In addition to predrawn objects, the tool palettes offer a way to add hatch patterns and other components quickly to your drawing. They're great tools to help you manage your library of custom, predrawn symbols. Chapter 25, "Managing and Sharing Your Drawings," shows you how to use and customize the tool palettes.

FIGURE 1.31
The tool palettes offer predrawn symbols that you can easily place in your drawings.

Select a tab containing predrawn symbols you want to use.

Click on a symbol.

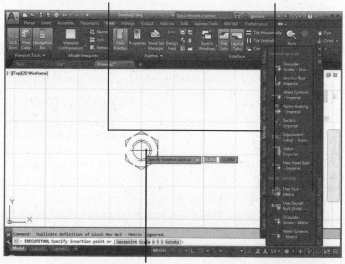

The symbol appears at the cursor ready to be placed in the drawing.

CAN'T FIND THE TOOL OR PANEL WE'RE DISCUSSING?

The AutoCAD interface is easy to customize, and sometimes tools and options are hidden from view due to changes other users have made or as a result of changes from our review software to the final release version. If you don't see a tool or icon we're asking you to use in this or other chapters, here are a few places to check.

Quick Access Toolbar   If you don't see an icon in the Quick Access toolbar, you can click the Customize Quick Access Toolbar tool at the right end of the toolbar to open a list of additional Quick Access toolbar options.

Customize Quick Access Toolbar

Options that already appear in the toolbar show a check mark next to their name in the menu. Click the option that you want to have visible in the toolbar to make it visible. Clicking on an option that shows a check mark will hide that option from the toolbar.

Status Bar   Items missing from the status bar can be found by clicking the Customization tool in the lower-right corner of the AutoCAD window.

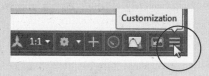

continues

continued

This opens a menu of tools that can be added to the status bar. Just as with the Quick Access toolbar, items that already appear in the status bar will display a check mark in the menu next to their name. If you need to check and uncheck multiple options, you can turn on the Lock UI option in the list. Lock UI keeps the menu open after you make a selection.

Ribbon   If a Ribbon panel or Ribbon tab is missing, you can right-click in the Ribbon panel to open a menu that offers a list of available panels and tabs.

If you select the Show Tabs option, you will see a list of all of the tabs that are available for the current workspace. If you select the Show Panels option, you will see a list of panels that are available for the current Ribbon tab.

USC Icon, ViewCube, and Navigation Bar   Some of the more useful panels in the AutoCAD interface can be turned on and off through tools in the Ribbon. The UCS icon, ViewCube, and Navigation bar can be controlled through tools in the View tab's Viewport Tools panel.

Reset AutoCAD to the Default Settings   Finally, if your version of AutoCAD looks completely different from what you see here, you can reset your AutoCAD profile to the default settings.

1. Type options↵.

2. In the Options dialog box, select the Profiles tab at the upper right.

3. Click the Reset button in the right-hand column.

4. Click OK to exit the Options dialog box.

See "The Profiles Tab" in Appendix B for more information on how to save and restore the way AutoCAD is set up. Note that AutoCAD LT 2018 does not have a Profiles tab.

The Bottom Line

Use the AutoCAD® window.   AutoCAD® is a typical Windows graphics program that makes use of menus, toolbars, Ribbon panels, and palettes. If you've used other graphics programs, you'll see at least a few familiar tools.

Master It   Name the components of the AutoCAD window that you can use to select a function.

Get a closer look with the Zoom command.   One of the first things that you'll want to learn is how to manipulate your views. The Zoom command is a common tool in graphics programs.

Master It   Name at least two ways of zooming into a view.

Save a file as you work.   Nothing is more frustrating than having a power failure that causes you to lose hours of work. It's a good idea to save your work frequently. AutoCAD offers an Automatic Save feature that can be a lifesaver if you happen to forget to save your files.

Master It   How often does the AutoCAD Automatic Save feature save your drawing?

Make changes and open multiple files.   As with other Windows programs, you can have multiple files open and exchange data between them.

Master It   With two drawings open, how can you copy parts of one drawing into the other?

Chapter 2

Creating Your First Drawing

This chapter examines some of the basic functions of the AutoCAD® software. You'll get a chance to practice with the drawing editor by building a simple drawing to use in later exercises. You'll learn how to give input to AutoCAD, interpret prompts, and get help when you need it. This chapter also covers the use of coordinate systems to give AutoCAD exact measurements for objects. You'll see how to select objects that you've drawn and how to specify base points for moving and copying.

If you're not a beginning AutoCAD user, you may want to move on to the more complex material in Chapter 3, "Setting Up and Using the Drafting Tools." You can use the files supplied at the book's web page (www.sybex.com/go/masteringautocad2018) to continue the tutorials at that point.

Beginning in this chapter, we'll be using a setup that displays a white drawing background instead of the dark gray background you see on your screen. We do this to keep the figures legible in the printed version of this book, but the difference should not hinder your understanding of the figures. If you like, you can set up your screen with a white background by following the instructions in Appendix B, "Installing and Setting Up AutoCAD," in the section "Set Up AutoCAD with a White Background."

In this chapter, you will learn to

- ◆ Specify distances with coordinates
- ◆ Interpret the cursor modes and understand prompts
- ◆ Select objects and edit with grips
- ◆ Use dynamic input
- ◆ Display data in a text window
- ◆ Display the properties of an object
- ◆ Get help

Getting to Know the Home Tab's Draw and Modify Panels

Your first task in learning how to draw in AutoCAD software is simply to draw a line. Since AutoCAD is designed as a precision drawing tool, you'll be introduced to methods that allow you to input exact distances. But before you begin drawing, take a moment to familiarize yourself with the features that you'll be using more than any other to create objects with AutoCAD: the Draw and Modify panels. Try these steps:

1. Start AutoCAD just as you did in Chapter 1, "Exploring the Interface," by choosing Start ➤ All Programs ➤ Autodesk ➤ AutoCAD 2018 ➤ AutoCAD 2018.

2. Click the Templates drop-down arrowhead in the Dashboard and select acad.dwt (see Figure 2.1). Metric users should use the acadiso.dwt template. You could also click the Start Drawing icon, but we ask you to use the acad.dwt or acadiso.dwt template to ensure that you are set up with the same defaults as in this exercise.

FIGURE 2.1
The Templates drop-down list

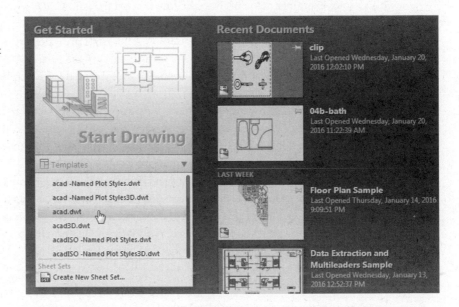

3. Make sure that you are in the Drafting & Annotation workspace. Click the Workspace Switching tool in the status bar, and select Drafting & Annotation.

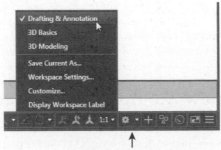

Workspace Switching tool.

4. Move the arrow cursor to the Line tool in the Home tab's Draw panel at the far upper-left portion of the AutoCAD window, and rest it there so that the tool tip appears. As you hold the cursor over the tool, first one tool tip appears and then another (see Figure 2.2).

FIGURE 2.2
The Draw panel

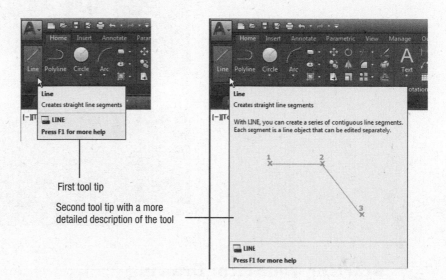

First tool tip

Second tool tip with a more
detailed description of the tool

5. Slowly move the arrow cursor to the right over the other tools in the Home tab's Draw panel, and read each tool tip.

In most cases, you'll be able to guess what each tool does by looking at its icon. The icon with an arc, for instance, indicates that the tool draws arcs; the one with the ellipse signifies that the tool draws ellipses; and so on. If you hover over the tool, you'll see the tool tip name and the keyboard command associated with the tool. Hold the cursor for a bit longer, and a cue card appears that gives a brief explanation of how to use the tool.

DON'T GET STUCK ON THE PROMPTS

In many of the exercises in this book, we'll mention the Command prompt that appears in the Command window. The prompts are shown for your reference, but don't let yourself get too bogged down by them. For example, we'll say, "At the `Specify lower left corner or [ON/OFF] <0.0000,0.0000>:` prompt, press ↵." The important part is to press ↵. You can skim over the prompt. Just keep in mind that the prompts can offer some direction and show the options for the current command. They can also serve as helpful reminders later when you're working on your own.

You see several tools in the Home tab's Draw and Modify panels. In Chapter 1, you saw that if you click the arrow in a panel's title bar, the panel expands to reveal more tools (see Figure 2.3). Once you've selected a tool from the expanded Draw or Modify panel, the expanded panel closes. If you want to keep the expanded panel open, click the pushpin icon at the left end of the expanded panel's title bar.

FIGURE 2.3
The Home tab's Draw
and Modify panel tools

Starting Your First Drawing

In Chapter 1, you looked at a preexisting sample drawing. This time, you'll begin to draw your own drawing by creating a door that will be used in later exercises. First, though, you must learn how to tell AutoCAD what you want, and, even more important, you must understand what AutoCAD wants from you.

IMPERIAL AND METRIC

In this chapter, you'll start to see instructions for both Imperial and metric measurements. In general, you'll see the instructions for Imperial measurement first, followed by the metric instructions. You won't be dealing with inches or centimeters yet, however. You're just getting to know the AutoCAD system.

You'll start by setting the size of the work area, known as the drawing *limits*. These limits aren't fixed in any way, and you aren't forced to stay within the bounds of the drawing limits unless the Limits command's ON/OFF option is turned on. But limits can help to establish a starting area from which you can expand your drawing.

You currently have a new blank file, but it's a little difficult to tell the size of your drawing area. Let's set up the work area so that you have a better idea of the space with which you're working:

1. Enter **Limits**↵.

2. At the Specify lower left corner or [ON/OFF] <0.0000,0.0000>: prompt, press ↵.

3. At the Specify upper right corner <12.0000,9.0000>: prompt, press ↵ to accept the default of 12.0000,9.0000. Metric users should enter **40,30**↵.

4. Type **Z↵ A↵** for the Zoom All command. You can also select Zoom All from the Zoom flyout on the Navigation bar.

5. Metric users do the following: Open the Application menu and choose Drawing Utilities ➤ Units or enter **Units↵**. In the Units dialog box, select Centimeters from the Insertion Scale panel's drop-down list and click OK. See "Inserted Drawings Not to Scale?" in Chapter 25, "Managing and Sharing Your Drawings," for more on the Insertion Scale setting.

In step 4, the All option of the Zoom command uses the limits you set up in steps 2 and 3 to determine the display area. In a drawing that contains objects, the Zoom tool's All option displays the limits plus the area occupied by the objects in the drawing if they happen to fall outside the limits. Now give your file a unique name:

1. Choose Save As from the Application menu or type **Saveas↵** to open the Save Drawing As dialog box.

2. Type **Door**. As you type, the name appears in the File Name text box.

3. Save your file in the My Documents folder or, if you prefer, save it in another folder of your choosing. Just remember where you put it because you'll use it later.

4. Click Save. You now have a file called Door.dwg, located in the My Documents folder. Of course, your drawing doesn't contain anything yet. You'll take care of that next.

UNDERSTANDING THE DRAWING AREA

The new file shows a drawing area roughly 12 inches wide by 9 inches high. Metric users have a file that shows an area roughly 40 centimeters (cm) wide by 30 cm high. This is just the area you're given to start with, but you're not limited to it in any way. No visual clues indicate the size of the area. To check the area size for yourself, move the crosshair cursor to the upper-right corner of the drawing area and observe the value in the coordinate readout in the lower-left corner. The coordinate readout won't show exactly 12'9 inches, or 40'30 cm for metric, because the proportions of your drawing area aren't likely to be exactly 12'9 or 40'30. AutoCAD does try to optimize the display for the drawing area when you choose the All option of the Zoom command.

Now you can start to explore the drawing process. To begin a drawing, follow these steps:

1. Click the Line tool on the Home tab's Draw panel, or type **L↵**.

   You've just issued the Line command. AutoCAD responds in two ways. First, you see the message

   `Specify first point:`

   in the Command prompt, asking you to select a point to begin your line. Also, the cursor changes its appearance; it no longer has a square in the crosshairs. This is a clue telling you to pick a point to start a line.

2. Using the left mouse button, select a point on the screen just a little to the left and below the center of the drawing area (see Figure 2.4). After you select the point, AutoCAD changes the prompt to this:

   `Specify next point or [Undo]:`

FIGURE 2.4
A rubber-banding
line

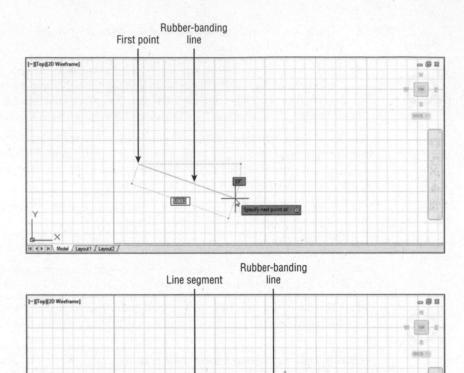

Now, as you move the mouse around, notice the line with one end fixed on the point you just selected and the other end following the cursor in a *rubber-banding* motion (see the first image in Figure 2.4). You also see a message at the cursor asking you to Specify next point or.

3. Move the cursor to a location directly to the left or right of the point you clicked, and you'll see a dashed horizontal line appear along with a different message at the cursor. This action also occurs when you point directly up or down. Your cursor seems to jump to a horizontal or vertical position.

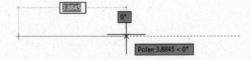

This feature is called *Polar Tracking*. Like a T square or triangle, it helps restrict your line to an exact horizontal or vertical direction. You can turn Polar Tracking on or off by clicking the Polar Tracking tool in the status bar. You'll learn more about this tool in Chapter 3.

4. Continue with the Line command. Move the cursor to a point below and to the right of the first point you selected and click again. You've just drawn a line segment, and a second rubber-banding line appears (see the second image in Figure 2.4).

5. If the line you drew isn't the exact length you want, you can back up during the Line command and change it. To do this, type **U↵**. The line you drew previously rubber-bands as if you hadn't selected the second point to fix its length.

6. Right-click and select Enter. This terminates the Line command.

The Undo and Redo tools in the Quick Access toolbar offer Undo and Redo drop-down lists from which you can select the exact command you want to undo or redo. See the sidebar "Getting Out of Trouble" later in this chapter for more information.

You've just drawn, and then undrawn, a line of an arbitrary length. In step 6 of the previous exercise, you were asked to terminate the Line command. If you happen to forget that a command is still active, two onscreen clues can remind you of the status of AutoCAD. If you don't see the words Type a Command in the Command window, a command is still active. Also, the cursor is the plain crosshair without the box at its intersection.

Many tools will display a small icon or *badge* next to the cursor. The badge will be similar to the tool's icon in most cases. A red X appears when you hover over an object while using the Erase tool. A question mark appears when you use the Measure, ID, or List tool.

From now on, we'll refer to the crosshair cursor without the small box as the Point Selection mode of the cursor. Figure 2.5 shows all the modes of the drawing cursor.

FIGURE 2.5
The drawing cursor's modes

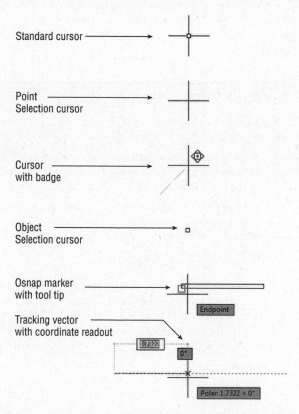

Standard cursor

Point Selection cursor

Cursor with badge

Object Selection cursor

Osnap marker with tool tip

Tracking vector with coordinate readout

Why Use the Keyboard Commands?

For many years, Autodesk has been encouraging users to move away from the command line and keyboard method of command entry, but it seems that AutoCAD users will have none of that. Although you would expect "grizzled veteran" users to stick with the keyboard entry method, you might be surprised to find that young, "fresh out of school" apprentice architects also prefer the keyboard over the newer palettes and ribbons in AutoCAD.

We made this observation to one of the designers of AutoCAD at a recent Autodesk function. Without hesitation, he answered that "keyboard entry is much faster." In our experience, it isn't just faster. Entering commands via the keyboard gives you a more "connected" feeling with AutoCAD. Work seems to flow much smoother. If you learn the keyboard commands, you'll also find that customizing AutoCAD is much easier. So for these reasons, we encourage you to try both the keyboard and the buttons to see which you prefer. You'll find that, wherever possible, we'll give the keyboard command equivalent to a tool selection in the exercises of this book. Remember that a tool's tool tip will also show its keyboard command.

Specifying Exact Distances with Coordinates

Certification
Objective

Next, you'll continue with the Line command to draw a plan view (an overhead view) of a door, to no particular scale. This will give you some practice in drawing objects to exact distances. Later, you'll resize the drawing for use in future exercises. The door will be 3 units long and 0.15 units thick. For metric users, the door will be 9 units long and 0.5 units thick. To specify these exact distances in AutoCAD, you can use either relative polar coordinates or Cartesian coordinates.

Getting Out of Trouble

Beginners and experts alike are bound to make a few mistakes. Before you get too far into the exercise, here are some powerful but easy-to-use tools to help you recover from accidents:

Backspace If you make a typing error, press the Backspace key to back up to your error and then retype your command or response. The Backspace key is in the upper-right corner of the main keyboard area.

Escape (Esc) This is perhaps the single most important key on your keyboard. When you need to exit a command or a dialog box quickly without making changes, press the Esc key in the upper-left corner of your keyboard. In most cases, you need to press Esc only once, although it won't hurt to press it twice. (Press Esc before editing with grips or issuing commands through the keyboard.)

U If you accidentally change something in the drawing and want to reverse that change, click the Undo tool in the Quick Access toolbar (the left-pointing curved arrow). You can also type **U↵** at the Command prompt. Each time you do this, AutoCAD undoes one operation at a time, in reverse order. The last command performed is undone first, then the next-to-last command, and so on. The prompt displays the name of the command being undone, and the drawing reverts to its state prior to that command being issued. If you need to, you can undo everything back to the beginning of an editing session. You can also select the exact command to back up to by using the Undo drop-down list in the Quick Access toolbar.

You can open the Undo drop-down list by clicking the down-pointing arrow found to the right of the Undo tool.

Undo If you want more control over the way Undo works, you can use the Undo command. This command allows you to "bookmark" places to which you can "undo" in your editing session. Type **Undo⏎**, and you'll see the Enter the number of operations to undo or [Auto/Control/BEgin/End/Mark/Back] <1>: prompt. Enter a number indicating the number of steps you want to undo. Use the Mark option to bookmark a location; then use Back to undo your work to that bookmark. You can use Begin and End to mark the beginning and ending of a set of operations that will be undone all at once. Control offers options to control the behavior of the Undo command. Auto is an option that is on by default and causes AutoCAD to undo the action of the whole command rather than the individual actions within a command.

Redo If you accidentally undo one too many commands, you can redo the last undone command by clicking the Redo tool (the right-pointing curved arrow) in the Quick Access toolbar, or you can type **Redo⏎**. You can redo several operations that you may have undone with the **Undo** command. You can also select the exact command to redo by using the Redo drop-down list in the Quick Access toolbar.

Oops If you've deleted something and gone on to use other commands, you can restore the last deleted object or objects by using the Oops command. Oops enables you to restore the last deleted set of objects without having to undo a series of commands.

The Imperial and metric distances aren't equivalent in the exercises in this chapter. For example, 3 units in the Imperial-based drawing aren't equal to 9 metric units. These distances are arbitrary and based on how they appear in the figures in this chapter.

Specifying Polar Coordinates

To enter the exact distance of 3 (or 9 metric) units to the right of the last point you selected, do the following:

1. Click the Line tool on the Home tab's Draw panel, or type **L⏎**.

2. Click a point slightly to the left of the center of the drawing area to select the start point.

3. Type **@3<0**. Metric users should type **@9<0**. As you type, the letters appear at the Command prompt.

4. Press ⏎. A line appears, starting from the first point you picked and ending 3 units to the right of it (see Figure 2.6). You've just entered a relative polar coordinate.

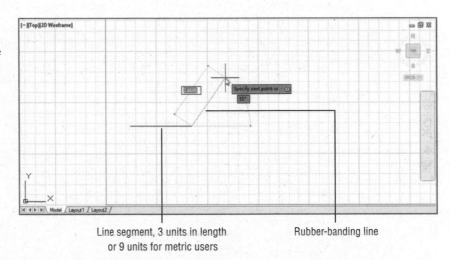

FIGURE 2.6
Notice that the rubber-banding line now starts from the last point selected. This indicates that you can continue to add more line segments.

Line segment, 3 units in length or 9 units for metric users   Rubber-banding line

The "at" sign (@) you entered tells AutoCAD that the coordinate you're specifying is from the last point you selected. The 3 (or 9, metric) is the distance, and the less-than symbol (<) tells AutoCAD that you're designating the angle at which the line is to be drawn. The last part is the value for the angle, which in this case is 0 for 0°. This is how to use polar coordinates to communicate distances and directions to AutoCAD.

If you're accustomed to a different method for describing directions, you can set AutoCAD to use a vertical direction as 0°. See Chapter 3 for details.

Angles are given based on the system shown in Figure 2.7, in which 0° is a horizontal direction from left to right, 90° is straight up, 180° is horizontal from right to left, and so on. You can specify degrees, minutes, and seconds of arc if you want to be that exact. You can also specify angles using negative values, which would mirror the direction around the x-axis. For example, a minus 45° angle would point in the direction shown as 315° in Figure 2.7. We'll discuss angle formats in more detail in Chapter 3.

Figure 2.7
AutoCAD default system for specifying angles

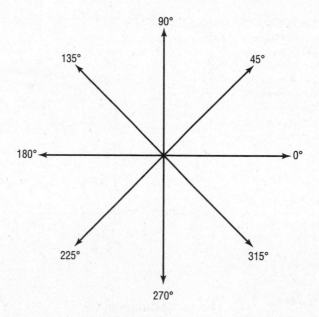

Specifying Relative Cartesian Coordinates

For the next line segment, let's try another method for specifying exact distances:

1. Enter @0,0.15↵. Metric users should enter @0,0.5↵. A short line appears above the end-point of the last line. Once again, @ tells AutoCAD that the coordinate you specify is from the last point picked. But in this example, you give the distance in X and Y values. The X distance, 0, is given first, followed by a comma, and then the Y distance, 0.15 or 0.5. This is how to specify distances in relative Cartesian coordinates.

> **COMMAS AND PERIODS**
>
> Step 1 indicates that metric users should enter **@0,0.5**↵ for the distance. Instead, you could enter **@0,.5** (zero comma point five). The leading zero is included for clarity. European metric users should be aware that the comma is used as a separator between the X and Y components of the coordinate. In AutoCAD, commas aren't used for decimal points; you must use a period to denote a decimal point.

2. Enter @-3,0↵. Metric users should enter @-9,0↵. This distance is also in X,Y values, but here you use a negative value to specify the X distance. The result is a drawing that looks like Figure 2.8.

   Positive values in the Cartesian coordinate system are from left to right and from bottom to top (see Figure 2.9). (You may remember this from your high school geometry class!) If you want to draw a line from right to left, you must designate a negative value. It's also helpful to know where the origin of the drawing lies. In a new drawing, the origin—or coordinate 0,0—is in the lower-left corner of the drawing.

FIGURE 2.8
The Line tool was used to draw these three sides of the door. Points are specified by using either relative Cartesian or polar coordinates.

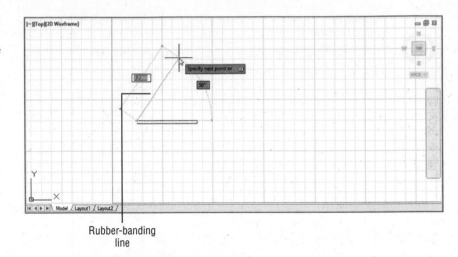

Rubber-banding
line

FIGURE 2.9
Positive and negative Cartesian coordinate directions

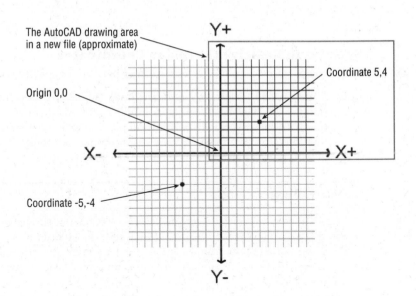

3. Type **C↵**. This C stands for the Close option. You can also click the Close option in the command line or right-click and select Close from the context menu. A line connecting the first and last points of a sequence of lines is drawn (see Figure 2.10), and the Line command terminates. The rubber-banding line also disappears, telling you that AutoCAD has finished drawing line segments. You can also use the rubber-banding line to indicate direction while simultaneously entering the distance through the keyboard. See the sidebar "Other Ways to Enter Distances" later in this chapter.

FIGURE 2.10

Distance and direction input for the door. Distances for metric users are shown in brackets.

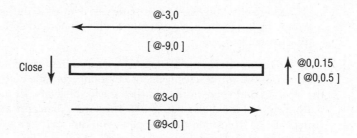

To finish drawing a series of lines without closing them, you can press Esc, ↵, or the spacebar.

Interpreting the Cursor Modes and Understanding Prompts

The key to working with AutoCAD successfully is understanding the way it interacts with you. The following sections will help you become familiar with some of the ways AutoCAD prompts you for input. Understanding the format of the messages in the Command window and recognizing other events on the screen will help you learn the program more easily.

Understanding Cursor Modes

As the Command window aids you with messages, the cursor gives you clues about what to do. Earlier in this chapter, Figure 2.5 illustrates the various modes of the cursor, and it gives a brief description of the role of each mode. Take a moment to study this figure.

Standard Cursor   The Standard cursor tells you that AutoCAD is waiting for instructions. You can also edit objects by using grips when you see this cursor. *Grips* are squares, rectangles, or arrowheads that appear at endpoints and at the midpoint of objects when they're selected. (You might know them as *workpoints* from other graphics programs.)

Point Selection Cursor   The Point Selection cursor appears whenever AutoCAD expects point input. It can also appear in conjunction with a rubber-banding line. You can either click a point or enter a coordinate through the keyboard.

Cursor with Badge   The Cursor with Badge lets you know at a glance which tool you are using. The badge will be similar to the tool icon currently being used. A red X badge appears when you hover over an object while using the Erase tool. A question mark badge appears when you use the Measure, ID, or List tool.

Object Selection or Pickbox Cursor   The Object Selection or Pickbox cursor tells you that you must select objects—either by clicking them or by using any of the object-selection options available.

Osnap (Object Snap) Marker   The osnap (object snap) marker appears along with the Point Selection cursor when you invoke an osnap. Osnaps let you accurately select specific points on an object, such as endpoints or midpoints.

Tracking Vector   The tracking vector appears when you use the Polar Tracking or Object Snap Tracking feature. Polar Tracking aids you in drawing orthogonal lines, and Object Snap

Tracking helps you align a point in space relative to the geometry of existing objects. Object Snap Tracking works in conjunction with osnaps. You'll learn more about the tracking vector in Chapter 3.

Certification
Objective

If you're an experienced AutoCAD user, you may prefer to use the old-style crosshair cursor that crosses the entire screen. Choose Options from the bottom of the Application menu to open the Options dialog box, and then click the Display tab. Set the Crosshair Size option near the bottom right of the dialog box to 100. The cursor then appears as it did in previous versions of AutoCAD. As the option name implies, you can set the crosshair size to any percentage of the screen you want. The default is 5 percent.

OTHER WAYS TO ENTER DISTANCES

Certification
Objective

A third method for entering distances is to point in a direction with a rubber-banding line and then enter the distance through the keyboard. For example, to draw a line 3 units long from left to right, click the Line tool on the Home tab's Draw panel, click a start point, and then move the cursor so that the rubber-banding line points to the right at some arbitrary distance. With the cursor pointing in the direction you want, type **3**↵. The rubber-banding line becomes a fixed line 3 units long. Using this method, called the *Direct Distance method*, along with the Ortho mode or Polar Tracking (described in Chapter 3), can be a fast way to draw orthogonal lines of specific lengths.

You can also specify an exact angle along with the distance. For example, start the Line command and then pick the first point. Type **3** for the length, but don't press ↵. Press the Tab key instead. The line segment will become fixed at 3 units, and as you move the cursor, the segment will rotate freely around the first point. Next, type an angle in degrees, **30**↵ for example, and the line will be drawn at 30 degrees. Or, instead of typing in an angle, just adjust the angle of the line visually until you see the angle you want on the Dynamic Input temporary angle dimension and then click.

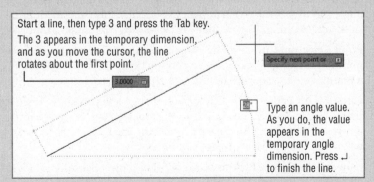

If you watch the temporary dimensions as you press the Tab key, you'll see that the Tab key lets you move from the length dimension to the angle dimension and back again. You can press the Tab key at any time to shift back and forth between dimensions. A lock appears next to a dimension that you have entered, telling you that the dimension is "locked" until you tab to it again.

You'll learn more about how to enter values with Dynamic Input's temporary dimensions later in this chapter.

Choosing Command Options

Many commands in AutoCAD offer several options, which are often presented to you in the Command window in the form of a prompt. This section uses the Arc command to illustrate the format of AutoCAD prompts.

Usually, in a floor plan drawing in the United States, an arc is drawn to indicate the direction of a door swing. Figure 2.11 shows other standard symbols used in architectural-style drawings.

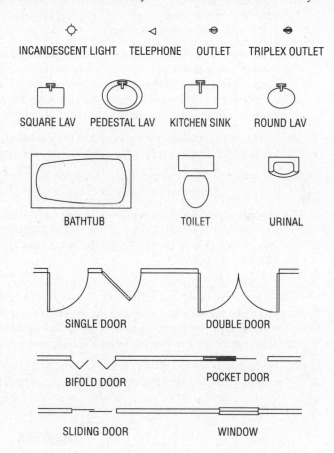

FIGURE 2.11

Samples of standard symbols used in architectural drawings

INCANDESCENT LIGHT   TELEPHONE   OUTLET   TRIPLEX OUTLET

SQUARE LAV   PEDESTAL LAV   KITCHEN SINK   ROUND LAV

BATHTUB   TOILET   URINAL

SINGLE DOOR   DOUBLE DOOR

BIFOLD DOOR   POCKET DOOR

SLIDING DOOR   WINDOW

Next, you'll draw the arc for the door you started in the previous exercise:

1. Click the 3-Point Arc tool in the Home tab's Draw panel. Click the Arc flyout and select 3-Point. The Specify start point of arc or [Center]: prompt appears in the Command window, and the cursor changes to Point Selection mode. You also see the prompt Specify start point of arc or prompt next to the cursor.

   Examine the Specify start point of arc or [Center]: prompt. The prompt contains two options. The default is stated in the main part of the prompt, which is to specify the start point of the arc. If other options are available, they appear within square brackets. In the Arc command, you see the word Center within brackets telling you that, if you prefer, you can also start your arc by selecting a center point instead of a start point. If multiple options are available, they appear within the brackets and are set off with a slightly darker background. This background tells you that the option is selectable using your cursor and also aids in separating option names. The default is the option AutoCAD assumes you intend to use unless you tell it otherwise.

2. Type C↵ to select the Center option or click the word Center in the command line. The Specify center point of arc: prompt appears. Notice that you had to type only the C and not the entire word Center.

When you see a set of options in the Command window, note their capitalization. If you choose to respond to prompts by using the keyboard, these capitalized letters are all you need to enter to select the option. In some cases, the first two letters are capitalized to differentiate two options that begin with the same letter, such as LAyer and LType. You can also just click the option name in the Command prompt to select the option.

3. Pick a point representing the center of the arc near the upper-left corner of the door (see Figure 2.12). The Specify start point of arc: prompt appears.

4. Type @3<0↵. Metric users should type @9<0↵. The Specify end point of arc (hold Ctrl to switch direction) or [Angle chord Length]: prompt appears.

5. Move the mouse and a temporary arc appears, originating from a point 3 units to the right of the center point you selected and rotating about that center, as shown in Figure 2.12. (Metric users will see the temporary arc originating 9 units to the right of the center point.)

As the prompt indicates, you now have three options. You can enter an angle, a chord length, or the endpoint of the arc. The prompt default, to specify the endpoint of the arc, picks the arc's endpoint. Again, the cursor is in Point Selection mode, telling you it's waiting for point input. To select this default option, you only need to pick a point on the screen indicating where you want the endpoint.

6. Move the cursor so that it points in a vertical direction from the center of the arc. You'll see the Polar Tracking vector snap to a vertical position.

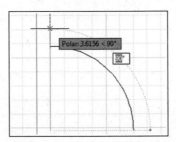

7. Click any location with the Polar Tracking vector in the vertical position. The arc is now fixed in place, as shown in Figure 2.12.

FIGURE 2.12
Using the Arc
command

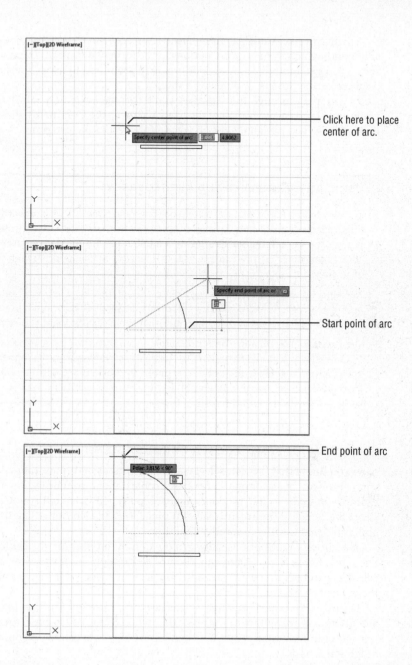

This exercise has given you some practice working with AutoCAD Command window prompts and entering keyboard commands—skills you'll need when you start to use advanced AutoCAD functions.

As you can see, AutoCAD has a distinct structure in its prompt messages. You first issue a command, which in turn offers options in the form of a prompt. Depending on the option you select, you get another set of options or you're prompted to take some action, such as picking a point, selecting objects, or entering a value.

As you work through the exercises, you'll become intimately familiar with this routine. After you understand the workings of the Ribbon panels, the Command window prompts, and the dialog boxes, you can almost teach yourself the rest of the program!

USING AUTOCOMPLETE AND AUTOCORRECT

You may have noticed that as you enter a command through the keyboard, the Command window offers suggestions to complete your typing in a way similar to many web browsers. For example, if you type **LI**, a list pops up offering a number of commands that start with *LI*. You can then click the option that you want to use. This feature can be helpful when you forget the full name of a command.

AutoCorrect works in a similar way, but instead of offering a list of commands that start with the letters you type, AutoCAD will try to "correct" a mistyped command. For example, if you type **crl**, AutoCAD will display several commands that come close to what you typed.

You can also control how the AutoComplete and AutoCorrect features work. Right-click in the Command window, and then point to the Input Settings option that appears in the context menu. You can then toggle several options on or off. The options are AutoComplete, AutoCorrect, Search System Variables, Search Content, Mid-string Search, and Delay Time.

SELECTING OPTIONS FROM A CONTEXT MENU

Now you know that you can select command options by typing them. You can also right-click at any time during a command to open a context menu containing those same options. For example, in step 2 in the previous exercise, you typed **C↵** to tell AutoCAD that you wanted to select the center of the arc. Instead of typing, you can also right-click to open a menu of options applicable to the Arc command at that time.

Certification Objective
In addition to the options shown in the Command prompt, the context menu shows you a few more: Enter, Cancel, Pan, and Zoom. The Enter option is the same as pressing ↵. Cancel cancels the current command. Pan and Zoom let you adjust your view as you're working through the current command.

The menu is context sensitive, so you see only those options that pertain to the command or activity that is currently in progress. Also, when AutoCAD is expecting a point, an object selection, or a numeric value, right-clicking doesn't display a context menu. Instead, AutoCAD treats a right-click as ↵.

The location of your cursor when you right-click determines the contents of the list of available operations. A right-click in the Command window displays a list of operations that you can apply to the command line, such as repeating one of the last several commands you've used or copying the most recent history of command activity to the Clipboard.

A right-click in the drawing area when no command is active displays a set of basic options for editing your file, such as the command most recently used, Undo, Redo, Pan, and Zoom, to name a few (see Figure 2.13). The Cut, Copy, and Paste commands can be found under the Clipboard option.

FIGURE 2.13
A set of basic options

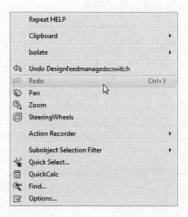

If you're ever in doubt about what to do in AutoCAD, you can right-click to see a list of options. You'll learn more about these options later in this book. For now, let's move on to the topic of selecting objects.

HOW WE'LL SHOW COMMAND OPTIONS

As mentioned earlier, the options in the command line are shown with a slightly darker background color so that you can easily determine the name of the options (see Figure 2.14).

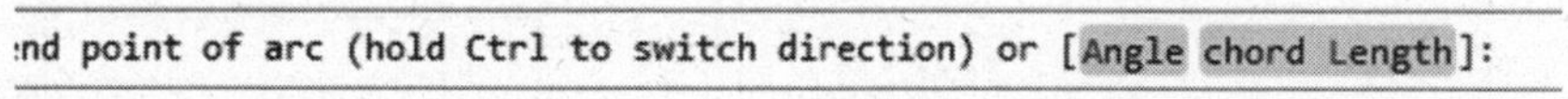

FIGURE 2.14
The Angle and chord Length options are separated by a gray background.

```
nd point of arc (hold Ctrl to switch direction) or [Angle chord Length]:
```

Unfortunately, it's a bit more difficult to show the options in the same way in this book. Thus, from now on when we show the command options, we'll use a forward slash mark to separate the options. For example, in the Arc command options discussed earlier, you saw this command prompt:

```
Specify end point of arc or [Angle chord Length]
```

We'll show it like this, using the / symbol to separate the command options:

```
Specify end point of arc or [Angle/chord Length]
```

Without the / symbol, you might confuse the option names as Angle chord and Length, or you may even think that there are three options named Angle, chord, and Length. Those of you familiar with older versions of AutoCAD will recognize this use of the / symbol as the way AutoCAD used to separate command options in the command line.

Selecting Objects

In AutoCAD, you can select objects in many ways. The following sections cover two ways: object-selection methods unique to AutoCAD and the Noun/Verb method, the more common selection method used in most popular graphics programs. Because these two methods play a major role in working with AutoCAD, it's a good idea to familiarize yourself with them early on.

If you need to select objects by their characteristics rather than by their location, see Chapter 14, "Advanced Editing and Organizing," which describes the Quick Select and Object Selection Filters tools. These tools let you easily select a set of objects based on their properties, including object type, color, layer assignment, and so on.

Selecting Objects in AutoCAD

With many AutoCAD commands, you'll see the Select objects: prompt. Along with this prompt, the cursor changes from crosshairs to the Object Selection cursor (look back at Figure 2.5). Whenever you see the Select objects: prompt and the square Pickbox cursor, you have several options while making your selection. Often, as you select objects on the screen, you'll change your mind about a selection or accidentally select an object that you don't want. Let's look at most of the selection options available in AutoCAD and learn what to do when you make the wrong selection.

Before you continue, you'll turn off two features that, although extremely useful, can be confusing to new users. These features are called Running Osnaps and Osnap Tracking. You'll get a chance to explore these features in depth later in this book, but for now follow these steps to turn them off:

1. Check to see if either Object Snap or Object Snap Tracking is turned on in the status bar. If they're turned on, they will be a light blue.

2. To turn off Object Snap, click the tool in the status bar. When turned off, it will change to gray.

Now, let's see how to select an object in AutoCAD:

1. Choose Move from the Home tab's Modify panel, or type **M↵**.

2. At the Select objects: prompt, click each of the two horizontal lines that constitute the door. As you know, whenever AutoCAD wants you to select objects, the cursor turns into the small square pickbox. This tells you that you're in Object Selection mode. As you place the cursor over an object, it appears thicker to give you a better idea of what you're about to select. As you click an object, it's highlighted, as shown in Figure 2.15.

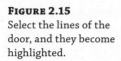

FIGURE 2.15
Select the lines of the door, and they become highlighted.

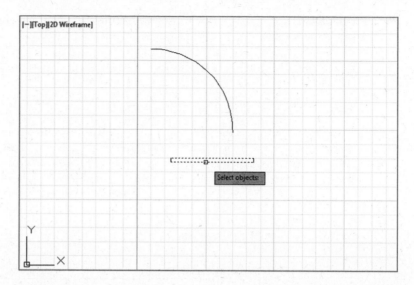

If objects don't become "thicker" as you roll over them with your selection cursor, the Selection preview system variable may be turned off. You can turn it back on by entering **selectionpreview**↵ 3↵. This setting can also be found in the Selection tab of the Options dialog box. See Appendix B for more on the Options dialog box, and see Bonus Chapter 4, "System Variables and Dimension Styles," for more on system variables, available at www.omura.com/chapters.

3. After making your selections, you may decide to deselect some items. Enter **U**↵ from the keyboard. Notice that one line is no longer highlighted. When you type **U**↵, objects are deselected, one at a time, in reverse order of selection.

4. You can deselect objects in another way. Hold down the Shift key and click the remaining highlighted line. It reverts to a solid line, showing you that it's no longer selected for editing.

5. By now, you've deselected both lines. Let's try another method for selecting groups of objects. To select objects with a window selection, type **W**↵. The cursor changes to a Point Selection cursor, and the prompt changes to

```
Specify first corner:
```

Certification
Objective

6. Click a point below and to the left of the rectangle representing the door. As you move your cursor across the screen, a selection window appears and stretches across the drawing area. Also notice that the window has a blue tint.

7. After the selection window completely encloses the door but not the arc, click this location to highlight the entire door. This window selects only objects that are completely enclosed by the window, as shown in Figure 2.16.

Don't confuse the selection window you're creating here with the zoom window you used in Chapter 1, which defines an area of the drawing you want to enlarge. Remember that the Window option works differently under the Zoom command than it does for other editing commands.

FIGURE 2.16
Selecting the door in a
selection window

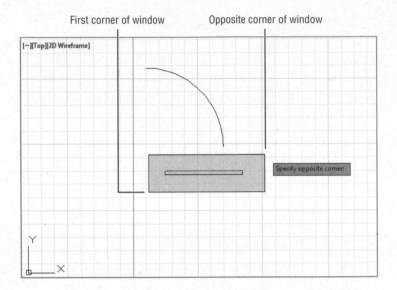

First corner of window   Opposite corner of window

[−][Top][2D Wireframe]

Specify opposite corner:

8. Press ↵. This tells AutoCAD that you've finished selecting objects. It's important to remember to press ↵ as soon as you finish selecting the objects you want to edit. A new prompt, `Specify base point or [Displacement] <Displacement>:`, appears. The cursor changes to its Point Selection mode.

Now you've seen how the selection process works in AutoCAD—but you're in the middle of the Move command. The next section discusses the prompt that's on your screen and describes how to enter base points and displacement distances.

CONTROLLING THE STATUS BAR DISPLAY

Toward the right side of the status bar, you'll see a tool icon with three horizontal lines. This tool opens a menu that controls the display of the status bar. You use this menu to turn the items in the status bar on or off. A check mark by an item indicates that it's currently on. If for some reason you don't see all of the buttons mentioned in the following exercise, check this menu to make sure all the status bar options are turned on. For the items in the left half of the status bar, choose Status Toggles from the menu.

Providing Base Points

When you move or copy objects, AutoCAD prompts you for a base point, which is a difficult concept to grasp. AutoCAD must be told specifically *from* where and *to* where the move occurs. The *base point* is the exact location from which you determine the distance and direction of the move. After the base point is determined, you can tell AutoCAD where to move the object in relation to that point.

Follow these steps to practice using base points:

1. To select a base point, press Shift+right-click. A menu appears, displaying the Object Snap options (see Figure 2.17).

FIGURE 2.17
The Object Snap options

When you right-click, make sure that the cursor is within the AutoCAD drawing area; otherwise, you won't get the results described in this book.

2. Choose Intersection from the Object Snap menu. The Object Snap menu closes.

3. Move the cursor to the lower-right corner of the door. Notice that as you approach the corner, a small x-shaped graphic appears on the corner. This is called an *osnap marker*.

4. After the x-shaped marker appears, hold the mouse motionless for a second or two. A tool tip appears, telling you the current osnap point that AutoCAD has selected.

5. Click the left mouse button to select the intersection indicated by the osnap marker. Whenever you see the osnap marker at the point you want to select, you don't have to point exactly at the location with your cursor. Just left-click to select the exact osnap point (see Figure 2.18). In this case, you selected the exact intersection of two lines.

FIGURE 2.18

Using the Point Selection cursor and osnap marker

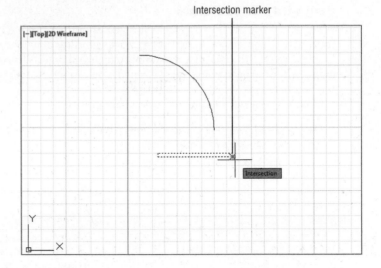

6. At the `Specify second point or <use first point as displacement>:` prompt, hold down the Shift key and right-click again to open the Object Snap menu.

7. This time, you'll use the Endpoint osnap, but instead of clicking the option with the mouse, type **E**.

8. Pick the lower-right end of the arc you drew earlier. (Remember that you need to move your cursor close to the endpoint just until the osnap marker appears.) The door moves so that the corner connects exactly with the endpoint of the arc (see Figure 2.19).

FIGURE 2.19

Moving the rectangle to its new position using the Endpoint osnap

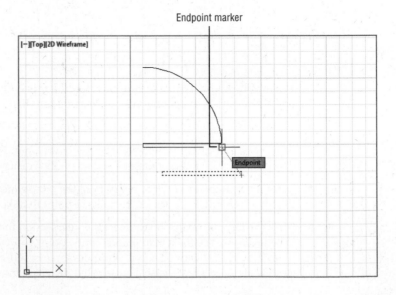

As you can see, the osnap options let you select specific points on an object. You used Endpoint and Intersection in this exercise, but other options are available. Chapter 3 discusses some of the other osnap options. You may have also noticed that the osnap marker is different for each of the options you used. You'll learn more about osnaps in Chapter 3. Now let's continue with our look at point selection.

You may have noticed the statement Use first point as displacement in the prompt in step 6 of the preceding exercise. This means that if you press ↵ instead of clicking a point, the object will move a distance based on the coordinates of the point you selected as a base point. If, for example, the point you click for the base point is at coordinate 2,4, the object will move 2 units in the x-axis and 4 units in the y-axis.

If you want to specify an exact distance and direction by typing a value, select any point on the screen as a base point. As an alternative, you can type @ followed by ↵ at the base point prompt; then, enter the second point's location in relative coordinates. Remember that @ means the last point selected. In the next exercise, you'll try moving the entire door an exact distance of 1 unit at a 45° angle. Metric users will move the door 3 units at a 45° angle. Here are the steps:

1. Click the Move tool on the Home tab's Modify panel.

2. Type **P**↵. The set of objects you selected in the previous exercise is highlighted. P is a selection option that selects the previously selected set of objects.

3. You're still in Object Selection mode, so click the arc to include it in the set of selected objects. The entire door, including the arc, is highlighted.

4. Press ↵ to tell AutoCAD that you've finished your selection. The cursor changes to Point Selection mode.

5. At the Specify base point or [Displacement] <Displacement>: prompt, choose a point on the screen between the door and the left side of the screen (see Figure 2.20).

FIGURE 2.20
The highlighted door and the base point just to the left of the door. Note that the base point doesn't need to be on the object that you're moving.

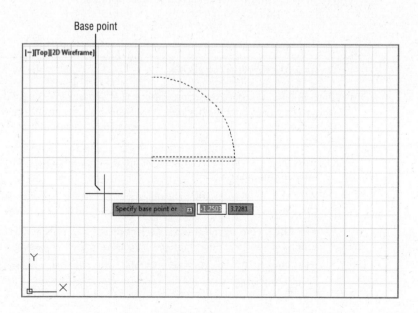

Base point

Specify base point or   -1.2503   3.7281

6. Move the cursor around slowly and notice that the door moves as if the base point you selected were attached to it. The door moves with the cursor, at a fixed distance from it. This demonstrates how the base point relates to the objects you select.

7. Type @1<-45↵. (Metric users should type @3<-45↵.) The door moves to a new location on the screen at a distance of 1 unit (3 for metric users) from its previous location and at an angle of minus 45°, which is a direction that is downward at a 45-degree angle.

If AutoCAD is waiting for a command, you can repeat the last command used by pressing the spacebar or pressing ↵. You can also right-click in the drawing area and select the option at the top of the list. If you right-click the Command window, a context menu offers an option for the most recent commands.

This exercise illustrates that the base point doesn't have to be on the object you're manipulating; it can be virtually anywhere on your drawing. You also saw how to reselect a group of objects that were selected previously without having to duplicate the selection process.

Using Noun/Verb Selection

Nearly all graphics programs today allow the Noun/Verb method for selecting objects. This method requires you to select objects before you issue a command to edit them—that is, you identify the "noun" (the object that you want to work on) before the "verb" (the action that you want to perform on it). The following exercises show you how to use the Noun/Verb method in AutoCAD.

You've seen that when AutoCAD is waiting for a command, it displays the crosshair cursor with the small square. As mentioned, this square is a pickbox superimposed on the cursor. It indicates that you can select objects even while the Command prompt appears at the bottom of the screen and no command is currently active. The square momentarily disappears when you're in a command that asks you to select points.

OTHER SELECTION OPTIONS

There are several other selection options that you haven't tried yet. You'll see how these options work in exercises later in this book. Or, if you're adventurous, try them now on your own. To use these options, type their keyboard abbreviations (shown in brackets in the following list) at any `Select objects:` prompt:

Add [A↵] Switches from Remove mode to the Add mode. See the description for Remove later in this sidebar.

All [ALL↵] Selects all of the objects in a drawing except those in frozen or locked layers. (See Chapter 5, "Keeping Track of Layers and Blocks," for information on layers.)

Box [B↵] Forces the standard selection window so that a left-to-right selection uses a standard window and a right-to-left selection uses a crossing window.

Crossing [C↵] Similar to the Window selection option (described later in this sidebar) but selects anything that is entirely within or crosses through the window that you define.

Crossing Polygon [CP↵]   Acts exactly like Window Polygon (described later in this sidebar), but like the Crossing selection option, selects anything that crosses through a polygon boundary.

Fence [F↵]   Selects objects that are crossed by a temporary line called a *fence*. This operation is like using a line to cross out the objects you want to select. After you invoke this option, you can then pick points, as when you're drawing a series of line segments. After you finish drawing the fence, press ↵, and then go on to select other objects or press ↵ again to finish your selection.

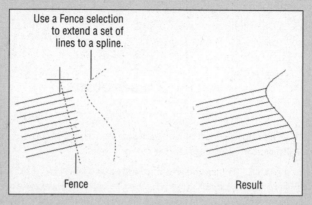

Use a Fence selection to extend a set of lines to a spline.

Fence   Result

Group [G↵]   Allows you to select a group by name.

Last [L↵]   Selects the last object you created.

Multiple [M↵]   Lets you select several objects first before AutoCAD highlights them. In a large file, selecting objects individually can cause AutoCAD to pause after each selection while it locates and highlights each object. The Multiple option can speed things up: First you select all of the objects quickly and then you highlight them all by pressing ↵. This has no menu equivalent.

Previous [P↵]   Selects the last object or set of objects that was edited or changed.

Remove [R↵]   Switches to a selection mode whereby the objects you click are removed from the selection set.

Subobject [SU↵]   Allows selection of faces, edges, and vertices of 3D solid objects. This can also be accomplished by pressing the Ctrl key while picking.

Object [O↵]   Ends selecting by Subobject and restores normal behavior.

Undo [U↵]   Removes the most recently added object from the selection set.

Window [W↵]   Forces a standard window selection. This option is useful when your drawing area is too crowded to use the Autoselect feature to place a window around a set of objects. (See the Auto entry later in this sidebar.) It prevents you from accidentally selecting an object with a single pick when you're placing your window.

Window Polygon [WP↵]   Lets you select objects by enclosing them in an irregularly shaped polygon boundary. When you use this option, you see the First polygon point: prompt. You then pick points to define the polygon boundary. As you pick points, the Specify endpoint of line or [Undo]: prompt appears. Select as many points as

continues

continued

you need to define the boundary. You can undo boundary line segments as you go by pressing **U**↵. With the boundary defined, press ↵. The bounded objects are highlighted and the `Select objects:` prompt returns, allowing you to use more selection options.

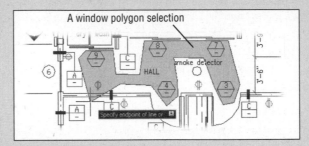

The following two selection options are also available but are seldom used. They're intended for use in creating custom menu options or custom tools:

Auto [AU↵]   Forces the standard automatic window or crossing window when a point is picked and no object is found. (See the section "Using Autoselect" later in this chapter.) You produce a standard window when you pick the two window corners from left to right, and you produce a crossing window when you pick the two corners from right to left. After you select this option, it remains active for the duration of the current command. Auto is intended for use on systems on which the Autoselect feature has been turned off.

Single [SI↵]   Forces the current command to select only a single object. If you use this option, you can pick a single object and the current command acts on that object as if you had pressed ↵ immediately after selecting it. This has no menu equivalent.

In addition to Noun/Verb selection, AutoCAD offers selection options that let you use familiar GUI techniques. See Appendix B to learn how you can control object-selection methods. This appendix also describes how to change the size of the Standard cursor.

Try moving objects by first selecting them and then using the Move command:

1. Press the Esc key twice to make sure that AutoCAD isn't in the middle of a command, which you might have accidentally issued. Then click the arc. The arc is highlighted, and you may also see squares appear at various points on the arc. As stated earlier, these squares are called *grips*. You'll get a chance to work with them later.

2. Choose Move from the Home tab's Modify panel. The cursor changes to Point Selection mode. Notice that the grips on the arc disappear but the arc is still selected.

3. At the `Specify base point or [Displacement] <Displacement>:` prompt, pick any point on the screen. The following prompt appears:

```
Specify second point or:
<use first point as displacement>:
```

4. Type **@1<0**↵. Metric users should type **@3<0**↵. The arc moves to a new location 1 unit (3 units for metric users) to the right.

If this exercise doesn't work as described here, chances are that the Noun/Verb setting has been turned off on your copy of AutoCAD. To turn on the Noun/Verb setting, choose Options from the Application menu to open the Options dialog box and then click the Selection tab. In the Selection Modes group, select the check box next to the Noun/Verb Selection option and click OK.

In this exercise, you picked the arc *before* issuing the Move command. Then, when you clicked the Move tool, you didn't see the `Select objects:` prompt. Instead, AutoCAD assumed that you wanted to move the arc that you selected and went directly to the `Specify base point or [Displacement] <Displacement>:` prompt.

USING AUTOSELECT

Next, you'll move the rest of the door in the same direction by using the Autoselect feature:

1. Pick a point just above and to the left of the rectangle representing the door. Be sure not to pick the door itself. A selection window appears that you can drag across the screen as you move the cursor. If you move the cursor to the left of the last point selected, the window outline appears dotted and there's a green tint inside the window (see the first image in Figure 2.21). If you move the cursor to the right of that point, the outline appears solid and there's a blue tint inside (see the second image in Figure 2.21).

FIGURE 2.21
The dotted window (first image) indicates a crossing selection; the solid window (second image) indicates a standard selection window.

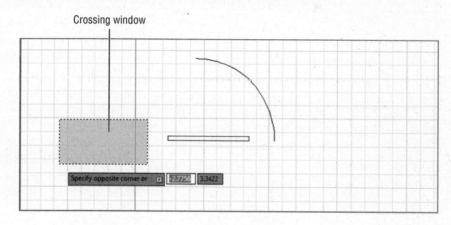

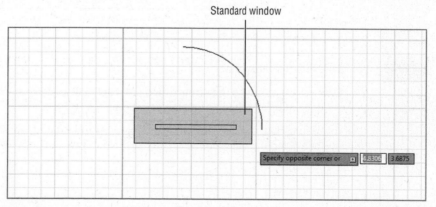

2. Pick a point below and to the right of the door so that the door, but not the arc, is completely enclosed by the window, as shown in the bottom image in Figure 2.21. The door is highlighted (and, again, you may see grips appear at the lines' endpoints and midpoints).

3. Click the Move tool again. Just as in the preceding exercise, the `Specify base point or [Displacement] <Displacement>:` prompt appears.

4. Pick any point on the screen; then enter **@1<0**↵. Metric users should enter **@3<0**↵. The door joins with the arc.

The two selection windows you've just seen—the blue solid one and the dotted green one—represent a standard window and a crossing window. If you use a *standard window,* anything completely within the window is selected. If you use a *crossing window,* anything that crosses through the window is selected. These two types of windows start automatically when you click any blank portion of the drawing area with a Standard cursor or a Point Selection cursor, hence the name *Autoselect.*

Next, you'll select objects with an automatic crossing window:

1. Pick a point below and to the right of the door. As you move the cursor left, the crossing (dotted) window appears.

2. Select the next point so that the window encloses the door and part of the arc (see Figure 2.22). The entire door, including the arc, is highlighted.

FIGURE 2.22
The door enclosed by a crossing window

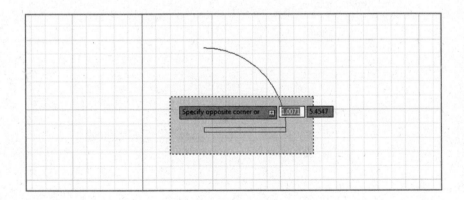

3. Click the Move tool.

4. Pick any point on the screen; then enter **@1<180**↵. Metric users should type **@3<180**↵. The door moves back to its original location.

You'll find that, in most cases, the Autoselect standard and crossing windows are all that you need when selecting objects. They really save you time, so you'll want to become familiar with these features.

MODIFYING AN AUTOSELECT WINDOW

Two settings, known as *system variables*, enable you to use the Autoselect feature in a more flexible way. These two settings, Pickdrag and Pickauto, control the behavior of the Autoselect window, giving you more options to select objects in your drawing.

Pickdrag   If you click to start a selection window and then decide that you want to use a window polygon, crossing polygon, or fence, you can type **W⏎** for a window polygon, **C⏎** for a crossing polygon, or **F⏎** for a fence. If this does not work, make sure that the Pickdrag system variable is set to 2 by typing **PICKDRAG⏎2⏎**.

Pickauto   In a crowded drawing, you may want to use a selection window, but objects close to the cursor may be selected instead. If you set Pickauto to 2 by typing **PICKAUTO⏎2⏎**, you can click and drag your mouse over an object in a crowded drawing without having the single object selected. AutoCAD will start a selection window instead. You can still use a single click to select a single object.

Before continuing, click the Save tool in the Quick Access toolbar to save the Door.dwg file. You won't want to save the changes you make in the next section, so saving now stores the current condition of the file on your hard disk for safekeeping.

RESTRICTIONS ON NOUN/VERB OBJECT SELECTION

For many of the modifying or construction-oriented commands, the Noun/Verb selection method is inappropriate because, for those commands, you must select more than one set of objects. You'll know whether a command accepts the Noun/Verb selection method right away. Commands that don't accept the Noun/Verb selection method clear the selection and then ask you to select an object or set of objects.

If you'd like to take a break, now is a good time to do so. If you want, exit AutoCAD, and return to this point in the chapter later. When you return, start AutoCAD and open the Door.dwg file.

CLICK AND DRAG TO LASSO OBJECTS

If you need to use an irregular-shaped window to select objects, you can use a click-and-drag motion to start a lasso selection. A lasso enables you to draw an irregular "freehand" selection window of any shape. Just as with the rectangular selection window, the direction of the lasso determines the method of selection. A clockwise lasso creates a standard window, and a counterclockwise lasso creates a crossing window.

Editing with Grips

Certification Objective

Earlier, when you selected the door, grips appeared at the endpoints, center points, and midpoints of the lines and arcs. You can use grips to make direct changes to the shape of objects or to move and copy them quickly.

If you didn't see grips on the door in the previous exercise, your version of AutoCAD may have the Grips feature turned off. To turn them on, refer to the information on grips in Appendix B.

So far, you've seen how operations in AutoCAD have a discrete beginning and ending. For example, to draw an arc, you first issue the Arc command and then go through a series of operations, including answering prompts and picking points. When you're finished, you have an arc and AutoCAD is ready for the next command.

The Grips feature plays by a different set of rules. Grips offer a small yet powerful set of editing functions that don't conform to the lockstep command/prompt/input routine that you've seen so far. As you work through the following exercises, it's helpful to think of grips as a subset of the standard method of operation in AutoCAD.

To practice using the Grips feature, you'll make some temporary modifications to the door drawing.

Stretching Lines by Using Grips

Certification
Objective

In this exercise, you'll stretch one corner of the door by grabbing the grip points of two lines:

1. Use the Zoom Realtime tool from the Zoom tool in the View tab's Navigate 2D panel to adjust your view so that the size of the door is similar to what is shown in Figure 2.23. You can click and drag the mouse wheel to pan the view if needed.

FIGURE 2.23
Stretching lines by using grips. The top image shows the rectangle's corner being stretched upward. The bottom image shows the new location of the corner at the top of the arc.

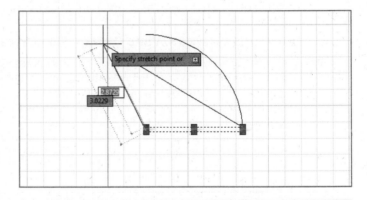

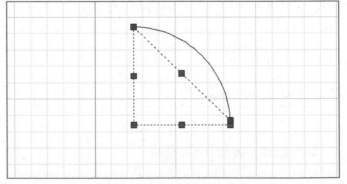

2. Press the Esc key to make sure that you're not in the middle of a command. Click a point below and to the left of the door to start a selection window.

3. Click above and to the right of the rectangular part of the door, placing the selection window around the door rectangle to select it.

4. Place the cursor on the lower-left corner grip of the rectangle, *but don't press the mouse button yet.* Notice that the cursor jumps to the grip point and that the grip is highlighted. You also see some dimensions related to the objects associated with the grip.

5. Move the cursor to another grip point. Notice again how the cursor jumps to it. When placed on a grip, the cursor moves to the exact center of the grip point. This means that, for example, if the cursor is placed on an endpoint grip, it's on the exact endpoint of the object.

6. Move the cursor to the upper-left corner grip of the rectangle and click. The grip becomes a solid color and is now a *hot grip.* The prompt displays the following message:

```
**STRETCH**
Specify stretch point or [Base point/Copy/Undo/eXit]:
```

This prompt tells you that Stretch mode is active. Notice the options in the prompt. As you move the cursor, the corner follows, and the lines of the rectangle stretch (see Figure 2.23).

You can control the size and color of grips by using the Selection tab in the Options dialog box; see Appendix B for details.

7. Move the cursor upward toward the top end of the arc and click that point. The rectangle deforms with the corner placed at your pick point (see Figure 2.23).

Here you saw that a command called Stretch is issued by clicking a grip point. As you'll see in these next steps, a handful of other hot-grip commands are also available:

1. Notice that the grips are still active. Click the grip point that you moved before to make it a hot grip again.

2. Right-click to open a context menu that contains a list of grip-edit options (see Figure 2.24).

FIGURE 2.24
A list of grip-edit options

When you click the joining grip point of two contiguous line segments, AutoCAD selects the overlapping grips of two lines. When you stretch the corner away from its original location, the endpoints of both lines follow.

3. Choose Base Point from the list, and then click a point to the right of the hot grip. Now as you move the cursor, the hot grip moves relative to the cursor.

4. Right-click again, choose Copy from the context menu, and enter @1<-30↵. (Metric users should enter @3<-30↵.) Instead of the hot grip moving and the lines changing, copies of the two lines are made with their endpoints 1 unit (or 3 units for metric users) below and to the right of the first set of endpoints.

5. Pick another point just below the last. More copies are made.

6. Press ↵ or enter X↵ to exit Stretch mode. You can also right-click again and choose Exit from the context menu.

In this exercise, you saw that you can select a base point other than the hot grip. You also saw how you can specify relative coordinates to move or copy a hot grip. Finally, you saw that with grips selected on an object, right-clicking opens a context menu that contains grip-edit options.

SELECTING MULTIPLE GRIPS

Suppose you want to stretch two grips together. You can select multiple grips by holding down the Shift key while selecting grips. For example, if you want to stretch the top two corners of a rectangle, select the rectangle, and then Shift-click the two top corner grips. Click one of the selected grips and move it to a new location. All of the selected grips will move together.

Moving and Rotating with Grips

As you've just seen, the Grips feature is an alternative method for editing your drawings. You've already seen how you can stretch endpoints, but you can do much more with grips. The next exercise demonstrates some other options. You'll start by undoing the modifications you made in the preceding exercise:

1. Type U↵. The copies of the stretched lines disappear.

2. Press ↵ again. The deformed door snaps back to its original form.

   Pressing ↵ at the Command prompt causes AutoCAD to repeat the last command entered—in this case, U.

3. Type Zoom↵0.6↵ to show more of the drawing's work area.

4. You are going to select the entire door. First, click a blank area below and to the right of the door.

5. Move the cursor to a location above and to the left of the rectangular portion of the door and click. Because you went from right to left, you created a crossing window. Recall that the crossing window selects anything enclosed and crossing through the window.

6. Click the lower-left grip of the rectangle to turn it into a hot grip. Just as before, as you move your cursor the corner stretches.

7. Right-click and choose Move from the context menu. The Command window displays the following:

```
**MOVE**
Specify move point or [Base point/Copy/Undo/eXit]
```

Now as you move the cursor, the entire door moves with it.

8. Position the door near the center of the screen and click. The door moves to the center of the screen. Notice that the Command prompt returns but the door remains highlighted, indicating that it's still selected for the next operation.

9. Click the lower-left grip again, right-click, and choose Rotate from the context menu. The Command window displays the following:

```
**ROTATE**
Specify rotation angle or [Base point/Copy/Undo/Reference/eXit]:
```

As you move the cursor, the door rotates about the grip point.

10. Position the cursor so that the door rotates approximately 180° (see Figure 2.25). Then Ctrl+click (hold down the Ctrl key and press the left mouse button). A copy of the door appears in the new rotated position, leaving the original door in place.

FIGURE 2.25
Rotating and copying the door by using a hot grip. Notice that more than one object is affected by the grip edit, even though only one grip is hot.

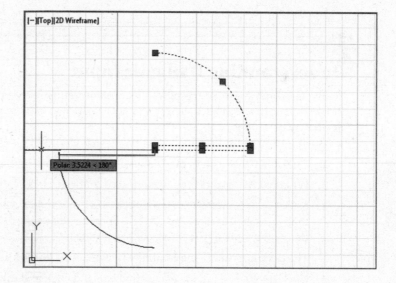

11. Press ↵ to exit Grip Edit mode.

You've seen how the Move command is duplicated in a modified way as a hot-grip command. Other hot-grip commands (Stretch, Rotate, Scale, and Mirror) have similar counterparts in the standard set of AutoCAD commands. You'll see how those work in Chapter 11, "Using Dimensions," and Chapter 13, "Copying Existing Drawings from Other Sources."

After you complete any operation by using grips, the objects are still highlighted with their grips active. To clear the grip selection, press the Esc key.

In this exercise, you saw how hot-grip options appear in a context menu. Several other options are available in that menu, including Exit, Base Point, Copy, and Undo.

You can access many of these grip-edit options by pressing the spacebar or ↵ while a grip is selected. With each press, the next option becomes active. The options then repeat if you continue to press ↵. The Ctrl key acts as a shortcut to the Copy option. You have to use it only once; then, each time you click a point, a copy is made.

SCALING WITH GRIPS

Grips can be used to scale an object graphically to fit between two other objects. For example, a door can be scaled to fit within a door frame. Place the door so that its hinge side is at the door frame and the door is oriented properly for the frame. With the door selected, click the grip at the hinge side. Right-click and select Scale. Type **R**↵ or select Reference from the command line, and then click the grip at the hinge again. Click the grip at the end of the arc representing the door swing. Finally, click the opposite side of the door frame.

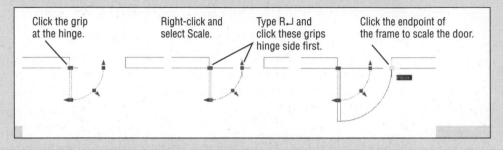

Click the grip at the hinge.

Right-click and select Scale.

Type R↵ and click these grips hinge side first.

Click the endpoint of the frame to scale the door.

Understanding Dynamic Input

You've seen how AutoCAD displays a lot of information at the cursor through its Dynamic Input display. In this section, you'll now get a chance to explore the Dynamic Input display through grip editing.

You'll start by going back to the original version of the Door.dwg drawing that you saved earlier:

1. Click the Close icon in the Drawing tab of the drawing area.

2. When you're asked if you want to save changes, click No.

3. Click Open from the Quick Access toolbar, and then locate and select the Door.dwg file that you saved earlier. You can also open the doorsample.dwg file from the sample files that you installed from this book's web page.

   The door appears in the condition in which you left it when you last saved the file.

Certification Objective

4. Click the Pan tool in the Navigation bar, and click and drag the mouse to pan the view to the center of the drawing area.

5. Right-click and select Exit to exit the Pan tool.

6. Click the arc to expose its grips.

DON'T SEE THE DYNAMIC INPUT DISPLAY?

If you don't see the Dynamic Input display at the cursor, type **Dynmode** ↵↵ to turn it on. You can also click the Customization tool at the far-right end of the status bar and select Dynamic Input to add the Dynamic Input tool to the status bar. This tool lets you toggle the Dynamic Input display on and off.

7. Place the cursor on the grip at the middle of the arc, but don't click it. (This is called *hovering* over a grip.) You see the dimensions of the arc appear as well as a menu offering two options: Stretch and Radius. The dimensions are useful when you need to check the size of objects you've drawn (see Figure 2.26).

FIGURE 2.26
Hovering over a grip

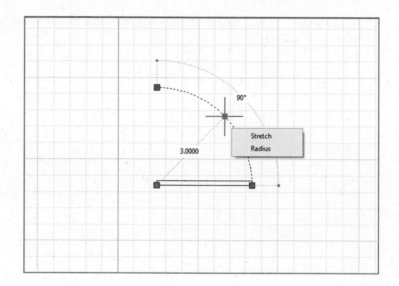

8. Click the Radius option in the grip menu. The Command prompt appears at the cursor, and the radius dimension changes to a text box.

9. Move the cursor toward the upper-right corner of the drawing area. The radius dimension of the arc changes as you move the cursor.

10. Enter 4↵. Metric users enter 12↵. As you type, the new value appears in the radius dimension. When you press ↵, the arc changes to the new radius.

11. Click the Undo button to revert to the original arc size.

Here you saw the basic methods for using the Dynamic Input display. You can hover over an object's grip to display its dimensions along with a grip menu. The menu appears for many but not all grips, and the contents of the menu depend on the object selected. Click the grip, and if available, the dimensions can be edited directly through the keyboard. In this example, you were able to change the radius of the arc to an exact value by selecting the Radius option from the grip menu and then entering a value. Depending on the grip you click, you can change a dimension through direct keyboard input. For example, if you want to change the degrees the arc covers instead of its radius, you can hover over the arrow grip at either end of the arc and select Lengthen. The dimensions that appear can then be edited to increase or decrease the length of the arc without affecting its radius.

Next, try Dynamic Input display on a line:

1. Click the bottommost line of the door, as shown in Figure 2.27. Hover over the rightmost grip on the selected line. Just as you saw with the arc, you can see the dimensions of the line, including its length and directional angle. You also see a menu that offers the Stretch and Lengthen options.

FIGURE 2.27
Selecting a line on the door

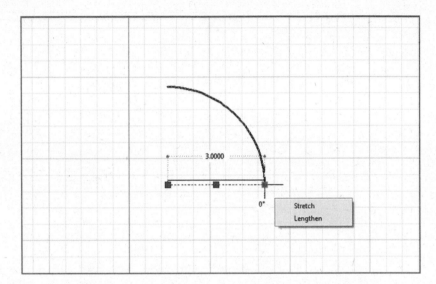

2. Click the grip over which you're hovering, and then move the cursor up and to the right. You see two dimensions: One indicates the overall length, and the other shows the change in length of the line. You also see the Command prompt at the cursor. Notice that the dimension indicating the change in length is highlighted (see Figure 2.28).

FIGURE 2.28
The overall length dimension and the change in length dimension

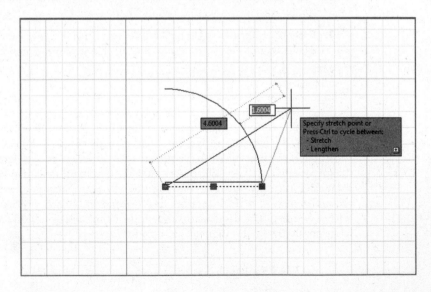

3. Type **1** and press the Tab key, not the Enter key, to increase the length of the line by 1 unit. Metric users should enter **3** and press the Tab key. Now, as you move the cursor, the line is locked at a new length that is 1 (or 3) units longer than its original length. Also notice that the overall dimension is highlighted. You also see a lock icon on the length dimension (see Figure 2.29).

FIGURE 2.29
The line locked at a new length

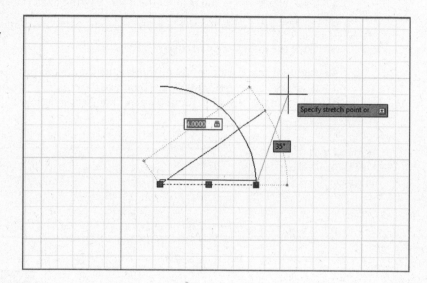

4. Press the Tab key again. The angle value is highlighted.

5. Type **45** and press the Tab key to lock the angle of the line at 45°.

6. Make sure that the cursor isn't too close to the locked endpoint of the line and then click the left mouse button. The line is now in its new orientation with a length of 4 (12 for metric users) and an angle of 45°, as shown in Figure 2.30.

FIGURE 2.30
The line's new length and orientation

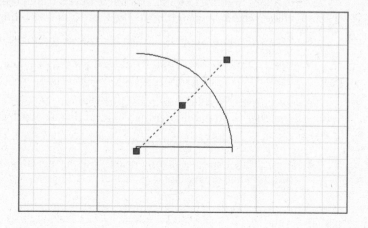

You can see that the Dynamic Input display lets you enter specific dimensions for the selected object, making possible precise changes in an object's size. Choose Lengthen from the grip menu if you just want to change the length of the line.

You can also use the Dynamic Input display while using other grip-editing features. Try the following exercise to see how the Dynamic Input display works while moving objects:

1. Click above and to the right of the door drawing to start a crossing selection window.

2. Click below and to the left to select the entire door drawing.

3. Click the middle grip of the arc.

4. Right-click and choose Move. You see the Command prompt at the cursor with the distance value highlighted. As you move the cursor, you can see the distance and angle values in the Dynamic Input display change (see Figure 2.31).

FIGURE 2.31
The Dynamic Input display

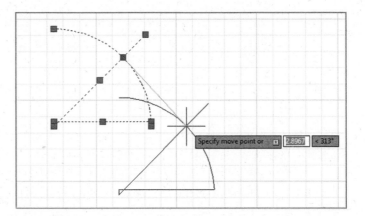

5. Type **4** (metric users enter **12**) and then press the Tab key. As you move the cursor, the distance from the original location of the arc's midpoint is locked at 4 (or 12) units. The angle value is now highlighted and available for editing.

6. Type **225** and then press the Tab key to lock the angle at 225°.

7. Click a location away from the door drawing. The door moves to its new location, exactly 4 units (**12** units for metric users) from its original location.

As you can see from these exercises, the Dynamic Input display adds some helpful methods for editing objects. To summarize, here is a rundown of the basic Dynamic Input display features:

◆ You can quickly check the dimensions of an object by selecting it and then hovering over a grip.

◆ You can alter an object's dimensions by entering values into the highlighted dimensions of the Dynamic Input display.

◆ To highlight a different dimension, press the Tab key.

◆ To accept any changes you've made using the Dynamic Input display, click at a location away from the grip you're editing. You can also press ↵ or the spacebar.

Not all grips offer dimensions that can be edited. If you click the midpoint grip on the line, for example, you won't see the dimensions of the line, although you'll see the Command prompt and you'll be able to enter a new coordinate for the midpoint.

As you've seen in the arc and line examples, each object offers a different set of dimensions. If you like the way that the Dynamic Input display works, you can experiment on other types of objects. AutoCAD offers a number of settings that let you control the behavior of the Dynamic Input display. You'll learn about those settings in Appendix B.

TYPING COORDINATES WITH DYNAMIC INPUT

When entering coordinates through the keyboard while Dynamic Input is enabled, you have to use a slightly different notation for relative and absolute coordinates. If you're entering relative coordinates for a series of points as in drawing a polygon with the Line command, you can leave off the @ sign after the first point is selected, so instead of typing **@12,9**↵, you can simply type **12,9**↵. If you are entering absolute coordinates, you need to precede your coordinate list with a # sign. So instead of entering **1,1**↵ to specify a point at coordinate 1,1, you would need to enter **#1,1**↵.

Displaying Data in a Text Window

You may have noticed that as you work in AutoCAD, the activity displayed in the Command window scrolls up. Sometimes, it's helpful to view information that has scrolled past the view shown in the Command window. For example, you can review the command activity from your session to check input values or to recall other data-entry information. Try the following exercise to see how the text window works:

1. From the Home tab's expanded Properties panel, click the List tool.

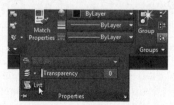

2. At the Select objects: prompt, click the arc and press ↵. A text window appears and displays information about the arc (see Figure 2.32). If your command window is undocked, it will expand to display the information. Toward the bottom is the list of the arc's properties. Don't worry if the meaning of some listed properties isn't obvious yet; as you work your way through this book, you'll learn what the properties of an object mean.

FIGURE 2.32
The expanded
AutoCAD Command
window showing the
data displayed by the
List tool

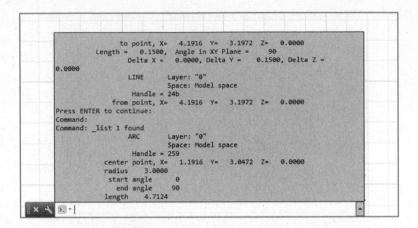

```
                          to point, X=  4.1916  Y=   3.1972  Z=   0.0000
               Length =  0.1500,  Angle in XY Plane =      90
                      Delta X =   0.0000, Delta Y =   0.1500, Delta Z =
0.0000
               LINE        Layer: "0"
                           Space: Model space
               Handle = 24b
         from point, X=  4.1916  Y=   3.1972  Z=   0.0000
Press ENTER to continue:
Command:
Command: _list 1 found
               ARC         Layer: "0"
                           Space: Model space
               Handle = 259
       center point, X=   1.1916  Y=   3.0472  Z=   0.0000
       radius    3.0000
        start angle      0
          end angle     90
          length     4.7124
```

3. If your command window is unlocked, you can dismiss the expanded Command window by clicking in the drawing area. To bring it back, press the F2 function key or click the up-pointing arrowhead at the far right of the unlocked Command window.

You can set the number of lines that AutoCAD retains by using the Options dialog box, or you can have AutoCAD record the AutoCAD Text Window information in a text file.

When you have more than one document open, the AutoCAD Command window displays a listing for the drawing that is currently active.

DOCKING THE COMMAND WINDOW

If you've used AutoCAD before, you may wonder if you can restore the old-style Command window. You can do this by docking the window to the bottom of the AutoCAD window. Once this is done, the Command window behaves the same way as in earlier versions of AutoCAD. You can open a separate Text Window by entering **TEXTSCR**↵ or by pressing F2.

Displaying the Properties of an Object

Certification
Objective

While we're on the subject of displaying information, you'll want to know about the Properties palette. In the preceding exercise, you saw how the List command showed some information regarding the properties of an object, such as the location of an arc's center and endpoints. You can also double-click an object to display the Quick Properties palette that shows other basic information about the object. (You might accidentally display the Quick Properties palette from time to time!) The Properties palette provides a more complete view of an object's properties with the additional feature of allowing you to make changes to those properties. The Properties palette is so useful that you may want to consider leaving it open all the time.

To see what the Properties palette is for, try the following exercise:

1. If you haven't done so already, select the arc in the drawing, right-click it, and select Properties to open the Properties palette, which displays a list of the arc's properties.

Don't worry if many of the items in this palette are undecipherable; you'll learn more about this palette as you work through the early chapters of this book. For now, just be aware that you can get to this palette with a right-click and that it displays the object's properties. You can also use it to modify many of the properties listed (see Figure 2.33).

FIGURE 2.33
Object Properties palette

2. Click the small Auto-hide box at the top of the Properties palette. It's the icon that looks like a double arrow. The icon changes to a single arrow. The Auto-hide option in the Properties palette lets you keep the palette open without having it take up too much of the drawing area. This can be useful when you need to edit the properties of many objects.

3. Move the cursor away from the Properties palette. The Properties palette collapses so that only the title bar remains.

4. Hover the cursor on the Properties palette title bar. The Properties palette opens to display all of the options again.

5. Click the Auto-hide box again to restore the "always open" mode of the palette.

6. Close the Properties palette by clicking the X in its upper corner. (The X appears in the upper-left or upper-right corner, depending on the placement of the palette in the AutoCAD window.) You can also right-click the title bar on the side of the Properties palette and then choose Close from the context menu.

Certification Objective

7. You're finished with the door drawing, so choose Close from the Application menu.

8. In the AutoCAD dialog box, click the No button. (You've already saved this file just as you want it, so you don't need to save it again.)

USING ROTATE REFERENCE TO ALIGN OBJECTS

You can use the Rotate command's Reference option to align a set of objects graphically to another object. For example, suppose you want to rotate a set of circles inside a hexagon to align with the corner of the hexagon.

To do this, you can use the Reference option as follows:

1. Start the Rotate command, and select the circles.

2. At the Specify base point: prompt, use the Center osnap to select the center of the hexagon as represented by the central circle. Once you do this, the objects rotate around the selected point as you move your cursor.

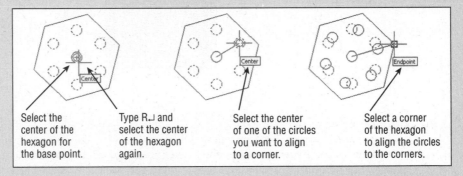

Select the center of the hexagon for the base point.

Type R↲ and select the center of the hexagon again.

Select the center of one of the circles you want to align to a corner.

Select a corner of the hexagon to align the circles to the corners.

3. At the Specify rotation angle or [Copy/Reference]: prompt, enter **R**↲.

4. At the Specify the reference angle <0>: prompt, use the Center osnap to select the center of the hexagon again. You can also enter **@**↲ since the last point you selected was the center.

5. At the Specify second point: prompt, use the Center osnap to select the center of one of the circles you want to align with the hexagon. Now, as you move the cursor, the circle whose center you selected is aligned with the cursor angle.

6. At the Specify the new angle or [Points]: prompt, use the Endpoint osnap to select one of the corners of the hexagon. The circles align with the corners.

You can also use grips to align objects. Here's how: Select the object or set of objects and then click a grip. The grip you select becomes the rotation point, so select this first grip carefully. Right-click and select Rotate. Type **R**↲ and select the grip you just selected and another point to determine the reference angle. Finally, select the new angle for the object or set of objects. If you want to rotate around a point other than the first grip, use the Grip Base right-click option. If you'd like to experiment with the Rotate Reference option, we've provided a sample file that you can use called rotatereference.dwg.

In many cases, you can open the Quick Properties palette by double-clicking an object (see Figure 2.34). Some objects, however, display a dialog box to allow you to edit them.

FIGURE 2.34
The Quick Properties palette

The Quick Properties palette lets you control just a few properties of an object (color, layer, linetype, and length). When turned on, it pops up every time you select an object, so you may want to limit its use to those times when you are adjusting the color, layer, and linetype of objects in your drawing.

Getting Help

Eventually, you'll find yourself somewhere without documentation and you'll have a question about an AutoCAD feature. AutoCAD provides an online help facility that gives you information on nearly any topic related to AutoCAD.

You can open the AutoCAD Help website by clicking the Help tool in the InfoCenter. There you'll find a comprehensive set of help topics and tools, including video tutorials and the standard help documentation. As with many other programs, you can obtain context-sensitive help by pressing the F1 function key.

If you're looking for more general information about AutoCAD, the Start tab offers some introductory videos and links to online training. Click the Learn option at the bottom of the Start tab to view these resources. Click the Create option at the bottom of the Start tab to return to the drawing file options.

Using the InfoCenter

If you want to find information about a topic based on a keyword, you can use the InfoCenter in the upper-right corner of the AutoCAD window. Follow these steps:

1. Type **change** in the InfoCenter text box at the top right of the AutoCAD window, and then click the Search tool to the right of the text box.

2. The AutoCAD Help window opens and lists topics that discuss change.

3. Click CHANGE (Command) from the list to the right. A description of the Change command appears (see Figure 2.35).

You can use Boolean AND, OR, NEAR, and NOT in conjunction with other keywords to help filter your searches, just as in a typical search engine that you might use in your web browser.

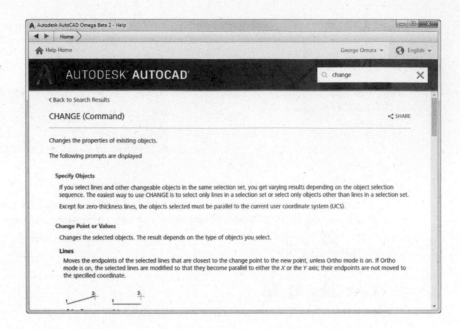

Finding Additional Sources of Help

The InfoCenter is the main online source for reference material, but you can also find answers to your questions through the other options in the InfoCenter's Help flyout menu. You can open this menu by clicking the arrowhead next to the InfoCenter Help tool. The following is a brief description of those options. Note that only the Help, Download Offline Help, and About Autodesk AutoCAD 2018 options are shown when no file is open:

Help This option opens the AutoCAD 2018 Help website.

Download Offline Help This option lets you select and download help files that can be stored locally on your PC. These help files can be useful if you find yourself in a location without Internet access.

Send Feedback Autodesk offers the product feedback web page, which enables you to send comments to Autodesk. The Send Feedback option takes you directly to this page.

Download Language Packs If you need to set up AutoCAD for a language other than English, you can download a language pack using this link.

Desktop Analytics Autodesk also provides an opt-in for its Desktop Analytics program. This program monitors your AutoCAD activity by collecting information about use, session length, country location, document type, size, and whether documents are open locally or from Autodesk® 360.

About Autodesk AutoCAD 2018 This option provides information about the version of AutoCAD you're using.

The Bottom Line

Specify distances with coordinates.   One of the most basic skills that you need to learn is how to indicate exact distances through the keyboard. AutoCAD uses a simple annotation system to indicate distance and direction.

> **Master It**   What would you type to indicate a relative distance of 14 units at a 45° angle?

Interpret the cursor modes and understand prompts.   The AutoCAD cursor changes its shape depending on the command that is currently active. These different cursor modes can give you a clue regarding what you should be doing.

> **Master It**   Describe the Point Selection cursor and the Pickbox cursor.

Select objects and edit with grips.   Grips are small squares or arrowheads that appear at key points on the object when they're selected. They offer a powerful way to edit objects.

> **Master It**   How do you select multiple grips?

Use Dynamic Input.   Besides grips, objects display their dimensional properties when selected. These dimensional properties can be edited to change an object's shape.

> **Master It**   How do you turn on the Dynamic Input display? And once it's on, what key lets you shift between the different dimensions of an object?

Display data in a text window.   AutoCAD offers the AutoCAD Text Window, which keeps a running account of the commands that you use. This can be helpful in retrieving input that you've entered when constructing your drawing.

> **Master It**   Name a command that displays its results in the AutoCAD Text Window.

Display the properties of an object.   The Properties palette is one of the most useful sources for drawing information. Not only does it list the properties of an object, it also lets you change the shape, color, and other properties of objects.

> **Master It**   How do you open the Properties palette for a particular object?

Get help.   The AutoCAD Autodesk Exchange website is thorough in its coverage of AutoCAD features. New and experienced users alike can often find answers to their questions through the Help window, so it pays to become familiar with it.

> **Master It**   What keyboard key do you press for context-sensitive help?

Chapter 3

Setting Up and Using the Drafting Tools

Chapter 1, "Exploring the Interface," and Chapter 2, "Creating Your First Drawing," covered the basic information you need to understand the workings of the AutoCAD® 2018 software. Now you'll put this knowledge to work. In this architectural tutorial, which begins here and continues through Chapter 14, "Advanced Editing and Organizing," you'll draw an apartment building composed of studios. We'll show you how to use AutoCAD commands and give you a solid understanding of the basic AutoCAD package. With these fundamentals, you can use AutoCAD to its fullest potential regardless of the kinds of drawings you intend to create or the enhancement products you may use in the future.

In this chapter, you'll start drawing an apartment's bathroom fixtures. In the process, you'll learn how to use the basic AutoCAD tools. You'll also be introduced to the concept of drawing scale and how the size of what you draw is translated into a paper sheet size.

In this chapter, you will learn to

- Set up a work area

- Explore the drawing process

- Plan and lay out a drawing

- Use the AutoCAD modes as drafting tools

Setting Up a Work Area

Before beginning most drawings, you should set up your work area. To do this, determine the measurement system, the drawing sheet size, and the scale you want to use. The default work area is roughly 16"×9" at full scale, given a decimal measurement system in which 1 unit equals 1 inch. Metric users will find that the default area is roughly 550×300 mm, in which 1 unit equals 1 mm. If these are appropriate settings for your drawing, you don't have to do any setting up. It's more likely, however, that you'll make drawings of various sizes and scales. For example, you might want to create a drawing in a measurement system in which you can specify feet, inches, and fractions of inches at 1' = 1" scale and print the drawing on an 8 1/2"×11" sheet of paper.

In the following sections, you'll learn how to set up a drawing exactly the way you want.

Specifying Units

You'll start by creating a new file called Bath. Then you'll set up the unit style.

Use these steps to create the file:

1. If you haven't done so already, start AutoCAD. If AutoCAD is already running, click the Templates drop-down list just below the Start Drawing icon in the Dashboard.

2. Select acad.dwt from the list. Metric users should select acadiso.dwt.

3. Type Z↵A↵ or select Zoom All from the Zoom flyout in the Navigation bar.

4. Choose Save As from the Application menu.

5. In the Save Drawing As dialog box, enter **Bath** for the filename.

6. Check to make sure that you're saving the drawing in the My Documents folder, or in the folder where you've chosen to store your exercise files, and then click Save.

USING THE IMPERIAL AND METRIC EXAMPLES

The exercises in this book are shown in both the metric and Imperial measurement systems. Be sure that if you start to work with the Imperial system, you continue with it throughout this book.

The metric settings described in this book are only approximations of their Imperial equivalents. For example, the drawing scale for the metric example is 1:10, which is close to the 1″ = 1′-0″ scale used in the Imperial example. In the grid example, you're asked to use a 30-unit grid, which is close to the 1′ grid of the Imperial example. Dimensions of objects are similar, but not exact. For example, the Imperial version of the tub measures 2′-8″×5′-0″ and the metric version of the tub is 81×152 cm. The actual metric equivalent of 2′-8″×5′-0″ is 81.28×152.4 cm. Measurements in the tub example are rounded to the nearest centimeter.

Metric users should also be aware that AutoCAD uses a period as a decimal point instead of the comma used in most European nations, South Africa, and elsewhere. Commas are used in AutoCAD to separate the X, Y, and Z components of a coordinate.

The next thing you want to tell AutoCAD is the *unit style* you intend to use. So far, you've been using the default, which is a generic decimal unit. This unit can be interpreted as inches, centimeters, feet, kilometers, or light-years—whatever you like. When it comes time to print your drawing, you can tell AutoCAD how to convert these units into a meaningful scale.

If you are a US user, decimal units typically represent inches. If you want to be able to enter distances in feet, you must change the unit style to a style that accepts feet as input. In this chapter, you'll do this through the Drawing Units dialog box, shown in Figure 3.1.

If you're a civil engineer, you should know that the Engineering unit style lets you enter feet and decimal feet for distances. For example, the equivalent of 12′-6″ is 12.5′. If you use the Engineering unit style, you'll ensure that your drawings conform to the scale of drawings created by your architectural colleagues.

FIGURE 3.1
The Drawing Units
dialog box

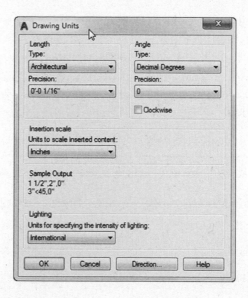

Follow these steps to set a unit style:

1. Choose Drawing Utilities ➢ Units from the Application menu or type **Un**↵ to open the Drawing Units dialog box. Remember that you can open the Application menu by clicking the red AutoCAD icon in the upper-left corner of the AutoCAD window.

2. Let's look at a few of the options available. Click the Type drop-down list in the Length group. Notice the unit styles in the list.

3. Click Architectural. The Sample Output group of the dialog box shows you what the Architectural style looks like in AutoCAD. Metric users should keep this setting as Decimal.

SHORTCUT TO SETTING UNITS

You can also control the Drawing Units settings by using several system variables. To set the unit style, you can type **'lunits**↵ at the Command prompt. (The apostrophe lets you enter this command while in the middle of other commands.) At the Enter new value for LUNITS <2>: prompt, enter **4** for Architectural.

---

4. Click the Precision drop-down list just below the Type list. Notice the options available. You can set the smallest unit AutoCAD will display in this drawing. For now, leave this setting at its default value of 0'-01/16". Metric users will keep the setting at 0.0000.

5. Click the drop-down list in the Insertion Scale group. The list shows various units of measure.

6. Click Inches; if you're a metric user, choose Centimeters. This option lets you control how AutoCAD translates drawing scales when you import drawings from outside the current

drawing. You'll learn more about this feature in Chapter 25, "Managing and Sharing Your Drawings."

7. Click OK in the Drawing Units dialog box to return to the drawing.

If you use the Imperial system of measurement, you selected Architectural measurement units for this tutorial, but your work may require a different unit style. You saw the unit styles available in the Drawing Units dialog box. Table 3.1 shows examples of how the distance 15.5 is entered in each of these styles.

TABLE 3.1: Measurement systems available in AutoCAD

MEASUREMENT SYSTEM	DISPLAY OF MEASUREMENT IN AUTOCAD
Scientific	1.55E+01 (inches or metric)
Decimal	15.5000 (inches or metric)
Engineering	1'-3.5" (input as 1'3.5")
Architectural	1'-31/2" (input as 1'3–1/2")
Fractional	151/2" (input as 15–1/2")

In the previous exercise, you needed to change only two settings. Let's look at the other Drawing Units settings in more detail. As you read, you may want to refer to Figure 3.1.

Fine-Tuning the Measurement System

Most of the time you'll be concerned only with the units and angles settings of the Drawing Units dialog box. But as you saw in the preceding exercise, you can control many other settings related to the input and display of units.

TAKING MEASUREMENTS

To measure the distance between two points, click Distance from the Measure flyout on the Home tab's Utilities panel, or type **Mea↵D↵** and then click the two points. (*Mea* is the shortcut for the Measuregeom command.) If this command doesn't give you an accurate distance measurement, examine the Precision option in the Drawing Units dialog box. If it's set too high, the value returned by the Measuregeom command may be rounded to a greater number than your tolerances allow, even though the distance is drawn accurately.

The Precision drop-down list in the Length group lets you specify the smallest unit value that you want AutoCAD to display in the status bar and in the prompts. If you choose a measurement system that uses fractions, the Precision list includes fractional units. You can also control this setting with the Luprec system variable.

The Angle group lets you set the style for displaying angles. You have a choice of five angle types: Decimal Degrees, Degrees/Minutes/Seconds, Grads, Radians, and Surveyor's Units. In the Angle group's Precision drop-down list, you can specify the degree of accuracy you want AutoCAD to display for angles. You can also control these settings with the `Aunits` and `Auprec` system variables.

You can find out more about system variables on the AutoCAD 2018 Help website. First, open the Help website by clicking the question mark icon in the Info Center at the top-right side of the AutoCAD window. Select the System Variables option in the right side of the page. You may need to scroll down to see it. In the System Variable Quick Reference, select the first letter of a system variable name from the list.

You can tell AutoCAD which direction is positive, either clockwise or counterclockwise. The default, which is counterclockwise, is used in this book. The Direction Control dialog box lets you set the direction of the 0 base angle. The default base angle (and the one used throughout this book) is a direction from left to right. However, at times you may want to designate another direction as the 0 base angle. You can also control these settings with the `Angbase` and `Angdir` system variables.

The Insertion Scale setting in the Drawing Units dialog box lets you control how blocks from the tool palettes or DesignCenter™ are scaled as they're imported into your current drawing. A *block* is a collection of drawing objects that form a single object. Blocks are frequently used to create standard symbols. You'll learn more about blocks in Chapter 4, "Organizing Objects with Blocks and Groups." The Insertion Scale setting lets you compensate for drawings of different scales by offering an automatic scale translation when importing blocks from an external file. The `Insunits` system variable also controls the Insertion Scale setting. You'll learn more about this setting in Chapter 25.

If you're new to AutoCAD, don't worry about the Insertion Scale setting right now. Make a mental note of it. It may come in handy in your work in the future.

Setting Up the Drawing Limits

One of the big advantages of using AutoCAD is that you can draw at full scale; you aren't limited to the edges of a piece of paper the way you are in manual drawing. But you may find it difficult to start drawing without knowing the drawing boundaries. You can set up some arbitrary boundaries using the Limits feature.

You'll be drawing a bathroom that is roughly 8' by 5' (230 cm by 150 cm for metric users). You'll want to give yourself some extra room around the bathroom, so your drawing limits should be a bit larger than that actual bathroom size. You'll use an area of 11' by 8'-6" for the limits of your drawing. Metric users will use an area 297 cm by 210 cm. These sizes will accommodate your bathroom with some room to spare.

Now that you know the area you need, you can use the Limits command to set up the area:

1. Type **LIMITS**↵.

2. At the `Specify lower left corner or [ON/OFF] <0'-0",0'-0.">`: prompt, specify the lower-left corner of your work area. Press ↵ to accept the default.

3. At the `Specify upper right corner <1'-0",0'-9.">`: prompt, you can specify the upper-right corner of your work area. (The default is shown in brackets.) Enter **132,102**. Or, if you prefer, you can enter **11',8'6** because you've set up your drawing for Architectural units. Metric users should enter **297,210**.

Zoom All

4. Select Zoom All from the Zoom flyout in the Navigation bar, or type **Z⏎A⏎**. Although it appears that nothing has changed, your drawing area is now set to a size that will enable you to draw your bathroom at full scale.

5. Move the cursor to the upper-right corner of the drawing area and watch the coordinate readout at the left end of the status bar. If you don't see the coordinate readout, select Coordinates from the Customize tool in the lower-right corner of the AutoCAD window. Notice that now the upper-right corner has a y-coordinate of approximately 8'-6", or 210 for metric users. The x-coordinate depends on the proportion of your AutoCAD window. The coordinate readout also displays distances in feet and inches.

6. Click the Grid Display tool in the status bar to turn off the grid.

THINGS TO WATCH FOR WHEN ENTERING DISTANCES

When you're using Architectural units, you should be aware of two points:

◆ Use hyphens only to distinguish fractions from whole inches.

◆ You can't use spaces while specifying a dimension. For example, you can specify eight feet, four and one-half inches as 8'4-1/2" or 8'4.5 but not as 8'-4 1/2".

These idiosyncrasies are a source of confusion to many architects and engineers new to AutoCAD because the program often displays architectural dimensions in the standard architectural format but doesn't allow you to enter dimensions that way.

Here are some tips for entering distances and angles in unusual situations:

◆ When entering distances in inches and feet, you can omit the inch (") sign. If you're using the Engineering unit style, you can enter decimal feet and forgo the inch sign entirely.

◆ You can enter fractional distances and angles in any format you like, regardless of the current unit style. For example, you can enter a distance as @1/2 <1.5708r, even if your current unit system is set for decimal units and decimal degrees (1.5708r is the radian equivalent of 90°).

◆ If you have your angle units set to grads, radians, or degrees, you don't need to specify *g*, *r*, or *d* after the angle. You do have to specify *g*, *r*, or *d*, however, if you want to use these units when they aren't the current default angle system.

◆ If your current base angle is set to something other than horizontal from left to right, you can use a double less-than symbol (<<) in place of the single less-than symbol (<) to override the current base angle. The << assumes the base angle of 0° to be a direction from left to right and the positive direction to be counterclockwise.

◆ If your current angle system uses a different base angle and direction and you want to specify an angle in the standard base direction, you can use a triple less-than symbol (<<<) to indicate angles. Note that this works only if Dynamic Input is turned off.

◆ You can specify a denominator of any size when specifying fractions. However, be aware that the value you've set for the maximum number of digits to the right of decimal points (under the Precision setting in the Length group of the Drawing Units dialog box) restricts the fractional value AutoCAD reports. For example, if your units are set for a maximum of two digits of decimals and you give a fractional value of 5/32, AutoCAD rounds this value to 3/16. Note that this doesn't affect the accuracy of the actual drawing dimensions.

◆ You can enter decimal feet for distances in the Architectural unit style. For example, you can enter 6'-6" as 6.5'.

In step 5, the coordinate readout shows you that your drawing area is larger than before. The background grid can help you visualize the area in which you're working. You can control the grid using the Grid Display tool in the status bar, which you'll learn about toward the end of this chapter. Grid Display shows a background grid that helps you visualize distances, and it can also show you the limits of your drawing. It can be a bit distracting for a new user, so we've asked you to turn it off for now.

Looking at an Alternative to Limits

As an alternative to setting up the drawing limits, you can draw a rectangle that outlines the same area used to define the drawing limits. For example, in the previous exercise you could use the Rectangle tool to draw a rectangle that has its lower-left corner at coordinate 0,0 and its upper-right corner at 132,102 (297,210 for metric users). You can set up the rectangle to be visible without printing using the Layer feature. You'll learn more about layers in Chapter 5, "Keeping Track of Layers and Blocks."

Coordinating with Paper Sizes

At this point, you may have questions about how your full-scale drawing will fit onto standard paper sizes. AutoCAD offers several features that give you precise control over the scale of your drawing. These features offer industry-standard scales to match your drawing with any paper size you need. You'll learn more about these features as you work through the chapters of this book. However, if you're anxious to find out about them, look at the sections on layouts in Chapter 8, "Introducing Printing, Plotting, and Layouts," and Chapter 15, "Laying Out Your Printer Output," and also check out the Annotative Scale feature in Chapter 9, "Adding Text to Drawings."

Understanding Scale Factors

If you've ever had to create a drawing to scale using pencil and paper, you rely on an architect's or engineer's scale to mark off distances on paper. You are working directly with the final media on which the drawing will appear. With a CAD program, you're a few steps removed from the finished product. Because of this, you need a deeper understanding of your drawing scale and how it's derived. In particular, you must understand *scale factors*. For example, one common use of scale factors is translating the size of a graphic symbol, such as a section symbol in an architectural drawing, to the final plotted text size. When you draw manually, you draw your symbol at the size you want. In a CAD drawing, you need to translate the desired final symbol size to the drawing scale.

When you start adding graphic symbols to your drawing (see Chapter 4), you have to specify a symbol height. The scale factor helps you determine the appropriate symbol height for a particular drawing scale. For example, you may want your symbol to appear 1/2" high in your final plot. But if you draw your symbol to 1/2" in your drawing, it appears as a dot when plotted. The symbol has to be scaled up to a size that, when scaled back down at plot time, appears 1/2" high. For a 1/4" scale drawing, you multiply the 1/2" text height by a scale factor of 48 to get 24". Your symbol should be 24" high in the CAD drawing in order to appear 1/2" high in the final plot. Where did the number 48 come from?

The scale factor for fractional inch scales is derived by multiplying the denominator of the scale by 12 and then dividing by the numerator. For example, the scale factor for 1/4" = 1'-0" is (4 times 12) / 1, or 48/1. For 3/16" = 1'-0" scale, the operation is (16 times 12) / 3, or 64. For whole-foot scales such as 1"= 10', multiply the feet side of the equation by 12. Metric scales require simple decimal conversions.

You can also use scale factors to determine your drawing limits. For example, if you have a sheet size of 11" by 17" and you want to know the equivalent full-scale size for a 1/4" scale drawing, you multiply the sheet measurements by 48. In this way, 11" becomes 528" (48 times 11"), and 17" becomes 816" (48 times 17"). Your work area must be 528" by 816" if you intend to have a final output of 11" by 17" at 1/4" = 1'. You can divide these inch measurements by 12" to get 44' by 68'.

Table 3.2 shows scale factors as they relate to standard drawing scales. These scale factors are the values by which you multiply the desired final printout size to get the equivalent full-scale size. If you're using the metric system, you can use the drawing scale directly as the scale factor. For example, a drawing scale of 1:10 has a scale factor of 10, a drawing scale of 1:50 has a scale factor of 50, and so on. Metric users need to take special care regarding the base unit. Centimeters are used as a base unit in the examples in this book, which means that if you enter a distance as 1, you can assume the distance to be 1 cm.

TABLE 3.2:   Scale conversion factors

SCALE FACTORS FOR ENGINEERING DRAWING SCALES	**DRAWING SCALE**							
$n = 1''$	10'	20'	30'	40'	50'	60'	100'	200'
Scale factor	120	240	360	480	600	720	1200	2400
$n = 1'$-0"	1/16"	1/8"	1/4"	1/2"	3/4"	1"	1–1/2"	3"
Scale factor	192	96	48	24	16	12	8	4

In older drawings, scale factors were used to determine text height and dimension settings. Chances are that you will eventually have to work with drawings created by older AutoCAD versions, so understanding scale factors will pay off later. Plotting to a particular scale is also easier with an understanding of scale factors.

Using Polar Tracking

In this section, you'll draw the first item in the bathroom: the toilet. It's composed of a rectangle representing the tank and a truncated ellipse representing the seat. To construct the toilet, you'll use Polar Tracking, which is one of the more versatile drafting tools. Polar Tracking helps you align your cursor to exact horizontal and vertical angles, much like a T-square and triangle.

In this exercise, you'll use Polar Tracking to draw a rectangular box:

1. Start a line at the coordinate 5'-7", 6'-3" by entering **L↵5'7",6'3"↵**. Metric users should enter **L↵171,189↵** as the starting coordinate. This starting point is somewhat arbitrary, but by entering a specific starting location, you're coordinated with the figures and instructions in this book. You can also use the Line tool in the Draw panel to start the line.

2. Make sure Polar Tracking is on (the Polar Tracking tool in the status bar should be blue), and then point the cursor directly to the right of the last point. The tracking vector appears at the cursor along with the Polar Tracking readout and dimensions.

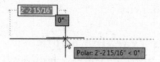

3. With the cursor pointing directly to the right, enter **1'-10"↵**. Metric users should enter **56↵**. You can use the spacebar in place of the ↵ key when entering distances in this way.

4. Point the cursor downward and enter **9↵** for 9". Metric users should enter **23↵**.

5. Continue drawing the other two sides of the rectangle by using Polar Tracking. After you've completed the rectangle, press ↵ or the Esc key to exit the Line tool. You should have a drawing that looks like 3.2.

FIGURE 3.2
A plan view of the toilet tank

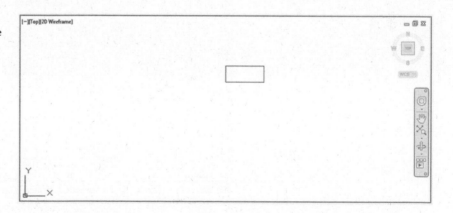

As you can see from the exercise, you can use Polar Tracking and the tracking vector to restrain your cursor to horizontal and vertical positions, just as you would use a T-square and triangle. Later, you'll learn how you can set up Polar Tracking to set the angle to any value you want in a way similar to an adjustable triangle.

In some situations, you may find that you don't want Polar Tracking on. You can turn it off by clicking the Polar Tracking tool in the status bar. You can also press the F10 function key to turn Polar Tracking on or off.

Although this exercise tells you to use the Line tool to draw the tank, you can also use the Rectangle tool. The Rectangle tool creates what is known as a polyline, which is a set of line or arc segments that act like a single object. You'll learn more about polylines in Chapter 18, "Drawing Curves."

By using the Snap modes in conjunction with the coordinate readout and Polar Tracking, you can locate coordinates and measure distances as you draw lines. This is similar to the way you draw when using a scale. The smallest distance registered by the coordinate readout and the Polar Tracking readout depends on the area you've displayed on your screen. For example, if you're displaying an area the size of a football field, the smallest distance you can indicate with your cursor may be 6", or 15 cm. On the other hand, if your view is enlarged to show an area of only one square inch or centimeter, you can indicate distances as small as 1/1000 of an inch or centimeter by using your cursor.

Setting the Polar Tracking Angle

You've seen how Polar Tracking lets you draw exact vertical and horizontal lines. You can also set Polar Tracking to draw lines at other angles, such as 30° or 45°. To change the angle Polar Tracking uses, you use the Polar Tracking tab in the Drafting Settings dialog box (see Figure 3.3).

FIGURE 3.3
The Polar Tracking
tab in the Drafting
Settings dialog box

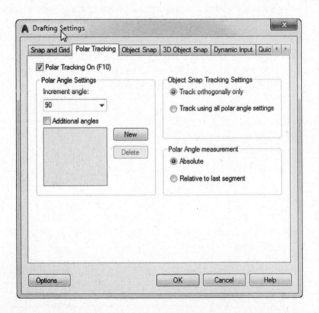

Right-click the Polar Tracking tool in the status bar, and then choose Settings from the context menu to open the Drafting Settings dialog box. As an alternative, you can type **DS.⏎** and then click the Polar Tracking tab.

To change the Polar Tracking angle, enter an angle in the Increment Angle text box or select a predefined angle from the drop-down list. You can set angles on the fly. Just right-click the Polar Tracking tool and select an angle from the drop-down list.

ORTHO MODE

Besides using Polar Tracking mode, you can restrain the cursor to a vertical or horizontal direction by using Ortho mode. To use Ortho mode, hold down the Shift key while drawing. You can also press F8 or click Ortho Mode in the status bar to keep Ortho mode on while you draw. When you move the cursor around while drawing objects, the rubber-banding line moves only vertically or horizontally. With Ortho mode turned on, Polar Tracking is automatically turned off.

Numerous other settings are available in the Polar Tracking tab. Here is a list of their functions:

Additional Angles   This setting lets you enter a specific angle for Polar Tracking. For example, if you want Polar Tracking to snap to 12 degrees, click the New button next to the Additional Angles list box and enter 12. The value you enter appears in the list box and, when the Additional Angles check box is selected, Polar Tracking snaps to 12°. To delete a value from the list box, highlight it and click the Delete button.

The Additional Angles option differs from the Increment Angle setting in that the latter causes Polar Tracking to snap to every increment of its setting, whereas Additional Angles snaps only to the angle specified. You can enter as many angles as you want in the Additional Angles list box. As a shortcut, you can use the Polarang system variable (Polarang↵) to set the incremental angle without using the dialog box. The Polarmode system variable lets you determine whether Polar Tracking uses the current UCS or a selected object as the basis for the angle.

Object Snap Tracking Settings   These settings let you control whether Object Snap Tracking (or Osnap Tracking) uses strictly orthogonal directions (0°, 90°, 180°, and 270°) or the angles set in the Polar Angle Settings group in this dialog box. (See the section "Aligning Objects by Using Object Snap Tracking" later in this chapter.)

Polar Angle Measurement   These radio buttons let you determine the zero angle on which Polar Tracking bases its incremental angles. The Absolute option uses the current AutoCAD setting for the 0° angle. The Relative To Last Segment option uses the last drawn object as the 0° angle. For example, if you draw a line at a 10° angle and the Relative To Last Segment option is selected with Increment Angle set to 90°, Polar Tracking snaps to 10°, 100°, 190°, and 280°, relative to the actual 0° direction.

NUDGING OBJECTS

If you need to move objects incrementally in an orthogonal direction, you can use the Nudge feature. Select the object or objects, and then hold down the Ctrl key and press an arrow key. Your selection moves in the direction of the arrow key in small increments.

Exploring the Drawing Process

The following sections present some common AutoCAD commands and show you how to use them to complete a simple drawing. As you draw, watch the prompts and notice how your responses affect them. Also notice how you use existing drawing elements as reference points.

While drawing with AutoCAD, you create simple geometric forms to determine the basic shapes of objects, and you can then modify the shapes to fill in detail.

AutoCAD offers a number of basic 2D drawing object types; lines, arcs, circles, text, dimensions, polylines, points, ellipses, elliptical arcs, spline curves, regions, hatches, and multiline text are the most common. All drawings are built on at least some of these objects. In addition, there are several 3D solids and meshes, which are three-dimensional shapes. You're familiar with lines and arcs; these, along with circles, are the most commonly used objects. As you progress through the book, you'll learn about the other objects and how they're used. You'll also learn about 3D objects in the chapters on AutoCAD 3D.

Locating an Object in Reference to Others

Continuing to draw the toilet, to define the seat you'll use an ellipse. Follow these steps:

1. Click the Axis, End Ellipse tool from the Ellipse flyout in the Home tab's Draw panel, or type **EL↵**.

2. At the `Specify axis endpoint of ellipse or [Arc/Center]:` prompt, pick the midpoint of the bottom horizontal line of the rectangle. To do this, Shift+right-click to open the Object Snap (Osnap) context menu and select Midpoint; then move the cursor toward the bottom line. (Remember, Shift+click the right mouse button to open the Object Snap menu.) When you see the Midpoint Osnap marker on the line, click the left mouse button.

3. At the `Specify other endpoint of axis:` prompt, point the cursor downward and enter **1'-10"↵**. Metric users should enter **55↵**.

4. At the `Specify distance to other axis or [Rotation]:` prompt, point the cursor horizontally from the center of the ellipse and enter **8"↵**. Metric users should enter **20↵**. Your drawing should look like Figure 3.4.

FIGURE 3.4
The ellipse added to the tank

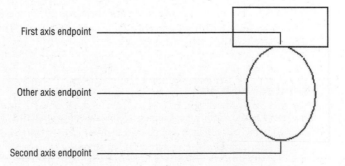

OBJECT SNAP AND OSNAP ARE THE SAME

You will see the terms *osnap* and *object snap* throughout this chapter and in other chapters. *Osnap* is just a shortened version of *object snap*. The two terms are interchangeable.

Getting a Closer Look

During the drawing process, you'll often want to enlarge areas of a drawing to edit its objects. In Chapter 1, you saw how to use the Zoom capability for this purpose. Follow these steps to enlarge the view of the toilet:

1. Click Zoom Window from the Zoom flyout in the Navigation bar, or type **Z↵W↵**. Next, you'll place a closely fitting window around your toilet.

2. At the Specify first corner: prompt, pick a point below and to the left of your drawing, at or near coordinate 5'-0",3'-6". Metric users should use the coordinate 150.0000,102.0000.

3. At the Specify opposite corner: prompt, pick a point above and to the right of the drawing, at or near coordinate 8'-3",6'-8" (246.0000,195.0000 for metric users). The toilet should be completely enclosed by the zoom window. You can also use the Zoom Realtime tool in conjunction with the Pan Realtime tool. The toilet enlarges to fill more of the screen. Your view should look similar to Figure 3.5.

FIGURE 3.5
The line copied down

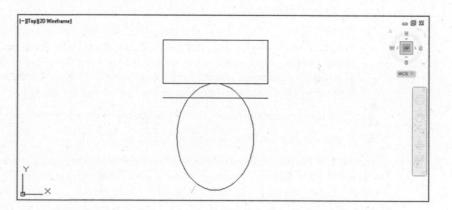

If you have a mouse with a scroll wheel, you can avoid using the Zoom command altogether. Just place the cursor on the toilet and turn the wheel to zoom into the image.

Modifying an Object

Now let's see how editing commands are used to construct an object. To define the back edge of the seat, let's put a copy of the line defining the front of the toilet tank 3" (7 cm for metric users) toward the center of the ellipse:

1. Click the Copy tool in the Home tab's Modify panel, or type **CO↵**.

2. At the Select objects: prompt, pick the horizontal line that touches the top of the ellipse. The line is highlighted. Press ↵ to complete your selection.

3. At the Specify base point or [Displacement/mOde] <Displacement>: prompt, pick a base point near the line. Then point the cursor down and enter 3"↵, or 7↵ if you're a metric user.

4. Press ↵ to exit the Copy command. Your drawing should look like Figure 3.5.

Notice that the Copy command acts exactly like the Move command you used in Chapter 2, except that Copy doesn't alter the position of the objects you select and you must press ↵ to exit Copy.

TRIMMING AN OBJECT

Now you must delete the part of the ellipse that isn't needed. You'll use the Trim command to trim off part of the ellipse:

1. Click the Trim tool in the Home tab's Modify panel. If you don't see the Trim tool, click the Trim/Extend flyout and select Trim. You'll see this prompt:

```
Current settings: Projection=UCS Edge=None
Select cutting edges ...
Select objects or <select all>:
```

2. Click the line you just created—the one that crosses through the ellipse—and press ↵ to finish your selection.

3. At the Select object to trim or shift-select to extend or [Fence/Crossing/ Project/Edge/eRase/Undo]: prompt, hover over the topmost portion of the ellipse above the line. Notice that you see a preview of how the ellipse will look when trimmed. The top portion of the ellipse dims to a gray line. Also notice the red X by the cursor. This indicates that the selected portion of the ellipse will be deleted.

4. Click the topmost portion of the ellipse above the line. This trims the ellipse back to the line.

5. Press ↵ to exit the Trim command.

In step 1 of the preceding exercise, the Trim command produces two messages in the prompt. The first message, Select cutting edges. . . ., tells you that you must first select objects to define *the edge to which you want to trim an object*. In step 3, you're again prompted to select objects, this time to select the *object to trim*. Here you see a preview of how the ellipse will look before you commit to your selection. The red X by the cursor, called a cursor badge, indicates the action that the current command will apply. You will see several cursor badges as you work in AutoCAD, each one offering a hint regarding the current activity.

Trim is one of a handful of AutoCAD commands that asks you to select two sets of objects: The first set defines a boundary, and the second is the set of objects that you want to edit. The two sets of objects aren't mutually exclusive. You can, for example, select the cutting-edge objects as objects to trim. The next exercise shows how this works.

First, you'll undo the trim you just did. Then, you'll use the Trim command again in a slightly different way to finish the toilet:

1. Click the Undo button in the Quick Access toolbar, or enter **U**↵ at the Command prompt. The top of the ellipse reappears.

2. Start the Trim tool again by clicking it in the Modify panel.

3. At the `Select objects or <select all>:` prompt, click the ellipse and the line crossing the ellipse. (See the first image in Figure 3.6.)

4. Press ↵ to finish your selection.

FIGURE 3.6
Trimming the ellipse and the line

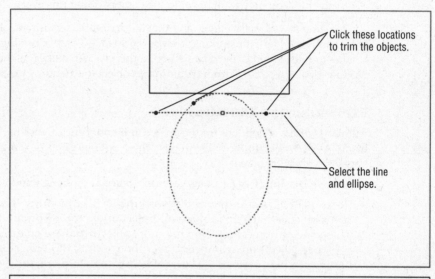

Click these locations to trim the objects.

Select the line and ellipse.

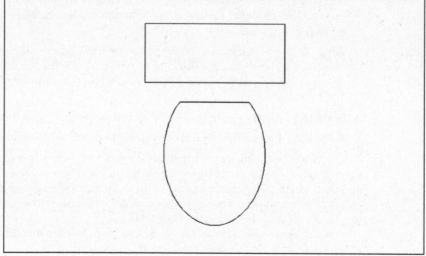

5. At the `Select object to trim or shift-select to extend or [Fence/Crossing/Project/Edge/eRase/Undo]:` prompt, click the top portion of the ellipse as you did in the previous exercise. The ellipse trims back.

6. Click a point near the left end of the trim line, outside the ellipse. The line trims back to the ellipse.

7. Click the other end of the line. The right side of the line trims back to meet the ellipse. Your drawing should look like the second image in Figure 3.6.

8. Press ↵ to exit the Trim command.

9. Click Save on the Quick Access toolbar to save the file in its current state, but don't exit the file. You may want to get in the habit of doing this every 20 minutes.

Here you saw how the ellipse and the line are both used as trim objects as well as the objects to be trimmed. The Trim options you've seen so far—Fence, Crossing, Project, Edge, Erase, and Undo—are described in the next section in this chapter. Also note that by holding down the Shift key, you can change from trimming an object to extending an object.

EXPLORING THE TRIM OPTIONS

Certification Objective

AutoCAD offers six options for the Trim command: Fence, Crossing, Project, Edge, Erase, and Undo. As described in the following list, these options give you a higher degree of control over how objects are trimmed:

Fence/Crossing [F or C] Lets you use a fence or crossing window to select objects.

Project [P] Useful when you're working on 3D drawings. It controls how AutoCAD trims objects that aren't coplanar. Project offers three options: None, UCS, and View. The None option causes Trim to ignore objects that are on different planes so that only coplanar objects are trimmed. If you choose UCS, the Trim command trims objects based on a plan view of the current UCS and then disregards whether the objects are coplanar. (See the middle of Figure 3.7.) View is similar to UCS but uses the current view's "line of sight" to determine how non-coplanar objects are trimmed. (See the bottom of Figure 3.7.)

Edge [E] Lets you trim an object to an apparent intersection, even if the cutting-edge object doesn't intersect the object to be trimmed (see the top of Figure 3.7). Edge offers two options: Extend and No Extend. You can also set these options by using the `Edgemode.` system variable.

Erase [R] Allows you to erase an object while remaining in the Trim command.

Undo [U] Causes the last trimmed object to revert to its original length.

You've just seen one way to construct the toilet. However, you can construct objects in many ways. For example, you can trim only the top of the ellipse, as you did in the first trim exercise, and then use the Grips feature to move the endpoints of the line to meet the endpoints of the ellipse. As you become familiar with AutoCAD, you'll start to develop your own ways of working, using the tools best suited to your style.

If you'd like to take a break, now is a good time. You can exit AutoCAD and then come back to the Bath drawing file when you're ready to proceed.

FIGURE 3.7
The Trim command's options

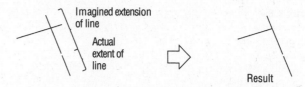

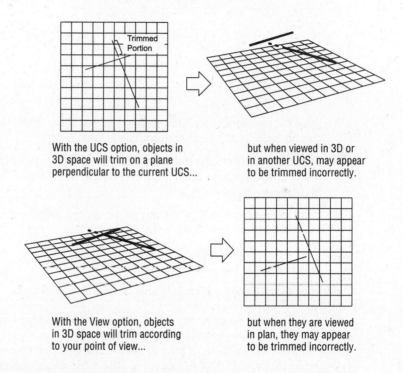

With the Extend option, objects will trim even if the trimmed object doesn't actually intersect with the object to be trimmed.

With the UCS option, objects in 3D space will trim on a plane perpendicular to the current UCS...

but when viewed in 3D or in another UCS, may appear to be trimmed incorrectly.

With the View option, objects in 3D space will trim according to your point of view...

but when they are viewed in plan, they may appear to be trimmed incorrectly.

Planning and Laying Out a Drawing

For the next object, the bathtub, you'll use some new commands to lay out parts of the drawing. This will help you get a feel for the kind of planning you must do to use AutoCAD effectively. You'll begin the bathtub by using the Line command to draw a rectangle 2'-8"×5'-0" (81×152 cm for metric users) on the left side of the drawing area. For a change this time, you'll use a couple of shortcut methods built into AutoCAD: the Line command's keyboard shortcut and the Direct Distance method for specifying distance and direction.

First, though, you'll go back to the previous view of your drawing and arrange some more room to work. Follow these steps:

1. Return to your previous view, shown in Figure 3.8. A quick way to do this is to type **Z↵P↵**, or if you are returning to the file after closing it, type **Z↵A↵** or use the Zoom All option. Your view returns to the one you had before the last Zoom command.

FIGURE 3.8
The view of the finished toilet after using the Zoom Previous tool. You can also obtain this view by using the Zoom All tool from the Zoom flyout.

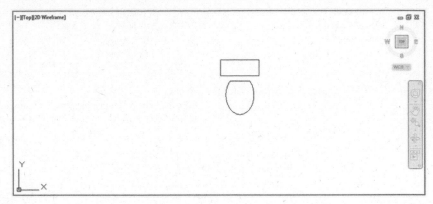

2. Type **L↵**, and then enter **9,10↵** to start the line at the 0'-9",0'-10"coordinate. Metric users should enter **24,27↵** for the coordinate 24.0000,27.0000.

3. Place your cursor to the right of the last point selected so that the rubber-banding line is pointing directly to the right, and type **2'8"**. Then press ↵ for the first side of the tub. Metric users should enter **81↵**.

4. Point the rubber-banding line up toward the top of the screen and type **5'**. Then press ↵ for the next side. Metric users should enter **152↵**.

5. Point the rubber-banding line directly to the left of the last point and type **2'8"** (**81** for metric users). Then press ↵ for the next side.

6. Type **C↵** to close the rectangle and exit the Line command.

Instead of pressing ↵ during the Direct Distance method, you can press the spacebar, or you can right-click and choose Enter from the context menu.

Now you have the outline of the tub. Notice that you don't have to enter the at sign (@) or angle specification. Instead, you use the Direct Distance method to specify direction and distance. You can use this method for drawing lines or moving and copying objects at right angles. The Direct Distance method is less effective if you want to specify exact angles other than right angles.

BE CAREFUL WITH HYPHENS

When you enter feet and inches in the Command window, you must avoid hyphens or spaces. Thus, 2 feet 8 inches is typed as 2'8". But be aware that hyphens are allowed when using the Direct Distance method.

The keyboard shortcuts for some of the tools or commands used in this chapter are CO (Copy), E (Erase), EL (Ellipse), F (Fillet), MI (Mirror), O (Offset), and TR (Trim). Remember that you can enter keyboard shortcuts and invoke commands only when Type a Command is visible in the Command window.

Making a Preliminary Sketch

Certification
Objective

In this section, you'll see how planning ahead will make your use of AutoCAD more efficient. When drawing a complex object, you'll often have to do some layout before you do the actual drawing. For those of you who have done manual drafting, this is similar to drawing an accurate pencil sketch using construction lines that you later trace over to produce a finished drawing. The advantage of doing this in AutoCAD is that your drawing doesn't lose any accuracy between the sketch and the final product. Also, AutoCAD enables you to use the geometry of your sketch to aid in drawing. While you're planning your drawing, think about what you want to draw and then decide which drawing elements will help you create that object.

You'll use the Offset command to establish reference lines to help you draw the inside of the tub. This is where the osnap overrides are useful. (See the sidebar "The Osnap Options" later in this chapter.)

You can use the Offset tool on the Home tab's Modify panel to make parallel copies of a set of objects, such as the lines forming the outside of your tub. Offset is different from the Copy command; although Offset allows only one object to be copied at a time, it can remember the distance you specify. The Offset option doesn't work with all types of objects. Only lines, arcs, circles, ellipses, splines, and 2D polylines can be offset.

Standard lines are best suited for the layout of the bathtub in this situation. In Chapter 6, "Editing and Reusing Data to Work Efficiently," you'll learn about two other objects, construction lines and rays, which are specifically designed to help you lay out a drawing. In this exercise, you'll use standard lines:

1. Click the Offset tool in the Home tab's Modify panel, or type O⏎.

2. At the Specify offset distance or [Through/Erase/Layer] <Through>: prompt, enter 3⏎. This specifies the distance of 3" as the offset distance. Metric users should enter 7 for 7 cm, which is roughly equivalent to 3".

3. At the Select object to offset or [Exit/Undo] <Exit>: prompt, click the bottom line of the rectangle you just drew. Remember that you can click and drag the wheel of your mouse to pan your view while in the middle of a command if needed.

4. At the Specify point on side to offset or [Exit/Multiple/Undo] <Exit>: prompt, pick a point inside the rectangle. A copy of the line appears. You don't have to be exact about where you pick the side to offset; AutoCAD only wants to know on which side of the line you want to make the offset copy.

5. The prompt Select object to offset or [Exit/Undo] <Exit>: appears again. Click another side to offset. Then click again on a point inside the rectangle.

6. Continue to offset the other two sides. Then offset these four new lines inside the rectangle toward the center. You'll have a drawing that looks like Figure 3.9.

FIGURE 3.9
The completed
layout

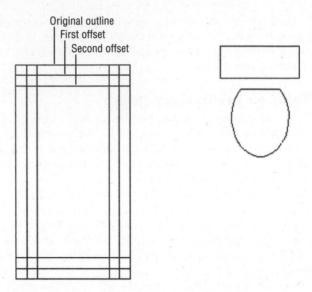

7. When you're done, exit the Offset command by pressing ↵.

Using the Layout

In step 4, you may have noticed that a "preview" line appears showing you where the offset line will appear should you select that point. This aids you in determining where to select points while using the Offset command.

Now you'll begin to draw the inside of the tub, starting with the narrow end. You'll use your offset lines as references to construct the arcs that make up the tub. Also in this exercise, you'll set up some of the osnap options to be available automatically whenever AutoCAD expects a point selection. Here are the steps:

1. Right-click the Object Snap tool in the status bar, and select Settings from the context menu. You can also type **OS**↵.

2. Click the Clear All button to turn off any options that may be selected.

   Look at the graphic symbols next to each of the osnap options in the Object Snap tab. These are the osnap markers that appear in your drawing as you select osnap points. Each osnap option has its own marker symbol. As you use the osnaps, you'll become more familiar with how they work.

3. Click the Endpoint, Midpoint, and Intersection check boxes so that a check mark appears in each box, and make sure that the Object Snap On option is selected. Click OK (see Figure 3.10).

FIGURE 3.10
The Object Snap tab in the Drafting Settings dialog box

You've just set up the Endpoint, Midpoint, and Intersection osnaps to be on by default. This is called a *running osnap*; AutoCAD automatically selects the nearest osnap point without your intervention. Now let's see how a running osnap works:

1. Click the 3-Point Arc tool in the Home tab's Draw panel or type **A**↵. See Figure 3.11 for other Arc options available from the Draw panel's Arc flyout.

FIGURE 3.11
Examples of how the Arc flyout options work

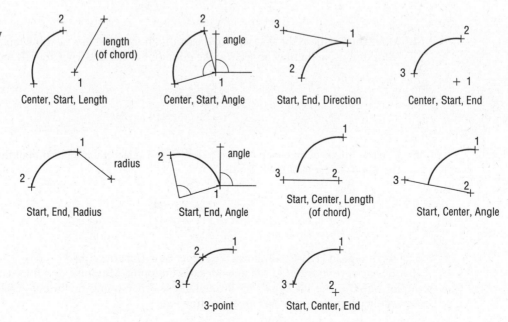

Center, Start, Length

Center, Start, Angle

Start, End, Direction

Center, Start, End

Start, End, Radius

Start, End, Angle

Start, Center, Length (of chord)

Start, Center, Angle

3-point

Start, Center, End

2. For the first point of the arc, move the cursor toward the intersection of the two lines as indicated in the top image in Figure 3.12. Notice that the Intersection osnap marker appears on the intersection.

FIGURE 3.12
Drawing the top, left side, and bottom of the tub

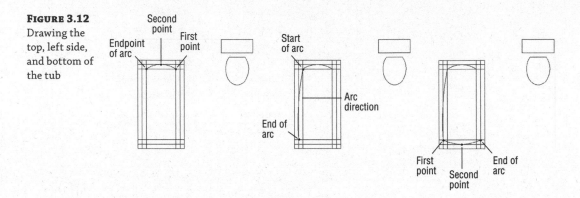

3. With the Intersection osnap marker on the desired intersection, click the left mouse button.

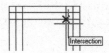

4. Move the cursor to the midpoint of the second horizontal line near the top. When the Midpoint osnap marker appears at the midpoint of the line, click the left mouse button.

5. Use the Intersection osnap marker to locate and select the intersection of the two lines at the upper-left side of the bathtub.

The top image in Figure 3.12 shows the sequence we just described.

If you have several running osnap modes on (Endpoint, Midpoint, and Intersection, for example), pressing the Tab key cycles through those osnap points on the object. This feature can be especially useful in a crowded area of a drawing.

ADJUSTING THE AUTOSNAP FEATURE

When you click the Options button in the Object Snap tab of the Drafting Settings dialog box, you'll see the Drafting tab of the Options dialog box. This tab offers a set of options pertaining to the AutoSnap™ feature. AutoSnap looks at the location of your cursor during osnap selections and locates the osnap point nearest your cursor. AutoSnap then displays a graphic called a *marker* showing you the osnap point it has found. If it's the one you want, left-click to select it.

The AutoSnap settings enable you to control various features:

Marker   Turns the graphic markers on or off.

Magnet   Causes the cursor to jump to inferred osnap points.

Display AutoSnap Tooltip   Turns the AutoSnap tool tip on or off.

Display AutoSnap Aperture Box   Turns the old-style Osnap cursor box on or off.

Colors   Controls the color of the AutoSnap marker. This option opens the Drawing Window Colors dialog box, which lets you select a color for your 2D and 3D AutoSnap markers.

AutoSnap Marker Size   Controls the size of the graphic marker.

Next, you'll draw an arc for the left side of the tub:

1. Click the Arc tool in the Draw panel again.

2. Type @↵ to select the last point you picked as the start of the next arc.

   It's easy for new users to select points inadvertently. If you accidentally selected additional points after the last exercise and prior to step 1, you may not get the results described here. If this happens, issue the Arc command again; then, use the Endpoint osnap and select the endpoint of the last arc.

3. Type E↵ or select the End option from the command line to tell AutoCAD that you want to specify the other end of the arc instead of the next point. You can also right-click anywhere in the drawing area and choose End from the context menu.

4. At the Specify end point of arc: prompt, use the Intersection osnap to pick the intersection of the two lines in the lower-left corner of the tub. The following image shows a close-up view.

5. Type D↵ or select the Direction option in the command line. You can also right-click anywhere in the drawing area and then choose Direction from the context menu. The arc drags, along with a rubber-banding line from the starting point of the arc, as you move the cursor.

6. Move the cursor to the left of the dragging arc until it touches the middle line on the left side of the tub. Pick that line as shown in the middle image in Figure 3.12. You may need to turn off osnaps temporarily to do this by using a Shift+right-click and selecting None.

In step 5 of the preceding exercise, the rubber-banding line indicates the direction of the arc. Be sure that Ortho mode is off because Ortho mode forces the rubber-banding line and the arc in a direction you don't want. Check the status bar; if the Ortho Mode tool is blue (on), press F8 or click the Ortho Mode tool to turn off Ortho mode.

Now you'll draw the bottom of the tub:

1. Click the Arc tool in the Draw panel again. You can also press ↵ to repeat the last command.

2. Using the Endpoint osnap marker, pick the endpoint of the bottom of the arc just drawn.

3. Using the Midpoint osnap marker, pick the middle horizontal line at the bottom of the tub.

4. Pick the intersection of the two lines in the lower-right corner of the tub. The following image shows a close-up view.

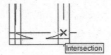

Next, create the right side of the tub by mirroring the left side:

1. Click the Mirror tool on the Home tab's Modify panel. You can also enter **MI**↵ at the Command prompt.

2. At the Select objects: prompt, pick the long arc on the left side of the tub to highlight the arc. Press ↵ to indicate that you've finished your selection.

3. At the Specify first point of mirror line: prompt, pick the midpoint of the top horizontal line. By now, you should know how to use the automatic osnap modes that you set up earlier.

4. At the Specify second point of mirror line: prompt, use Polar Tracking mode to pick a point directly below the last point selected.

5. At the Erase source objects? [Yes/No] <N>: prompt, press ↵ to accept the Mirror command's default Erase source objects option (No) and exit the Mirror command. A mirror image of the arc you picked appears on the right side of the tub. Your drawing should look like Figure 3.13.

In this exercise, you were able to use osnaps in Running Osnap mode. You'll find that you'll use osnaps constantly as you create your drawings. For this reason, you may want running osnaps on all of the time. Even so, at times, running osnaps can get in the way. For example, they may be a nuisance in a crowded drawing when you want to use a zoom window. The osnaps can cause you to select an inappropriate window area by automatically selecting osnap points.

FIGURE 3.13
The inside of the tub completed with the layout lines still in place

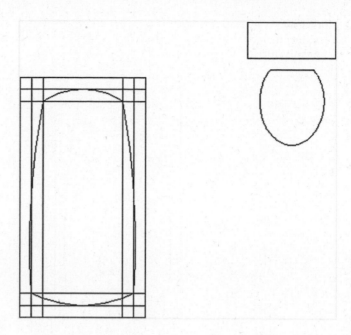

Fortunately, you can toggle Running Osnaps on and off easily by clicking the Object Snap tool in the status bar. If you don't have any running osnaps set, right-click the Object Snap tool and select Settings from the context menu that appears.

Erasing the Layout Lines

Next, you'll erase the layout lines you created using the Offset command. But this time, you'll try selecting the lines *before* issuing the Erase command.

Follow these steps:

1. Click each internal layout line individually.

   If you have problems selecting just the lines, try using a selection window to select single lines. (Remember, a window selects only objects that are completely within it.)

2. After all of the layout lines are highlighted, enter E↵ to use the keyboard shortcut for the Erase command, or right-click and choose Erase from the context menu. Your drawing will look like Figure 3.14.

If you right-clicked to use the context menu in step 2, you'll notice that you have several options besides Erase. You can move, copy, scale, and rotate the objects that you selected. These options are similar to the tools on the Home tab's Modify panel in the way they act. But be aware that they act somewhat differently from the hot-grip options described in Chapter 2.

FIGURE 3.14
The drawing after
erasing the layout
lines

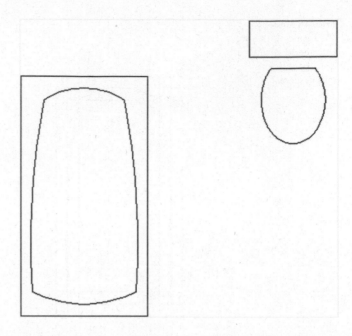

THE OSNAP OPTIONS

Earlier, you made several of the osnap settings automatic so that they're available without having to select them from the Osnap context menu. Another way to invoke the osnap options is to type their keyboard equivalents while selecting points or to Shift+right-click and type the capital letter shown in the Osnap context menu for the option you want to use.

The following is a summary (in alphabetic order) of all the available osnap options, including their command-line keyboard shortcuts. You can type the command-line keyboard shortcuts to bypass the context menu. You've already used many of these options in this chapter and in the previous one. Pay special attention to those options that you haven't yet used in the exercises but may find useful to your style of work. The full name of each option is followed by its keyboard shortcut name in brackets. To use these options, you can enter either the full name or the abbreviation at any point prompt. You can also select these options from the context menu you open by Shift+right-clicking the mouse.

Apparent Intersection [APP]   Selects the apparent intersection of two objects. This is useful when you want to select the intersection of two objects that don't actually intersect. You'll be prompted to select the two objects.

Center [CEN]   Selects the center of an arc or circle.

Endpoint [ENDP or END]   Selects the endpoints of lines, polylines, arcs, curves, and 3D Face vertices.

Extension [EXT]   Selects a point that is aligned with an imagined extension of a line. For example, you can pick a point in space that is aligned with an existing line but that isn't on that line. To use that point, type **ext↵** during point selection or select Extension from the Osnap context menu. Then move the cursor to the line whose extension you want to use and hold it there until you see a small, cross-shaped marker on the line. The cursor also displays a tool tip with the word *extension*, letting you know that the Extension osnap is active.

From [FRO]   Selects a point relative to a picked point. For example, you can select a point that is 2 units to the left and 4 units above a circle's center. This option is usually used in conjunction with another osnap option, such as From Endpoint or From Midpoint.

Geometric Center [GCEN]   Finds the geometric center of a closed polyline or polygon. For irregularly shaped closed polylines where the center is not obvious, you can hover over the polyline and a center marker will appear after a second or two.

Insert [INS]   Selects the insertion point of text, blocks, Xrefs, and overlays.

Intersection [INT]   Selects the intersection of objects.

Mid Between 2 Points [M2P]   Selects a point that is midway between two other points.

Midpoint [MID]   Selects the midpoint of a line or an arc. In the case of a polyline, it selects the midpoint of the polyline segment.

Nearest [NEA]   Selects a point on an object nearest the pick point.

Node [NOD]   Selects a point object.

None [NON]   Temporarily turns off Running Osnaps for a single point selection.

Parallel [PAR]   Lets you draw a line segment that is parallel to another existing line segment. To use this option, type **par**⏎ during point selection or select Parallel from the Osnap context menu. Then move the cursor to the line that you want to be parallel and hold it there until you see a small cross-shaped marker on the line. The cursor also displays a tool tip with the word *parallel*, letting you know that the Parallel osnap is active.

Perpendicular [PER]   Selects a position on an object that is perpendicular to the last point selected.

Point Filters   Not really object snaps, but point-selection options that let you filter x-, y-, or z-coordinate values from a selected point. (See Chapter 20, "Creating 3D Drawings," for more on point filters.)

Quadrant [QUA]   Selects the nearest cardinal (north, south, east, or west) point on an arc or a circle.

Tangent [TAN]   Selects a point on an arc or a circle that represents the tangent from the last point selected.

Temporary Track Point [TT]   Provides an alternate method for using the Object Snap Tracking feature described later in this chapter.

3D Osnap   Offers additional osnaps for 3D modeling. With these osnap options, you can select a vector that is perpendicular to a surface or find the midpoint of an edge of a 3D object.

Sometimes you'll want one or more of these osnap options available as the default selection. Remember that you can set Running Osnaps to be on at all times. Type **DS**, and then click the Object Snap tab. You can also right-click the Object Snap tool in the status bar and choose Settings from the context menu to open the Drafting Settings dialog box, or just select osnap options directly from the context menu.

If you need more control over the selection of objects, you'll find the Add/Remove Selection Mode setting useful. This setting lets you deselect a set of objects within a set of objects you've already selected. While in Object Selection mode, enter **R↵**, and then proceed to use a window or other selection tool to remove objects from the selection set. Enter **A↵** to continue to add options to the selection set. Or, if you need to deselect only a single object, Shift+click it.

Putting on the Finishing Touches

The inside of the tub still has some sharp corners. To round out these corners, you can use the versatile Fillet tool on the Home tab's Modify panel. *Fillet* enables you to join lines and arcs end to end, and it can add a radius where they join so there is a smooth transition from arc to arc or line to line. Fillet can join two lines that don't intersect, and it can trim two crossing lines back to their point of intersection.

Another tool, called *Chamfer*, performs a similar function, but instead of joining lines with an arc, Chamfer joins lines with another line segment. Since they perform similar functions, Fillet and Chamfer occupy the same location on the Modify panel. If you don't see the Fillet tool, click the Chamfer flyout and select Fillet.

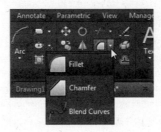

Continue with your tutorial by following these steps:

1. Click the Fillet tool on the Home tab's Modify panel, or type **F↵**.

2. At the prompt

   ```
   Current settings: Mode = TRIM, Radius = 0'-0 1/2"
   Select first object or [Undo/Polyline/Radius/Trim/Multiple]:
   ```

   enter **R↵**, or right-click and choose Radius from the context menu. You can also click Radius from the command line.

3. At the `Specify fillet radius <0'-0.">:` prompt, enter **4↵**. This tells AutoCAD that you want a 4" radius for your fillet. Metric users should enter **10↵**.

4. Pick two adjacent arcs. The fillet arc joins the two larger arcs.

5. Press **↵** again, and fillet another corner. Repeat until all four corners are filleted. Your drawing should look like Figure 3.15.

FIGURE 3.15
A view of the finished
toilet and tub with the
tub corners filleted

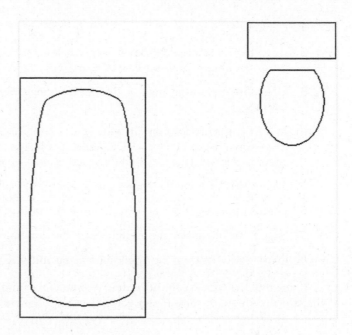

You may have noticed that the Fillet tool offers a preview of the resulting arc. After you click the first of the two lines to be filleted, you can hover over the second line to see a temporary arc appear where the fillet will occur. This feature can help you determine whether the radius of your fillet is really the radius you want.

As you will see in later chapters, the Fillet tool is also used to join two lines quickly end to end to form a corner. You can accomplish this, even if you have the Fillet tool set to join two lines with an arc, by holding down the Shift key while clicking the second line.

Aligning Objects by Using Object Snap Tracking

You saw how to use lines to construct an object such as the bathtub. In many situations, using these *construction lines* is the most efficient way to draw, but they can also be a bit cumbersome. AutoCAD offers another tool that helps you align locations in your drawing to existing objects without having to draw intermediate construction lines. The tool is called *Object Snap Tracking*, or *Osnap Tracking*.

Osnap Tracking is like an extension of object snaps that enables you to *align* a point to the geometry of an object instead of just selecting a point on an object. For example, with Osnap Tracking, you can select a point that is exactly at the center of a rectangle.

In the following exercises, you'll draw a plan view of a bathroom sink as an introduction to the Osnap Tracking feature. This drawing will be used as a symbol in later chapters.

GETTING SET UP

First, as a review, you'll open a new file and use the tools with which you are already familiar to set up the next drawing.

1. Click the Start tab.

2. Open the Templates drop-down list just below the Star Drawings icon and select `acad.dwt` (metric users select `acadiso.dwt`).

3. Open the Application menu, and select Drawing Utilities ➤ Units. You can also type **UNITS**↵.

4. In the Length group of the Drawing Units dialog box, select Architectural from the Type drop-down list and then click OK. Metric users should leave this setting as Decimal but should select Centimeters from the Insert Scale drop-down list.

5. Enter **LIMITS**↵, and then press ↵ to accept the default lower-left corner coordinates.

6. For the upper-right corner of the limits, enter **48,26**↵. Metric users should enter **122,92**↵.

7. Type **Z**↵**A**↵ to display the overall area of the drawing set by the limits.

8. Choose Save As from the Application menu and save the file under the name **Sink**.

If you find that you use the same drawing setup over and over, you can create template files that are already set up to your own way of working. Templates are discussed in Chapter 6.

DRAWING THE SINK

You're ready to draw the sink. First, you'll draw the sink countertop. Then, you'll make sure that Running Osnaps and Osnap Tracking are turned on. Finally, you'll draw the bowl of the sink. Here are the steps for drawing the outline of the sink countertop:

1. If the grid is on, click the Grid Display tool in the status bar to turn it off.

2. Click the Rectangle tool in the Draw panel, or type **REC**↵.

3. At the prompt

   ```
   Specify first corner point or [Chamfer/Elevation/Fillet/Thickness/Width]:
   ```

   enter **0,0**↵. This places one corner of the rectangle in the origin of the drawing.

4. At the `Specify other corner point or [Area/Dimensions/Rotation]:` prompt, enter **@2′4,1′6**↵ to place the other corner of the rectangle. Metric users should enter **@71,46**↵. This makes the rectangle 2′-4″ wide and 1′-6″ deep, or 71 cm wide and 46 cm deep for metric users. The rectangle appears in the lower half of the drawing area.

5. Choose Zoom Extents from the Zoom flyout on the Navigation bar, or type **Z**↵**E**↵. This enlarges the view of the sink outline so it fits in the drawing area.

6. Use the Zoom Realtime tool in the Zoom flyout to adjust your view so it looks similar to the one shown in Figure 3.16. You can also enter **Z**↵↵ to start the real-time zoom feature or just use your scroll wheel.

FIGURE 3.16
The view of the sink countertop after making some adjustments

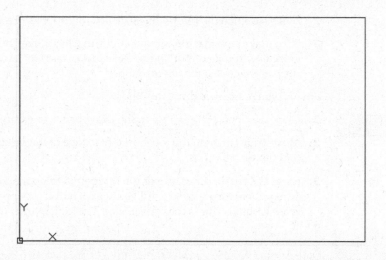

When you draw the bowl of the sink, an ellipse will represent the bowl. You want to place the center of the ellipse at the center of the rectangle that you've just drawn. To do this, you'll use the midpoint of two adjoining sides of the rectangle as alignment locations. This is where the Osnap Tracking tool will be useful.

You need to make sure that the Object Snap tool is turned on and that the Midpoint Object Snap option is also turned on. Then you'll make sure that Osnap Tracking is turned on. Use these steps:

1. Right-click the Object Snap tool in the status bar and choose Settings from the context menu to open the Drafting Settings dialog box at the Object Snap tab (see Figure 3.17).

FIGURE 3.17
The Object Snap tab in the Drafting Settings dialog box

2. Make sure that the Midpoint check box in the Object Snap Modes group is selected.

3. Also make sure that Object Snap On and Object Snap Tracking On are both selected. Click OK. You'll notice that the Object Snap and Object Snap Tracking buttons in the status bar are now in the On position.

Finally, you're ready to draw the ellipse:

1. Click the Center Ellipse tool in the Draw panel, or enter **EL↵C↵**.

2. Move your cursor to the top, horizontal edge of the rectangle until you see the Midpoint tool tip.

3. Move the cursor directly over the Midpoint Osnap marker. Without clicking, hold the cursor there for a second until you see a small cross appear. Look carefully because the cross is small. This is the Object Snap Tracking marker (see Figure 3.18).

FIGURE 3.18
The Object Snap
Tracking marker

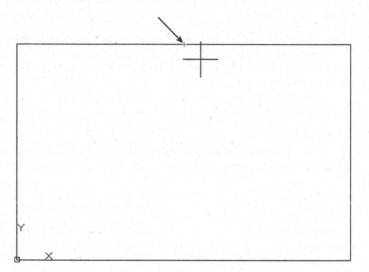

You can alternately insert and remove the Object Snap Tracking marker by passing the cursor over the osnap marker.

4. As you move the cursor downward, a dotted line appears, emanating from the midpoint of the horizontal line. The cursor also shows a small X following the dotted line as you move it (see Figure 3.19).

5. Move the cursor to the midpoint of the left vertical side of the rectangle. Don't click, but hold it there for a second until you see the small cross. Now, as you move the cursor away, a horizontal dotted line appears with an X following the cursor (see Figure 3.20).

FIGURE 3.19
A vertical dotted
line appears.

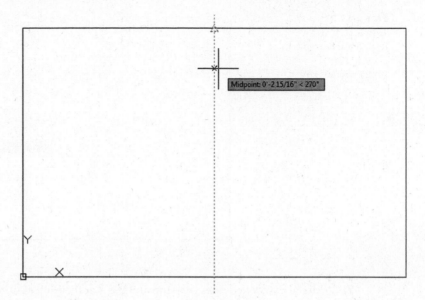

FIGURE 3.19
A vertical dotted
line appears.

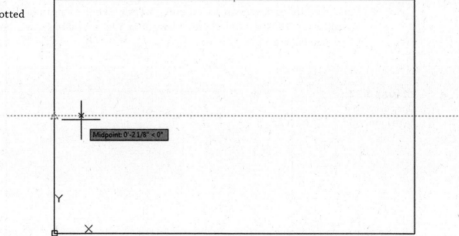

FIGURE 3.20
A horizontal dotted
line appears.

6. Move the cursor to the center of the rectangle. The two dotted lines appear simultane-ously and a small *X* appears at their intersection (see Figure 3.21).

FIGURE 3.21
The vertical and horizontal dotted lines appear simultaneously.

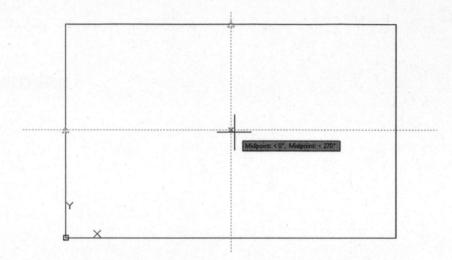

7. With the two dotted lines crossing and the X at their intersection, click the left mouse button to select the exact center of the rectangle.

8. Point the cursor to the right, and enter **8⏎** to make the width of the bowl 16″. Metric users should enter **20⏎** for a bowl 40 cm wide.

9. Point the cursor downward, and enter **6⏎** to make the length of the bowl 12″. Metric users should enter **15⏎** for a bowl with a length of 30 cm. The basic symbol for the sink is complete (see Figure 3.22).

FIGURE 3.22
The completed bathroom sink

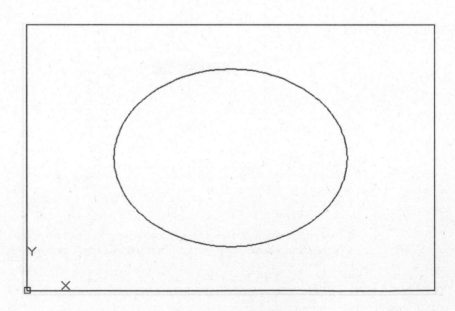

10. Click Save in the Quick Access toolbar and close the current file. You can also save and close the Bath file and exit AutoCAD.

You could have used the Geometric Center Osnap to find the center of the rectangle, but we wanted to show how Object Snap Tracking enables you to align two locations to select a point in space. Although you used only the Midpoint osnap setting in this exercise, you aren't limited to one osnap setting. You can use as many as you need to select the appropriate geometry. You can also use as many alignment points as you need, although in this exercise you used only two. If you like, erase the ellipse and repeat this exercise until you get the hang of using the Object Snap Tracking feature.

As with all of the other tools in the status bar, you can turn Object Snap Tracking on or off by clicking the Object Snap Tracking tool.

Using the AutoCAD Modes as Drafting Tools

Before you finish this chapter, you'll want to know about a few of the other drafting tools that are common to drawing programs. These tools may be compared to a background grid (*Grid mode*) and the ability to "snap" to grid points (*Snap mode*). These drawing modes can be indispensable tools under certain conditions. Their use is fairly straightforward. You can experiment with them on your own using the information in the following sections.

Using Grid Mode as a Background Grid

Using Grid mode is like having a grid under your drawing to help you with layout, as shown in Figure 3.23. In this figure, the grids are set to a 1′ spacing with major grid lines at 5′. The grid also shows, in darker lines, the x- and y-axes that start at the origin of the drawing.

FIGURE 3.23
A sample drawing showing the grids turned on

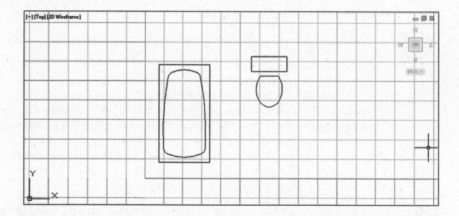

USING OBJECT SNAP TRACKING AND POLAR TRACKING TOGETHER

In addition to selecting as many tracking points as you need, you can use different angles besides the basic orthogonal angles of 0°, 90°, 180°, and 270°. For example, you can have AutoCAD locate a point that is aligned vertically to the top edge of the sink and at a 45° angle from a corner.

continues

continued

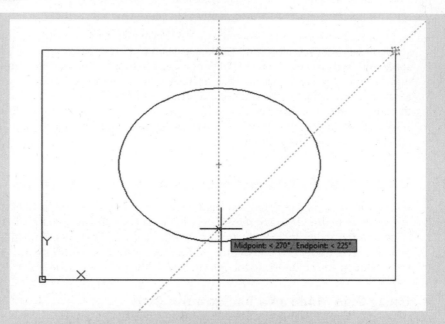

Midpoint: < 270°, Endpoint: < 225°

This can be accomplished by using the settings in the Polar Tracking tab of the Drafting Settings dialog box. (See the section "Setting the Polar Tracking Angle" earlier in this chapter.) If you set the increment angle to 45° and turn on the Track Using All Polar Angle Settings option, you'll be able to use 45° in addition to the orthogonal directions. You'll see firsthand how this works in Chapter 6.

Grids will not print in your final output. They are a visual aid to help you gauge distances. In AutoCAD, Grid mode can also let you see the limits of your drawing because the grid can be set to display only within the limits setting of your drawing. Grid mode can help you visually determine the distances with which you're working in any given view. In this section, you'll learn how to control the grid's appearance. The F7 key toggles Grid mode on and off. You can also click the Grid Display tool in the status bar.

To set up the grid spacing, follow these steps:

1. Right-click the Snap Mode tool in the status bar and select Snap Settings (or type **DS↵**) to open the Drafting Settings dialog box showing all of the mode settings.

2. Click the Snap And Grid tab if it isn't already selected. You will see six groups: Snap Spacing, Grid Style, Grid Spacing, Polar Spacing, Grid Behavior, and Snap Type. Notice that the Grid X Spacing text box contains a value of 1/2", or 0.5. Metric users see a value of 10 (see Figure 3.24).

FIGURE 3.24
The Snap And
Grid tab of the
Drafting Settings
dialog box

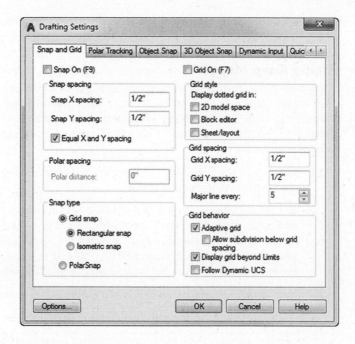

3. Enter the grid spacing you want in the Grid X Spacing and Grid Y Spacing input boxes.

4. Click the Grid On check box to make the grid visible. Notice the F7 in parentheses: This tells you that the F7 function key also controls the Grid On/Off function. Click OK to dismiss the Drafting Settings dialog box and save your settings.

If you prefer, you can use the Gridunit system variable to set the grid spacing. Enter **Gridunit**⏎, and at the Enter new value for GRIDUNIT <0'-0 1/2",0'-0 1/2">: prompt, enter a grid spacing in x-,y-coordinates. You must enter the Gridunit value as an x-,y-coordinate.

There are several other grid options in the Drafting Settings dialog box. The Grid Style group lets you display the grid as a series of dots instead of the graph paper–style lines. Place a check mark by the view name where you want to display dots instead of grid lines.

The Adaptive Grid option adjusts the grid spacing depending on how much of the view is displayed. If you zoom out to a point where the grid becomes too dense for you to view the drawing, the grid automatically increases its interval. The Major Line Every option in the Grid Spacing group lets you control how frequently the major grid lines (lines that appear darker than the others) appear. The Display Grid Beyond Limits option does what it says—it lets the grid appear beyond the drawing limits. Turn this option off to limit the grid display to the drawing limits. The Follow Dynamic UCS option causes the grid to align with the dynamic UCS. See Chapter 20 for more on the Dynamic UCS.

Once you've set up your grid, you can press F7 or click Grid Display in the status bar to turn the grid on and off. (You can also hold down the Ctrl key and press G.)

Using Snap Modes

Certification
Objective

Snap mode forces the cursor to move in steps of a specific distance. Snap mode is useful when you want to select points on the screen at a fixed interval. Two Snap mode options are available in the Snap And Grid tab's Snap type group: *Grid Snap* and *Polar Snap*. The F9 key toggles Grid Snap mode on and off, or you can click the Snap tool in the status bar. Follow these steps to access Snap mode:

1. Right-click the Snap Mode tool in the status bar and select Settings (or type **DS↵**) to open the Drafting Settings dialog box.

2. In the Snap Spacing group of the dialog box, double-click the Snap X Spacing text box and enter a value for your snap spacing. Then press the Tab key to move to the next option. AutoCAD assumes that you want the X and Y snap spacing to be the same unless you specifically ask for a different Y setting. If you want the X snap spacing to be different from the Y, uncheck the Equal X And Y spacing option.

3. You can click the Snap On check box to turn on Snap mode from this dialog box.

4. Click OK to save your settings and close the dialog box.

With Snap mode on, the cursor seems to move in steps rather than in a smooth motion. The Snap Mode tool in the status bar appears blue, indicating that Snap mode is on. Press F9 or click Snap Mode in the status bar (you can also hold down the Ctrl key and press B) to turn Snap mode on or off.

Note that you can use the Snapunit system variable to set the snap spacing. Enter **Snapunit↵**. Then, at the Enter new value for SNAPUNIT <0'0",0'0">: prompt, enter a snap distance value as an x-,y-coordinate.

In the Snap Type group, you can change the snap and grid configuration to aid in creating 2D isometric drawings by clicking the Isometric Snap radio button. The PolarSnap option enables you to set a snap distance for the PolarSnap feature. When you click the PolarSnap radio button, the Polar Distance option at the middle left of the dialog box changes from gray to black and white to allow you to enter a Polar Snap distance.

You can also set up the grid to follow the snap spacing automatically. To do this, set Grid X Spacing and Grid Y Spacing to 0.

CONTROLLING THE COLOR OF GRID LINES

If you find that the colors of the grid lines are too strong and they obscure your drawing, you can set them so that they blend into the background. To do this, you use the Options dialog box (see Appendix B, "Installing and Setting Up AutoCAD," for more on this dialog box):

1. Right-click and select Options, or type **Options↵**.

2. Select the Display tab.

3. Click the Colors button in the Window Elements group.

4. Make sure that 2D Model Space is selected in the Context list, and then select Grid Minor Lines from the Interface Element list.

5. Select a color for your grid line from the Color drop-down list.

6. Select Grid Major Lines from the Interface Element list, and select a color from the Color drop-down list.

7. Click Apply & Close, and then click OK in the Options dialog box.

In steps 5 and 6, you can select from the list of colors or choose the Select Color option at the bottom of the list to select a custom color.

The Bottom Line

Set up a work area.   A blank AutoCAD drawing offers few clues about the size of the area with which you're working, but you can get a rough idea of the area shown in the AutoCAD window.

Master It   Name two ways to set up the area of your work.

Explore the drawing process.   To use AutoCAD effectively, you'll want to know how the different tools work together to achieve an effect. The drawing process often involves many cycles of adding objects and then editing them.

Master It   Name the tool that causes the cursor to point in an exact horizontal or vertical direction.

Plan and lay out a drawing.   If you've ever had to draw a precise sketch with just a pencil and pad, you've probably used a set of lightly drawn guidelines to lay out your drawing first. You do the same thing in AutoCAD, but instead of lightly drawn guidelines, you can use any object you want. In AutoCAD, objects are easily modified or deleted, so you don't have to be as careful when adding guidelines.

Master It   What is the name of the feature that lets you select exact locations on objects?

Use the AutoCAD modes as drafting tools.   The main reason for using AutoCAD is to produce precision technical drawings. AutoCAD offers many tools to help you produce a drawing with the precision you need.

Master It   What dialog box lets you set both the grid and snap spacing?

Chapter 4

Organizing Objects with Blocks and Groups

Drawing the tub, toilet, and sink in Chapter 3, "Setting Up and Using the Drafting Tools," may have taken what seemed to you an inordinate amount of time. As you continue to use the AutoCAD® 2018 software, however, you'll learn to draw objects more quickly. You'll also need to draw fewer of them because you can save drawings as symbols and then use those symbols like rubber stamps, duplicating drawings instantaneously wherever they're needed. This saves a lot of time when you're composing drawings.

To make effective use of AutoCAD, begin a *symbol library* of drawings you use frequently. A mechanical designer might have a library of symbols for fasteners, cams, valves, or even complete assemblies used in their application. An electrical engineer might have a symbol library of capacitors, resistors, switches, and the like. A circuit designer will have yet another unique set of frequently used symbols. In Chapter 3, you drew three objects that architects often use—a bathtub, a toilet, and a sink. In this chapter, you'll see how to create symbols from those drawings.

In this chapter, you will learn to

- ◆ Create and insert a symbol

- ◆ Modify a block

- ◆ Understand the annotation scale

- ◆ Group objects

Creating and Using a Symbol

To save a drawing as a symbol, you use the tools in the Home tab's Block panel or the Insert tab's Block Definition panel. In word processors, the term *block* refers to a group of words or sentences selected for moving, saving, or deleting. You can copy a block of text elsewhere within the same file, to other files, or to a separate location on a server or USB storage device for future use. AutoCAD uses blocks in a similar fashion. In a file, you can turn parts of your drawing into blocks that can be saved and recalled at any time. You can also use entire existing files as blocks.

You'll start by opening the file you worked on in the previous chapter and selecting the objects that will become a block:

1. Start AutoCAD, and open the existing Bath file. Use the one you created in Chapter 3, or open the 04-bath.dwg sample file from this book's web page (www.sybex.com/go/masteringautocad2018). Metric users can use the 04-bath-metric.dwg file. The drawing appears just as you left it in the last session.

2. In the Home tab's Block panel, click the Create tool or type **B↵**, the keyboard shortcut for the Create tool. This opens the Block Definition dialog box (see Figure 4.1).

FIGURE 4.1
The Block Definition
dialog box

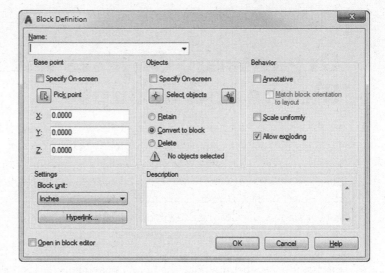

3. In the Name text box, type **Toilet**.

4. In the Base Point group, click the Pick Point button. This option enables you to select a base point for the block by using your cursor. (The *insertion base point* of a block is a point of reference on the block that is used like a grip.) When you've selected this option, the Block Definition dialog box temporarily closes.

Notice that the Block Definition dialog box gives you the option to specify the x-, y-, and z-coordinates for the base point instead of selecting a point.

5. Using the Midpoint osnap, pick the midpoint of the back of the toilet as the base point. Remember that you learned how to set up running osnaps in Chapter 3; all you need to do is point to the midpoint of a line to display the Midpoint Osnap marker and then left-click.

After you've selected a point, the Block Definition dialog box reappears. Notice that the X, Y, and Z values in the Base Point group now display the coordinates of the point you picked. For two-dimensional drawings, the z-coordinate should remain at 0.

Next, you need to select the objects that you want as part of the block.

6. Click the Select Objects button in the Objects group. Once again, the dialog box momentarily closes. You now see the familiar `Select objects:` prompt in the Command window, and the cursor becomes a Pickbox cursor. Click a point below and to the left of the toilet. Then use a selection window to select the entire toilet. The toilet is now highlighted.

Make sure that you use the Select Objects option in the Block Definition dialog box to select the objects that you want to turn into a block. AutoCAD lets you create a block that contains no objects. If you try to proceed without selecting objects, you'll get a warning message. This can cause confusion and frustration, even for an experienced user.

7. Press ↵ to confirm your selection. The Block Definition dialog box opens again.

8. Select Inches from the Block Unit drop-down list. Metric users should select Centimeters.

9. Click the Description list box, and enter **Standard Toilet**.

10. Make sure the Retain radio button in the Objects group is selected, and then click OK. The toilet drawing is now a block with the name Toilet.

11. Repeat the blocking process for the tub, but this time use the upper-left corner of the tub as the insertion base point and give the block the name **Tub**. Enter **Standard Tub** for the description.

You can press ↵ or right-click and choose Repeat BLOCK from the context menu to start the Create Block tool.

When you turn an object into a block, it's stored in the drawing file, ready to be recalled at any time. The block remains part of the drawing file even when you end the editing session. When you open the file again, the block is available for your use. In addition, you can access blocks from other drawings by using the AutoCAD DesignCenter™ and the tool palettes. You'll learn more about the DesignCenter and the tool palettes in Chapter 25, "Managing and Sharing Your Drawings."

A block acts like a single object, even though it's made up of several objects. One unique characteristic of a block is that when you modify it, all instances of it are updated to reflect the modifications. For example, if you insert several copies of the toilet into a drawing and then later decide the toilet needs to be a different shape, you can edit the Toilet block, and all of the other copies of the toilet are updated automatically.

You can modify a block in a number of ways after it has been created. In this chapter, you'll learn how to make simple changes to individual blocks by modifying the block's properties. For more detailed changes, you'll learn how to redefine a block after it has been created. Later, in Chapter 17, "Using Dynamic Blocks," you'll learn how to use the Block Editor to make more interactive blocks.

Understanding the Block Definition Dialog Box

The Block Definition dialog box offers several options that can help make using blocks easier. If you're interested in these options, take a moment to review the Block Definition dialog box as you read the descriptions. If you prefer, you can continue with the tutorial and come back to this section later.

You've already seen how the Name option lets you enter a name for your block. AutoCAD doesn't let you complete the block creation until you enter a name.

You've also seen how to select a base point for your block. The base point is like the grip of the block: It's the reference point you use when you insert the block back into the drawing. In the exercise, you used the Pick Point option to indicate a base point, but you also have the option to enter x-, y-, and z-coordinates just below the Pick Point option. In most cases, however, you'll want to use the Pick Point option to indicate a base point that is on or near the set of objects that you're converting to a block.

The Objects group of the Block Definition dialog box lets you select the objects that make up the block. You use the Select Objects button to select visually the objects that you want to include in the block you're creating. The QuickSelect button to the right of the Select Objects button lets you filter out objects based on their properties. You'll learn more about Quick Select in Chapter 14, "Advanced Editing and Organizing." Once you select a set of objects for your block, you'll see a thumbnail preview of the block's contents near the top center of the Block Definition dialog box.

Other options in the Objects group and Settings group let you specify what to do with the objects you're selecting for your block. Table 4.1 shows a list of those other options and what they mean.

TABLE 4.1:   The Block Definition dialog box options

OPTION	PURPOSE
Base Point group	
Specify On-Screen	Lets you select the base point for the block after you click OK.
Pick Point	Lets you select the base point for the block before you click OK to dismiss the dialog box.
X, Y, and Z text boxes	Enable you to enter exact coordinates for the block's base point.
Objects group	
Specify On-Screen	Lets you select the objects for the block after you click OK.
Select Objects/Quick Select	Lets you select the objects for the block before you click OK to dismiss the dialog box.
Retain	Keeps the objects you select for your block as they are, or unchanged.
Convert To Block	Converts the objects you select into the block you're defining. The block then acts like a single object after you've completed the Create Block command.
Delete	Deletes the objects you selected for your block. A warning message appears at the bottom of the Objects group if you haven't selected objects for the block. After you've selected objects, the warning changes to tell you how many objects you've selected.
Behavior group	
Annotative	Turns on the annotation scale feature for blocks. This feature lets you use a single block for different scale views of a drawing. With this feature turned on, AutoCAD can be set to adjust the size of the block to the appropriate scale for the viewport.

TABLE 4.1:   The Block Definition dialog box options   *(CONTINUED)*

OPTION	PURPOSE
Match Block Orientation To Layout	With the Annotative option activated, this option is available. This option causes a block to appear always in its normal orientation regardless of the orientation of the layout view.
Scale Uniformly	By default, blocks can have a different X, Y, or Z scale. This means that they can be stretched in any of the axes. You can lock the X, Y, and Z scales of the block by selecting this option. That way, the block will always be scaled uniformly and can't be stretched in one axis.
Allow Exploding	By default, blocks can be exploded or reduced to their component objects. You can lock a block so that it can't be exploded by turning off this option. You can always turn on this option later through the Properties palette if you decide that you need to explode a block.
Settings group	
Block Unit	Lets you determine how the object is to be scaled when it's inserted into the drawing using the DesignCenter feature discussed in Chapter 25. By default, this value is the same as the current drawing's insert value.
Hyperlink	Lets you assign a link to a block. This option opens the Insert Hyperlink dialog box, where you can select a location or file for the link.
Description and Open In Block Editor	
Description	Lets you include a brief description or keyword for the block. This option is helpful when you need to find a specific block in a set of drawings. You'll learn more about searching for blocks later in this chapter and in Chapter 25.
Open In Block	If you turn on this option, the block is created and then opened in the Block Editor, described in Chapter 17.

Inserting a Symbol

You can recall the Tub and Toilet blocks at any time—as many times as you want. You'll draw the interior walls of the bathroom first, and then you'll insert the tub and toilet. Follow these steps to draw the walls:

1. Delete the original tub and toilet drawings. Click the Erase tool in the Modify Ribbon panel, and then enter **All**⏎ to erase the entire visible contents of the drawing. (Doing so has no effect on the blocks you created previously.)

2. Draw a rectangle 7'-6" by 5'-0". Metric users should draw a 228 cm by 152 cm rectangle. Orient the rectangle so the long sides go from left to right and the lower-left corner is at coordinate 1'-10",1'-10" (or coordinate 56.0000,56.0000 for metric users).

If you use the Rectangle tool to draw the rectangle, make sure that you explode it by using the Explode command. This is important for later exercises. (See the section "Unblocking and

Redefining a Block" later in this chapter if you aren't familiar with the Explode command.) Your drawing should look like Figure 4.2.

FIGURE 4.2
The interior walls of
the bathroom

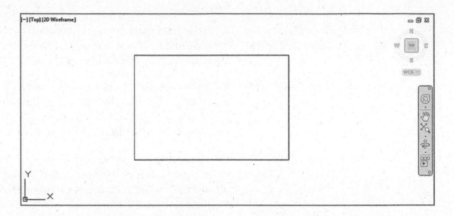

Now you're ready to place your blocks. Start by placing the tub in the drawing. Although there is a fairly simple way to do this, you'll use a resizable dialog box so that you become familiar with some of the options available:

1. In the Block Ribbon panel, click the Insert tool. You'll see a flyout with icons of the blocks you have just created. You could click the icon of the block you want to insert from this flyout, but in this exercise, you'll look at the options available through the Insert dialog box. If you do not see the flyout with icons, type **Galleryview⤶1⤶**.

2. From the flyout, select More Options. Or instead of clicking the Insert tool, you can type **I⤶** to open the Insert dialog box (see Figure 4.3).

FIGURE 4.3
The Insert dialog box

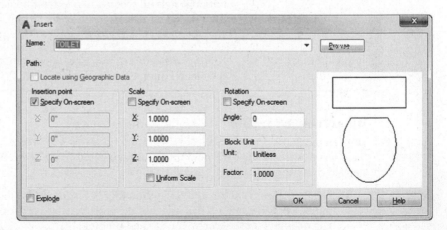

3. Click the Name drop-down list to display a list of the available blocks in the current drawing.

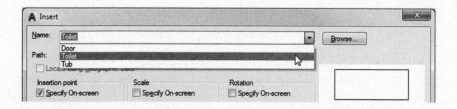

4. Click the block named Tub.

5. In the Insertion Point and Rotation groups, turn on the Specify On-Screen option. With this option turned on in the Insertion Point group, you're asked to specify an insertion point using your cursor. The Specify On-Screen option in the Rotation group lets you specify the rotation angle of the block graphically as you insert it.

6. Click OK and you will see a preview image of the tub attached to the cursor. The upper-left corner that you picked for the tub's base point is now on the cursor intersection.

7. At the `Specify insertion point or [Basepoint/Scale/X/Y/Z/Rotate]:` prompt, pick the upper-left intersection of the room as your insertion point.

8. At the `Specify rotation angle <0>:` prompt, notice that you can rotate the block. This lets you visually specify a rotation angle for the block. You won't use this feature at this time, so press ↵ to accept the default of 0. The tub should look like the one in the top image of Figure 4.4.

FIGURE 4.4
The bathroom, first with the tub and then with the toilet inserted

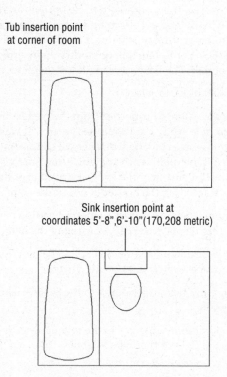

Tub insertion point
at corner of room

Sink insertion point at
coordinates 5'-8",6'-10"(170,208 metric)

You've got the tub in place. Now place the Toilet block in the drawing:

1. Open the Insert dialog box again, but this time select Toilet in the Name drop-down list.

2. Clear the Specify On-Screen check box in the Rotation group.

3. Place the toilet at the midpoint of the line along the top of the rectangle representing the bathroom wall, as shown in the bottom image in Figure 4.4. The toilet appears in the drawing.

You've just used two methods for inserting a block. When you used the Insert dialog box to place the Tub block, you saw a number of options that you could use to fine-tune the block while you insert it. Note that this dialog box can be enlarged by dragging one of its corners or sides.

Scaling and Rotating Blocks

When you insert the tub, you can see it rotate as you move the cursor. You can pick a point to fix the block in place, or you can enter a rotation value. This is the result of selecting the Specify On-Screen option in the Insert dialog box. You may find that you want the Rotation group's Specify On-Screen option turned on most of the time so that you can adjust the rotation angle of the block while you're placing it in the drawing.

The options in the Insert dialog box that you didn't use are the Scale group options. These options let you scale the block to a different size. You can scale the block uniformly, or you can distort the block by individually changing its X, Y, or Z scale factor. With the Specify On-Screen option unchecked, you can enter specific values in the X, Y, and Z text boxes to stretch the block in any direction. If you turn on the Specify On-Screen option, you can visually adjust the X, Y, and Z scale factors in real time. Although these options aren't used often, they can be useful in special situations when a block needs to be stretched one way or another to fit in a drawing.

You aren't limited to scaling or rotating a block when it's being inserted into a drawing. You can always use the Scale or Rotate tool or modify an inserted block's properties to stretch it in one direction or another. The next exercise shows you how this is done:

1. Click the Toilet block to select it.

2. Right-click, and choose Properties from the context menu to open the Properties palette. Take a moment to study the Properties palette. Toward the bottom, under the Geometry heading, you see a set of labels that show Position and Scale. These labels may appear as Posi and Scal if the width of the palette is too narrow to show the entire label. Remember that you can click and drag the left or right edge of the palette to change its width. You can also click and drag the border between the columns in the palette.

3. If the first item label under the Geometry heading isn't visible, place the cursor on the label. A tool tip displays the full wording of the item, which is Position X.

4. Move the cursor down one line to display the tool tip for Position Y. This shows how you can view the label even if it isn't fully visible.

5. Continue to move the cursor down to the Scale X label. The tool tip displays the full title and description.

6. Let's try making some changes to the toilet properties. Click the Scale X value in the column just to the right of the Scale X label.

7. Enter **1.5**↵. Notice that the toilet changes in width as you do this.

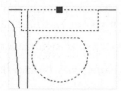

8. You don't really want to change the width of the toilet, so click the Undo tool in the Quick Access toolbar or enter **U**↵ at the command line.

9. Close the Properties palette by clicking the X at the top of the Properties palette title bar.

If a block is created with the Scale Uniformly option turned on in the Block Definition dialog box, you can't scale the block in just one axis as shown in the previous exercise. You can only scale the block uniformly in all axes.

SYMBOLS FOR PROJECTS LARGE AND SMALL

A symbol library was a crucial part of the production of the San Francisco Main Library construction documents. Shown here is a portion of an AutoCAD floor plan of the library in which some typical symbols were used:

Notice the familiar door symbols, such as the one for the door you created in Chapter 2, "Creating Your First Drawing." And yes, there are even toilets in the lower half of the plan in the public restrooms. Symbol use isn't restricted to building components. Room number labels, diamond-shaped interior elevation reference symbols, and the hexagonal column grid symbols are all common to an architectural drawing, regardless of the project's size. As you work through this chapter, keep in mind that all of the symbols used in the library drawing were created using the tools presented here.

You've just seen how you can modify the properties of a block by using the Properties palette. In the exercise, you changed the X scale of the Toilet block, but you could have just as easily changed the Y value. You may have noticed other properties available in the Properties palette. You'll learn more about those properties as you work through this chapter.

You've seen how you can turn a drawing into a symbol, known as a block in AutoCAD. Now let's see how you can use an existing drawing file as a symbol.

Using an Existing Drawing as a Symbol

You need a door into the bathroom. Because you've already drawn a door and saved it as a file, you can bring the door into this drawing file and use it as a block:

1. If Object Snaps are on, turn them off to avoid selecting any default Osnap points.

2. In the Block Ribbon panel, click the Insert tool and select More Options. You can also just type I↵.

3. In the Insert dialog box, click the Browse button to open the Select Drawing File dialog box.

4. This is a standard Windows file browser dialog box. Locate the Door.dwg file and double-click it. If you didn't create a door file, you can use the Door.dwg file from the Chapter 4 project files at this book's web page.

5. You can also browse your hard disk by looking at thumbnail views of the drawing files in a folder.

6. When you return to the Insert dialog box, make sure the Specify On-Screen option is checked in the Insertion Point, Scale, and Rotation groups, and then click OK. As you move the cursor around, notice that the door appears above and to the right of the cursor intersection, as shown in Figure 4.5.

FIGURE 4.5
The door drawing being inserted in the Bath file

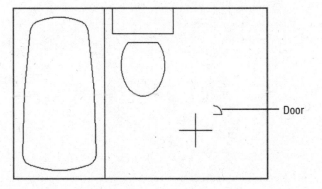

Door

7. At this point, the door looks too small for this bathroom. This is because you drew it 3 units long, which translates to 3″. Metric users drew the door 9 cm long. Pick a point near coordinates 7′-2″,2′-4″ so that the door is placed in the lower-right corner of the room. Metric users should use the coordinates 210,70.

8. If you take the default setting for the X scale of the inserted block, the door will remain 3″ long, or 9 cm long for metric users. However, as mentioned earlier, you can specify a smaller or larger size for an inserted object. In this case, you want a 3′ door. Metric users want a 90 cm door. To get that from a 3″ door, you need an X scale factor of 12, or 10 for metric users. (You may want to review "Understanding Scale Factors" in Chapter 3 to see how this is determined.) At the Enter X scale factor, specify opposite corner, or [Corner/XYZ] <1>: prompt, enter 12↵. Metric users should enter 10↵.

9. Press ↵ twice to accept the default Y = X and the rotation angle of 0°.

The Command prompt appears, but nothing seems to happen to the drawing. This is because when you enlarged the door, you also enlarged the distance between the base point and the object. This raises another issue when you consider using drawings as symbols: All drawings have base points. The default base point is the absolute coordinate 0,0, otherwise known as the *origin*, which is located in the lower-left corner of any new drawing. When you drew the door in Chapter 2, you didn't specify the base point. When you try to bring the door into this drawing, AutoCAD uses the origin of the door drawing as its base point (see Figure 4.6).

FIGURE 4.6
By default, a drawing's origin is also its insertion point. You can change a drawing's insertion point by using the Base command.

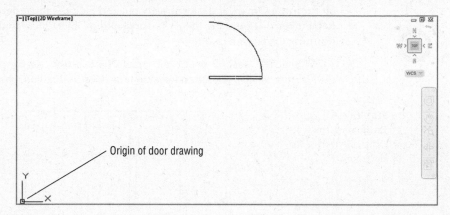

AutoCAD also uses the inserted drawing's Insertion scale setting in the Units dialog box to apply the proper scale (see Chapters 3 and 25 for more on the Insert Scale setting). This feature is important when the unit type of the inserted drawing differs from the current drawing. For example, you could insert a door drawn in centimeters into a floor plan drawn in feet and inches and, as long as the insertion scale is set correctly in the door drawing, the door will appear at the correct size for the floor plan.

Because the door appears outside the bathroom, you must first choose Zoom All from the Zoom flyout on the Navigation bar to show more of the drawing and then use the Move command on the Modify panel to move the door to the right-side wall of the bathroom. Let's do so now:

1. Click Zoom All from the Zoom flyout on the Navigation bar. The view of the room shrinks, and the door is displayed. Notice that it's now the proper size for your drawing (see Figure 4.7).

FIGURE 4.7
The enlarged door

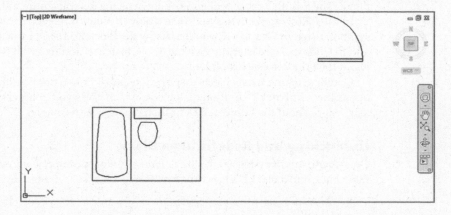

2. Choose the Move tool from the Modify Ribbon panel, or type **M**↵.

3. To pick the door you just inserted, at the `Select objects:` prompt, click a point anywhere on the door and press ↵. Notice that now the entire door is highlighted. This is because a block is treated like a single object, even though it may be made up of several lines, arcs, and so on.

4. At the `Specify base point or [Displacement] <Displacement>:` prompt, turn on Running Osnaps if it isn't already on, and pick the lower-left corner of the door. Remember that pressing the F3 key or clicking Object Snap in the status bar toggles Running Osnaps on or off.

5. At the `Specify second point or <use first point as displacement>:` prompt, use the Nearest osnap override and position the door so that your drawing looks like Figure 4.8.

FIGURE 4.8
The door on the right-side wall of the bathroom

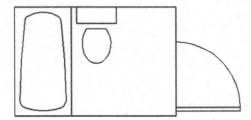

Because the door is an object that you'll use often, it should be a common size so that you don't have to specify an odd value every time you insert it. It would also be helpful if the door's insertion base point were in a more convenient location—that is, a location that would let you place the door accurately within a wall opening. Next, you'll modify the Door block better to suit your needs.

Modifying a Block

You can modify a block in three ways. One way is to redefine it completely. In earlier versions of AutoCAD, this was the only way to make changes to a block. A second way is to use the Block Editor. A third way is to use the Edit Reference tool on the Insert tab's expanded Reference panel. The Edit Reference tool is also known as the Refedit command.

In the following sections, you'll learn how to redefine a block by making changes to the door symbol. Later, in Chapter 17, you'll see how the Block Editor lets you add adjustability to blocks, and in Chapter 7, "Mastering Viewing Tools, Hatches, and External References," you'll learn about the Edit Reference tool.

Double-clicking most objects displays the Quick Properties palette. Double-clicking a block opens the Edit Block Definition dialog box, which gives you another way to edit blocks. You'll learn more about the Edit Block Definition dialog box in Chapter 17.

Unblocking and Redefining a Block

One way to modify a block is to break it down into its components, edit them, and then turn them back into a block. This is called *redefining* a block. If you redefine a block that has been inserted in a drawing, each occurrence of that block in the current file changes to reflect the new block definition. You can use this block-redefinition feature to make rapid changes to a design.

To separate a block into its components, use the Explode command:

1. Click Explode from the Home tab's Modify panel. You can also type **X**↵ to start the Explode command.

2. Click the door, and press ↵ to confirm your selection.

   You can simultaneously insert and explode a block by clicking the Explode check box in the lower-left corner of the Insert dialog box.

Now you can edit the individual objects that make up the door, if you desire. In this case, you want to change only the door's insertion point because you've already made it a more convenient size. You'll turn the door back into a block, this time using the door's lower-left corner for its insertion base point:

1. In the Block Ribbon panel, select Create Block, or type **B**↵.

2. In the Block Definition dialog box, select Door from the Name drop-down list.

3. Click the Pick Point button, and pick the lower-left corner of the door.

4. Click the Select Objects button, and select the components of the door, including the small, vertical lines at each end of the door. Press ↵ when you've finished making your selection.

5. Select the Convert To Block option in the Objects group to convert the selected objects automatically in the drawing into a block.

6. Select Inches (or cm for metric users) from the Block Unit drop-down list, and then enter **Standard door** in the Description box.

7. Click OK. You see a warning message that reads, "The block definition has changed. Do you want to redefine it?" You don't want to redefine an existing block accidentally. In this case, you know that you want to redefine the door, so click the Redefine button to proceed.

The Select Objects and Pick Point buttons appear in other dialog boxes. Make note of their appearance and remember that when you select them, the dialog box temporarily closes to let you select points or objects and otherwise perform operations that require a clear view of the drawing area.

In step 7, you received a warning message that you were about to redefine the existing Door block. But originally you inserted the door as a file, not as a block. Whenever you insert a drawing file by using the Insert Block tool, the inserted drawing automatically becomes a block in the current drawing. When you redefine a block, however, you don't affect the drawing file you imported. AutoCAD changes only the block in the current file.

You've just redefined the door block. Now place the door in the wall of the room:

1. Choose Erase from the Modify Ribbon panel and then click the door. Notice that the entire door is one object instead of individual lines and an arc. Had you not selected the Convert To Block option in step 5 of the previous exercise, the components of the block would have remained individual objects.

2. Press ↵ to erase the door.

3. Click the Insert tool on the Home tab's Block panel, and select More Options.

4. In the Insert dialog box, select Door from the Name drop-down list and make sure that the Specify On-Screen option for Scale is not checked. This will save time while inserting subsequent blocks, since AutoCAD will not prompt you for a scale after selecting a location.

5. This time, use the Nearest osnap override and pick a point on the right-side wall of the bathroom near coordinate 9'-4",2'-1". Metric users should insert the door near 284,63.4.

6. At the `Specify rotation angle <0>:` prompt, press ↵ to accept the default angle.

7. Use the Grips feature to mirror the door, using the wall as the mirror axis so that the door is inside the room. To mirror an object using grips, select the objects to mirror, click a grip, and right-click. Select Mirror from the context menu; then, indicate a mirror axis with the cursor. Press Esc when you're done.

Your drawing will look like Figure 4.9.

FIGURE 4.9
The bathroom floor plan thus far

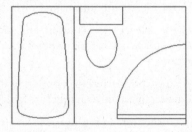

Next, you'll see how you can update an external file with a redefined block.

Saving a Block as a Drawing File

You've seen that, with little effort, you can create a symbol and place it anywhere in a file. Suppose you want to use this symbol in other files. When you create a block by using the Block command, the block exists in the current file only until you specifically instruct AutoCAD to save it as a separate drawing file. When you have an existing drawing that has been brought in and modified, such as the door, the drawing file associated with that door isn't automatically updated. To update the Door file, you must take an extra step and use the Export option on the Application menu. Let's see how this works.

Start by turning the Tub and Toilet blocks into individual files:

1. Press the Esc key to make sure that nothing is selected and that no command is active.

2. From the Application menu, choose Export ➤ Other Formats to open the Export Data dialog box, which is a simple file dialog box.

3. Open the Files Of Type drop-down list, and select Block (*.dwg).

   If you prefer, you can skip step 3 and instead enter the full filename, including the .dwg extension, as in Tub.dwg.

4. Select the entire contents of the File Name text box and enter **Tub**.

5. Click the Save button to close the Export Data dialog box.

6. At the [= (block=output file)/* (whole drawing)] <define new drawing>: prompt, enter the name of the block you want to save to disk as the tub file—in this case, **Tub**⏎.

   The Tub block is now saved as a file.

7. Repeat steps 1 through 6 for the Toilet block. Give the file the same name as the block.

OPTIONS FOR SAVING BLOCKS

AutoCAD gives you the option to save a block's file under the same name as the original block or save it with a different name. Usually, you'll want to use the same name, which you can do by entering an equal sign (=) after the prompt.

Normally, AutoCAD saves a preview image with a file. This enables you to preview a drawing file before opening it.

Replacing Existing Files with Blocks

The Wblock command does the same thing as choosing Export ➤ Other Formats, but output is limited to AutoCAD DWG files. Let's try using the Wblock command this time to save the Door block you modified:

1. Issue the Wblock command by typing **Wblock**⏎, or use the keyboard shortcut by typing **W**⏎. This opens the Write Block dialog box (see Figure 4.10).

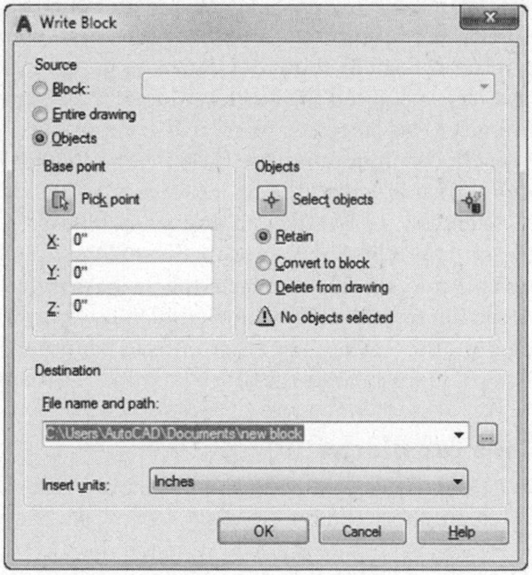

FIGURE 4.10
The Write Block dialog box

2. In the Source group, click the Block radio button.

3. Select Door from the drop-down list. You can keep the old name or enter a different name if you prefer.

4. In this case, you want to update the door you drew in Chapter 2. Click the Browse button to the right of the File Name And Path text box in the Destination group.

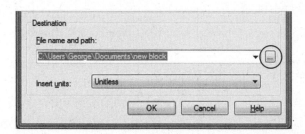

5. Locate and select the original Door.dwg file that you inserted earlier. Click Save to close the dialog box.

6. Click OK. A warning message tells you that the Door.dwg file already exists. Go ahead and click the "Replace the existing. . ." option to confirm that you want to overwrite the old door drawing with the new door definition.

In this exercise, you typed the Wblock command at the Command prompt instead of choosing Export ➤ Other Formats. The results are the same regardless of which method you use. If you're in a hurry, the Export ➤ Other Formats command is a quick way to save part of your drawing as a file. The Wblock option might be easier for new users because it offers options in a dialog box.

Understanding the Write Block Dialog Box Options

The Write Block dialog box offers a way to save parts of your current drawing as a file. As you can see from the dialog box shown in the previous exercise, you have several options.

In that exercise, you used the Block option of the Source group to select an existing block as the source object to be exported. You can also export a set of objects by choosing the Objects option. If you choose this option, the Base Point and Objects groups become available. These options work the same way as their counterparts in the Block Definition dialog box, which you saw earlier when you created the Tub and Toilet blocks.

The other option in the Source group, Entire Drawing, lets you export the whole drawing to its own file. This may seem to duplicate the Save As option in the Application menu, but saving the entire drawing from the Write Block dialog box performs some additional operations, such as stripping out unused blocks or other unused components. This has the effect of reducing file size. You'll learn more about this feature later in this chapter.

Other Uses for Blocks

So far you've used the Block tool to create symbols, and you've used the Export and Wblock commands to save those symbols to disk. As you can see, you can create symbols and save them at any time while you're drawing. You've made the tub and toilet symbols into drawing files that you can see when you check the contents of your current folder.

However, creating symbols isn't the only use for the Block, Export, and Wblock commands. You can use them in any situation that requires grouping objects (though you may prefer to use the more flexible Object Grouping dialog box discussed later in this chapter). You can also use blocks to stretch a set of objects along one axis by using the Properties palette. Export and Wblock also enable you to save a part of a drawing to disk. You'll see instances of these other uses of the Block, Export, and Wblock commands throughout the book.

Block, Export, and Wblock are extremely versatile commands and, if used judiciously, can boost your productivity and simplify your work. If you aren't careful, however, you can get carried away and create more blocks than you can track. Planning your drawings helps you determine which elements will work best as blocks and recognize situations in which other methods of organization are more suitable.

Another way of using symbols is to use the external reference capabilities. External reference files, known as *Xrefs*, are files inserted into a drawing in a way similar to how blocks are inserted. The difference is that Xrefs don't become part of the drawing's database. Instead, they're loaded along with the current file at startup time. It's as if AutoCAD opens several drawings at once: the main file you specify when you start AutoCAD and the Xrefs associated with the main file.

By keeping the Xrefs independent from the current file, you make sure that any changes made to the Xrefs automatically appear in the current file. You don't have to update each inserted copy of an Xref. For example, if you use the Attach tool on the Insert tab's Reference panel (discussed in Chapter 7) to insert the tub drawing and later you make changes to the tub, the next time you open the Bath file, you'll see the new version of the tub. Or if you have both the tub and the referencing drawing open and you change the tub, AutoCAD will notify you that a change has been made to an external reference. You can then update the tub Xref using the External Reference palette.

Xrefs are especially useful in workgroup environments where several people are working on the same project. One person might be updating several files that have been inserted into a variety of other files. Before Xrefs were available, everyone in the workgroup had to be notified of the changes and had to update all the affected blocks in all the drawings that contained them. With Xrefs, the updating is automatic. Many other features are unique to these files. They're discussed in more detail in Chapters 7 and 14.

Understanding the Annotation Scale

Certification
Objective

One common use for the AutoCAD block feature is creating *reference symbols*. These are symbols that refer the viewer to other drawings or views in a set of drawings. An example would be a building-section symbol on a floor plan that directs the viewer to look at a location on another sheet to see a cross-sectional view of a building. Such a symbol is typically a circle with two numbers: one is the drawing sheet number, and the other is the view number on the sheet (see Figure 4.11).

In the past, AutoCAD users had to insert a reference symbol block multiple times to accommodate different scales of the same view. For example, the same floor plan might be used for a 1/4" = 1'-0" scale view and a 1/8" = 1'-0" view. An elevation symbol block that works for the 1/4" = 1'-0" scale view would be too small for the 1/8" = 1'-0" view, so two copies of the same block were inserted, one for each scale. The user then had to place the two blocks on different layers to control their visibility. In addition, if sheet numbers changed, the user had to make sure that every copy of the elevation symbol block was updated to reflect the change.

FIGURE 4.11
A single block is used to create building section symbols of different sizes in these layout views. Both views show the same floor plan displayed at different scales.

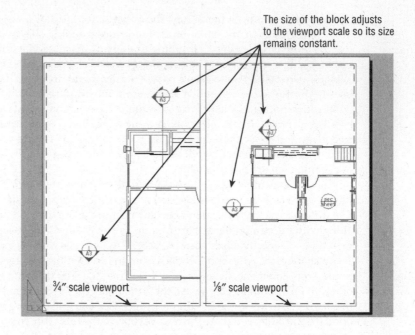

The size of the block adjusts to the viewport scale so its size remains constant.

¾" scale viewport   ⅛" scale viewport

The annotation scale feature does away with this need for redundancy. You can now use a single instance of a block even if it must be displayed in different scale views. To do this, you must take some additional steps when creating and inserting the block. Here's how you do it:

1. Draw your symbol at the size it should appear when plotted. For example, if the symbol is supposed to be a 1/4" circle on a printed sheet, draw the symbol as a 1/4" circle.

2. Open the Block Definition dialog box by choosing the Create Block tool from the Insert tab's Block Definition Ribbon panel.

3. Turn on the Annotative option in the Behavior section of the Block Definition dialog box. You can also turn on the Match Block Orientation To Layout option if you want the symbol always to appear in a vertical orientation (see Figure 4.12).

FIGURE 4.12
Select the Annotative option in the Block Definition dialog box.

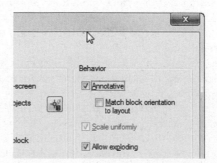

4. Select the objects that make up the block, and indicate an insertion point as usual.

5. Give the block a name and then click OK.

After you've followed these steps, you need to apply an annotation scale to the newly created block:

1. Click the new block to select it.

2. Right-click and choose Annotative Object Scale ➢ Add/Delete Scales. The Annotation Object Scale dialog box appears (see Figure 4.13).

FIGURE 4.13
The Annotation Object
Scale dialog box

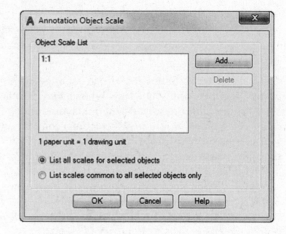

3. Click the Add button. The Add Scales To Object dialog box appears (see Figure 4.14).

FIGURE 4.14
The Add Scales To
Object dialog box

4. Select from the list the scale you'll be using with this block. You can Ctrl+click to select multiple scales. When you've finished selecting scales, click OK. The selected scales appear in the Annotation Object Scale dialog box.

5. Click OK to close the Annotation Object Scale dialog box.

At this point, the block is ready to be used in multiple scale views. You need only to select a scale from the model view's Annotation Scale drop-down list or the layout view's Viewport Scale drop-down list, which are both in the lower-right corner of the AutoCAD window (see Figure 4.15). For you to select a scale while in a layout, a viewport border needs to be selected.

FIGURE 4.15
The Annotation Scale and the layout view's Viewport Scale drop-down lists

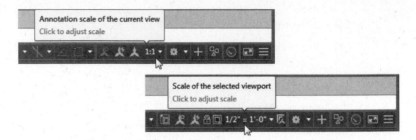

The Annotation Scale drop-down list appears in model view, and the Viewport Scale drop-down list appears in layout view when a viewport is selected. (See Chapter 15, "Laying Out Your Printer Output," for more about layouts and viewports.) Note that the list has a scroll bar to the right, enabling you to select from a comprehensive list of scales. In layout view, you can set the Viewport Scale value for each individual viewport so that the same block can appear at the appropriate size for different scale viewports (see Figure 4.15).

If you want to use several copies of a block that is using multiple annotation scales, you should insert the block and assign the additional annotation scales and then make copies of the block. If you insert a new instance of the block, the block acquires only the annotation scale that is current for the drawing. You'll have to assign additional annotation scales to each new insertion of the block.

If you're uncertain whether an annotation scale has been assigned to a block, you can click the block and you'll see the different scale versions of the block as ghosted images. Also, if you hover over a block, triangular symbols appear next to the cursor for blocks that have been assigned annotation scales.

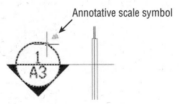

Annotative scale symbol

If you need to change the position of a block for a particular layout viewport scale, go to Model view, select the appropriate scale from the Annotation Scale drop-down list, and then adjust the position of the block.

Grouping Objects

Blocks are extremely useful tools, but for some situations, they're too restrictive. At times, you'll want to group objects so that they're connected but can still be edited individually. For example, consider a space planner who has to place workstations on a floor plan. Although each workstation is basically the same, some slight variations in each station could make the use of blocks unwieldy. For instance, one workstation might need a different configuration to accommodate special equipment, and another workstation might need to be slightly larger than the standard size. You would need to create a block for one workstation and then, for each variation, explode the block, edit it, and create a new block.

A better way is to draw a prototype workstation and turn it into a group. You can copy the group into position and then edit it for each individual situation without losing its identity as a group. The AutoCAD LT® software offers a different method for grouping objects. If you're using AutoCAD LT, skip this exercise and continue with the section "Working with the AutoCAD LT Group Manager" later in this chapter.

The following exercise demonstrates how grouping works:

1. Save the Bath file, and then open the drawing Office1.dwg from the sample files at this book's web page. Metric users should open Office1-metric.dwg.

2. Use the Zoom command to enlarge just the view of the workstation, as shown in the first image in Figure 4.16.

FIGURE 4.16
A workstation in an office plan

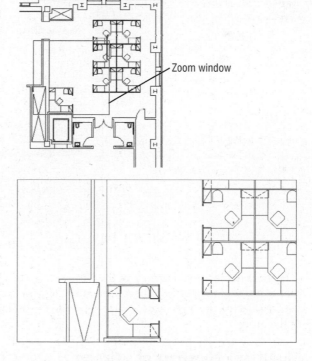

Zoom window

3. Click Group in the Home tab's Groups panel, or type **G**↵ or **Group**↵.

4. Type **N**↵**Station1**↵ or select Name from the Command window and type **Station1**↵ to name your group.

5. At the `Select objects or [Name/Description]:` prompt, use a selection window to select the entire workstation in the lower-left corner of the plan and press ↵. You've just created a group.

Now whenever you want to select the workstation, you can click any part of it to select the entire group. At the same time, you can still modify individual parts of the group—the desk, partition, and so on—without losing the grouping of objects (see the next section, "Modifying Members of a Group").

Another way to create a group is to use the Object Grouping dialog box (see Figure 4.17). Click Group Manager on the Home tab's expanded Groups panel or type **classicgroup**↵ to open it.

FIGURE 4.17
Object Grouping dialog box

Enter a name for your group in the Group Name text box, and then click the New button. The dialog box will temporarily disappear, allowing you to select the objects for your group. Once you've selected the objects, press ↵ to return to the dialog box. Click OK to complete the creation of the group.

Modifying Members of a Group

Next you'll make copies of the original group and modify the copies. Figure 4.18 is a sketch of the proposed layout that uses the new workstations. Look carefully and you'll see that some of the workstations in the sketch are missing a few of the standard components that exist in the Station1 group. One pair of stations has a partition removed; another station has one fewer chair.

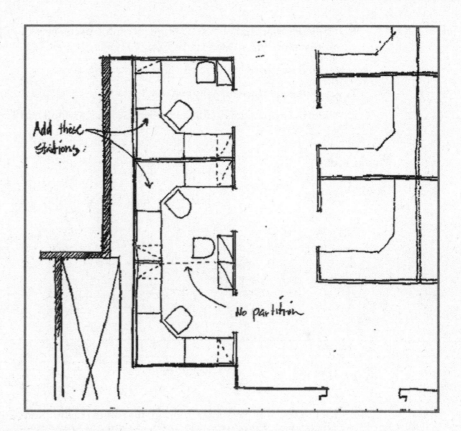

FIGURE 4.18
A sketch of the new office layout

The exercises in this section show you how to complete your drawing to reflect the design requirements of the sketch.

Start by making a copy of the workstation:

1. Click Copy on the Modify Ribbon panel or type **Co**↵; then click the Station1 group you just created. Notice that you can click any part of the station to select the entire station. If only a single object is selected, press Shift+Ctrl+A and try clicking another part of the group.

2. Press ↵ to finish your selection.

3. At the `Specify base point or [Displacement/mOde] <Displacement>:` prompt, type @↵.

4. At the `Specify second point or [Array] <use first point as displacement>:` prompt, enter **@8'2"<90** to copy the workstation 8'-2" vertically. Metric users should enter **@249<90**. Press ↵ to exit the Copy command.

   You can also use the Direct Distance method by typing @↵ and then pointing the rubber-banding line 90° and typing **8'2"**↵. Metric users should type **249**↵.

5. Issue the Copy command again, but this time click the copy of the workstation that you just created. Notice that it too is a group.

6. Copy this workstation 8'-2" (249 cm for metric users) vertically, just as you did the original workstation. Press ↵ to exit the Copy command.

Next you'll use grips to mirror the first workstation copy:

1. Click the middle workstation to highlight it.

2. Click the grip in the middle of the workstation, as shown in Figure 4.19.

FIGURE 4.19
Selecting the grip to
mirror the group

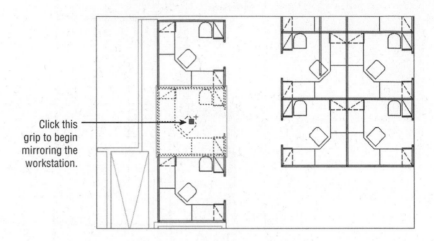

Click this
grip to begin
mirroring the
workstation.

3. Right-click and choose Mirror from the context menu. Notice that a temporary mirror image of the workstation follows the movement of your cursor.

4. Turn on Ortho mode, and pick a point directly to the right of the hot grip you picked in step 2. The workstation is mirrored to a new orientation.

5. Press the Esc key twice to clear the grip selection. Also, turn off Ortho mode.

Now that you've got the workstations laid out, you need to remove some of the partitions between the new workstations. If you had used blocks for the workstations, you would first need to explode the workstations that have partitions that you want to edit. Groups, however, let you make changes without undoing their grouping.

Use these steps to remove the partitions:

1. Click the Group Select On/Off tool in the Home tab's Groups panel. You can also press Shift+Ctrl+A. Notice that the icon changes from being highlighted to not being high-lighted. The Group Select On/Off tool turns groupings on or off so that you can select and edit individual objects within a group.

2. Erase the short partition that divides the two workstations, as shown in Figure 4.20. Since you made a mirror copy of the original workstation, you'll need to erase two partitions that are overlapping each other, the original and the copy.

3. Press Shift+Ctrl+A again to turn Group back on.

FIGURE 4.20
Remove the partitions between the two workstations.

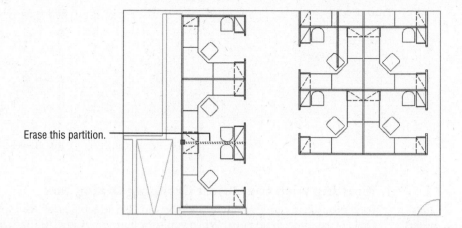

Erase this partition.

4. To check your workstations, click one of them to see whether all of its components are highlighted together.

5. Close the file when you're finished. You don't need to save your changes.

Besides pressing Shift+Ctrl+A to turn groups on and off, you can click the Group Selection On/Off tool in the Home tab's Groups panel. This tool changes the setting for Pickstyle. Pickstyle is a system variable that controls how groups are selected.

Ungrouping, Adding, and Subtracting from a Group

There are a few other tools in the Groups panel that will come in handy when working with groups (see Figure 4.21). The Ungroup tool does exactly what it says: It will "ungroup" a group. Click the Ungroup tool or type **ungroup.**↵, and then select the group or groups you want to ungroup.

FIGURE 4.21
The tools on the Home tab's Groups panel

The Group Edit tool enables you to add or subtract objects from a group. You can also rename a group with this tool. Click the Group Edit tool or enter **groupedit**↵, select the group you want to edit, and then use the Add, Remove, or Rename option from the Dynamic Input menu that appears at the cursor. You can also type **A**↵, **R**↵, or **Ren**↵ to add to, remove from, or rename a group, respectively.

The Groups panel can be expanded to display the Group Manager and Group Bounding Box options. The Group Manager tool opens the Object Grouping dialog box. If you've used the Group command in earlier versions of AutoCAD, you'll recognize this as the old Group command. The Group Bounding Box option toggles the way groups are displayed. You can view groups with the grips of all objects displayed, which is how groups were displayed in prior releases of AutoCAD, or you can display groups with a single grip and a bounding box (see Figure 4.22).

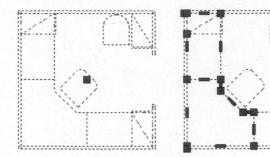

FIGURE 4.22
Groups in a bounding box (left) and with all the grips displayed (right)

Working with the Object Grouping Dialog Box

Each group has a unique name, and you can also attach a brief description of a group in the Object Grouping dialog box. When you copy a group, AutoCAD assigns an arbitrary name to the newly created group. Copies of groups are considered unnamed, but you can still list them in the Object Grouping dialog box by clicking the Include Unnamed check box. You can click the Rename button in the Object Grouping dialog box to name unnamed groups appropriately (see Figure 4.23). Click the Group Manager tool in the Home tab's Groups panel or type **classicgroup**.⏎ to open the Object Grouping dialog box.

FIGURE 4.23
The Object Grouping dialog box

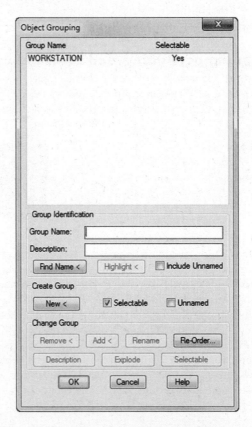

Objects in a group aren't bound solely to that group. One object can be a member of several groups, and you can have nested groups (groups within groups).

AutoCAD LT users have a different set of options. See the next section, "Working with the AutoCAD LT Group Manager."

Table 4.2 gives a rundown of the options available in the Object Grouping dialog box.

TABLE 4.2: Object Grouping dialog box options

OPTION	PURPOSE
Group Name list	Shows the names of groups in the drawing. You can click the name to edit a group.
Group Identification	Identifies your groups with unique elements that let you remember the purpose of each group.
Group Name	Lets you create a new group by naming it first.
Description	Lets you include a brief description of the group.
Find Name <	Finds the name of a group. The Object Grouping dialog box temporarily closes so that you can click a group.
Highlight <	Highlights a group that has been selected from the Group Name list. This helps you locate a group in a crowded drawing.
Include Unnamed	Determines whether unnamed groups are included in the Group Name list. Check this box to display the names of copies of groups for processing by this dialog box.
Create Group	Controls how a group is created.
New <	Creates a new group. The Object Grouping dialog box closes temporarily so that you can select objects for grouping. To use this button, you must have either entered a group name or selected the Unnamed check box.
Selectable	Lets you control whether the group you create is selectable. See the description of the Selectable button in the Change Group panel later in this table.
Unnamed	Lets you create a new group without naming it.
Change Group	These buttons are available only when a group name is highlighted in the Group Name list at the top of the dialog box.
Remove <	Removes objects from a group.
Add <	Adds objects to a group. While you're using this option, grouping is temporarily turned off to allow you to select objects from other groups.
Rename	Renames a group.

TABLE 4.2: Object Grouping dialog box options *(CONTINUED)*

OPTION	PURPOSE
Re-Order	Changes the order of objects in a group. The order refers to the order in which you selected the objects to include in the group. You can change this selection order for special purposes such as tool-path machining.
Description	Modifies the description of a group.
Explode	Separates a group into its individual components.
Selectable	Turns individual groupings on and off. When a group is selectable, it can be selected only as a group. When a group isn't selectable, the individual objects in a group can be selected, but not the group.

If a group is selected, you can remove individual items from the selection with a Shift+click. In this way, you can isolate objects within a group for editing or removal without having to turn off groups temporarily.

Working with the AutoCAD LT Group Manager

If you're using AutoCAD LT, you use the Group Manager to manage groups. Table 4.3 offers a rundown of the tools that are available in the Group Manager.

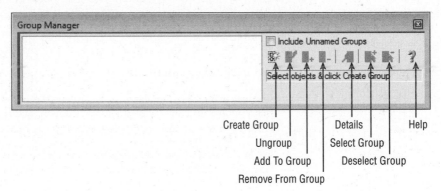

TABLE 4.3: AutoCAD LT 2018 Group Manager options

OPTION	PURPOSE
Create Group	Lets you convert a set of objects into a group. Select a set of objects, and then click Create Group.
Ungroup	Removes the grouping of an existing group. Select the group name from the list, and then select Ungroup.

TABLE 4.3: AutoCAD LT 2018 Group Manager options *(CONTINUED)*

OPTION	PURPOSE
Add To Group	Lets you add an object to a group. At least one group and one additional object must be selected before this option is available.
Remove From Group	Lets you remove one or more objects from a group. To isolate individual objects in a group, first select the group and then Shift+click to remove individual objects from the selection set. After you isolate the object you want to remove, click Remove From Group.
Details	Lists detailed information about the group, such as the number of objects in the group and whether it's in model space or a layout. Select the group name from the group list, and then click Details.
Select Group	Lets you select a group by name. Highlight the group name in the group list, and then click Select Group.
Deselect Group	Removes a group from the current selection set. Highlight the group name in the group list, and then click Deselect Group.
Help	Opens the AutoCAD LT Help website and displays information about the Group Manager.

You've seen how you can use groups to create an office layout. You can also use groups to help you keep sets of objects temporarily together in a complex drawing. Groups can be especially useful in 3D modeling when you want to organize complex assemblies together for easy selection.

The Bottom Line

Create and insert a symbol.   If you have a symbol that you use often in a drawing, you can draw it once and then turn it into an AutoCAD block. A block can be placed in a drawing multiple times in any location, like a rubber stamp. A block is stored in a drawing as a block definition, which can be called up at any time.

   Master It   Name the dialog box used to create a block from objects in a drawing, and also name the tool used to open this dialog box.

Modify a block.   Once you've created a block, it isn't set in stone. One of the features of a block is that you can change the block definition and all of the copies of the block are updated to the new definition.

   Master It   What is the name of the tool used to "unblock" a block?

Understand the annotation scale.   In some cases, you'll want to create a block that is dependent on the drawing scale. You can create a block that adjusts itself to the scale of your drawing through the annotation scale feature. When the annotation scale feature is turned on for a block, the block can be set to appear at the correct size depending on the scale of your drawing.

Master It What setting in the Block Definition dialog box turns on the annotation scale feature, and how do you set the annotation scale of a block?

Group objects. Blocks can be used as a tool to group objects together, but blocks can be too rigid for some grouping applications. AutoCAD offers groups, which are collections of objects that are similar to blocks but aren't as rigidly defined.

Master It How are groups different from blocks?

Chapter 5

Keeping Track of Layers and Blocks

Imagine a filing system that has only one category into which you put all of your records. For only a handful of documents, such a filing system might work. However, as soon as you start to accumulate more documents, you would want to start separating them into meaningful categories, perhaps alphabetically or by their use, so that you could find them more easily.

The same is true for drawings. If you have a simple drawing with only a few objects, you can get by without using layers. But as soon as your drawing gets the least bit complicated, you'll want to start sorting your objects into layers to keep track of what's what. Layers don't restrict you when you're editing objects, such as blocks or groups, and you can set up layers so that you can easily identify which object belongs to which layer.

In this chapter, you'll learn how to create and use layers to keep your drawings organized. You'll learn how color can play an important role while you're working with layers, and you'll also learn how to include linetypes such as dashes and center lines through the use of layers.

In this chapter, you will learn to

◆ Organize information with layers

◆ Control layer visibility

◆ Keep track of blocks and layers

Organizing Information with Layers

Certification Objective

You can think of layers as overlays on which you keep various types of information (see Figure 5.1). In a floor plan of a building, for example, you want to keep the walls, ceiling, plumbing fixtures, wiring, and furniture separate so that you can display or plot them individually or combine them in different ways. It's also a good idea to keep notes and reference symbols, as well as the drawing's dimensions, on their own layers. As your drawing becomes more complex, you can turn the various layers on and off to allow easier display and modification.

For example, one of your consultants might need a plot of just the dimensions and walls, without all the other information; another consultant might need only a furniture layout. In the days of manual drafting, you would have had to redraw your plan for each consultant or use overlay drafting techniques, which could be cumbersome. With the AutoCAD® 2018 software, you can turn off the layers you don't need and plot a drawing containing only the required information. A carefully planned layering scheme helps you produce a document that combines the types of information needed in each case.

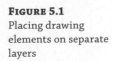

FIGURE 5.1
Placing drawing
elements on separate
layers

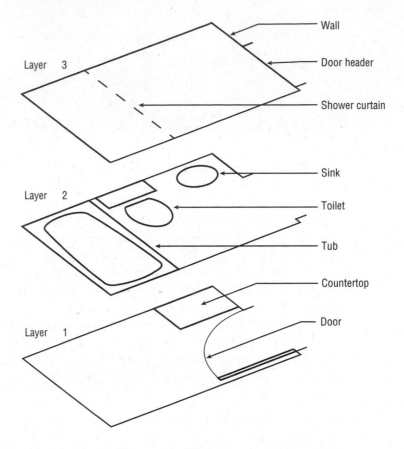

Using layers also lets you modify your drawings more easily. For example, suppose you have an architectural drawing with separate layers for the walls, the ceiling plan, and the floor plan. If any change occurs in the wall locations, you can turn on the ceiling plan layer to see where the new wall locations will affect the ceiling, make the proper adjustments, and then turn it off again to see the walls more clearly.

AutoCAD allows an unlimited number of layers, and you can name each layer anything you want, using any characters, with the exception of these: < > / \ ":; ? * |, = '..

Creating and Assigning Layers

You'll start your exploration of layers by using a palette to create a new layer, giving your layer a name, and assigning it a color. Then you'll look at alternate ways of creating a layer through the command line. Next you'll assign the new layer to the objects in your drawing. Start by getting familiar with the Layer Properties Manager:

1. Open the Bath file you created in Chapter 4, "Organizing Objects with Blocks and Groups." (If you didn't create one, use either 04b-bath.dwg or 04b-bath-metric.dwg from this book's companion web page, www.sybex.com/go/masteringautocad2018.)

2. To display the Layer Properties Manager, click the Layer Properties tool in the Home tab's Layers panel, or type **LA**↵ to use the keyboard shortcut.

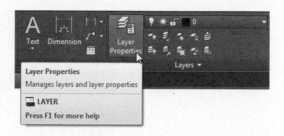

The Layer Properties Manager shows you, at a glance, the status of your layers. Right now, you have only one layer, but as your work expands, so too will the number of layers. You'll then find this palette indispensable.

3. Click the New Layer button at the top of the palette. The button has an icon that looks like a star next to a sheet.

A new layer named Layer1 appears in the list box. Notice that the name is highlighted. This tells you that, by typing, you can change the default name to something better suited to your needs.

4. Type **Wall**. As you type, your entry replaces the Layer1 name in the list box.

5. With the Wall layer name highlighted, click the Color icon in the Wall layer listing to display a dialog box in which you can assign a color to the Wall layer. You will find the Color icon under the Color column; it currently shows White as its value. The icon is just to the left of the word *white*, which doesn't appear in its entirety in the following image.

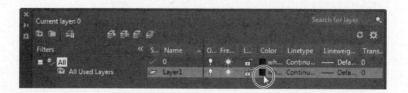

The Select Color dialog box opens to the Index Color tab (see Figure 5.2).

FIGURE 5.2
The Select Color dialog
box

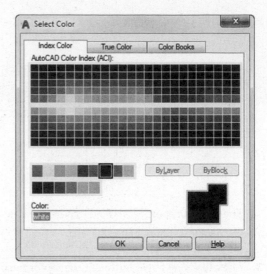

6. In the row of standard colors next to the ByLayer button, click the green square and then click OK. Notice that the color swatch in the Wall layer listing is now green.

7. Click the X at the top of the Layer Properties Manager's title bar to close it.

From this point on, any object assigned to the Wall layer will appear green, unless the object is specifically assigned a different color.

USING AUTO-HIDE WITH THE LAYER PROPERTIES MANAGER

The Layer Properties Manager is a non-modal (or modeless) palette, which means that any change you make within the palette will take effect immediately in the drawing. It also means that the palette can stay open even while you perform other operations that aren't layer related. Throughout this chapter, we'll ask you to open or close the Layer Properties Manager, but if you prefer, you can keep it open all the time. If you decide to keep it open, you may want to use the palette's Auto-Hide feature. Click the Auto-Hide icon toward the top of the palette's title bar so that it changes to a single-sided arrowhead.

With Auto-Hide on, the palette will minimize to display only its title bar. To open the palette, click the title bar. To minimize it, point the cursor anywhere outside of the palette for a moment. You can also force the palette to the left or right margin of the AutoCAD window. To do this, right-click the palette title bar and select Anchor Left or Anchor Right.

USING TRUE OR PANTONE COLORS

In the preceding exercise, you chose a color from the Index Color tab of the Select Color dialog box. Most of the time, you'll find that the Index Color tab includes enough colors to suit your needs. But if you're creating a presentation drawing in which color selection is important, you can choose colors from either the True Color or the Color Books tab of the Select Color dialog box.

The True Color tab offers a full range of colors through a color palette similar to the one found in Adobe Photoshop and other image-editing programs (see Figure 5.3).

FIGURE 5.3
The True Color tab

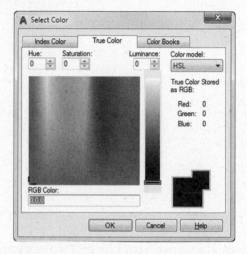

You have the choice of using hue, saturation, and luminance, which is the HSL color model, or you can use the RGB (red, green, blue) color model. You can select HSL or RGB from the Color Model drop-down list in the upper-right corner of the dialog box (see Figure 5.4).

FIGURE 5.4
The Color Model drop-down list

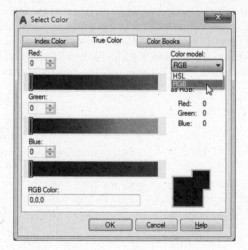

You can also select from DIC, PANTONE, and RAL *color books*, to match those widely used print color systems, by using the Color Books tab (see Figure 5.5).

FIGURE 5.5
The Color Books tab

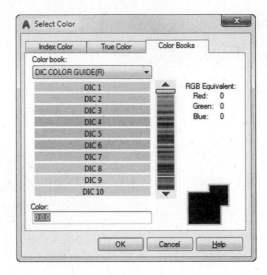

Let's continue with our look at layers in AutoCAD.

UNDERSTANDING THE LAYER PROPERTIES MANAGER PALETTE

The Layer Properties Manager conforms to the Windows interface standard. The most prominent feature of this palette is the layer list box, as you saw in the previous exercise. Notice that the bar at the top of the list offers several columns for the various layer properties. Just as in File Explorer, you can adjust the width of each column in the list by clicking and dragging either side of the column headings. You can also sort the layer list based on one of these properties by clicking the property name at the top of the list. Also, just as with other Windows list boxes, you can Shift+click to select a block of layer names, or you can Ctrl+click individual names to select multiple layers throughout the list. These features will become helpful as your list of layers grows.

Above the layer list, you can see four tool buttons.

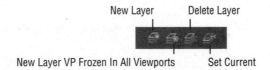

You've already seen how the New Layer tool works. The tool next to it, New Layer VP Frozen In All Viewports, looks similar to the New Layer tool and performs a similar function. The main difference is that the New Layer VP Frozen In All Viewports tool freezes the newly created layer. To delete layers, you select a layer or group of layers and then click the Delete Layer tool. Be aware that you can't delete layer 0, locked layers, or layers that contain objects. The Set Current tool enables you to set the current layer, the one on which you want to work. You can also see at a glance which layer is current by the green check mark in the Status column of the layer list.

Another way to create or delete layers is to select a layer or set of layers from the list box and then right-click. A menu appears that includes the same functions as the tools above the layer list.

You'll also notice another set of three tools farther to the left of the New Layer tool. Those tools offer features to organize your layers in a meaningful way. You'll get a closer look at them a little later in this chapter in the section "Taming an Unwieldy List of Layers."

CONTROLLING LAYERS THROUGH THE LAYER COMMAND

You've seen how the Layer Properties Manager makes it easy to view and edit layer information and how you can select layer colors from the Select Color dialog box. But you can also control layers through the Command prompt.

Use these steps to control layers via the Command prompt:

1. Press the Esc key to make sure any current command is canceled.

2. At the Command prompt, enter **-Layer**↵. Make sure you include the hyphen in front of the word *Layer*. The following prompt appears:

```
Enter an option
[?/Make/Set/New/Rename/ON/OFF/Color/Ltype/
LWeight/TRansparency/MATerial/
Plot/ Freeze/Thaw/LOck/Unlock/stAte/
Description/rEconcile]:
```

You'll learn about many of the options in this prompt as you work through this chapter.

3. Enter **N**↵ to select the New option.

4. At the Enter name list for new layer(s): prompt, enter **Wall2**↵. The [?/Make/Set/New/Rename/ON/OFF/Color/Ltype/LWeight/TRansparency/MATerial/Plot/Freeze/Thaw/LOck/Unlock/stAte/rEconcile]: prompt appears again.

5. Enter **C**↵.

6. At the New color [Truecolor/COlorbook]: prompt, enter **Yellow**↵. Or, you can enter **2**↵, the numeric equivalent of the color yellow in AutoCAD.

7. At the Enter name list of layer(s) for color 2 (yellow) <0>: prompt, enter **Wall2**↵. The [?/Make/Set/New/Rename/ON/OFF/Color/Ltype/LWeight/TRansparency/MATerial/Plot/Freeze/Thaw/LOck/Unlock/stAte/rEconcile]: prompt appears again.

8. Press ↵ to exit the Layer command.

Each method of controlling layers has its own advantages. The Layer Properties Manager offers more information about your layers at a glance. On the other hand, the Layer command offers a quick way to control and create layers if you're in a hurry. Also, if you intend to write custom macros, you'll want to know how to use the Layer command, as opposed to using the Layer Properties Manager, because palettes can't be controlled through custom toolbar buttons or scripts.

ASSIGNING LAYERS TO OBJECTS

Certification
Objective

When you create an object, that object is assigned to the current layer. Until now, only one layer has existed—layer 0—and it contains all of the objects that you've drawn so far. Now that you've created some new layers, you can reassign objects to them by using the Properties palette:

1. Select the four lines that represent the bathroom walls. If you have trouble singling out the wall to the left, use a window to select the wall line. You can also select everything with a selection window and then Shift+click the tub, toilet, and door.

2. With the cursor in the drawing area, right-click and choose Properties from the context menu to open the Properties palette. This palette lets you modify the properties of an object or a set of objects. (See the upcoming sidebar "Understanding Object Properties.")

3. Click the Layer option on the list in the Properties palette. Notice that an arrow appears in the layer name to the right of the Layer option.

4. Click the down-pointing arrow to the far right of the Layer option to display a list of all of the available layers.

5. Select the Wall layer from the list. Notice that the wall lines you selected change to a green color. This tells you that the objects have been assigned to the Wall layer. (Remember that you assigned a green color to the Wall layer.)

6. Close the Properties palette by clicking the X at the top of its title bar.

7. Press the Esc key to clear your selection.

The bathroom walls are now on the new layer called Wall and are green. Layers are more easily distinguished from one another when you use colors to set them apart.

Certification
Objective

USING THE QUICK PROPERTIES PANEL

This chapter focuses on the tools in the Ribbon and the Properties palette to set the properties of an object. You can also use the Quick Properties panel to change the color, layer, and linetype of objects. The Quick Properties panel appears when you double-click most objects. For a block you have to select the block, right-click, and select Quick Properties from the context menu.

Next, you'll practice the commands you learned in this section and try some new ones by creating new layers and changing the layer assignments of the rest of the objects in your bathroom:

1. Click the Layer Properties tool in the Home tab's Layers panel to open the Layer Properties Manager. Create a new layer called **Fixture**, and give it the color blue.

You can change the name of a layer in the Layer Properties Manager. Select the layer name that you want to change and click it again so that the name is highlighted, or press the F2 key. You can then rename the layer. This works in the same way as renaming a file or folder in Windows.

2. Press the Esc key to clear any selections and then click the Tub and Toilet blocks.

3. Right-click and choose Properties from the context menu to open the Properties palette.

4. Click Layer in the list of properties, and then select Fixture from the drop-down list to the right of the layer listing.

5. Click the X at the top of the title bar of the Properties palette to dismiss it, and then press the Esc key to clear your selection.

6. Create a new layer for the door, name the layer **Door**, and make it red.

7. Just as you've done with the walls and fixtures, use the Properties palette to assign the door to the Door layer.

8. Use the Layer Properties Manager to create three more layers: one for the ceiling, one for the doorjambs, and one for the floor. Create these layers, and set their colors as indicated (remember that you can open the Select Color dialog box by clicking the color swatch of the layer listing):

Ceiling	Magenta (6)
Jamb	Green (3)
Floor	Cyan (4)

In step 3 of the previous exercise, you opened the Properties palette, which offered several options for modifying the block. The options displayed in the Properties palette depend on the objects you've selected. With only one object selected, AutoCAD displays options that apply specifically to that object. With several objects selected, you'll see a more limited set of options because AutoCAD can change only those properties that are common to all of the objects selected.

UNDERSTANDING OBJECT PROPERTIES

It helps to think of the components of an AutoCAD drawing as having properties. For example, a line has geometric properties, such as its length and the coordinates that define its endpoints. An arc has a radius, a center, and beginning and ending coordinates. Even though a layer isn't an object that you can grasp and manipulate, it can have properties such as color, linetypes, and lineweights.

By default, objects take on the color, linetype, and lineweight of the layer to which they're assigned, but you can also assign these properties directly to individual objects. These general properties can be manipulated through both the Properties palette and the Home tab's Properties panel.

Although many of the options in the Properties palette may seem cryptic, don't worry about them at this point. As you work with AutoCAD, these properties will become more familiar. You'll find that you won't be too concerned with the geometric properties because you'll be manipulating them with the standard editing tools in the Modify panel. The other properties will be explained in the rest of this chapter and in other chapters.

Note that in a block, you can change the color assignment and linetype of only those objects that are on layer 0. See the sidebar "Controlling Colors and Linetypes of Blocked Objects" in the next section.

Working on Layers

So far, you've created layers and then assigned objects to them. In this section, you'll learn how to use the layer drop-down list in the Layers panel to assign layers to objects. In the process, you'll make some additions to the drawing.

CONTROLLING COLORS AND LINETYPES OF BLOCKED OBJECTS

Layer 0 has special importance to blocks. When objects assigned to layer 0 are used as parts of a block and that block is inserted on another layer, those objects take on the characteristics of their new layer. However, if those objects are on a layer other than layer 0, they maintain their original layer characteristics even if you insert or change that block to another layer. For example, suppose the tub is drawn on the Door layer instead of on layer 0. If you turn the tub into a block and insert it on the Fixture layer, the objects the tub comprises will maintain their assignment to the Door layer even though the Tub block is assigned to the Fixture layer.

It may help to think of the block function as a clear plastic bag that holds together the objects that make up the tub. The objects inside the bag maintain their assignment to the Door layer even while the bag itself is assigned to the Fixture layer. This concept may be a bit confusing at first, but it should become clearer after you use blocks for a while.

AutoCAD also enables you to have more than one color or linetype on an object. For example, you can use the Color and Linetype drop-down lists in the Properties palette to alter the color or linetype of an object on layer 0. That object then maintains its assigned color and linetype—no matter what its layer assignment. Likewise, objects specifically assigned a color or linetype aren't affected by their inclusion in blocks.

The current layer is still layer 0, and unless you change the current layer, every new object you draw will be on layer 0. Here's how to change the current layer:

1. Press the Esc key to clear any selections, and then click the layer drop-down list on the Home tab's Layers panel.

The list shows you all of the layers available in the drawing. Notice the icons that appear next to the layer names; they control the status of the layer. You'll learn how to work with these icons later in this chapter. Also notice the box directly to the left of each layer name. This shows you the color of the corresponding layer.

Momentarily placing the cursor on an icon in the layer drop-down list displays a tool tip that describes the icon's purpose.

2. Click the Jamb layer name. The drop-down list closes, and the name *Jamb* appears in the panel's layer name box. Jamb is now the current layer.

   You can also use the Layer command to reset the current layer. To do this using the keyboard, enter **-Layer↵S↵** and then type **Jamb↵↵**.

3. Zoom in on the door and draw a 5" line; start at the lower-right corner of the door, and draw toward the right. Metric users should draw a 13 cm line.

4. Draw a similar line from the top-right end of the arc. Your drawing should look like Figure 5.6.

FIGURE 5.6
Door at wall with doorjambs added

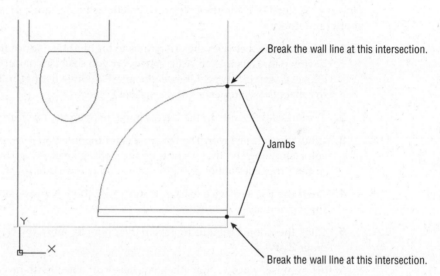

Break the wall line at this intersection.

Jambs

Break the wall line at this intersection.

Because you assigned the color green to the Jamb layer, on your own screen you'll see that the two lines you just drew to represent the doorjambs are green. This gives you a visual cue about which layer you're on as you draw.

Now you'll use the part of the wall between the jambs as a line representing the door header (the part of the wall above the door). To do this, you'll have to cut the line into three line segments and then change the layer assignment of the segment between the jambs:

Certification
Objective

1. Click the Break At Point tool in the Home tab's expanded Modify panel.

2. At the Select object: prompt, click the wall between the two jambs.

3. At the Specify first break point: prompt, use the Endpoint osnap override to pick the endpoint of the door's arc that is touching the wall, as shown previously in Figure 5.6.

4. Click Break At Point on the expanded Modify panel again, and then repeat steps 2 and 3, this time using the jamb near the door hinge location to locate the break point (see Figure 5.6).

Although it may not be obvious, you've just broken the right-side wall line into three line segments: one at the door opening and two more on either side of the jambs. You can also use the Break tool (below the Break At Point tool) to produce a gap in a line segment.

The Break At Point tool won't work on a circle. You can, however, use the Break tool to place a small gap in the circle. If you create a small enough gap, the circle will still look like a full circle.

Next you'll change the Layer property of the line between the two jambs to the Ceiling layer. However, instead of using the Properties palette as you've done in earlier exercises, you'll use a shortcut method:

1. Click the line between the doorjambs to highlight it. Notice that the layer listing in the Layers panel changes to Wall. Whenever you select an object to expose its grips, the Object Color, Linetype, Lineweight, and Plot Style listings in the Properties panel change to reflect those properties of the selected object.

2. Click the layer name in the Layers panel to open the layer drop-down list.

3. Click the Ceiling layer. The list closes and the line you selected changes to the magenta color, showing you that it's now on the Ceiling layer. Also notice that the Object Color list in the Properties panel changes to reflect the new color for the line.

4. Press the Esc key twice to clear the grip selection. Notice that the layer returns to Jamb, the current layer.

5. Click the Zoom Previous tool from the Zoom flyout in the Navigation bar. You can also enter Z↵P↵.

In this exercise, you saw that when you select an object with no command active, the object's properties are immediately displayed in the Properties palette under Object Color, Linetype, and Lineweight. Using this method, you can also change an object's color, linetype, and line-weight independent of its layer. Just as with the Properties palette, you can select multiple objects and change their layers through the layer drop-down list. These options in the Home tab's Properties panel offer a quick way to edit some of the properties of objects.

Now you'll finish the bathroom by adding a sink to a layer named Casework:

1. Open the Layer Properties Manager, and create a new layer called **Casework**.

2. With the Casework layer selected in the layer list, click the Set Current button at the top of the palette.

3. Click the color swatch for the Casework layer listing, and then select Blue from the Select Color dialog box. Click OK to exit the dialog box.

4. Click X in the Layer Properties Manager palette. Notice that the layer drop-down list in the Layers panel indicates that the current layer is Casework.

   Next you'll add the sink. As you draw, the objects will appear in blue, the color of the Casework layer.

5. Choose Zoom All from the Zoom flyout on the Navigation bar, or type Z↵A↵.

6. Click the Insert tool on the Home tab's Block panel, More Options, and then click the Browse button in the Insert dialog box to open the Select Drawing File dialog box.

7. Locate the sink.dwg file that you drew in the previous chapter, or the sample from this book's companion web page, and double-click it.

8. In the Insert dialog box, make sure that the Specify On-Screen options in both the Scale and Rotation groups aren't selected; then click OK.

9. Place the sink roughly in the upper-right corner of the bathroom plan, and then use the Move command to place it accurately in the corner, as shown in Figure 5.7.

FIGURE 5.7
The bathroom with
sink and counter added

Counter and sink

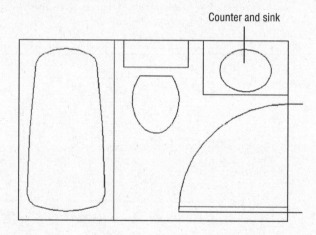

Controlling Layer Visibility

We mentioned earlier that you'll sometimes want to display only certain layers to work within a drawing. A door header is in this bathroom that would normally appear only in a reflected ceiling plan. To turn off a layer so that it becomes invisible, you click the lightbulb icon in the Layer Properties Manager, as shown in these steps:

1. Open the Layer Properties Manager by clicking the Layer Properties tool in the Layers panel.

2. Click the Ceiling layer in the layer list.

3. Click the lightbulb icon in the layer list next to the Ceiling layer name. The lightbulb icon changes from yellow to gray to indicate that the layer is off.

4. Click the X at the top of the Layer Properties Manager's title bar to close it. The door header (the line across the door opening) disappears because you've made it invisible by turning off its layer.

GETTING MULTIPLE USES FROM A DRAWING USING LAYERS

Layering lets you use a single AutoCAD drawing for multiple purposes. A single drawing can show both the general layout of the plan and more detailed information, such as the equipment layout and the floor-paving layout.

The following two images are reproductions of the San Francisco Main Library's lower level and show how one floor plan file was used for two purposes. The first view shows the layout of furnishings, and the second view shows a paving layout. In each case, the same floor plan file was used, but in the first panel, the paving information is on a layer that is turned off. Layers also facilitate the use of differing scales in the same drawing. Frequently, a small-scale drawing of an overall plan will contain the same data for an enlarged view of other portions of the plan, such as a stairwell or an elevator core. The detailed information, such as notes and dimensions, might be on a layer that is turned off for the overall plan.

You can also control layer visibility by using the layer drop-down list on the Layers panel:

1. On the Home tab's Layers panel, click the layer drop-down list.

2. Find the Ceiling layer, and note that its lightbulb icon is gray. This tells you that the layer is off and not visible.

3. Click the lightbulb icon to make it yellow; the door header reappears.

4. Click the drawing area to close the layer drop-down list.

Figure 5.8 explains the roles of the other icons in the layer drop-down list. The figure also shows the Freeze Or Thaw In Current Layout Viewport icon, which appears only when you are in a layout. You'll learn more about layouts in Chapter 15, "Laying Out Your Printer Output."

FIGURE 5.8
The layer drop-down list icons

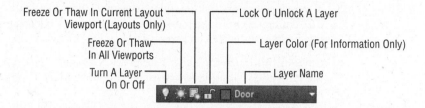

When you start to work with layouts in Chapter 8, "Introducing Printing, Plotting, and Layouts," and Chapter 15, you'll learn about *viewports*. A viewport is like a custom view of your drawing. You can have multiple viewports in a layout, each showing a different part of your drawing. Layer properties can be controlled for each viewport independently, so you can set up different linetypes, colors, and layer visibility for each viewport.

Finding the Layers You Want

With only a handful of layers, it's fairly easy to find the layer you want to turn off. It becomes much more difficult, however, when the number of layers exceeds a couple of dozen. The Layer Properties Manager offers some useful tools to help you find the layers you want quickly.

Suppose that you have several layers whose names begin with C, such as C-lights, C-header, and C-pattern, and you want to find those layers quickly. You can click the Name button at the top of the layer list to sort the layer names in alphabetic order. (Click the Name button again to reverse the order.) To select those layers for processing, click the first layer name that starts with C, and then scroll down the list until you find the last layer of the group and Shift+click it. All of the layers between those layers are selected. If you want to deselect some of those layers, hold down the Ctrl key while clicking the layer names that you don't want to include in your selection. Another option is to Ctrl+click the names of other layers you want selected.

The Color and Linetype headings at the top let you sort the list by the color or linetype assignments of the layers. Other columns sort the list by status: On/Off, Freeze/Thaw, Lock/Unlock, and so forth. (See the sidebar "Freeze, Lock, Transparency, and Other Layer Options" later in this chapter.)

Now try changing the layer settings again by turning off all the layers except Wall and Ceiling, leaving just a simple rectangle. In this exercise, you'll get a chance to experiment with the On/Off options of the Layer Properties Manager:

1. Click the Layer Properties tool in the Layers panel.

2. Click the top layer name in the list box; then Shift+click the last layer name. All of the layer names are highlighted.

Another way to select all of the layers at once in the Layer Properties Manager is to right-click the layer list and then choose the Select All option from the context menu. If you want to clear your selections, right-click the layer list and choose Clear All.

3. Ctrl+click the Wall and Ceiling layers to deselect them and thus exempt them from your next action.

4. Click the lightbulb icon of any of the highlighted layers.

5. A message appears, asking if you want the current layer on or off. Select Turn The Current Layer Off in the message box. The lightbulb icons turn gray to show that the selected layers have been turned off.

6. Close or minimize the Layer Properties Manager. The drawing now appears with only the Wall and Ceiling layers displayed. It looks like a simple rectangle of the room outline.

7. Open the Layer Properties Manager again, select all of the layers as you did in step 2, and then click any of the gray lightbulbs to turn on all the layers at once.

8. Click the X at the top of the Layer Properties Manager's title bar to close it.

In this exercise, you turned off a set of layers by clicking a lightbulb icon. You can freeze/thaw, lock/unlock, or change the color of a group of layers in a similar manner by clicking the appropriate layer property. For example, clicking a color swatch of one of the selected layers opens the Select Color dialog box, in which you can set the color for all the selected layers.

Taming an Unwieldy List of Layers

Certification
Objective

Chances are that you'll eventually end up with a fairly long list of layers. Managing such a list can become a nightmare, but AutoCAD provides some tools to help you organize layers so that you can keep track of them more easily.

On the left side of the Layer Properties Manager is a set of tools and a list box designed to help you with your layer-management tasks (see Figure 5.9).

FIGURE 5.9
Tools in the Layer Properties Manager that help you manage your layers

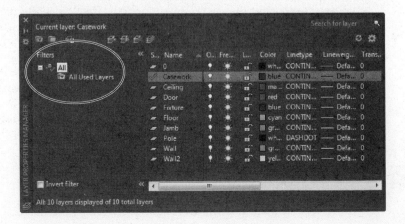

In the upper-left corner of the palette is a toolbar with three tools:

New Property Filter Tool Lets you filter your list of layers to display only layers with certain properties, such as specific colors or names.

New Group Filter Tool Lets you create named groups of layers that can be quickly recalled at any time. This tool is helpful if you often work with specific sets of layers. For example, you might have a set of layers in an architectural drawing that pertains to the electrical layout. You could create a group filter called Electrical that filters out all layers except those pertaining to the electrical layout. The filters don't affect the layers in any way; they just limit which layers are displayed in the main layer list.

Layer States Manager Tool Lets you create sets of layer states. For example, if you want to save the layer settings that have only the Wall and Door layers turned on, you can do so by using this tool.

FREEZE, LOCK, TRANSPARENCY, AND OTHER LAYER OPTIONS

You may have noticed the Freeze and Thaw icons in the Layer Properties Manager. These options are similar to On and Off icons. However, Freeze not only makes layers invisible, it also tells AutoCAD to ignore the contents of those layers when you select the All response at the Select objects: prompt. Freezing layers can save time when you issue a command that regenerates a complex drawing. This is because AutoCAD ignores objects on frozen layers during a drawing regen. You'll get firsthand experience with Freeze and Thaw in Chapter 7, "Mastering Viewing Tools, Hatches, and External References."

Another pair of Layer Properties Manager options, Lock and Unlock, offers functionality similar to Freeze and Thaw. If you lock a layer, you can view and snap to objects on that layer, but you can't edit those objects. This feature is useful when you're working on a crowded drawing and you don't want to edit portions of it accidentally. You can lock all of the layers except those you intend to edit and then proceed to work without fear of making accidental changes. The expanded Layers Ribbon panel offers a Locked Layer Fading slider that allows you to distinguish locked layers more easily by fading them. The slider does not affect plotter output because it is only a visual aid to use when you are editing your drawings.

Three more options—Lineweight, Plot Style, and Plot—offer control over the appearance of printer or plotter output. Lineweight lets you control the width of lines in a layer. Plot Style lets you assign plotter configurations to specific layers. (You'll learn more about plot styles in Bonus Chapter 5, "Understanding Plot Styles," available at www.omura.com/chapters.) Use the Plot option to specify whether you want a layer to be printed in hard-copy output. This can be useful for setting up layers you may use for layout purposes only. The Linetype option allows you to control line patterns, such as dashed or center lines.

Transparency enables you to make a layer transparent. You can enter a value from 0, which is completely opaque, to 90, which is the maximum transparency allowed. After setting the transparency value, you may need to enter **Re**↵ to regenerate the drawing and see the transparency of the layer.

Finally, you can save layer settings for later recall by using the Layer States Manager tool in the upper-left corner of the Layer Properties Manager. This feature is extremely useful when you want to save different layer combinations. Chapter 14, "Advanced Editing and Organizing," shows you how to use this feature. This option is also accessible from the stAte option in the command-line version of the Layer command.

FILTERING LAYERS BY THEIR PROPERTIES

Below the New Property Filter, New Group Filter, and Layer States Manager tools is a filter list, which is a hierarchical list displaying the different sets of layer properties and group filters. Right now, you don't have any filters in place, so you see only All and All Used Layers.

In this section, you'll learn how the tools and the filter list box work. You'll start with a look at the New Property Filter tool:

1. Open the Layer Properties Manager by clicking the Layer Properties tool in the Layers panel.

2. Click the New Property Filter tool in the upper-left corner of the Layer Properties Manager to open the Layer Filter Properties dialog box. You see two list boxes. The Filter Definition list box at the top is where you enter your filter criteria. The Filter Preview list box below is a preview of your layer list based on the filter options. Right now, there are no filter options, so the Filter Preview list shows all the layers.

3. In the Filter Definition list box, click the blank box just below the Color label. A button appears in the box (see Figure 5.10).

FIGURE 5.10
The Layer Filter Properties dialog box

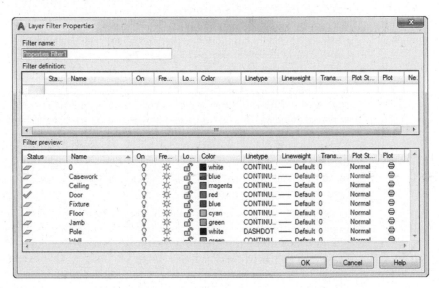

4. Click in the blank box again; then enter **red**↵. The Filter Preview changes to show only layers that are red. In the current drawing, only one layer has been assigned the color red.

5. Click twice in the blank box below the one you just edited. Again, a button appears.

6. This time, enter **green**↵. The layers that are green appear in the Filter Preview list.

   You can also select a color from the Select Color dialog box by clicking the button that appears in the box.

7. In the Filter Definition list, click in the Name column in the third row down. A cursor appears followed by an asterisk.

8. Type **F**. Two new layers that have names beginning with *F* are added to the Filter Preview list.

9. In the Filter Name text box at the upper-left corner of the dialog box, change the name Properties Filter1 to **My List**, and then click OK.

Now you see the My List filter in the list box on the left side of the Layer Properties Manager.

The layer list shows only the layers that have properties conforming to those you selected in the Layer Filter Properties dialog box. Notice that My List is highlighted in the filter list to the left. This tells you that My List is the current layer property filter being applied to the layer list to the right.

You can change the layer list display by selecting different options in the filter list. Try these steps:

1. Click the All option in the filter list at the left side of the dialog box. The layer list to the right changes to display all the layers in the drawing. Also note that a brief description of the current layer filter is displayed at the bottom of the dialog box.

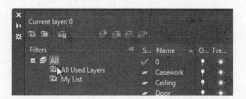

2. Click the All Used Layers option in the filter list. Now all the layers continue to be displayed.

3. Click My List. The layer list changes back to the limited set of layers from your filter list.

4. Double-click My List. The Layer Filter Properties dialog box opens and displays the list of layer properties that you set up earlier for My List. You can edit the criteria for your filter by making modifications in this dialog box.

5. Click Cancel to exit the Layer Filter Properties dialog box.

CREATING LAYER GROUPS

The preceding exercise shows how you can filter out layer names based on the properties that you specify in the Layer Filter Properties dialog box. But suppose you want to create a layer filter list by graphically selecting objects on the screen. You can use the New Group Filter tool to do just that:

1. Click the New Group Filter tool in the upper-left corner of the Layer Properties Manager, and then press ↵ to accept the default name for the group. You see a new listing appear called Group Filter1.

2. Right-click the Group Filter1 listing to the left, and then choose Select Layers ➢ Add from the context menu. Notice that your cursor is now a Pickbox cursor.

3. Click a line representing a wall of the bathroom; then click the door. Press ↵ when you're finished with your selection. The layers of the two objects you selected are displayed in the layer list. Also note that Group Filter1 is highlighted in the filter list to the left.

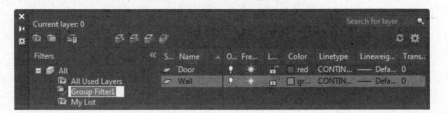

You may have noticed the Select Layers ➢ Replace option in the context menu in step 2. This option lets you completely replace an existing group filter with a new selection set. It works just like the Select Layers ➢ Add option. You can also click and drag layers from the All layer list to the group filter list name in the left column.

Earlier you saw how you can double-click a properties filter to edit a properties filter list. But group filters work in a slightly different way. If you want to add layers to your group filter, you can click and drag them from the layer list to the group filter name. Here's how it's done:

1. In the Layer Properties Manager, select All from the filter list to the left.

2. Click the Fixture layer in the layer list; then Ctrl+click the Jamb layer in the list. These are the layers that you'll add to the Group Filter1 layer group.

3. Click and drag the Fixture and Jamb layers to the Group Filter1 listing in the filter list.

4. To check the addition to Group Filter1, click it in the filter list. The Fixture and Jamb layers have been added to the Group Filter1 list.

If you want to delete a layer from a group filter, you can use the context menu, as shown in these steps:

1. With the Group Filter1 list selected, select the Jamb layer from the layer list and then right-click it.

2. Select Remove From Group Filter from the context menu. (Make sure that you don't select Delete Layer.) Jamb is removed from the Group Filter1 list.

You can also convert a layer property filter into a group filter. Select the layer property filter from the filter list, right-click, and then select Convert To Group Filter. The icon for the layer property filter changes to a group filter icon, indicating that it's now a group filter.

You've seen how you can add property and group filters to the Layer Properties Manager by using the tools on the left side of the palette. One tool that you haven't explored yet is the Layer

States Manager. To understand how this tool works, you'll need to learn a little more about AutoCAD; look for a discussion of the Layer States Manager in Chapter 14.

Before you move on, you'll want to know about a few other options that appear in the Layer Properties Manager (see Figure 5.11).

FIGURE 5.11
Invert Filter, Refresh tool, and Settings button in the Layer Properties Manager

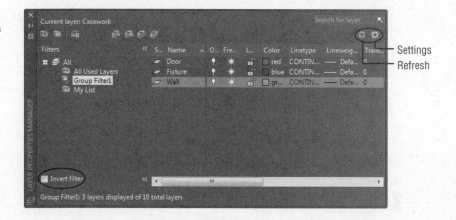

The Invert Filter Check Box   Located at the bottom of the Filters list, this option changes the list of layers to show all layers *excluding* those in the selected filter. For example, if the My List filter contains layers that are red and you select Invert Filter, the layer list will display all layers *except* those that are red.

The Refresh Tool   Located in the upper-right corner, this tool updates the layer information in the Layer Properties Manager.

The Settings Button   Located in the upper-right corner, the Settings button opens the Layer Settings dialog box. This dialog box controls the way that you're notified when new layers are added to a drawing (see Figure 5.12).

In the next section, you'll find some tips for how to use layer names so that you can use text filters more effectively.

NAMING LAYERS TO STAY ORGANIZED

In the previous section, you saw how to create a layer property filter by using the name of a layer. If you name layers carefully, you can use them as a powerful layer-management tool. For example, suppose that you have a drawing whose layer names are set up to help you easily identify floor-plan data versus ceiling-plan data, as in the following list:

1. A-FP-WALL-JAMB

2. A-FP-WIND-JAMB

3. A-CP-WIND-HEAD

4. A-CP-DOOR-HEAD

5. L-FP-CURB

6. C-FP-ELEV

FIGURE 5.12
The Layer Settings
dialog box

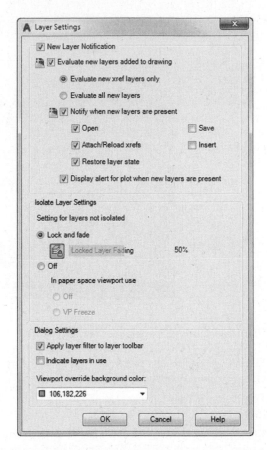

The first character in the layer name designates the discipline related to that layer: *A* for architectural, *L* for landscape, and *C* for civil. In this example, layers with names containing the two characters *FP* signify floor-plan layers. *CP* designates ceiling-plan information.

These layer examples are loosely based on a layer-naming convention devised by the American Institute of Architects (AIA). As you can see from this example, careful naming of layers can help you manage them.

If you want to isolate only those layers that have to do with floor plans, regardless of their discipline, enter **??FP*** in the Name column of the Layer Filter Properties dialog box (see Figure 5.13). You can then give this layer property filter the name Floor Plan by entering **Floor Plan** in the Filter Name text box.

After you've created the Floor Plan layer properties list, you can pick Floor Plan from the filter list on the right side of the Layer Properties Manager, and only those layers with names containing the letters *FP* as their third and fourth characters will appear in the list of layers. You can turn off all of these layers, change their color assignment, or change other settings quickly without having to wade through layers you don't want to touch. You can create other filter properties to isolate other groups of layers. AutoCAD keeps these filter lists for future use until you delete them by using the Delete option in the context menu. (Right-click the name of the property filter and choose Delete.)

FIGURE 5.13
Enter **??FP*** in the Name column and Floor Plan in the Filter Name box as shown.

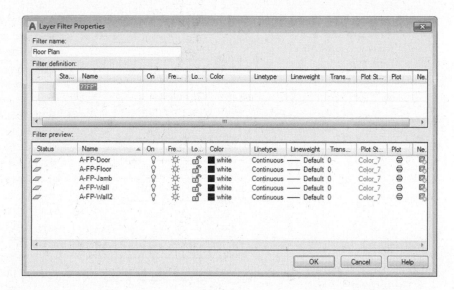

In the ??FP* example, the question marks (??) tell AutoCAD that the first two characters in the layer name can be anything. The *FP* tells AutoCAD that the layer name must contain *F* and *P* in these two places of the name. The asterisk (*) at the end tells AutoCAD that the remaining characters can be anything. The question marks and asterisk are known as *wildcard characters*. They're commonly used filtering tools for the Unix, Linux, and Windows operating systems.

As the number of layers in a drawing grows, you'll find layer filters an indispensable tool. Bear in mind, however, that the successful use of layer filters can depend on a careful layer-naming convention. If you're producing architectural plans, you may want to consider the AIA layer-naming guidelines.

Assigning Linetypes to Layers

Certification
Objective

You'll often want to use different linetypes to show hidden lines, center lines, fence lines, or other noncontinuous lines. You can assign a color and a linetype to a layer. You then see International Organization for Standardization (ISO) and complex linetypes, including lines that can be used to illustrate gas and water lines in civil work or batt insulation in a wall cavity.

AutoCAD comes with several linetypes, as shown in Figure 5.14. ISO linetypes are designed to be used with specific plotted line widths and linetype scales. For example, if you're using a pen width of 0.5 mm, set the linetype scale of the drawing to 0.5 as well. (See Chapter 15 for more information on plotting and linetype scale.) You can also create your own linetypes (see Chapter 25, "Managing and Sharing Your Drawings").

Linetypes that contain text, such as the gas line sample at the bottom of Figure 5.14, use the current text height and font to determine the size and appearance of the text displayed in the line. A text height of 0 displays the text properly in most cases. See Chapter 9, "Adding Text to Drawings," for more on text styles.

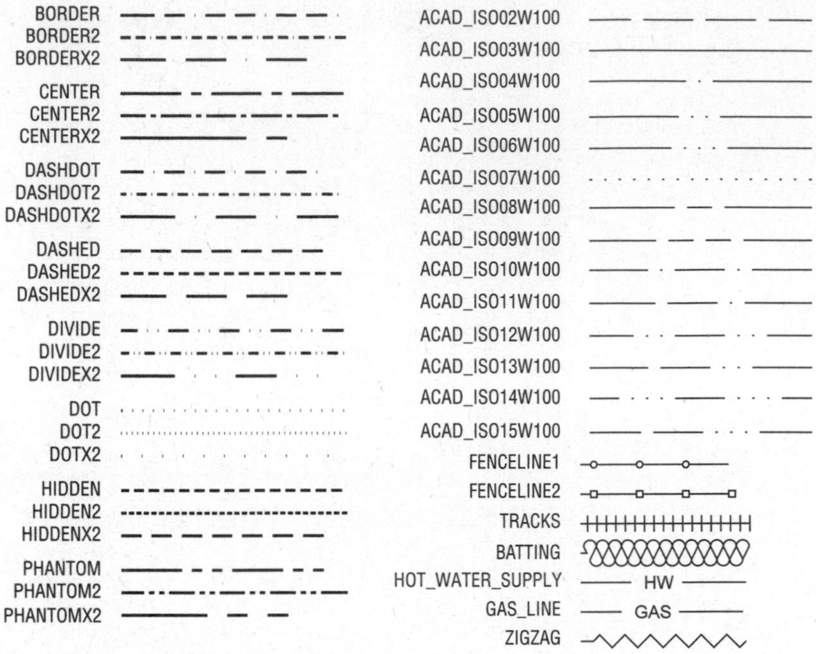

FIGURE 5.14

Standard, ISO, and complex AutoCAD linetypes

BORDER	ACAD_ISO02W100
BORDER2	ACAD_ISO03W100
BORDERX2	ACAD_ISO04W100
CENTER	ACAD_ISO05W100
CENTER2	ACAD_ISO06W100
CENTERX2	ACAD_ISO07W100
DASHDOT	ACAD_ISO08W100
DASHDOT2	ACAD_ISO09W100
DASHDOTX2	ACAD_ISO10W100
DASHED	ACAD_ISO11W100
DASHED2	ACAD_ISO12W100
DASHEDX2	ACAD_ISO13W100
DIVIDE	ACAD_ISO14W100
DIVIDE2	ACAD_ISO15W100
DIVIDEX2	FENCELINE1
DOT	FENCELINE2
DOT2	TRACKS
DOTX2	BATTING
HIDDEN	HOT_WATER_SUPPLY
HIDDEN2	GAS_LINE
HIDDENX2	ZIGZAG
PHANTOM	
PHANTOM2	
PHANTOMX2	

AutoCAD stores linetype descriptions in an external file named Acad.lin, or Acadiso.lin for metric users. You can edit this file in a text editor like Notepad to create new linetypes or to modify existing ones. You'll see how this is done in Chapter 24, "Customizing Toolbars, Menus, Linetypes, and Hatch Patterns."

Adding a Linetype to a Drawing

Certification Objective

To see how linetypes work, you'll add a DASHDOT line in the bathroom plan to indicate a shower curtain rod:

1. Open the Layers Properties Manager, and select All from the filter list.

2. Click New Layer, and then type **Pole**↵ to create a new layer called Pole.

3. Change the color of the Pole layer to **Black/White**.

4. In the Pole layer listing, under the Linetype column, click the word *Continuous* to open the Select Linetype dialog box (see Figure 5.15). To find the Linetype column, you may need to scroll the list to the right by using the scroll bar at the bottom of the list (see Figure 5.11).

   The word *Continuous* truncates to *Contin* when the Linetype column is at its default width and the Continuous option is selected.

FIGURE 5.15

The Select Linetype
dialog box

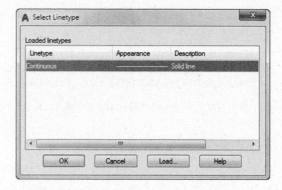

5. The Select Linetype dialog box offers a list of linetypes from which to choose. In a new
   file, such as the Bath file, only one linetype is available by default. You must load any
   additional linetypes you want to use. Click the Load button at the bottom of the dialog
   box to open the Load Or Reload Linetypes dialog box. Notice that the list of linetype
   names is similar to the layer drop-down list. You can sort the names alphabetically or
   by description by clicking the Linetype or Description heading at the top of the list (see
   Figure 5.16).

FIGURE 5.16

The Load Or Reload
Linetypes dialog box

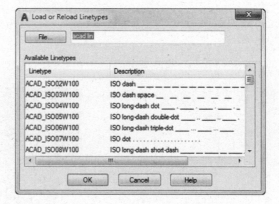

6. In the Available Linetypes list, scroll down to locate the DASHDOT linetype, click it,
   and then click OK. Do not select the ISO dash dot linetype that appears in the first part
   of the list.

   Notice that the DASHDOT linetype is added to the linetypes available in the Select
   Linetype dialog box.

7. Click DASHDOT to highlight it; then click OK. DASHDOT appears in the Pole layer listing under Linetype.

   If you're in a hurry, you can simultaneously load a linetype and assign it to a layer by using the Layer command. In this exercise, you enter **-Layer**↵ at the Command prompt. Then enter **L**↵, **DASHDOT**↵, and **Pole**↵, and press ↵ to exit the Layer command.

8. With the Pole layer still highlighted, click the Set Current button to make the Pole layer current.

9. Exit the Layer Properties Manager.

10. Click the Line tool in the Home tab's Draw panel.

11. Enter **4'4,1'10**↵ for the first point and **#4'4,6'10**↵ for the second point of the line. Metric users should enter **133,56**↵ for the first point and **#133,208**↵ for the second point. The # sign before the second coordinate is needed when Dynamic Input is active, and it tells AutoCAD that the second coordinate is an absolute coordinate and not relative to the last point.

12. Press ↵ to finish the line.

CONTROLLING LINETYPE SCALE

Although you've designated this as a DASHDOT line, it appears solid. Zoom in to a small part of the line and you'll see that the line is indeed as you specified.

Because your current drawing is at a scale of 1″ = 1′, you must adjust the scale of your linetypes accordingly. This too is accomplished in the Linetype Manager dialog box. Here are the steps:

1. Click the Linetype drop-down list in the Home tab's Properties panel and select Other.

2. The Linetype Manager dialog box opens. Click the Show Details button in the upper-right corner of the dialog box. Some additional options appear at the bottom (see Figure 5.17).

   The Linetype Manager dialog box offers Load and Delete buttons that let you load or delete a linetype directly without having to go through a particular layer's linetype setting.

FIGURE 5.17
The Linetype
Manager dialog
box

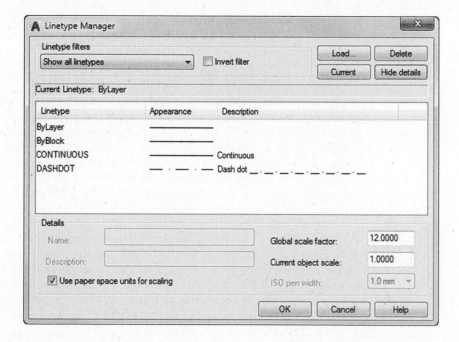

FIGURE 5.17
The Linetype
Manager dialog
box

3. Double-click the Global Scale Factor text box, and then type **12**. This is the scale conversion factor for a 1″ = 1′ scale (see the discussion of scale factors in Chapter 3, "Setting Up and Using the Drafting Tools"). If you are a metric user and the line appears solid, set Global Scale Factor to 30.

4. Click OK. The drawing regenerates and the shower curtain rod is displayed in the linetype and at the scale you designated.

5. Click the Zoom Previous tool from the Navigation bar or the Previous tool from the View tab's Navigate 2D panel so that your drawing looks like Figure 5.18.

FIGURE 5.18
The completed
bathroom

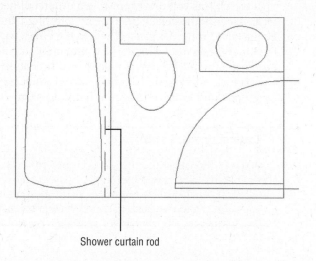

Shower curtain rod

You can also use the Ltscale system variable to set the linetype scale. Type **LTSCALE**↵, and at the Enter new linetype scale factor <1.0000>: prompt, enter **12**↵.

LINETYPES TROUBLESHOOTING

If you change the linetype of a layer or an object but the object remains a continuous line, check the Ltscale system variable. It should be set to your drawing scale factor. If this doesn't work, set the Viewres system variable to a higher value (see Appendix B, "Installing and Setting Up AutoCAD"). Viewres can also be set by the Arc And Circle Smoothness option in the Display tab of the Options dialog box. The behavior of linetype scales depends on whether you're in model space or in a drawing layout. If your efforts to control linetype scale have no effect on your linetype's visibility, you may be in a drawing layout. See Chapter 15 for more on model space and layouts.

Remember that if you assign a linetype to a layer, everything you draw on that layer will be of that linetype. This includes arcs, polylines, and circles. As explained in the sidebar "Assigning Colors, Linetypes, and Linetype Scales to Individual Objects" later in this chapter, you can also assign different colors and linetypes to individual objects rather than relying on their layer assignment to define color and linetype. However, you may want to avoid assigning colors and linetypes directly to objects until you have some experience with AutoCAD and a good grasp of your drawing's organization.

In the previous exercise, you changed the global linetype scale setting. This affects all noncontinuous linetypes within the current drawing. You can also set the default linetype scale for all new objects with the Current Object Scale option in the Linetype Manager dialog box.

When individual objects are assigned a linetype scale, they're still affected by the global linetype scale set by the Ltscale system variable. For example, say you assign a linetype scale of 2 to the curtain rod in the previous example. This scale is then multiplied by the global linetype scale of 12, for a final linetype scale of 24.

You can also set the default linetype scale for individual objects by using the Celtscale system variable. After it's set, only newly created objects are affected. You must use the Properties palette to change the linetype scale of individual existing objects.

If the objects you draw appear in a different linetype from that of the layer on which they're located, check the default linetype by selecting Other from the Linetype drop-down list on the Home tab's Properties panel. Then, in the Linetype Manager dialog box, highlight ByLayer in the Linetype list and click the Current button. In addition, check the linetype scale of the object itself by using the Properties palette. A different linetype scale can make a line appear to have an assigned linetype that might not be what you expect. (See the sidebar "Assigning Colors, Linetypes, and Linetype Scales to Individual Objects.")

LINETYPES IN LAYOUTS

A system variable called Psltscale affects how layout viewports display linetypes. When the Psltscale system variable is set to 1, layout viewports display linetypes at the Ltscale setting, which is usually incorrect for the 1-to-1 scale of the layout. When Psltscale is set to 0, linetypes appear in layout viewports in the same way that they appear in the Model tab.

ADDING THE FINAL DETAIL

If you're working through the tutorial, your final task is to set up an insertion point for the current drawing to facilitate its insertion into other drawings in the future. Follow these steps:

1. Type **BASE**↵.

2. At the Enter base point <0'-0",0'-0",0'-0">: prompt, use the Endpoint object snap to pick the upper-left corner of the bathroom. The bathroom drawing is complete.

3. Click the Save tool in the Quick Access toolbar to record your work up to now.

Controlling Lineweights

You may have noticed a Lineweight column in the Layer Properties Manager. If you click this option for a given layer, the Lineweight dialog box opens, which enables you to control the plotted thickness of your lines. Plotted lineweights can also be set through direct object property assignment. You can view lineweights as they will appear in your final plot by making setting changes in the Lineweight Settings dialog box, which you'll learn about in Chapter 15.

With the Lineweight option and Lineweight Settings dialog box, you have greater control over the look of your drawings. This can save time because you don't have to print your drawing just to check for lineweights. You'll be able to see how thick or thin your lines are as you edit your drawing. You'll get a chance to delve into lineweights in Chapter 15.

Keeping Track of Blocks and Layers

The Insert dialog box and the Layer Properties Manager let you view the blocks and layers available in your drawing by listing them in a window. The Layer Properties Manager also includes information about the status of layers. However, you may forget the layer on which an object resides. You've seen how the Properties option on the context menu shows you the properties of an object. The List tool in the Properties panel also enables you to get information about individual objects.

Use these steps to see an alternate way to view the properties of a block:

1. Click the List tool from the Home tab's expanded Properties panel.

If you just want to check quickly to see where an object is located, click it. Its layer will appear in the layer drop-down list of the Layers panel.

2. At the Select objects: prompt, click the Tub block and then press ↵ to open the AutoCAD Text Window.

3. The Command window expands to display a list that shows not only the layer on which the tub is located but also its space, insertion point, name, rotation angle, and scale. If the Command window is in its docked position, the AutoCAD Text Window appears with the list.

The information in the expanded Command window or the AutoCAD Text Window, except the handle listing, is duplicated in the Properties palette. However, having the data in the Command window or Text Window gives you the flexibility to record it in a text file in case you need to store data about parts of your drawing. You can also use the AutoCAD Text Window to access and store other types of data regarding your drawings.

The Space property listed for the Tub block designates whether the object resides in model space or paper space. You'll learn more about these spaces in Chapter 8 and Chapter 15.

Getting a Text File List of Layers or Blocks

With complex drawings, it can be helpful to get a text file that lists the layers or blocks in your drawing. You can do this by using the log-file feature in AutoCAD. At the Command prompt, enter **Logfilemode**↵ and then enter **1**↵. Type **-La.↵?.↵↵** (don't forget the hyphen at the beginning of the La command). If your list of layers is extensive, you may be asked to press ↵ to continue. Do so. Your list of layers appears in the AutoCAD Text Window. For a list of blocks, enter **-Insert.↵?.↵↵**. When you've obtained your list, close the log-file feature by typing **Logfilemode.↵0.↵**.

ASSIGNING COLORS, LINETYPES, AND LINETYPE SCALES TO INDIVIDUAL OBJECTS

If you prefer, you can set up AutoCAD to assign specific colors and linetypes to objects instead of having objects take on the color and linetype settings of the layer on which they reside. Normally, objects are given a default color and linetype called *ByLayer*, which means that each object takes on the color or linetype of its assigned layer. (You've probably noticed the word *ByLayer* in the Properties panel and in various dialog boxes and tool palettes.)

Use the Properties panel to change the color or linetype of existing objects. This panel lets you set the properties of individual objects. For new objects, use the Object Color drop-down list on the Properties panel to set the current default color to red (for example) instead of ByLayer. Then everything you draw will be red, regardless of the current layer color. The Object Color drop-down list also offers a Select Colors option that opens the Select Color dialog box you saw earlier in this chapter.

For linetypes, you can use the Linetype drop-down list in the Properties panel to select a default linetype for all new objects. The list shows only linetypes that have already been loaded into the drawing, so you must first load a linetype before you can select it.

Another possible color and linetype assignment is *ByBlock*, which you also set with the Properties panel. ByBlock makes everything you draw white until you turn your drawing into a block and then insert the block on a layer with an assigned color. The objects then take on the color of that layer. This behavior is similar to that of objects drawn on layer 0. The ByBlock linetype works similarly to the ByBlock color.

You can set an object or set of objects to ByLayer or ByBlock using the SETBYLAYER command. Click the Set To ByLayer tool in the Home tab's expanded Modify panel or type **SETBYLAYER**↵, select the objects that you want to modify, and follow the prompt.

Finally, if you want to set the linetype scale for each individual object instead of relying on the global linetype scale (the Ltscale system variable), you can use the Properties palette to modify the linetype scale of individual objects. In place of using the Properties palette, you can set the Celtscale system variable to the linetype scale you want for new objects.

As mentioned earlier, stay away from assigning colors and linetypes to individual objects until you're comfortable with AutoCAD; even then, use color and linetype assignments carefully. Other users who work on your drawing may have difficulty understanding your drawing's organization if you assign color and linetype properties indiscriminately.

Once the log-file feature is closed, you can use Windows Notepad to open the AutoCAD log file located in the C:\Users\User Name\AppData\Local\Autodesk\AutoCAD 2018\R22.0\enu\ folder. You'll need to change the Text Document (*.txt) option to All Files. The name of the log file will start with the name of the current drawing, followed by a series of numbers and the .log filename extension, as in 04c-bath-metric_1_1_6500.log.

If you have difficulty finding the log file, enter **(getvar "logfilepath")** at the AutoCAD Command prompt to get a listing of the log-file location. The log file may also be in a hidden folder, so you may have to turn off the hidden folder setting in File Explorer. See Appendix B for instructions on how to do this.

With the log-file feature, you can record virtually anything that appears at the Command prompt. You can even record an entire AutoCAD session. The log file can also be helpful in constructing script files to automate tasks. (See Chapter 24 for more information on scripts.) If you want a hard copy of the log file, print it from an application such as Windows Notepad or your favorite word processor.

USING EXCEL TO ANALYZE LARGE LAYER LISTS

You may encounter a drawing that has a very long list of layers. To help you analyze the layers in a drawing, you can copy the layer list into Microsoft Excel by doing the following: Open the Layer Properties Manager and press Ctrl+A to select the entire layer list. Press Ctrl+C to copy the list to the Clipboard, and then open Excel. Press Ctrl+V to paste the list into Excel.

The Bottom Line

Organize information with layers.   Layers are perhaps the most powerful feature in AutoCAD. They help to keep drawings well organized, and they give you control over the visibility of objects. They also let you control the appearance of your drawing by setting colors, lineweights, and linetypes.

Master It   Describe the process of creating a layer.

Control layer visibility.   When a drawing becomes dense with information, it can be difficult to edit. If you've organized your drawing using layers, you can reduce its complexity by turning off layers that aren't important to your current session.

Master It   Describe at least two methods for hiding a layer.

Keep track of blocks and layers.   At times, you may want a record of the layers or blocks in your drawing. You can create a list of layers using the log-file feature in AutoCAD.

Master It   Where do you go to turn on the log-file feature?

Part 2

Mastering Intermediate Skills

- Chapter 6: Editing and Reusing Data to Work Efficiently
- Chapter 7: Mastering Viewing Tools, Hatches, and External References
- Chapter 8: Introducing Printing, Plotting, and Layouts
- Chapter 9: Adding Text to Drawings
- Chapter 10: Using Fields and Tables
- Chapter 11: Using Dimensions

Chapter 6

Editing and Reusing Data to Work Efficiently

If you're an experienced drafter, you know that you frequently have to draw the same item several times in many drawings. The AutoCAD® 2018 software offers a variety of ways to reuse existing geometry, thereby automating much of the repetitive work usually associated with manual drafting. That's why at least 5 commands are devoted to duplicating objects—10 if you include the grips options.

In this chapter, as you finish drawing the studio apartment unit, you'll explore some of the ways to exploit existing files and objects while constructing your drawing. For example, you'll use existing files as prototypes for new files, eliminating the need to set up layers, scales, and sheet sizes for similar drawings. With AutoCAD, you can also duplicate objects in multiple arrays. In Chapter 3, "Setting Up and Using the Drafting Tools," you saw how to use the object snap (osnap) overrides on objects to locate points for drawing complex forms. This chapter describes other ways of using lines to aid your drawing.

Because you'll begin to use the Zoom command more in the exercises in this chapter, you'll review this command as you go along. You'll also discover the Pan command, another tool to help you get around in your drawing.

You're already familiar with many of the commands you'll use to draw the apartment unit. So, rather than going through every step of the drawing process, the exercises will sometimes ask you to copy the drawing from a figure and, using notes and dimensions as guides, put objects on the indicated layers. If you have trouble remembering a command you've already learned, go back and review the appropriate section of the book.

In this chapter, you will learn to

- ◆ Create and use templates
- ◆ Copy an object multiple times
- ◆ Develop your drawing
- ◆ Find an exact distance along a curve
- ◆ Change the length of objects
- ◆ Create a new drawing by using parts from another drawing

Creating and Using Templates

Most programs today include what are called *templates*. A template is a file that is already set up for a specific application. For example, in your word processor, you might want to set up a document with a logo, a return address, and a date so that you don't have to add these elements each time you create a letter. You might also want to format invoices in a slightly different way. You can set up a template for the needs of each type of document. That way, you don't have to spend time reformatting each new document you create.

Similarly, AutoCAD offers templates, which are drawing files that contain custom settings designed for a particular function. Out of the box, AutoCAD has templates for ISO, ANSI, DIN, GB, and JIS standard drawing formats that include generic title blocks. But you aren't limited to these "canned" templates. You can create your own templates for your particular style and method of drawing.

If you find that you use a particular drawing setup frequently, you can turn one or more of your typical drawings into a template. For example, you might want to create a set of drawings with the same scale and sheet size as an existing drawing. By turning a frequently used drawing into a template, you can save a lot of setup time for subsequent drawings.

Creating a Template

The following exercise guides you through creating and using a template drawing for your studio's kitchenette. Because the kitchenette will use the same layers, settings, scale, and sheet size as the bathroom drawing, you can use the Bath file as a prototype. Follow these steps:

1. Start AutoCAD in the usual way.

2. Choose Open from the Quick Access toolbar to open the Select File dialog box.

3. Locate the Bath file you created in the previous chapter. You can also use 06-bath.dwg from the companion web page at www.sybex.com/go/masteringautocad2018.

THE FILE DIALOG BOX REMEMBERS SORT ORDERS

When using the File dialog box in AutoCAD, you can sort the file list by name, date, size, or another criteria. AutoCAD will remember the last used sort order you specify.

---

4. Click the Erase button on the Home tab's Modify panel, or enter E↵; then type all↵↵. This erases all the objects that make up the bathroom, but other elements, such as layers, linetypes, and stored blocks, remain in the drawing.

5. Choose Save As from the Application menu to open the Save Drawing As dialog box.

6. Open the File Of Type drop-down list, and select AutoCAD Drawing Template (*.dwt). The file list window changes to display the current template files in the \Template\ folder.

7. In the File Name text box, enter the name **Arch8x11h**. If you're a metric user, enter the name **A4plan**.

8. Click Save to open the Template Options dialog box (see Figure 6.1).

FIGURE 6.1
The Template Options
dialog box

9. Enter the following description: **Architectural one-inch scale drawing on 8 1/2 by 11 inch media**. Metric users should enter the description **Architectural 1:10 scale drawing on A4 media**.

10. Select English or Metric from the Measurement drop-down list, depending on the unit system you're using.

11. Click the Save All Layers As Reconciled option.

12. Click OK to save your new file and create a template. The template file you saved becomes the current file. (As with other Windows programs, choosing File ➤ Save As makes the saved file current.) This exercise shows that you can edit template files just as you would regular drawing files.

13. Close the template file.

Using a Template

Now let's see how a template is used. You'll use the template you just created as the basis for a new drawing that you'll work on in this chapter:

1. Click the New tool from the Quick Access toolbar to open the Select Template dialog box. This is a typical file dialog box, which should be familiar to you by now.

2. In the Select Template list box, click the filename Arch8x11h.dwt. Metric users should click the filename A4plan.dwt. Because this file is blank, you won't see anything in the preview window.

3. Click Open. It may not be obvious, but your new file is set up with the same architectural units and drawing limits as the bathroom drawing. It also contains the Door, Toilet, and Tub blocks.

4. You need to give your new file a name. Choose Save As from the Application menu to open the Save Drawing As dialog box. (Make sure that you choose Save As, or you won't get the Save Drawing As dialog box.) Enter **Kitchen** for the filename, and select the folder in which to save your new kitchen file. For example, you can save your file in the My Documents folder by clicking the My Documents shortcut in the left column.

5. Click Save to create the Kitchen file, and close the dialog box.

You've created and used your own template file. Later, when you've established a comfortable working relationship with AutoCAD, you can create a set of templates that are custom-made to your particular needs.

However, if you're in a hurry, you don't need to create a template every time you want to reuse settings from another file. You can use an existing file as the basis or prototype for a new file without creating a template. Open the prototype file, and choose Save As from the Application menu to create a new version of the file under a new name. You can then edit the new version without affecting the original prototype file.

LOCATING THE *TEMPLATE* FOLDER

When you choose the AutoCAD Drawing Template option in the Save Drawing As dialog box, AutoCAD automatically opens the folder containing the template files. The standard AutoCAD installation creates the folder named Template to contain the template files. If you want to place your templates in a different folder, you can change the default template location by using the Options dialog box (choose Options from the bottom of the Application menu). Click the Files tab, double-click to expand Template Settings, and then double-click Drawing Template File Location in the list. Double-click the folder name that appears just below Drawing Template File Location; then select a new location from the Browse For Folder dialog box that appears.

Copying an Object Multiple Times

 Let's explore the tools that let you quickly duplicate objects. In the following sections, you'll begin to draw parts of a small kitchen. The first set of exercises introduces the Array command, which you can use to draw the gas burners of a range top.

As you'll see, an array can be either in a circular pattern, called a *polar array*, or a matrix of columns and rows, called a *rectangular array*. You can also create arrays that follow a curved or straight path, such as a spline curve, arc, or polyline.

Making Circular Copies

To start the range top, first set the layer on which you want to draw, and then draw a circle representing the edge of one burner:

1. Set the current layer to Fixture by selecting Fixture from the layer drop-down list in the Home tab's Layers panel.

Because you used the Bath file as a template, Running Osnap is already turned on for Endpoint, Midpoint, and Intersection, but check the running osnap settings to make sure that they are turned on.

 2. Click the Center, Radius Circle tool on the Home tab's Draw panel, or type **C⏎**.

3. At the Specify center point for circle or [3P/2P/Ttr (tan tan radius)]: prompt, pick a point at coordinate 4′,4′. Metric users should pick a point at coordinate 120,120.

4. At the Specify radius of circle or [Diameter]: prompt, enter **3**↵. Metric users should enter **7.6**↵. The circle appears.

Certification
Objective

Now you're ready to use the Array command to draw the burner grill. You'll first draw one line representing part of the grill and then use the Array command to create the copies:

1. Zoom into the circle you just drew, and then make sure Snap mode is off by unchecking the Snap Mode tool in the status bar.

2. Draw a 4″ line starting from the coordinate 4′-1″,4′-0″ and ending to the right of that point. Metric users should draw a 10 cm line starting at coordinate 122,120 and ending to the right of that point.

3. Adjust your view so it looks similar to Figure 6.2.

FIGURE 6.2
A close-up of the
circle and line

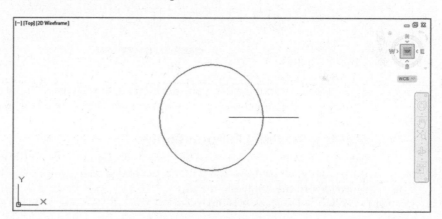

You've got the basic parts needed to create the burner grill. You're ready to make multiple copies of the line. For this part, you'll use the Array command:

1. Make sure Ortho mode is off and Polar Tracking is on.

Polar Array

2. Click the Polar Array tool from the Array flyout on the Modify panel, as shown in Figure 6.3, or type **ARRAYPOLAR**↵.

FIGURE 6.3
The Array flyout

3. At the Select Objects: prompt, click the horizontal line and press ↵.

4. At the `Specify center point of array or [Base point/Axis of rotation]:` prompt, Shift+right-click and select Center. To select the center of the circle, hover over the circle perimeter until you see the Center osnap marker. When the marker appears, click. A circular array of the line appears.

5. At the `Select grip to edit array or [Associative/Base point/Items/Angle between/Fill angle/ROWs/Levels/ROTate items/eXit]<eXit>:` prompt, enter **I↵** or select Items from the command line.

6. At the `Enter number of items in array or [Expression]:` prompt, enter **8↵**. The lines appear evenly spaced in a circular array (see Figure 6.4).

FIGURE 6.4
The lines evenly spaced in a polar array

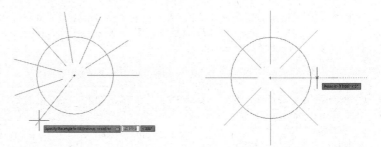

7. Press ↵ to exit the Arraypolar command, or if Dynamic Input is on, choose eXit from the menu that appears at the cursor. Your drawing should look like Figure 6.4.

Making Row and Column Copies

Now you'll draw the other three burners of the gas range by creating a rectangular array from the burner you just drew. You'll first zoom back a bit to get a view of a larger area. Then you'll proceed with the Array command.

Follow these steps to zoom back:

Zoom Scale

1. Click Zoom Scale from the Navigation bar. You can also type **Z↵S↵**.

2. Enter **0.5x↵**. Your drawing will look like Figure 6.5.

FIGURE 6.5
The preceding view reduced by a factor of 0.5

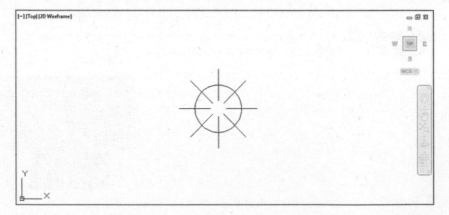

If you're not too fussy about the amount that you want to zoom out, you can click Out from the Zoom flyout on the View tab's Navigate 2D panel to reduce your view quickly.

Entering 0.5x for the Zoom Scale factor tells AutoCAD that you want a view that reduces the width of the current view to fill half of the display area, enabling you to see more of the work area. If you specify a scale value greater than 1 (5, for example), you'll magnify your current view. If you leave off the *x*, your new view will be in relation to the drawing limits rather than the current view.

Next you'll finish the range top. You'll get a chance to use the Rectangular Array option to create three additional burners:

1. Click the Rectangular Array tool on the Array flyout on the Modify panel, as shown in Figure 6.6, or type **ARRAYRECT**↵.

FIGURE 6.6
The Rectangular Array tool on the Array flyout

2. Select the entire burner, including the lines and the circle, and then press ↵ to confirm your selection.

3. At the Select grip to edit array or [Associative/Base point/COUnt/Spacing/ COLumns/Rows/Levels/eXit]<eXit>: prompt, type **COU**↵ or select COUnt from the command line.

4. At the Enter number of columns or [Expression] <4>: prompt, enter **2**↵.

5. At the Enter number of rows or [Expression] <4>: prompt, enter **2**↵ again.

6. To set the array dimensions, type **S**↵ or select Spacing from the command line.

7. At the Specify the distance between columns or [Unit cell] <1'-3">: prompt, type **1'-4"**↵. Metric users enter **40.6**↵.

8. At the Specify the distance between rows <1'-3">: prompt, type **1'-2"**↵. Metric users enter **35.5**↵.

9. Press ↵, or right-click and select the eXit option in the context menu.

10. The array appears in the drawing, but a few of the array elements are off the top of the screen, as shown in Figure 6.7. In the next section, "Fine-Tuning Your View," you'll learn about the Pan tool, which will enable you to adjust the view so that the array is centered in the drawing area.

FIGURE 6.7
The burners arrayed

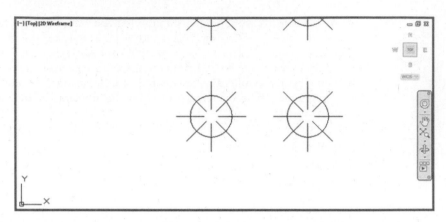

QUICK ARRAY COPIES WITH GRIPS

Sometimes the Array tool can be overkill if you need to make only a few evenly spaced copies. Fortunately, grip editing offers a feature that lets you quickly make evenly spaced copies. Here's how it's done:

1. Press the Esc key to make sure that you aren't in the middle of a command; then select the objects that you want to copy.

2. Click a grip point as your base point.

3. Right-click and select Move.

4. Ctrl+click a location at which to place a copy of the selected object. This first copy will determine the interval distance for additional copies.

5. Continue to hold down the Ctrl key, and select additional points to make copies at regularly spaced intervals.

The copies snap to the distance that you indicate with the first Ctrl+click point (in step 4). You can use osnaps to select a distance based on the position of another object. Once you've made the first copy with the Ctrl+click, you can release the Ctrl key to make multiple copies at random intervals.

Another option is to use PolarSnap while making grip edit copies. With PolarSnap, you can enter a specific distance for the intervals. To turn on Polar snap, right-click the snap mode icon in the status bar and select Polar Snap.

Fine-Tuning Your View

Certification
Objective

Back in Figure 6.7, you may have noticed that parts of the burners don't appear on the display. To move the view over so that you can see all the burners, use the Pan command. Pan is similar to Zoom in that it changes your view of the drawing. However, Pan doesn't alter the magnification of the view the way Zoom does. Rather, Pan maintains the current magnification while moving your view across the drawing, just as you would pan a camera across a landscape.

To activate the Pan command, follow these steps:

1. Click the Pan tool on the Navigation bar, or type **P↵**. A small hand-shaped cursor appears in place of the AutoCAD cursor.

2. Place the hand cursor in the center of the drawing area, and then click and drag it down and to the left. The view follows the motion of your mouse.

3. Continue to drag the view until it looks similar to Figure 6.8; then release the mouse button.

FIGURE 6.8
The panned view of the range top

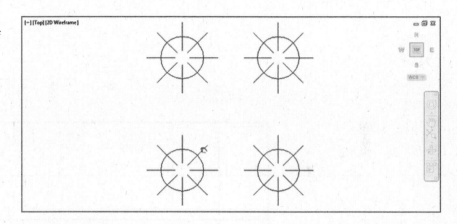

Zoom Realtime

4. To finish the kitchen, you want a view that shows more of the drawing area. Click the Zoom Realtime option in the Navigation bar's zoom flyout. The cursor changes to the Zoom Realtime cursor. The Zoom/Pan context menu also appears when you right-click during the Zoom Realtime command.

5. Place the cursor close to the top of the screen, and click and drag the cursor down to zoom out until your view looks like the top panel of Figure 6.9. You may need to click and drag the Zoom Realtime cursor a second time to achieve this view.

6. Right-click again, and choose Exit from the context menu. Press Esc twice to cancel the Zoom command. You're now ready to add more information to the kitchen drawing.

You can also exit the Pan or Zoom Realtime command without opening the context menu; just press the Esc key twice.

This exercise showed how you can fine-tune your view by easily switching between Pan and Zoom Realtime. After you get the hang of these two tools working together, you'll be able to access the best view for your needs quickly. The other options in the context menu—Zoom Window, Zoom Original, and Zoom Extents—perform the same functions as the options in the Zoom flyout on the View tab's Navigate 2D panel or in the Navigation bar.

The Zoom Window option in the Zoom/Pan context menu functions in a slightly different way from the standard Zoom Window option. Instead of clicking two points, you click and drag a window across your view.

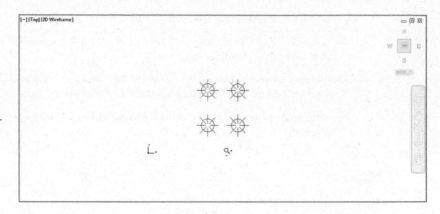

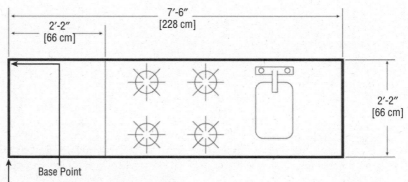

Finishing the Kitchenette

Before you save and close the Kitchen file, you need to do one more thing. You'll be using this drawing as a symbol and inserting it into the overall plan of the studio apartment unit. To facilitate accurate placement of the kitchen, you'll change the location of the base point of this drawing to the upper-left corner of the kitchen. This will then be the drawing's *grip*:

1. Complete the kitchenette as indicated in the bottom panel of Figure 6.9, shown earlier in this chapter. As the figure indicates, make sure that you put the kitchenette on the Fixture layer. This will help you control the visibility of the kitchenette in future edits of this file. Draw the sink roughly as shown in the figure.

2. Click the Set Base Point tool in the Insert tab's expanded Block Definition panel.

3. At the Enter base point: prompt, pick the upper-left corner of the kitchen, as indicated in the bottom image of Figure 6.9. The kitchen drawing is complete.

4. Select Save from the Quick Access toolbar, but keep the file open because you'll use it later.

USING THE COPY COMMAND TO CREATE AN ARRAY

In the previous section, you learned how you can quickly make an array of objects using the Array command. You can also create simple arrays using the Copy command. To see firsthand how this works, see "Copying and Editing Attribute Definitions" in Chapter 12, "Using Attributes."

Array Along a Path

Before you continue with the apartment drawings you're working on for the main part of the tutorial, we'd like to introduce you to one more Array feature. In AutoCAD 2018, you can create an array that follows a curved or straight path, such as an arc, spline curve, or complex polyline. Try the following exercise to see how it works:

1. Open the file called seating.dwg. You'll see a drawing of a chair in the lower-left corner along with an arc drawn across the width of the drawing area.

2. Click the Path Array tool in the Array flyout (see Figure 6.10), or type **ARRAYPATH.**↵.

FIGURE 6.10
Select the Path Array tool from the Array flyout on the Home tab's Modify panel.

3. At the Select objects: prompt, click the chair at the left end of the arc in the drawing and then press ↵ (see Figure 6.11).

FIGURE 6.11
Click the chair at the left end of the arc.

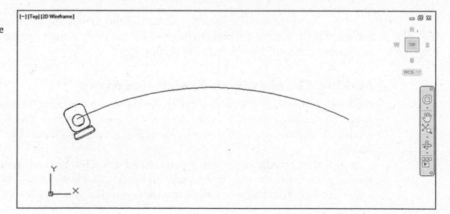

4. At the Select Path curve: prompt, select the arc toward the left end.

5. At the Select grip to edit array or [Associative/Method/Base point/Tangent direction/Items/Rows/Levels/Align items/Z direction/eXit] <eXit>: prompt, press ↵ to exit the command.

In this exercise, you made an array of a chair that follows the path of an arc. Note that the chair had been set up facing away from the center of the arc. In a later exercise, you'll see how you can easily rotate the chairs to face the center.

You could have used a spline curve or polyline (see Chapter 18, "Drawing Curves," for more on spline curves and polylines) instead of the arc and the results would have been similar.

Now suppose that you want to adjust the curvature of your array. This is just a simple matter of adjusting the shape of the arc, as in the following steps:

1. Click the arc to expose its grips.

2. Click the middle grip, drag it up until the arc dimension shows an Ortho value close to 30.0000 < 90 degrees, and then click. The array of chairs follows the arc (see Figure 6.12).

FIGURE 6.12

Change the radius of the arc and the array follows.

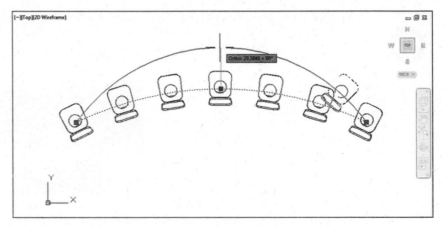

3. Press the Esc key twice to clear your selection of the arc.

Here you see how the associative feature of the Arraypath command enables you to control the array by adjusting the object you used for the path. Arrays can be edited through a variety of methods, as you'll see in the next section.

Making Changes to an Associative Array

Now let's take a look at how you can make changes to an array. You may have noticed the Associative option in the Array command's prompt. By default, the Associative option is turned on, which enables you to edit array objects as a group. You'll see how this works in the following exercises.

You'll start by editing the array you created using the Path Array tool. Since you've changed the arc array path, the chairs no longer fill the arc. The last chair to the right is no longer at the end of the arc. This happened because when you changed the arc's radius, you made it a bit longer. By default, the chair array is set up to maintain the chairs' distance from each other. You can change that setting so that the chairs fill the arc. Here's how it's done:

1. Click the array of chairs. Notice that the Array contextual Ribbon tab appears (see Figure 6.13).

FIGURE 6.13
The Array tab displays a different set of panels and options when an array is selected.

2. Click the Measure flyout in the Array tab's Properties panel and then select the Divide Method option. The chairs are now evenly spaced along the arc.

The Divide and Measure options in the Array tab's Properties panel are similar to the Divide and Measure commands. Divide marks off an object into equal parts, whereas Measure marks off an object based on a distance between the marks. You'll learn more about Divide and Measure in the section "Finding an Exact Distance Along a Curve" later in this chapter.

You may have also noticed that the chairs are pointing away from the center of the arc. You can realign them so that they face the center of the arc by making a simple change to the original chair.

The following steps show you how this is done:

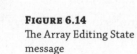

1. Click the Edit Source tool in the Array tab's Options panel.

2. Click the middle chair in the array. The Array Editing State message appears, informing you that you need to enter **ARRAYCLOSE** to exit the array editing state (see Figure 6.14).

FIGURE 6.14
The Array Editing State message

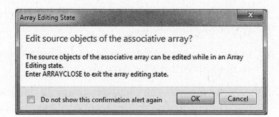

3. Click OK.

4. Press the Esc key to clear the selection of chairs.

5. Click the middle chair again, and then click the Rotate tool in the Home tab's Modify panel.

6. For the rotation base point, click the center of the circle in the chair seat, using the Center osnap.

7. Rotate the chair so that all of the chairs are facing the center of the arc, as shown in Figure 6.15.

FIGURE 6.15
Rotating the chairs

8. When the chairs are oriented so that they are pointing toward the center of the arc, click to fix their location.

9. Click the Save Changes tool in the Edit Array panel to save the changes and exit the array editing state. You can also type **ARRAYCLOSE**↵ and choose Yes in the dialog box that appears.

In this exercise, you saw how editing the source object of an array affects the other array copies. This is the Associative array feature at work. You could have made any number of other changes to the array.

Next, you'll make changes to the chair array spacing and add a few additional rows. Then you'll revisit the kitchenette to see how you can edit a nested array.

Try the following exercise to see how the Ribbon can be used to edit an array:

1. Click any chair in the array. Notice again that the Ribbon changes to show the Array tab with some new panels.

2. In the Rows panel, change the Row Count value in the top text box to **3**. Two more rows of chairs appear for a total of three rows.

3. Adjust your view so that you can see all of the rows. If this action closes the Array contextual ribbon, just click the chair again to get back to it.

4. In the Items panel, change the Item Count value at the top to **10**. If you are unable to change the item count value, open the Properties panel, click Measure, and select Divide.

5. Press the Esc key to clear your selection.

6. Exit the file without saving it so that you can come back and practice with it again.

UNABLE TO CHANGE THE ITEM COUNT?

If you can't change the Item Count value in the Items panel, select Divide Method from the Divide/Measure flyout in the Properties panel of the Array tab. The Measure option does not allow you to change the item count because Measure forces a fixed distance between objects in the array. Since the Divide option doesn't care about the distance between objects, it allows you to change the item count.

As you can see from these exercises, you can easily make changes to an array through the Ribbon panel options in the Array tab. Many of these options are also available through the multifunction grip menus when you have Dynamic Input turned on.

Several other tools become available on the Ribbon panel when you select an associative array. Table 6.1 gives you a rundown of the panels and tools and their function. The tools that appear in the Ribbon will be slightly different depending on whether the array is a polar, rectangular, or path array, but the features they offer are similar to those in the table.

TABLE 6.1: The panels and tools on the Array tab

PANEL OR TOOL	PURPOSE
Items	Controls the number of items, their distance, and the overall width of the array.
Rows	Controls the number of rows, the distance between rows, and the overall distance between the first and last row. A fourth option, Incremental Elevation in the expanded Rows panel, enables you to control the z-axis height of rows for 3D models.
Levels	Controls the number of levels in the z-axis, their spacing, and the overall distance from the first to the last level.
Base Point	Enables you to adjust the base point of the array objects.
Measure/Divide	Controls how the arrayed objects behave when the path is modified. Measure Method maintains the distance between objects when the path object changes in length. Divide Method causes the distance between objects to adjust to changes in the path object's length.
Align Items	Controls whether the array objects are aligned with the path object.
Z Direction	Controls whether array objects are "banked" with a 3D path object.
Edit Source	Enables you to edit the source object in an array.
Replace Item	Enables you to replace the source object in the array.
Reset Array	Restores erased items and removes overrides.

In the next exercise, you'll return to the kitchen drawing to see how you can use grips to modify an array:

1. If you have closed the kitchen drawing, open it again.

2. Click the array of burners that you created earlier. The grips appear for the array, and you see the Array tab in the Ribbon as you did earlier.

3. Hover over the grip in the upper-right burner. A menu appears.

4. Select the Row And Column Count option from the menu. Now, as you move the cursor up and to the right, additional burners appear. The farther to the upper right you move the cursor, the more rows and columns will appear (see Figure 6.16).

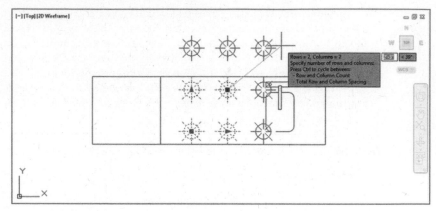

FIGURE 6.16
The rows and columns increase as you move the cursor farther from the base point.

5. When you see one additional row and column, click and then press the Esc key to clear your selection. The additional burners are added to the drawing.

6. You don't want the changes to be permanent, so click the Undo tool to revert to the four burners of the original drawing.

7. Close the kitchen drawing without saving it.

In step 4, you used the Row And Column Count multifunction grip option to add rows and columns to an array. This option combines the function of the Rows and Columns panels in the Array tab.

Developing Your Drawing

As mentioned briefly in Chapter 3, when you're using AutoCAD, you first create the basic geometric forms used in your drawing, and then you refine them. In the following sections, you'll create two drawings—the studio apartment unit and the lobby—that demonstrate this process in more detail.

First, you'll construct a typical studio apartment unit by using the drawings you've created thus far. In the process, you'll explore the use of lines as reference objects.

You'll also further examine how to use existing files as blocks. In Chapter 4, "Organizing Objects with Blocks and Groups," you inserted a file into another file. The number of files you can insert is limitless, and you can insert files of any size. As you may already have guessed, you can also *nest* files and blocks—that is, you can insert blocks or files in other blocks or files. Nesting can help reduce your drawing time by enabling you to build one block out of smaller blocks. For example, you can insert your door drawing into the bathroom plan. In turn, you can insert the bathroom plan into the studio unit plan, which also contains doors. Finally, you can insert the unit plan into the overall floor plan for the studio apartment building.

Importing Settings

In this exercise, you'll use the Bath file as a prototype for the studio unit plan. However, you must make a few changes to it first. After the changes are made, you'll import the bathroom and thereby import the layers and blocks contained in the bathroom file.

As you go through this exercise, observe how the drawings begin to evolve from simple forms to complex, assembled forms.

Use these steps to modify the Bath file:

1. Open the Bath file you worked on earlier. If you skipped drawing the Bath file in Chapter 5, "Keeping Track of Layers and Blocks," use the file 05c-bath.dwg (or 05c-bath-metric.dwg) from this book's companion web page.

2. Click the Set Base Point tool in the Insert tab's expanded Block Definition panel, and select the upper-left corner of the bathroom as the new base point for this drawing so that you can position the Bath file more accurately.

3. Save the Bath file. If you use the sample from the book's web page, choose Save As from the Application menu and save it as Bath. You can save it to your Documents folder to keep the original in its unedited state.

4. Click the Close icon in the Drawing tab, or choose Close from the Application menu to close the bath drawing.

Next you'll create a new file. Use the New option from the Quick Access toolbar to create a file from a template:

1. Click New from the Quick Access toolbar to open the Select Template dialog box.

2. Locate and select the acad.dwt template file. Metric users should select the acadiso.dwt template file.

3. Click Open to open the new file, and when the file opens, turn off the background grid.

4. If you're using Imperial measurements, choose Drawing Utilities ➢ Units from the Application menu; then, in the Drawing Units dialog box, select Architectural from the Length group's Type drop-down list and click OK. Metric users should use the default decimal length type and should select Centimeters in the Insertion Scale drop-down list.

5. Type **LIMITS**↵. At the Specify lower left corner or [ON/OFF] <0'-0",0'-0">: prompt, press ↵ to accept the default drawing origin for the lower-left corner.

6. If you're using Imperial measurements, enter **528,408**↵ at the next prompt. These are the appropriate dimensions for an 8–1/2" × 11" drawing at 1/4" = 1'-0" scale. Metric users should enter **1485,1050**. This is the work area for a 1:50 scale drawing on an A4 sheet.

7. Click Zoom All from the Navigation bar.

Let's continue by laying out a typical studio unit. You'll discover how importing a file also imports a variety of drawing items such as layers and linetypes. Follow these steps:

1. Begin the unit by drawing two rectangles, one 14' long by 24' wide and the other 14' long by 4' wide. Metric users should make the rectangles 426 cm long by 731 cm wide and 426 cm long by 122 cm wide. For the first rectangle, click the Rectangle tool in the Home tab's Draw panel, enter the coordinate for the lower-left corner as shown in Figure 6.17, and then enter **@14',24'**↵. Metric users should enter **@426,731**↵. Repeat the process using the coordinates for the second, smaller rectangle.

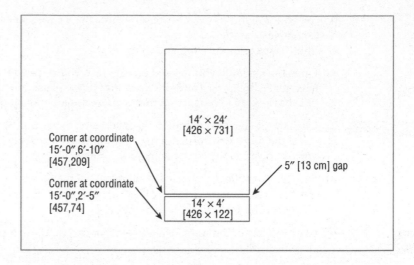

FIGURE 6.17
The apartment unit interior and balcony. Metric locations and dimensions are shown in brackets.

The rectangles should be placed as shown in Figure 6.17. The large rectangle represents the interior of the apartment unit, and the small rectangle represents the balcony. The size and location of the rectangles are indicated in the figure.

2. Click the Explode tool on the Home tab's Block panel, select the two rectangles, and then press ↵.

3. Click the Insert tool on the Home tab's Block panel to open the Insert dialog box.

4. Click the Browse button, and locate and select the bath drawing by using the Select Drawing File dialog box; then click Open. If you haven't saved a bathroom drawing from earlier exercises, you can use 05c-bath.dwg or 05c-bath-metric.dwg if you are working in the metric system.

5. If you're using the 05c-bath.dwg or the 05c-bath-metric.dwg file, do the following: After selecting 05c-bath.dwg or 05c-bath.dwg in step 4, change the name that appears in the Name text box to Bath before you click OK in step 6. This gives the inserted file a block name of Bath, even though its originating filename is 05c-bath or 05c-bath.dwg.

IF YOU USED THE RECTANGLE TOOL TO DRAW THE INTERIOR AND BALCONY...

....of the apartment unit, make sure that you use the Explode tool on the Modify panel to explode the rectangles. The Rectangle tool draws a polyline rectangle instead of simple line segments, so you need to explode the rectangle to reduce it to its component lines. You'll learn more about polylines in Chapter 18.

---

6. Click OK in the Insert dialog box, and then click the upper-left corner of the unit's interior as the insertion point (see Figure 6.18). You can use the Endpoint osnap to place the bathroom accurately. If you are prompted for scale and rotation, use a scale factor of 1.0 and a rotation angle of 0°.

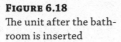

FIGURE 6.18
The unit after the bathroom is inserted

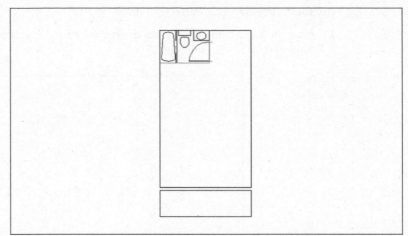

7. If running osnaps haven't been set up in this file, you need to use the Osnap context menu (Shift+right-click) to access the Endpoint osnap. You can set up running osnaps to take advantage of the AutoSnap functions by right-clicking the Object Snap button in the status bar and selecting Settings. Set the running osnaps as described in Chapter 3.

8. Assign the two rectangles that you drew earlier to the Wall layer. To do this, select the two rectangles so that they're highlighted and then open the layer drop-down list in the Layers panel and select Wall. Press the Esc key to clear the selection.

By inserting the bathroom, you imported the layers and blocks contained in the Bath file. You were then able to move previously drawn objects to the imported layers. If you're in a hurry, this can be a quick way to duplicate layers that you know exist in another drawing. This method is similar to using an existing drawing as a template, but it lets you start work on a drawing before deciding which template to use.

Using Osnap Tracking to Place Objects

You'll draw lines in the majority of your work, so it's important to know how to manipulate lines to your best advantage. In the following sections, you'll look at some common ways to use and edit these fundamental drawing objects. The following exercises show you the process of drawing lines rather than just how individual commands work. While you're building walls and adding doors, you'll get a chance to become more familiar with Polar Tracking and Osnap Tracking.

ROUGHING IN THE LINE WORK

The bathroom you inserted in the preceding section has only one side of its interior walls drawn. (Walls are usually shown by double lines.) In this next exercise, you'll draw the other side. Rather than trying to draw the wall perfectly the first time, you'll sketch in the line work and then clean it up in the next section, in a way similar to manual drafting.

Use these steps to rough in the wall lines:

1. Zoom in to the bathroom so that the entire bathroom and part of the area around it are displayed, as shown in Figure 6.19.

FIGURE 6.19
The enlarged view of the bathroom

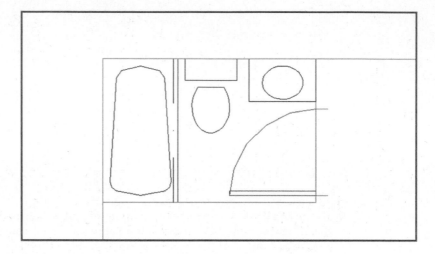

2. Select Wall from the layer drop-down list in the Layers panel to make Wall the current layer.

3. Make sure that the Object Snap Tracking and Object Snap tool options on the status bar are selected.

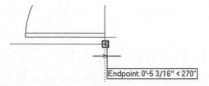

4. Select Line from the Draw panel, or type **L**↵.

5. At the Specify first point: prompt, hover your cursor over the lower-right corner of the bathroom so that the Endpoint Osnap marker appears, but don't click it.

6. Now move the cursor down and, as you do, the tracking vector appears. (If the tracking vector doesn't appear at first, hover your cursor over the corner again until it does appear.)

Remember that a little cross appears at the osnap location, telling you that Osnap Tracking has "locked on" to that location.

7. With the tracking vector visible, point the cursor directly downward from the corner and then type **5**⏎. Metric users should type **13**⏎. A line starts 5″ (or 13 cm) below the lower-right corner of the bathroom.

8. Point the cursor to the left to cross the left wall of the apartment unit slightly, as illustrated in the top image in Figure 6.20. Click to place the line in this position, and then press ⏎ to exit the Line command.

FIGURE 6.20
The first wall line and the wall line by the door

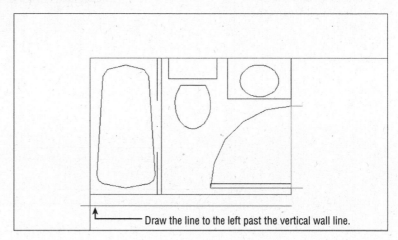

Draw the line to the left past the vertical wall line.

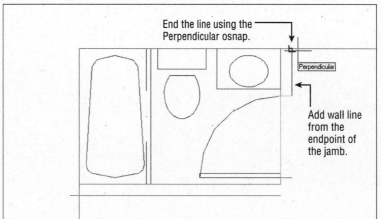

End the line using the Perpendicular osnap.

Perpendicular

Add wall line from the endpoint of the jamb.

9. Draw another line up from the endpoint of the top doorjamb to meet the top wall of the unit (see the bottom image in Figure 6.20). Use the Perpendicular osnap to pick the top wall of the unit. This causes the line to end precisely on the wall line in a perpendicular position, as seen in the bottom image in Figure 6.20.

You can also use the Perpendicular osnap override to draw a line perpendicular to a non-orthogonal line—one at a 45° angle, for instance.

10. Draw a line connecting the two doorjambs. Then assign that line to the Ceiling layer. (See the top panel in Figure 6.21.)

11. Draw a line 6″ down from the endpoint of the doorjamb nearest the corner. (See the top panel in Figure 6.21.) Metric users should draw a line 15 cm down.

FIGURE 6.21
The corner of the bathroom wall and the filleted wall around the bathroom

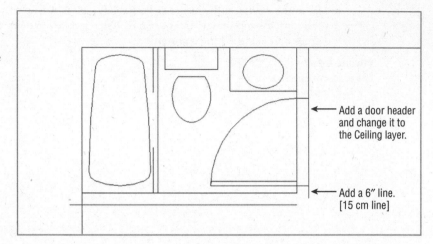

← Add a door header and change it to the Ceiling layer.

← Add a 6″ line. [15 cm line]

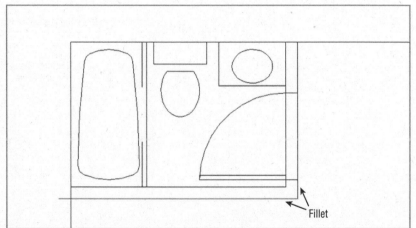

Fillet

SMOOTHING THE ARC

You may notice that some of the arcs in your bathroom drawing aren't smooth. Don't be alarmed; this is how AutoCAD displays arcs and circles in enlarged views. The arcs will be smooth when they're plotted. If you want to see them now as they're stored in the file, you can regenerate the drawing by typing **RE**↵ at the Command prompt. Chapter 7, "Mastering Viewing Tools, Hatches, and External References," discusses regeneration in more detail.

In the previous exercise, Osnap Tracking mode enabled you to specify the starting point of a line at an exact distance from the corner of the bathroom. In step 7, you used the Direct Distance method for specifying distance and direction.

SELECTING POINTS FROM A KNOWN LOCATION

Instead of using a tracking vector in step 6 of the previous exercise, you could choose From on the Osnap context menu and then open the context menu again and select Endpoint. Select the corner and enter a polar coordinate such as **@5<-90** to accomplish the same task as this exercise.

CLEANING UP THE LINE WORK

Certification
Objective

You've drawn some of the wall lines, approximating their endpoint locations. Next, you'll use the Fillet command to join lines exactly end to end and then import the kitchen drawing.

UNDERSTANDING THE OSNAP TRACKING VECTOR

The Osnap Tracking vector comes into play only after you've placed an osnap marker on a location—in this case, the corner of the bathroom. It won't appear at any other time. If you have both Running Osnaps and Osnap Tracking turned on, you'll get the tracking vector every time the cursor lands on an osnap location. This can be confusing to novice users, so you may want to use Osnap Tracking sparingly until you become more comfortable with it.

Because Polar Tracking also uses a tracking vector, you may get the two confused. Remember that Polar Tracking lets you point the cursor in a specific direction while selecting points. If you're an experienced AutoCAD user, you can think of it as a more intelligent Ortho mode. On the other hand, Osnap Tracking lets you align points to osnap locations. Experienced AutoCAD users can think of Osnap Tracking as a more intelligent XYZ filter option.

Follow these steps to join the lines:

1. Click the Fillet tool on the Modify panel or type **F⏎**.

   The Fillet, Chamfer, and Blend Curves tools share the same location in the Modify toolbar, so the tool tip may say any of these. If it does, then click the flyout arrowhead next to the tool and select Fillet.

2. Type **R⏎0⏎** to make sure that the fillet radius is set to 0.

3. Fillet the two lines by picking the vertical and horizontal lines, as indicated in the bottom panel in Figure 6.21. Notice that these points lie on the portion of the line you want to keep. Your drawing will look like the bottom panel in Figure 6.21.

CHAMFER VS. FILLET VS. BLEND CURVES

The Chamfer command performs a similar function to the Fillet command, but unlike Fillet, it enables you to join two lines with an intermediate beveled line rather than with an arc. Chamfer can be set to join two lines at a corner in exactly the same manner as Fillet.

The Blend Curves command will also join lines, but it does so by inserting a curved spline to intuitively bridge a gap between the ends of various types of objects.

4. Fillet the bottom wall of the bathroom with the left wall of the unit, as shown in Figure 6.22. Make sure that the points you pick on the wall lines are on the side of the line that you want to keep, not on the side that you want trimmed.

5. Fillet the top wall of the unit with the right-side wall of the bathroom, as shown in Figure 6.22.

FIGURE 6.22
The cleaned-up wall intersections

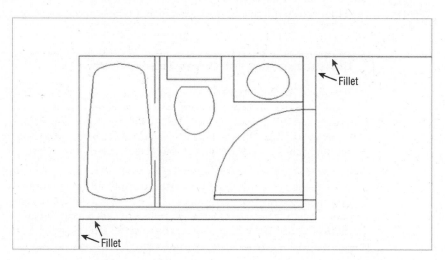

You can select two lines at once for the fillet operation by using a crossing window; to do so, type **C↵** at the Select first object or ...: prompt and then use a crossing window to select the two endpoints you want to join. The two endpoints closest to the fillet location are trimmed.

Where you select the lines affects the way the lines are joined. As you select objects to fillet, the side of the line where you click is the side that remains when the lines are joined. Figure 6.23 illustrates how the Fillet command works and shows what the Fillet options do.

If you select two parallel lines during the Fillet command, the two lines are joined with an arc. Now import the kitchen plan you drew earlier in this chapter:

1. Click Insert on the Block panel, and select More Options.

2. In the Insert dialog box, click the Browse button to locate the kitchen drawing that you created earlier in this chapter. Make sure that you leave the Specify On-Screen check box deselected under the Scale and Rotation groups of the Insert dialog box.

FIGURE 6.23
Where you click the object to select it determines which part of an object will be filleted.

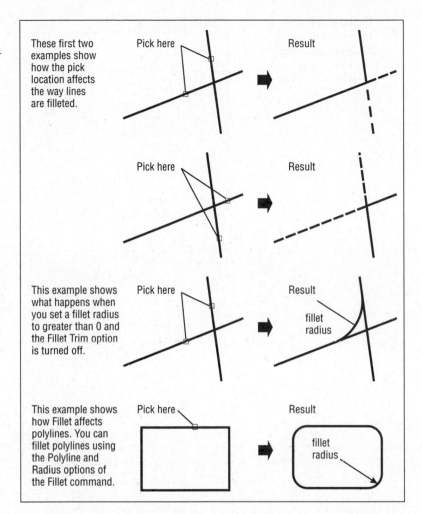

These first two examples show how the pick location affects the way lines are filleted.

Pick here   Result

Pick here   Result

This example shows what happens when you set a fillet radius to greater than 0 and the Fillet Trim option is turned off.

Pick here   Result

fillet radius

This example shows how Fillet affects polylines. You can fillet polylines using the Polyline and Radius options of the Fillet command.

Pick here   Result

fillet radius

3. Place the kitchen drawing at the wall intersection below the bathtub. (See the top image in Figure 6.24.)

If you didn't complete the kitchen earlier in this chapter, you can use the `06a-kitchen` `.dwg` file. Metric users can use `06-kitchen-metric.dwg`. Rename the file to **kitchen.dwg** to stay consistent with the tutorials in this book.

4. Adjust your view with Pan and Zoom so that the upper portion of the apartment unit is centered in the drawing area, as illustrated in the top image in Figure 6.24.

FIGURE 6.24
The view after using
Pan and Zoom, with
the door inserted and
the jamb and header
added

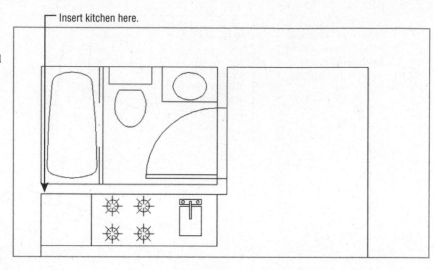

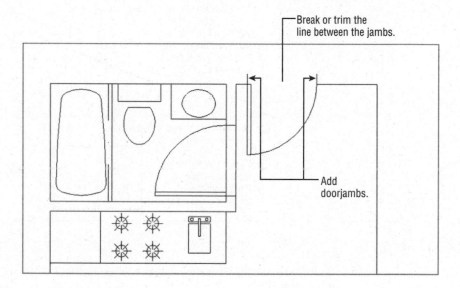

PLACING THE DOOR ACCURATELY

The next step is to add the entry door shown in the bottom image in Figure 6.24. In doing that, you'll use a number of new tools together to streamline the drawing process.

In this exercise, you'll practice using the Osnap Tracking feature and the From Osnap option to place the entry door at an exact distance from the upper corner of the floor plan:

1. Make sure that the Object Snap and Object Snap Tracking options on the status bar are selected; then right-click in the drawing area, and choose Recent Input ➤ Insert from the context menu to open the Insert dialog box.

2. Select Door from the Name drop-down list.

3. Make sure that the Specify On-Screen option is checked in the Rotation group but not in the Scale group, and then click OK. You'll see the door follow the cursor in the drawing window.

4. Shift+right-click to open the Osnap context menu, and then choose From.

5. Use the Endpoint running osnap to hover over the corner where the upper horizontal wall line meets the bathroom wall.

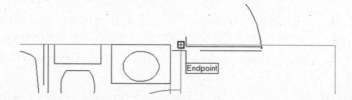

6. Now move the cursor to the right, and you'll see the Osnap Tracking vector extend from the corner.

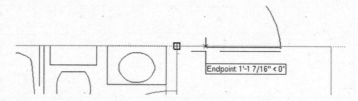

7. Continue to move the cursor to the right so that the polar tracking vector readout shows roughly 6", or 15 cm for metric users.

8. With the cursor in this position, enter 5↵. Metric users should enter 13↵. The door is placed exactly 5 (or 13) units to the right of the corner.

9. At the <offset> prompt enter @↵.

10. At the Specify rotation angle <0>: prompt, enter 270↵. Or, if you prefer, turn on Polar Tracking to orient the door so that it's swinging *into the studio*. You've now accurately placed the entry door in the studio apartment.

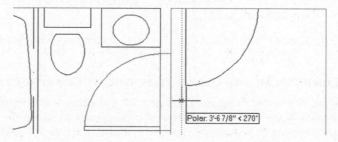

11. Make sure that the door is on the Door layer and the kitchen block is on the Fixture layer.

For a shortcut to setting an object's layer, you can select the object or objects and then select a layer from the layer drop-down list in the Layers panel.

Next, add the finishing touches to the entry door:

Certification Objective

1. Add 5" (13 cm for metric users) doorjambs, as shown in the bottom image in Figure 6.24, and change their Layer property to the Jamb layer.

2. Choose the Break tool in the expanded Modify panel, and then select the header over the entry door. (See the bottom image in Figure 6.24.)

3. Type F↵ to use the first-point option; then select the endpoint of one of the doorjambs.

4. At the Specify second break point: prompt, select the endpoint of the other jamb, as shown in the bottom image in Figure 6.24. The line between the points disappears.

5. Draw the door header on the Ceiling layer, as shown in Figure 6.25.

FIGURE 6.25
The other side of the wall

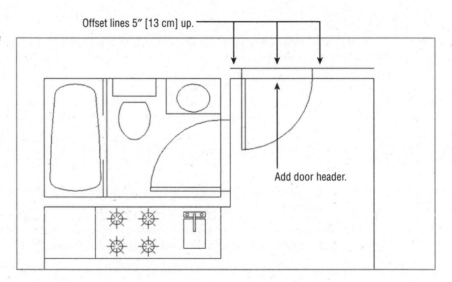

Offset lines 5" [13 cm] up.

Add door header.

6. Click Offset on the Modify panel, and offset the top wall lines of the unit and the door header up 5" (13 cm for metric users) so that they connect with the top end of the door-jamb, as shown in Figure 6.25. Remember to include the short wall line from the door to the bathroom wall.

7. Choose Save As from the Application menu and save your file as **Unit**.

USING POLAR AND OSNAP TRACKING AS CONSTRUCTION LINE TOOLS

Certification Objective

So far, you've been using existing geometry to place objects in the plan accurately. In this section, you'll use the Polar and Osnap Tracking tools to extend the upper wall line 5" (13 cm for metric users) beyond the right interior wall of the unit. You'll also learn how to use the Construction Line tool to locate doorjambs accurately near the balcony.

> **OTHER METHODS FOR USING THE BREAK COMMAND**
>
> In the exercise for finishing the unit plan, you used the Break command to place a gap in a line accurately over the entry door. In Chapter 5, you broke a line at a single point to create multiple, contiguous line segments.
>
> In this chapter, you used the Break command's first-point (F) option, which allows you to specify the first point of a break. You can also break a line without the F option, but with a little less accuracy. When you don't use the F option, the point at which you select the object is used as the first breakpoint. If you're in a hurry, you can dispense with the F option and place a gap in an approximate location. You can later use other tools to adjust the gap.
>
> In addition, you can use locations on other objects to select the first and second points of a break. For example, you might want to align an opening with another opening some distance away. After you've selected the line to break, you can then use the F option and select two points on the existing opening to define the first and second breakpoints. The breakpoints will align in an orthogonal direction to the selected points.

Start by changing the Polar Tracking setting to include a 45° angle:

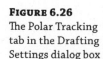

1. Right-click the Polar Tracking button in the status bar at the bottom of the AutoCAD window, and choose Settings to open the Drafting Settings dialog box at the Polar Tracking tab (see Figure 6.26).

FIGURE 6.26
The Polar Tracking tab in the Drafting Settings dialog box

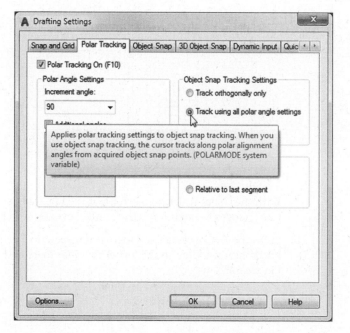

2. Select 45 from the Increment Angle drop-down list in the Polar Angle Settings group.

3. In the Object Snap Tracking Settings group, make sure that the Track Using All Polar Angle Settings option is selected and click OK.

You're ready to extend the wall line. For this operation, you'll use grip editing:

1. Click the wall line at the top of the plan and to the right of the door to select the line and expose its grips.

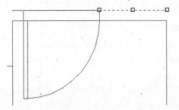

2. Click the Ortho Mode button in the status bar to turn on Ortho mode. This keeps the wall line straight as you edit it.

3. Click the rightmost grip of the line to make it hot.

4. Place the cursor on the upper-right corner of the inner wall on the plan until you see the Endpoint osnap marker; then move the cursor up and to the right of the corner at a 45° angle. The Osnap Tracking vector appears at a 45° angle. Notice the small X that appears at the intersection of the Osnap Tracking vector and the line (see Figure 6.27).

FIGURE 6.27
The Osnap Tracking vector

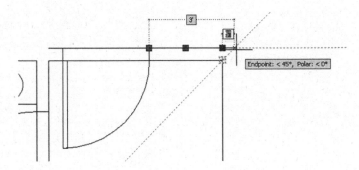

With the Osnap Tracking vector and the line intersecting, click the mouse button. The line changes to extend exactly 5 units beyond the vertical interior wall of the plan.

5. Press the Esc key twice to clear your selection. Then repeat steps 1 through 4 for the horizontal wall line to the left of the door to extend that line to the left corner (see Figure 6.28).

FIGURE 6.28
Extend the wall line
using the Osnap
Tracking vector.

FIGURE 6.28
Extend the wall line
using the Osnap
Tracking vector.

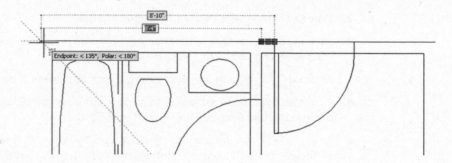

6. Click Zoom All from the Zoom flyout on the Navigation bar, or type **Z⏎A⏎** to view the entire drawing. It looks like Figure 6.29.

FIGURE 6.29
The studio unit so far

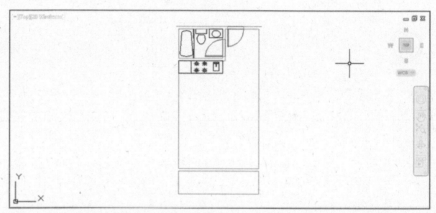

With Polar Tracking set to 45° and Osnap Tracking turned on in a crowded drawing, you may find that you're selecting points that you don't really want to select. Just remember that if a drawing becomes too crowded, you can turn off these options temporarily by clicking the Object Snap Tracking or Polar Tracking button in the status bar.

In this exercise, you used Polar Tracking and Ortho mode to position the two lines used for the exterior walls of the studio unit accurately. This shows how you can take advantage of existing geometry with a combination of tools in the status bar.

Now you'll finish the balcony by adding a sliding glass door and a rail. This time, you'll use lines for construction as well as for parts of the drawing. First, you'll add the doorjamb by drawing a construction line. A *construction line* is a line that has an infinite length, but unlike a ray, it extends in both directions. After drawing the construction line, you'll use it to position the doorjambs quickly.

Certification
Objective

Follow these steps:

1. Zoom in to the balcony area, which is the smaller rectangle at the bottom of the drawing.

Click the Construction Line tool on the expanded Draw panel. You can also type **XL⏎**. You'll see this prompt:

```
Specify a point or [Hor/Ver/Ang/Bisect/Offset]:
```

2. Type **O**↵ or select Offset from the command line.

3. At the `Specify offset distance or [Through] <0'-5">:` prompt, type **4'**↵. Metric users should type **122**↵.

4. At the `Select a line object:` prompt, click the wall line at the right of the unit.

5. At the `Specify side to offset:` prompt, click a point to the left of the wall to display the construction line. (See the top image of Figure 6.30.)

6. At the `Select a line object:` prompt, click the left wall line and then click to the right of the selected wall to create another construction line. Your drawing should look like the top image in Figure 6.30.

FIGURE 6.30
Drawing the door opening

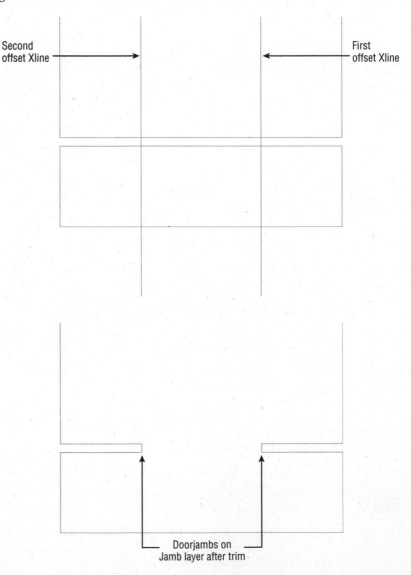

Second offset Xline

First offset Xline

Doorjambs on Jamb layer after trim

Next, you'll edit the construction lines to form the jambs.

7. Press the Esc key to exit the Xline command.

8. Click Trim on the Modify panel or type **Tr↵**.

9. Select the construction lines and the two horizontal lines representing the wall between the unit and the balcony and press ↵. You can either use a crossing window or select each line individually. You've just selected the objects to trim.

   You can also use the Fence selection option to select the lines to be trimmed.

10. Click the horizontal lines at any point between the two construction lines. Then click the construction lines above and below the horizontal lines to trim them. Your drawing should look like the bottom image in Figure 6.30.

11. Assign the trimmed construction lines to the Jamb layer.

12. Add lines on the Ceiling layer to represent the door header.

13. Draw lines between the two jambs (on the Door layer) to indicate a sliding glass door (see Figure 6.31).

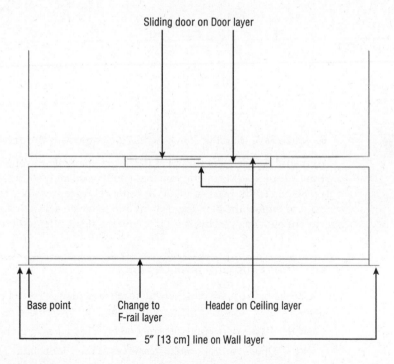

FIGURE 6.31
Finishing the sliding glass door and the railing

The wall facing the balcony is now complete. To finish the unit, you need to show a handrail and the corners of the balcony wall:

1. Offset the bottom line of the balcony 3" toward the top of the drawing. Metric users should offset the line 7.6 units.

2. Create a new layer called **F-rail**, and assign this offset line to it.

3. Add a 5″ (13 cm for metric users) horizontal line to the lower corners of the balcony, as shown in Figure 6.31.

4. Select the Set Base Point tool from the Insert tab's expanded Block Definition panel to set the base point at the lower-left corner of the balcony at the location shown in Figure 6.31.

5. Zoom back to the previous view. Your drawing should now look like Figure 6.32.

FIGURE 6.32
The completed studio apartment unit

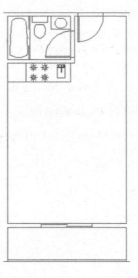

6. Click Save from the Quick Access toolbar to save the drawing, and then close the file.

Your studio apartment unit plan is now complete. The exercises you've just completed demonstrate a typical set of operations that you'll perform while building your drawings. In fact, nearly 80 percent of what you'll do in AutoCAD is represented here.

Now, to review the drawing process and to create a drawing you'll use later, you'll draw the apartment building's lobby. As you follow the steps, refer to Figure 6.33.

THE CONSTRUCTION LINE OPTIONS

There is more to the Construction Line command than you've seen in the exercises in this chapter. Here is a list of the Construction Line options and their uses:

Hor Draws horizontal construction lines as you click points

Ver Draws vertical construction lines as you click points

Ang Draws construction lines at a specified angle as you pick points

Bisect Draws construction lines bisecting an angle or an area between two points

Offset Draws construction lines offset at a specified distance from an existing line

FIGURE 6.33
Drawing the lobby plan. Metric dimensions are shown in brackets.

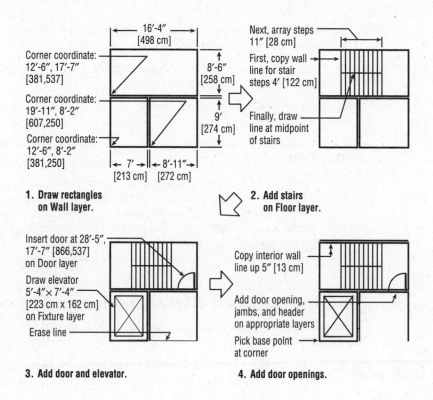

As is usual in floor plans, the elevator shaft is indicated by the box with the large X through it, and the stair shaft is indicated by the box with the row of parallel lines through it. If you're in a hurry, use the finished version of this file, called Lobby.dwg (Lobby-metric.dwg for metric users).

To draw the apartment building lobby, follow these steps:

1. Create a new file called Lobby.dwg using the Unit.dwg file as a prototype. (Open the Unit.dwg file, choose Save As from the Application menu, and enter **Lobby** for the new filename.)

2. Erase the entire unit (select the Erase tool from the Modify panel, and then type **All**↵).

3. Draw the three main rectangles that represent the outlines of the stair shaft, the elevator shaft, and the lobby.

4. To draw the stairs, copy or offset the stair shaft's left wall to the right a distance of 4 feet (122 cm). This creates the first line representing the steps.

5. Array this line in one row of 10 columns, using an 11" (28 cm) column offset.

6. Draw the center line dividing the two flights of stairs.

7. Draw the elevator, insert the door, and assign the door to the Door layer. Practice using construction lines here.

8. Draw the doorjambs. Edit the door openings to add the doorjambs and headers and add the interior walls to the stairwell.

9. Use the Base command to set the base point of the drawing. Your plan should resemble the one in Figure 6.33, step 4.

10. Save the Lobby.dwg file and close it.

USING RAYS

If you like the Construction Line tool but you would like to have one endpoint, you can use a ray (click Ray in the expanded Draw panel). A *ray* is like a line that starts from a point you select and continues off to an infinite distance. You specify the start point and angle of the ray. You can place a ray at the corner at a 45° angle and then fillet the ray to the horizontal wall line to shorten or lengthen the line to the appropriate length.

Finding an Exact Distance Along a Curve

To find an exact distance along a curve or to mark off specific distance increments along a curve, do the following:

1. With a file open, click the Point Style tool in the Home tab's expanded Utilities panel, or enter **ddptype**↵ to open the Point Style dialog box (see Figure 6.34).

FIGURE 6.34
The Point Style dialog box

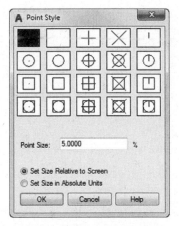

2. Click the X icon in the top row. Also be sure the Set Size Relative To Screen radio button is selected and then click OK. You can also set the point style by setting the Pdmode system variable to 3.

3. Select Measure from the expanded Draw panel, or type **ME**↵ (see Figure 6.35).

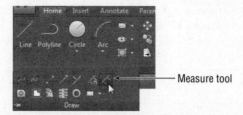

Measure tool

THE DIFFERENCE BETWEEN DIVIDE AND MEASURE

The Divide tool (Divide from the expanded Draw panel) marks off a line, an arc, or a curve into equal divisions as opposed to divisions of a length you specify. You might use Divide to divide an object into 12 equal segments, for example. Aside from this difference in function, Divide works exactly the same as Measure.

---

4. At the Select object to measure: prompt, click the end of the curve that you want to use as the starting point for your distance measurement.

5. At the Specify length of segment or [Block]: prompt, enter the distance you want. A series of Xs appears on the curve, marking off the specified distance along the curve. You can select the exact location of the Xs by using the Node osnap override (see Figure 6.36).

FIGURE 6.36
Finding an exact dis-
tance along a spline
curve by using points
and the Measure
command

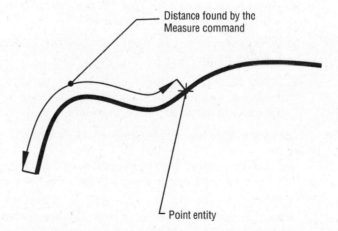

Distance found by the
Measure command

Point entity

USING BLOCKS INSTEAD OF POINTS

With the Block option of the Measure command, you can specify a block to be inserted at the specified segment length in place of point objects on the arc. You can align the block with the arc as it's inserted. Or you can use the Arraypath command described earlier in this chapter.

The Measure command also works on most objects, including arcs and polylines. You'll get a more detailed look at the Measure command in Chapter 18.

As you work with AutoCAD, you'll find that constructing temporary geometry will help you solve problems in new ways. Don't hesitate to experiment! Remember, you always have the Save and Undo commands to help you recover from your mistakes.

DIVIDE AND MEASURE AS AUTOLISP CUSTOMIZATION TOOLS

Divide and Measure are great tools for gathering information about objects in a drawing. A colleague of ours found it to be an excellent way to find the length of a complex object while working on an AutoLISP® macro. In AutoLISP, you have to write some elaborate code just to find the length of a complex polyline. After struggling with his program code, our colleague realized that he could use the Measure command to mark off known distances along a polyline and then count the points to find the overall length of the polyline.

Changing the Length of Objects

Suppose that, after finding the length of an arc, you realize you need to lengthen the arc by a specific amount. The Lengthen tool in the expanded Modify panel lets you lengthen or shorten arcs, lines, polylines, splines, and elliptical arcs. Here's how to lengthen an arc:

1. Select Lengthen from the expanded Modify panel, or type **LEN**↵.

2. At the Select an object or [DElta/Percent/Total/DYnamic]: prompt, type **T**↵, or select Total from the command line.

3. At the Specify total length or [Angle] <1.0000)>: prompt, enter the length you want for the arc.

4. At the Select an object to change or [Undo]: prompt, click the arc that you want to change. Be sure to click at a point nearest the end that you want to lengthen. The arc increases in length to the size that you specified.

The Lengthen command also shortens an object if it's currently longer than the value you enter.

In this short example, you've learned how to change an object to a specific length. You can use other criteria to change an object's length using these options available for the Lengthen command:

Delta Lengthens or shortens an object by a specific length. To specify an angle rather than a length, use the Angle suboption.

Percent Increases or decreases the length of an object by a percentage of its current length.

Total Specifies the total length or angle of an object.

Dynamic Lets you graphically change the length of an object using your cursor.

Creating a New Drawing by Using Parts from Another Drawing

Next, we'll explain how to use the Export command. Export can be used to turn parts of a drawing into a separate file in a way similar to the Wblock command described in Chapter 4. Here you'll use the Export command to create a separate staircase drawing by using the staircase you've already drawn for the lobby.

Follow these steps:

1. If you closed the lobby drawing, open it now. If you didn't create the drawing, open the 06-Lobby.dwg (or 06-Lobby-metric.dwg) file.

2. Choose Export ➢ Other Formats from the Application menu, or type **export**⏎ to open the Export Data dialog box.

3. Enter stair.dwg in the File Name text box, and click Save. By including the .dwg filename extension, you let AutoCAD know that you want to export to a drawing file and not a file in some other file format, such as DXF or WMF.

4. At the Enter name of existing block or [= (block=output file)/* (whole drawing)] <define new drawing>: prompt, press ⏎. When you export to a DWG format, AutoCAD assumes that you want to export a block. Bypassing this prompt by pressing ⏎ tells AutoCAD that you want to create a file from part of the drawing rather than from a block.

5. At the Specify insertion base point: prompt, pick the lower-right corner of the stair shaft. This tells AutoCAD the base point for the new drawing.

6. At the Select objects: prompt, use a standard window (not a crossing window) to select the stair shaft, as shown in Figure 6.37.

FIGURE 6.37
A selection window enclosing the stair shaft

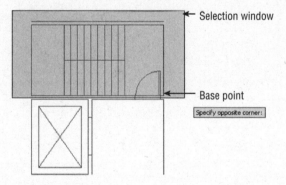

7. When the stair shaft, including the door, is highlighted, press ⏎ to confirm your selection. The stairs disappear.

8. Because you want the stairs to remain in the lobby drawing, click the Undo button to bring them back. Undo doesn't affect any files that you might export by choosing Export ➢ Other Formats from the Application menu, by using Wblock, or by using the Block tool.

Eliminating Unused Blocks, Layers, Linetypes, Shapes, Styles, and More

A template can contain blocks and layers that you don't need in your new file. For example, the lobby you just completed contains the bathroom block because you used the Unit file as a prototype. Even though you erased this block, it remains in the drawing file's database. It's considered unused because it doesn't appear as part of the drawing. Such extra blocks can slow you down by increasing the amount of time needed to open the file. They also increase the size of your file unnecessarily. You can eliminate unused elements from a drawing by using the Purge command.

SELECTIVELY REMOVING UNUSED ELEMENTS

You use the Purge command to remove unused individual blocks, layers, linetypes, shapes, text styles, and other drawing elements from a drawing file. To help keep the file size small and to make layer maintenance easier, you should purge your drawing of unused elements. Bear in mind, however, that the Purge command doesn't delete certain primary drawing elements—namely, layer 0, the Continuous linetype, and the Standard text style.

Use these steps to practice using the Purge command:

1. In the lobby drawing, choose Drawing Utilities ➤ Purge from the Application menu to open the Purge dialog box (see Figure 6.38). You'll see a listing of drawing components that can be purged. If the drawing contains any of the types of components listed, a plus sign appears to the left of the component name.

FIGURE 6.38

The Purge dialog box

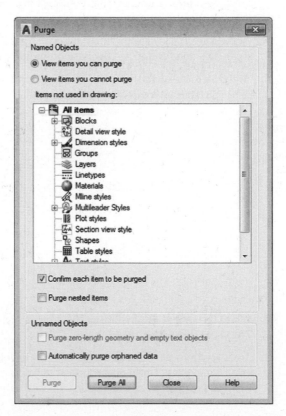

2. Click the plus sign of the component that you want to purge. In this exercise, click the plus sign next to the Blocks listing. The list expands to show the names of the items under the component category.

3. Select the name BATH from the expanded list. If you want to select more than one item, you can Ctrl+click individual names or Shift+click to select a group of names.

4. After the components are selected, click the Purge button in the lower-left corner of the dialog box. You then see a message box asking you to confirm that you want to purge the block.

5. Click Purge This Item, and then click Close to close the Purge dialog box.

REMOVING ALL UNUSED ELEMENTS

In the previous exercise, you selected a single block for removal from the lobby drawing. If you want to clear all the unused elements from a file at once, you can click the Purge All button at the bottom of the Purge dialog box (see Figure 6.38).

Here are the steps:

1. Choose Drawing Utilities ➢ Purge from the Application menu to open the Purge dialog box again.

2. Click the Purge Nested Items check box to turn on this option.

3. Click Purge All to open the Confirm Purge dialog box, which asks whether you want to purge a block.

4. Click Purge This Item. The Confirm Purge dialog box displays the name of another block, asking you to confirm the purge. You can continue to click Purge This Item, and AutoCAD will display the Confirm Purge dialog box for each unused element still in the drawing.

5. Click the Purge All Items option to purge everything at once. The Confirm Purge dialog box closes.

6. In the Purge dialog box, click Close.

7. Close and save the Lobby file, and exit AutoCAD.

The Lobby file is now trimmed down to the essential data it needs and nothing else. You may have noticed that when you returned to the Purge dialog box in step 6, the items in the list box no longer showed plus signs. This indicates that there are no longer any unused items in the drawing.

In this last exercise, you used the Purge Nested Items option at the bottom of the dialog box. The Purge Nested Items option automatically purges unused blocks, including those nested within other blocks. If this option isn't checked, you might have to repeat the Purge operation to remove all unused elements in a drawing.

PURGING ZERO-LENGTH GEOMETRY AND BLANK TEXT

At the very bottom of the Purge dialog box, you'll see the option Purge Zero-Length Geometry And Empty Text Objects. This has long been on the wish list of AutoCAD users, and it does just what it says: It purges objects that have no length as well as text objects that do not contain any text. They are offered in the Purge dialog box because they cannot be selected and deleted like normal AutoCAD objects. The Automatically Purge Orphaned Data Option purges DGN linestyle data.

The Bottom Line

Create and use templates.   If you find that you're using the same settings when you create a new drawing file, you can set up an existing file the way you like and save it as a template. You can then use your saved template for any new drawings you create.

Master It   Describe the method for saving a file as a template.

Copy an object multiple times.   Many tools in AutoCAD allow you to create multiple copies. The Array command offers a way to create circular copies, row and column copies, and copies that follow a path.

Master It   What names are given to the three types of arrays offered in the Modify panel?

Develop your drawing.   When laying down simple line work, you'll use a few tools frequently. The exercises in the early part of this book showed you some of these commonly used tools.

Master It   What tool can you use to join two lines end to end?

Find an exact distance along a curve.   AutoCAD offers some tools that allow you to find an exact distance along a curve.

Master It   Name the two tools that you can use to mark off exact distances along a curve.

Change the length of objects.   You can accurately adjust the length of a line or arc in AutoCAD using a single command.

Master It   What is the keyboard alias for the command that changes the length of objects?

Create a new drawing by using parts from another drawing.   You can save a lot of time by reusing parts of drawings. The Export command can help.

Master It   True or false: The Export command saves only blocks as drawing files.

Chapter 7

Mastering Viewing Tools, Hatches, and External References

Now that you've created drawings of a typical apartment unit and the apartment building's lobby and stairs, you can assemble them to complete the first floor of the apartment building. In this chapter, you'll take full advantage of the features of the AutoCAD® 2018 software to enhance your drawing skills and to reduce the time to create accurate drawings.

As your drawing becomes larger, you'll find that you need to use the Zoom and Pan commands more often. Larger drawings also require some special editing techniques. You'll learn how to assemble and view drawings in ways that will save you time and effort as your design progresses. Along the way, you'll see how you can enhance the appearance of your drawings by adding hatch patterns.

In this chapter, you will learn to

- ◆ Assemble the parts
- ◆ Take control of the AutoCAD display
- ◆ Use hatch patterns in your drawings
- ◆ Understand the boundary hatch options
- ◆ Use external references

Assembling the Parts

One of the best timesaving features of AutoCAD is its ability to duplicate repetitive elements quickly in a drawing. In this section, you'll assemble the drawings you've been working on into the complete floor plan of a fictitious apartment project. Doing so will demonstrate how you can quickly and accurately copy your existing drawings in a variety of ways.

> **DON'T SEE THE NAVIGATION BAR?**
>
> In this chapter, you'll be asked to use the Zoom and Pan tools on the Navigation bar frequently. If you don't see it in the AutoCAD window, then go to the View tab's Viewport Tools panel and turn on the Navigation Bar option.

Start by creating a new file for the first floor:

1. Create a new file named Plan to contain the drawing of the apartment building's first floor. This is the file you'll use to assemble the unit plans into an apartment building. If you want to use a template file, use acad.dwt. Metric users can use the acadiso.dwt template file. (These are AutoCAD template files that appear in the Select Template dialog box when you choose New from the Quick Access toolbar.)

2. In the Length group of the Drawing Units dialog box, set the unit Type to Architectural (choose Drawing Utilities ➤ Units from the Application menu). Metric users can leave Type as Decimal but change the insertion scale to centimeters.

3. Set up the drawing for a 1/8" = 1'-0" scale on a 24" by 18" drawing area. (You can use the Limits command for this.) Such a drawing requires an area 2,304 units wide by 1,728 units deep. Metric users should set up a drawing at 1:100 scale on an A2 sheet size. Your drawing area should be 5940 cm by 4200 cm.

4. Create a layer called **Plan1**, and make it the current layer.

5. Right-click the Snap Mode tool in the status bar and select Settings.

6. Set Snap Spacing to **1** for both Imperial and metric users.

7. Choose Zoom All from the Navigation bar or type **Z↵A↵** to get an overall view of the drawing area.

Now you're ready to start building a floor plan of the first floor from the unit plan you created in the previous chapter. You'll begin by creating a mirrored copy of the apartment plan:

1. Make sure that the Object Snap tool is turned off, and then insert the 07a-unit.dwg drawing at coordinate 31'-5",43'-8". Metric users should insert the 07a-unit-metric.dwg drawing at coordinate 957,1330. If you don't already have them, you can download these and other exercise files for this book at www.sybex.com/go/masteringautocad2018.

2. Accept the Insert defaults. 07a-unit and 07a-unit-metric are the same drawings as the Unit.dwg file that you were asked to create in earlier chapters.

If you prefer, you can specify the insertion point in the Insert dialog box by removing the check mark from the Specify On-Screen check box. The input options in the Insertion Point group then become available to receive your input.

If you happen to insert a block in the wrong coordinate location, you can use the Properties palette to change the insertion point for the block.

Continue the drawing by making mirrored copies of the inserted plan:

1. Zoom into the apartment unit plan.

2. Click Mirror on the Home tab's Modify panel, select the unit plan, and press ↵.

3. At the Specify first point of the mirror line: prompt, Shift+right-click and choose From.

4. Shift+right-click again, and choose Endpoint.

5. Select the endpoint of the upper-right corner of the apartment unit, as shown in Figure 7.1.

FIGURE 7.1
The unit plan mirrored

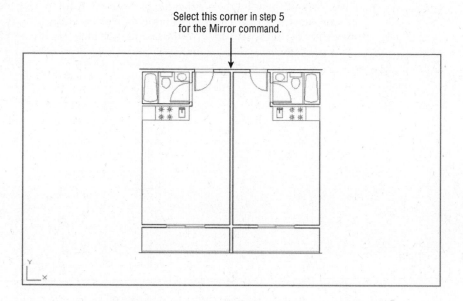

Select this corner in step 5 for the Mirror command.

6. At the <Offset>: prompt, enter **@2.5<0**↵. Metric users should enter **@6.5<0**↵. A rubber-banding line appears, indicating the mirror axis.

7. Turn on the Ortho mode tool, and select any point to point the mirror axis in a vertical orientation. You can also hold down the Shift key as you make your point selection to turn on Ortho mode temporarily.

8. At the Erase Source Objects? [Yes/No] <N>: prompt, press ↵. You'll get a 5" wall thickness between two studio units. Your drawing should be similar to the one shown in Figure 7.1.

You now have a mirror-image copy of the original plan in the exact location required for the overall plan. Next, make some additional copies for the opposite side of the building:

1. Press ↵ to reissue the Mirror command and select both units.

2. Use the From osnap option again, and using the Endpoint osnap, select the same corner you selected in step 5 of the previous exercise.

3. Enter **@24<90** to start a mirror axis 24" directly above the selected point. Metric users should enter **@61<90**.

4. With Ortho mode on, select a point so that the mirror axis is exactly horizontal.

5. At the Erase source objects? [Yes/No] <N>: prompt, press ↵ to keep the two unit plans you selected in step 1 and complete the mirror operation.

With the tools you've learned about so far, you've quickly and accurately set up a fairly good portion of the floor plan. Continue with the next few steps to "rough in" the main components of the floor:

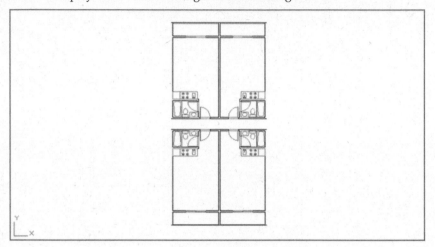

Zoom Extents

1. Click Zoom Extents on the Navigation bar's Zoom flyout to get a view of the four plans, or you can type **Z↵E↵**. The Extents option forces the entire drawing to fill the screen at the center of the display area. Your drawing will look like Figure 7.2.

FIGURE 7.2
The unit plan, duplicated four times

2. Copy the four units to the right at a distance of 28'-10" (878 cm for metric users), which is the width of two units from center line to center line of the walls.

3. Insert the Lobby.dwg file from Chapter 6, "Editing and Reusing Data to Work Efficiently," at coordinate 89'-1",76'-1" (2713,2318 for metric users).

4. Copy all of the unit plans to the right 74'-5" (2267 cm for metric users), the width of 4 units plus the width of the lobby.

Zoom All

5. Click Zoom All on the Navigation bar's Zoom flyout or type **Z↵A↵** to view the entire drawing, which should look like Figure 7.3.

FIGURE 7.3
The Plan drawing

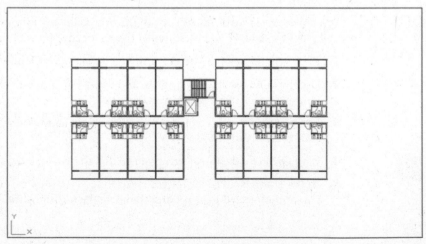

6. Click Save on the Quick Access toolbar to save this Plan.dwg file.

Taking Control of the AutoCAD Display

By now, you should be familiar with the Pan and Zoom functions in AutoCAD. Many other tools can also help you get around in your drawing. In the following sections, you'll get a closer look at the ways you can view your drawing.

Understanding Regeneration and Redrawing

AutoCAD uses two commands for refreshing your drawing display: Regen (drawing regeneration) and Redraw. Each command serves a particular purpose, although it may not be clear to a new user.

To understand the difference between Regen and Redraw, keep in mind that AutoCAD stores drawing data in two ways:

◆ In a database of highly accurate coordinate information that is part of the properties of objects in your drawing

◆ In a simplified database used just for the display of the objects in your drawing

As you draw, AutoCAD starts to build an accurate, core database of objects and their properties. At the same time, it creates a simpler database that it uses just to display the drawing quickly. AutoCAD uses this second database to allow quick manipulation of the display of your drawing. For the purposes of this discussion, we'll call this simplified database the *virtual display* because it's like a computer model of the overall display of your drawing. This virtual display is, in turn, used as the basis for what is shown in the drawing area. When you issue a Redraw command, you're telling AutoCAD to reread this virtual display data and display that information in the drawing area. A Regen command, on the other hand, tells AutoCAD to rebuild the virtual display based on information from the core drawing database.

You may notice that the Pan and Zoom Realtime commands don't work beyond a certain area in the display. When you reach a point where these commands seem to stop working, you've come to the limits of the virtual display data. To go beyond these limits, AutoCAD must rebuild the virtual display data from the core data; in other words, it must regenerate the drawing. You can usually do this by zooming out to the extents of the drawing.

Sometimes, when you zoom in to a drawing, arcs and circles may appear to be faceted instead of smooth curves. This faceting is the result of the virtual display simplifying curves to conserve memory. You can force AutoCAD to display smoother curves by typing **RE↵**, which is the shortcut for the Regen command.

CREATING MULTIPLE VIEWS

So far, you've looked at ways that will help you get around in your drawing while using a single view window. You can also set up multiple views of your drawing, called *viewports*. With viewports, you can display more than one view of your drawing at a time in the AutoCAD drawing area. For example, one viewport can display a close-up of the bathroom, another can display the overall plan view, and yet another can display the unit plan.

When viewports are combined with the Paper Space feature, you can plot multiple views of your drawing. Paper Space is a display mode that lets you arrange multiple views of a drawing. To find out more about viewports and Paper Space mode, see Chapter 15, "Laying Out Your Printer Output," and Chapter 22, "Editing and Visualizing 3D Solids."

Saving Views

Another way to control your views is by saving them. You might think of saving views as a way of creating a bookmark or a placeholder in your drawing.

CONTROLLING DISPLAY SMOOTHNESS

As you work in AutoCAD, you may notice that linetypes sometimes appear continuous even when they're supposed to be dotted or dashed. You may also notice that arcs and circles occasionally appear to be segmented lines although they're always plotted as smooth curves. A command called Viewres controls how smoothly linetypes, arcs, and circles are displayed in an enlarged view. The lower the Viewres value, the fewer the segments and the faster the redraw and regeneration. However, a low Viewres value causes noncontinuous linetypes, such as dashes or center lines, to appear as though they're continuous, especially in drawings that cover very large areas (for example, civil site plans).

Finding a Viewres value that best suits the type of work you do will take some experimentation. The default Viewres setting is 1000. You can try increasing the value to improve the smoothness of arcs and see if a higher value works for you. Enter **Viewres**↵ at the Command prompt to change the value. If you work with complex drawings, you may want to keep the value at 1000 and then, when you zoom in close to a view, use the Regen command to display smooth arcs and complete linetypes.

For example, a few walls in the Plan drawing aren't complete. To add the lines, you'll need to zoom into the areas that need work, but these areas are spread out over the drawing. AutoCAD lets you save views of the areas in which you want to work and then jump from one saved view to another saved view. This technique is especially helpful when you know you'll often want to return to a specific area of your drawing.

You'll see how to save and recall views in the following set of exercises. Here's the first one:

1. Click the View Manager tool in the View tab's Views panel. If you don't see the Views panel, right-click in the View tab and select Show Panel ➤ Views. You can also type **V**↵ to open the View Manager dialog box (see Figure 7.4).

FIGURE 7.4
The View Manager
dialog box

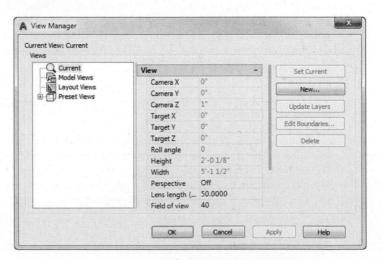

MANAGING SAVED VIEWS

In the View Manager dialog box, you can call up an existing view (Set Current), create a new view (New), or get detailed information about a view. You can also select from a set of predefined views that include orthographic and isometric views of 3D objects. You'll learn more about these options in Chapter 20, "Creating 3D Drawings."

---

2. Make sure that the Current option is selected in the list to the left, and then click the New button to open the New View / Shot Properties dialog box (see Figure 7.5). You'll notice some options related to the User Coordinate System (UCS) plus an option called View Category. You'll get a chance to look at the UCS in Chapter 20 and Chapter 21, "Using Advanced 3D Features." The View Category option relates to the Sheet Set feature described in Bonus Chapter 7, "Keeping a Project Organized with Sheet Sets," available at www.omura.com/chapters. Other options, including Visual Style, Background, and Boundary, give you control over the appearance of the background and layout of a saved view. For now, you'll concentrate on creating a new view.

FIGURE 7.5
The New View / Shot Properties dialog box

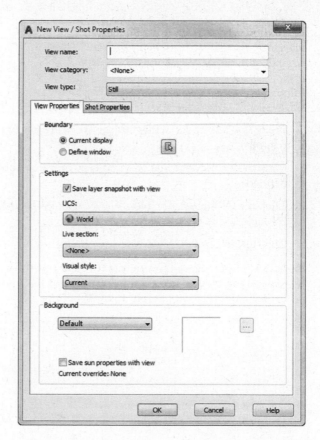

3. Click the Define Window radio button. The dialog boxes momentarily disappear, and the Dynamic Input display turns on.

4. At the `Specify first corner:` prompt, click two points to place a selection window around the area that surrounds the elevator lobby, as shown in Figure 7.6. Notice that the display changes so that the nonshaded area shows the area you selected. If you aren't satisfied with the selection area, you can place another window in the view.

FIGURE 7.6
Select this area for your saved view.

Elevator lobby

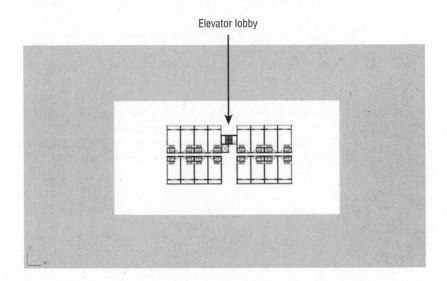

5. When you're satisfied with your selection, press ↵ or right-click. The dialog boxes reappear.

6. Click the View Name text box, and type **Elevator Lobby** for the name of the view you just defined.

7. Click the OK button. The New View / Shot Properties dialog box closes, and you see Elevator Lobby in the Views list.

8. Click OK to close the View Manager dialog box.

9. Let's see how to recall the view that you've saved. Type **V↵** to open the View Manager, expand the Model Views option in the Views list, and select Elevator Lobby. Click Set Current and then click Apply and OK.

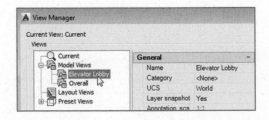

Your view changes to a close-up of the area you selected in step 4.

If you need to make adjustments to a view after you've created it, you can do so by following these steps: Right-click the view name in the View Manager dialog box, select Edit Boundaries, and then select a window as you did in steps 2 and 3.

REPEAT THE LAST COMMAND

Remember that when no command is active, you can right-click the drawing area and then select Recent Input to repeat a recently issued command. You can also right-click the drawing area when AutoCAD is idle and repeat the last command.

If you prefer, you can use the keyboard to invoke the View command and thus avoid all the dialog boxes:

1. Click Zoom Extents on the Navigation bar's Zoom flyout, or type Z⏎E⏎.

2. Enter -View⏎S⏎ at the Command prompt, or use the -V⏎S⏎ shortcut. (Remember to use the minus sign in front of *View* or *V*.)

3. At the Enter view name to save: prompt, enter **Overall**⏎.

4. Save the Plan file.

As you can see, this is a quick way to save a view. With the name Overall assigned to this view, you can easily recall it at any time. (Choosing the Zoom All flyout option from the Navigation bar gives you an overall view too, but it may zoom out too far for some purposes, or it may not show what you consider an overall view.)

OPENING A FILE TO A PARTICULAR VIEW

The Select File dialog box contains a Select Initial View check box. If you open a drawing with this option selected, you're greeted with a Select Initial View dialog box just before the opened file appears on the screen. This dialog box lists any views saved in the file. You can then go directly to a view by double-clicking the view name. If you've saved views and you know the name of the view you want, using Select Initial View saves time when you're opening large files.

Understanding the Frozen Layer Option

As mentioned earlier, you may want to turn off certain layers to plot a drawing containing only selected layers. But even when layers are turned off, AutoCAD still takes the time to redraw and regenerate them. The Layer Properties Manager offers the Freeze option; this acts like the Off option, except that Freeze causes AutoCAD to ignore frozen layers when redrawing and regenerating a drawing. By freezing layers that aren't needed for reference or editing, you can reduce the time AutoCAD takes to perform regens. You'll find this capability helpful when working with large files.

Be aware, however, that the Freeze option affects blocks in an unusual way. Try the following exercise to see how the Freeze option makes entire blocks disappear:

1. Close the Plan file, and open the 07b-plan.dwg file from the sample files. Metric users should open 07b-plan-metric.dwg. This file is similar to the Plan file you created but with a few walls and stairs added to finish off the exterior. Also note that the individual units are blocks named 07a-unit or 07a-unit-metric. This will be important in a later exercise.

2. Open the Layer Properties Manager dialog box, and then set the current layer to 0.

3. Click the yellow lightbulb icon in the Plan1 layer listing to turn off that layer. Nothing changes in your drawing. Even though you turned off the Plan1 layer, the layer on which the unit blocks were inserted, the unit blocks remain visible.

4. Right-click in the layer list, choose Select All from the context menu, and then click a lightbulb icon (not the one you clicked in step 3). You see a message warning you that the current layer will be turned off. Click Turn The Current Layer Off. Now everything is turned off, including objects contained in the unit blocks.

5. Right-click in the layer list, choose Select All from the context menu, and then click a lightbulb icon to turn all the layers back on.

6. Click the Plan1 layer to select it and then click its Freeze/Thaw icon. (You can't freeze the current layer.) The yellow sun icon changes to a gray snowflake, indicating that the layer is now frozen (see Figure 7.7). Only the unit blocks disappear.

FIGURE 7.7
Freezing the Plan1 layer

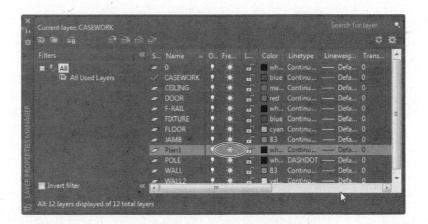

Even though none of the objects in the unit blocks were drawn on the Plan1 layer, the entire contents of the blocks assigned to the Plan1 layer are frozen when Plan1 is frozen. Another way to freeze and thaw individual layers is by clicking the Freeze/Thaw icon (which looks like a sun) in the layer drop-down list in the Home tab's Layers panel.

You don't really need the Plan1 layer frozen. You froze it to see the effects of Freeze on blocks. Do the following to turn Plan1 back on:

1. Thaw layer Plan1 by going back to the Layer Properties Manager and clicking the snow-flake icon in the Plan1 layer listing.

2. Turn off the Ceiling layer. Exit the dialog box by clicking the X in the Layer Properties Manager's title bar.

The previous exercise showed the effect of freezing on blocks. When a block's layer is frozen, the entire block is made invisible regardless of the layer assignments of the objects contained in the block.

Keep in mind that when blocks are on layers that aren't frozen, the individual objects that are part of the block are still affected by the status of the layer to which they're assigned. This means that if some objects in a block are on a layer called Wall and the Wall layer is turned off or frozen, then those objects become invisible. Objects within the block that aren't on the layer that is off or frozen remain visible.

Using Hatch Patterns in Your Drawings

Certification
Objective

To help communicate your ideas to others, you'll want to add graphic elements that represent types of materials, special regions, or textures. AutoCAD provides hatch patterns for quickly placing a texture over an area of your drawing. In the following sections, you'll add a hatch pattern to the floor of the studio apartment unit, thereby instantly enhancing the appearance of one drawing. In the process, you'll learn how to update all the units in the overall floor plan quickly to reflect the changes in the unit.

Placing a Hatch Pattern in a Specific Area

It's always a good idea to provide a separate layer for hatch patterns. By doing so, you can turn them off if you need to do so. For example, the floor paving pattern might be displayed in one drawing but turned off in another so that it won't distract from other information.

In the following exercises, you'll set up a layer for a hatch pattern representing floor tile and then add that pattern to your drawing. This will give you the opportunity to learn the different methods of creating and controlling hatch patterns.

Follow these steps to set up the layer:

1. Open the 07a-unit.dwg file. Metric users should open 07a-unit-metric.dwg. These files are similar to the Unit drawing that you created in earlier chapters, and they are used to create the overall plan in the 07b-plan and 07b-plan-metric files. Remember that you also still have the 07b-plan or 07b-plan-metric file open.

2. Zoom into the bathroom and kitchen area.

3. Create a new layer called **FLR-PAT**.

4. Make FLR-PAT the current layer.

Now that you've set up the layer for the hatch pattern, you can place the pattern in the drawing:

1. Click the Hatch tool on the Home tab's Draw panel, or type **H**↵. The Hatch Creation Ribbon tab appears (see Figure 7.8).

FIGURE 7.8
The Hatch Creation
Ribbon tab

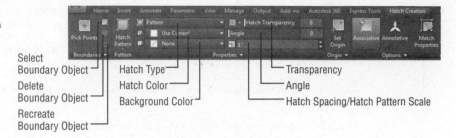

Select
Boundary Object

Delete
Boundary Object

Recreate
Boundary Object

Hatch Type

Hatch Color

Background Color

Transparency

Angle

Hatch Spacing/Hatch Pattern Scale

2. In the Pattern drop-down list box of the Properties panel, select User Defined. The User Defined option lets you define a simple crosshatch pattern by specifying the line spacing of the hatch and whether it's a single- or double-hatch pattern.

3. Click the Hatch Spacing text box in the lower-right corner of the Properties panel (see Figure 7.8), and enter **6** (metric users should enter **15**). This tells AutoCAD that you want the hatch's line spacing to be 6″, or 15 cm. Leave the Hatch Angle value at 0 because you want the pattern to be aligned with the bathroom.

4. Expand the Properties panel, and click the Double button. This tells AutoCAD that you want the hatch pattern to run both vertically and horizontally.

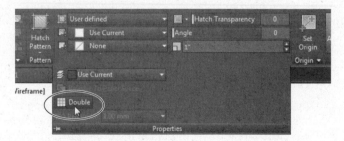

5. Hover the cursor over different parts of the bathroom layout, but don't click anything. You will see a preview of your hatch pattern appear in each area over which you hover. If you don't see a preview, check the Command line and click Pick Internal Point if it is not the default option.

6. Click inside the area representing the bathroom floor. The hatch pattern is placed in the floor area. Notice that the area inside the door swing is not hatched. This is because the door swing area is not a contiguous part of the floor.

7. Click inside the door swing to place the hatch pattern.

8. Right-click and select Enter to exit the Hatch command, or press the Enter key.

HATCHING AROUND TEXT

If you have text in the hatch boundary, AutoCAD will avoid hatching over it unless the Ignore option is selected in the Island Display Style options of the Advanced Hatch settings. See the section "Using Additional Hatch Features" later in this chapter for more on the Ignore setting.

As you saw from the exercise, AutoCAD gives you a preview of your hatch pattern before you place it in the drawing. In the previous steps, you set up the hatch pattern first by selecting the User Defined option, but you can reverse the order if you like. You can click in the areas you want to hatch first and then select a pattern, adjust the scale, and apply other hatch options.

NOTE Also note that in step 3, you are asked to change the Hatch Spacing setting. The name of this setting changes from Hatch Spacing to Hatch Pattern Scale when you use a predefined pattern instead of a user-defined one.

Certification
Objective

MATCHING PATTERNS

Say you want to add a hatch pattern that you've previously inserted in another part of the drawing. With the Match Properties tool in the Options panel of the Hatch Creation tab, you can select a previously inserted hatch pattern as a prototype for the current hatch pattern. However, this feature doesn't work with exploded hatch patterns.

Adding Predefined Hatch Patterns

In the previous exercise, you used the User Defined option to create a simple crosshatch pattern. You also have a number of other predefined hatch patterns from which to choose. You can find other hatch patterns on the Internet, and if you can't find the pattern you want, you can create your own (see Chapter 24, "Customizing Toolbars, Menus, Linetypes, and Hatch Patterns").

Try the following exercise to see how you can add one of the predefined patterns available in AutoCAD:

1. Pan your view so that you can see the area below the kitchenette. Using the Rectangle tool in the Draw panel, draw the 8'-0" by 3'-0" outline of the floor tile area, as shown in Figure 7.9. Metric users should create a rectangle that is 228 cm by 91 cm. You can also use a closed polyline.

FIGURE 7.9
The area below the kitchen, showing the outline of the floor tile area

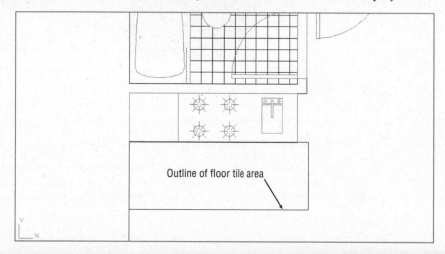

Outline of floor tile area

2. Click the Hatch tool in the Draw panel.

3. In the Properties panel of the Hatch Creation Ribbon tab, select the Pattern option in the Hatch Type drop-down list.

4. Click the Hatch Pattern tool in the Pattern panel. (If you don't see the Hatch Pattern tool, skip to step 6.) A flyout appears that displays a selection of hatch patterns (see Figure 7.10). This list has a scroll bar to the right that lets you view additional patterns.

5. Scroll down the flyout, and locate and select AR-PARQ1 (see Figure 7.10).

6. If you didn't see the Hatch Pattern tool in step 4, scroll through the patterns in the Pattern panel using the down arrow to the right of the panel to locate and select the AR-PARQ1 pattern. You can also expand the list by clicking the arrowhead below the scroll arrows (see Figure 7.10).

FIGURE 7.10
The Hatch Pattern flyout (left) and the Hatch Pattern panel in a full-screen AutoCAD window (right)

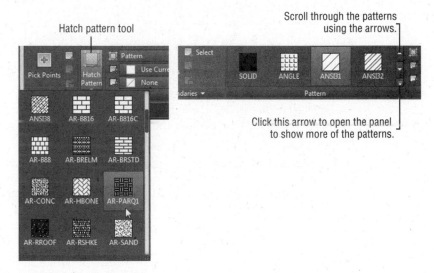

7. Click inside the rectangle you just drew.

8. If you are a metric user, set the Hatch Pattern Scale to 2.5. The Hatch Pattern Scale is the bottom option in the right-hand column in the Hatch Creation tab's Properties panel.

9. Right-click and select Enter, or press the Enter key.

The predefined patterns with the *AR* prefix are architectural patterns that are drawn to full scale. In general, you should leave their Hatch Pattern Scale settings at 1. You can adjust the scale after you place the hatch pattern by using the Properties palette, as described later in this chapter.

Certification
Objective

> ### ADDING SOLID FILLS
>
> You can use the Solid option from the Hatch Type drop-down list in the Hatch Creation tab's Properties panel to create solid fills. The Hatch Color drop-down list lets you set the color of your solid fill. Remember that you can drag and drop solid fills and hatch patterns from the tool palettes you saw in Chapter 1, "Exploring the Interface."

Positioning Hatch Patterns Accurately

If you've ever laid tile in a bathroom, you know that you have to select the starting point for your tiles carefully in order to get them to fit in an area with pleasing results. If you need to fine-tune the position of a hatch pattern within an enclosed area, you can do so by using the options in the Origin panel of the Hatch Creation tab.

The main tool in the panel, Set Origin, lets you select an origin point for your hatch pattern. You can also use the Hporigin system variable to accomplish this. Or you can expand the Origin panel for a set of predefined origin locations. These locations are Bottom Left, Bottom Right, Top Left, Top Right, Center, and Use Current Origin. The Use Current Origin option refers to the X,Y origin of the drawing.

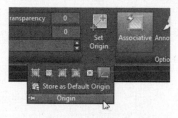

If you are hatching an irregular shape, these origin locations are applied to the *boundary extents* of the shape. An imaginary rectangle represents the outermost boundary, or the boundary extents of the shape, as shown in Figure 7.11.

FIGURE 7.11
The origin options shown in relation to the boundary extents of an irregular shape

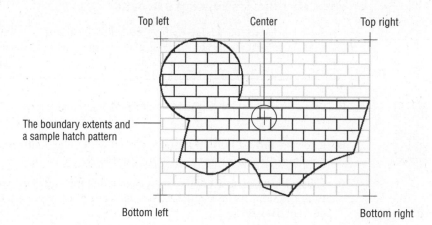

The boundary extents and a sample hatch pattern

The Store As Default Origin option lets you save your selected origin as the default origin for future hatch patterns in the current drawing.

Now that you've learned how to add a hatch pattern, let's continue with a look at how your newly edited plan can be used. In the next exercise, you'll use this updated 07a-unit file to update all the units in the Plan file.

Updating a Block from an External File

As you progress through a design project, you make countless revisions. With traditional drafting methods, revising a drawing, such as the studio apartment floor plan, takes a good deal of time. If you changed the bathroom layout, for example, you would have to erase every occurrence of the bathroom and redraw it 16 times. With AutoCAD, revising this drawing can be a quick operation. You can update the studio unit you just modified throughout the overall Plan drawing by replacing the current Unit block with the updated Unit file. AutoCAD can update all occurrences of the Unit block. The following exercise shows how this is accomplished.

For this exercise, remember that the blocks representing the units in the 07b-plan and 07b-plan-metric files are named 07a-unit and 07a-unit-metric:

1. Make sure that you've saved the 07a-unit (07a-unit-metric for metric users) file with the changes, and then return to the 07b-plan file that is still open. Click the Open Documents tool from the Application menu, and then select 07b-plan.dwg. Metric users should use 07b-plan-metric.dwg.

> #### YOU CAN'T UPDATE EXPLODED BLOCKS
>
> Exploded blocks won't be updated when you update blocks from an external file. If you plan to use this method to update parts of a drawing, don't explode the blocks you plan to update. See Chapter 4, "Organizing Objects with Blocks and Groups."

2. Click the Insert tool on the Home tab's Block panel, and select More Options to open the Insert dialog box.

3. Click the Browse button. In the Select Drawing File dialog box, double-click the 07a-unit filename (07a-unit-metric for metric users).

4. Click OK in the Insert dialog box. A warning message tells you that a block already exists with the same name as the file. You can cancel the operation or redefine the block in the current drawing.

5. Click Redefine Block. The drawing regenerates.

6. At the `Specify insertion point or [Basepoint/Scale/X/Y/Z/Rotate]:` prompt, press the Esc key. You do this because you don't want to insert the `07a-unit` file into your drawing; you're just using the Insert feature to update an existing block.

7. Zoom into one of the units. The floor tile appears in all the units as you drew it in the `Unit` file (see Figure 7.12).

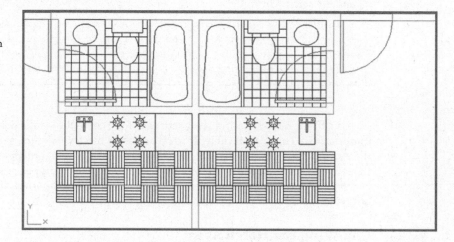

FIGURE 7.12
The Plan drawing with the tile pattern

Nested blocks must be updated independently of the parent block. For example, if you modified the Toilet block while editing the `07a-unit` file and then updated the `07a-unit` drawing in the `07b-plan` file, the old Toilet block wouldn't be updated. Even though the toilet is part of the `07a-unit` file, it's still a unique, independent block in the `Plan` file, and AutoCAD won't modify it unless specifically instructed to do so. In this situation, you must edit the original Toilet block and then update it in both the `Plan` and `Unit` files.

SUBSTITUTING BLOCKS

In the exercise in "Updating a Block from an External File," you updated a block in your `Plan` file by using the Browse option in the Insert dialog box. In that exercise, the block name and the filename were the same. You can also replace a block with another block or a file of a different name. Here's how to do it:

1. Open the Insert dialog box.

2. Click the Browse button next to the Name text box, locate and select the file that you want to use as a substitute, and then click Open to return to the Insert dialog box.

continues

continued

3. Change the name in the Name text box to the name of the block you want replaced.

4. Click OK. A warning message appears, telling you that a block with this name already exists. Click OK to proceed with the block substitution.

Another method is to type **-Insert**↵. (Don't forget the minus sign in front of *Insert*.) At the Enter Block name or [?]: prompt, enter the block name followed by an equal sign (=), and then enter the name of the new block or the filename. Don't include spaces between the name and the equal sign.

You can use this method of replacing blocks if you want to see how changing one element of your project can change your design. You might, for example, draw three different apartment unit plans and give each plan a unique name. You could then generate and plot three apartment building designs in a fraction of the time that it would take you to do so by hand.

Also, block references and layer settings of the current file take priority over those of the imported file. For example, if a file to be imported has layers of the same name as the layers in the current file, but those layers have color and linetype assignments that are different from those in the current file, the current file's layer color and linetype assignments determine those of the imported file. This doesn't mean, however, that the imported file on disk is changed—only that the insertion in the active drawing is affected.

Changing the Hatch Area

You may have noticed the Associative option in the Hatch Creation tab's Options panel. When this option is turned on, AutoCAD creates an associative hatch pattern. *Associative* hatches adjust their shapes to any changes in their associated boundary, hence the name. The following exercise demonstrates how this works.

Suppose that you want to enlarge the tiled area of the kitchen by one tile. Here's how it's done:

1. Click the 07a-unit Drawing tab to switch to that drawing.

2. Click the outline border of the hatch pattern that you created earlier. Notice the grips that appear around the hatch-pattern area.

3. Shift+click the grip in the lower-left corner of the hatch area.

4. With the lower-left grip highlighted, Shift+click the lower-right grip.

5. Click the lower-right grip again, but don't Shift+click this time.

SELECTING HATCH GRIPS

If the boundary of the hatch pattern consists of line segments, you can use a crossing window or polygon-crossing window to select the corner grips of the hatch pattern.

6. Enter **@12<–90**↵↵ (**@30<–90** for metric users) to widen the hatch pattern by 1', or 30 cm for metric users. The hatch pattern adjusts to the new size of the hatch boundary.

7. Press the Esc key twice to clear any grip selections.

8. Choose Save from the Quick Access toolbar to save the Unit file.

9. Return to the 07b-plan file using the Drawing tab, and repeat the steps in the section "Updating a Block from an External File" earlier in this chapter to update the units again.

The Associative feature of hatch patterns can save time when you need to modify your drawing, but you need to be aware of its limitations. A hatch pattern can lose its associativity when you do any of the following:

♦ Erase or explode a hatch boundary

♦ Erase or explode a block that forms part of the boundary

♦ Move a hatch pattern away from its boundary

These situations frequently arise when you edit an unfamiliar drawing. Often, boundary objects are placed on a layer that is off or frozen, so the boundary objects aren't visible. Also, the hatch pattern might be on a layer that is turned off and you proceed to edit the file not knowing that a hatch pattern exists. When you encounter such a file, take a moment to check for hatch boundaries so that you can deal with them properly.

Modifying a Hatch Pattern

Certification
Objective

Like everything else in a project, a hatch pattern may eventually need to be changed in some way. Hatch patterns are like blocks in that they act like single objects. You can explode a hatch pattern to edit its individual lines. The Properties palette contains most of the settings that you'll need to make changes to your hatch patterns. But the most direct way to edit a hatch pattern is to use the Hatch Editor Ribbon tab.

EDITING HATCH PATTERNS FROM THE HATCH EDITOR TAB

Follow these steps to modify a hatch pattern by using the Hatch Editor Ribbon tab:

1. Return to the Unit drawing.

2. Press the Esc key to clear any grip selections that may be active from earlier exercises.

3. Click the hatch pattern in the kitchen to open the Hatch Editor Ribbon tab. It's the same as the Hatch Creation Ribbon tab.

RIGHT-CLICK TO OPEN THE PROPERTIES PALETTE

Clicking a hatch pattern opens a Ribbon tab in which you can edit the pattern using the same tools that you used to create it. If you prefer, you can right-click and select Properties to access the Properties palette.

---

4. In the Pattern panel, locate and click the pattern named AR-BRSTD. It's the pattern that looks like a brick wall.

5. Press the Esc key to clear your selection of the hatch pattern. The AR-BRSTD pattern appears in place of the original parquet pattern.

6. Save and exit your file.

In this exercise, you were able to change the hatch just by clicking it. Although you changed only the pattern type, other options are available. You can, for example, modify a predefined pattern to a user-defined one by selecting User Defined from the Hatch Type drop-down list in the Properties panel of the Hatch Editor tab.

You can then enter angle and scale values for your hatch pattern in the options provided in the Properties panel of the Hatch Editor tab.

The other items in the Hatch Editor Ribbon tab are duplicates of the options in the Hatch Creation tab. They let you modify the individual properties of the selected hatch pattern. The upcoming section "Understanding the Boundary Hatch Options" describes these other properties in detail.

EDITING HATCH PATTERNS FROM THE PROPERTIES PALETTE

Certification
Objective

If you prefer, you can use the older method to edit a hatch pattern. To open the Properties palette, select and right-click the hatch pattern that you want to edit and then select Properties. The Properties palette displays a Pattern category, which offers a Pattern Name option (see Figure 7.13). The actual pattern name appears to the right of the option.

FIGURE 7.13
The Pattern category in
the Properties palette

When you click this option, an ellipsis button appears, enabling you to open the Hatch Pattern Palette dialog box (see Figure 7.14). You can then select a new pattern from the dialog box. The Type option in the Properties palette lets you change the type of hatch pattern from Predefined to User Defined or Custom.

FIGURE 7.14
The Hatch Pattern
Palette dialog box

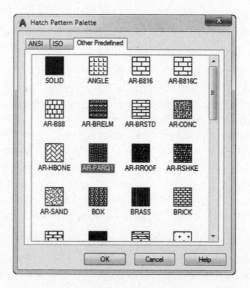

Understanding the Boundary Hatch Options

The Hatch Creation and Hatch Editor Ribbon panels offer many other options that you didn't explore in the previous exercises. For example, instead of clicking in the area to be hatched, you can select the objects that bound the area you want to hatch by clicking the Select Boundary Objects tool in the Boundaries panel. You can use the Select Boundary Objects tool to add boundaries to existing hatch patterns as well.

Controlling Boundaries with the Boundaries Panel

The previous exercises in this chapter have just touched upon the tools in the Boundaries panel. Other options in the Boundaries panel are Pick Points, Select Boundary Objects, Remove Boundary Objects, and Recreate Boundary.

Pick Points   Lets you place a hatch pattern across several enclosed areas by clicking inside the areas. This is the default selection mode.

Select Boundary Objects   Lets you select objects to define a hatch boundary.

Remove Boundary Objects   Lets you remove a bounded area, or *island*, in the area to be hatched. An example is the toilet seat in the bathroom. This option is available only when you select a hatch area by using the Pick Points option and an island has been detected.

Recreate Boundary   Draws a region or polyline around the current hatch pattern. You're then prompted to choose between a region and a polyline and to specify whether to reassociate the pattern with the re-created boundary. (See the Associative option discussed in a moment.)

Fine-Tuning the Boundary Behavior

The Boundary Hatch feature is view dependent—that is, it locates boundaries based on what is visible in the current view. If the current view contains a lot of graphic data, AutoCAD can have difficulty finding a boundary or can be slow in finding a boundary. If you run into this problem or if you want to single out a specific object for a point selection boundary, you can further limit the area that AutoCAD uses to locate hatch boundaries by using the Boundary Set options found in the expanded Boundaries panel:

Display Boundary Objects   Highlights the objects that have been selected as the hatch boundary by AutoCAD.

Don't Retain/Retain Boundary Objects   Retains outlines used to create the hatch pattern, a capability that can be helpful if you want to duplicate the shape of the boundary for other purposes. Typically, this option is set to Don't Retain Boundaries, but you can use two other settings: Retain Boundaries – Polyline and Retain Boundaries – Regions.

Select New Boundary Set   Lets you select the objects that you want AutoCAD to use to determine the hatch boundary instead of searching the entire view. The screen clears and lets you select objects. This option discards previous boundary sets. It's useful for hatching areas in a drawing that contains many objects that you don't want to include in the hatch boundary.

Use Current Viewport   Uses the current viewport extents to define the boundary set.

The Boundary Set options give you more control over the way a point selection boundary is created. These options have no effect when you use the Select Boundary Objects button to select specific objects for the hatch boundary.

BOUNDARY RETENTION

The Hatch command can also create an outline of the hatch area by using one of two objects: 2D regions, which are like 2D planes, or polyline outlines. Hatch creates such a polyline boundary temporarily to establish the hatch area. These boundaries are automatically removed after the hatch pattern is inserted. If you want to retain the boundaries in the drawing, make sure that the Retain Boundaries – Polyline option is selected. Retaining the boundary can be useful if you know that you'll be hatching the area more than once or if you're hatching a fairly complex area.

Retaining a hatch boundary is useful if you want to know the hatched area's dimensions in square inches or feet because you can find the area of a closed polyline by using the List command. See Chapter 2, "Creating Your First Drawing," for more on the List command.

Controlling Hatch Behavior with the Options Panel

The Options panel offers a set of tools that control some additional features of the Hatch command. These features affect the way a hatch pattern fills a boundary area as well as how it behaves when the drawing is edited. Note that the Gap Tolerance, Create Separate Hatches, Normal Island Detection, and Send Behind Boundary options are on the expanded Options panel. The following gives you a brief description of each of the Options panel's options:

Associative   Allows the hatch pattern to adjust to changes in its boundary. With this option turned on, any changes to the associated boundary of a hatch pattern cause the hatch pattern to flow with the changes in the boundary.

Annotative Scale   Allows the hatch pattern to adjust to different scale views of your drawing. With this option turned on, a hatch pattern's size or spacing adjusts to the annotation scale of a viewport layout or Model Space mode. See Chapter 4 for more on the annotation scale.

Match Properties   This group allows you to use an existing hatch pattern when inserting additional hatch patterns into a drawing. Select Use Current Origin when you want to use the current default hatch origin. Select Use Source Hatch Origin when you want to use the origin from the existing hatch pattern.

Gap Tolerance   Lets you hatch an area that isn't completely enclosed. The Gap Tolerance value sets the maximum gap size in the perimeter of an area that you want to hatch. You can use a value from 0 to 5000.

Create Separate Hatches   Creates separate and distinct hatches if you select several enclosed areas while selecting hatch areas. With this option off, separate hatch areas behave as a single hatch pattern.

Outer Island Detection   Controls how islands within a hatch area are treated. Islands are enclosed areas that are completely inside a hatch boundary. There are four options in this list:

Normal Island Detection   This causes the hatch pattern to alternate between nested boundaries. The outer boundary is hatched; if there is a closed object within the boundary, it isn't hatched. If *another* closed object is inside the first closed object, *that* object is hatched.

Outer Island Detection   This applies the hatch pattern to an area defined by the outermost boundary and a closed object within that boundary. Any boundaries nested in that closed object are ignored.

Ignore Island Detection   This supplies the hatch pattern to the entire area within the outermost boundary, ignoring any nested boundaries.

No Island Detection   This turns off island detection. This option is not available if you have already added a hatch pattern to your drawing.

Send Behind Boundary (Draw Order)   Allows you to specify whether the hatch pattern appears on top of or underneath its boundary. This is useful when the boundary is of a different color or shade and must read clearly or when the hatch pattern must cover the boundary. The options in this list are self-explanatory and are Do Not Assign, Send To Back, Bring To Front, Send Behind Boundary, and Bring In Front Of Boundary. See "Overlapping Objects with Draw Order" later in this chapter.

Controlling Hatch Default Layer, Layout Scale, and ISO Line Weight

The expanded Properties panel contains a few items that you'll want to be aware of as you become more familiar with AutoCAD. You've already seen how the Double option works when you are creating user-defined hatch patterns. The following list describes several other options that are available:

Hatch Layer Override   Allows you to select the default layer for hatch patterns. Select a layer name from the drop-down list. New hatch patterns you add to the drawing will be placed on the selected layer instead of the current one.

Relative To Paper Space   Allows you to change a hatch pattern's scale to one that is relevant to the current Paper Space view. This option is available only while you are in a layout tab and when you're using a pattern that is not user defined.

ISO Pen Width   Allows you to select an ISO pen width for the lines of a hatch pattern. This option is available only when you are using ISO patterns.

ANNOTATIVE HATCH PATTERNS

In Chapter 4, you learned about a feature called the *annotation scale*. With this tool, you can assign several scales to certain types of objects and AutoCAD displays the object to the proper scale of the drawing. You can take advantage of this feature to allow hatch patterns to adjust their spacing or pattern size to the scale of your drawing. The Annotative option in the Options panel of the Hatch Creation Ribbon tab turns on the annotation scale feature for hatch patterns. Once this capability is turned on for a hatch pattern, you can set up the drawing scales that you want to apply to the hatch pattern using the same methods described for blocks in Chapter 4.

Using Additional Hatch Features

The Hatch command has a fair amount of "intelligence." As you saw in an earlier exercise, it was able to detect not only the outline of the floor area but also the outline of the toilet seat that represents an island in the pattern area. If you prefer, you can control how AutoCAD treats these island conditions and other situations by selecting options available in the Hatch Creation and Hatch Editor Ribbon tab. You can also create and edit hatch patterns using the Hatch And Gradient dialog box (see Figure 7.15), which should be familiar to anyone who has used AutoCAD before.

FIGURE 7.15

The expanded Hatch And Gradient dialog box

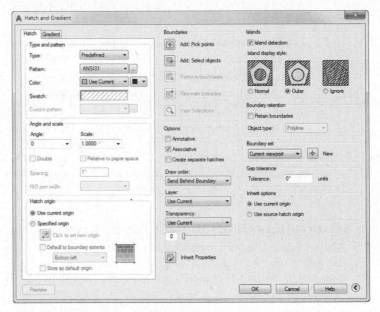

To open the Hatch And Gradient dialog box, start the Hatch command by clicking the Hatch tool in the Home tab's Draw panel, and then click the Hatch Settings tool in the right side of the Options panel title bar. This opens the Hatch And Gradient dialog box. Click the More Options button in the lower-right corner of this dialog box.

This button expands the dialog box to show additional hatch options (see Figure 7.15).

Nearly all of the settings and tools in the Hatch And Gradient dialog box are repeated in the Hatch Creation and Hatch Editor Ribbon tabs. They are just presented in a different way.

HATCH BOUNDARIES WITHOUT THE HATCH PATTERN

The Boundary command creates a polyline outline or region in a selected area. It works much like the Retain Boundary – Polyline option but doesn't add a hatch pattern.

Using Gradient Shading

Certification Objective

You may have noticed Solid and Gradient options in the Pattern drop-down list. The solid hatch pattern lets you apply a solid color instead of a pattern to a bounded area. AutoCAD also offers a set of gradient patterns that let you apply a color gradient to an area.

You can apply a gradient to an area using the same method that you used to apply a hatch pattern, but when you select the Gradient option, you'll see a slight change in the Hatch Creation tab panels. The Hatch Pattern Scale text box in the Properties panel changes to a Tint slider, and the Pattern panel changes to show a set of different gradient patterns. The Origin panel also changes to show Centered as the only option (see Figure 7.16). The Hatch Color and Background Color options in the Properties panel change to Gradient Color 1 and Gradient Color 2, enabling you to set the gradient colors.

FIGURE 7.16
The Gradient Shading feature

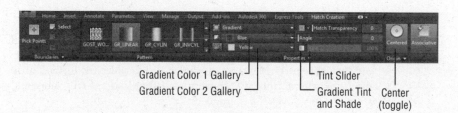

Gradient Color 1 Gallery
Gradient Color 2 Gallery

Tint Slider
Gradient Tint and Shade
Center (toggle)

Instead of offering hatch patterns, the Pattern panel offers a variety of gradient patterns. If you don't see the gradient patterns, you can click the Hatch Pattern tool to open a flyout of the gradient patterns. The Properties panel lets you control the colors of the gradient. You can select the colors from the two color drop-down lists in the Properties panel.

If you don't see a color that you want, you can click the Select Colors option at the bottom of the list to open the Select Color dialog box. This dialog box lets you choose from Index, True Color, or Color Books colors (see Figure 7.17).

FIGURE 7.17
The True Color options
in the More Colors
dialog box

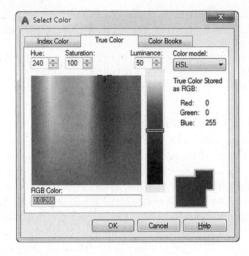

The Gradient Tint And Shade slider just to the right of the color drop-down lists lets you control the shade of the single-color gradient.

CHOOSING BETWEEN A SINGLE COLOR OR TWO COLORS

You can choose a gradient that transitions between shades of a single color by clicking the Gradient Tint And Shade tool in the Properties panel just to the left of the Tint slider. This turns on the Gradient Tint And Shade slider and disables the Color 2 drop-down list. When you turn off the Gradient Tint And Shade button, the Gradient Tint slider is disabled and the Gradient Color 2 drop-down list is enabled.

SELECTING GRADIENT PATTERNS

As mentioned earlier, you can choose from a set of gradient patterns in the Pattern panel. The Angle slider gives you further control over the gradient pattern by allowing you to rotate the angle of the pattern. The Centered option in the Origin panel places the center of the gradient at the center of the area selected for the pattern. This option is a toggle that is either on or off.

To place a gradient pattern, select a set of objects or a point in a bounded area, just as you would for a hatch pattern.

Tips for Using Hatch

Here are a few tips for using the Hatch feature:

◆ Watch out for boundary areas that are part of a large block. AutoCAD examines the entire block when defining boundaries. This can take time if the block is large. Use the Specify

Boundary Set option to focus on the set of objects that you want AutoCAD to use for your hatch boundary.

◆ The Hatch feature is view dependent—that is, it locates boundaries based on what is visible in the current view. To ensure that AutoCAD finds every detail, zoom in to the area to be hatched.

◆ If the area to be hatched is large yet requires fine detail, first outline the hatch area by using a polyline. (See Chapter 18, "Drawing Curves," for more on polylines.) Then use the Select Boundary Objects option in the Hatch Creation tab's Boundaries panel to select the polyline boundary manually instead of depending on Hatch to find the boundary for you.

◆ Consider turning off layers that might interfere with the ability of AutoCAD to find a boundary.

◆ Hatch works on nested blocks as long as the nested block entities are parallel to the current User Coordinate System. You'll learn more about the User Coordinate System in Chapter 20 and Chapter 21.

Space Planning and Hatch Patterns

Suppose that you're working on a plan in which you're constantly repositioning equipment and furniture or you're in the process of designing the floor covering. You might be a little hesitant to place a hatch pattern on the floor because you don't want to have to rehatch the area each time you move a piece of equipment or change the flooring. You have two options in this situation: You can use the Hatch feature's associative capabilities to include the furnishings in the boundary set, or you can use the Display Order feature.

USING ASSOCIATIVE HATCH

Associative Hatch is the most straightforward method. Make sure that the Associative option is selected in the Hatch Creation tab's Options panel, and include your equipment or furniture in the boundary set. You can do this by using the Select option in the Boundaries panel.

After the pattern is in place, the hatch pattern automatically adjusts to its new location when you move the furnishings in your drawing. One drawback, however, is that AutoCAD attempts to hatch the interior of your furnishings if they cross the outer boundary of the hatch pattern. Also, if any boundary objects are erased or exploded, the hatch pattern no longer follows the location of your furnishings. To avoid these problems, you can use the method described in the next section.

OVERLAPPING OBJECTS WITH DRAW ORDER

The Draw Order feature lets you determine how objects overlap. In the space-planning example, you can create furniture by using a solid hatch to indicate horizontal surfaces (see Figure 7.18).

FIGURE 7.18
Using Draw Order to create an overlapping effect over a hatch pattern

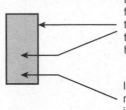

Draw an outline of the furniture or equipment; then use the Hatch tool to fill the outline with a Solid hatch pattern.

In the Hatch And Gradient dialog box, make sure that Send Behind Boundary is selected in the Draw Order drop-down list before you add the hatch pattern.

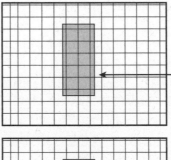

Place the drawing of the equipment on the floor pattern; then click the Send To Back tool from the Draworder flyout on the Home tab's Modify panel.

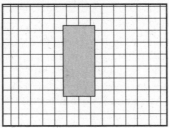

The equipment will appear to sit on top of the floor pattern.

Certification
Objective

MATCHING A HATCH PATTERN AND OTHER PROPERTIES QUICKLY

Another tool to help you edit hatch patterns is Match Properties, which is similar to Format Painter in Microsoft Office. This tool lets you change an existing hatch pattern to match another existing hatch pattern. Here's how to use it:

1. Choose Match Properties from the Home tab's Properties panel or type **Matchprop**↵.

2. Click the source hatch pattern that you want to copy.

3. Click the target hatch pattern that you want to change. The target pattern changes to match the source pattern.

The Match Properties tool transfers other properties as well, such as layer, color, and linetype settings. You can select the properties that are transferred by opening the Property Settings dialog box.

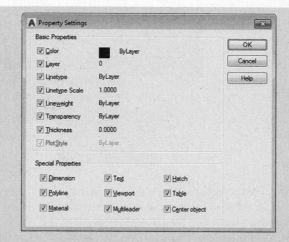

To open this dialog box, type **S**↵ after selecting the object in step 2, or right-click and choose Settings from the context menu. You can then select the properties that you want to transfer from the options shown. All of the properties are selected by default. You can also transfer text and dimension style settings. You'll learn more about text and dimension styles in Chapter 9, "Adding Text to Drawings," and Chapter 11, "Using Dimensions."

You can then place the furniture on top of a floor-covering pattern and the pattern will be covered and hidden by the furniture. Here's how to do that. (These steps aren't part of the regular exercises of this chapter. They're shown here as general guidelines when you need to use the Draw Order feature.)

1. Draw the equipment outline, and make sure that the outline is a closed polygon.

2. Start the Hatch tool described earlier in this chapter, and place a solid hatch pattern inside the equipment outline.

3. In the Hatch Creation tab's expanded Options panel, make sure that Send To Back is selected in the Draw Order drop-down list.

4. Turn the outline and solid hatch into a block, or use the Group command to group them.

5. Move your equipment drawing into place over the floor pattern.

6. Click the floor hatch pattern and then, in the Hatch Editor tab's expanded Options panel, select Send To Back from the Draw Order drop-down list.

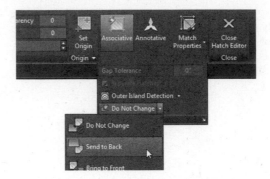

After you take these steps, the equipment will appear to rest on top of the pattern. (See the bottom panel in Figure 7.18.) You can also change the display order of objects relative to other objects in the drawing using the Draworder flyout in the Home tab's Modify panel.

The Draworder options are all part of the Draworder command. As an alternative to using the Ribbon, you can type **Draworder.⏎** at the Command prompt, select an object, and then enter an option at the prompt:

```
Enter object ordering option
[Above objects/Under objects/Front/Back]:
```

For example, the equivalent of choosing the Send To Back tool from the Draworder flyout is entering **Draworder.⏎B.⏎**. You can also select the object that you want to edit, right-click, and then choose Draw Order from the context menu.

You've now had a detailed look at hatch patterns and fills. Remember that you can also use the tool palettes to help organize and simplify access to your favorite hatch patterns, or you can use the patterns already available in the tool palettes. The patterns in the tool palettes can be edited and manipulated in the same way as described in this chapter. If you want to know how to make full use of the tool palettes, check out the discussion on the AutoCAD DesignCenter™ in Chapter 25, "Managing and Sharing Your Drawings."

TAKE A BREAK

If you're working through the tutorial in this chapter, this would be a good place to take a break or stop. You can pick up the next exercise in the section "Attaching a Drawing as an External Reference" at another time.

Using External References

Certification Objective

AutoCAD allows you to import drawings in a way that keeps the imported drawing independent from the current one. A drawing imported in this way is called an *external reference* (*Xref*). Unlike drawings that have been imported as blocks, Xref files don't become part of the drawing's database. Instead, they're loaded along with the current file at startup time. It's as if AutoCAD were opening several drawings at once: the currently active file you specify when you start AutoCAD and any file inserted as an Xref.

If you keep Xref files independent from the current file, any changes you make to the Xref automatically appear in the current file. You don't have to update the Xref file manually as you do blocks. For example, if you use an Xref to insert the Unit file into the Plan file and you later make changes to the Unit file, you will see the new version of the Unit file in place of the old one the next time you open the Plan file. If the Plan file was still open while edits were made, AutoCAD will notify you that a change has been made to an Xref.

BLOCKS AND XREFS CAN'T HAVE THE SAME NAME

You can't use a file as an Xref if the file has the same name as a block in the current drawing. If this situation occurs but you still need to use the file as an Xref, you can rename the block of the same name by using the Rename command. You can also use Rename to change the name of various objects and named elements.

Another advantage of Xref files is that, because they don't become part of a drawing's database, drawing size is kept to a minimum. This results in more efficient use of your hard disk space.

Xref files, like blocks, can be edited only by using special tools. You can, however, use osnaps to snap to a location in an Xref file, or you can freeze or turn off the Xref file's insertion layer to make it invisible.

Attaching a Drawing as an External Reference

The next exercise shows how to use an Xref in place of an inserted block to construct the studio apartment building. You'll first create a new unit file by copying the old one. Then you'll bring a new feature, the External References palette, to the screen. Follow these steps to create the new file:

1. Use the Drawing tab at the top of the drawing area to return to the 07a-unit file.

2. Choose Save As from the Application menu to save it under the name unitxref.dwg, and then close the unitxref.dwg file. This will make a copy of the 07a-unit.dwg file for the following steps. Or, if you prefer, you can use the unitxref.dwg file for the following steps.

3. Return to the 07b-plan file, choose Save As, and save the file under the name Planxref. The current file is now Planxref.dwg.

4. Ensure that you are on layer 0. Erase all of the unit plans (E↵All↵↵). In the next step, you'll purge the unit plans from the file. (By completing steps 2 through 4, you save yourself from having to set up a new file.)

5. Choose Drawing Utilities ➤ Purge from the Application menu to open the Purge dialog box.

6. Select the Purge Nested Items option and then click the Purge All button to open the Confirm Purge dialog box. This blocks any layers that aren't in use in the drawing.

7. Click Purge All Items and close the Purge dialog box.

Now you're ready to use the External References palette:

1. Click the External References tool in the Insert tab's Reference panel title bar or type **XR.⏎** to open the External References palette (see Figure 7.19).

FIGURE 7.19
The External
References palette

2. Click the Attach DWG button in the upper-left corner of the palette to open the Select Reference File dialog box. This is a typical AutoCAD file dialog box complete with a preview window.

3. Locate and select the unitxref.dwg file, and then click Open to open the Attach External Reference dialog box (see Figure 7.20). Notice that this dialog box looks similar to the Insert dialog box. It offers the same options for insertion point, scale, and rotation.

4. You'll see a description of the options presented in this dialog box in "The Attach External Reference Dialog Box" later in this chapter. For now, click OK.

5. Enter **31′-5″,43′-8″.⏎** (metric users enter **957,1330**) for the insertion point.

6. The inserted plan may appear faded. If it does, click the Xref Fading tool in the Insert tab's expanded Reference panel to turn off the Xref Fading feature. This will give the plan a more solid appearance.

FIGURE 7.20
The Attach External
Reference dialog box

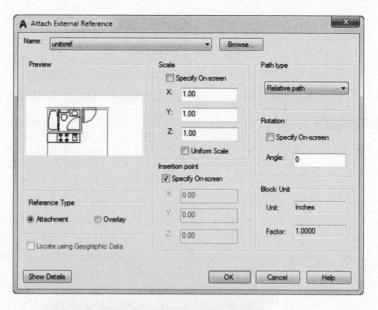

7. After `unitxref.dwg` is inserted, re-create the same layout of the floor plan that you created in the first section of this chapter by copying and mirroring the `unitxref.dwg` external reference.

8. Save the `Planxref` file.

You now have a drawing that looks like the `07b-plan.dwg` file that you worked with earlier in this chapter, but instead of blocks that are detached from their source file, you have a drawing composed of Xrefs. These Xrefs are the actual `unitxref.dwg` file, and they're loaded into AutoCAD at the same time you open the `Planxref.dwg` file. An icon in the lower-right corner of the AutoCAD window tells you that the current drawing contains Xrefs.

Not only does this icon alert you to Xrefs, but it also enables you to open the External References palette, as you'll see in the next exercise.

FADING XREFS

In step 6 of the previous exercise, you saw the Xref Fading tool. This tool is an aid to help you visualize which objects in your drawing are Xrefs. To the right of the Xref tool is the Xref Fading slider, which lets you control the amount of fading that is applied to the Xrefs in your drawing. You can either move the slider or enter a fading value in the text box to the far right. The Xref Fading tool affects only the appearance of the Xref in the drawing. It does not cause the Xref to fade in your printed or plotted output.

Next, you'll modify the unitxref.dwg file and see the results in the Planxref.dwg file:

1. To open the unitxref.dwg file, from the current Planxref file, select and then right-click a unit and choose Open Xref from the context menu. You can also enter **Xopen**↵ at the Command prompt and then select the unit plan Xref.

2. Erase the hatch patterns and kitchen outline for the floors, and save the unitxref.dwg file.

3. Use the Drawing tab to return to the Planxref.dwg file. You see a message balloon pointing to the Manage Xrefs icon in the lower-right corner of the AutoCAD window. The balloon warns you that an Xref has changed. Right-click the Manage Xrefs icon in the lower-right corner of the AutoCAD window, and then choose External References from the pop-up menu to open the External References palette.

4. Right-click the unitxref name in the list box and then click Reload. Notice that the units in the Planxref drawing have been updated to include the changes that you made to the unitxref file.

You may have noticed that there is a Reload DWG Xrefs option in the Manage Xrefs icon context menu. This option will reload all Xrefs in the current drawing without requiring you to select the individual file to reload in the External References palette.

Also, you may have noticed the Open option in step 4 when you used the right-click menu in the External References palette. This option performs the same function as the Xopen command, which opens the selected Xref for editing.

Be aware that when an Xref has been modified, the Manage Xrefs icon at the lower right of the AutoCAD window changes to show an exclamation point. This alerts you to changes in an Xref being used by the current drawing.

Click the Manage Xrefs icon to open the External References palette. The Xref that has been changed is indicated by a warning icon in the Status column of the list box along with the "Needs reloading" message.

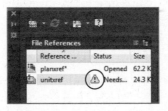

You can then select the Xref that needs to be updated, right-click, and choose the Reload option from the context menu to reload the selected Xref. You can also select multiple Xrefs if more than one needs updating. Another option is to select Reload All References from the Refresh flyout at the top of the External References palette.

Here you saw how an Xref file is updated in a different way than a block. Because Xrefs are loaded along with the drawing file that contains them, the containing file, which in this case was the Planxref file, automatically displays any changes made to the Xref when it's opened. Also, you avoid having to update nested blocks because AutoCAD updates nested Xrefs as well as non-nested Xrefs. When an Xref is modified while you're editing a file, you're alerted to the change through the Xref icon located in the lower-right corner of the AutoCAD window. You can click the balloon message that appears from that icon to update any modified Xrefs.

Other Differences Between External References and Blocks

Here are a few other differences between Xrefs and inserted blocks that you'll want to keep in mind:

◆ Any new layers, text styles, or linetypes brought in with Xref files don't become part of the current file. If you want to import any of these items, you can use the Xbind command (described in Chapter 14, "Advanced Editing and Organizing").

◆ If you make changes to the layers of an Xref file, those changes aren't retained when the file is saved unless you checked the Retain Changes To Xref Layers option in the Open And Save tab of the Options dialog box. This option, found in the External References (Xrefs) group, instructs AutoCAD to remember any layer color or visibility settings from one editing session to the next. In the standard AutoCAD settings, this option is on by default.

◆ Another way to ensure that layer settings for Xrefs are retained is to enter **Visretain**⏎ at the Command prompt. At the New value for VISRETAIN<0>: prompt, enter **1**.

◆ To segregate layers in Xref files from layers in the current drawing, AutoCAD prefixes the names of the Xref file's layers with their file's name. A vertical bar separates the filename prefix and the layer name when you view a list of layers in the layer drop-down list or the Layer Properties Manager dialog box (as in unitxref | wall).

◆ You can't explode Xrefs. You can, however, convert an Xref into a block and then explode it. To do so, select the Xref in the External References palette, then right-click and choose Bind to open another dialog box that offers two ways of converting an Xref into a block. See the section "Other External Reference Options" later in this chapter for more information.

◆ If an Xref is renamed or moved to another location on your hard disk, AutoCAD won't be able to find that file when it opens other files to which the Xref is attached. If this happens, you must select the path in the Found At field at the bottom of the External References palette and then click the Browse button (the ellipsis) to tell AutoCAD where to find the cross-referenced file.

◆ Take care when retargeting an Xref file with the Browse button. The Browse button can assign a file of a different name to an existing Xref as a substitution.

◆ Xref files are especially useful in workgroup environments in which several people are working on the same project. For example, one person might be updating several files that are inserted into a variety of other files. If blocks are used, everyone in the workgroup would have to be notified of the changes and would have to update all the affected blocks in all the drawings that contained them. With Xref files, however, the updating is automatic; you avoid confusion about which files need their blocks updated.

IMPORTING BLOCKS, LAYERS, AND OTHER NAMED ELEMENTS FROM EXTERNAL FILES

You can use the Xbind command to import blocks and other named elements from another file. First, use the External References palette to cross-reference a file; type **Xbind** at the Command

continues

continued

prompt. In the Xbind dialog box, click the plus sign next to the Xref filename, and then click the plus sign next to Block. Select the name of the block that you want to import, click the Add button, and click OK. Finally, open the External References palette, select the Xref filename from the list, right-click, and select Detach to remove the Xref file. The imported block remains as part of the current file. (See Chapter 14 for details on importing named elements.) You can also use the AutoCAD Content Explorer™ to import named elements from external files. Content Explorer is described in Chapter 25.

The tool palettes give you access to frequently used blocks and hatch patterns that reside in other drawings. You can open the tool palettes by clicking the Tool Palettes tool in the View tab's Palettes panel.

In standard AutoCAD installations, the tool palette window is configured with sample 3D commands (not in the AutoCAD LT® software), blocks, and hatch patterns that you can drag and drop into your current drawing. Select a tab for the tool palette that contains the block or pattern that you want, and then click and drag the item into your drawing. In the case of hatch patterns, click and drag the pattern into an area that is bounded on all sides by objects. When you're ready to customize the tool palette window, you do so by clicking and dragging objects or tools into a new or existing palette. See Chapter 24 for more on customizing tool palettes.

Other External Reference Options

Many other features are unique to external reference files. Let's briefly look at some of the other options in the External References palette.

OPTIONS IN THE EXTERNAL REFERENCES PALETTE

Several options are available when you right-click an external reference name listed in the External References palette, as shown in Figure 7.19 earlier in this chapter. You saw the Reload option in an earlier exercise. The following other options are available:

Attach   Opens the Attach External Reference dialog box, in which you can select a file to attach and set the parameters for the attachment.

Detach   Detaches an Xref from the current file. The file is then completely disassociated from the current file.

Reload   Restores an unloaded Xref.

Unload   Similar to Detach, but maintains a link to the Xref file so that it can be quickly reattached. This has an effect similar to freezing a layer and can reduce redraw, regeneration, and file-loading times.

Bind   Converts an Xref into a block. Bind offers two options: Bind and Insert. The Bind option maintains the Xref's named elements (layers, linetypes, and text and dimension styles) by creating new layers in the current file with the Xref's filename prefix (discussed again in Chapter 14). The Insert option doesn't attempt to maintain the Xref's named elements but merges them with named elements of the same name in the current file. For example, if both the Xref and the current file have layers of the same name, the objects in the Xref are placed in the layers of the same name in the current file.

Open   Lets you open an Xref. Select the Xref from the list, and then click Open. The Xref opens in a new window when you close the External References palette.

Change Path Type   Enables you to remove the path to the Xref file (shown in the Found At option of the Details panel) or change it from a full path to a relative path.

Select New Path. . .   Lets you browse to a new path for selected Xrefs. This can be useful for lost or missing Xrefs. You are given the option to apply the path to all missing Xrefs.

Find and Replace. . .   Lets you replace an Xref file path with a new one. This option locates reference file paths from the selected Xrefs and replaces the path with one you select.

Details   A panel at the bottom of the External References palette. It's similar to the Properties palette in that it displays the properties of a selected external reference and also allows you to modify some of those properties. For example, the Reference Name option in the Details panel lets you give the external reference a name that is different from the Xref filename. Table 7.1 gives you a rundown of the options in the Details panel.

TABLE 7.1:   The Details panel of the External References palette

OPTION	FUNCTION
Reference Name	Lets you give the Xref a different name from the Xref's filename. This can be helpful if you want to use multiple external references of the same file.
Status	Tells you whether the Xref is loaded, unloaded, or not found (read only).
Size	Gives you the file size information (read only).
Type	Lets you choose between the Attach and Overlay attachment methods for the Xref file. Xrefs attached as overlays don't include nested Xrefs.
Date	Gives you the date and time that the file was attached (read only).
Found At	Tells you where AutoCAD expects to find the Xref file (read only).
Saved Path	Lets you select the location of the Xref file. When you click the text box for this option, a Browse button appears to the right. You can click this button to locate a lost Xref or use a different file from the original attached Xref.

THE ATTACH EXTERNAL REFERENCE DIALOG BOX

The Attach External Reference dialog box, shown in Figure 7.20 earlier in this chapter, offers these options:

Browse   Opens the Select Reference File dialog box to enable you to change the file you're importing as an Xref.

Attachment   Tells AutoCAD to include other Xref attachments that are nested in the selected file.

Overlay   Tells AutoCAD to ignore other Xref attachments that are nested in the selected file. This avoids multiple attachments of other files and eliminates the possibility of circular references (referencing the current file into itself through another file).

Path Type Offers options for locating Xrefs. Xref files can be located anywhere on your system, including network servers. For this reason, you can easily lose links to Xrefs either by moving them or by rearranging file locations. To help you manage Xrefs, the Path Type option offers three options: Full Path, Relative Path, and No Path.

Full Path Retains the current full path.

Relative Path Maintains paths in relation to the current drawing. The current drawing must be saved before using the Relative Path option.

No Path Used for drawings in which Xrefs are located in the same folder as the current drawing or in the path specified in Support File Search Path in the Files tab of the Options dialog box (choose Options from the Application menu).

Specify On-Screen Appears in three places. It gives you the option to enter an insertion point, scale factors, and rotation angles in the dialog box or in the Command window, in a way similar to inserting blocks. If you clear this option for any of the corresponding parameters, the parameters change to allow input. If they're selected, you're prompted for those parameters after you click OK to close the dialog box. With all three Specify On-Screen check boxes cleared, the Xref is inserted in the drawing using the settings indicated in the dialog box.

Show Details/Hide Details Displays or hides the path information for the selected Xref file.

Block Unit Displays the insert scale setting for the external reference. Values are shown as the unit type and scale factor.

Clipping Xref Views and Improving Performance

Xrefs are frequently used to import large drawings for reference or backgrounds. Multiple Xrefs, such as a floor plan, column grid layout, and site-plan drawing, might be combined into one file. One drawback to multiple Xrefs in earlier versions of AutoCAD was that the entire Xref was loaded into memory even if only a small portion of it was used for the final plotted output. For computers with limited resources, multiple Xrefs could slow the system to a crawl.

AutoCAD offers two tools that help make display and memory use more efficient when using Xrefs: the Clip command and the Demand Load option in the Options dialog box.

CLIPPING VIEWS

The Clip command, found in the Insert tab's Reference panel, lets you clip the display of an Xref or a block to any shape you want, as shown in Figure 7.21. For example, you might want to display only an L-shaped portion of a floor plan to be part of your current drawing. Clip lets you define such a view. To access the command, choose Clip from the Insert tab's Reference panel.

You can clip blocks and multiple Xrefs as well. You can also specify a front and back clipping distance so that the visibility of objects in 3D space can be controlled. You can define a clip area by using polylines or spline curves, although curve-fitted polylines revert to de-curved polylines. (See Chapter 18 for more on polylines and spline curves.)

FIGURE 7.21
The first panel shows a polyline outline of the area to be isolated with the Clip option. The second panel shows how the Xref appears after Clip is applied. The last panel shows a view of the plan with the polyline's layer turned off.

a.

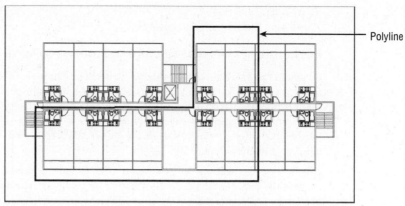

Polyline

b.

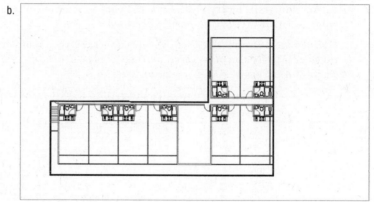

c.

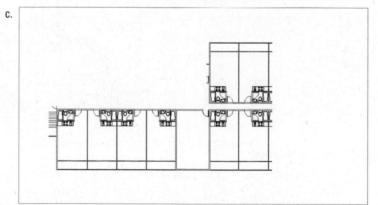

CONTROLLING XREF SETTINGS IN THE OPTIONS DIALOG BOX

The External References (Xrefs) group in the Open And Save tab of the Options dialog box offers some tools to help you manage memory use and other features related to Xrefs. If you're working on large projects with others in a workgroup, you should be aware of these settings and what they do.

Real World Scenario

EXTERNAL REFERENCES IN THE SAN FRANCISCO MAIN LIBRARY PROJECT

Although the exercises in this chapter demonstrate how Xrefs work, you aren't limited to using them in the way shown here. Perhaps one of the most common ways of using Xrefs is to combine a single floor plan with different title block drawings, each with its own layer settings and title block information. In this way, single-drawing files can be reused in several drawing sheets of a final construction document set. This helps keep data consistent across drawings and reduces the number of overall files needed.

This is exactly how Xrefs were used in the San Francisco Main Library drawings. One floor plan file contained most of the main information for that floor. The floor plan was then used as an Xref in another file that contained the title block as well as additional information such as furnishings or floor finish reference symbols. Layer visibility was controlled in each title block drawing so that only the data related to that drawing appeared.

Multiple Xref files were also used by segregating the structural column grid layout drawings from the floor plan files. In other cases, portions of plans from different floors were combined into a single drawing by using Xrefs, as shown here:

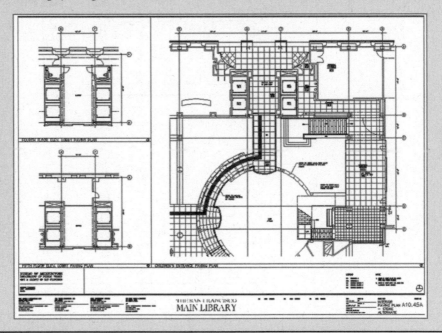

The Demand Load Xrefs drop-down list offers three settings: Disabled, Enabled, and Enabled With Copy. Demand Load is set to Enabled With Copy by default in the standard AutoCAD setup. In addition to reducing the amount of memory an Xref consumes, Demand Load prevents other users from editing the Xref while it's being viewed as part of your current drawing. This helps aid drawing version control and drawing management. The Enabled With Copy option creates a copy of the source Xref file and then uses the copy, thereby enabling other AutoCAD users to edit the source Xref file.

Demand loading improves performance by loading only the parts of the referenced drawing that are needed to regenerate the current drawing. You can set the location for the Xref copy in the Files tab of the Options dialog box under Temporary External Reference File Location.

Two other options are also available in the Options dialog box:

Retain Changes To Xref Layers   Instructs AutoCAD to remember any layer color or visibility settings of Xrefs from one editing session to the next. In the standard AutoCAD settings, this option is on by default.

Allow Other Users To Refedit Current Drawing   Lets others edit the current drawing by choosing Edit Reference from the Insert tab's expanded Reference panel (Refedit). You'll learn about this command in the next section.

Editing Xrefs in Place

You've seen different methods for editing blocks and Xrefs as external files. There is also a way to edit a block or an Xref directly in a file without having to edit an external file: You can use the Edit Reference option in the Insert tab's expanded Reference panel or the Edit Reference In-Place option in the External Reference tab's Edit panel. These options issue the Refedit command.

The following exercise demonstrates how Refedit works. If you are a metric user, note that for this exercise we're using a file set up with Imperial units. The unit type is not important to the exercise:

1. Open the 07-planxref.dwg file. This file is set up like the Planxref.dwg file you created in the previous exercises. 07-planxref uses a file called 07-unitxref.dwg instead of the unitxref.dwg file for the Xref units.

2. Zoom into the unit plan in the lower-left corner of the drawing so that you see a view similar to Figure 7.22.

FIGURE 7.22
The enlarged view of the unitxref in the Planxref drawing

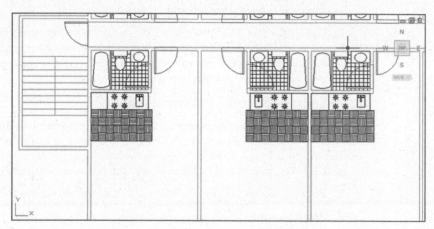

3. Click the hatch pattern of the corner unit to select the unit. Notice that the External Reference Ribbon tab appears, offering several options that allow you to edit the Xref. You'll learn more about these options later.

4. Double-click the hatch pattern corner unit. You can also right-click and select Edit Xref In-place. The Reference Edit dialog box appears (see Figure 7.23).

FIGURE 7.23
The Reference
Edit dialog box

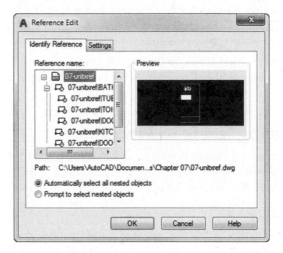

The Reference Edit dialog box contains two main areas. The right side shows a thumbnail view of the items that you're editing. The left side shows a list of the specific items you selected in the Xref. Notice that the list box shows the hierarchical relationship of the kitchenette block in relation to the 07-unitxref Xref.

5. In the list, click the 07-unitxref|KITCHEN listing and then click OK. The Edit Reference panel appears in the current Ribbon tab. You may see a "previous release warning" message. Click OK at the warning.

6. Use a selection window to select the entire lower-left corner unit. Notice that only the grips in the kitchenette appear, indicating that the objects in the kitchenette are selected. Although the rest of the unit appears to be selected, it appears lighter in color. This shows you that only the kitchen is available for editing.

7. Press the Esc key to clear your selection.

In step 5 of the previous exercise, the Refedit command isolates the objects that you select for editing. You can't edit anything else in the Xref until you exit the Refedit command and start over.

At this point, you can edit a block in an Xref. Now let's continue editing the kitchenette:

1. Zoom in on the kitchenette, and move the four burners to the right 8".

2. Erase the sink.

3. Click the Save Changes tool on the Edit Reference panel. If your screen resolution is fairly low, you may have to expand the Edit Reference panel to see the Save Changes tool.

SPECIAL SAVE AS OPTIONS THAT AFFECT DEMAND LOADING

AutoCAD offers a few additional settings that boost the performance of the Demand Load feature. When you choose Save As from the Application menu to save a file in the standard DWG format, you see the Tools button in the upper-right corner of the Save Drawing As dialog box. Choosing Tools ➢ Options opens the Save As Options dialog box. Using the options in the Index Type drop-down list on the DWG Options tab can help improve the speed of demand loading. The index options are as follows:

None No index is created.

Layer AutoCAD loads only layers that are both turned on and thawed.

Spatial AutoCAD loads only portions of an Xref or raster image within a clipped boundary.

Layer & Spatial This option turns on both the Layer and Spatial options.

---

4. A warning message appears, telling you that the changes you've made to the Xref will be saved. Click OK.

5. Zoom back to your previous view. Notice that the other units reflect the changes you made to the 07-unitxref Xref (see Figure 7.24).

FIGURE 7.24
The Xrefs after being edited

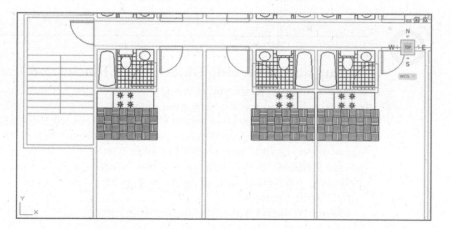

6. Open the 07-unitxref.dwg file, which can be found in the Chapter 7 sample file folder. The kitchen reflects the changes that you made to the Xref of the unit in the 07-planxref file. This shows you that by choosing to save the reference edit in step 3, you saved the changes back to the Xref's source file.

As you saw from these two exercises, it's possible to edit a specific block in an Xref, but to do that you must select the block name in the Reference Edit dialog box.

In these exercises, you edited a block contained in an Xref, but you could have just as easily edited a block in the current drawing. You can also edit nested blocks by using the Refedit command. Changes in blocks in the current file don't affect other files because blocks aren't linked to external files. The changes to blocks remain in the current file until you explicitly export the changed block to a file, as you saw in earlier exercises.

Using the External Reference Tab

Earlier, you saw that when you click an Xref, the External Reference tab appears. This tab offers several tools divided into three panels: Edit, Clipping, and Options. See Table 7.2 for a complete description of these tools.

TABLE 7.2:   The External Reference tab options

TOOL NAME	FUNCTION
Edit Reference In-Place	Starts the Refedit command, which allows you to edit an Xref within the current drawing.
Open Reference	Opens the selected Xref.
Create Clipping Boundary	Starts the Xclip command, which allows you to hide portions of an Xref. This feature is similar to the image clipping command described in Chapter 13, "Copying Existing Drawings from Other Sources."
Remove Clipping	Removes a clipping boundary.
External References	Opens or closes the External References palette.

Adding and Removing Objects from Blocks and Xrefs

In the previous exercises, you removed objects from the Kitchen block by using the Erase command. You can also move objects from a block or an Xref into the current drawing without erasing them. To do this, choose Remove From Working Set from the Edit Reference panel while in the Refedit command. This removes the objects from the block or Xref without erasing them. Likewise, you can add new objects to the block or Xref by choosing Add To Working Set from the Edit Reference panel. Both menu options invoke the Refset command, with different options applied. Also note that the Edit Reference panel appears in all of the Ribbon tabs when you are in the Refedit command.

To see how Refset works, try the following exercise:

1. Close the 07-unitxref.dwg file.

2. In the 07-planxref file, zoom in to the kitchenette to get a view similar to the top panel of Figure 7.25.

FIGURE 7.25
Moving the burners out of the Kitchen block and adding the rectangle

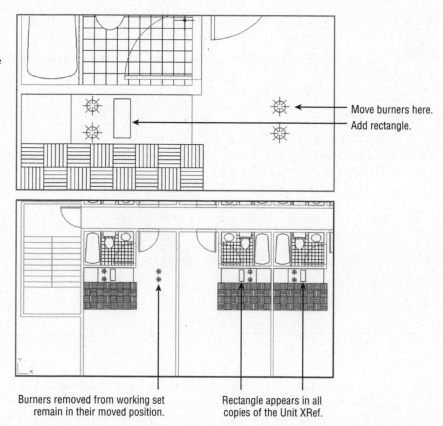

Move burners here.
Add rectangle.

Burners removed from working set remain in their moved position.

Rectangle appears in all copies of the Unit XRef.

3. Double-click the unit plan drawing. You can also choose Edit Reference from the Insert tab's expanded Reference panel and then click the unit plan.

4. Click the 07-unitxref | KITCHEN listing in the Reference Edit dialog box, and then click OK.

5. Use the Move tool to move the two burners on the right just to the right of the kitchenette, as shown in Figure 7.25.

6. Click the Remove From Working Set tool in the expanded Edit Reference panel.

7. Select the two burners you just moved, and then press ↵.

Notice that the burners become grayer to show that they're removed from the working set. They remain as part of the Planxref drawing, but they're no longer part of the Kitchen block. Now add a rectangle to the Kitchen block in place of the burners:

1. Draw a 7″ by 16″ rectangle in place of the moved burners, as shown in the top panel of Figure 7.25. Anything you add to the drawing automatically becomes part of the working set.

2. Click Save Changes in the Edit Reference panel. You'll see a warning message stating that all reference edits will be saved. Click OK.

3. Zoom out enough to see the other units in the drawing (see Figure 7.26).

FIGURE 7.26
The Planxref drawing with the changes made to the `07-unitxref` Xref

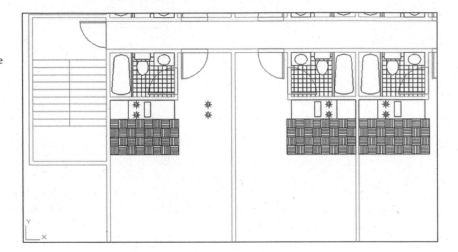

You can see that the burners have been replaced by the rectangle in all of the other Xref units. The burners you moved are still there in the lower-left corner unit, but they have been removed from all of the Xrefs. It's as if you extracted them from the block and placed them in the Plan drawing.

While you were using the Refedit command, any new objects that you created were added to the working set automatically. When you drew the rectangle in step 1, for example, it was automatically included in the *working set*, which is the set of objects included in the block or Xref on which you're currently working. You didn't have to add it specifically to the working set.

If you want to include existing objects in the working set, choose the Add To Working Set tool from the Edit Reference panel.

You've completed the exercises in this chapter, so you can exit AutoCAD without saving these changes.

Understanding the Reference Edit Dialog Box Options

The Reference Edit dialog box offers you the option to isolate specific blocks in the Xref by selecting them from the hierarchy list. You may have noticed the two radio button options: Automatically Select All Nested Objects and Prompt To Select Nested Objects. The default option, Automatically Select All Nested Objects, lets you select any object contained in the selected object in the hierarchy listing. If you select the Prompt To Select Nested Objects option, you're prompted to select objects on the screen before the Edit Reference panel appears.

In addition to the options you used in the exercises, the Reference Edit dialog box includes the Settings tab, which provides a few options (see Figure 7.27).

FIGURE 7.27
The Settings tab of the Reference Edit dialog box

CREATE UNIQUE LAYER, STYLE, AND BLOCK NAMES

When you use the Refedit command with the Automatically Select All Nested Objects option turned on, you can import nested blocks into the current drawing. For example, if you selected the Bath block in the hierarchy list in the previous exercise, you would have access to the Tub and Toilet blocks in the Bath block. You could then copy either of those blocks into the current file.

When you make a copy of a block from an Xref, AutoCAD needs to assign that block a name. The Create Unique Layer, Style, And Block Names option tells AutoCAD to use the original block name and append a $#$ prefix to the name (# is a numeric value starting with 0). If you were to import the Bath block, for example, it would become 0bath in the current drawing. This ensures that the block maintains a unique name when it's imported, even if there is a block with the same name in the current drawing. If you turn off the Create Unique Layer, Style, And Block Names option, the original name is maintained. If the current drawing contains a block of the same name, the imported block uses the current file's definition of that block.

DISPLAY ATTRIBUTE DEFINITIONS FOR EDITING

If your drawing contains attributes (see Chapter 12, "Using Attributes," for more on attributes), this option is offered. If you turn on this option, you can then edit attribute definitions by using the Refedit command. If you select a block that contains an attribute definition while you're using the Refedit command, the attribute definition is exposed, enabling you to make changes. Changes to attribute definitions affect only new attribute insertions. Except for the attribute of the edited block, existing attributes aren't affected. If you want to update existing attributes to a newly edited definition, use the Sync option of the Block Attribute Manager (choose Manage Attributes from the Home tab's expanded Block panel).

LOCK OBJECTS NOT IN WORKING SET

In the Refedit exercises, you saw that objects that aren't selected in the Reference Edit dialog box are grayed out and aren't selectable. The Lock Objects Not In Working Set option controls this feature and is turned on by default.

The Bottom Line

Assemble the parts.   Technical drawings are often made up of repetitive parts that are drawn over and over. AutoCAD makes quick work of repetitive elements in a drawing, as shown in the first part of this chapter.

Master It   What is the object used as the basic building block for the floor plan drawing in the beginning of this chapter?

Take control of the AutoCAD display.   Understanding the way the AutoCAD display works can save you time, especially in a complex drawing.

Master It   Name the dialog box used to save views in AutoCAD. Describe how to recall a saved view.

Use hatch patterns in your drawings.   Patterns can convey a lot of information at a glance. You can show the material of an object or you can indicate a type of view, like a cross section, by applying hatch patterns.

Master It   How do you open the Hatch And Gradient dialog box?

Understand the boundary hatch options.   The hatch options give you control over the way that hatch patterns fill an enclosed area.

Master It   Describe an island as it relates to boundary hatch patterns.

Use external references.   External references are drawing files that you've attached to the current drawing to include as part of the drawing. Because external references aren't part of the current file, they can be worked on at the same time as the referencing file.

Master It   Describe how drawing files are attached as external references.

Chapter 8

Introducing Printing, Plotting, and Layouts

Getting hard-copy output from the AutoCAD® 2018 software is something of an art. You'll need to be intimately familiar with both your output device and the settings available in AutoCAD. You'll probably spend a good deal of time experimenting with the plotter settings in AutoCAD and with your printer or plotter to get your equipment set up just the way you want.

With the huge array of output options available, this chapter can provide only a general discussion of plotting and printing. As a rule, the process for using a plotter isn't much different from that for a printer; you just have more media-sized options with plotters. Still, every output device is different. It's up to you to work out the details and fine-tune the way you and AutoCAD together work with your particular plotter or printer.

This chapter describes the features available in AutoCAD and discusses some general rules and guidelines to follow when setting up your plots. We'll start with an overview of the plotting features in AutoCAD and then delve into the finer details of setting up your drawing and controlling your plotter or printer.

In this chapter, you will learn to

◆ Understand the plotter settings

◆ Use layout views to control how your plots look

◆ Add an output device

◆ Store a page setup

Plotting the Plan

Certification
Objective

To see firsthand how the Plot command works, you'll plot the plan drawing by using the default settings on your system. You'll start by getting a preview of your plot before you commit to printing your drawing. As an introduction, you'll plot from the model view of an AutoCAD drawing, but be aware that typically you should plot from a layout view. Layout views give you a greater degree of control over how your output will look. You'll be introduced to layout views later in this chapter. Now let's get started!

First, try plotting your drawing to no particular scale:

1. Be sure that your printer or plotter is connected to your computer and is turned on.

2. Start AutoCAD, and open the plan.dwg file; open plan-metric.dwg if you are using the metric system. These files can be found in the Chapter 8 sample files.

3. Select Zoom All from the Zoom flyout in the navigation bar to display the entire drawing, or type **Z↵A↵**.

4. Click the Plot tool from the Quick Access toolbar. You may see a message asking if you want to use the Batch Plot feature. Select Continue to plot a single sheet to open the Plot dialog box (see Figure 8.1). If your dialog box looks like it has more information than what is shown in Figure 8.1, don't worry—you'll learn about the expanded portion of the dialog box in the next exercise.

FIGURE 8.1
The Plot dialog box

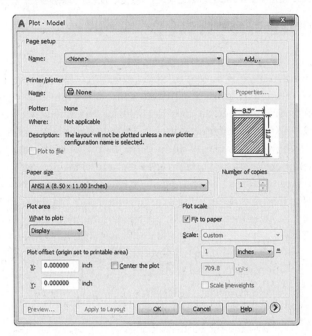

5. If the Name option in the Printer/Plotter group shows None, click the drop-down arrow and select your current Windows system printer.

6. In the Plot Area group, select the Display option from the What To Plot drop-down list (see Figure 8.2). This tells AutoCAD to plot the drawing as it appears in the drawing window. You also have the option to plot the limits of the drawing or to select an area to plot with a window. In addition, you can choose to plot the extents of a drawing or a saved view.

FIGURE 8.2
Choose the Display option.

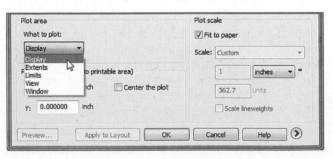

7. Select the Fit To Paper option in the Plot Scale group.

8. Click the Preview button in the lower-left corner of the dialog box. AutoCAD works for a moment and then displays a sample view of how your drawing will appear when printed. Notice that the view also shows the Zoom Realtime cursor. You can use the Zoom/Pan Realtime tools to get a close-up of your print preview.

9. Go ahead and plot the file: Right-click and choose Plot from the context menu. AutoCAD sends the drawing to your printer.

10. Your plotter or printer prints the plan to no particular scale.

You've just plotted your first drawing to see how it looks on paper. You used the minimal settings to ensure that the complete drawing appears on the paper.

You may notice that a message bubble appears in the lower-right corner of the AutoCAD window (see Figure 8.3). If you click the text that reads "Click to view plot and publish details," the Plot And Publish Details dialog box opens to display some detailed information about your plot.

FIGURE 8.3
Click the message text to open the Plot And Publish Details dialog box.

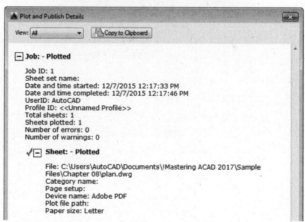

As you become more experienced with AutoCAD and your projects become more demanding, the information presented in the Plot And Publish Details dialog box may be useful to you. For now, make a mental note that this information is available should you need it.

> **SET THE APPROPRIATE UNITS**
>
> It's important to make sure that you use the appropriate unit settings in this chapter. For example, if you've been using the metric measurements for previous exercises, make sure that you use the metric settings in the exercises of this chapter; otherwise, your results won't coincide.

Next, try plotting your drawing to an exact scale. This time, you'll expand the Plot dialog box to show a few more options:

1. In the status bar, click the Annotation Scale tool and select 1/16″ = 1′-0″ from the flyout. Metric users should select 1:20.

2. Click Plot on the Quick Access toolbar again to open the Plot dialog box. If the Name option in the Printer/Plotter group shows None, click the drop-down arrow and select your current Windows system printer.

3. Click the More Options button. You'll see some additional options appear on the right side of the dialog box (see Figure 8.4).

FIGURE 8.4
Open the additional
options on the right.

New options
appear to
the right.

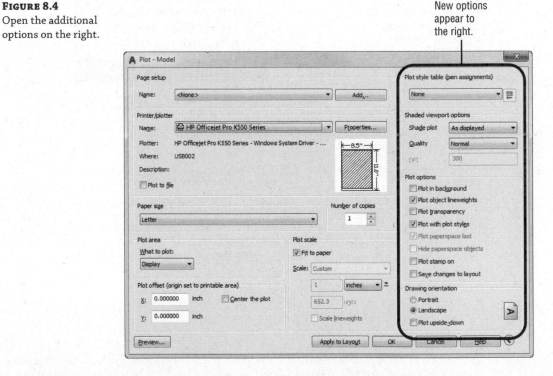

4. If your last printout wasn't oriented correctly on the paper, select the Landscape option in the Drawing Orientation group.

PRINT PREVIEW DEPENDENCIES

The appearance of the print preview depends on the type of output device that you chose when you installed AutoCAD or when you last selected a Plotter Device option (described in the section "Plotting Using Layout Views" later in this chapter). The print preview is also affected by other settings in the Plot dialog box, such as those in the Drawing Orientation, Plot Offset, and Plot Area groups. This example shows a typical preview view using the Windows default system printer in Landscape mode.

---

5. In the Plot Scale group, clear the Fit To Paper check box. Then select 1/16″ = 1′-0″ from the Scale drop-down list. Metric users should select 1:20. As you can see, you have several choices for the scale of your output.

6. In the Paper Size group, select Letter. Metric users should select A4. The options in this drop-down list depend on your Windows system printer or the output device you configured for AutoCAD.

7. In the Plot Area group, select Limits from the drop-down list. This tells AutoCAD to use the limits of your drawing to determine which part of your drawing to plot.

8. Click the Preview button again to get a preview of your plot.

9. Right-click and choose Plot from the context menu. This time, your plot is to scale.

Here, you were asked to specify a few more settings in the Plot dialog box. Several settings work together to produce a drawing that is to scale and that fits properly on your paper. Here is where it pays to understand the relationship between your drawing scale and your paper's size, discussed in Chapter 3, "Setting Up and Using the Drafting Tools." You also saw how you could expand the options in the Plot dialog box.

The following sections are lengthy and don't contain many exercises. If you prefer to continue with the exercises in this chapter, skip to the section "Plotting Using Layout Views." Be sure to come back and read the following sections while the previous exercises are still fresh in your mind.

Understanding the Plotter Settings

In the following sections, you'll explore all of the settings in the Plot dialog box. These settings give you control over the size and orientation of your image on the paper. They also let you control which part of your drawing gets printed. All of these settings work together to give you control over how your drawing fits on your printed output.

AUTOCAD REMEMBERS PLOTTER SETTINGS

AutoCAD 2018 relies mainly on the Windows system printer configuration instead of its own plotter drivers. However, it does remember printer settings that are specific to AutoCAD, so you don't have to adjust your printer settings each time you use AutoCAD. This gives you more flexibility and control over your output. Be aware that you'll need to understand the Windows system printer settings in addition to those offered by AutoCAD.

Paper Size

You use the options in the Paper Size group to specify the paper size for your output. You can select a paper size from the Paper Size drop-down list. These sizes are derived from those available from your selected system printer. You'll find out how to select a different printer later in this chapter.

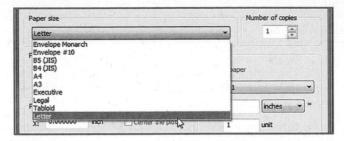

AutoCAD 2018 offers sheet sizes in both Imperial and metric measurements in the Paper Size group. AutoCAD assumes that if you pick a metric sheet size such as A4 or A5, you'll want the sheet dimensions specified in metric measurements, so it adjusts the dialog box settings accordingly.

Drawing Orientation

When you used the Preview button in the first exercise in this chapter, you saw your drawing as it would be placed on the paper. In that example, it was positioned in a *landscape orientation*, which places the image on the paper so that the width of the paper is greater than its height. You can rotate the image on the paper 90° into what is called a *portrait orientation* by selecting the Portrait radio button in the Drawing Orientation group. A third option, Plot Upside-Down, lets you change the orientation further by turning the landscape or portrait orientation upside down. These three settings allow you to print the image in any one of four orientations on the sheet.

In AutoCAD, the preview displays the paper in the orientation it's in when it leaves the printer. For most small-format printers, if you're printing in the portrait orientation, the image appears in the same orientation that you see when you're editing the drawing. If you're using the landscape orientation, the preview image is turned sideways. For large-format plotters, the preview may be oriented in the opposite direction. The graphic in the Drawing Orientation group displays a capital *A* on a sheet showing the orientation of your drawing on the paper output.

Remember that you need to click the More Options button in the lower-right corner of the Plot dialog box, as shown earlier, to access the Drawing Orientation group. The More Options button looks like a circle with a greater-than sign. You can also press Alt+Shift+>.

Plot Area

The What To Plot drop-down list in the Plot Area group lets you specify which part of your drawing you want to plot. You may notice some similarities between these settings and the Zoom command options. The Plot Area options are described next. Most of these options are used only in a model view. Typically, when plotting from a layout view, you'll use the Layout option.

Display   Display is the default option; it tells AutoCAD to plot what is currently displayed on the screen. If you let AutoCAD fit the drawing onto the sheet (that is, you select the Fit To Paper check box in the Plot Scale group), the plot is exactly the same as what you see on your screen, adjusted for the width and height proportions of your display.

Extents   The Extents option uses the extents of the drawing to determine the area to print. If you let AutoCAD fit the drawing onto the sheet (by selecting the Fit To Paper check box in the Plot Scale group), the plot displays exactly the same image that you would see on the screen if you chose the Zoom Extents tool from the Zoom flyout in the Navigation bar.

Layout   The Layout option (available in layout views only) replaces the Limits option when you plot from a layout view. (See the section "Plotting Using Layout Views" later in this chapter.) This option plots everything displayed within the paper margins shown in the layout view. Typically, this is the only option you'll use when printing from a layout.

Limits   The Limits option (available in model space only) uses the limits of the drawing to determine the area to print. If you let AutoCAD fit the drawing onto the sheet (by selecting the Fit To Paper check box in the Plot Scale group), the plot displays exactly the same image that you would see on the screen if you selected Zoom All from the Zoom flyout on the Navigation bar.

GETTING A BLANK PLOT?

Do you get a blank printout even though you selected Extents or Display? Chances are that the Fit To Paper check box isn't selected or the Inches = Units (mm = Units for metric users) setting is inappropriate for the sheet size and scale of your drawing. If you don't care about the scale of the drawing, make sure the Fit To Paper option is selected. Otherwise, make sure the Plot Scale settings are set correctly. If you select Display for the plot area, try Extents instead. The next section, "Plot Scale," describes how to set the scale for your plots.

View   The View option is available when you've saved a view in the drawing by using the View command. When you select View from the What To Plot drop-down list, another drop-down list appears offering a list of views available in the drawing. You can then select the view that you want to plot. If you let AutoCAD fit the drawing onto the sheet (by selecting Fit To Paper from the Plot Scale group), the plot displays exactly the same thing that you would see on the screen if you recalled the view that you're plotting. Objects that don't appear in the view are clipped in the plotted view.

Window   The Window option enables you to use a window to indicate the area that you want to plot. Nothing outside the window prints. When you select this option, the Plot dialog box temporarily closes to allow you to select a window. After you've done this the first time, a Window button appears next to the drop-down list. You can click the Window button and then indicate a window in the drawing area, or AutoCAD will use the last indicated window. If you use the Fit To Paper option in the Plot Scale group to let AutoCAD fit the drawing onto the sheet, the plot displays exactly what you enclose in the window.

Plot Scale

In the previous section, you could select Fit To Paper for several of the Plot Area options. Bear in mind that when you apply a scale factor to your plot instead, the results of the Plot Area settings change and some problems can arise. This is where most new users have difficulty.

For example, the apartment plan drawing fits nicely on the paper when you use Fit To Paper. But if you try to plot the drawing at a scale of 1″ = 1′, you'll probably get a blank piece of paper because, at that scale, hardly any of the drawing fits on your paper. AutoCAD will tell you that it's plotting and then tell you that the plot is finished. You won't have a clue as to why your sheet is blank.

If an image is too large to fit on a sheet of paper because of improper scaling, the plot image is placed on the paper differently, depending on whether the plotter uses the center of the image or the lower-left corner for its origin. Keep this in mind as you specify scale factors in this area of the dialog box.

SCALE

You can select a drawing scale from a set of predefined scales in the Scale drop-down list. These options cover the most common scales you'll need to use.

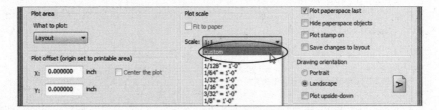

You've already seen how the Fit To Paper option lets you avoid giving a scale and forces the drawing to fit on the sheet when you're plotting from the model view. This works fine if you're plotting illustrations that aren't to scale. If you select another option, such as 1/8″= 1′-0″, the inches and units text boxes change to reflect this scale. The Inches = text box changes to 0.125, and the Units text box changes to 12.

If you're plotting from a layout, you'll use the 1:1 scale option or perhaps a 1:2 scale if you're plotting a half-size drawing. In a layout, the drawing scale is typically set up through the viewport. While you're plotting from a layout, AutoCAD automatically determines the area to plot based on the printer and sheet size you select. For more information, see "Plotting Using Layout Views" later in this chapter.

CUSTOM SCALE

In some cases, you may need to set up a nonstandard scale (not shown in the drop-down list) to plot your drawing. If you can't find the scale you want in the Scale drop-down list, you can select Custom and then enter custom values in the Inches or mm and Units text boxes.

Through these text boxes, you can indicate how the drawing units in your drawing relate to the final plotted distance in inches or millimeters. For example, if your drawing is of a scale factor of 96, you would follow these steps:

1. In the Plot Scale group of the Plot dialog box, double-click the text box just below the Scale drop-down list, and enter **1**.

2. Double-click the Units text box, enter **96**, and press the Tab key. Metric users who want to plot to a scale of 110 should enter **1** in the mm text box and **10** in the Units text box.

If you're more used to the Architectural unit style in the Imperial measurement system, you can enter a scale as a fraction. For example, for a 1/8″ scale drawing, do this:

1. Double-click the Inches = text box, enter **1/8**, and press the Tab key. The value in the text box changes to 0.125, which is the decimal equivalent of 1/8″.

2. Double-click the Units text box, enter **12**, and press the Tab key.

If you specify a different scale than the one you chose while setting up your drawing, AutoCAD plots your drawing to that scale. You aren't restricted in any way as to scale, but entering the correct scale is important: If it's too large, AutoCAD will think your drawing is too large to fit on the sheet, although it will attempt to plot your drawing anyway. See Chapter 3 for a discussion of unit styles and scale factors.

Don't Forget Your Annotation Scale

You may see a message saying that the "annotation scale is not equal to the plot scale" when you attempt to plot your drawing. You can click Continue at the message and your drawing will still be plotted to the scale you specify. If you are using any text or blocks that use the annotation scale feature, those items will be plotted at the Annotation scale setting for the model view or layout that you are trying to plot. See Chapter 4, "Organizing Objects with Blocks and Groups," for more on the annotation scale.

If you plot to a scale that is different from the scale you originally intended, objects and text appear smaller or larger than is appropriate for your plot. You'll need to edit your text size to match the new scale. You can do so by using the Properties palette. Select the text whose height you want to change, right-click and choose Properties from the context menu, and then change the Height setting in the Properties palette.

Adding a Custom Scale to the Scale Drop-Down List

If you use a custom scale frequently, you may find it annoying to have to input the scale every time you plot. AutoCAD offers the ability to add your custom scale to the Scale drop-down list shown earlier. You can then easily select your custom scale from the list instead of entering it through the text box.

Certification Objective

Here are the steps you use to add a custom scale to the Scale drop-down list:

1. Choose Options from the Application menu to open the Options dialog box.

2. Select the User Preferences tab, and then click the Default Scale List button at the bottom of the dialog box.

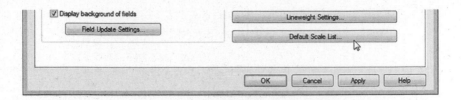

3. In the Default Scale List dialog box, click the Add button.

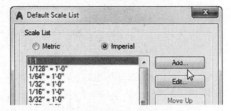

4. In the Add Scale dialog box, enter a name for your custom scale in the Name Appearing In Scale List text box, and then enter the appropriate values in the Scale Properties text boxes.

5. Click OK in each dialog box to close it.

There are several options besides Add in the Default Scale List dialog box. Clicking the Edit button lets you edit an existing scale in the list. Clicking the Move Up and Move Down buttons lets you change the location of an item in the list. Clicking Delete deletes an item or a set of items from the list. Clicking the Reset button restores the list to its default condition and removes any custom items that you may have added.

SCALE LINEWEIGHTS

AutoCAD offers the option to assign lineweights to objects either through their layer assignments or by directly assigning a lineweight to individual objects. The lineweight option, however, doesn't have any meaning until you specify a scale for your drawing. After you specify a scale, the Scale Lineweights option becomes available. Select this check box if you want the lineweight assigned to layers and objects to appear correctly in your plots. You'll get a closer look at lineweights and plotting later in this chapter.

Shaded Viewport Options

Most of your plotting will probably involve 2D technical line drawings, but occasionally you may need to plot a shaded or rendered 3D view. You may need to include such 3D views combined with 2D or 3D Wireframe views. AutoCAD offers the Shaded Viewport Options group, which enables you to plot shaded or rendered 3D views of your AutoCAD drawing. These options give you control over the quality of your rendered output. (Users of the AutoCAD LT® software don't have the Shaded Viewport Options group.)

Remember that you need to click the More Options button in the lower-right corner of the Plot dialog box to get to the Shaded Viewport Options group. You also need be in a model space view before these options are made available.

SHADE PLOT

The Shade Plot and Quality drop-down lists let you control how a Model Space view or layout is plotted. You can choose from the following options:

As Displayed   Plots the Model Space view as it appears on your screen.

Legacy Wireframe   Plots the Model Space view of a 3D object as a Wireframe view.

Legacy Hidden   Plots your Model Space view with hidden lines removed.

3D Hidden/3D Wireframe/Conceptual/Hidden/Realistic. . .   Plots the Model Space using one of several visual styles. These selections override the current Model Space visual style. See Chapter 20, "Creating 3D Drawings," for more on visual styles.

Rendered   Renders your Model Space view before plotting (see Bonus Chapter 6, "Rendering 3D Drawings," available at www.omura.com/chapters).

Low/Medium/High   Sets the quality of the plot.

The Shade Plot options aren't available if you're plotting from a layout view. You can control the way each layout viewport is plotted through the viewport's Properties settings. You'll learn more about layout viewport properties later in this chapter.

QUALITY AND DPI

The Quality drop-down list determines the dots per inch (dpi) setting for your output. These options aren't available if you select Legacy Wireframe or Legacy Hidden from the Shade Plot drop-down list:

Draft   Plots 3D views as wireframes.

Preview   Offers 150 dpi resolution.

Normal   Offers 300 dpi resolution.

Presentation   Offers 600 dpi resolution.

Maximum   Defers dpi resolution to the current output device's settings.

Custom   Lets you set a custom dpi setting. When you select Custom, the DPI text box is made available for your input.

If some of the terms discussed for the Shaded Viewport Options group are unfamiliar, don't be alarmed. You'll learn about 3D shaded views in Part 4 of this book. When you start to explore 3D modeling in AutoCAD, come back and review the Shaded Viewport Options group.

Plot Offset

Sometimes, your first plot of a drawing shows the drawing positioned incorrectly on the paper. You can fine-tune its location by using the Plot Offset settings. To adjust the position of your drawing on the paper, enter the location of the view origin in relation to the plotter origin in x- and y-coordinates (see Figure 8.5).

FIGURE 8.5
Adjusting the image
location on a sheet

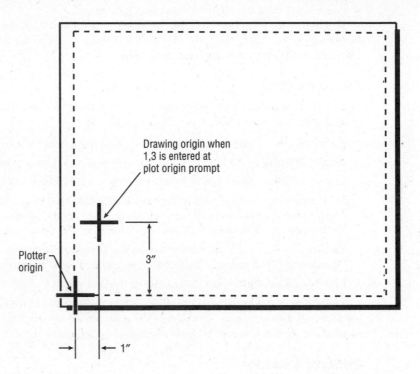

For example, suppose that you plot a drawing and then realize that it needs to be moved 1" to the right and 3" up on the sheet. You can replot the drawing by making the following changes:

1. Double-click the X text box, type **1**, and press the Tab key.

2. Double-click the Y text box, type **3**, and press the Tab key.

Now proceed with the rest of the plot configuration. With these settings, the image is shifted on the paper exactly 1" to the right and 3" up when the plot is done.

The Center The Plot option does just what it says: It centers the plot on the sheet. This option is not available when you're plotting a layout.

You can also tell AutoCAD the location from which the offset is to occur. The Plot And Publish tab of the Options dialog box (choose Application ➢ Options) offers the Specify Plot Offset Relative To button group. This group offers two radio buttons: Printable Area and Edge Of Paper. You can select the option that makes the most sense for you.

Plot Options

The options in the Plot Options group provide you with greater control over your output and require some detailed instruction. Here is a brief description of these options.

Plot In Background   If you think your plot will take some time to complete, this option plots your drawing in the background so that, after you begin a plot, you can immediately return to your drawing work. You can also control this option through the Backgroundplot system variable.

Plot Object Lineweights   As mentioned earlier, AutoCAD lets you assign lineweights to objects either through their layer assignment or by assigning them directly. If you use this feature in your drawing, this option lets you turn lineweights on or off in your output.

Plot With Transparency   You can apply a transparency of objects and layers in your drawing. This option lets you control whether transparency is used when your drawing is plotted.

Plot With Plot Styles   Plot styles give you a high degree of control over your drawing output. You can control whether your output is in color or black and white, and you can control whether filled areas are drawn in a solid color or a pattern. You can even control the way lines are joined at corners. You can learn more about these options and how they affect your work in Bonus Chapter 5, "Understanding Plot Styles," available at www.omura.com/chapters.

Plot Paperspace Last   When you're using a layout view, otherwise known as Paper Space, this option determines whether objects in paper space are plotted before or after objects in model space.

Hide Paperspace Objects   This option pertains to 3D models in AutoCAD. When you draw in 3D, you can view your drawing as a *Wireframe view*. In a Wireframe view, your drawing looks like it's transparent even though it's made up of solid surfaces. Using hidden-line removal, you can view and plot your 3D drawings so that solid surfaces are opaque. To view a 3D drawing in the drawing area with hidden lines removed, use the Hide command or use one of the visual styles other than Wireframe. To plot a 3D drawing with hidden lines removed, choose the Hidden option or a visual style from the Shade Plot drop-down list.

Hide Paperspace Objects doesn't work for views in the Layout viewport described later. Instead, you need to set the viewport's Shade Plot setting to Hidden. (Click the viewport border, right-click, and choose Shade Plot ➤ Hidden from the context menu.)

Plot Stamp On   The Plot Stamp feature lets you place pertinent data on the drawing in a location you choose. This includes the drawing name, date and time, scale, and other data. When you click the Plot Stamp On check box to turn on this option, the Plot Stamp Settings button appears.

Click this button to gain access to the Plot Stamp dialog box (see Figure 8.6). This dialog box offers many controls over the plot stamp. It is a fairly extensive tool, so rather than us filling this chapter with a description of all of its features, see Bonus Chapter 3, "Hardware and Software Tips," available at www.omura.com/chapters, for a complete rundown of the Plot Stamp options.

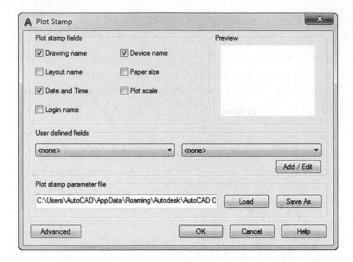

Save Changes To Layout   When this option is turned on, the changes you make to Plot dialog box settings are saved with the current layout. You'll learn more about layouts in the section "Plotting Using Layout Views."

Exit Options

The Plot dialog box has the usual OK, Cancel, and Help buttons at the bottom. You'll also see the Apply To Layout button. This button lets you save the plot settings that you make without sending your drawing to the printer or plotter for output. It is convenient for those times when you decide halfway through your plot setup not to plot your drawing.

Plotting Using Layout Views

Certification
Objective

So far, you've done all of your work in the model space view, also known as model space. There are other views to your drawing that are specifically geared toward printing and plotting. The *layout* views enable you to control drawing scale, add title blocks, and set up layer settings different from those in the model view. You can think of the layout views as page layout spaces that act like a desktop publishing program.

This part of the chapter introduces you to layout views as they relate to plotting. You'll also learn more about layout views in Chapter 15, "Laying Out Your Printer Output."

You can have as many layout views as you like, each set up for a different type of output. You can, for example, have two or three layout views, each set up for a different scale drawing or with different layer configurations for reflected ceiling plans, floor plans, or equipment plans. You can even set up multiple views of your drawing at different scales in a single layout view. In addition, you can draw and add text and dimensions in layout views just as you would in model space.

To get familiar with the layout views, try the following exercise:

1. Hover over the Plan file's Drawing tab at the top of the drawing area (see Figure 8.7), and then click the Layout1 preview panel.

FIGURE 8.7
Choose the
Layout1 panel.

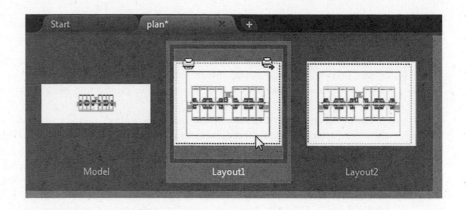

OPTIONS IN THE PREVIEW PANEL

When you hover over a Drawing tab, you see two printer icons along the top of the preview images. The icon in the upper-left corner lets you plot the layout. The icon in the upper-right corner lets you start the Publish feature. See Chapter 25, "Managing and Sharing Your Drawings," for more on the Publish feature.

A view of your drawing appears on a gray background, as shown in Figure 8.8. This is a view of your drawing as it will appear when plotted on your current default printer or plotter. The white area represents the printer or plotter paper.

FIGURE 8.8
A view of Layout1

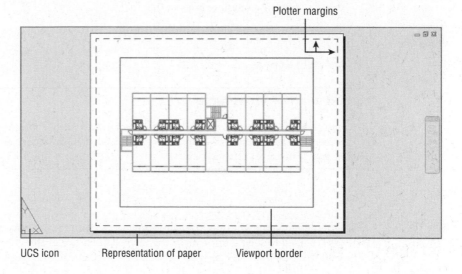

2. Try zooming in and out using the Zoom Realtime tool or the scroll wheel of your mouse. Notice that the entire image zooms in and out, including the area representing the paper.

Layout views give you full control over the appearance of your drawing printouts. You can print a layout view just as you did the view in model space. Note that the ViewCube® is absent since layout views are strictly 2D. However, you can double-click inside a layout viewport and use the ViewCube to select a 3D view.

Let's take a moment to look at the elements in the Layout1 view. As mentioned previously, the white area represents the paper on which your drawing will be printed. The dashed line immediately inside the edge of the white area represents the limits of your plotter's margins. Finally, the solid rectangle that surrounds your drawing is the outline of the viewport border. A *viewport* is an AutoCAD object that works like a window into your drawing from the layout view. Also notice the triangular symbol in the lower-left corner of the view; this is the UCS icon for the layout view. It tells you that you're currently in layout view space. You'll see the significance of this icon in the following exercise:

1. Try using a selection window to select the lobby area of your drawing. Nothing is selected.

2. Click the viewport border, which is the rectangle surrounding the drawing, as shown in Figure 8.8. This is the viewport into model space. Notice that you can select it.

3. Open the Properties palette by clicking the Properties arrow icon in the title bar of the Home tab's Properties panel. You can see from the Properties palette that the viewport is just like any other AutoCAD object with layer, linetype, and color assignments. You can even hide the viewport outline by turning off its layer.

4. Close the Properties palette.

5. With the viewport still selected, click the Erase tool in the Modify toolbar. The view of your drawing disappears when you erase the viewport. Remember that the viewport is like a window into the drawing that you created in the model view. After the viewport is erased, the drawing view goes with it.

 6. Type U⏎ or click the Undo button in the Quick Access toolbar to restore the viewport.

CREATING NEW VIEWPORTS

You can create new viewports using the Vports command (the Rectangular/Polygonal/Object tool in the Layout tab's Layout Viewports panel). See the section "Creating New Paper Space Viewports" in Chapter 15 for more information.

---

7. Double-click anywhere within the viewport's boundary. Notice that the UCS icon that you're used to seeing appears in the lower-left corner of the viewport. The Layout UCS icon disappears. The Navigation bar and ViewCube also appear inside the viewport.

8. Click the lobby in your drawing. You can now select parts of your drawing.

9. Try zooming and panning your view. Changes in your view take place only within the boundary of the viewport.

10. Click Zoom All from the Zoom flyout in the Navigation bar or type **Z↲A↲** to display the entire drawing in the viewport.

11. To return to paper space, double-click an area outside the viewport. You can also type **PS↲** to return to paper space or **MS↲** to access the space within the viewport.

This exercise shows you the unique characteristics of layout views. The objects in the viewport are inaccessible until you double-click the interior of the viewport. You can then move about and edit your drawing in the viewport, just as you would while in the model view.

Layout views can contain as many viewports as you like, and each viewport can hold a different view of your drawing. You can size and arrange each viewport any way you like, or you can create multiple viewports, giving you the freedom to lay out your drawing as you would a page in a page layout program. You can also draw in the layout view or import Xrefs and blocks for title blocks and borders.

Setting Plot Scale in the Layout Viewports

In the first part of this chapter, you plotted your drawing from the model view. You learned that to get the plot to fit on your paper, you had to either use the Fit To Paper option in the Plot dialog box or indicate a specific drawing scale, plot area, and drawing orientation.

The layout view works in a different way: It's designed to enable you to plot your drawing at a 1-to-1 scale. Instead of specifying the drawing scale in the Plot dialog box, as you did when you plotted from the model view, you let the size of your view in the layout view viewport determine the drawing scale. You can set the viewport view to an exact scale by making changes to the properties of the viewport.

To set the scale of a viewport in a layout view, try the following exercise:

1. Press the Esc key to clear any selections. Then click the viewport border to select it. You'll see the Viewport Scale tool appear in the status bar.

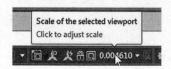

2. Click the Viewport Scale tool, and a list of common drawing scales appears (see Figure 8.9).

3. Select 1/16″ = 1′ (metric users should select 1:20). The view in the drawing window changes to reflect the new scale for the viewport. Now most of the drawing fits into the viewport, and it's to scale. The scale of 1/16″ = 1′ is similar to the metric 1:200 scale, but because you used centimeters instead of millimeters as the base unit for the metric version of the plan drawing, you drop the second 0 in 200. The metric scale becomes 1:20.

FIGURE 8.9
Choose a viewport
scale.

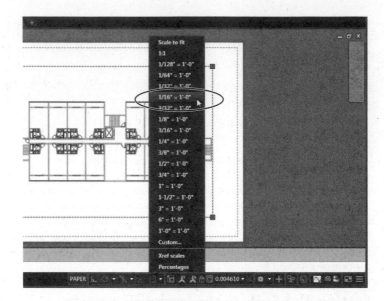

4. Use the viewport grips to enlarge the viewport enough to display all of the drawing, as shown in Figure 8.10. As you move a corner grip, notice that the viewport maintains a rectangular shape.

FIGURE 8.10
The enlarged
viewport

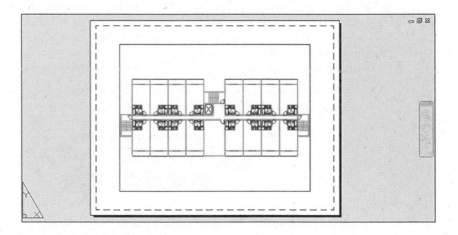

5. Click Plot from the Quick Access toolbar, and in the Plot dialog box, make sure that the Scale option is set to 1:1 and your system printer is selected in the Printer/Plotter group; then click OK. Your drawing is plotted as it appears in the Layout tab, and it's plotted to scale.

In step 2, you used the Viewport Scale tool in the status bar to select a scale for a viewport. If you look just below the Standard Scale option, you see the Custom Scale option. Both options work like their counterparts, the options in the Plot Scale group in the Plot dialog box.

Layout views and viewports work in conjunction with your plotter settings to give you a better idea of how your plots will look. There are numerous plotter settings that can dramatically change the appearance of your layout view and your plots. Next, you'll learn how some of the plotter settings can enhance the appearance of your drawings. You'll also learn how layout views can display those settings, letting you see on your computer screen exactly what will appear on your paper output.

Adding an Output Device

We mentioned earlier that you can set up AutoCAD for more than one output device. You can do this even if you have only one printer or plotter connected to your computer. You might want multiple printer configurations in AutoCAD for many reasons. You might want to set up your system so that you can print to a remote location over a network or the Internet. Some printer configurations are strictly file oriented, such as the AutoCAD DWF format for Internet web pages or raster file output. (See Chapter 25 for more on DWF files.)

AutoCAD works best with printers and plotters configured as Windows system devices. Although you can add devices through the AutoCAD Plot Manager, Autodesk recommends that you set up your plotters and printers as Windows devices and then use the System Printer option in AutoCAD to select your output device. (In Windows 7, choose Start ➤ Devices And Printers, and then select Add A Printer from the menu bar to configure a new printer.) You can use the Add-A-Plotter Wizard in AutoCAD to create predefined settings for your system printer so that you can quickly choose a printer or plotter setup.

You can also configure additional printers through the AutoCAD Plot Manager; this method also uses the Add-A-Plotter Wizard. Here's how it's done:

1. Click the Plotter Manager tool on the Output tab's Plot panel to open the Plotters window (see Figure 8.11). Your view of the Plotters window may look a little different, depending on your operating system, but the same basic information is there.

FIGURE 8.11
The Plotters window

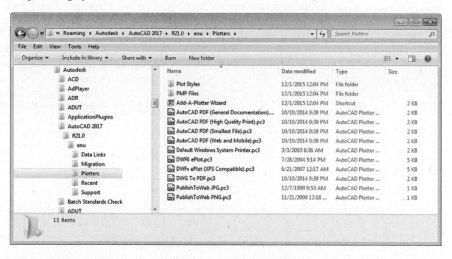

You can also open this window by clicking the Add Or Configure Plotters button in the Plot And Publish tab of the Options dialog box. It's just a File Explorer window showing you the contents of the Plotters folder that is buried in the Users folder for your

Windows 10, Windows 8, or Windows 7 user profile (C:\Users\User Name\AppData\Roaming\ Autodesk\AutoCAD 2018\R22.0\enu\Plotters, where User Name is your login name).

2. Double-click the Add-A-Plotter Wizard icon to open the Add Plotter dialog box. You see the Introduction screen, which describes the purpose of the wizard.

3. Click Next. The next screen lets you select the type of setup you want. You're offered three options: My Computer, Network Plotter Server, and System Printer. The first two options offer plotter options based on drivers specific to AutoCAD. They offer the same set of options, except the Network Plotter Server option asks you for a network server name. The System Printer option uses the existing Windows system printer as the basis for the setup.

4. Click the My Computer radio button and click Next, and you will see a listing of plotter models that are supported by AutoCAD directly through its own drivers. If you use a PostScript device or if you want to convert drawings to raster formats, this is the place to select those options. You can select the plotter or printer manufacturer name from the Manufacturers list on the left and then select a specific model from the list on the right. If you have a driver for a specific plotter or printer that isn't listed, you can click the Have Disk button to browse to your driver location.

5. After you've made a printer or plotter selection, click Next. You're then asked if you want to use an existing PCP or PC2 configuration file for the selected plotter. PCP and PC2 configuration files are plotter configuration files from earlier releases of AutoCAD.

6. Unless you plan to use one of those files, click Next on the Import PCP Or PC2 screen. If you selected My Computer in step 3, the Ports screen opens (see Figure 8.12). With the Plot To A Port option selected, you can use the list to select a port to which your printer or plotter is connected. The Configure Port button lets you set up the port if you have a specific requirement for it. If you intend to plot to a file instead of to a port, you can select the Plot To File radio button at the top as an alternative. An AutoSpool option is also offered if your printer requires this feature.

FIGURE 8.12
The Ports screen of the Add-A-Plotter Wizard

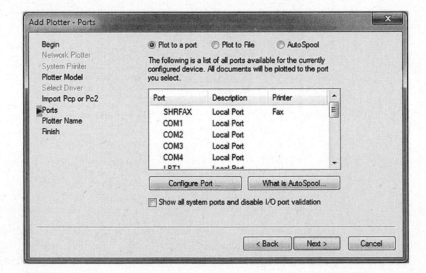

If you selected an option in step 4 that doesn't require a port setup, click the Next button to skip this option; the Plotter Name screen opens.

7. Enter a name for this configuration in the space provided, and then click Next to open the Finish screen. You can enter a descriptive name in the Plotter Name text box. This name will appear in the Printer Name drop-down list of the Plot Or Page Setup dialog box.

8. From this screen you can make adjustments to the configuration you've just created by clicking the Edit Plotter Configuration button. Click Finish to exit the Add-A-Plotter Wizard. Your new configuration appears in the Plotters window.

The Edit Plotter Configuration button lets you fine-tune your plotter settings. For example, you can calibrate your plotter for more accurate scaling of your plots, or if you're creating a raster file output configuration, you can create a custom page setting for extremely high-resolution raster images.

After you've set up a plotter, the plotter information is stored as a file with the .pc3 filename extension in the Plotters folder described earlier.

Editing a Plotter Configuration

In step 8 of the previous exercise, you exited the Add-A-Plotter Wizard without editing the newly created plotter configuration. You can always go back and edit the configuration by opening the Plotters window (choose Plotter Manager on the Output tab's Plot panel) and double-clicking the configuration that you want to edit. You can recognize a plotter configuration file by its .pc3 filename extension.

Most users use their Windows system printer or plotter for other applications besides AutoCAD, and frequently the AutoCAD settings for that printer are different from the settings used for other applications. You can set up AutoCAD to use its own settings automatically so that you don't have to reconfigure your Windows system printer every time you switch applications. To do so, follow these steps:

1. Click the Page Setup Manager tool on the Output tab's Plot panel to open the Page Setup Manager dialog box. You can also right-click a layout or model tab and choose Page Setup Manager from the context menu.

2. Click the Modify button to open the Page Setup dialog box.

3. Select the printer that you want to configure in the Name drop-down list of the Printer/ Plotter group.

4. Click the Properties button just to the right of the drop-down list to open the Plotter Configuration Editor dialog box. A list box displays all the properties of the printer or plotter. Not all these properties are editable, however. Each time you click a property in the list box, the lower half of the dialog box displays the options associated with that property.

5. Click the Custom Properties item in the list box. In the lower half of the dialog box, you'll see the Custom Properties button (see Figure 8.13).

6. Click the Custom Properties button. You'll see the Windows system printer options. These are the same options that you see when you edit the properties of your printer by choosing Start ➤ Printers And Faxes or Start ➤ Control Panel ➤ Printers And Other Hardware.

FIGURE 8.13
Click Custom Properties.

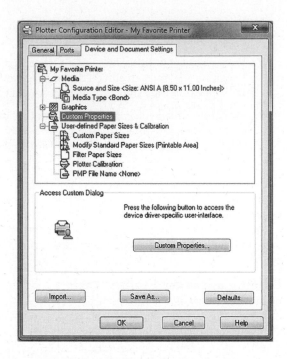

CONTROLLING THE APPEARANCE OF THE LAYOUT VIEWS

The Options dialog box offers a set of controls dedicated to the layout views. If you don't like some of the graphics in the layout views, you can turn them off. Open the Options dialog box, and click the Display tab to see a set of options in the Layout Elements group in the lower-left side of the dialog box.

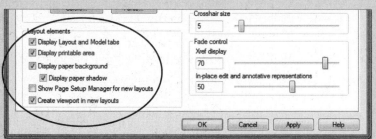

As you can see, you can control the display of the tabs themselves, the margins, the paper background, and the paper shadow. In addition, you can specify whether AutoCAD automatically creates a viewport or opens the Page Setup dialog box when you open a layout view for the first time.

7. Adjust these settings the way that you want them when you plot from AutoCAD and then click OK.

8. Back in the Plotter Configuration Editor dialog box, click the Save As button. A standard Save As dialog box appears.

9. Enter the name of the plot configuration that you've set up or accept the default name (which is usually the name of the Windows printer or plotter), and click Save.

10. Click OK in the Plotter Configuration Editor dialog box; then click OK in the Page Setup dialog box and close the Page Setup Manager.

The Plotter Configuration Editor offers a wide variety of options that are fairly technical in nature. If you want to know more about the Plotter Configuration Editor, see Bonus Chapter 3, available at www.omura.com/chapters.

Storing a Page Setup

Certification
Objective

Unlike most other programs, AutoCAD offers hundreds of page setup options. It can be quite a chore to keep track of and maintain all these options. But as you settle into using AutoCAD, you'll probably find that you'll set up a few plotter configurations and stick to them. AutoCAD 2018 lets you save a page setup under a name to help you store and manage the settings that you use most often.

You've already seen the Page Setup Manager dialog box on your way to preparing a page for printing. In this section, you'll take a closer look at this useful tool.

Follow these steps to create a page setup:

1. In AutoCAD, click the Page Setup Manager tool in the Output tab's Plot panel. The Page Setup Manager dialog box opens (see Figure 8.14). So far, you've used only the Modify option in this dialog box to modify an existing page setup. Now you'll try creating a new setup.

FIGURE 8.14
The Page Setup Manager

2. Click the New button to open the New Page Setup dialog box (see Figure 8.15).

FIGURE 8.15

Naming a new page setup

3. To create a new page setup, first enter a name in the New Page Setup Name text box and then select a setup from the Start With list box. AutoCAD will use the setup that you select as the basis for the new setup. Notice that AutoCAD offers the name Setup1 as a default name for a new setup.

4. Click OK when you're finished. AutoCAD opens the Page Setup dialog box, where you can choose the settings for your new page setup.

5. Click OK to return to the Page Setup Manager and then close it. Your new page setup is listed in the Current Page Setup list box. From here, you can select a page setup from the list box and then click the Set Current button to make it the current page setup for the layout.

You can also import other user-defined page setups by clicking the Import button. Because page setups are stored in the drawing, the Import button opens a standard file dialog box that displays drawing files. You can then select a file from which you want to import a page setup.

The current page setup applies to the current Layout tab, but after you create a new page setup, it's offered as an option in the Page Setup Manager dialog box for all of the other Layout tabs in this file. You can also select a page setup directly from the Plot dialog box by using the Name drop-down list in the Page Setup group.

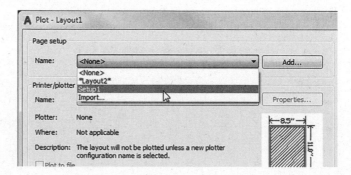

Page setups can be used with the Publish feature described in Chapter 25 to set up batch plots or in the Sheet Set feature described in Bonus Chapter 7, "Keeping a Project Organized with Sheet Sets," available at www.omura.com/chapters. You can also create an entirely new page setup on the fly while in the Plot dialog box. To do this, click the Plot tool in the Quick Access toolbar and then click the Add button in the Page Setup group of the Plot dialog box. This opens a simple dialog box where you can enter a name for your new setup. After you enter a new name and click OK, you can proceed to choose your page settings. Then click OK or Apply To Layout, and the setup will be saved under the new name.

UNDERSTANDING THE PLOT AND PUBLISH TAB IN THE OPTIONS DIALOG BOX

We mentioned the Plot And Publish tab in the Options dialog box earlier in this chapter. This tab contains several options related to plotting that can be useful. Here's a summary of those options and their purposes.

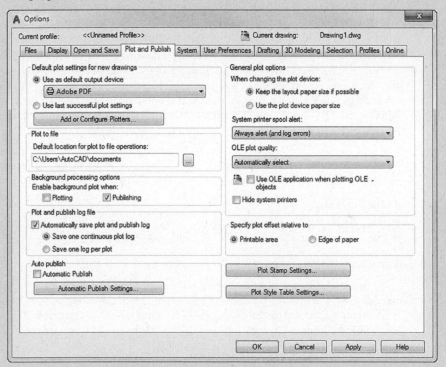

DEFAULT PLOT SETTINGS FOR NEW DRAWINGS

The options in this group let you control the default plot settings for new drawings and for drawings from earlier versions of AutoCAD that are opened for the first time in AutoCAD 2018. The Use As Default Output Device radio button and drop-down list let you select the default plotter or printer to be used with new drawings. When the Use Last Successful Plot Settings radio button is selected, the last successful plotter settings for subsequent plots are used. This is how earlier

continues

continued

versions of AutoCAD worked. The Add Or Configure Plotters button opens the Plotters window. This is the same as choosing the Plot Manager tool from the Output tab's Plot panel. From the Plotters window, you can launch the Add-A-Plotter Wizard to add new plotter configurations. You can also edit existing plotter configurations.

GENERAL PLOT OPTIONS

These options control some of the general plotter parameters. The Keep The Layout Paper Size If Possible radio button causes AutoCAD to attempt to plot to the paper size specified in the Plot dialog box, regardless of the paper size in the plotter. If the specified size is larger than the capacity of the plotter, a warning message is displayed. The Use The Plot Device Paper Size option causes AutoCAD to use the paper size specified by the system printer or the PC3 plot configuration file currently in use. Both settings are also controlled by the Paperupdate system variable.

The System Printer Spool Alert drop-down list offers control over printer-spooling alert messages. The OLE Plot Quality drop-down list lets you control the quality of OLE objects embedded in or linked to a drawing. This setting can also be controlled through the Olequality system variable.

When the Use OLE Application When Plotting OLE Objects check box is selected, AutoCAD launches any application that is associated with an OLE object embedded or linked to the AutoCAD drawing that is currently being plotted. This helps improve the plot quality of Object Linking and Embedding (OLE) objects. You can also set this option through the Olestartup system variable. See Chapter 19, "Getting and Exchanging Data from Drawings," for more information about OLE.

The Hide System Printers option affects the Printer/Plotter group's Name drop-down list in the Plot and Page Setup dialog boxes. With this option turned on, you see only printers that have a .pc3 filename extension associated with them. These include printers that have been set up using the Add-A-Plotter Wizard discussed earlier in this chapter.

PLOT TO FILE

You have the option to plot to a file that can be downloaded to your printer or plotter at a later date. The Plot To File group lets you specify the default destination for the plot files.

PLOT AND PUBLISH LOG FILE

You can maintain a plot log file that records information about each plot you make. This can be helpful when you must keep records of hard-copy output for billing purposes. You can specify the location of the plot and publishing log file in the Files tab of the Options dialog box under the Plot And Publishing Log File Location listing. The log file has a .csv filename extension.

BACKGROUND PROCESSING OPTIONS

AutoCAD performs background plots so that after you begin a plot, you can immediately return to your drawing work instead of waiting for the plot to be completed. The options in this group let you turn on this feature either for standard plotting or for the Publish feature discussed in Chapter 25. You can also control this option through the Backgroundplot system variable.

PLOT STAMP SETTINGS

This button opens the Plot Stamp dialog box, which you saw in the section "Plot Options" earlier in this chapter. The Plot Stamp dialog box lets you determine what information is displayed in a plot stamp, which is a label placed on the print of a drawing to provide information about the source file.

PLOT STYLE TABLE SETTINGS

When you click this button, the Plot Style Table Settings dialog box opens. This dialog box controls the type of plot styles used in AutoCAD. In the case of named plot styles, you can also select a default plot style for layer 0 and a default plot style for objects. Note that the Use Color Dependent Plot Styles and Use Named Plot Styles radio buttons don't have an effect on the current drawing; they affect only new drawings and pre–AutoCAD 2000 drawings being opened for the first time in AutoCAD 2018. The Default Plot Style Table drop-down list lets you select a default plot style table for new and pre–AutoCAD 2000 drawings. These settings are also controlled by the `Pstylepolicy` system variable.

The Add Or Edit Plot Style Tables button in the Plot Style Table Settings dialog box opens the Plot Styles dialog box. From there, you can double-click an existing plot style table file or start the Add-A-Plot Style Table Wizard to create a new plot style.

SPECIFY PLOT OFFSET RELATIVE TO

Here you can determine whether the plot offset is set in relation to the printable area of your printer or to the edge of the paper. The printable area is determined by the printer margin.

AUTO PUBLISH

You can set up AutoCAD to publish your file to a DWF, DWFx, or PDF file automatically when you save or close a drawing. Place a check mark in the Automatic Publish check box to enable this feature. The Automatic Publish Settings button gives you control over the location of the published files as well as the file format and other file features. Note that this feature will increase the time it takes to save or close a file.

Using Electronic Plots

The focus of this chapter has been printer or plotter hard-copy output. But a major part of your work will involve the transmission of electronic versions of your documents. More than ever, architects and engineers are using the Internet to exchange documents of all types, so AutoCAD offers several tools to make the process easier.

We've mentioned that you can control some of your output settings through the Plot And Publish tab of the Options dialog box. The Publish feature includes items that enable you to "print" your drawings as a file that can be emailed to clients and consultants or posted on an FTP site or website. The Publish feature lets you create a single file that contains multiple pages so that you can combine several drawing sheets into one file.

The Publish feature also enables you to plot several drawings at once without having to load and print each one individually. This can be helpful when you've finished a set of drawings and want to plot them during a break or overnight. Chapter 25 gives you a detailed look at the Publish feature.

Exporting to PDF Through the Plot Dialog Box

More than ever, designers and engineers rely on the PDF file format to transfer and view technical drawings. AutoCAD supports the PDF format in a number of ways.

When you select a printer from the Page Setup or Plot dialog box, you have the option to select from four types of PDF printers: General Documentation, High Quality Print, Smallest File, and Web And Mobile. These options appear in the Printer/Plotter Name drop-down list, as shown in Figure 8.16.

FIGURE 8.16
The PDF options in the
Printer/Plotter Name
drop-down list

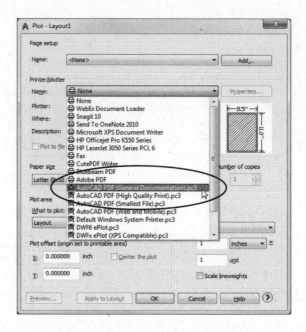

The High Quality Print, Smallest File, and Web And Mobile options are self-explanatory and offer predefined settings for these three types of PDF files. The General Documentation option is similar to the High Quality Print option, but with a slightly lower image resolution. When you select one of these PDF options, a PDF Options button appears, which you can click to open the PDF Options dialog box shown in Figure 8.17. This dialog box enables you to make changes to PDF output. For example, you can adjust the vector and raster quality or change the type of data that you want to include in the PDF file.

FIGURE 8.17
The PDF Options
dialog box

Exporting to PDF Through the Export To DWF/PDF Ribbon Panel

PDF output is also offered in the Export To DWF/PDF panel of the Output tab (see Figure 8.18). This panel offers a quick alternative to the Plotter dialog box when you want to produce a PDF of your drawing.

FIGURE 8.18

The Export To DWF/ PDF panel

If you click the Export flyout on the panel and choose PDF, the Save As PDF dialog box opens. This dialog box enables you to select the location for your files, choose one of the four PDF presets mentioned earlier, or make custom changes to a selected preset. The Save As PDF dialog box also offers some of the same options found in the Plot dialog box, such as the Output Controls options, including the plot stamp feature and a page setup override (see Figure 8.19).

FIGURE 8.19

Save As PDF dialog box

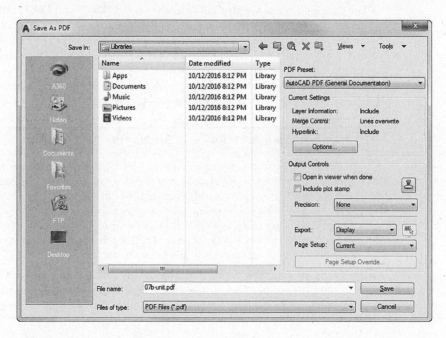

The Options button opens the PDF Options dialog box shown in Figure 8.17. The Export: Current Layout drop-down list lets you select which layout to convert to PDF. The Page Setup: Override drop-down list lets you select between the current setup or a custom setup using the Page Setup Override dialog box shown in Figure 8.20.

FIGURE 8.20

Page Setup Override
dialog box

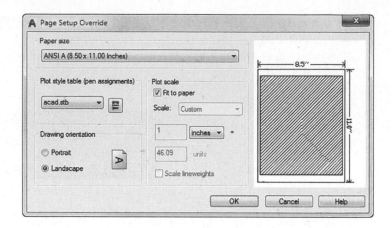

The Page Setup Override dialog box lets you change the paper size, plot scale, drawing orientation, and plot style.

Exporting Autodesk DWF and DWFx Files

The Output Ribbon tab also offers tools to export DWF and DWFx files. The Autodesk DWF file formats allow you to exchange drawing data with others. They offer features that are more focused toward AutoCAD users. You can import DWF and DWFx files as external references, and using a free DWF viewer, you can gather information about a drawing such as block information, attribute data, and distance measurements.

The process to create DWF files is similar to the process for creating PDFs, with some differences in the options available for the output file. See Chapter 25 for more on DWF.

PLOTTING IMAGE FILES AND CONVERTING 3D TO 2D

If your work involves producing manuals, reports, or similar documents, you may want to add the Raster File Export option to your list of plotter configurations. The Raster File Export option lets you plot your drawings to a wide range of raster file formats, including CALS, JPEG, PCX, Targa, Tiff, and BMP. You can then import your drawings into documents that accept bitmap images. Images can be up to 8,000×8,000 pixels (set through the Plotter Configuration Editor) and can contain as many colors as the file format allows. If you need several raster formats, you can use multiple instances of this or any plotter configuration.

To convert your 3D wireframe models into 2D line drawings, use the Flatshot tool described in Chapter 20. You can then include your 2D line drawings with other 2D drawings for plotting and printing.

The Bottom Line

Understand the plotter settings.   Unlike other types of documents, AutoCAD drawings can end up on nearly any size sheet of paper. To accommodate the range of paper sizes, the AutoCAD plotter settings are fairly extensive and give you a high level of control over your output.

Master It   Name at least two of the settings available in the Plot Scale panel of the Plot dialog box.

Use layout views to control how your plots look.   The Layout tabs in AutoCAD offer a way to let you set up how a drawing will be plotted. You can think of the layout views as paste-up areas for your drawings.

Master It   Name some of the items that you see in a layout view.

Add an output device.   Typically, AutoCAD will use the Windows system printer as an output device, but often you will find that the printer you use is a dedicated plotter that is not connected to Windows in the usual way. AutoCAD lets you add custom plotters and printers through the Add-A-Plotter Wizard.

Master It   How do you start the Add-A-Plotter Wizard?

Store a page setup.   Most of the time, you will use the same plotter settings for your drawings. You can save plotter settings using the Page Setup feature.

Master It   Describe a way to create a page setup. Describe how to retrieve a setup.

Chapter 9

Adding Text to Drawings

One of the most tedious drafting tasks is applying notes to your drawing. The AutoCAD® 2018 software makes this job faster by enabling you to type your notes, insert text from other sources, and copy notes that repeat throughout a drawing. It also helps you to create professional-looking notes using a variety of fonts, type sizes, and type styles.

In this chapter, you'll add notes to your apartment building plan. In the process, you'll explore some of the AutoCAD text-creation and text-editing features. You'll learn how to control the size, slant, type style, and orientation of text and how to import text files. You'll start by working through some exercises that show you the process of preparing a drawing for text. You'll then add a few lines of text to the drawing and learn how text size and drawing scale interrelate. The rest of the chapter shows you the tools available for formatting text to fit your application.

In this chapter, you will learn to

- ◆ Prepare a drawing for text

- ◆ Set the annotation scale and add text

- ◆ Explore text formatting in AutoCAD

- ◆ Add simple single-line text objects

- ◆ Use the Check Spelling feature

- ◆ Find and replace text

Preparing a Drawing for Text

Certification Objective

In these first sections, you'll go through the process of adding text to a drawing that currently has none. By doing so, you'll gain firsthand experience in using all the tools that you'll need for adding text to a drawing. Start by setting up a drawing to prepare it for the addition of text:

1. Start AutoCAD and open the Unit file. If you haven't created this file, you can use the file called 9a-unit.dwg (metric users should use 9a-unit-metric.dwg), which you'll find among this chapter's files at the book's web page, www.sybex.com/go/masteringautocad2018. After the file is open, choose Save As from the Application menu to save the Unit drawing to a file called Unit.dwg.

2. Create a layer called **Notes**, and make it the current layer. Notes is the layer on which you'll keep all your text information.

3. If the FLR-PAT layer is on, turn it off. Otherwise, the floor pattern you added previously will obscure the text you enter during the exercises in this chapter.

4. Set up your view so that it looks similar to the top image in Figure 9.1.

FIGURE 9.1
The top image shows the points to pick to place the text boundary window. The bottom image shows the completed text.

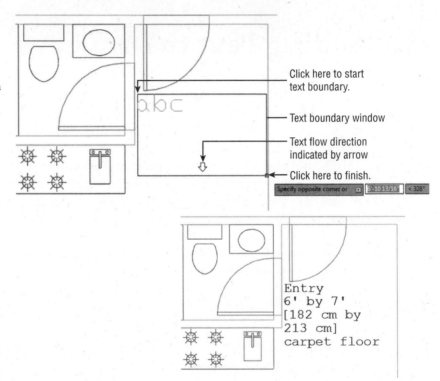

Click here to start text boundary.

Text boundary window

Text flow direction indicated by arrow

Click here to finish.

ORGANIZE TEXT WITH LAYERS

It's a good idea to keep your notes on a separate layer so that you can plot drawings containing only the graphics information.

Organizing Text by Styles

Certification
Objective

Before you begin to add text to your drawing, you should set up a text style or two. You can think of text styles as a tool to store your most common text formatting. Styles store text height and font information, so you don't have to set these options every time you enter text. Generally, you'll need only a few text styles.

Even if you started to add text without creating your own text style, you would still be using a text style. That's because every text object must have a style, so AutoCAD includes the Standard text style in every new drawing. The Standard style uses an AutoCAD font called Txt, and it includes numerous other settings that you'll learn about in this section. These other settings include width factor, oblique angle, and default height.

SET UP DEFAULT FONTS IN TEMPLATES

If you don't like the way the AutoCAD default style is set up, open the `acad.dwt` template file and change the Standard text style settings to your liking. You can also add other styles that you use frequently. Remember, AutoCAD files with the `.dwt` filename extension in their name are just AutoCAD DWG files with a slightly different extension to set them apart as templates.

In this next exercise, you'll create a text style called Note1, which you'll use to add notes to the unit plan on which you've been working:

1. Click the Text Style drop-down list from the Home tab's expanded Annotation panel and select Manage Text Styles, or type **St⏎**. This opens the Text Style dialog box (see Figure 9.2).

FIGURE 9.2
The Text Style dialog box

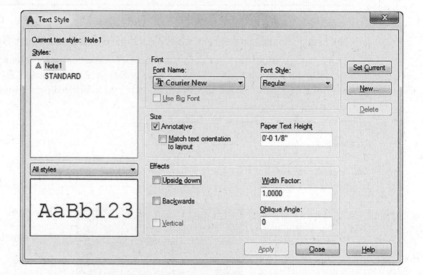

2. Click the New button to the right in the dialog box to open the New Text Style dialog box.

3. Enter **Note1** for the name of your new style, and then click OK.

4. In the Text Style dialog box again, click the Font Name drop-down list in the Font group and select a font for your style.

5. Locate the Courier New TrueType font and select it. A quick way to locate the font is to click in the list and start typing the font name.

6. Select the Annotative option in the Size group (see Figure 9.3).

FIGURE 9.3
The Annotative option in the Text Style dialog box

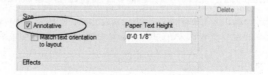

7. In the Paper Text Height box, enter **0.1**. You'll see your input change to 1/8" if you are using the architectural unit style. Metric users should enter **0.15**.

8. Close the dialog box.

The Annotative option you turned on in step 6 is an important feature for keeping your text at the proper size for your drawing scale. You'll see how it works in the exercises later in the section "Setting the Annotation Scale and Adding Text."

MAKING A STYLE THE DEFAULT

Once you've created a style, you can make it the default current style by selecting it from the Text Style drop-down list in the Annotate tab's Text panel.

Getting Familiar with the Text and Annotation Scale Control Panels

Before you go much further into the AutoCAD text features, take a moment to familiarize yourself with the Annotate tab's Text and Annotation Scaling panels (see Figure 9.4). You'll be using a few of these panel tools in this chapter. If you need to, you can refer to this figure as you work through the exercises.

FIGURE 9.4
The Text panel (left) and the Annotation Scaling panel (right)

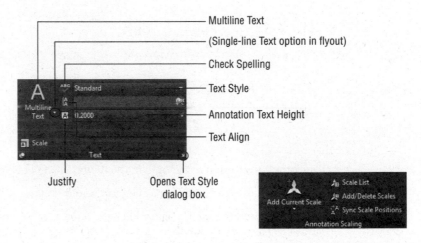

If your Annotation panel doesn't look like the one in this figure, hover over it and the panel will expand to display the options.

Setting the Annotation Scale and Adding Text

You've got a text style set up and ready to use. Now you'll add some text to your unit plan. Before you begin, you should determine a drawing scale. This is important because with the

Annotative feature turned on, AutoCAD needs to know the drawing scale in order to set the size of the text. Follow these steps:

1. In the right side of the status bar, click the drop-down arrow next to Annotation Scale.

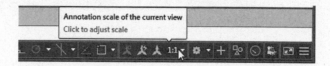

2. Select 1/4″ = 1′-0″. Metric users, select 1:100.

You've just set the drawing scale for the Model Space view. This isn't a permanent setting; you can change it at any time, as you'll see later. The settings you used for the annotation scale are somewhat arbitrary for the purposes of demonstrating the Annotative Scale feature.

Inserting Text

Finally, you can begin to add text. To start, you'll add some text to label the entrance to the floor plan. The process is similar to the process in other graphics programs that offer a text feature. You draw a boundary in the area where you want the text to appear, and then you start typing:

1. Turn off the Object Snap tool in the status bar.

2. Click the Multiline Text tool in the Annotate tab's Text panel. You can also type **MT**↵. You see a prompt that tells you the current text style and height.

```
Current text style: "Note1" Text height: 4 13/16"
Annotative: Yes
Specify first corner:
```

3. Click the first point indicated in the top image in Figure 9.1 to start the text boundary window. This boundary window indicates the area in which you'll place the text. Notice the arrow near the bottom of the window; it indicates the direction of the text flow. You don't have to be too precise about where you select the points for the boundary because you can adjust the location and size later.

4. At the `Specify opposite corner or [Height/Justify/Line spacing/Rotation/Style/Width/Columns]:` prompt, click the second point indicated in the top image in Figure 9.1. The Text Editor tab appears with the text editor superimposed over the area you just selected (see Figure 9.5).

5. Click the text editor and type **Entry**. As you type, the word appears in the text editor just as it will appear in your drawing.

6. Press ↵ to advance one line; then enter **6′ by 7′**.

7. Press ↵ to advance another line, and enter **[182 cm by 213 cm]**.

8. Press ↵ again to advance another line, and enter **carpet floor**.

FIGURE 9.5
The text editor floats over the selected area.

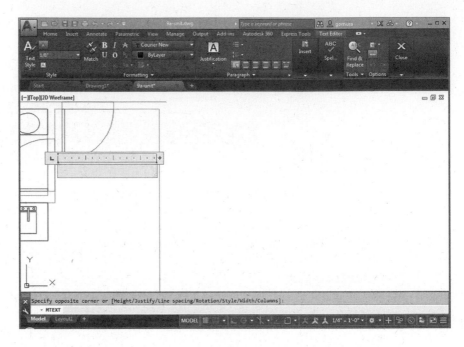

9. Click Close Text Editor on the Close panel. The text appears in the drawing just as it did in the text editor. (See the bottom image in Figure 9.1.)

After you've added text, if the text doesn't quite fit in the area you've indicated, you can make adjustments to the text boundary. Click the text to expose the text boundary, including the boundary grips. Then click and drag the grips to resize the boundary. The word-wrap feature automatically adjusts the text formatting to fit the text boundary.

You may have noticed that the Text Editor tab and text editor work like any text editor; if you make a typing error, you can highlight the error and retype the letter or word. You can perform other word processing functions too, such as using search and replace, importing text, and changing fonts.

You also saw that the text editor shows how your text will appear in the location you selected using the text boundary. If your view of the drawing is such that the text is too small to be legible, the text editor enlarges the text so that you can read it clearly. Likewise, if you're zoomed in too closely to see the entire text, the text editor adjusts the text to enable you to see all of it.

MAKING TEXT READABLE OVER HATCH PATTERNS

If text is included in a selection where a hatch pattern is to be placed, AutoCAD automatically avoids hatching over the text. If you add text over a hatched area, you can use the Background Mask tool in the Text Editor tab to make the text more readable. Another option is to use the Select Boundary Objects tool in the Hatch Edit tab to add text to a hatch selection.

Exploring Text and Scale

Even though your text height is 0.1′, or 0.15 cm, it appears at the appropriately enlarged size for the current scale. If the text were drawn to the size of 0.1′, it would be very small and barely visible. However, the Annotative Scale feature makes the adjustment to your text size based on the Annotation Scale setting.

You can see how the Annotation Scale setting affects your text:

1. First, make sure the Show Annotation Objects tool is turned on in the status bar, or type **Annoallvisible.⏎1⏎**.

2. Click the Annotation Scale setting, and select 1/2″ = 1′-0″. Metric users should select 1:50.

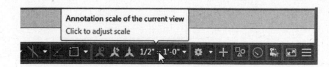

3. Click the Add/Delete Scales tool in the Annotate tab's Annotation Scaling panel, or enter **Objectscale⏎**.

4. At the `Select annotative objects:` prompt, select the text and press ⏎. You see the Annotation Object Scale dialog box (see Figure 9.6) listing the annotation scales that you have used for this drawing.

FIGURE 9.6

The Annotation Object Scale dialog box

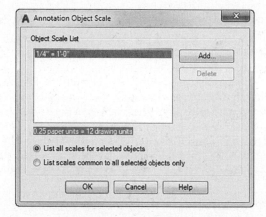

5. You can add additional scales to your text object. Click the Add button, which opens the Add Scales To Object dialog box (see Figure 9.7).

FIGURE 9.7

The Add Scales To Object dialog box

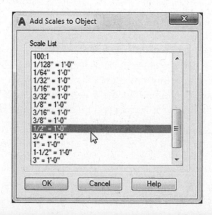

6. Select 1/2″ = 1′-0″ from the list (metric users should select 1:50) and click OK, and then click OK again in the Annotation Object Scale dialog box. The new text changes to the appropriate size for the selected scale.

Now test your settings by changing the Annotation Scale value back to the previous setting:

1. In the status bar, click the Annotation Scale setting and select 1/4″ = 1′-0″. Metric users should select 1:100.

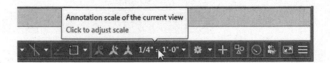

2. The text changes back to its original size.

In steps 2 through 4 of the first exercise in this section, you added a new annotation scale to the text. This is necessary for the text to be aware of the new annotation scale that you want to use. Each time you include a new scale for your drawing, you need to add an annotation scale to the text in your drawing.

If you prefer, you can turn on the Automatically Add Scales To Annotative Objects tool in the status bar, which does just what its name says. The keyboard command for this tool is **Annoautoscale.**↵↵. Once a scale is added, you can quickly change between scales by selecting a scale from the Annotation Scale list.

So far, you've used only a single multiline text object. However, if you have many notes distributed throughout a drawing, you'll need to add an annotation scale to all of them before they can automatically adjust themselves to the different scales that you'll use with your drawing. If you have the Automatically Add Scales To Annotative Objects tool turned on in the status bar, this happens automatically. Otherwise, you'll have to add the scales to each annotative object. This is easy to do because you have the option to select as many objects as you need when adding annotation scales.

TEXT AND SCALE IN LEGACY DRAWINGS

AutoCAD 2018 offers the Annotative Scale feature to automate the scaling of text and other objects to their proper size based on the drawing's annotation scale. However, there is a good chance you'll encounter drawings that were created before the Annotative Scale feature was available. For that reason, you should have a basic understanding of scale factors as they apply to text.

As you know by now, AutoCAD lets you draw at full scale—that is, you can represent distances as values equivalent to the actual size of the object. When you plot the drawing later, you tell AutoCAD the scale at which you want to plot and the program reduces the drawing accordingly. This gives you the freedom to enter measurements at full scale and not worry about converting them to various scales every time you enter a distance. Unfortunately, in earlier versions of AutoCAD this feature created problems when users entered text and dimensions. You had to make the text height very large in order for it to be readable when scaled down.

To illustrate this point, imagine that you're drawing the unit plan at full size on a very large sheet of paper. When you're finished with this drawing, it will be reduced to a scale that enables it to fit on an 8-1/2″ × 11″ sheet of paper. Thus you have to make your text large to keep it legible after it's reduced. If you want text to appear 1/8″ high when the drawing is plotted, you must convert it to a considerably larger size when you draw it. To do so, you multiply the desired height of the final plotted text by a scale conversion factor. (See Chapter 3, "Setting Up and Using the Drafting Tools," for more on scale conversion factors.)

For example, if your drawing is at a 1/8″ = 1′-0″ scale, you multiply the desired text height, 1/8″, by the scale conversion factor of 96 to get a height of 12″. This is the height you must make your text to get 1/8″-high text in the final plot.

With AutoCAD 2018, you don't have to work through the math to get the right text size for your drawing. But if you encounter a drawing that was created in an earlier version of AutoCAD and you notice that the text size is very large, you'll know why.

Understanding the Text Style Dialog Box Options

You've just taken nearly all the steps you'll need to know to add text to any drawing. Now let's take a step back and look more closely at some of the finer points of adding text, starting with text styles. The following sections give you more detailed information about the text style settings you saw in the early part of this chapter. They explain those settings and their purposes. Some of them, such as Width Factor, can be quite useful. Others, such as the Backwards and Vertical options, are rarely used. Take a moment to study these settings to become familiar with what is available and make a mental note of these items for future reference.

Styles

In the Styles list box, you'll see a list showing the current style. This list also contains other styles that may be present in the drawing. The drop-down list below the Styles list box lets you control whether all styles are listed or just those that are being used in the drawing. In addition, there are the Set Current, New, and Delete buttons and options in the Font and Effects groups. You have already seen the Size group.

Set Current/New/Delete

Set Current makes the selected style the current one. New lets you create a new text style. Delete lets you delete the selected style.

The Delete option isn't available for the Standard style.

Font

In the Font group, you have the following options:

Font Name   Lets you select a font from a list of available fonts. The list is derived from the font resources available to Windows 10, Windows 8, and Windows 7, plus the standard AutoCAD fonts.

Font Style   Offers variations of a font, such as italic or bold, when they're available.

Use Big Font   Applicable to Asian fonts. This option is offered only with AutoCAD fonts.

Size

The Size group offers settings relating to text size, scale, and orientation.

Annotative   Causes the text size to adjust automatically to the current annotation scale setting.

Match Text Orientation To Layout   Causes the text orientation to match the orientation of a layout view. This option is available only when the Annotative option is on.

Height/Paper Text Height   Lets you enter a font size. With the Annotative option turned off, this option is named *Height* and will set the absolute height of the text. With the Annotative option turned on, it shows *Paper Text Height* and will set the height of the text when printed. A 0 height has special meaning when you use the Text command to enter single-line text as described later in this chapter.

Effects

In the Effects group, you have the following options:

Upside Down   Displays text upside down.

Backwards   Displays text backward.

Vertical   Displays text in a vertical column (not available with TrueType fonts).

Width Factor   Adjusts the width and spacing of the characters in the text. A value of 1 keeps the text at its normal width. Values greater than 1 expand the text, and values less than 1 compress the text.

> This is the Simplex font expanded by 1.4
> This is the Simplex font using a width factor of 1
> This is the Simplex font compressed by .6

Oblique Angle   Skews the text at an angle. When this option is set to a value greater than 0, the text appears italicized. A value of less than 0 (–12, for example) causes the text to lean to the left.

> *This is the Simplex font*
> *using a 12–degree oblique angle*

You can also set the width factor and oblique angle directly for text using the Width Factor and Oblique Angle tools in the expanded Formatting panel under the Text Editor Ribbon panel. This tab is available when you create new text or double-click existing text.

RENAMING A TEXT STYLE OR OTHER NAMED OBJECT

If you need to rename a text style or other named object in AutoCAD, you can do so using the Rename command. Enter **Ren⏎** at the Command prompt to open the Rename dialog box. In the Named Objects list box to the left, choose Text Styles. Click the name of the style that you want to change from the Items list on the right; the name appears in the Old Name box below the list. In the box next to the Rename To button, enter the new name. Click the Rename To button, and click OK.

Exploring Text Formatting in AutoCAD

You've seen how you can set up a style and make scale adjustments. AutoCAD also offers a wide range of text-formatting options that are typical of the options in most word processing programs. You can control fonts, text height, justification, line spacing, and width. You can even include special characters such as degree symbols or stacked fractions. With these additional formatting tools, you can make adjustments to the text style with which you started.

Adjusting the Text Height and Font

To get some experience using the text-formatting tools in AutoCAD, try the following exercise. You'll use the Multiline Text tool again, but this time you'll get to try some of its other features.

In this exercise, you'll see how you can use the Ribbon tools to adjust the size and font of text:

1. Pan your view so that the kitchen is just at the top of the drawing, as shown in the first image in Figure 9.8.

FIGURE 9.8
Placing the text-boundary window for the living-room label and the final label

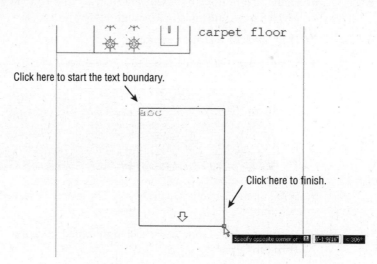

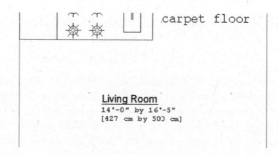

2. In the status bar, make sure that Annotation Scale is set to 1/4" = 1'-0" (1:100 for metric users).

3. Click the Multiline Text tool on the Annotate tab's Text panel, and then select a text boundary window, as shown in the first image in Figure 9.8.

4. In the text editor, type the following:

```
Living Room
14'-0" by 16'-5" [427 cm by 500 cm]
```

Be sure that you press ↵ after *Living Room*, but make the rest of the text a continuous string. As you type, the words wrap. AutoCAD uses word wrap to fit the text inside the text boundary area.

5. Highlight the text *14'-0" by 16'-5" [427 cm by 500 cm]* as you would in any word processor. For example, you can click the end of the line to place the cursor there and then Shift+click the beginning of the line to highlight the whole line.

6. In the Text Editor tab's Style panel, click in the Text Height text box and enter **1/16**↵. Metric users, enter **0.08**↵. The highlighted text changes to a smaller size.

7. Highlight the words *Living Room*.

8. In the Formatting panel, click the Font drop-down list to display a list of font options.

9. Scroll up the list until you find Arial. The text in the text editor changes to reflect the new font.

10. With the words *Living Room* still highlighted, click the Underline button in the Formatting panel.

11. Click Close Text Editor in the Close panel. The label appears in the area you indicated in step 3 (see the bottom image in Figure 9.8).

12. To see how you can go back to the Text Editor tab, double-click the text. The Text Editor tab and text editor appear, enabling you to change the text.

13. Click Close Text Editor in the Close panel.

While using the Multiline Text tool, you may have noticed the [Height/Justify/Line spacing/Rotation/Style/Width/Columns]: prompt immediately after you picked the first point of the text boundary. You can use any of these options to make on-the-fly modifications to the height, justification, line spacing, rotation style, or width of the multiline text.

For example, after clicking the first point for the text boundary, you can type **R**↵ and then specify a rotation angle for the text window, either graphically with a rubber-banding line or by entering an angle value. After you've entered a rotation angle, you can resume selecting the text boundary.

Understanding the Text Editor Tab

You've just experimented with a few of the Text Formatting features of the Text Editor tab. A variety of additional formatting tools are available. Figure 9.9 shows where these tools are, and Table 9.1 describes their uses. Note that Figure 9.9 shows the Ribbon with the AutoCAD window at a 1024-pixel width. The Style panel will display the text styles as a list in large displays. These Ribbon tools are fairly straightforward, and if you've used other word processing programs, you should find them easy to use. Most are common to the majority of word processors, although a few—such as Symbol, Oblique Angle, and Width Factor—are unique to AutoCAD. Look at Table 9.1 and see if there are any tools that you think you'll find useful.

FIGURE 9.9
Additional features of the Text Editor tab

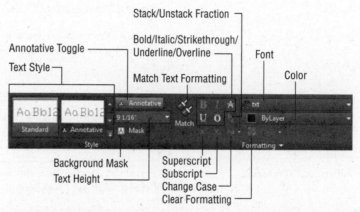

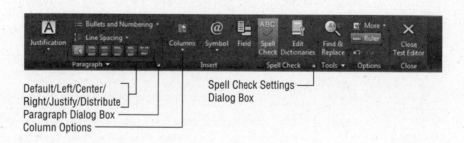

TABLE 9.1: Text formatting tools

TOOL	USE
Text Style (appears when the AutoCAD window is 1024 pixels wide or smaller)	Select a text style.
Annotative Toggle	Turn the Annotative feature on or off.
Text Height	Set the paper text height of text currently being entered or edited.
Stack/Unstack Fraction	Change fractions to stacked or unstacked.

TABLE 9.1:   Text formatting tools   *(CONTINUED)*

TOOL	USE
Bold/ Italic/ Strikethrough/ Underline/Overline	Select text, and then select one of these options to add bold, italic, underline, overline, or strikethrough to the text.
Match Text Formatting	Select text with desired formatting, click Match, and then select text to change format.
Color	Select text, and then choose a color from this drop-down list.
Font	Select a font different from the font for the current text style.
Background Mask	Control the background mask feature, which places a background behind text to make it more readable when placed over hatch patterns.
Change Case	Change the case of text.
Line Spacing	Set the line spacing in paragraphs. You can also set line spacing in the Properties palette for an Mtext object or by using the Paragraph dialog box. (See "Setting Indents and Tabs" later in this chapter.)
Bullets And Numbering	Select a text list, click this tool, and then select Lettered, Numbered, or Bulleted to add letters, numbers, or bullets to the list.
Default/Left/Center/Right/ Justify/Distribute	Click the appropriate tool to align the text to the left, center, or right side of the text boundary. Justify adds space between words to force left and right alignment. Distribute adds space between letters to force left and right alignment.
Paragraph Dialog Box	Open a dialog box that lets you set up paragraph formatting, including tabs, indents, and paragraph spacing.
Columns	Indicate the number of columns and how the columns are set up.
Symbol	Place the cursor at a location for the symbol, and then click the Symbol tool to find and add a symbol. (See Figure 9.10 later in this chapter for the available symbols.)
Field	Click to open the Field dialog box, where you can add a text field. See "Adding Formulas to Cells" in Chapter 10, "Using Fields and Tables," for more about fields.
More	Use Character Set to insert foreign language characters, such as Cyrillic or Greek. Use Editor Settings to choose settings for the text editor.
Ruler	Click to turn the ruler at the top of the Text panel on or off.

Adding Symbols and Special Characters

The Text Editor tab also offers a tool called Symbol. This tool lets you add special symbols common to technical drawing and drafting. Figure 9.10 shows the symbols that are offered in the Symbol tool in the form of a drop-down list.

FIGURE 9.10
The AutoCAD symbols

Degrees	$x°$	Identity	≡
Plus/Minus	±	Initial Length	⌒
Diameter	⌀	Monument Line	ℳ
Almost Equal	≈	Not Equal	≠
Angle	∠	Ohm	Ω
Boundary Line	ℬℒ	Omega	Ω
Center Line	℄	Property Line	ℙ
Delta	Δ	Subscript 2	x_2
Electrical Phase	Φ	Squared	x^2
Flow Line	ℱℒ	Cubed	x^3

At the bottom of the Symbol drop-down list is an option called Other. By clicking the Other option, you open the Windows Character Map dialog box (see Figure 9.11). Characters such as the trademark (™) and copyright (©) symbols are often available in the fonts offered in the Character Map. The contents of the Character Map depend on the font currently selected.

FIGURE 9.11
The Character Map

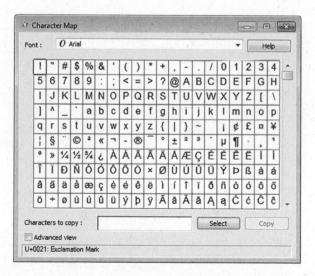

The Character Map is a Windows accessory. If it doesn't appear when you choose Other from the Symbol tool menu, you may need to install the Character Map from your Windows installation DVD.

Finally, if your application requires music, math, astronomy, Greek, or other symbols, AutoCAD offers a set of fonts with special symbols. Figure 9.17, later in this chapter, shows these fonts and the symbols that they contain. You can set up text styles with these fonts or call them up directly from the Formatting panel's Font option.

ADDING A FRAME AROUND TEXT

If you need to place a rectangular frame around text, you can draw a rectangle to enclose the text. However, if the text is edited, the box must be adjusted to fit the changes in the text size. To make life a little easier, AutoCAD offers a text property that will draw a frame that automatically adjusts to the size of the text whenever it is edited.

To add a frame to text, select the text and then right-click and select Properties from the context menu. Scroll down the list of properties until you find the Text frame option. Select Yes from the Text frame option drop-down list.

TEXT JUSTIFICATION AND OSNAPS

Certification Objective

You may have noticed that the object-justification list offers three center options: Top Center, Middle Center, and Bottom Center. All three of these options have the same effect on the text's appearance, but they each have a different effect on how osnaps act on the text. Figure 9.12 shows where the osnap point occurs on a text boundary depending on which justification option is selected. A multiline text object has only one insertion point on its boundary, which you can access with the Insert osnap.

FIGURE 9.12
The location of the Insert osnap point on a text boundary, based on its justification setting

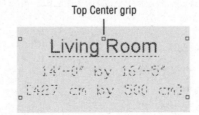

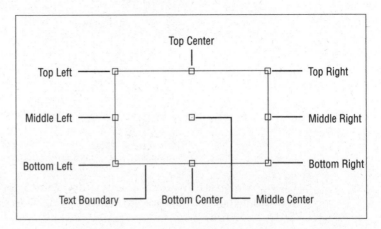

The osnap point also appears as an extra grip point on the text boundary when you click the text. If you were to center-justify the text that you just entered, you would see that a grip point appears at the top center of the text boundary.

Knowing where the osnap points occur can be helpful when you want to align the text with other objects in your drawing. In most cases, you can use the grips to align your text boundary, but the Top Center and Middle Center justification options enable you to use the center and middle portions of your text to align the text with other objects.

CHANGING JUSTIFICATION OF MULTIPLE TEXT OBJECTS

You've seen how you can change the justification of an individual text object, but you'll often find that you need to change the justification of several text objects at one time. AutoCAD offers the Justifytext command for this purpose. To use it, click the Justify tool in the Annotate tab's Text panel, or type **Justifytext↵** at the Command prompt. At the Select objects: prompt, select the text that you want to change and then press ↵ to confirm your selection. You'll see the following prompt in the command line (or at the cursor if Dynamic Input is on):

```
[Left/Align/Fit/Center/Middle/Right/TL/TC/TR/ML/MC/MR/BL/BC/BR] <Left>:
```

Enter the letters corresponding to the type of justification that you want to use for the text. (See the section "Justifying Single-Line Text Objects" later in this chapter for a description of these options.) After you enter an option, the selected text changes to conform to the selected justification option.

Setting Indents and Tabs

You should also know about the indent and tab features of the text editor. You may have noticed the ruler at the top of the text editor. Figure 9.13 shows that ruler, including tabs and indent markers.

FIGURE 9.13
The ruler at the top of the text editor lets you quickly set tabs and indents for text.

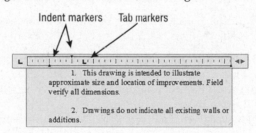

The indent markers let you control the indention of the first line and the rest of the paragraph. The tab markers give you control over tab spacing. For new text, the tab markers don't appear until you add them by clicking the ruler. The following exercises will demonstrate the use of these markers.

Start by practicing with the indent markers:

1. Save the unit drawing, and then open the indent.dwg file. This file contains some text with which you'll experiment.

2. Double-click the text at the top of the drawing to open the Text Editor tab.

3. Press Ctrl+A to highlight all the text in the text editor. This is necessary to indicate the text group to be affected by your indent settings.

4. Click and drag the top indent marker two spaces to the right. The indent of the first line moves with the marker. A note appears above the ruler showing you how much indent you're applying. Also notice that the text at the first tab remains at its starting location.

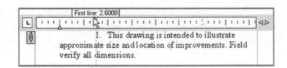

5. Click and drag the bottom indent marker two spaces to the left. The rest of the paragraph moves with the marker. Again, you see a note by the ruler showing how much indent you're applying.

6. Click the Close Text Editor tool in the Text Editor tab to exit.

Here you see how you can control the indents of the selected text with the indent markers. You can set paragraphs of a single Mtext object differently, giving you a wide range of indent-formatting possibilities. Just select the text you want to set, and then adjust the indent markers.

Now try the tab markers. For this exercise, you'll try the text-import feature to import a tab-delimited text file:

1. Click the Multiline Text tool on the Annotate tab's Text panel.

2. For the first corner of the text boundary, click the upper-left corner of the large rectangle in the drawing, just below the paragraph.

3. For the opposite corner of the text boundary, click the lower-right corner of the rectangle.

4. Right-click in the text editor, and select Import Text.

5. In the Select File dialog box, locate and select the `tabtest.txt` file and then click Open. The contents of the `tabtest.txt` file are displayed in the text editor.

The file you just imported was generated from the Attribute Extraction Wizard in AutoCAD. You'll learn more about this feature in Chapter 12, "Using Attributes." This file contains tabs to align the columns of information. You can adjust those tabs in the Text Formatting toolbar, as you'll see in the next set of steps.

Now use the tab markers to adjust the tab spacing of the columns of text:

1. Press Ctrl+A to select all the text.

2. Click the ruler at a point that is at the 12th mark from the left (that's three of the taller tick marks in the ruler). An L-shaped marker appears, and the first tab column of text moves to this position.

3. Click the ruler again at the 20th mark. The second tab column aligns to this position.

4. Continue to click the ruler to add more tab markers so that the text looks similar to Figure 9.14. Don't worry about being exact; this is just for practice. After you've placed a marker, you can click and drag it to make adjustments.

FIGURE 9.14
Add tab markers so that your text looks similar to this figure.

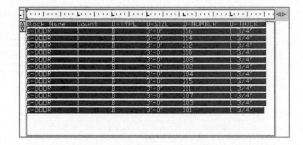

5. Click Close Text Editor in the Text Editor tab's Close panel. The text appears in the drawing as a door schedule.

Here you saw how you can create a table or a schedule from an imported text file. You can also create a schedule from scratch by composing it directly in the text editor of the Multiline Text command. AutoCAD also offers the Table feature, which is specifically designed for creating tables (see Chapter 10). Still, the previous example offers a way to demonstrate the tab feature in the Multiline Text tool, and you may encounter a file in which a table is formatted in the way described here.

In addition to using the indent and tab markers on the ruler, you can control indents and tabs through the Paragraph dialog box. Do the following to get a firsthand look:

1. Double-click the text at the top of the indent.dwg drawing (the one you edited in the first part of this section), and then press Ctrl+A to select all the text.

2. Right-click the ruler above the text editor, and select Paragraph to open the Paragraph dialog box (see Figure 9.15). The Paragraph dialog box also lets you set other paragraph settings, such as alignment, spacing between paragraphs, and line spacing in the paragraph.

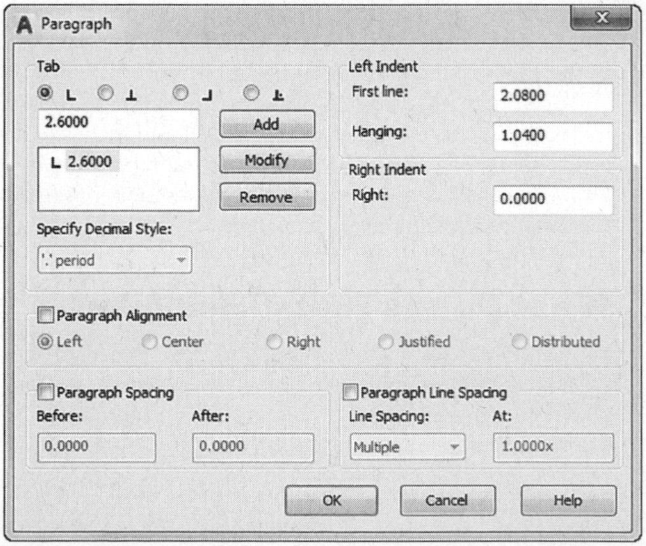

FIGURE 9.15
The Paragraph dialog box

3. Change the value in the First Line box to **1.5** and the Hanging box to **2.2**.

4. Double-click the tab position box in the upper-left corner, just below the row of tab symbols in the Tab group. Enter **2.2**, and click the Add button.

5. Click OK. The text now appears indented from the numbers.

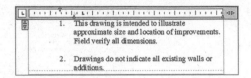

6. Click the Close Text Editor tool in the Close panel. The text in the drawing is now formatted as it appeared in the text editor.

7. Close but do not save the `indent.dwg` file.

In this exercise, you used the Paragraph dialog box to set the paragraph indent and the first tab marker to be the same value. This causes the text portion of the list to be aligned at a distance of 2.2 drawing units from the left text boundary, leaving the list number extended farther to the left. This gives the list a more professional appearance.

SETTING EXACT MTEXT WIDTH AND HEIGHT

You may have noticed the options Set Mtext Width and Set Mtext Height in the right-click context menu in step 2 of the exercise using the Paragraph dialog box. The Set Mtext Width option opens a dialog box that enables you to enter a width for paragraph columns where there are multiple columns. Set Mtext Height allows you to enter an exact height for columns.

The Paragraph dialog box gives you fine control over the formatting of your text. It lets you delete tabs by highlighting them in the list and clicking the Remove button. You can also add tabs at specific distances from the left margin of the text boundary by entering new tab locations in the Tab box and clicking the Add button.

You specify distances in drawing units. If your drawing is set up to use architectural units, for example, you can enter values in feet and inches or just inches. In the First Line and Hanging boxes, you enter a numeric value for paragraph indents. As you've just seen, you can use the First Line and Hanging boxes to create a numbered list by setting the Hanging box value to be the same as the first tab stop position.

What Do the Fonts Look Like?

You've already seen a few of the fonts available in AutoCAD. Chances are that you're familiar with the TrueType fonts available in Windows. You have some additional AutoCAD fonts from which to choose. You may want to stick with the AutoCAD fonts for all but your presentation drawings because other fonts can consume more memory.

IMPORTING TEXT FILES

With multiline text objects, AutoCAD enables you to import ASCII text (TXT) or Rich Text Format (RTF) files. RTF files can be exported from Microsoft Word and most other word processing programs, and they retain most of their formatting in AutoCAD. Here's how you import text files:

1. With the Multiline Text tool open, right-click in the text area and choose Import Text.

2. In the Select File dialog box, locate a valid text file. It must be a file in either a raw text (ASCII) format, such as a Notepad file (with the filename extension .txt), or RTF (with the filename extension .rtf). RTF files can store formatting information such as boldface and varying point sizes.

3. After you've highlighted the file you want, double-click it or click Open. The text appears in the text editor window.

4. Click the Close Text Editor button, and the text appears in your drawing.

You can use the Windows Clipboard and the Cut and Paste functions to add text to a drawing. To do this, follow these steps:

1. Select some text and then choose Cut or Copy in any Windows program to place the text on the Windows Clipboard.

2. Open AutoCAD. Right-click in the drawing area, and choose Clipboard ➤ Paste. Click a point in the drawing to place the text; the pasted text appears in your drawing. However, it isn't editable in AutoCAD. You can adjust the size of the text using grips.

Additionally, you may drag and drop TXT and RTF files directly from Windows File Explorer into AutoCAD with the same results.

If the text is from a text editor like Windows Notepad, it is inserted as AutoCAD text. If the text contains formatting from a word processor, like Microsoft Word, the text is an OLE object.

Because AutoCAD is an OLE client, you can also attach other types of documents to an AutoCAD drawing file. See Chapter 19, "Getting and Exchanging Data from Drawings," for more on OLE support in AutoCAD.

Figure 9.16 shows the basic AutoCAD text fonts. The Romans font is perhaps the most widely used because it offers a reasonable appearance while consuming little memory. Figure 9.17 lists some of the symbols and Greek fonts.

FIGURE 9.16

Some of the standard AutoCAD text fonts

This is Txt
This is Monotxt
This is Simplex   (Old version of Roman Simplex)
This is Complex   (Old version of Roman Complex)
This is Italic   (Old version of Italic Complex)
This is Romans   (Roman Simplex)
This is Romand   (Roman double stroke)
This is Romanc   (Roman Complex)
This is Romant   (Roman triple stroke)
This is Scripts   (Script Simplex)
This is Scriptc   (Script Complex)
This is Italicc   (Italic Complex)
This is Italict   (Italic triple stroke)
Τηισ ισ Γρεεκσ   (This is Greeks - Greek Simplex)
Τηισ ισ Γρεεκχ   (This is Greekc - Greek Complex)
This is Gothice   (Gothic English)
This is Gothicg   (Gothic German)
This is Gothici   (Gothic Italian)

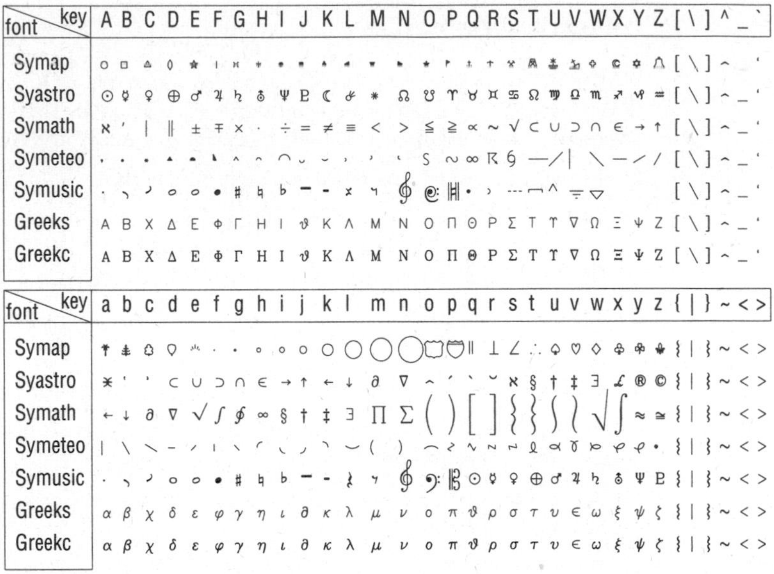

FIGURE 9.17
Some of the AutoCAD symbols and Greek fonts

In the following sections, you'll work with some of the AutoCAD fonts. You can see samples of all the fonts, including TrueType fonts, in the preview window of the Text Style dialog box. If you use a word processor, you're probably familiar with at least some of the TrueType fonts available in Windows and AutoCAD.

THE *TEXTFILL* SYSTEM VARIABLE

Unlike the standard sticklike AutoCAD fonts, TrueType and PostScript fonts have filled areas. These filled areas take more time to generate, so if you use these fonts for a lot of text, your redraw and regen times will increase. To help reduce redraw and regen times, you can set AutoCAD to display and plot these fonts as outline fonts while still printing them as solid fonts.

To change this setting, type **Textfill**↵ and then type **0**↵. Doing so turns off text fill for PostScript and TrueType fonts.

Adding Simple Single-Line Text Objects

Certification Objective

You might find that you're entering a lot of single words or simple labels that don't require all the bells and whistles of the multiline text editor. AutoCAD offers the *single-line text object*, which is simpler to use and can speed text entry if you're adding only small pieces of text.

Continue the tutorial on the Unit.dwg or 9b-unit.dwg sample file by trying the following exercise:

1. Adjust your view so that you see the part of the drawing shown in Figure 9.18.

2. Make sure that Note1 is the current text style, and then, from the Multiline Text flyout on the Annotate tab's Text panel, click the Single Line tool, or enter **Dt**↵.

3. At the `Specify start point of text or [Justify/Style]:` prompt, pick the starting point for the text that you're about to enter, just below the kitchen at coordinate 17'-2",22'-5" (490,664 for metric users). Note that the prompt offers the Justify and Style options.

4. At the `Specify rotation angle of text <0>:` prompt, press ⏎ to accept the default, 0. You can specify any angle that you like at this prompt (for example, if you want your text aligned with a rotated object). You see a text I-beam cursor at the point that you picked in step 3.

5. Type **Kitchenette**. As you type, the word appears directly in the drawing.

PASTING TEXT FROM OTHER SOURCES

You can paste text from the Clipboard into the cursor location by using the Ctrl+V keyboard shortcut or by right-clicking in the drawing area to access the context menu.

---

6. This time, you want to label the bathroom. Pick a point to the right of the door swing; you can approximate the location since you can always adjust the text location later. The text cursor moves to that point.

7. Type **Bathroom**⏎. Figure 9.18 shows how your drawing should look now.

FIGURE 9.18
Adding simple labels to the kitchen and bath by using the Text command

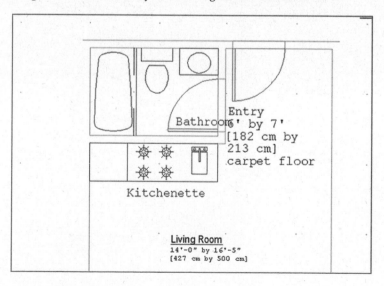

8. Press ⏎ again to exit the Text command.

> **CONTINUING WHERE YOU LEFT OFF**
>
> If for some reason you need to stop entering single-line text objects to do something else in AutoCAD, you can continue the text where you left off by starting the Text command and then pressing ↵ at the Specify start point of text or [Justify/Style]: prompt. The text continues immediately below the last line of text entered.

Here you were able to add two single lines of text in different parts of your drawing fairly quickly. Text uses the current default text style settings. If you want to create a column of single-line text, you can press ↵ to move the cursor down to start a new line below the one you just entered.

To edit single-line text, you can double-click the text. The text is highlighted, and you can begin typing to replace it all, or you can click a location in the text to make single word or character changes.

This is the end of the tutorial section of this chapter. The rest of this chapter offers additional information about text. You can close the Unit.dwg file.

Justifying Single-Line Text Objects

Certification
Objective

Justifying single-line text objects is slightly different than justifying multiline text. For example, if you change the justification setting to Center, the text moves so that the center is placed at the text-insertion point. In other words, the insertion point stays in place while the text location adjusts to the new justification setting. Figure 9.19 shows the relationship between single-line text and the insertion point based on different justification settings.

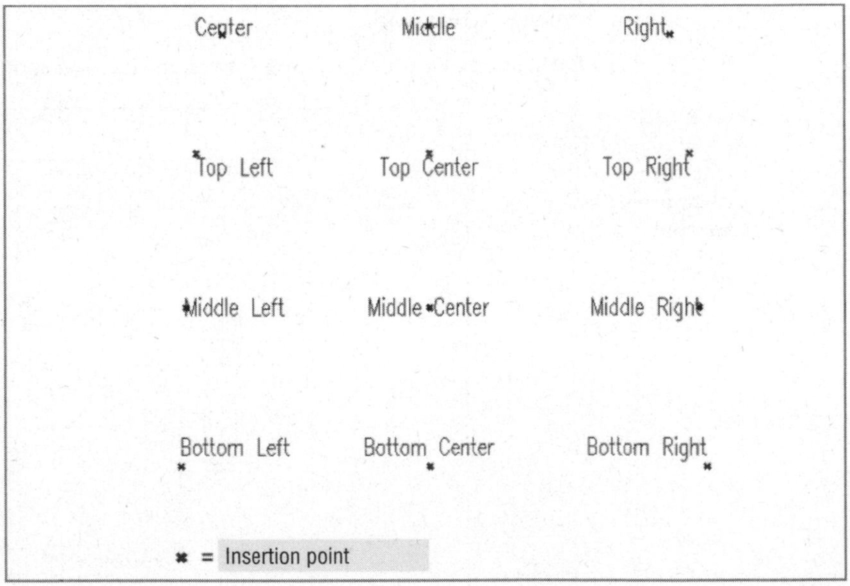

FIGURE 9.19
Text inserted using the various justification options

Center   Middle   Right

Top Left   Top Center   Top Right

Middle Left   Middle Center   Middle Right

Bottom Left   Bottom Center   Bottom Right

✳ = Insertion point

To set the justification of text as you enter it, you must enter **J**↵ at the `Specify start point of text or [Justify/Style]:` prompt after issuing the Text command. You can also change the current default style by entering **S**↵ and then the name of the style at the `Specify start point of text or [Justify/Style]:` prompt.

After you've issued Text's Justify option, you get the following prompt:

```
Enter an option
[Left/Center/Right/Align/Middle/Fit/TL/TC/TR/ML/MC/MR/BL/BC/BR]:
```

Here are descriptions of each of these options. (We've left Fit and Align until last because they require more explanation.)

Left   This justifies the text on the start point with the baseline on the start point.

Center   This centers the text on the start point with the baseline on the start point.

Right   This justifies the text to the right of the start point with the baseline on the start point.

Middle   This centers the text on the start point with the baseline slightly below the start point.

TL, TC, and TR   TL, TC, and TR stand for Top Left, Top Center, and Top Right. When you use these justification styles, the text appears entirely below the start point, justified left, center, or right, depending on which option you choose.

ML, MC, and MR   ML, MC, and MR stand for Middle Left, Middle Center, and Middle Right. These styles are similar to TL, TC, and TR, except that the start point determines a location midway between the baseline and the top of the lowercase letters of the text.

BL, BC, and BR   BL, BC, and BR stand for Bottom Left, Bottom Center, and Bottom Right. These styles too are similar to TL, TC, and TR, but here the start point determines the bottommost location of the letters of the text (the bottom of letters that have descenders, such as *p*, *q*, and *g*).

Align and Fit   With the Align and Fit justification options, you must specify a dimension in which the text is to fit. For example, suppose that you want the word *Refrigerator* to fit in the 26"-wide box representing the refrigerator. You can use either the Fit or the Align option to accomplish this. With Fit, AutoCAD prompts you to select start and end points and then stretches or compresses the letters to fit within the two points you specify. You use this option when the text must be a consistent height throughout the drawing and you don't care about distorting the font. Align works like Fit, but instead of maintaining the current text style height, the Align option adjusts the text height to keep it proportional to the text width without distorting the font. Use this option when it's important to maintain the font's shape and proportion. Figure 9.20 demonstrates how Fit and Align work.

A Justify   You can change the justification of single-line text by using the Properties palette, but the text moves from its original location while maintaining its insertion point. If you want to change the justification of text without moving the text, you can use the Justifytext command. Click the Justify tool in the Annotate tab's Text panel, or type **Justifytext** at the Command prompt and then select the text that you want to change. Justifytext works on both multiline and single-line text.

FIGURE 9.20
The word *Refrigerator* as it appears normally and with the Fit and Align options selected

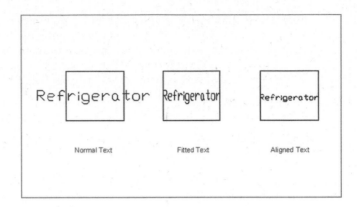

Using Special Characters with Single-Line Text Objects

Just as with multiline text, you can add a limited set of special characters to single-line text objects. For example, you can place the degree symbol (°) after a number, or you can *underscore* (underline) text. To accomplish this, you use double percent signs (%%) in conjunction with a special code. For example, to underscore text, you enclose that text with %% followed by the letter *u*, which is the underscore code. So to create the text "This is underscored text," you enter the following at the prompt:

```
This is %%uunderscored%%u text.
```

Overscoring (putting a line above the text) operates in the same manner. To insert codes for symbols, you place the codes in the correct positions for the symbols they represent. For example, to enter 100.5°, you type **100.5%%d**. Table 9.2 shows some other examples of special character codes.

TABLE 9.2:   Special character codes

CODE	WHAT IT DOES
%%o	Toggles overscore on and off.
%%u	Toggles underscore on and off.
%%c	Places a diameter symbol where the code occurs.
%%d	Places a degree sign (°) where the code occurs.
%%p	Places a plus/minus sign where the code occurs.
%%%	Forces a single percent sign. This is useful when you want a percent sign in conjunction with another code.
%%*nnn*	Allows the use of extended characters or Unicode characters when these characters are available for a given font. *nnn* is the three-digit value representing the ASCII extended character code.

KEEPING TEXT FROM MIRRORING

At times, you'll want to mirror a group of objects that contain some text. This operation causes the mirrored text to appear backward. You can change a setting in AutoCAD to make the text read normally even when it's mirrored:

1. At the Command prompt, enter **Mirrtext**↵.

2. At the Enter new value for MIRRTEXT <1>: prompt, enter **0**↵.

Now any mirrored text that isn't in a block will read normally. The text's position, however, will still be mirrored, as shown in the following example. Mirrtext is set to 0 by default.

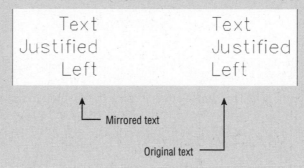

Using the Character Map Dialog Box to Add Special Characters

You can add special characters to a single line of text in the same way that you add special characters to multiline text. You may recall that to access special characters, you use the Character Map dialog box.

To open the Character Map dialog box, choose Start ➤ All Programs ➤ Accessories ➤ System Tools ➤ Character Map. You can then use the procedure discussed in the section "Adding Symbols and Special Characters" earlier in this chapter to cut and paste a character from the Character Map dialog box. If you use the Character Map dialog box often, create a shortcut for it and place the shortcut in your Start menu or on your Desktop.

Using the Check Spelling Feature

Although AutoCAD is primarily a drawing program, you'll find that some of your drawings contain more text than graphics, and so AutoCAD does include a spell-checking tool. If you've ever used the spelling checker in a typical word processor, such as Microsoft Word, the operation in AutoCAD will be familiar to you.

How Check Spelling Works

The hardest part to using the Check Spelling tool is locating it in the Ribbon. Try the following to see how it works:

1. Click the Check Spelling tool in the Annotate tab's Text panel. You can also type **Sp**↵. The Check Spelling dialog box appears (see Figure 9.21).

FIGURE 9.21
The Check Spelling
dialog box

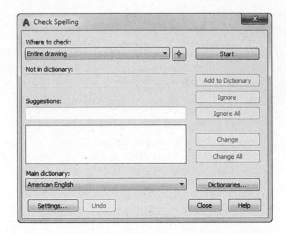

2. You can click the Start button to check the spelling in the entire drawing. Or, if you prefer, you can be more selective by choosing an option from the Where To Check drop-down list. You can select a mixture of multiline and single-line text as well as dimension text, attributes, and text in Xrefs.

When the spelling checker finds a word that it doesn't recognize, the Check Spelling dialog box shows you the word along with a suggested spelling. If the spelling checker finds more than one spelling, a list of suggested alternate words appears below the box. You can then highlight the desired replacement and click the Change button to change the misspelled word, or you can click Change All to change all occurrences of the word in the selected text. If the suggested word is inappropriate, choose another word from the replacement list (if any) or enter your own spelling in the Suggestions box. Then click Change or Change All.

Here is a list of the options available in the Check Spelling dialog box:

Add To Dictionary   Adds the word in question to the current dictionary.

Ignore   Skips the word.

Ignore All   Skips all occurrences of the word in the text being checked.

Change   Changes the word in question to the word you've selected from (or entered into) the Suggestions box.

Change All   Changes all occurrences of the current word when there are multiple instances of the misspelling.

Dictionaries   Lets you use a different dictionary to check spelling. This option opens the Dictionaries dialog box, described in the upcoming section.

The Check Spelling feature includes types of notations that are more likely to be found in technical drawings. It also checks the spelling of text that is included in block definitions, externally referenced files, and dimensions.

Choosing a Dictionary

Clicking the Dictionaries button in the Check Spelling dialog box opens the Dictionaries dialog box (see Figure 9.22), where you can select a main dictionary for foreign languages or create or choose a custom dictionary. The names of main dictionary files have the .dct extension. The main dictionary for the US version of AutoCAD is Enu.dct.

FIGURE 9.22

Choosing a dictionary

FIGURE 9.22

Choosing a dictionary

In the Dictionaries dialog box, you can also add or delete words from a custom dictionary. Custom dictionary files are ASCII files with names that end with the .cus extension. Because they're ASCII files, you can edit them outside AutoCAD. Click the Current Custom Dictionary drop-down list to view a list of existing custom dictionaries.

If you prefer, you can select a main or custom dictionary by using the Dctmain system variable. Click the Help button and then, in the Autodesk® Exchange window, select the Search tab. Enter **Dctmain** to learn more about the Dctmain system variable.

You can also select a dictionary from the Files tab of the Options dialog box (see Figure 9.23; choose Options from the Application menu). You can find the dictionary list under Text Editor, Dictionary, And Font File Names. Click the plus sign next to this item, and then click the plus sign next to the Main Dictionary item to display the dictionary options. From here, you can double-click the dictionary that you prefer.

FIGURE 9.23

Choosing a dictionary via the Options dialog box

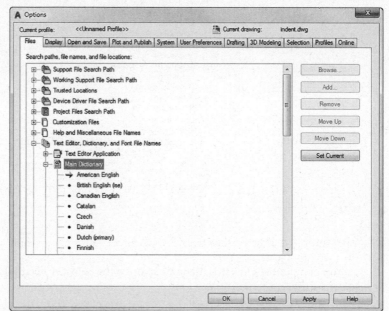

Substituting Fonts

At times, you'll want to change all the fonts in a drawing quickly. For instance, you might need to convert the font of a drawing received from another office to a font that conforms to your own office standards. The Fontmap system variable works in conjunction with a font-mapping table, enabling you to substitute fonts in a drawing easily.

The font-mapping table is an ASCII file called Acad.fmp, which is located in the C:\Users*User Name*\AppData\Roaming\Autodesk\AutoCAD 2018\R22.0\enu\Support folder. You can also use a file that you create yourself. You can give this file any name you choose, as long as it has the .fmp extension.

This font-mapping table contains one line for each font substitution that you want AutoCAD to make. A typical line in this file reads as follows:

```
romant; C:\Program Files\Autodesk\AutoCAD 2018\Fonts\txt.shx
```

In this example, AutoCAD is directed to use the txt.shx font in place of the romant.shx font. To execute this substitution, you type **Fontmap↵***Fontmap_filename***↵**.

Fontmap_filename is the font-mapping table that you created. This tells AutoCAD where to look for the font-mapping information. Then you issue the Regen command to view the font changes. To disable the font-mapping table, type **Fontmap↵**.

You can also specify a font-mapping file in the Files tab of the Options dialog box. Look for the Text Editor, Dictionary, And Font File Names listing. Click the plus sign next to this listing, and then click the plus sign next to the Font Mapping File listing to display the name and location of the current default font-mapping file. If you hold the cursor over the name, AutoCAD displays the full location of the file (see Figure 9.24).

FIGURE 9.24
AutoCAD shows
the full path to the
font-mapping file.

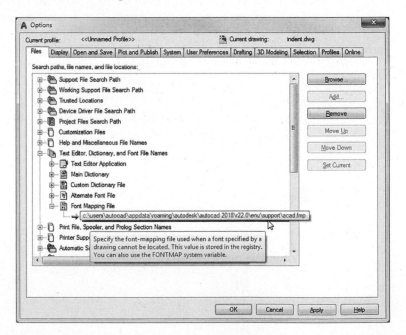

You can double-click this filename to open the Select A File dialog box. From there, you can select a different font-mapping file.

Finding and Replacing Text

One of the most time-consuming tasks in drafting is replacing text that appears repeatedly throughout a drawing. Fortunately, you have a Find And Replace tool to help simplify this task. Find And Replace in AutoCAD works like any other find-and-replace tool in a word processing program. A few options work specifically with AutoCAD. Here's how it works:

1. Enter the text that you want to locate in the Find Text box located in the middle of the Annotate tab's Text panel (see Figure 9.25), and then click the magnifying glass to the right. The Find And Replace dialog box opens, and the drawing area displays the part where the text has been found.

FIGURE 9.25
Using Find And Replace

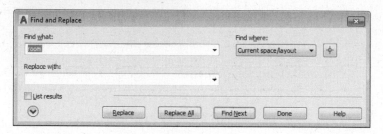

2. Enter the replacement text in the Replace With box.

3. When you've made certain that this is the text that you want to change, click Replace. If you want to replace all occurrences of the text in the drawing, click Replace All.

4. If you want to skip over the found text, click Find Next to locate the next instance of the text in your drawing. If the text is not found, AutoCAD returns to your original view.

You can also enter **Find**⏎ at the Command prompt to open the Find And Replace dialog box and then enter the text that you want in the Find What text box.

To limit your find-and-replace operation to a specific set of objects in your drawing, choose Selected Objects from the Find Where drop-down list. Once you've selected this option, click the Select Objects tool in the upper-right corner of the Find And Replace dialog box (see Figure 9.26).

FIGURE 9.26
The Select Objects tool

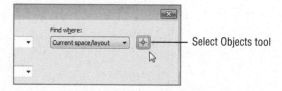

Select Objects tool

When you click the Select Objects tool, the Find And Replace dialog box closes temporarily to enable you to select a set of objects or a region of your drawing. Find And Replace then limits its search to those objects or the region you select.

MAKING SUBSTITUTIONS FOR MISSING FONTS

When text styles are created, the associated fonts don't become part of the drawing file. Instead, AutoCAD loads the needed font file at the same time the drawing is loaded. If a text style in a drawing requires a particular font, AutoCAD looks for the font in the AutoCAD search path; if the font is there, it's loaded. Usually this isn't a problem if the drawing file uses the standard fonts that come with AutoCAD or Windows. But occasionally, you'll encounter a file that uses a custom font.

In earlier versions of AutoCAD, you saw an error message when you attempted to open such a file. This missing-font message often sent new AutoCAD users into a panic.

Fortunately, now AutoCAD automatically substitutes an existing font for the missing font in a drawing. By default, AutoCAD substitutes the `simplex.shx` font, but you can specify another font by using the `Fontalt` system variable. Type **Fontalt.⏎** at the Command prompt, and then enter the name of the font that you want to use as the substitute.

You can also select an alternate font through the Files tab of the Options dialog box. Locate the Text Editor, Dictionary, And Font File Names listing, and then click the plus sign at the left. Locate the Alternate Font File item, and click the plus sign at the left. The current alternate is listed. You can double-click the font name to select a different font through the Alternate Font dialog box.

Be aware that the text in your drawing will change in appearance, sometimes radically, when you use a substitute font. If the text in the drawing must retain its appearance, substitute a font that is as similar in appearance to the original font as possible.

You can further control the types of objects that Find And Replace looks for by clicking the More Options tool in the lower-left corner of the Find And Replace dialog box. The dialog box expands to show more options (see Figure 9.27).

FIGURE 9.27
More extensive options for Find And Replace

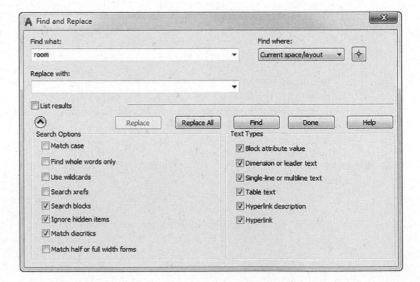

With this dialog box, you can refine your search by limiting it to blocks, dimension text, standard text, or hyperlink text. You can also specify whether to match the case and find whole words only.

SPEEDING UP AUTOCAD WITH QTEXT

If you need to edit a large drawing that contains a lot of text but you don't need to edit the text, you can use the Qtext command to help accelerate redraws and regenerations when you're working on the drawing. Qtext turns lines of text into rectangular boxes, saving AutoCAD from having to form every letter. This enables you to see the note locations so that you don't accidentally draw over them. To use it, enter **qtext**⏎ at the Command prompt and enter **On** or select the On option from the Dynamic Input display.

CREATE PARAGRAPH COLUMNS

You can format Mtext into multiple columns. This can be useful for long lists or to create a newspaper column appearance for your text. Text formatted into columns will automatically flow between columns as you add or remove text.

To format text into columns, do the following:

1. Create the text using the Mtext tool as usual.

2. Click and drag the corner resizer at the bottom-right corner of the text upward. As you do this, a second column appears.

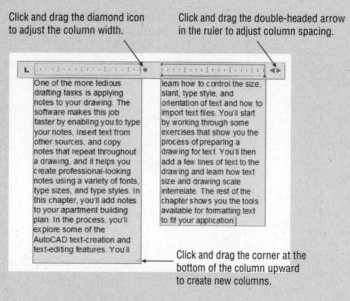

Click and drag the diamond icon to adjust the column width.

Click and drag the double-headed arrow in the ruler to adjust column spacing.

Click and drag the corner at the bottom of the column upward to create new columns.

3. If you want to create another column, click and drag the bottom edge of the rightmost column upward.

continues

continued

4. To adjust the column width, click and drag the diamond icon that appears just to the right of the first column in the ruler. All of the columns will adjust to the width of the first column.

Once you've set up your columns, click the Close Text Editor tool. You can adjust the column width and spacing by using grips that appear when you click the text.

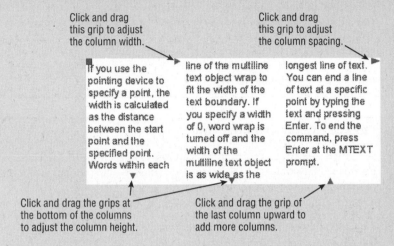

Click and drag this grip to adjust the column width.

Click and drag this grip to adjust the column spacing.

Click and drag the grips at the bottom of the columns to adjust the column height.

Click and drag the grip of the last column upward to add more columns.

To adjust the column width of existing Mtext, click and drag the arrow grip at the top and to the right of the first column. To adjust the width between columns (the column spacing), click and drag the arrow grip at the top and to the right of the last column. The grips at the bottom of each column allow you to adjust the height of the columns.

You can manually set column features through the Column Settings dialog box. To open it, double-click the Mtext and then choose Column Settings from the Columns flyout in the Text Editor tab's Insert panel.

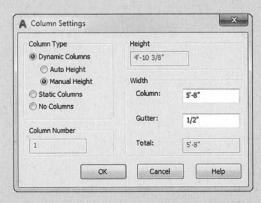

The Dynamic Columns option is the default for the Column Type group, and it allows you to adjust the column size using grips.

The Bottom Line

Prepare a drawing for text.   AutoCAD offers an extensive set of features for adding text to a drawing, but you need to do a little prep work before you dive in.

Master It   Name two things that you need to do to prepare a drawing for text.

Set the annotation scale and add text.   Before you start to add text, you should set the annotation scale for your drawing. Once this is done, you can begin to add text.

Master It   In a sentence or two, briefly describe the purpose of the annotation scale feature. Name the tool that you use to add text to a drawing.

Explore text formatting in AutoCAD.   Because text styles contain font and text-size settings, you can usually set up a text style and then begin to add text to your drawing. For those special cases where you need to vary the text height and font or other text features, you can use the Formatting panel of the Text Editor tab.

Master It   What text formatting tool can you use to change text to boldface type?

Add simple single-line text objects.   In many situations, you need only a single word or a short string of text. AutoCAD offers the single-line text object for these instances.

Master It   Describe the methods for starting the single-line text command.

Use the Check Spelling feature.   It isn't uncommon for a drawing to contain the equivalent of several pages of text, and the likelihood of having misspelled words can be high. AutoCAD offers the Check Spelling feature to help you keep your spelling under control.

Master It   What option do you select in the Check Spelling dialog box when it finds a misspelled word and you want to accept the suggestion it offers?

Find and replace text.   A common activity when editing technical drawings is finding and replacing a word throughout a drawing.

Master It   True or false: The Find And Replace feature in AutoCAD works very differently from the find-and-replace feature in other programs.

Chapter 10

Using Fields and Tables

Adding text to a set of drawings can become a large part of your work. You'll find that you're editing notes and labels almost as frequently as you're editing the graphics in your drawings. To make some of those editing tasks easier, the AutoCAD® 2018 software provides a few special text objects.

In this chapter, we'll look at fields and tables, two features that can help automate some of the most common tasks in AutoCAD.

Fields are a special type of text object that can automatically update to reflect changes in the drawing. The Table feature is a tool that helps automate the process of creating and editing tables and schedules. Tables are a common part of technical drawings and are similar to spreadsheets. In fact, AutoCAD tables behave much like spreadsheets, giving you the ability to add formulas to cells.

We'll start this chapter with an introduction to fields and then go on to explore tables. Toward the end, we'll revisit fields to see how they can be used to add formulas to tables.

In this chapter, you will learn to

- Use fields to associate text with drawing properties

- Add tables to your drawing

- Edit the table line work

- Add formulas to cells

- Import and export tables

- Create table styles

Using Fields to Associate Text with Drawing Properties

The text labels you worked with in Chapter 9, "Adding Text to Drawings," are static and don't change unless you edit them by using the tools described in that chapter. Another type of text object, called a *field*, behaves in a more dynamic way than the multiline text. A field can be linked to the properties of other objects so that it updates itself automatically as the associated properties change. For example, you can create a field that is associated with a block name. If the block name changes, the field text automatically changes as well.

Try the following exercise to see how this works:

1. Open the 10c-unit.dwg file. This file is similar to the drawing you worked on in Chapter 9.

2. Double-click the Kitchen text to highlight it and make it available for editing.

3. Right-click the highlighted Kitchen text, and then choose Insert Field to open the Field dialog box (see Figure 10.1). A list to the left shows the types of fields available. Don't worry if your dialog box looks different from Figure 10.1. The appearance will change in the following steps.

FIGURE 10.1
Choose the field you want to insert.

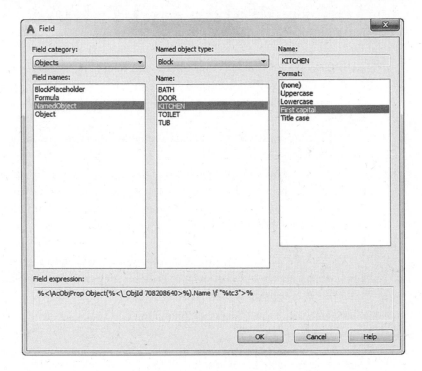

4. In the Field Category drop-down list, select Objects. This limits the display of field types to object fields.

5. In the Field Names list, select NamedObject.

6. Make sure that Block is selected in the Named Object Type drop-down list in the top of the dialog box, and then select KITCHEN from the Name list. This associates the field with the KITCHEN block name.

7. In the Format list to the far right, select First Capital. This causes the field text to be lowercase with a capital first letter (also referred to as sentence case), regardless of how the block name is spelled.

8. Click OK to exit the Field dialog box, and then press ↵ twice to return to the Command prompt.

When you return to the drawing, the text appears in a gray background. This tells you that the text is a field rather than an Mtext or text object. The gray background is a device to help you keep track of field text; it doesn't plot.

You've converted existing text into a field that is linked to a block name. Now let's see how the field works:

1. Enter **Rename**↵ at the Command prompt to open the Rename dialog box.

2. Make sure Blocks is selected in the Named Objects list, and then select KITCHEN from the Items list. The word *KITCHEN* appears in the Old Name box near the bottom of the dialog box.

3. Enter **Kitchenette** in the box just below the Old Name box, and then click the Rename To button.

4. Click OK to close the Rename dialog box.

5. Type **Re**↵. The field you created changes to reflect the new block name.

Fields can be associated with a wide variety of properties. You've just seen how a block name can be associated with a field. In this exercise, you'll use a field to display the area of an object:

1. Click Zoom Extents from the Zoom flyout on the Navigation bar or type **Z**↵**E**↵ to view the entire plan.

2. Use the Rectangle command to place a rectangle in the living room area, as shown in Figure 10.2.

FIGURE 10.2
Place a rectangle that fills the living room.

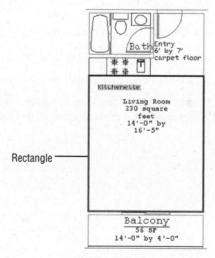

3. Double-click the Living Room text to open the Text Editor tab and the text editor.

4. Highlight the text that reads *230 square feet*. Right-click the selected text, and choose Insert Field from the context menu.

5. In the Field dialog box, select Object from the Field Names list.

6. Click the Select Object button next to the Object Type box at the top of the Field dialog box (see Figure 10.3). The Field dialog box momentarily closes to enable you to select an object.

FIGURE 10.3
Click the Select
Object button.

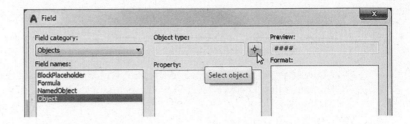

7. Select the rectangle that you just added. The Field dialog box returns.

8. In the Property list just below the Object Type box, select Area.

9. Select Architectural from the Format list to the far right (see Figure 10.4).

FIGURE 10.4
The Architectural
option in the
Format list

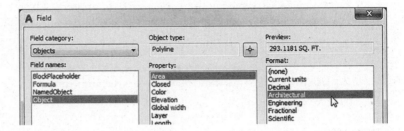

10. Click OK. The field you just added appears in the drawing as the area of the rectangle.

11. Click Close Text Editor in the Text Editor tab's Close panel.

Next, you'll alter the rectangle to see how it affects the field:

1. Click the rectangle to expose its grips (see Figure 10.5). Then select the top-middle grip of
the rectangle, and move it upward so that the top edge aligns with the bathroom wall.

FIGURE 10.5
Expose the grips.

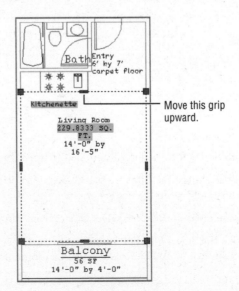

Move this grip
upward.

2. Type **Re**↲. The field that you just added updates to reflect the new area of the rectangle.

3. After reviewing the results, close 10c-unit.dwg without saving it.

In previous exercises, you changed existing text into fields. You can create new fields in either the Text or Mtext command by selecting Insert Field from the context menu whenever you're typing the text content.

In this exercise, you used a rectangle, but you can use any closed polyline to create an area field.

We've touched on just two of the many possible uses for fields. You can associate other types of properties, including the current layer, the drawing name, linetypes, and more. You can include DIESEL macros as part of fields. (You'll learn about DIESEL macros in Chapter 24, "Customizing Toolbars, Menus, Linetypes, and Hatch Patterns.") Fields can also be used in the Table feature (described in the next section), which enables you to create tables and schedules quickly. Fields are used to coordinate sheet labels with reference symbols in the AutoCAD Sheet Set feature described in Bonus Chapter 7, "Keeping a Project Organized with Sheet Sets," available at www.omura.com/chapters.

For most of your projects, the standard text objects will work just fine, but you may find fields useful when you know that a label has to be associated with specific types of data in your drawing. In later chapters, you'll have more opportunities to work with fields.

Adding Tables to Your Drawing

One of the most common text-related tasks that you'll do for your drawings is to create schedules, such as door and window schedules or parts schedules. Such schedules are tables used to provide detailed information about the elements in your design.

In the past, AutoCAD users used Mtext or Text to create the content of schedules and then used line-drawing tools to create the cells of the schedule. Since AutoCAD 2006, you have been able to use tables to help you generate schedules more quickly. Tables allow you to format the columns and rows of text automatically, similar to formatting in spreadsheet programs.

Creating a Table

The first step in creating a table is to determine the number of rows and columns you want. Don't worry if you aren't certain of the exact number of rows and columns; you can add or subtract them at any time. In this exercise, you'll create a table that contains 12 rows and 9 columns, as shown in Figure 10.6.

FIGURE 10.6
A sample table created with the Table tool

Number	Room	Finish				Ceiling Ht.	Area	Remarks
		Floor	Base	Wall	Ceiling			
110	Lobby	B	1	A	1	10'-0"	200sf	
111	Office	A	1	B	2	8'-0"	96sf	
112	Office	A	1	B	2	8'-0"	96sf	
113	Office	A	1	B	2	8'-0"	96sf	
114	Meeting	C	1	B	2	8'-0"	150sf	
115	Breakout	C	1	B	2	8'-0"	150sf	
116	Womens	D	2	C	3	8'-0"	50sf	
117	Mens	D	2	C	3	8'-0"	50sf	

Room Finish Schedule

Start by creating the basic table layout:

1. Click New on the Quick Access toolbar, and use the standard acad.dwt drawing template. You may also want to turn off the background grid to get a clear view of your work.

2. Click Table in the Home tab's Annotation panel to open the Insert Table dialog box (see Figure 10.7). You can also click the Table tool in the Annotate tab's Tables panel or type Tb↵.

FIGURE 10.7
The Insert Table dialog box

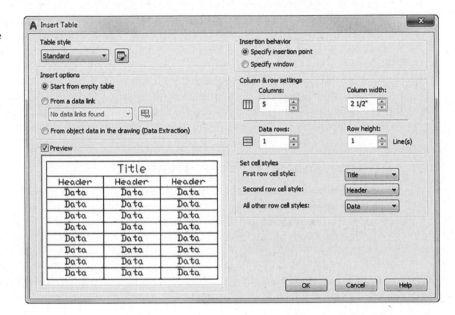

3. In the Column & Row Settings group, enter **9** for Columns and **12** for Data Rows.

4. Click OK. The dialog box closes, and the outline of a table follows your cursor.

5. Position the table in the center of your drawing area, and click to place it. The table appears with a cursor in the top cell. You also see the Text Editor tab in the Ribbon.

6. Enter **Room Finish Schedule**, and press ↵. The cursor moves to the next cell.

7. Click Close Text Editor in the Text Editor tab's Close panel.

Adding Cell Text

You've just created a table and added a title. Notice that the table actually contains 14 rows, including the title row at the top and an additional row for the headings of each column. You can delete these additional rows if you don't need them, but for now you'll start to add some text to the table:

1. Adjust your view so that the table fills most of the drawing area.

2. Double-click in the first cell at the top left, just below the Room Finish Schedule label (see Figure 10.8). The cell turns gray, and the Text Editor tab appears in the Ribbon. You also see labels across the top and left side showing the row and column addresses.

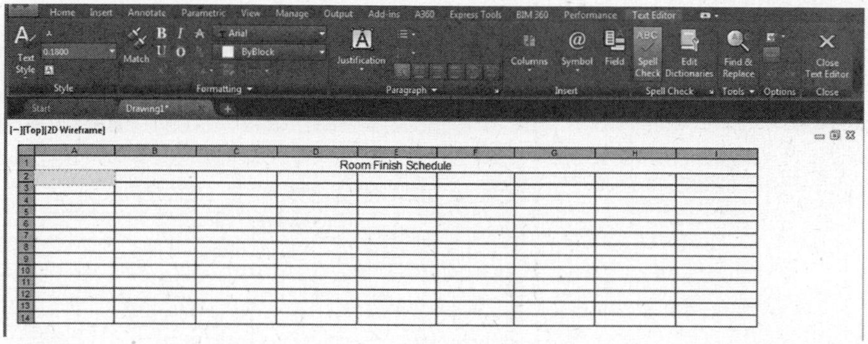

FIGURE 10.8
Double-click the first cell shown here.

3. Enter **Number** for the room number column at the far left, and then press the Tab key to advance to the next cell to the right.

4. Enter **Room**, and press the Tab key again.

5. Enter **Finish**, and press the Tab key four times to advance four columns. You do this because the Finish heading shown earlier in Figure 10.6 has four columns under it: Floor, Base, Wall, and Ceiling. In the next exercise, you'll learn how to format those four columns under the single heading.

6. Enter **Ceiling Ht.** and press the Tab key again.

7. Enter **Area**, press the Tab key, and enter **Remarks**.

8. Click Close Text Editor in the Text Editor tab's Close panel.

You have the column headings in place. Now you need to do a little extra formatting. In step 5, you left three cells blank because four of the columns will be combined under one heading: the Finish heading covers the Floor, Base, Wall, and Ceiling columns. Next, you'll combine the blank cells with the Finish heading:

1. Click in the center of the cell with the Finish label to select it.

2. Shift+click in the third cell to the right of the Finish cell to select all four cells (see Figure 10.9).

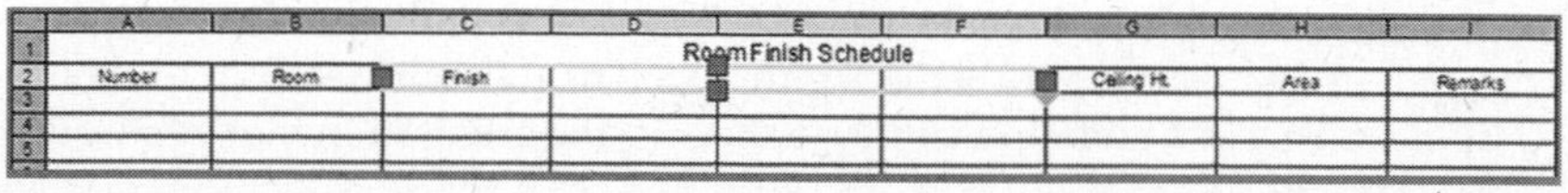

FIGURE 10.9
Select a group of four cells.

3. Right-click in the selected cells, and choose Merge ➢ All. The four selected cells merge into a single cell with the word *Finish*.

Now you need to add the subheads under the Finish header:

1. Double-click in the leftmost cell below the Finish cell. The Text Editor tab appears in the Ribbon (see Figure 10.10).

FIGURE 10.10
Double-click this cell and the Text Editor tab appears.

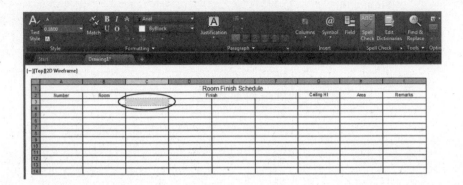

2. Enter **Floor**, and press the Tab key.

3. Enter **Base**, **Wall**, and **Ceiling** in each of the following columns as you've been doing. Remember that the Tab key advances you to the next cell to the right. Your table should look like Figure 10.11.

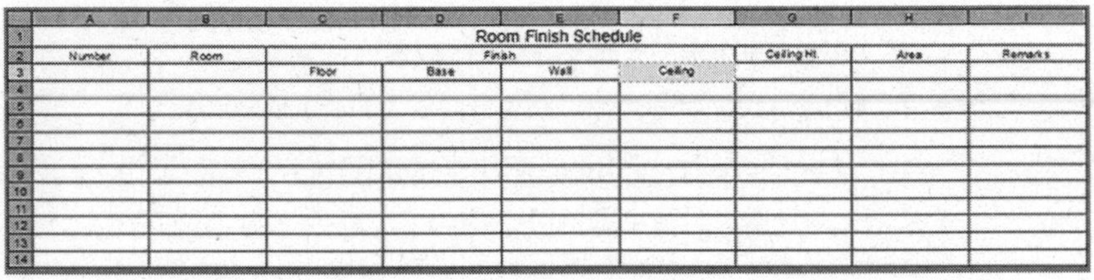

FIGURE 10.11
The table so far

4. Click Close Text Editor in the Text Editor tab's Close panel.

Adjusting Table Text Orientation and Location

You now have the basic layout of the table, with one difference: The Floor, Base, Wall, and Ceiling labels that you just added are oriented horizontally, but you want them oriented vertically, as shown earlier in Figure 10.6. The following steps will show you how to rotate a set of labels in a table so that they appear in the orientation that you want:

1. Click in the cell labeled Floor to select it. The Table Cell tab appears in the Ribbon.

2. Shift+click in the cell labeled Ceiling to select all four of the cells below the Finish heading. The combined cells have four grips, one on each side of the group.

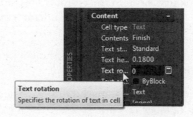

The table header showing:

A	B	C	D	E	F	G	H	I
				Room Finish Schedule				
Number	Room			Finish		Ceiling Ht.	Area	Remarks
		Floor	Base	Wall	Ceiling			

3. Click the grip at the bottom of the selected group, and move it down about four rows. At this point, the entire table will be highlighted, but you will affect only the cells you selected. Click to "fix" the row height in place. The entire row becomes taller. This provides room for the text when you rotate it.

4. Right-click in the selected cells, and choose Properties from the context menu to open the Properties palette.

5. In the Properties palette, click the Text Rotation box under the Content group.

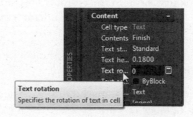

Content
Cell type   Text
Contents   Finish
Text st...   Standard
Text he...   0.1800
Text ro...   0
ByBlock
Text

Text rotation
Specifies the rotation of text in cell

6. Enter **90.↵** for a 90° rotation of the text. The text rotates into a vertical orientation.

7. Close the Properties palette.

With the text in this orientation, the columns are too wide, so you'll change the cell width for the selected cells.

8. Move the right grip to the left to decrease the width of the cells.

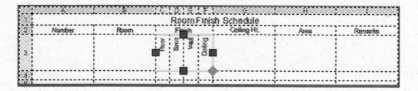

9. For the final touch, you'll center the text in the cells. With the cells still selected, right-click in the selected cells, and choose Alignment ➢ Bottom Center. The text becomes centered in the cells and aligned at the bottom of the cells.

A table showing:

A	B	C D E F	G	H	I
		Room Finish Schedule			
Number	Room	Finish	Ceiling Ht.	Area	Remarks
		Floor Base Wall Ceiling			

SETTING MARGINS WITH THE PROPERTIES PALETTE

You can also control the margin between the text and the cell border by using the Cell Margin options in the Properties palette. Select a group of cells in the table, right-click, and choose Properties. In the Properties palette, click the Vertical Cell Margin option or the Horizontal Cell Margin option in the Cell group.

In the previous exercise, you learned how you could adjust the text orientation through the Properties palette. You can also adjust the width of cells through the Properties palette. Or, if you prefer, you can adjust the width of multiple cells by adjusting the grip location of selected cells. Now continue to add text to the cells and adjust their sizes:

1. Double-click in the cell in the Number column just below the row that contains the Floor, Base, Wall, and Ceiling cells. A text cursor appears in the cell, and the Text Editor tab appears in the Ribbon.

2. Enter **110**, and press ↵. Instead of advancing to the next cell to the right, you advance to the next cell below.

3. Enter **111**, and press ↵ again. Continue to enter each room number in this way until you reach room number 117. When you've finished entering the room numbers, click Close Text Editor in the Text Editor tab's Close panel.

   Next, you'll reduce the width of the column to fit the text a bit better.

4. Click in the cell with the Number text label. It's the first column heading in the table.

5. Shift+click in the bottom cell of the Number column to select the entire column.

6. Click the grip to the left of the column, and move the grip to the right so that the column width is approximately half the width of the Room column. You can zoom in on the column to allow more control over the positioning of the grip.

7. Press Esc to exit the selection and view your table so far (see Figure 10.12).

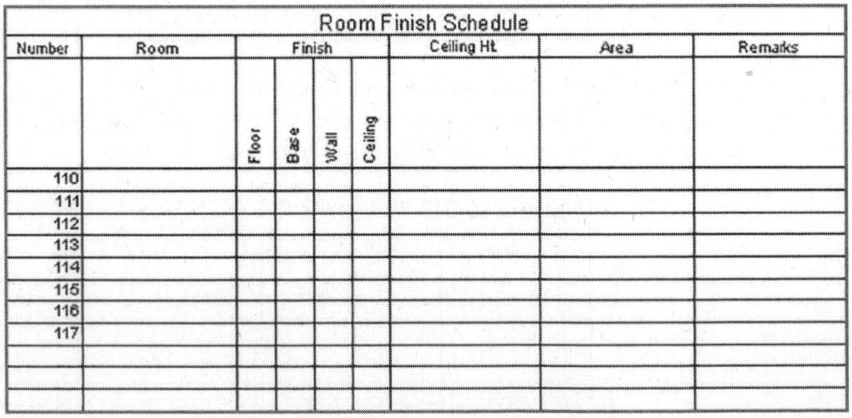

FIGURE 10.12

The table with the columns resized

Number	Room	Finish				Ceiling Ht.	Area	Remarks
		Floor	Base	Wall	Ceiling			
110								
111								
112								
113								
114								
115								
116								
117								

Room Finish Schedule

Now, suppose that you want to delete one of the extra rows of cells at the bottom of the table or add a new row. Here's how:

1. Click the bottom-left cell of the table to select it.

2. Right-click, and choose Rows ➤ Delete from the context menu. The row disappears.

3. To add a row, select a cell, right-click, and choose Rows ➤ Insert Above or Rows ➤ Insert Below, depending on where you want the new row. (You don't have to do this last step.)

You may notice the Delete Columns and Insert Columns options in the context menu that let you add or delete columns. These options function in a way that's similar to how the Delete Rows and Insert Rows options function. You can also use the tools in the Rows and Columns panels of the contextual Table Cell tab to insert and delete rows and columns.

Editing the Table Line Work

So far, you've concentrated on how you can format text and cells in a table, but you'll also want some control over the lines in the table. Typically, heavier lines are used around the border of the table and between the title and the rest of the table.

Selecting a cell, right-clicking, and selecting Borders from the context menu option lets you modify the outline of the border. When you select this option, the Cell Border Properties dialog box opens (see Figure 10.13).

FIGURE 10.13
Setting border properties

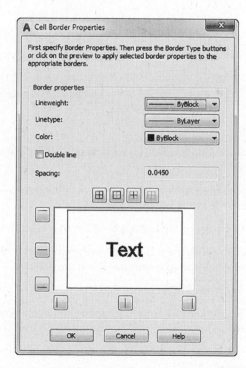

You can use this dialog box to fine-tune the appearance of the line work of the table. Try the following exercise to see how this dialog box works:

1. Make sure you do not have a cell selected, and then turn on the display of lineweights by typing **LW**↵.

2. In the Lineweight Settings dialog box, select the Display Lineweight setting and then click OK.

3. Click in the title cell at the top of the table to select the cell, and then right-click and choose Borders to open the Cell Border Properties dialog box.

4. Click the Lineweight drop-down list, and select 0.30 mm.

5. Click the Outside Borders button that appears just above the preview panel to tell AutoCAD to change the borders of the cell to the selected lineweight (see Figure 10.14).

FIGURE 10.14
Click to display
outside borders.

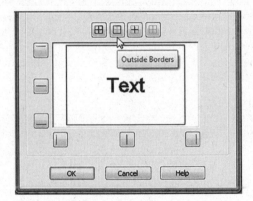

6. Click OK. The title cell is now outlined in a heavier line. To see it clearly, press the Esc key.

You can also adjust the lineweights of the borders that encircle a group of cells, as demonstrated in the following exercise:

1. Click the cell in the upper-left corner with the Number label.

2. Shift+click the cell in the lower-right corner of the table so that all of the cells from the second-from-the-top row down are selected.

3. Right-click and choose Borders.

4. Select 0.30 mm from the Lineweight drop-down list. Then click the Outside Borders button as you did in step 5 of the previous exercise.

5. Click OK. The outlines of the selected cells are given the new lineweight setting (see Figure 10.15).

FIGURE 10.15
The borders updated

			Room Finish Schedule				
Number	Room	Finish					
					Ceiling Ht.	Area	Remarks
		Floor	Base	Wall	Ceiling		
110							
111							
112							
113							
114							
115							
116							
117							

6. Save this file for future reference.

CHANGING THE BACKGROUND COLOR

In addition to the table borders, you can change the background color for the cells of the table using the Table Cell Background Color drop-down list in the Cell Styles panel of the contextual Table Cell tab, which appears when a cell, or range of cells, is selected. You can also use the Background Fill option in the Properties palette to set cell background colors.

The Cell Border Properties dialog box also lets you set the line colors by selecting a color from the Color drop-down list before selecting an Apply To option. In addition, there are several other buttons around the preview panel (see Figure 10.16) that let you select the lines that are affected by the Cell Border Properties settings.

FIGURE 10.16
Setting which borders will be affected

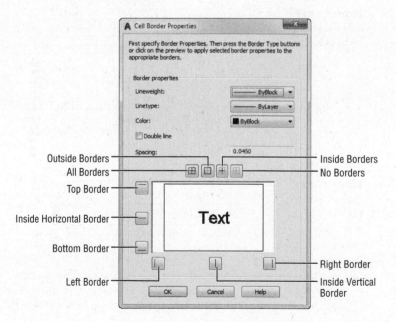

You can also use the preview panel to select individual borders by clicking the sample border in the preview panel. The sample changes to show you which border lines are affected.

Adding Formulas to Cells

In the beginning of this chapter, we mentioned that you can include formulas in cells of AutoCAD tables. This can be a great time-saver because you can set up a table with quantities that automatically adjust to changes in values in individual cells. You don't have to calculate the changes manually.

You may recall that formulas are a type of field and that a field can be linked with objects in a drawing so that the field displays the linked object's properties. The formula field can be linked to several numeric text values.

Although fields are the tools you use for formulas, you don't have to choose deliberately to add a field to a cell every time that you want to add a formula. The exercise in the following section will demonstrate how you can add a formula by typing directly in a cell. AutoCAD takes care of converting your input into a field.

Using Formulas Directly in Cells

The simplest way to add a formula to a cell is to double-click the cell and then, when the Text Editor tab appears in the Ribbon, enter the formula directly in the cell with the addition of an = (equal sign) at the beginning. Try the following exercise to see how it works:

1. Open the FieldSample.dwg file.

2. Double-click in the cell, as shown in Figure 10.17, to select the location for your formula.

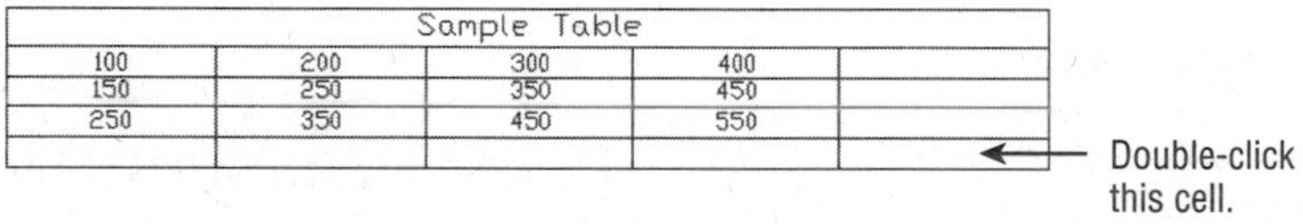

FIGURE 10.17
Selecting the cell
for your formula

Sample Table				
100	200	300	400	
150	250	350	450	
250	350	450	550	
				←— Double-click this cell.

3. Enter =A2+D4 in the cell to add the values in cell A2 and cell D4.

4. Press ↵ after you enter the formula. The value of A2 plus D4 appears in the cell (see Figure 10.18).

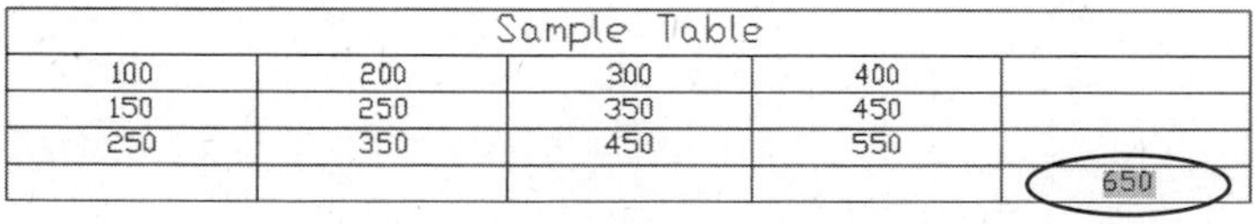

FIGURE 10.18
The cell with
the sum of two
other cells

Sample Table				
100	200	300	400	
150	250	350	450	
250	350	450	550	
				650

In step 3, the equal sign tells AutoCAD to convert the text into a formula field. You may have noticed that when you start to edit a cell in a table, the row and column labels appear along the top and left side of the table. You can use these labels to determine the cell addresses for your formula.

In typical spreadsheet fashion, you can change the formula in a cell at any time. Double-click the cell containing the formula, and then edit the formula values and operators.

You can also use the Formula drop-down list from the Table Cell tab's Insert panel to select from a set of predefined math operations (see Figure 10.19).

FIGURE 10.19
The Formula drop-down
list in the Insert panel

Click in the cell where you want to place the formula; then in the Table Cell tab, click the Formula drop-down list in the Insert panel and select the operation that you want to use. Next, place a selection window around the cells that you want to include in the formula. Click in the first cell that you want to include in the formula, and then click in the second cell. As you do this, a selection window appears. All of the cells that are included in the selection window are included in the formula.

Using Other Math Operations

In the previous exercise, you used the plus sign to add the value of two cells. You can string together several cells' addresses to add multiple cells as follows:

```
=A2+A3+A4...
```

You can also subtract, multiply, or divide by using the – (subtract or minus), * (multiply or asterisk), or / (divide) sign. To perform multiple operations on several cells, you can group operations within parentheses in a way similar to how you would do it in a typical spreadsheet formula. For example, if you want to add two cells together and then multiply their sum by another cell, use the following format:

```
=(A2+A3)*A4
```

The Average, Sum, and Count buttons that appear in the Formula flyout on the Table Cell tab's Insert panel give you quick access to these frequently used functions. You can add to a cell the average value of a set of cells, the sum of a set of cells, or the count of the number of cells. When you click one of these options after selecting a cell, you're prompted to select several cells with a selection window. Once you've selected a set of cells, you see the appropriate formula in the currently selected cell. Clicking the Average button, for example, produces a formula similar to the following:

```
=Average(A1:B5)
```

Clicking the Sum button produces a formula like this one:

```
=Sum(A1:B5)
```

In both cases, a range of cells is indicated by a colon, as in A1:B5. You can use this format when entering formulas manually. You can also include a single cell with a range by using a comma:

```
=Sum(A1:B5,C6)
```

Importing and Exporting Tables

Data of the kind found in tables is often shared with others who may not be AutoCAD users. For this reason, you'll want to be able to move table data to and from your drawing to other applications so that it can be viewed and edited by others. AutoCAD offers the following methods for importing and exporting tables.

Importing a Table

Frequently, tables are created outside AutoCAD in a spreadsheet program such as Microsoft Excel. You can import an Excel worksheet as an AutoCAD table by using the AutoCAD Entities option in the Paste Special feature. The ability to import tables lets non-AutoCAD users create the table data while you concentrate on the drawing.

Try the following exercise to see how you can import a table from a worksheet:

1. Open a new drawing; then open the Excel worksheet called `10a-plan.xls` and highlight the door data, as shown in Figure 10.20. You may see a security message in Excel. If you do, go ahead and close it.

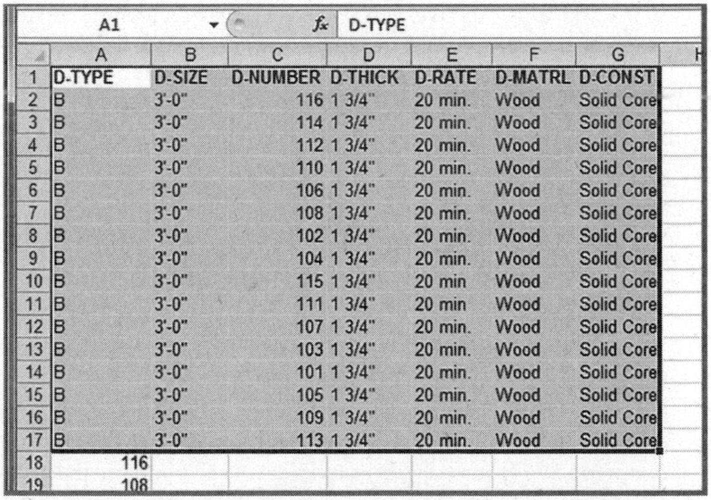

A1 | fx D-TYPE

	A	B	C	D	E	F	G	H
1	D-TYPE	D-SIZE	D-NUMBER	D-THICK	D-RATE	D-MATRL	D-CONST	
2	B	3'-0"	116	1 3/4"	20 min.	Wood	Solid Core	
3	B	3'-0"	114	1 3/4"	20 min.	Wood	Solid Core	
4	B	3'-0"	112	1 3/4"	20 min.	Wood	Solid Core	
5	B	3'-0"	110	1 3/4"	20 min.	Wood	Solid Core	
6	B	3'-0"	106	1 3/4"	20 min.	Wood	Solid Core	
7	B	3'-0"	108	1 3/4"	20 min.	Wood	Solid Core	
8	B	3'-0"	102	1 3/4"	20 min.	Wood	Solid Core	
9	B	3'-0"	104	1 3/4"	20 min.	Wood	Solid Core	
10	B	3'-0"	115	1 3/4"	20 min	Wood	Solid Core	
11	B	3'-0"	111	1 3/4"	20 min	Wood	Solid Core	
12	B	3'-0"	107	1 3/4"	20 min.	Wood	Solid Core	
13	B	3'-0"	103	1 3/4"	20 min.	Wood	Solid Core	
14	B	3'-0"	101	1 3/4"	20 min.	Wood	Solid Core	
15	B	3'-0"	105	1 3/4"	20 min.	Wood	Solid Core	
16	B	3'-0"	109	1 3/4"	20 min.	Wood	Solid Core	
17	B	3'-0"	113	1 3/4"	20 min.	Wood	Solid Core	
18	116							
19	108							

FIGURE 10.20 Selecting the door data in the `10a-plan.xls` spreadsheet

2. Right-click and select Copy to place a copy of the selected data into the Windows Clipboard, and then switch back to AutoCAD.

3. Choose Paste Special from the Paste flyout on the Home tab's Clipboard panel (see Figure 10.21) to open the Paste Special dialog box. If you don't see the Clipboard panel, enter **PASTESPEC**↵.

FIGURE 10.21
The Paste flyout

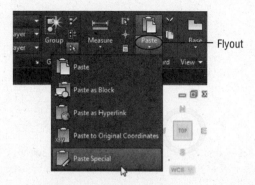

4. With the Paste radio button selected, click AutoCAD Entities in the list and then click OK.

5. At the Specify insertion point or [paste as Text]: prompt, click a point in the lower-right area of the drawing. The worksheet data appears in the drawing as a table.

If the text is difficult to read because of a dark drawing area background, you can change the background color of the table to white.

1. Select all the cells of the table by selecting cell 1A and then Shift+clicking cell 17G. Note that the Table Cell tab appears automatically in the ribbon.

2. In the Table Cell tab's Cell Style panel, select white from the Table Cell Background Color drop-down list.

In this exercise, you imported the worksheet by using the default standard table style. This gives you a simple-looking table using the AutoCAD Txt font. You can set up a custom table style, as described later in this chapter, with the fonts and borders that you want and then import the table for a more customized appearance. Make sure that your custom table style is the current style before you import the worksheet.

ADDING GRAPHICS TO TABLE CELLS

One of the most interesting features of the Table tool is its ability to include blocks in a cell. This ability can be useful if you want to include graphic elements in your table. Adding a block to a cell is a simple process. Here are the steps:

1. Click in a cell to select it.

2. Right-click, and choose Insert ➤ Block from the context menu to open the Insert A Block In A Table Cell dialog box.

continues

continued

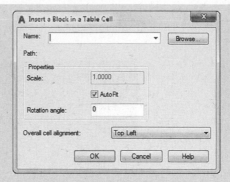

3. Select a block name from the Name drop-down list. You can also click the button to the right of the list to open the Select Drawing File dialog box, which lets you select a drawing file for import to the cell.

4. After you've selected a block and specified the settings in the Properties group of the dialog box, click OK. The block appears in the cell that you've selected.

The dialog box enables you to specify the alignment (Overall Cell Alignment) and size (Scale) of the inserted block. By default, the AutoFit option is turned on. This option adjusts the size of the block to make it fit in the current cell size.

Exporting Tables

You might want to export your AutoCAD table to a spreadsheet program or database. You can do this using a somewhat hidden option in a context menu. Follow these steps:

1. Select the entire table. You can do so by clicking in a spot above and to the right of the table. With the crossing selection window, completely enclose the table and click.

2. Right-click anywhere in the table, and choose Export from the context menu to open the Export Data dialog box.

3. Specify a name and location for your exported table data, and click Save.

The file is saved with a .csv filename extension. This type of file is comma delimited and can be read by most spreadsheet programs, including Excel. Unfortunately, the CSV file doesn't retain the AutoCAD table formatting.

To open the exported file from Excel, choose File ➤ Open in the Excel menu bar; then, in the Open dialog box, select Text Files (*.prn, *.txt, *.csv) in the Files Of Type drop-down list. You can then locate the exported table and open it.

Creating Table Styles

If you find that you're creating the same table layout over and over, you can set up predefined table styles. You can set up the properties of the title, column headings, and data in advance so that you don't have to set them up each time you create a table. For example, if you prefer to use Arial bold at 0.25" for the title and standard Arial at 0.125" for the column headings, you can create a table style with those settings. The next time you need to create a table, you can select your custom table style and specify the number of columns and rows; then you'll be ready to add the data without having to format the text.

Adding or Modifying a Table Style

The method that you use to create a table style in AutoCAD is similar to the method used to modify an existing one.

To create a table style, follow these steps:

1. Click Table Style in the Home tab's expanded Annotation panel to open the Table Style dialog box.

You can also select the Table Style tool from the Annotate tab's Tables panel title bar. The Table Style tool is the arrowhead at the right end of the Tables panel title bar. You see the Standard table style in the Styles list box (see Figure 10.22). This is the one you used in the previous exercises.

FIGURE 10.22
The Table Style dialog box

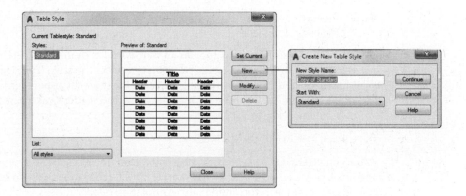

2. Click the New button to open the Create New Table Style dialog box. This is where you give your new table style a name.

3. Enter **My Table Style**, and click Continue to open the New Table Style dialog box (see Figure 10.23).

FIGURE 10.23
The New Table
Style dialog box

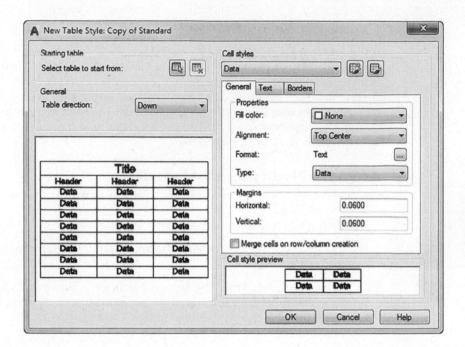

4. You'll learn more about the options in this dialog box next. For now, click OK to close the dialog box.

5. Your new table style now appears in the Styles list of the Table Style dialog box. If you want to edit an existing table style, you can select the style from the list and click the Modify button. The Modify Table Style dialog box will appear, enabling you to edit the existing style. The Modify Table Style dialog box is identical to the New Table Style dialog box shown in Figure 10.23.

6. Click Close to exit the dialog box.

After you've created a style, you can select it from the Table Style group of the Insert Table dialog box that you used to create the sample table (see Figure 10.24). To open the Insert Table dialog box, click Table in the Home tab's Annotation panel.

FIGURE 10.24
Select the table style
in the Insert Table
dialog box.

You can also open the New Table Style dialog box by clicking the Launch The Table Style Dialog button just to the right of the Table Style drop-down list in the Insert Table dialog box.

The Table Style Options

Let's take a closer look at the New Table Style dialog box, shown earlier in Figure 10.23. It may seem a bit bewildering at first, but once you take the time to explore the parts of this dialog box, it's fairly straightforward. The following offers a description of the parts of the New Table Style dialog box by group:

Starting Table Typically, you can set up a new table style using the settings in the other groups of this dialog box, but the Starting Table group gives you the ability to use an existing table in the drawing as the basis for your new table style. This can be helpful if you've already done some work formatting a table in your drawing. This group includes two buttons. The one on the left lets you select an existing table in the drawing for your new style. If you click this button, the dialog box closes temporarily to allow you to select a table in your drawing. The button on the right removes your in-drawing table selection and reverts to the settings in the dialog box.

General The General group offers only one setting: the direction for the table. Typically, you'll use the Down option, which means that the table reads from top to bottom. If for some reason you need a table with titles at the bottom, choose the Up option.

Cell Styles You have a high degree of control over the appearance of individual cells through the cell styles. By default, your new table style will have three cell styles, called Data, Header, and Title. You can select these cell styles from the drop-down list at the top of the Cell Styles group. You can then edit the selected style using the three tabs below the drop-down list. Here are brief descriptions of the function of each tab:

General The General tab gives you control over the fill color, alignment, format, and type of information presented in the cell. The Margins options control the margins in the cell. The Merge Cells On Row/Column Creation option at the bottom of the General tab causes the cells to merge into a single cell for the selected cell style.

Text The Text tab gives you control over the default text style, the height and color, and the angle of the text in the cell.

Borders The Borders tab lets you control the lineweight for the borders of the cell.

You can also create your own cell style using the two buttons to the right of the Cell Styles drop-down list. The left button lets you create a new cell style. The button on the right lets you create, rename, or delete a cell style through the Manage Cell Styles dialog box.

Cell Style Preview This window gives you a preview of what the cell style will look like with the settings you make in the tabs of the Cell Styles group. This preview changes in real time as you change the settings in the General, Text, or Borders tab.

The Bottom Line

Use fields to associate text with drawing properties. Fields are a special type of text object that can be linked to object properties. They can help to automate certain text-related tasks.

Master It Name two uses for fields that you learned about in the first part of this chapter.

Add tables to your drawing. The Tables feature can help you make quick work of schedules and other tabular data that you want to include in a drawing.

Master It What is the name of the dialog box that appears when you click the Table tool in the Annotate tab's Tables panel?

Edit the table line work. Because tables include line work to delineate their different cells, AutoCAD gives you control over table borders and lines.

Master It How do you get to the Cell Border Properties dialog box?

Add formulas to cells. Tables can also function like a spreadsheet by allowing you to add formulas to cells.

Master It What type of text object lets you add formulas to cells?

Import and export tables. The Table feature allows you to import Microsoft Excel spreadsheets into AutoCAD.

Master It Describe how to import a spreadsheet from Excel into AutoCAD.

Create table styles. Table styles can save time by enabling you to set up preformatted tables with a title, column headings, and other data.

Master It Name the four groups in the New Table Style dialog box.

Chapter 11

Using Dimensions

Before you determine the dimensions of a project, your design is in flux and many questions may be unanswered. After you begin dimensioning, you'll start to see whether things fit or work together. Dimensioning can be crucial to how well a design works and how quickly it develops. The dimensions answer questions about code conformance if you're an architect; they answer questions about tolerances, fit, and interference if you're involved in mechanical applications. After you and your design team reach a design on a schematic level, communicating even tentative dimensions to others on the team can accelerate design development. Dimensions represent a point from which you can develop your ideas further.

With the AutoCAD® 2018 software, you can easily add tentative or final dimensions to any drawing. AutoCAD gives you an accurate dimension without your having to take measurements. You pick the two points to be dimensioned and the dimension line location, and AutoCAD does the rest. The associative dimensioning capability of AutoCAD automatically updates dimensions whenever the size or shape of the dimensioned object changes. These dimensioning features can save you valuable time and reduce the number of dimensional errors in your drawings.

In this chapter, you will learn to

- Understand the components of a dimension
- Create a dimension style
- Draw linear dimensions
- Edit dimensions
- Dimension nonorthogonal objects
- Add a note with a leader arrow
- Apply ordinate dimensions
- Add tolerance notation

Understanding the Components of a Dimension

Before you start the exercises in this chapter, it will help to know the names of the parts of a dimension. Figure 11.1 shows a sample of a dimension with the parts labeled. The *dimension line* is the line that represents the distance being dimensioned. It's the horizontal line with the diagonal tick marks on either end. The *extension lines* are the lines that originate from the object being dimensioned. They show you the exact location from which the dimension is taken. The *dimension text* is the dimension value, usually shown inside or above the dimension line.

FIGURE 11.1
The components
of a dimension

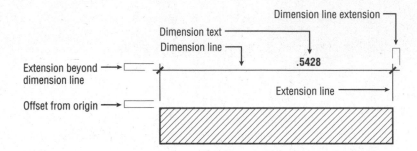

Another component of a dimension line is the *dimension line extension*. This is the part of the dimension line that extends beyond the extension line. Dimension line extensions are usually used only on architectural dimensions. The extension lines typically extend beyond the dimension lines in all types of dimensions. The extension line *offset from origin* is the distance from the beginning of the extension line to the object being dimensioned. The *extension beyond dimension line* is the distance the dimension line extends past the extension line.

You can control each of these components by creating or editing dimension styles. *Dimension styles* are the settings that determine the look of your dimensions. You can store multiple styles in a single drawing. The first exercise in this chapter will show you how to create a dimension style.

DIMENSIONING STANDARDS

In addition to the components of a dimension, you should know about the standards that govern the placement and style of dimensions in a drawing. Each industry has a different set of standards for text size, text style, arrow style, dimension placement, and general dimensioning methods. These issues are beyond the scope of this book; however, we urge you to become familiar with the standards associated with your industry. Many resources are available to you if you want to find out more about dimension standards. Here are a few resources on the subject:

◆ For mechanical drafting in the United States, check the American Society of Mechanical Engineers (ASME) website: www.asme.org.

◆ For European standards, see the International Organization for Standardization (ISO) website: www.iso.org.

◆ For architectural standards in the United States, see the American Institute of Architects (AIA) website: www.aia.org.

Creating a Dimension Style

Certification
Objective

Dimension styles are similar to text styles. They determine the look of your dimensions as well as the size of dimensioning features, such as the dimension text and arrows. You can set up a dimension style to have special types of arrows, for instance, or to position the dimension text above or in line with the dimension line. Dimension styles also make your work easier by enabling you to store and duplicate your most common dimension settings.

AutoCAD gives you one of two default dimension styles, *ISO-25* or *Standard,* depending on whether you use the metric or Imperial (also called English) measurement system. You'll probably add many other styles to suit the types of drawings you're creating. You can also create variations of a general style for those situations that call for only minor changes in the dimension's appearance.

In this section, you'll learn how to set up your own dimension style based on the Standard dimension style (see Figure 11.2). For metric users, the settings are different, but the overall methods are the same.

FIGURE 11.2

The AutoCAD Standard dimension style compared with an architectural-style dimension

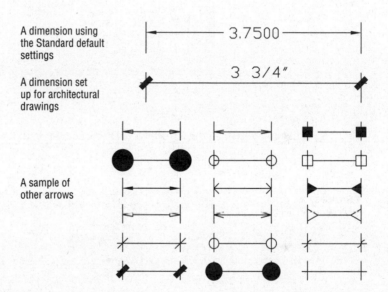

Follow these steps to create a dimension style:

1. Open the 11a-unit.dwg file and rename it **Unit.dwg**. Metric users should open 11a-unit-metric.dwg and rename it **Unit.dwg**. These files are the same as the Unit.dwg file that you used in the previous chapter before the exercises.

2. Choose Zoom Extents from the Zoom flyout in the Navigation bar or type Z↵E↵ to display the entire floor plan.

3. Click the Dimension Style tool on the Annotate tab's Dimensions panel title bar. You can also choose the Dimension Style tool from the Home tab's expanded Annotation panel (it looks like a dimension with a paintbrush) or type D↵ at the Command prompt to open the Dimension Style Manager.

4. Select Standard from the Styles list box. Metric users should select ISO-25 (see Figure 11.3).

FIGURE 11.3
The Dimension Style
Manager

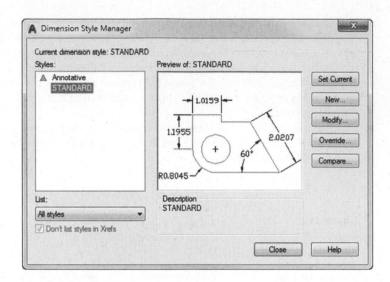

5. Click New to open the Create New Dimension Style dialog box (see Figure 11.4).

FIGURE 11.4
The Create New Dimension
Style dialog box

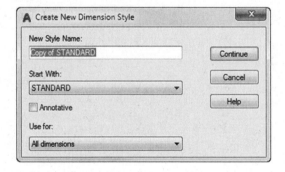

6. With the Copy of Standard or ISO-25 name highlighted in the New Style Name box, enter **My Architectural**.

7. Click Continue to open the detailed New Dimension Style dialog box (see Figure 11.5).

You've just created a dimension style called My Architectural, but at this point it's identical to the Standard style on which it's based. Nothing has happened to the Standard style; it's still available if you need to use it.

FIGURE 11.5
The New Dimension
Style dialog box

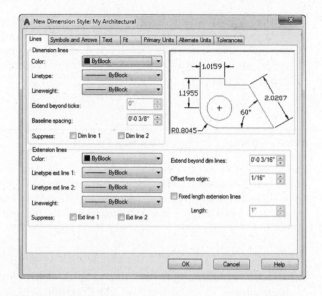

FIGURE 11.5
The New Dimension
Style dialog box

Setting Up the Primary Unit Style

Now you need to set up your new dimension style so that it conforms to the US architectural style of dimensioning. Let's start by changing the unit style for the dimension text. Just as you changed the overall unit style of AutoCAD to a feet-and-inches style for your bath drawing in Chapter 3, "Setting Up and Using the Drafting Tools," you must change your dimension styles. Setting the overall unit style doesn't automatically set the dimension unit style. Follow these steps:

1. In the New Dimension Style dialog box, click the Primary Units tab (see Figure 11.6).

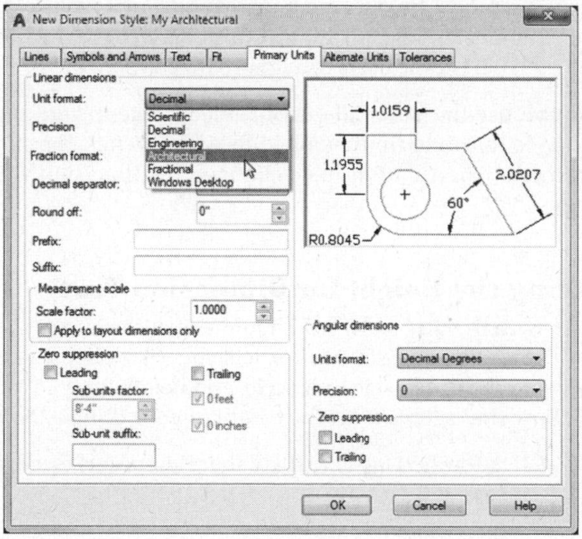

FIGURE 11.6
The Primary Units
options

2. In the Linear Dimensions group, open the Unit Format drop-down list and choose Architectural. Notice that this drop-down list contains the same unit styles as the main Drawing Units dialog box (choose Drawing Utilities ➤ Units from the Application menu), with the addition of the Windows Desktop option. Metric users can skip this option.

USING COMMAS OR PERIODS FOR DECIMALS

The Decimal Separator option, which is found a few settings below the Unit Format option, lets you choose between a period and a comma for decimal points. Metric users often use the comma for a decimal point, and US users use a period. This option doesn't have any meaning for measurements other than decimal, so it's dimmed when the Architectural unit format is selected.

---

3. Select 0'-0 1/4" from the Precision drop-down list, just below the Unit Format list. Metric users should select 0.00. The Precision option enables you to set the level of precision that is displayed in the dimension text. It doesn't limit the precision of the AutoCAD drawing database. This value is used to limit only the display of dimension text values.

4. Just below the Precision drop-down list, open the Fraction Format drop-down list and select Diagonal. Notice what happens to the graphic: The fractional dimensions change to show how your dimension text will look. Metric users can skip this step because it isn't available when the Decimal unit format is selected.

5. In the Zero Suppression group in the lower-left corner, click 0 Inches to deselect this check box. If you leave it turned on, indications of 0 inches will be omitted from the dimension text. (In architectural drawings, 0 inches are shown as in this dimension: 12'-0".) Metric users can ignore this option.

If you use the Imperial measurement system, you've set up My Architectural's dimension unit style to show dimensions in feet and inches, the standard method for US construction documents. Metric users have changed the Precision value and have kept the Decimal unit system.

Setting the Height for Dimension Text

Along with the unit style, you should adjust the size of the dimension text. The Text tab of the New Dimension Style dialog box lets you set a variety of text options, including text location relative to the dimension line, style, and height.

Follow these steps to set the height of your dimension text:

1. Click the Text tab to display the text options (see Figure 11.7).

FIGURE 11.7

The Text options

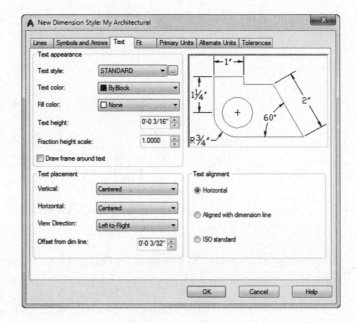

FIGURE 11.7

The Text options

2. Highlight the contents of the Text Height box.

3. The Text Height box can accept typed values, or you can use the up and down arrows on the right side of the input to increase or decrease the value. Press the down arrow to reach the 1/8" setting. Metric users should enter **0.3↵** for the text height.

Unlike with the text you created in Chapter 9, "Adding Text to Drawings," you specify dimension text height by its final plot size. You then specify an overall dimension scale factor that affects the sizing of all dimensioning settings, such as text and arrows.

If you want to use a specific text style for your dimensions, select a text style in the Text Style drop-down list in the Text tab. If the style you select happens to have a height specification greater than 0, that height will override any text height settings that you enter in the Text tab.

Setting the Location and Orientation of Dimension Text

The default AutoCAD setting for the placement of dimension text puts the text in line with the dimension line, as shown in the example at the top of Figure 11.2 earlier in this chapter. Suppose that you want the new My Architectural style to put the text above the dimension line instead, as shown in the second example in Figure 11.2. To do that, you'll use the Text Placement and Text Alignment group options in the Text tab of the New Dimension Style dialog box:

1. In the Text Alignment group in the lower-right corner of the dialog box, click the Aligned With Dimension Line radio button.

2. In the Text Placement group, open the Vertical drop-down list and select Above. The appearance of the sample image changes to show how your new settings will look.

3. Again in the Text Placement group, change the Offset From Dim Line value to 1/16". Metric users can leave this setting at 0.624. This setting controls the size of the gap between the dimension line and the dimension text.

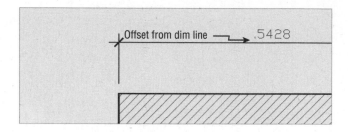

Each time you change a setting, the graphic gives you immediate feedback about how your changes will affect your dimension style.

Choosing an Arrow Style and Setting the Dimension Scale

Next you'll specify a different type of arrow for your new dimension style. For linear dimensions in architectural drawings, a diagonal line, or *tick* mark, is typically used instead of an arrow.

In addition, you want to set the scale for the graphical components of the dimension, such as the arrows and text. Recall from Chapter 9 that text must be scaled up in order to appear at the proper size in the final output of the drawing. Dimensions too must be scaled so that they look correct when the drawing is plotted. The arrows are controlled by settings in the Symbols And Arrows tab, and the overall scale of the dimension style is set in the Fit tab.

Here are the steps for specifying the arrow type and scale:

1. Click the Symbols And Arrows tab to display the options for controlling the arrow style and dimension line extensions (see Figure 11.8).

FIGURE 11.8
The Symbols And
Arrows options

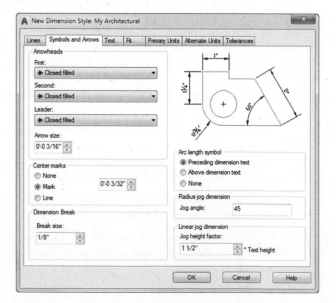

2. In the Arrowheads group, open the First drop-down list and choose Architectural Tick. The graphic next to the arrowhead name shows you what the arrowhead looks like. Note that the Second drop-down list automatically changes to Architectural Tick to maintain symmetry on the dimension.

3. In the Arrowheads group, change the Arrow Size setting to 1/8″. Metric users should enter **0.3**.

Next you need to set the behavior of the dimension line and extension lines:

1. Click the Lines tab to display the options for controlling the dimension and extension lines (see Figure 11.9).

FIGURE 11.9
The options for controlling the dimension and extension lines

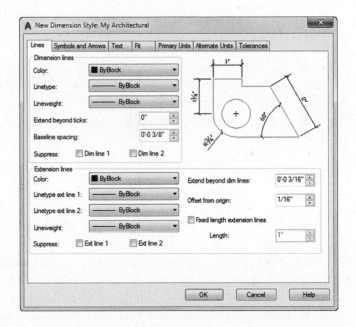

2. In the Dimension Lines group, highlight the value in the Extend Beyond Ticks box and change the value to **1/16**. (Metric users should enter **0.15**.) This causes the dimension lines to extend past the tick arrows. This is a standard graphic practice used for dimensioning linear dimensions in architectural plans.

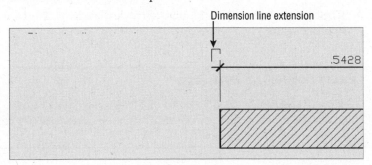

3. In the Extension Lines group, change the Extend Beyond Dim Lines setting to **1/8″**. Metric users should change this to **0.3**. This setting determines the distance the extension line extends past the dimension line.

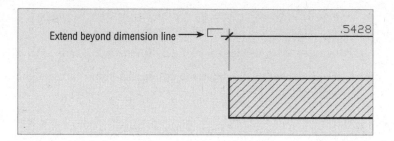

4. Again in the Extension Lines group, change the Offset From Origin setting to **1/8″**. Metric users should change this to **0.3**. This sets the distance from the point being dimensioned to the beginning of the dimension extension line.

5. Make sure that the Fixed length extension lines option is unchecked.

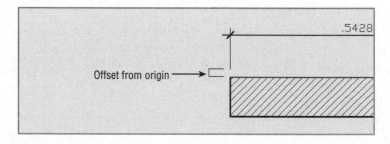

6. Click the Fit tab of the New Dimension Style dialog box to display the options for overall dimension scale and miscellaneous settings (see Figure 11.10).

Certification
Objective

7. Turn on the Annotative option in the Scale For Dimension Features group. You may recall from Chapter 9 that the Annotative option allows AutoCAD to scale an object automatically to the drawing's annotation scale.

8. Click OK to close the New Dimension Style dialog box. The Dimension Style Manager appears again.

CREATE CUSTOM ARROWHEADS

See Bonus Chapter 4, "System Variables and Dimension Styles," available at www.omura.com/chapters, for details on how you can create your own arrowheads. AutoCAD also lets you set up a separate arrow style for leaders.

FIGURE 11.10

The Fit options

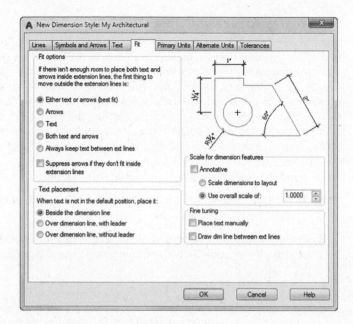

SCALE FOR DIMENSIONS IN LEGACY DRAWINGS

Drawings created prior to AutoCAD 2008 relied on scale factors to determine the scaling of dimensions. Because it's likely that you'll run into legacy drawing files, here is some information about the settings used for those earlier dimensions.

Instead of the Annotative option, the Use Overall Scale Of option is used in the Scale For Dimension Features group. You select the Use Overall Scale Of radio button and enter a drawing scale factor in the Use Overall Scale Of box.

All of the values that you enter for the options in the New Dimension Style dialog box are multiplied by this Use Overall Scale Of value to obtain the final size of the dimension components. For example, the text height that you entered earlier, 1/8", is multiplied by 48 for a dimension text height of 6". For metric users, the text height of 0.3 is multiplied by 50 for a text height of 15 cm. For more on the scaling of text and other objects in AutoCAD, see Chapter 3.

USING THE LAYOUT VIEWPORT SCALE FOR DIMENSIONS

If you use the Scale Dimensions To Layout option in the Scale For Dimension Features group of the Fit tab, AutoCAD uses the layout viewport scale to size the dimension components. See Chapter 8, "Introducing Printing, Plotting, and Layouts," for more information about viewport scale settings. The Scale Dimension To Layout option can be useful if you have a drawing that you want to print at multiple scales.

Setting Up Alternate Units

You can use the Alternate Units tab of the New Dimension Style dialog box to set up AutoCAD to display a second dimension in centimeters or millimeters. Likewise, if you're a metric user, you can set up a second dimension to display feet and inches. The following exercise shows you how to set up alternate dimensions. You don't have to do this exercise now; it's here for your information. If you like, come back later and try it to see how it affects your dimensions. You can pick up the exercise in the next section, "Setting the Current Dimension Style."

If you decide later that you don't want the alternate units to be displayed, you can turn them off by returning to the Modify Dimension Style dialog box and removing the check mark from the Display Alternate Units check box.

Here are the steps for setting up alternate dimensions:

1. In the Dimension Style Manager, select a style and then click Modify. Or, if you want to create a new style, click New.

2. In the Modify Dimension Style dialog box, click the Alternate Units tab (see Figure 11.11). This is virtually identical to the New Dimension Style dialog box with which you've been working.

FIGURE 11.11
The Alternate
Units options

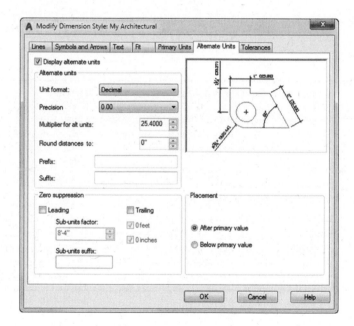

3. Click the Display Alternate Units check box. The options in the tab become available for your input.

4. Select the appropriate option from the Unit Format drop-down list. Imperial users should select Decimal to show metric alternate units. Metric users should select Architectural.

5. Select an appropriate precision value from the Precision drop-down list.

6. Enter a scale factor for your alternate dimension in the Multiplier For Alt Units box. For Imperial users, the default value is 25.4. This value converts feet-and-inch dimensions to

millimeters. In our metric examples, you've been using centimeters, so change this setting to **2.54**. Metric users should enter **0.3937** to convert centimeters to feet and inches.

7. In the Placement group, select where you want the alternate dimension to appear in relation to the main dimension.

8. You don't want to display alternate units now, so turn off the Display Alternate Units setting.

9. Click OK to close the Modify Dimension Style dialog box. The Dimension Style Manager
   appears again.

Setting the Current Dimension Style

Before you can begin to use your new dimension style, you must make it the current default:

1. Click My Architectural in the Styles list box in the Dimension Style Manager.

2. Click the Set Current button at the far right.

3. Click Close to exit the Dimension Style Manager.

You can also select a dimension style from the drop-down list in the Annotate tab's
Dimensions panel or the Home tab's expanded Annotation panel. You're now ready to use your
new dimension style.

FITTING TEXT AND ARROWS IN TIGHT PLACES

Every now and then, you'll need to dimension a small gap or a small part of an object in which
dimension text won't fit. The Fit tab includes a few settings (other than the ones with which you've
already worked) that control how dimensions act when the extension lines are too close. The Text
Placement group contains three options to place the text in tight situations:

Beside The Dimension Line   Places text next to the extension line but close to the dimension line. You'll see how this affects your dimension later.

Over Dimension Line, With Leader   Places the dimension text farther from the dimension line and includes an arrow or a leader from the dimension line to the text.

Over Dimension Line, Without Leader   Does the same as the previous setting, but
doesn't include the leader.

The options in the Fit Options group let you control how text and arrows are placed when there
isn't enough room for both between the extension lines.

In the next set of exercises, you'll use the My Architectural style that you just created. To
switch to another style, open the Dimension Style Manager again, select the style you want from
the Styles list, and click Set Current, as you did in the previous exercise.

Modifying a Dimension Style

Certification
Objective

To modify an existing dimension style, open the Dimension Style Manager dialog box, highlight the style that you want to edit, and then click Modify to open the Modify Dimension Style
dialog box. You can then make changes to the various components of the selected dimension
style. When you've finished making changes and closed both dialog boxes, all of the dimensions

associated with the edited style update automatically in your drawing. For example, if you're not using the Annotative Scale feature and you decide that you need to change the dimension scale of a style, you can open the Modify Dimension Style dialog box and change the Use Overall Scale Of value in the Scale For Dimension Features group of the Fit tab.

So far, you've been introduced to the various settings that let you determine the appearance of a dimension style. We haven't discussed every option; to learn more about the other dimension style options, consult Bonus Chapter 4. There you'll find descriptions of all the items in the New Dimension Style and Modify Dimension Style dialog boxes, plus reference material covering the system variables associated with each option.

If your application is strictly architectural, you may want to make these same dimension-style changes to the acad.dwt template file or create a set of template files specifically for architectural drawings of different scales.

Drawing Linear Dimensions

Certification Objective

The most common type of dimension that you'll be using is the *linear dimension*. The linear dimension is an orthogonal dimension measuring the width and length of an object. AutoCAD provides three dimensioning tools for this purpose: Linear (Dimlinear), Continue (Dimcont), and Baseline (Dimbase). These options are readily accessible from the Annotate tab's Dimensions panel.

In the following set of exercises, you'll see figures displaying dimensions in both Imperial and metric units. We've included both measurements so that both Imperial and metric users can more easily follow the exercise. But in your own drawing, you'll see only one dimension value displayed above the dimension line.

Understanding the Dimensions Panel

Before you apply any dimension, you should study the Annotate tab's Dimensions panel (see Figure 11.12). This panel contains nearly all of the tools necessary to draw and edit your dimensions.

FIGURE 11.12
The Annotate tab's Dimensions panel

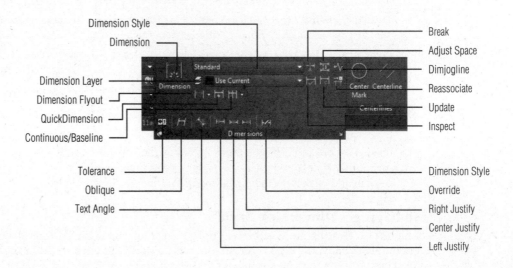

Many of the dimensioning tools discussed in this chapter can be found in the Home tab's Annotation panel. However, since the focus of this chapter is on dimensioning, unless otherwise noted, use the panels on the Annotate tab.

SELECTING OPTIONS FROM THE DIMENSION FLYOUT

As an introduction to dimensions, you'll be selecting options from the flyout on the bottom row of the Dimensions panel. This flyout starts out showing the Linear tool, but since the flyout name changes depending on the last tool selected, we'll refer to this flyout as the Dimension flyout. You'll learn about the larger Dimension tool later in this chapter.

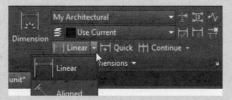

Placing Horizontal and Vertical Dimensions

Let's start by looking at the basic dimensioning tool, Linear. The Linear button (the Dimlinear command) on the Annotate tab's Dimensions panel accommodates both the horizontal and vertical dimensions.

In this exercise, you'll add a vertical dimension to the right side of the unit plan:

1. Before you start to dimension your drawing, you need to set its scale. Select 1/4"= 1'-0" from the Annotation Scale drop-down list. Metric users should select 1:50.

2. To start either a vertical or horizontal dimension, choose Linear from the Dimension flyout in the Annotate tab's Dimensions panel, or enter **DLI**↵ at the Command prompt.

3. The Specify first extension line origin or <select object>: prompt asks you for the first point of the distance to be dimensioned. An extension line connects the object being dimensioned to the dimension line. Use the Endpoint osnap override, and pick the upper-right corner of the entry, as shown in Figure 11.13.

4. At the Specify second extension line origin: prompt, pick the lower-right corner of the living room, as shown in Figure 11.13.

SELECTING OBJECTS TO BE DIMENSIONED

The prompt in step 3 gives you the option of pressing ↵ to select an object. If you do this, you're prompted to pick the object that you want to dimension rather than the distance to be dimensioned. This method is discussed later in this chapter.

FIGURE 11.13
The dimension line added to the Unit drawing

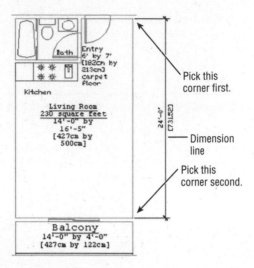

5. At the next prompt, `Specify dimension line location or [Mtext/Text/Angle/Horizontal/Vertical/Rotated]:`, the dimension line indicates the direction of the dimension and contains the arrows or tick marks. Move your cursor from left to right to display a temporary dimension. Doing so enables you to select a dimension-line location visually.

6. Enter **@4'<0↵** to tell AutoCAD that you want the dimension line to be 4' to the right of the last point that you selected. Metric users should enter **@122<0↵**. (You could pick a point by using your cursor, but this doesn't let you place the dimension line as accurately.) After you've done this, the dimension is placed in the drawing as shown in Figure 11.13.

Continuing a Dimension

You'll often want to enter a group of dimensions strung together in a line. For example, you may want to continue dimensioning the balcony and align the continued dimension with the dimension that you just entered.

To do this, use the Continue option found in the Dimensions panel's Continue/Baseline flyout:

1. Click the Continue tool on the Dimensions panel, or enter **DCO↵**.

2. At the `Specify second extension line origin or [Select/Undo] <Select>:` prompt, pick the upper-right corner of the balcony. (See the top image in Figure 11.14.)

3. Pick the right end of the rail on the balcony. See the bottom image in Figure 11.14 for the results.

4. Press ↵ twice to exit the command.

If you select the wrong location for a continued dimension, you can click the Undo tool or press **U↵** to undo the last dimension.

FIGURE 11.14
The dimension string, continued and completed

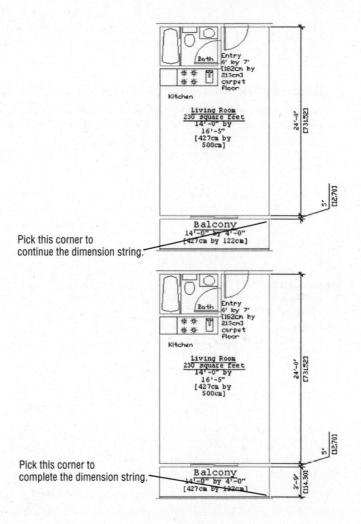

Pick this corner to continue the dimension string.

Pick this corner to complete the dimension string.

The Continue option adds a dimension from where you left off. The last-drawn extension line is used as the first extension line for the continued dimension. AutoCAD keeps adding dimensions as you continue to pick points, until you press ↵.

You probably noticed that the 5″ dimension is placed away from the dimension line with a leader line pointing to it. This is the result of the 5″ dimension's text not having enough space to fit between the dimension extension lines. You'll learn about dimension style settings that can remedy this problem. For now, let's continue adding dimensions to the plan.

CONTINUING A DIMENSION FROM A PREVIOUS DIMENSION

If you need to continue a string of dimensions from an older linear dimension instead of the most recently added one, press ↵ at the Specify second extension line origin or

[Select/Undo] <Select>: prompt that you saw in step 2 of the previous exercise. Then, at the Select continued dimension: prompt, click the extension line from which you want to continue.

Drawing Dimensions from a Common Base Extension Line

Another way to dimension objects is to have several dimensions originate from the same extension line. To accommodate this, AutoCAD provides the Baseline option on the Dimensions control panel and the Dimension drop-down menu.

To see how this works, you'll start another dimension—this time a horizontal one—across the top of the plan:

1. Use the Zoom Realtime and Pan tools in the Navigation bar to adjust your view so that you can add dimensions above the bathroom. See the dimensions at the top of the drawing in Figure 11.15 to get an idea of how much space you'll need.

FIGURE 11.15

The bathroom with horizontal dimensions

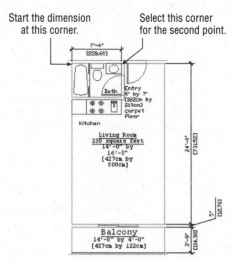

Start the dimension at this corner.

Select this corner for the second point.

2. Click the Linear tool in the Dimension flyout on the Dimensions panel. Or, as you did for the vertical dimension, type **DLI**⏎ to start the horizontal dimension.

3. At the Specify first extension line origin or <select object>: prompt, use the Endpoint osnap to pick the upper-left corner of the bathroom, as shown in Figure 11.15.

4. At the Specify second extension line origin: prompt, pick the upper-right corner of the bathroom, as shown in Figure 11.15.

5. At the Specify dimension line location or [Mtext/Text/Angle/ Horizontal/ Vertical/Rotated]: prompt, pick a point above the unit plan, like the 7'-6" dimension in Figure 11.15. If you need to, pan your view downward to fit the dimension in.

USE OSNAPS WHILE DIMENSIONING

Because you usually pick exact locations on your drawing as you dimension, you may want to turn on the Object Snap tool in the status bar to avoid the extra step of selecting osnaps from the Osnap context menu.

6. You're set to draw another dimension continuing from the first extension line of the dimension that you just drew. Click the Baseline tool on the Continue/Baseline flyout of the Dimensions panel, or type **DBA**↵ at the Command prompt to start a baseline dimension.

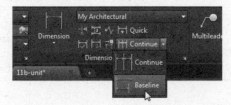

7. At the `Specify second extension line origin or [Select/Undo] <Select>:` prompt, click the upper-right corner of the entry, as shown in Figure 11.16.

FIGURE 11.16
The overall width dimension

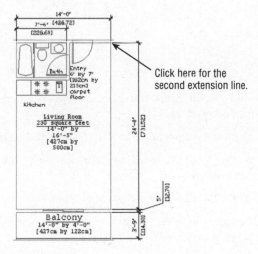

8. Press ↵ twice to exit the Baseline command.

In this example, you see that the Baseline option is similar to the Continue option, except that the Baseline option enables you to use the first extension line of the previous dimension as the base for a second dimension. The distance between the two horizontal dimension lines is controlled by the Baseline Spacing setting in the Lines tab of the New Dimension Style and Modify Dimension Style dialog boxes.

CONTINUING FROM AN OLDER DIMENSION

You may have noticed in step 8 that you had to press ↵ twice to exit the command. As with Continue, you can draw the baseline dimension from an older dimension by pressing ↵ at the `Specify second extension line origin [Select/Undo] <Select>:` prompt. You then get the `Select base dimension:` prompt, at which you can either select another dimension or press ↵ again to exit the command.

CONTROL THE STYLE USED WITH CONTINUE OR BASELINE

A system variable called `DIMCONTINUEMODE` lets you control the style of a continue or baseline dimension. At the `Type a Command` prompt, enter **dimcontinuemode**↵**1**↵ to have the baseline or continue dimension use the style of the selected dimension. Type **dimcontinuemode**↵**0**↵ to have the baseline or continue dimension use the current dimension style.

Adjusting the Distance Between Dimensions

As you work toward a deadline, you may find that you cut a few corners, or someone else does, when adding dimensions, and a set of parallel dimension lines isn't accurately placed.

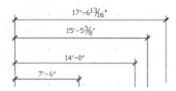

You can quickly adjust the spacing between dimension lines using the Adjust Space tool in the Dimensions panel:

1. Click the Adjust Space tool in the Dimensions panel or type **Dimspace**↵.

2. At the `Select base dimension:` prompt, click the dimension closest to the feature being dimensioned.

3. At the `Select dimensions to space:` prompt, click the next dimension.

4. Continue to select the other parallel dimensions. When you're finished with your selections, press ↵.

5. You see this prompt:

   ```
   Select dimensions to space:
   Enter value or [Auto] :
   ```

   Enter a value for the distance between the dimension lines. This value should be in full-scale distances. You can also press ↵ and AutoCAD will adjust the distance between dimensions for you.

Editing Dimensions

As you add more dimensions to your drawings, you'll find that AutoCAD occasionally places the dimension text or line in an inappropriate location or that you may need to modify the dimension text. In the following sections, you'll take an in-depth look at how you can modify dimensions to suit those special circumstances that always seem to crop up.

Appending Data to Dimension Text

So far in this chapter, you've been accepting the default dimension text. You can append information to the default dimension value or change it entirely if you need to do so. At the point when you see the temporary dimension dragging with your cursor, enter T↵. Then, using the less-than and greater-than (< and >) symbols, you can add text either before or after the default dimension, or you can replace the symbols entirely to replace the default text. The Properties palette lets you modify the existing dimension text in a similar way (see Chapter 2, "Creating Your First Drawing," for more on the Properties palette). You can open the Properties palette for a dimension by selecting the dimension and then right-clicking to open the context menu. Select Properties from there.

Let's see how this works by changing an existing dimension's text in your drawing:

1. Type **ED**↵. This starts the Ddedit command.

2. Click the last horizontal dimension that you added to the drawing at the top of the screen. The Text Editor tab appears in the Ribbon (see Figure 11.17).

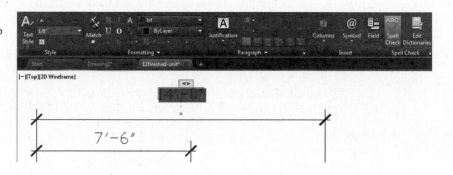

3. Press the End key to place the cursor at the end of the 14'-0" text, and then type **to face of stud** beginning with a space. The space is included to ensure that the dimension doesn't run into the text.

4. Click Close Text Editor in the Close panel of the Text Editor tab. The dimension changes to read 14'-0" to face of stud.

5. Because you don't need the new appended text for the exercise, click the Undo button in the Quick Access toolbar to remove the appended text.

If you need to restore the original dimension text for a dimension whose value has been completely replaced, you can use the steps shown in the previous exercise. However, in step 3, replace the text with the <> bracket symbols.

EDITING MULTIPLE DIMENSIONS

In the exercise where you changed an existing dimension's text, you were able to edit only a single dimension. To append text to several dimensions at once, you need to use the Dimension Edit tool. See the sidebar "Making Changes to Multiple Dimensions" later in this chapter for more on this command.

You can also have AutoCAD automatically add a dimension suffix or prefix to all dimensions instead of just a chosen few by using the Suffix or Prefix option in the Primary Units tab of the New Dimension Style or Modify Dimension Style dialog box. See the Bonus Chapter 4 for more on this feature.

AutoCAD provides the associative dimensioning capability to update dimension text automatically when a drawing is edited. Objects called *definition points* determine how edited dimensions are updated.

The definition points are located at the same points that you pick when you determine the dimension location. For example, the definition points for linear dimensions are the extension line origins. The definition points for a circle diameter are the points used to pick the circle and the opposite side of the circle. The definition points for a radius are the points used to pick the circle plus the center of the circle.

Definition points are point objects. They're difficult to see because they're usually covered by the feature that they define. You can, however, see them indirectly by using grips. The definition points of a dimension are the same as the dimension's grip points. You can see them by clicking a dimension. Try the following:

1. Make sure that the Grips feature is turned on. (See Chapter 2 to refresh your memory on the Grips feature.)

2. Click the longest of the three vertical dimensions that you drew in the earlier exercise. You'll see the grips of the dimension, which is shown in Figure 11.18.

FIGURE 11.18
The grip points are the same as the definition points on a dimension.

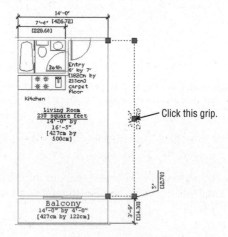

Using Grips to Make Minor Adjustments to Dimensions

The definition points, whose location you can see through their grips, are located on their own unique layer called *Defpoints*. Definition points are displayed regardless of whether the Defpoints layer is on or off.

To give you an idea of how these definition points work, the following exercises show you how to manipulate the definition points directly.

In this exercise, you'll use coordinates to move a dimension line:

1. With the grips visible, click the grip near the dimension text.

2. Move the cursor around. When you move the cursor vertically, the text moves along the dimension line. When you move the cursor horizontally, the dimension line and text move together, keeping their parallel orientation to the dimensioned floor plan. Here, the entire dimension line, including the text, moves. In a later exercise, you'll see how you can move the dimension text independently of the dimension line.

3. Enter @9'<0.⏎. Metric users should enter @275<0.⏎. The dimension line, text, and dimension extensions stretch to the new location to the right of the text (see Figure 11.19).

FIGURE 11.19
Moving the dimension
line by using its grip

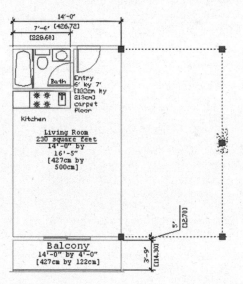

MOVING SEVERAL DIMENSION LINES AT ONCE

If you need to move several dimension lines, select them all and then Shift+click one set of dimension-line grips from each dimension. After you've selected the grips, click one of the hot grips again. You can then move all of the dimension lines at once.

In step 3 of the previous exercise, you saw that you could specify an exact distance for the dimension line's new location by entering a relative polar coordinate. Cartesian coordinates work just as well. You can even use object snaps to relocate dimension lines.

Next, try moving the dimension line back by using the Perpendicular osnap:

1. Click the grip at the bottom of the dimension line that you just edited.

2. Shift+right-click and choose Perpendicular from the Osnap context menu.

3. Place the cursor on the vertical dimension line that dimensions the balcony and click it. The selected dimension line moves to align with the other vertical dimension, back to its original location.

4. Press ↵ and then choose Zoom All from the Zoom flyout on the Navigation bar, and then click Save in the Quick Access toolbar to save this file in its current state.

MAKING CHANGES TO MULTIPLE DIMENSIONS

You can use the Dimension Edit tool to edit existing dimensions quickly. This tool gives you the ability to edit more than one dimension's text at one time. One common use for the Dimension Edit tool is to change a string of dimensions to read *Equal* instead of showing the actual dimensioned distance. The following example shows an alternative to using the Properties palette for appending text to a dimension:

1. Type **DED**↵.

2. At the prompt

   ```
   Enter type of dimension editing [Home/New/Rotate/Oblique]:
   ```

   type **N**↵ to use the New option. The Text Editor opens, showing 0 in the text box.

3. Use the arrow keys to move the cursor behind or in front of the 0, and then enter the text that you want to append to the dimension. You can remove the 0 and replace the dimension with your text as an alternative.

4. Click Close Text Editor in the Close panel of the Text Editor tab.

5. At the `Select objects:` prompt, pick the dimensions that you want to edit. The `Select objects:` prompt remains, enabling you to select several dimensions.

6. Press ↵ to finish your selection. The dimension changes to include your new text or to replace the existing dimension text.

The Dimension Edit tool is useful in editing dimension text, but you can also use this tool to make graphical changes to the text. Here is a list of the other Dimension Edit tool options:

Home Moves the dimension text to its standard default position and angle.

Rotate Rotates the dimension text to a new angle.

Oblique Skews the dimension extension lines to a new angle. (See the section "Skewing Dimension Lines" later in this chapter.)

Changing Style Settings of Individual Dimensions

In some cases, you have to change an individual dimension's style settings in order to edit it. For example, if you try to move the text of a typical linear dimension, you may find that the text and dimension lines are inseparable. You need to make a change to the dimension style setting that controls how AutoCAD locates dimension text in relation to the dimension line. The following section describes how you can change the style settings of individual dimensions to facilitate changes in the dimension.

Moving Fixed Dimension Text

You've seen how dimension text is attached to the dimension line so that when the text is moved, the dimension line follows. You may encounter situations in which you want to move the text independently of the dimension line. The following steps show how you can separate dimension text from its dimension line. These steps also show how you can change a single dimension's style settings:

1. Make sure that Dynamic Input is turned on in the status bar.

2. Click the dimension that you want to edit to expose its grips.

3. Hover over the grip nearest the dimension text. The multifunction grip menu appears (see Figure 11.20).

FIGURE 11.20

The multifunction grip menu for a dimension text

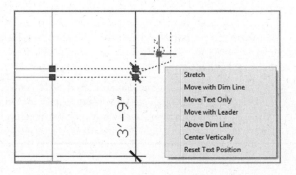

4. Select the option that you want to use to move the text. For example, to move the 5" dimension text in Figure 11.20, select Move Text Only (which removes the leader, as explained later) or Move With Leader.

5. Move the text, and when you are satisfied with the new location, press the Esc key to clear your selection.

As you saw in Figure 11.20, you have a number of options for moving dimension text. The multifunction grip options are self-explanatory, but you might want to experiment with them to see how each one behaves.

When you use some of the dimension text multifunction grip options, you are changing the property of that dimension. In fact, the old way of moving dimension text involved changing a setting in the Properties palette for a selected dimension. The Move Text, Add Leader option in the Text Movement listing of the Fit category of the Properties palette lets you move the dimension text independently of the dimension line. This option is similar to the Move With Leader option in the multifunction grip menu. It also draws a leader from the dimension line to the text. Another option—Move Text, No Leader—does the same thing but doesn't include a leader. This option has the same effect as the Move Text Only option in the multifunction grip menu. You can also set these options for a dimension style by using the Text Placement options in the Fit tab of the New Dimension Style or Modify Dimension Style dialog box.

The Properties palette gives you access to many of the settings that you saw for setting up dimension styles. The main difference here is that the Properties palette affects only the dimensions that you've selected.

In a previous exercise, you changed the format setting of a single dimension *after* it was placed. These settings can be made a standard part of your Architectural dimension style by using the Modify button in the Dimension Style Manager.

If you have multiple dimension styles and you want to change an existing dimension to the current dimension style, use the Update tool. Choose Update on the Dimensions panel or type **-Dimstyle↵A↵**. Make sure that you include the hyphen in front of the Dimstyle command. Then select the dimensions that you want to change and press ↵. The selected dimensions will be converted to the current style.

> ### ROTATING AND POSITIONING DIMENSION TEXT
>
> Once in a while, dimension text works better if it's kept in a horizontal orientation, even if the dimension itself isn't horizontal. To rotate dimension text, click the Text Angle tool from the Annotate tab's expanded Dimensions panel, select the dimension text, and then enter an angle or select two points to indicate an angle graphically. You can also enter **0↵** to return the dimension text to its default angle.
>
> If you need to move the dimension text to the left, center, or right of the dimension line, you can use the Left Justify, Center Justify, or Right Justify tool in the Annotate tab's expanded Dimensions panel. Note that if these Justify options are used on vertical dimensions, Right will shift the dimension to the top and Left will shift it to the bottom.

Editing Dimensions and Other Objects Together

It's helpful to be able to edit a dimension directly by using its grips. However, the key feature of dimensions in AutoCAD is their ability to adjust themselves *automatically* to changes in the drawing.

To see how this works, try moving the living room closer to the bathroom wall. You can move a group of lines and vertices by using the Stretch command and the Crossing option:

1. Click the Stretch tool in the Home tab's Modify panel, or type **S↵C↵**. You'll see the following prompts:

```
At the Select objects to stretch
by crossing-window or crossing-polygon...
Select objects: C
Specify first corner:
```

2. Pick a crossing window, as illustrated in Figure 11.21, and then press ↵ to confirm your selection.

FIGURE 11.21
The Stretch crossing window

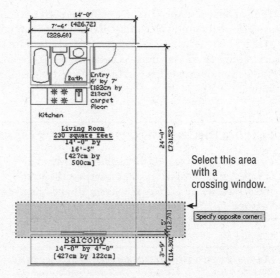

3. At the Specify base point or [Displacement] <Displacement>: prompt, pick any point on the screen.

4. At the Specify second point or <use first point as displacement>: prompt, enter @2'<90↵ to move the wall 2' in a 90° direction. Metric users should enter @61<90↵. The wall moves, and the dimension text changes to reflect the new dimensions, as shown in Figure 11.22.

FIGURE 11.22
The moved wall, with the updated dimensions

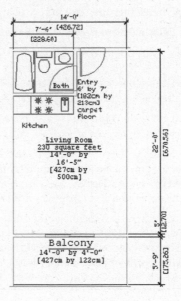

5. After viewing the result of using the Stretch tool, click the Undo tool in the Quick Access toolbar or type **U**↵ to change the drawing back to its previous state.

You can also use the Mirror, Rotate, and Stretch commands with dimensions. The polar arrays also work, and you can use Extend and Trim with linear dimensions.

When you're editing dimensioned objects, be sure to select the dimension associated with the object being edited. As you select objects, using the crossing window (C) or crossing polygon (CP) selection option helps you include the dimensions. For more on these selection options, see Chapter 2.

PLACING DIMENSIONS OVER HATCH PATTERNS

If a hatch pattern or solid fill completely covers a dimension, you can use the Draworder command to have AutoCAD draw the dimension over the hatch or solid fill. See Chapter 7, "Mastering Viewing Tools, Hatches, and External References," and Chapter 13, "Copying Existing Drawings from Other Sources," for more on various uses of the Draworder command.

MODIFYING THE DIMENSION STYLE SETTINGS BY USING OVERRIDE

In the section "Moving Fixed Dimension Text," you used the Properties palette to facilitate moving the dimension text. You can also choose the Override tool in the Annotate tab's expanded Dimensions panel (Dimoverride command) to accomplish the same thing. The Override option enables you to change an individual dimension's style settings. Here's an example that shows how you can use the Override option in place of the Properties palette in the exercise in "Moving Fixed Dimension Text":

1. Press the Esc key twice to make sure that you aren't in the middle of a command. Then choose Override from the Annotate tab's expanded Dimensions panel.

2. At the following prompt, type **Dimtmove**↵:

    Enter dimension variable name to override or [Clear overrides]:

3. At the `Enter new value for dimension variable <0>:` prompt, enter **2**↵. This has the same effect as selecting Move Text, Add Leader from the Fit category of the Properties palette.

4. The `Enter dimension variable name to override:` prompt appears again, enabling you to enter another dimension variable. Press ↵ to move to the next step.

5. At the `Select objects:` prompt, select the dimension that you want to change. You can select a group of dimensions if you want to change several dimensions at once. Press ↵ when you've finished with your selection. The dimension settings change for the selected dimensions. In this case, the dimension text can be moved independently of the dimension line.

As you can see from this example, the Dimoverride command requires that you know exactly which dimension variable to edit in order to make the desired modification. In this case, setting the Dimtmove variable to 2 lets you move the dimension text independently of the dimension line. If you find the Dimoverride command useful, consult Bonus Chapter 4 to determine which system variable corresponds to the Dimension Style dialog box settings.

Associating Dimensions with Objects

You've seen how dimensions and the objects with which they're associated can move together so that the dimension remains connected to the object. When you're in the process of editing a drawing, dimensions may lose their association with objects, so you may need to re-create an association between a dimension and an object. The following steps show you how this is done:

1. Choose Reassociate from the Annotate tab's expanded Dimensions panel. You can also type **Dimreassociate**↵ at the Command prompt.

2. At the following prompt, select the dimension that you want to reassociate with an object, and then press ↵:

   ```
   Select dimensions to reassociate
   Select Objects or [Disassociated]:
   ```

3. At the Specify first extension line origin or [Select object] <next>: prompt, note that an X appears at one of the dimension's definition points.

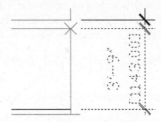

4. Use the Endpoint osnap, and click the end of the object that you want to have connected to the definition point indicated in step 3.

5. An X appears at the dimension's other definition point. Use the Endpoint osnap again, and click the other endpoint of the object that you want associated with the dimension. You now have the dimension associated with the endpoints of the object. You may have to adjust the location of the dimension line at this point.

In step 3, you see an X at the location of a dimension definition point. If the definition point is already associated with an object, the X appears with a box around it. The box is a reminder that the definition point is already associated with an object and that you'll be changing its association. In this situation, you can press ↵ to switch to the dimension's other definition point.

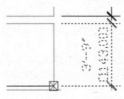

Also in step 3, you have the option to select an object. This option enables you to associate the dimension with an entire object instead of with just one endpoint. If you type **S**↵ at that prompt in step 3, you can then select the object that you want to associate with the dimension. The dimension changes so that its definition points coincide with the endpoints of the object. The dimension remains in its original orientation. For example, a vertical dimension remains vertical even if you associate the dimension with a horizontal line. In this situation, the dimension dutifully dimensions the endpoints of the line but shows a distance of 0.

REMOVING DIMENSION ASSOCIATIONS

You can remove a dimension's association with an object by using the Dimdisassociate command. Type **Dimdisassociate**↵ at the Command prompt, select the dimension(s), and then press ↵.

Adding a String of Dimensions with a Single Operation

In AutoCAD you can create a string of dimensions using a single operation. The Qdim command lets you select a set of objects instead of having to select points. The following exercise demonstrates how the Qdim command works:

1. If you haven't done so already, zoom out so that you have an overall view of the Unit floor plan.

2. Click Quick Dimension on the Dimensions panel.

3. At the Select geometry to dimension: prompt, place a selection window around the entire left-side wall of the unit.

4. Press ↵ to finish your selection. The following prompt appears:

```
Specify dimension line position, or
[Continuous/Staggered/Baseline/Ordinate/Radius/Diameter/
datumPoint/Edit/seTtings] :
```

5. Click a point to the left of the wall to place the dimension. A string of dimensions appears, displaying all of the dimensions for the wall (see Figure 11.23).

6. When you've finished reviewing the results of this exercise, exit the file without saving it.

The prompt in step 4 indicates several types of dimensions from which you can choose. For example, if you want the dimensions to originate from a single baseline, you can enter **B**↵ in step 4 to select the Baseline option.

The Qdim command can be a time-saver when you want to dimension a wall quickly. It may not work in all situations, but if the object that you're dimensioning is fairly simple, it can be all that you need.

In this exercise, you used a simple window to select the wall. For more complex shapes, try using a crossing polygon selection window. See Chapter 2 for more on crossing polygons.

FIGURE 11.23
The dimensions for
the wall

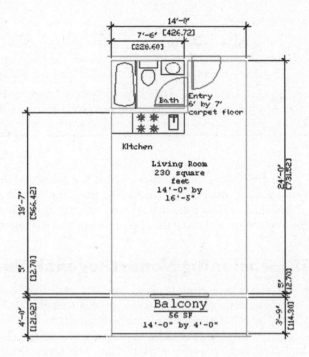

Adding or Removing the Alternate Dimensions

You may eventually encounter a drawing that contains alternate dimensions, as shown in some of the figures earlier in this chapter. You can remove those alternate dimensions by turning off the alternate dimension features. Here's how it's done:

1. Click the Dimension Style tool in the Annotate tab's Dimensions panel title bar or enter **D↵** to open the Dimension Style Manager.

2. Select the style that uses the alternate units. In the Styles list box, choose Modify.

3. Select the Alternate Units tab.

4. Click the Display Alternate Units check box to remove the check mark.

5. Click OK, and then click Close to close the Dimension Style Manager.

USING OBJECT SNAP WHILE DIMENSIONING

When you pick intersections and endpoints frequently, as you do during dimensioning, it can be inconvenient to use the Osnap context menu. If you know that you'll be using certain osnaps frequently, you can use running osnaps. (See the sidebar "The Osnap Options" in Chapter 3 for more on setting up running osnaps.)

continues

continued

After you've designated your running osnaps, the next time you're prompted to select a point, the selected osnap modes are automatically activated. You can still override the default settings by using the Osnap context menu (Shift+right-click the mouse).

There is a drawback to setting a running osnap mode: When your drawing gets crowded, you can end up picking the wrong point by accident. However, you can easily toggle the running osnap mode off by clicking Object Snap in the status bar or by pressing F3.

The dimensions that use the style that you just edited change to remove the alternate dimensions. You can also perform the reverse operation and add alternate dimensions to an existing set of dimensions. Follow the steps shown here, but instead of removing the check mark in step 4, add the check mark and make the appropriate setting changes to the rest of the Alternate Units tab.

Dimensioning Nonorthogonal Objects

So far, you've been reading about how to work with linear dimensions. You can also dimension nonorthogonal objects, such as circles, arcs, triangles, and trapezoids. In the following sections, you'll practice dimensioning a nonorthogonal object.

For the following exercises, you'll use a drawing of a hexagonal-shaped window. Open the 11a-wind.dwg file from the sample files. This file is set up for Imperial users but also displays metric measurements as alternative units. You can use this file to follow along.

Dimensioning Nonorthogonal Linear Distances

 Now you'll dimension the window. The unusual shape of the window prevents you from using the horizontal or vertical dimensions that you've used already. However, choosing Aligned from the Dimension flyout in the Dimensions panel enables you to dimension at an angle. Note that the drawing used for this exercise is set up to show alternate units in metric measurements with primary units in Imperial.

1. Click the Aligned tool in the Dimension flyout on the Dimensions panel. You can also enter **DAL**↵ to start the aligned dimension.

2. At the Specify first extension line origin or <select object>: prompt, press ↵. You could pick extension-line origins as you did in earlier examples, but pressing ↵ shows you how the Select Object option works.

3. At the Select object to dimension: prompt, pick the upper-right face of the hexagon near coordinate 29,22. As the prompt indicates, you can also pick an arc or a circle for this type of dimension.

4. At the Specify dimension line location or [Mtext/Text/Angle]: prompt, pick a point near coordinate 34,24. The dimension appears in the drawing, as shown in Figure 11.24.

FIGURE 11.24
The aligned dimension
of a nonorthogonal line

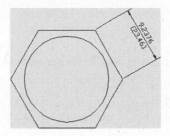

Just as with linear dimensions, you can enter **T.** in step 4 to enter alternate text for the dimension.

Next, you'll dimension a face of the hexagon. Instead of its actual length, however, you'll dimension a distance at a specified angle—the distance from the center of the face:

1. Select the Linear tool from the Dimension flyout on the Dimensions panel or type **DLI.**.

2. At the `Specify first extension line origin or <select object>:` prompt, press ↵.

3. At the `Select object to dimension:` prompt, pick the lower-right face of the hexagon near coordinate 29,14.

4. At the `Specify dimension line location or [Mtext/Text/Angle/Horizontal/ Vertical/Rotated]:` prompt, type **R.** to select the Rotated option.

5. At the `Specify angle of dimension line <0>:` prompt, enter **30.**.

6. At the `Specify dimension line location or [Mtext/Text/Angle/Horizontal/ Vertical/Rotated]:` prompt, pick a point near coordinate 33,7. Your drawing will look like Figure 11.25.

FIGURE 11.25
A linear dimension using
the Rotated option

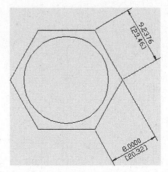

The Dimrotated command accomplishes the same thing with a slight change in the sequence of steps.

Dimensioning Radii, Diameters, and Arcs

To dimension circular objects, you use another set of options from the Dimension menu:

1. Select the Angular tool from the Dimension flyout on the Dimensions panel, or enter **DAN**↵ at the Command prompt.

2. At the `Select arc, circle, line, or <specify vertex>:` prompt, pick the upper-left face of the hexagon near coordinate 15,22.

3. At the `Select second line:` prompt, pick the top face at coordinate 22,26.

4. At the `Specify dimension arc line location or [Mtext/Text/Angle/Quadrant]:` prompt, notice that as you move the cursor around the upper-left corner of the hexagon, the dimension changes, as shown in the top images of Figure 11.26.

5. Pick a point near coordinate 21,20. The dimension is fixed in the drawing. (See the bottom image of Figure 11.26.)

FIGURE 11.26
The angular dimension added to the window frame

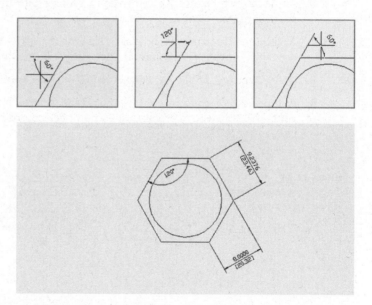

If you need to make subtle adjustments to the dimension line or text location, you can do so by using grips after you place the angular dimension.

Now try the Diameter option, which shows the diameter of a circle:

1. Click the Diameter tool in the Dimension flyout on the Dimensions panel, or enter **DDI**↵ at the Command prompt.

2. At the Select arc or circle: prompt, pick the circle.

3. At the Specify dimension line location or [Mtext/Text/Angle]: prompt, you see the diameter dimension drag along the circle as you move the cursor. If you move the cursor outside the circle, the dimension line and text also move outside the circle. (See the top image in Figure 11.27.)

If the dimension text can't fit in the circle, AutoCAD gives you the option to place the dimension text outside the circle as you drag the temporary dimension to a horizontal position.

4. Place the cursor inside the circle so that the dimension arrow points in a horizontal direction, as shown in the bottom image of Figure 11.27.

FIGURE 11.27
Dimension showing the diameter of a circle

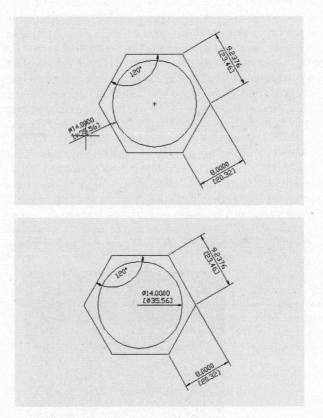

5. With the text centered, click the mouse.

The Radius tool in the Dimension flyout on the Dimensions panel gives you a radius dimension, just as the Diameter tool provides a circle's diameter. Figure 11.28 shows a radius dimension on the outside of the circle, but you can place it inside in a manner similar to how you place the diameter dimension.

FIGURE 11.28
A radius dimension
shown on the outside of
the circle

FIGURE 11.28
A radius dimension
shown on the outside of
the circle

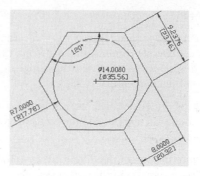

The Center Mark tool on the Centerlines panel places a center mark in the center of the selected arc or circle. This center mark is *associative*, meaning that it will follow changes in the location and size of the circle or arc with which it is associated. The center mark extension lines can also be edited using grips. The Centerdisassociate command can be used to "disassociate" the center mark from the circle or arc. Once disassociated, the center mark behaves as an independent object until the Centerreassociate command is used to re-associate it.

Properties of the center mark, such as the center mark size, the extension line visibility, or the extension line linetype, can be modified through the Properties palette. Select the center mark, and right-click and select Properties to open the Properties palette. Here you can set values such as the rotation angle of the center mark, the cross size, or the gap between the cross and extension line. You can also set the length of the extension line beyond the dimensioned object using the Left, Right, Top, and Bottom extension options. Figure 11.29 shows an example of a center mark placed on a circle object, along with the Properties palette. You can also double-click the center mark to open the Quick Properties palette, which gives you access to the extension line properties, such as length and display. You can also adjust the extension lines individually by clicking on the Center Mark's grips or all at the same time by hovering over the center grip and clicking Change extension length from the context menu.

FIGURE 11.29
The center mark
Properties
palette and the
components of
the center mark

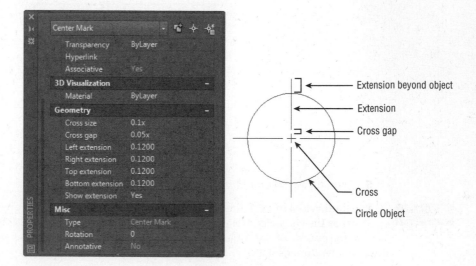

If you want to modify the default values for the center mark properties, you can do so using a set of system variables. Table 11.1 describes these system variables and their use.

TABLE 11.1:   The center mark system variables

SYSTEM VARIABLE	FUNCTION
Centerexe	Controls the distance at which the center mark line extends beyond the dimensioned object
Centermarkexe	Controls the display of the center mark extension lines
Centerlayer	Specifies the layer for the center mark
Centerltype	Controls the linetype used by the center mark extension lines
Centerltscale	Controls the linetype scale used by the center mark extension lines
Centercrosssize	Controls the size of the central cross of the center mark
Centercrossgap	Controls the gap between the central cross and the center mark extension lines

If you need to dimension an arc or a circle whose center isn't in the drawing area, you can use the jogged dimension. Here are the steps:

1. Click the Jogged tool from the Dimension flyout on the Annotate tab's Dimensions panel, or enter **DJO**↵ at the Command prompt.

2. At the Select arc or circle: prompt, select the object that you want to dimension.

3. At the Specify center location override: prompt, select a point that indicates the general direction to the center of the arc or circle. A dimension line appears and follows the movement of your cursor.

4. Position the dimension line where you want it, and then click.

5. Position the dimension line jog where you want it, and then click. The jogged dimension is placed in the drawing (see Figure 11.30).

FIGURE 11.30
The jogged dimension
in the drawing

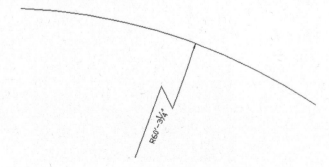

Arc lengths can also be given a dimension using the Arc Length tool. Choose the Arc Length tool from the Dimension flyout on the Dimensions panel, or enter **DAR**⏎ at the Command prompt. At the Select Arc or polyline arc segment: prompt, select the arc that you want to dimension. It can be either a plain arc or a polyline arc. Once you've selected the arc, the arc dimension appears and moves with the cursor. You can then select the location for the dimension.

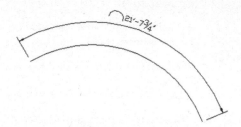

Skewing Dimension Lines

At times, you may need to force the extension lines to take on an angle other than 90° to the dimension line. This is a common requirement of isometric drawings, in which most lines are at 30° or 60° angles instead of 90°. To facilitate nonorthogonal dimensions like these, AutoCAD offers the Oblique option:

1. Choose Oblique from the expanded Dimensions panel, or type **DED**⏎**O**⏎.

2. At the Select objects: prompt, pick the aligned dimension in the upper-right portion of the drawing and press ⏎ to confirm your selection.

3. At the Enter obliquing angle (Press ENTER for none): prompt, enter **60**⏎ for 60°. The dimension will skew so that the extension lines are at 60° (see Figure 11.31).

4. Save the drawing.

FIGURE 11.31
The extension lines
at 60°

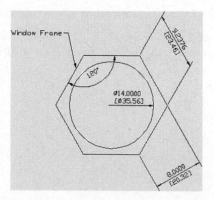

Using the Dimension Tool

Dimensions are often added to a drawing after the drawing has reached a fairly high level of completion. Most of the dimensions are then added all at once without using other tools. AutoCAD offers the Dimension tool, which lets you apply sets of dimensions without having to stop to select multiple tools. This can help to streamline your dimensioning work.

With the Dimension tool, you can add a radius dimension to a circle and then go on to dimension a polygon or add a set of linear dimensions without having to select another tool.

To get a better idea of how the Dimension tool works, try the following exercise. This is an exercise similar to the one you saw under "Drawing Linear Dimensions" earlier in this chapter, but this time you will use the Dimension tool in the Dimensions panel.

1. Open the 11b-unit.dwg drawing from the sample files. This file is set up to display both Imperial and metric dimensions.

2. Click the Dimension tool in the Annotate tab's Dimensions panel or type **DIM**↵.

3. Hover over the line representing the interior wall on the right side of the plan. You see a temporary dimension appear (see Figure 11.32).

FIGURE 11.32

The temporary dimension appears as you hover over the line.

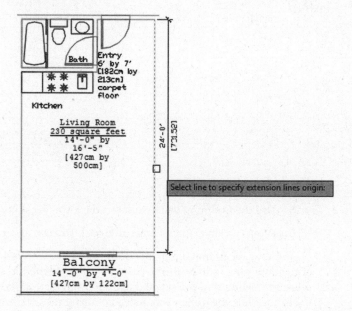

4. Move the cursor slightly to the left of the line, and then move it back to the right. The temporary dimension shifts position depending on the side of the line you point to.

5. Adjust the cursor so that the temporary dimension appears on the right side of the line, and then click that location. The dimension now follows the cursor.

6. Enter @4′<0↵. The dimension is placed in the drawing. Notice that the cursor and the command line still display the Select object prompt. This tells you that you are still in the Dim command. Also notice that the prompt offers several options (see Figure 11.33).

FIGURE 11.33
The Dimension
tool prompt

[Angular Baseline Continue Ordinate aliGn Distribute Layer Undo]:

7. Type **C**↵ and then select the dimension extension line toward the bottom of the dimension that you just added.

8. Use the Endpoint osnap to select the upper-right corner of the balcony (see Figure 11.34). Another dimension is added.

FIGURE 11.34
Select these endpoints
to continue the
dimension.

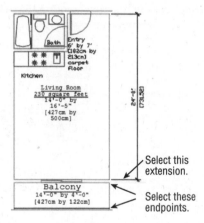

9. Use the Endpoint osnap to select the lower-right corner of the balcony (see Figure 11.34).

10. Press ↵↵↵ to exit the Dimension tool. You can also press the Esc key.

You may recall that in the first dimensioning exercise in this chapter, you selected the corners of the floor plan to indicate the points that you wanted to dimension. In the last exercise, you selected the line that you wanted to dimension instead of the points. In addition, you just typed **C**↵ to continue the dimension instead of using the Continue tool in the Dimensions panel. These differences may seem minor, but they can help to streamline your work as you add dimensions to your drawing.

Take a look at the options for the Dimension tool shown earlier in Figure 11.33. Most of these options offer the same functionality as tools that you've already seen enabling you to add different types of dimensions without leaving the Dimension tool. A few of the options are unique to the Dimension tool. Table 11.2 gives you a list of those options and their use.

TABLE 11.2:   The Dimension tool options

OPTION	FUNCTION
Angular	Draws an angular dimension between two nonparallel lines. This option is similar to the Angular tool in the Dimension flyout and the Dimangular command.
Baseline	Draws a dimension or set of dimensions from a dimension extension. This is similar to the Baseline tool or the Dimbaseline command.
Continue	Draws a string of dimensions from an existing dimension extension line. This is similar to the Continue tool or the Dimcontinue command.
Ordinate	Draws ordinate dimensions. This is similar to the Ordinate tool or the Dimordinate command (see "Applying Ordinate Dimensions" later in this chapter).
Align	Aligns a dimension to another dimension. This can be used to "straighten" a series of dimensions that are not in line with each other.
Distribute	Adjusts the vertical spacing of dimensions to be equidistant. This can be used to adjust stacked baseline dimensions so that they are evenly spaced.
Layer	Sets the layer for dimensions by entering a layer name or by selecting an object whose layer you want to use.
Undo	Undoes the last Dim command operation.

Another feature of the Dimension tool is its ability to recognize an object and apply the appropriate dimension type to that object. To see how this works, try the following exercise:

1. Close the 11b-unit.dwg file without saving it, and then open the 11b-wind.dwg file.

2. Click the Dimension tool, or type **DIM↵**, and then hover over the line in the upper-right side of the hexagon (see Figure 11.35).

FIGURE 11.35
Use the Dimension tool to select objects to be dimensioned.

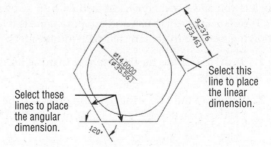

3. Adjust the temporary dimension so that it appears above and to the right of the line and click.

4. Click again to place the dimension, as shown in Figure 11.35.

5. Hover over the circle. You see a temporary diameter dimension. You can change the location of the dimension from the inside to the outside of the circle by adjusting the cursor

location. Also notice that the prompt offers the Radius, Jogged, and Angular options. You can enter the uppercase letter of the option to control the type of dimension that will be applied to the circle.

6. With the dimension on the inside of the circle, click the mouse. The dimension is now fixed inside the circle.

7. Adjust the location where the dimension touches the circle and click the mouse. The Diameter dimension is fixed in position.

8. Click the bottommost line of the hexagon, and then click the lower-left line of the hexagon (see Figure 11.35). A temporary angular dimension appears.

9. Slowly rotate the cursor around the corner where the two lines meet. Notice that a temporary angular dimension follows the cursor, offering a different dimension based on the location of the cursor, as shown earlier in Figure 11.26.

10. Place the cursor on the outside of the hexagon to display the 120-degree angle and click the mouse. The angular dimension is placed in the drawing.

11. Right-click and click Enter to exit the Dimension tool.

12. Close the 11b-wind.dwg file without saving it.

In this exercise, you saw how the Dimension tool offered the appropriate dimension type when hovering over an object. You also saw how you can continue to add dimensions without having to select a tool from the Ribbon panel.

As you work with the dimensioning tools in AutoCAD, you may find that you only need the Dimension tool for most of your dimensions. The Dimension tool may offer a faster way to add dimensions, depending on the type of drawing you are working on.

Adding a Note with a Leader Arrow

Certification
Objective

One type of dimension is something like a text-dimension hybrid. The AutoCAD Multileader tool lets you add a text note combined with an arrow, which points to an object in your drawing. Multileaders are easy to use and offer the same text formatting tools as the Mtext tool. Try the following exercise to get familiar with multileaders:

1. Turn off Osnaps for this exercise to make it easier to select points in a crowded area of the drawing.

2. Return to the 11a-wind.dwg file, and click the Multileader tool in the Annotate tab's Leaders panel (see Figure 11.36), or enter **MLD**↵.

FIGURE 11.36
The Leaders panel

3. At the `Specify leader arrowhead location or [leader Landing first/Content first/Options] <Options>:` prompt, pick a point near the top-left edge of the hexagon at coordinate 16,24 (45,59 for metric users).

4. At the `Specify leader landing location:` prompt, enter **@6<110↵**. The Text Editor tab appears, along with the text cursor at the note location.

5. Enter **Window Frame** for the note, and then click Close Text Editor in the Text Editor tab's Close panel. Your note appears with the leader arrow similar to the one shown in Figure 11.37.

FIGURE 11.37
The leader with a
note added

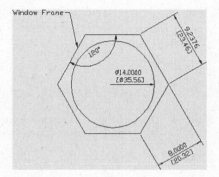

The text in the note is in the current text style unless you specify another style in the Text tab of the New Dimension Style or Modify Dimension Style dialog box. (See the section "The Text Tab" in Bonus Chapter 4 for more information.)

SETTING THE SCALE OF LEADERS

Multileaders have an Annotative option that allows them to adjust automatically to the scale of the drawing. You can find the Annotative option setting in the properties for a specific multileader in the drawing or in the multileader style setting. See the Scale option in Table 11.4, later in this chapter, under the Leader Structure tab.

The Multileader tool offers a lot of options that aren't obvious when you're using it. In step 2 of the previous example, after choosing Multileader, you can press ↵ to modify the behavior of the Multileader tool. You'll see the following prompt:

```
Enter an option [Leader type/leader lAnding/Content
type/Maxpoints/First angle/Second angle/eXit options]:
```

Table 11.3 gives you a rundown of these options and their functions.

TABLE 11.3: The Multileader options

OPTION	FUNCTION
Leader type	Allows you to choose between straight-line leaders, spline (curved) leaders, or no leaders.
leader lAnding	Determines whether a leader landing is used. The *leader landing* is the short line that connects the arrow to the note. It also lets you set landing distance.
Content type	Lets you select between Mtext or a block for the leader note. You also have the option to choose None.
Maxpoints	Lets you set the number of points that you select for the leader. The default is 2.
First angle	Lets you constrain the angle of the leader line to a fixed value.
Second angle	Lets you constrain the angle of the arrow's second line segment if you're using more than two points for the Maxpoints option.
eXit options	Lets you return to the main part of the Multileader command to draw the leader.

Creating Multileader Styles

Besides using the options shown in Table 11.3, you can create multileader styles to control the appearance of multileaders. Multileader styles are similar in concept to text and dimension styles. They allow you to set up the appearance of the leader under a name that you can call up at any time. For example, you may want to have one type of leader that uses a block instead of text for the note and another leader that uses a dot in place of an arrow. Alternatively, you may want to set up a style that uses curved lines instead of straight ones for the leader line. You can create a multileader style for each of these types of leader features and then switch between the leader styles, depending on the requirements of your leader note.

To set up or modify a multileader style, click the Multileader Style Manager tool in the Annotate tab's Leaders panel title bar. You can also enter **MLS**⏎ at the Command prompt. Doing so opens the Multileader Style Manager, shown in Figure 11.38. From here, you can select an existing style from the list on the left and click Modify to edit it, or you can click New to create a new one. If you click New, you're asked to select an existing style as a basis for your new style.

FIGURE 11.38
The Multileader
Style Manager

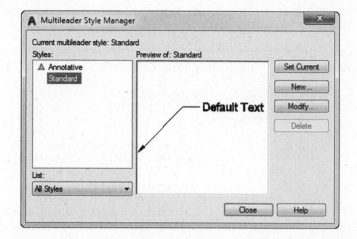

When you click Modify or New, the Modify Multileader Style (see Figure 11.39) dialog box opens.

FIGURE 11.39
The Modify Multileader
Style dialog box

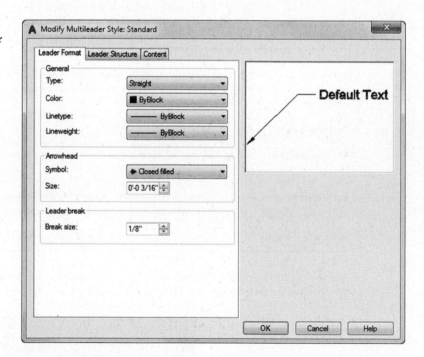

Table 11.4 describes the options in each of the tabs of the Modify Multileader Style dialog box. Some of these options are the same as those for the Multileader command.

TABLE 11.4: The Modify Multileader Style dialog box options

TAB AND GROUP	FUNCTION
Leader Format tab	
General	Lets you set the leader line to straight or curved. You can also set the color, lineweight, and linetype for the leader line.
Arrowhead	Controls the size and shape of the arrowheads.
Leader Break	Controls the size of the gap in a leader line when the Leaderbreak command is applied. Leaderbreak places a break on a leader line where two leader lines cross.
Leader Structure tab	
Constraints	Determines the number of line segments in the leader line. You can also apply angle constraints to the leader-line segments.
Landing Settings	Controls the leader-line landing segment. This is the last line segment that points to the note.
Scale	Lets you control the scale of the leader components. You can either apply a fixed scale or use the Annotative option to have the drawing annotation scale apply to the leader.
Content tab	
Multileader Type	Lets you select the type of object that will be used for the leader note. The options are Mtext, Block, and None.
Text Options	Gives you control over the way the leader note appears. You can control color, text style, size, justification, and orientation.
Leader Connection	Determines the position between the leader line and the note.

Once you've set up a multileader style, you can make it the default style by selecting it from the Multileader Style drop-down list on the Annotate tab's Leaders panel.

The selected style will be applied to any new multileader that you add to your drawing. You can also change the style of an existing multileader. To do this, click the multileader to select it, and then select the multileader style that you want from the Leaders panel drop-down list.

Editing Multileader Notes

If you need to make changes to the note portion of a multileader, you can do so by double-clicking the note. Doing so brings up the Text Editor tab in the Ribbon, allowing you to make changes as you would in a word processor.

At other times, you may want to change the leader line, arrows, or other graphic features of the multileader. For example, you may want to have all of the notes aligned vertically for a neater appearance. As another option, you may want to add more leader arrows so that the note points to several objects in the drawing instead of just one.

The Leaders panel offers several tools that let you make these types of changes to your leader notes (refer back to Figure 11.36). The Add Leader and Remove Leader tools let you add or remove leaders from a multileader. Add Leader is a handy tool if you want a single note to point to several objects. The Align tool lets you align the note portion of several multileaders. Finally, the Collect tool lets you collect several multileaders that use blocks for notes into a single note.

Breaking a Dimension Line for a Leader

In a crowded drawing, your multileader arrow may have to cross over a dimension line. In many drafting conventions, when a leader line crosses over a dimension line, the dimension line must be shown with a gap.

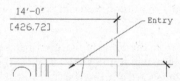

You can apply a gap to a dimension line using the Dimbreak tool. Here's how it works:

1. Choose Break from the Dimensions panel.

2. At the Select dimension to add/remove break or [Multiple]: prompt, select a dimension line, or enter **M**↵ and select multiple dimension lines.

3. When you're finished with your selection, press ↵. Note that this ↵ is necessary only when using the Multiple option.

4. At the Select object to break dimension or [Auto/Manual/Remove] <Auto>: prompt, press ↵. A gap appears wherever a leader line or other dimension line crosses over the selected dimension line.

If you prefer to indicate a break manually, enter **M**↵ at the prompt in step 4. Doing so allows you to select two points on the dimension, indicating where the gap is to occur. The drawback to adding a break manually is that the break will not follow the leader line if the leader line is moved. The break will have to be removed and replaced.

If additional dimension or leader lines are added that cross over the dimension line, repeat your use of the Dimbreak tool. To remove an existing break, use the Remove option in step 4 by entering **R**↵.

Applying Ordinate Dimensions

In mechanical drafting, *ordinate dimensions* are used to maintain the accuracy of machined parts by establishing an origin on the part. All major dimensions are described as x-coordinates or y-coordinates of that origin. The origin is usually an easy-to-locate feature of the part, such as a machined bore or two machined surfaces.

Figure 11.40 shows a typical application of ordinate dimensions. In the lower-right corner, note the two dimensions whose leaders are jogged. Also note the origin location in the center circle.

FIGURE 11.40
A drawing
using ordinate
dimensions

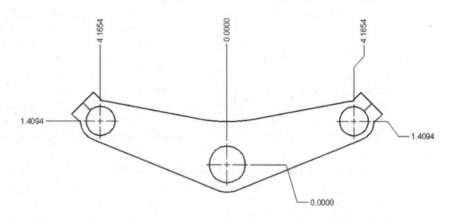

To use the Ordinate command, you can practice on the `Ord Sample.dwg` file to perform the following steps:

1. Select Origin from the View tab's Coordinates panel, or type **UCS↵Or↵**. If you don't see the Coordinates panel in the View tab, go to the View tab, right-click in the Ribbon, and select Show Panels ➤ Coordinates.

2. At the `Specify new origin point <0,0,0>:` prompt, click the exact location of the origin of your part.

3. Toggle Ortho mode on in the status bar.

4. Click the Ordinate tool in the Dimension flyout on the Annotate tab's Dimensions panel. You can also enter **DOR↵** to start the ordinate dimension.

5. At the `Specify feature location:` prompt, click the item that you want to dimension. The direction of the leader determines whether the dimension will be of the Xdatum or the Ydatum.

6. At the `Specify leader endpoint or [Xdatum/Ydatum/Mtext/Text/Angle]:` prompt, indicate the length and direction of the leader. Do this by positioning the rubber-banding leader perpendicular to the coordinate direction that you want to dimension and then clicking that point.

In steps 1 and 2, you used the UCS feature to establish a second origin in the drawing. The Ordinate Dimension tool then uses that origin to determine the ordinate dimensions. You'll get a chance to work with the UCS feature in Chapter 21, "Using Advanced 3D Features." You may have noticed options in the Command window for the Ordinate Dimension tool. The Xdatum and Ydatum options force the dimension to be of the x- or y-coordinate no matter what direction the leader takes. The Mtext option opens the Text Editor tab in the Ribbon, enabling you to append or replace the ordinate dimension text. The Text option lets you enter replacement text directly through the Command window.

If you turn off Ortho mode, the dimension leader is drawn with a jog to maintain the orthogonal line segment to the dimension text (look back at Figure 11.40).

Adding Tolerance Notation

In mechanical drafting, *tolerances* are a key part of a drawing's notation. They specify the allowable variation in size and shape that a mechanical part can have. To help facilitate tolerance notation, AutoCAD provides the Tolerance command, which offers common ISO tolerance symbols together with a quick way to build a standard feature-control symbol. *Feature-control symbols* are industry-standard symbols used to specify tolerances. If you're a mechanical engineer or drafter, the AutoCAD tolerance notation options will be a valuable tool. However, a full discussion of tolerances requires a basic understanding of mechanical design and drafting, and it is beyond the scope of this book.

Inserting Tolerance and Datum Values

To use the Tolerance command, choose Tolerance from the expanded Dimensions panel or type **TOL**↵ at the Command prompt to open the Geometric Tolerance dialog box (see Figure 11.41).

FIGURE 11.41
The Geometric
Tolerance dialog box

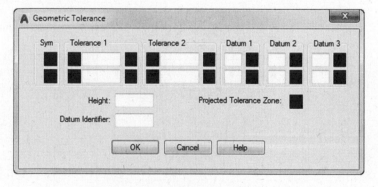

This is where you enter tolerance and datum values for the feature-control symbol. You can enter two tolerance values and three datum values. In addition, you can stack values in a two-tiered fashion.

Click a box in the Sym group to open the Symbol dialog box.

The top section of Figure 11.42 shows what each symbol in the Symbol dialog box represents. The bottom image shows a sample drawing with a feature symbol used on a cylindrical object. The symbols in the sample drawing show that the upper cylinder needs to be parallel within 0.003" of the lower cylinder. Note that mechanical drawings often use measurements in thousandths, so 0.3 means 0.003.

FIGURE 11.42
The tolerance symbols

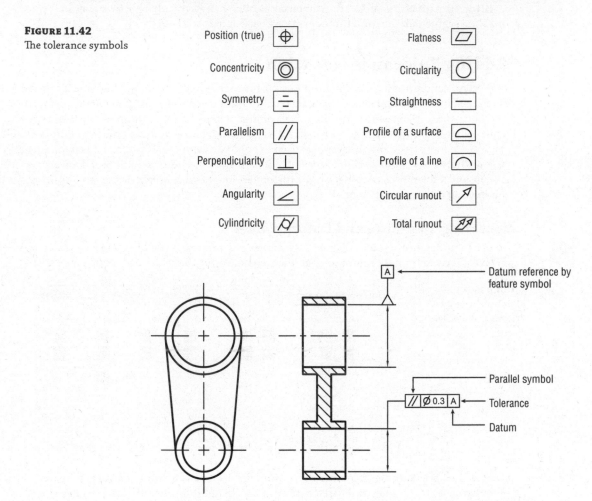

In the Geometric Tolerance dialog box, you can click a box in any of the Datum groups or a box in the right side of the Tolerance groups to open the Material Condition dialog box. This dialog box contains standard symbols relating to the maximum and minimum material conditions of a feature on the part being dimensioned.

Adding Inspection Dimensions

Another type of dimension related to tolerances is the *inspection dimension*. This is a type of dimension notation that indicates how often the tolerances of a dimension should be checked.

To add an inspection dimension, first add a regular linear dimension as described in the early part of this chapter. Next, follow these steps:

1. Choose Inspect from the Dimensions panel or type **Diminspect**⏎. The Inspection Dimension dialog box appears (see Figure 11.43).

FIGURE 11.43
The Inspection
Dimension dialog box

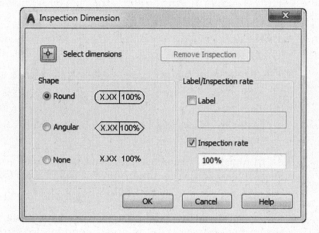

2. Click the Select Dimensions tool. The dialog box temporarily closes to allow you to select a dimension. Press ⏎ when you have selected the dimension that you want to edit.

3. Select a shape option from the Shape group.

4. Enter a value for the Label and Inspection Rate boxes, and then click OK.

The dimension appears with the additional changes from the dialog box (see Figure 11.44).

FIGURE 11.44
The dimension
with the additional
changes

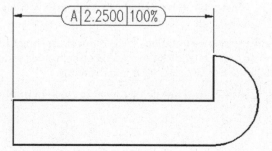

The Bottom Line

Understand the components of a dimension. Before you start to dimension with AutoCAD, become familiar with the different parts of a dimension. Doing so will help you set up your dimensions to fit the style you need.

Master It Name a few of the dimension components.

Create a dimension style. As you become more familiar with technical drawing and drafting, you'll learn that there are standard formats for drawing dimensions. Arrows, text size, and even the way dimension lines are drawn are all subject to a standard format. Fortunately, AutoCAD offers dimension styles that let you set up your dimension format once and then call up that format whenever you need it.

Master It What is the name of the dialog box that lets you manage dimension styles and how do you open it?

Draw linear dimensions. The most common dimension that you'll use is the linear dimension. Knowing how to place a linear dimension is a big first step in learning how to dimension in AutoCAD.

Master It Name the three locations for which you are prompted when placing a linear dimension.

Edit dimensions. Dimensions often change in the course of a project, so you should know how to make changes to dimension text or other parts of a dimension.

Master It How do you start the command to edit dimension text?

Dimension nonorthogonal objects. Not everything you dimension will use linear dimensions. AutoCAD offers a set of dimension tools for dimensioning objects that aren't made up of straight lines.

Master It Name some of the types of objects for which a linear dimension isn't appropriate.

Add a note with a leader arrow. In addition to dimensions, you'll probably add lots of notes with arrows pointing to features in a design. AutoCAD offers the multileader for this purpose.

Master It What two types of objects does the multileader combine?

Apply ordinate dimensions. When accuracy counts, ordinate dimensions are often used because they measure distances that are similar to coordinates from a single feature.

Master It What AutoCAD feature do you use for ordinate dimensions that aren't strictly associated with dimensions?

Add tolerance notation. Mechanical drafting often requires the use of special notation to describe tolerances. AutoCAD offers some predefined symbols that address the need to include tolerance notation in a drawing.

Master It How do you open the Geometric Tolerance dialog box?

Part 3

Mastering Advanced Skills

- Chapter 12: Using Attributes
- Chapter 13: Copying Existing Drawings from Other Sources
- Chapter 14: Advanced Editing and Organizing
- Chapter 15: Laying Out Your Printer Output
- Chapter 16: Making "Smart" Drawings with Parametric Tools
- Chapter 17: Using Dynamic Blocks
- Chapter 18: Drawing Curves
- Chapter 19: Getting and Exchanging Data from Drawings

Chapter 12

Using Attributes

Earlier in this book, you learned how to create blocks, which are assemblies of objects in the AutoCAD® 2018 program. Blocks enable you to form parts or symbols that can be easily reproduced. Furniture, bolts, doors, and windows are a few common items that you can create with blocks. Whole rooms and appliances can also be made into blocks. There is no limit to a block's size.

AutoCAD also offers a feature called *attributes*, which allows you to store text information as a part of a block. For example, you can store the material specifications for a bolt or other mechanical part that you've converted into a block. If your application is architecture, you can store the material, hardware, and dimensional information for a door or window that has been converted into a block. You can then quickly gather information about that block that may not be obvious from the graphics.

Attribute text can be set up to be invisible, or it can be displayed as text in the drawing. If it's invisible, you can easily view the attribute information by double-clicking the block that contains the attribute. The attribute information is displayed in a dialog box. This information can also be extracted to a database or spreadsheet, letting you keep an inventory of the blocks in your drawing. You can even convert attribute information into tables in an AutoCAD drawing. Doing so can help you make quick work of parts lists or door and window schedules. By using attributes, you can keep track of virtually any object in a drawing or maintain textual information in the drawing that can be queried.

Keeping track of objects is just one way to use attributes. You can also use them in place of text objects when you must keep text and graphic items together. One common example is the reference symbol in an architectural drawing. Reference symbols are used to indicate the location of more detailed information in a drawing set, such as the elevation views of a room or a cross-section of a wall or other part of a building.

In this chapter, you'll use attributes for one of their common functions: maintaining lists of parts. In this case, the parts are doors. This chapter also describes how to import these attributes into a database management program. As you go through the exercises, think about the ways that attributes can help you in your particular application.

In this chapter, you will learn to

- ♦ Create attributes
- ♦ Edit attributes
- ♦ Extract and export attribute information

Creating Attributes

Attributes depend on blocks. You might think of an attribute as text information attached to a block. The information can be a description of the block or some other pertinent text. For example, you can include an attribute definition with the Door block that you created in Chapter 4, "Organizing Objects with Blocks and Groups." Subsequently, every time you insert the Door block, you'll be prompted for a value associated with that door. The value can be a number, a height or width value, a name, or any type of text information that you want. After you enter a value, it's stored as part of the Door block in the drawing database. This value can be displayed as text attached to the Door block or it can be invisible. You can change the value at any time. You can even specify the prompts for the attribute value.

However, suppose that you don't have the attribute information when you design the Door block. As an alternative, you can add the attribute to a *symbol* that is later placed by the door when you know enough about the design to specify what type of door goes where. Figure 12.1 shows a sample door symbol and a table to which the symbol refers. The standard door-type symbol suits this purpose nicely because it's an object that you can set up and use as a block independent of the Door block.

FIGURE 12.1
A door symbol tells you what type of door goes in the location shown. Usually, the symbol contains a number or a letter that is keyed to a table that shows more information about the door.

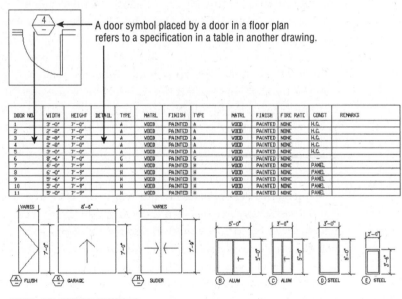

A door symbol placed by a door in a floor plan refers to a specification in a table in another drawing.

DOOR AND WINDOW SCHEDULE

Adding Attributes to Blocks

In the following exercise, you'll create a door-type symbol, which is commonly used to describe the size, thickness, and other characteristics of any given door in an architectural drawing. The symbol is usually a circle, a hexagon, or a diamond with a number in it. The number is generally cross-referenced to a schedule that lists all the door types and their characteristics.

You'll create a new block containing attribute definitions in the file for which the block is intended: the Plan.dwg file. You will use the 12a-plan.dwg file from the sample drawings, which is similar to the Plan file on which you've been working in previous chapters. You'll create the block in the file so that you can easily insert it where it belongs in the plan.

First, open the Plan file and set up a view appropriate for creating the block with the attribute:

1. Open the 12a-plan.dwg file. Metric users can use the file 12a-plan-metric.dwg. These are similar to the Plan.dwg file that you've created on your own with a few additions to facilitate the exercises in this chapter.

 Zoom Window

2. Select the Zoom Window option on the Navigation bar.

3. At the Specify first corner: prompt, enter **0,0**↵.

4. At the Specify opposite corner: prompt, enter **12,9** (**30.5,22.8** for metric users). This causes your view to zoom in to a location near the origin of the drawing in a 12″ × 9″ area (30.5 cm × 22.8 cm for metric users).

You zoom into this small area because you'll draw the block at its paper size of 1/4″ (or 0.6 cm for metric users). Now you're ready to create the block and attribute. You'll start by drawing the graphics of the block, and then you'll add the attribute definition:

1. Draw a circle with its center at coordinate 7,5 (15,11 for metric users) and a diameter of 0.25 (0.6 for metric users). The circle is automatically placed on layer 0, which is the current layer. Remember that objects in a block that are on layer 0 take on the color and linetype assignment of the layer on which the block is inserted.

2. Zoom into the circle so that it's about the same size as that shown in Figure 12.2.

FIGURE 12.2
The attribute definition inserted in the circle

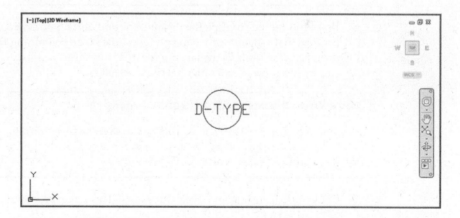

3. If the circle looks like an octagon, type **RE**↵ to regenerate your drawing.

4. Click the Define Attributes tool in the Home tab's expanded Block Definition panel, or type **ATT**↵ to open the Attribute Definition dialog box (see Figure 12.3).

FIGURE 12.3
The Attribute
Definition dialog box

5. In the Attribute group, click the Tag box and enter **D-TYPE**.

UNDERSTANDING THE ATTRIBUTE TAG

The attribute tag is equivalent to a field name in a database. You can also think of the tag as the attribute's name or ID. It can help to identify the purpose of the attribute. The tag can be a maximum of 255 characters but can't contain spaces. If you plan to use the attribute data in a database program, check that program's documentation for other restrictions on field names.

---

6. Press the Tab key or click the Prompt box and enter **Door type**. This is the text for the prompt that will appear when you insert the block containing this attribute. Often the prompt is the same as the tag, but it can be anything you like. Unlike the tag, the prompt can include spaces and other special characters.

GIVE YOUR PROMPTS MEANINGFUL NAMES

Use a prompt that gives explicit instructions so that the user will know exactly what is expected. Consider including an example in the prompt. (Enclose the example in square brackets to imitate the way AutoCAD prompts often display defaults.)

---

7. Click the Default box, and enter a hyphen (-). This is the default value for the door-type prompt.

MAKE YOUR DEFAULTS USEFUL

If an attribute will contain a number that is to be used later for sorting in a database, use a default attribute value such as 000 to indicate the number of digits required. The zeros can also remind the user that values less than 100 must be preceded by a leading zero, as in 099.

8. Click the Justification drop-down list, and select Middle Center. This enables you to center the attribute on the circle's center. The Text Settings group includes several other options. Because attributes appear as text, you can apply the same settings to them as you would to single-line text.

9. In the Text Height box, make sure that the value is 1/8" or **0.125**. (Metric users should enter **0.3**.) This makes the attribute text 0.125" (0.3 cm) high.

10. Select the Annotative option. Doing so allows the attribute to adjust in size automatically according to the annotation scale of the drawing.

11. In the Insertion Point group, make sure that the Specify On-Screen check box is selected.

12. Click OK to close the dialog box.

13. Using the Center osnap, pick the center of the circle. The attribute definition appears at the center of the circle (see Figure 12.2).

You've just created your first attribute definition. The attribute definition displays its tag in all uppercase letters to help you identify it. When you later insert this file into another drawing, the tag turns into the value you assign to it when it's inserted. If you want only one attribute, you can stop here and save the file. The next section shows you how to add several more attributes quickly to your drawing.

Copying and Editing Attribute Definitions

Next, you'll add a few more attribute definitions, but instead of using the Attribute Definition dialog box, you'll make an arrayed copy of the first attribute and then edit the attribute definition copies. This method can save you time when you want to create several attribute definitions that have similar characteristics. By making copies and editing them, you'll also get a chance to see firsthand how to change an attribute definition.

Follow these steps to make copies of the attribute:

1. Click Copy in the Home tab's Modify panel or type **CO**↵ to start the Copy command.

2. At the Select objects: prompt, select the attribute definition that you just created and press ↵ to confirm your selection.

3. At the Specify base point or [Displacement/mOde] <Displacement>: prompt, select the center of the circle.

4. At the Specify second point or [Array] <use first point as displacement>: prompt, type **A**↵ to enter the Array option.

5. At the Enter number of items to array: prompt, type **7**↵.

6. At the Specify second point or [Fit]: prompt, point the cursor directly downward and enter **0.18**↵ (**0.432** for metric users). You can use the Polar Tracking tool in the status bar to help align the cursor in a downward direction.

7. The Specify second point: prompt appears again, allowing you to create another set of copies. Press ↵ to exit the Copy command.

8. Pan your view upward to center the attribute definition copies in the view. You may also need to zoom out to view all the copies.

Now you're ready to modify the copies of the attribute definitions:

1. Press Esc twice to clear any selections or commands, and click all the attribute definitions just below the original.

2. Right-click and choose Properties from the context menu to open the Properties palette.

3. Scroll down the list of properties until you see the Invisible option in the Misc category.

4. Select Yes from the Invisible option's drop-down list.

5. Press the Esc key to clear your selection, and close the Properties palette.

You've just turned off Visibility mode for all but the first attribute definition. Now change the Tag, Prompt, and Default values for the attribute definitions:

1. Double-click the attribute definition just below the original one in the center of the circle. The Edit Attribute Definition dialog box appears.

2. Highlight the Tag text box, and type **D-SIZE**↵.

3. Highlight the Prompt text box, and type **Door size**↵.

4. In the Default text box, type **3'-0"**↵. Metric users should type **90**↵.

You've just learned how to edit an attribute definition. Now you'll make changes to the other attribute definitions:

1. Continue to edit the rest of the attribute definition properties by using the attribute settings listed in Table 12.1. To do so, click the next attribute definition and repeat steps 2 through 4 of the preceding exercise, replacing the Tag and Prompt values with those shown in Table 12.1. Use a hyphen for the Default values. Also, make sure that all but the original attributes have the Invisible option set to Yes.

2. When you've finished editing the last attribute definition, click OK or press ↵ on your last entry.

TABLE 12.1:   Attributes for the door-type symbol

TAG	PROMPT	DEFAULT VALUE
D-NUMBER	Door number	-
D-THICK	Door thickness	-
D-RATE	Fire rating	-
D-MATRL	Door material	-
D-CONST	Door construction	-

Note: Make sure that the Invisible option is selected for the attributes in this table.

When you later insert a file or a block containing attributes, the attribute prompts will appear in the order in which their associated definitions were created. If the order of the prompts at insertion time is important, you can control it by editing the attribute definitions so that their creation order corresponds to the desired prompt order. You can also control the order by using the Block Attribute Manager, which you'll look at later in this chapter.

> **USING PROPERTIES TO EDIT ATTRIBUTE DEFINITIONS**
>
> If you prefer, you can use the Properties palette to change an attribute definition's Tag, Prompt, or Default value (shown as Value). These values can be found under the Text group of the palette after an attribute definition is selected.

Certification
Objective

Turning the Attribute Definitions into a Block

You need to perform one more crucial step before these attribute definitions can be of any use. You must turn the attribute definitions into a block, along with the circle:

1. Click the Create Block tool in the Home tab's Block panel, or enter **B.↵**.

2. In the Block Definition dialog box, enter **S-DOOR** for the name.

3. In the Base Point group, click the Pick Point tool and then use the Center osnap to select the center of the circle.

4. In the Objects group, click the Select Objects tool and select the circle and all of the attributes. Press ↵ when you've completed your selection. Leave Convert To Block highlighted in the object group.

5. In the Behavior group, select the Annotative option. This ensures that the block is scaled to the appropriate size for the scale of the drawing into which it's inserted.

6. Click OK. When the Edit Attribute dialog box opens, click OK to close it.

7. The attributes and the circle are now a block called S-DOOR. You can delete the S-DOOR block on your screen.

UNDERSTANDING ATTRIBUTE DEFINITION MODES

The Attribute Definition dialog box includes several choices in the Mode group; you've used one of these modes to see what it does. You won't use any of the other modes in this exercise, but here is a list describing all of the modes for your reference:

Invisible   Controls whether the attribute is shown as part of the drawing.

Constant   Creates an attribute that doesn't prompt you to enter a value. Instead, the attribute has a constant, or fixed, value that you give it during creation. Constant mode is used when you know that you'll assign a fixed value to an object. After constant values are set in a block, you can't change them by using the standard set of attribute-editing commands.

Verify   Causes AutoCAD to review the attribute values that you enter at insertion time and to ask you whether they're correct. This option appears only when the Attribute dialog box is turned off (the Attdia system variable is set to 0).

Preset   Causes AutoCAD to assign the default value to an attribute automatically when its block is inserted. This saves time because a preset attribute won't prompt you for a value. Unlike attributes created in Constant mode, a preset attribute can be edited.

Lock Position   Prevents the attribute from being moved from its original location in the block when you're grip editing. This is on by default.

Multiple Lines   Allows the attribute to contain multiple lines of text, similar to Mtext objects. When this option is turned on, you can specify a text boundary width.

With the exception of Invisible mode, none of these modes can be altered after the attribute becomes part of a block. Later in this chapter, we'll show you how to make an invisible attribute visible.

Once you've created the block, you can place it anywhere in the drawing using the Insert command or the Insert tool in the Home tab's Block panel. You'll insert this block in another location in the drawing. If you want to use the block in other drawings, you can use the Wblock command to save the block as a drawing file, or you can use the DesignCenter™ palette to drag and drop blocks from a drawing file. (See Chapter 25, "Managing and Sharing Your Drawings," for more on DesignCenter.)

Inserting Blocks Containing Attributes

In the preceding section, you created a door-type symbol at the desired size for the plotted symbol. This size is known as the *paper size*. Because you turned on the Annotative option for the attribute and block, you can use the Annotation Scale setting to have the block insert at the appropriate size for the scale of the drawing. The following steps demonstrate the process of inserting a block that contains attributes. First, set up your view and annotation scale in preparation to insert the blocks:

1. Make sure that the Attribute Dialog mode is on by entering **Attdia**↵**1**↵ at the Command prompt. This enables you to enter attribute values through a dialog box in the next exercise. Otherwise, you'd be prompted for the attribute values in the command-line interface.

2. Select 1/8″=1′-0″ (1:100 for metric users) from the Annotation Scale drop-down list in the lower-right corner of the AutoCAD window. This ensures that the block appears at the proper size for the drawing scale.

3. Type **View**⏎ to open the View Manager dialog box.

4. Click the plus sign (+) to the left of the Model Views option to expand the Model Views list; then select FIRST from the list, select Set Current, and click OK. This is a view that has been saved in this drawing. (See "Taking Control of the AutoCAD Display" in Chapter 7, "Mastering Viewing Tools, Hatches, and External References," for more on saving views.)

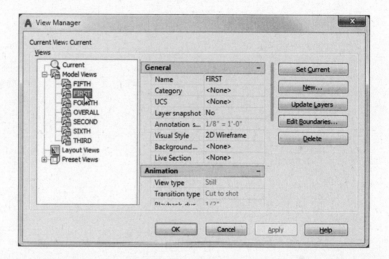

5. Be sure that the CEILING and FLR-PAT layers are off. Normally in a floor plan the door headers aren't visible anyway, and their appearance will interfere with the placement of the door-reference symbol.

6. Finally, you can begin to place the blocks in the drawing. Click the Insert tool in the Home tab's Block panel, then More Options, or type **I**⏎ to open the Insert dialog box.

7. Select S-DOOR from the Name drop-down list.

8. In the Insertion Point group, make sure that the Specify On-Screen option is turned on.

9. In the Scale group, make sure that the Uniform Scale check box is selected.

10. In the Rotation group, make sure that the Specify On-Screen option is turned off, and then click OK.

Now you're ready to place the block in your drawing in the appropriate location and enter the attribute values. AutoCAD is waiting for you to select a location for the symbol.

11. Click in the doorway of the lower-left unit, near coordinate 41'-3",72'-4". Metric users should use coordinate 1256,2202. You may want to turn off Osnaps temporarily to avoid accidentally clicking an object. When you click the location, the Edit Attributes dialog box opens (see Figure 12.4).

FIGURE 12.4
The Edit Attributes
dialog box

12. In the Door Construction box, enter **Solid core**↵. Note that this is the prompt that you created. Note also that the default value is the hyphen that you specified. Attribute data is case sensitive, so any text that you enter in all capital letters is stored in all capital letters.

13. In the Door Material box, change the hyphen to **Wood**. Continue to change the values for each box, as shown in Table 12.2.

14. When you've finished changing values, click OK and the symbol appears. The only attribute that you can see is the one that you selected to be visible: the door type.

15. Add the rest of the door-type symbols for the apartment entry doors by copying or arraying the door symbol that you just inserted. You can use the previously saved views found in the Views drop-down list in the View tab's Views panel to help you get around the drawing quickly. Don't worry that the attribute values aren't appropriate for each unit; you'll see how to edit the attributes in the next section.

TABLE 12.2:   Attribute values for the typical studio entry door

PROMPT	VALUE
Door Construction	Solid core
Door Material	Wood
Fire Rating	20 min.
Door Thickness	1 3/4″ (4 cm for metric)
Door Number	(Same as room number; see Figure 12.6, later in this chapter)
Door Size	3′-0″ (90 cm for metric)
Door Type	A

In addition to the S-DOOR block, you'll need a block for the room number. To save some time, we've included a block called S-APART that contains a rectangle and a single attribute definition for the room number (see Figure 12.5).

FIGURE 12.5

The apartment number symbol

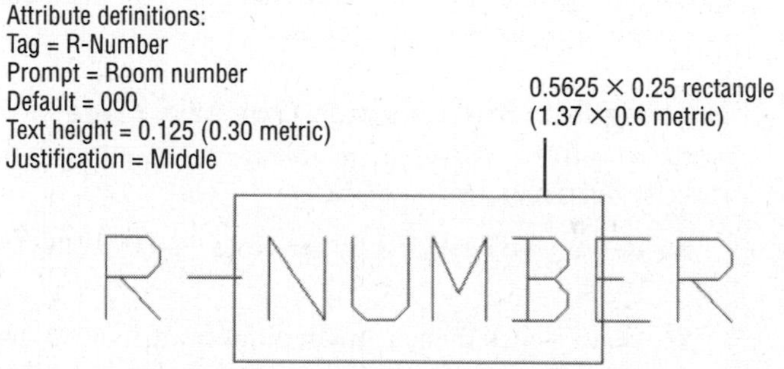

Attribute definitions:
Tag = R-Number
Prompt = Room number
Default = 000
Text height = 0.125 (0.30 metric)
Justification = Middle

0.5625 × 0.25 rectangle
(1.37 × 0.6 metric)

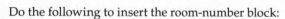

Do the following to insert the room-number block:

1. Choose Insert from the Home tab's Block panel, click more options, and then select S-APART from the Name drop-down list.

2. Make sure that the Specify On-Screen setting is turned on only for the Insertion point, and then click OK.

3. Insert the S-APART block into the lower-left unit. Give the attribute of this block the value **116**.

4. Copy or array the S-APART block so that there is one S-APART block in each unit. You'll learn how to modify the attributes to reflect their proper values in the following section. Figure 12.6 shows what the view should look like after you've entered the door symbols and the apartment numbers.

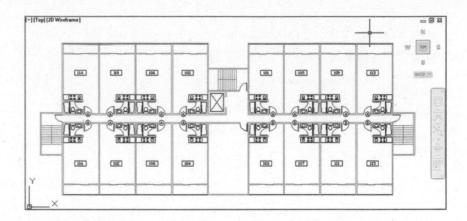

FIGURE 12.6
An overall view
of the plan with
door symbols
and apartment
numbers added

Editing Attributes

Because drawings are usually in flux even after construction or manufacturing begins, you'll eventually have to edit previously entered attributes. In the example of the apartment building, many things can change before the final set of drawings is completed.

Attributes can be edited individually or *globally*—you can edit several occurrences of a particular attribute tag all at one time. In the following sections, you'll use both individual and global editing techniques to make changes to the attributes that you've entered so far. You'll also practice editing invisible attributes.

Editing Attribute Values One at a Time

AutoCAD offers an easy way to edit attributes one at a time through a dialog box. The following exercise demonstrates this feature:

1. Restore the First view by selecting First from the Views flyout in the View tab's Views panel.

2. Double-click the apartment number attribute in the unit just to the right of the first unit in the lower-left corner to open the Enhanced Attribute Editor (see Figure 12.7).

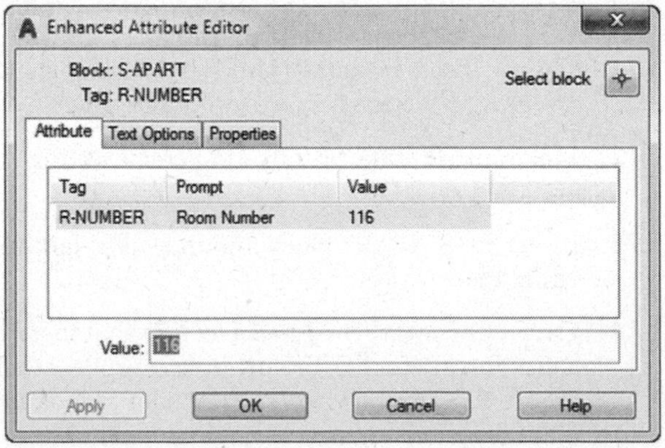

FIGURE 12.7
The Enhanced
Attribute Editor

3. Change the value in the Value box to **112**, and click OK to make the change.

4. Do this for each room, using Figure 12.8 as a reference for assigning room numbers.

5. Go back and edit the door number attribute for the S-DOOR blocks. Give each door the same number as the room number with which it's associated. See Figure 12.8 for the room numbers.

FIGURE 12.8
Apartment numbers for one floor of the studio apartment building

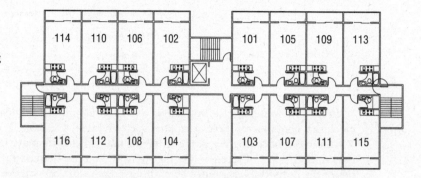

Editing Attribute Text Formats and Properties

You may have noticed that the Enhanced Attribute Editor in the preceding exercise has three tabs: Attribute, Text Options, and Properties. When you double-click a block containing attributes, the Enhanced Attribute Editor dialog box opens at the Attribute tab. You can use the other two tabs to control the size, font, color, and other properties of the selected attribute.

The Text Options tab (see Figure 12.9) lets you alter the attribute text style, justification, height, rotation, width factor, and oblique angle. (See Chapter 9, "Adding Text to Drawings," for more on these text options.)

FIGURE 12.9
The Enhanced Attribute Editor's Text Options tab

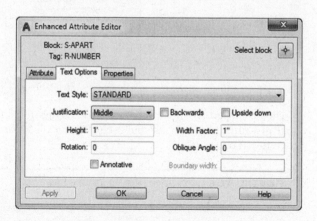

The Properties tab (see Figure 12.10) lets you alter the attribute's layer, linetype, color, line-weight (effective only on AutoCAD fonts), and plot-style assignments.

FIGURE 12.10
The Enhanced
Attribute Editor's
Properties tab

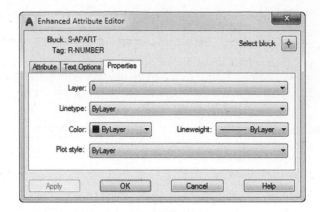

In the previous exercise, you edited a block containing a single attribute. Double-clicking a block that contains multiple attributes, such as the S-DOOR block, opens the resizable Enhanced Attribute Editor dialog box at the Attribute tab. This tab displays all of the attributes, whether they're visible or not, as shown in Figure 12.11. You can then edit the value, formats, and properties of the individual attributes by highlighting the attribute in the Attribute tab and using the other tabs to make changes. The changes you make affect only the attribute that you've highlighted in the Attribute tab.

FIGURE 12.11
The Enhanced
Attribute Editor show-
ing the contents of a
block that contains
several attributes

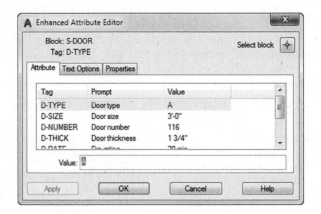

The Enhanced Attribute Editor lets you change attribute values, formats, and properties one block at a time. However, as you'll see in the next section, you can also make changes to several attributes at once.

MOVING THE LOCATION OF ATTRIBUTES

If you want to change the location of individual attributes in a block, you can do so by using grips. Click the block to expose the grips, and then click the grip connected to the attribute. Or, if you've selected several blocks, Shift+click the attribute grips, and then move the attributes to their new location. They are still attached to their associated blocks. If you don't see grips appear for the attributes, then the attribute definition has its Lock Position property turned on. This is a setting that is available when you create the attribute in the Attribute Definition dialog box.

Making Global Changes to Attribute Values

**Certification
Objective**

At times, you'll want to change the value of several attributes in a file so that they're all the same value. You can use the Edit Attribute Globally option to make global changes to the attribute values.

Suppose you decide that you want to change all of the entry doors to a type designated as B rather than A. Perhaps door-type A was an input error or type B is better suited for an entry door. The following exercise demonstrates how this is done:

1. Type **View**↵ to open the View Manager dialog box, and select the view named FOURTH from the Views list.

2. Click the Set Current option, and then click OK.

3. Pan your view down so that you can see all of the "A" door-reference symbols for this view.

4. Select Multiple from the Edit Attributes flyout on the Home tab's Block panel or the Insert tab's Block panel. You can also type **-Attedit**↵ at the Command prompt. Make sure that you include the hyphen at the beginning of the command.

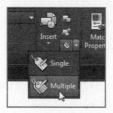

5. At the Edit Attributes one at a time? [Yes/No] <Y>: prompt, enter **N**↵ for No. You see the message Performing global editing of attribute values. This tells you that you're in Global Edit mode.

6. At the Edit only attributes visible on screen? [Yes/No] <Y>: prompt, press ↵. As you can see from this prompt, you have the option to edit all attributes, including those out of the view area. You'll get a chance to work with this option later in this chapter.

7. At the Enter block name specification <*>: prompt, press ↵. Optionally, you can enter a block name to narrow the selection to specific blocks.

8. At the Enter attribute tag specification <*>: prompt, press ↵. Optionally, you can enter an attribute tag name to narrow your selection to specific tags.

9. At the Enter attribute value specification <*>: prompt, press ↵. Optionally, you can narrow your selection to attributes containing specific values.

10. At the Select Attributes: prompt, select the door-type symbol's attribute value for units 103 to 115. You can use a window to select the attributes if you prefer. Press ↵ when you've finished your selection.

11. At the Enter string to change: prompt, enter **A**↵.

12. At the Enter new string: prompt, enter **B**↵. The door-type symbols all change to the new value.

In step 10, you were asked to select the attributes to be edited. AutoCAD limits the changes to those attributes that you select. If you know that you need to change every attribute in your drawing, you can do so by answering the series of prompts in a slightly different way, as demonstrated in the following exercise:

1. Try the same procedure again, but this time enter **N** for the first prompt and again at the `Edit only attributes visible on screen? [Yes/No] <Y>:` prompt (step 6 in the previous exercise). The message `Drawing must be regenerated afterwards` appears. The AutoCAD Text Window appears.

2. Once again, you're prompted for the block name, the tag, and the value (steps 7, 8, and 9 in the previous exercise). Respond to these prompts as you did earlier.

3. You then get the message `128 attributes selected`. This tells you the number of attributes that fit the specifications that you just entered.

4. At the `Enter string to change:` prompt, enter **A**↵ to indicate that you want to change the rest of the A attribute values.

5. At the `Enter new string:` prompt, enter **B**↵. The As change to Bs in the drawing.

In this exercise, AutoCAD skipped the `Select Attribute:` prompt and went directly to the `String to change:` prompt. AutoCAD assumes that you want it to edit every attribute in the drawing, so it doesn't bother asking you to select specific attributes.

Making Invisible Attributes Visible

You can globally edit invisible attributes, such as those in the door-reference symbol, by using the tools just described. You may, however, want to be more selective about which invisible attribute you want to modify. Optionally, you may want to make invisible attributes temporarily visible for other editing purposes.

This exercise shows you how to make invisible attributes visible:

1. On the Insert tab's expanded Block panel, click the Retain Display flyout and select Display All Attributes. You can also enter **Attdisp**↵**On**↵. Your drawing looks like Figure 12.12.

FIGURE 12.12
The drawing with all the attributes visible. (Door-type symbols are so close together that they overlap.)

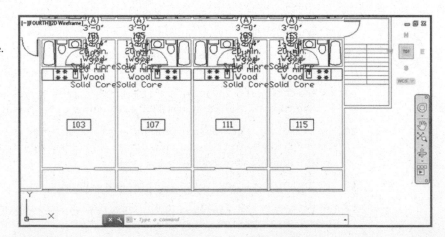

2. At this point, you could edit the invisible attributes individually as in the first attribute-editing exercise. For now, set the attribute display back to Normal. On the Insert tab's Expanded Block panel, click the Display All Attributes flyout and select Retain Attribute Display. You can also enter **Attdisp↵N↵**.

USING SPACES IN ATTRIBUTE VALUES

At times, you may want the default value to begin with a blank space. This enables you to specify text strings more easily when you edit the attribute globally. For example, suppose that you have an attribute value that reads 3334333. If you want to change the first 3 in this string of numbers, you have to specify 3334 when prompted for the string to change. Then, for the new string, you enter the same set of numbers again with the first 3 changed to the new number. If you specify only 3 for the string to change, AutoCAD will change all of the 3s in the value. If you start with a space, as in _3334333 (we're using an underscore here only to represent the space; it doesn't mean that you type an underscore character), you can isolate the first 3 from the rest by specifying _3 as the string to change (again, enter a space instead of the underscore).

You must enter a backslash character (\) before the space in the default value to tell AutoCAD to interpret the space literally rather than as a press of the spacebar (which is equivalent to pressing ↵).

You've seen the results of the On and Normal options. The Off option makes all attributes invisible regardless of the mode used when they were created.

Because the attributes weren't intended to be visible, they appear to overlap and cover other parts of the drawing when they're made visible. Remember to turn them back off when you're done reviewing them.

Making Global Format and Property Changes to Attributes

While we're on the subject of global editing, you should know how to make global changes to the format and properties of attributes. Earlier, you saw how to make format changes to individual attributes using the Enhanced Attribute Editor dialog box. You can also use the Edit Attribute dialog box to make global changes, as the following exercise demonstrates.

Follow these steps to make the global changes:

1. Click the Block Attribute Manager in the Home tab's expanded Block panel to open the Block Attribute Manager dialog box. You can also enter **battman↵**.

2. Select S-APART from the Block drop-down list at the top of the dialog box. This list displays all of the blocks that contain attributes. The only attribute defined for the selected block is displayed in the list box below it.

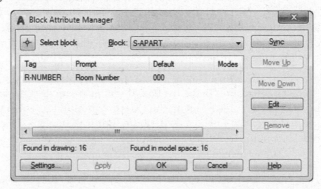

3. Click the attribute value in the list, and click the Edit button to open the Edit Attribute dialog box. The Edit Attribute dialog box is nearly identical to the Enhanced Attribute Editor that you saw earlier.

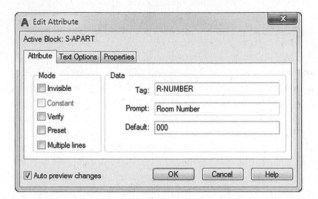

4. Click the Properties tab, select Red from the Color drop-down list, and click OK.

5. Click OK to exit the Block Attribute Manager dialog box.

The Edit Attribute dialog box that you saw in this exercise offers a slightly different set of options from those in the Enhanced Attribute Editor dialog box. In the Attribute tab of the Edit Attribute dialog box, you can change some of the mode settings for the attribute, such as visibility and the Verify and Preset modes. You can also change the Tag, Prompt, and Default values. In contrast, the Attribute tab in the Enhanced Attribute Editor dialog box enables you to change the attribute value but none of the other attribute properties.

Other Block Attribute Manager Options

The Block Attribute Manager dialog box includes a few other options that weren't covered in the exercises. Here's a rundown of the Settings, Move Up, Move Down, Remove, and Sync buttons:

Settings Click this button to open the Block Attribute Settings dialog box (see Figure 12.13), which lets you control which attribute properties are displayed in the list box of the Block Attribute Manager.

The Emphasize Duplicate Tags option highlights duplicate tag names by showing them in red. The Apply Changes To Existing References option forces any changes that you make to the attribute properties to be applied to existing attributes. If this setting is turned off, you have to use the Sync button in the Block Attribute Manager dialog box to update existing attributes, and the changes that you make to attribute properties are applied only to new attributes added after the change. You can also enter **Attsync**↵ at the Command prompt to synchronize older attributes.

Move Up and Move Down Clicking these buttons moves a selected attribute up or down the list of attributes in the list box. If you move an item down the list, the item changes its position when viewed using the Ddatte command or when you're viewing the attribute's properties in the Enhanced Attribute Editor dialog box. Of course, this has an effect only on blocks containing multiple attributes.

FIGURE 12.13
The Block Attribute
Settings dialog box

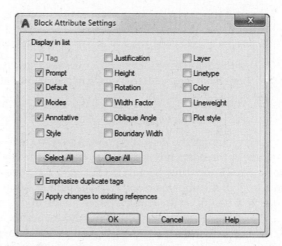

FIGURE 12.13
The Block Attribute
Settings dialog box

Remove   Clicking this button removes the selected attribute from the block, so make sure that you mean it before you click.

Sync   This option updates attribute properties such as order, text formatting, mode, and so on. It can also be used to update blocks globally that have had new attribute definitions added or deleted. It doesn't affect the individual attribute values.

Redefining Blocks Containing Attributes

Attributes act differently from other objects when they're included in redefined blocks. Normally, blocks that have been redefined change their configuration to reflect the new block definition. But if a redefined block contains attributes, the attributes maintain their old properties, including their position in relation to other objects in the block. This means that the old attribute position, style, and so on don't change even though you may have changed them in the new definition.

Fortunately, AutoCAD offers a tool that's specifically designed to let you update blocks with attributes. The following steps describe how to update attribute blocks:

1. Before you use the command to redefine an attribute block, you must create the objects and attribute definitions that will make up the replacement attribute block. The simplest way to do this is to explode a copy of the attribute block that you want to update. This ensures that you have the same attribute definitions in the updated block.

2. Make your changes to the exploded attribute block.

EXPLODE ATTRIBUTE BLOCKS AT A 1-TO-1 SCALE

Before you explode the attribute block copy, be sure that it's at a 1-to-1 scale. This is important because if you don't use the original size of the block, you could end up with all of your new attribute blocks at the wrong size. Also be sure you use a marker device, such as a line, to locate the insertion point of the attribute block before you explode it. Doing so will help you locate and maintain the original insertion point for the redefined block.

3. Type **Attredef**↵.

4. At the Enter name of block you wish to redefine: prompt, enter the appropriate name.

5. At the Select objects: prompt, select all of the objects, including the attribute definitions, that you want to include in the revised attribute block. Press ↵.

6. At the Specify insertion base point of new Block: prompt, pick the same location used for the original block.

After you pick the insertion point, AutoCAD takes a few seconds to update the blocks. The amount of time depends on the complexity of the block and the number of times the block occurs in the drawing. If you include a new attribute definition with your new block, it too is added to all the updated blocks with its default value. Attribute definitions that are deleted from your new definition are removed from all the updated blocks.

You can also use the Refedit command to modify an attribute definition. Click the Edit Reference tool in the Insert tab's expanded Reference panel to modify attribute definitions. After editing, you must use the Sync option in the Block Attribute Manager to update all instances of the modified block.

Extracting and Exporting Attribute Information

After you enter the attributes in your drawing, you can extract the information contained in the attributes and use it to generate reports or to analyze the attribute data in other programs. You might, for example, want to keep track of the number and type of doors in your drawing through a database manager. This is especially useful if you have a project such as a large hotel that contains thousands of doors.

When you extract attribute data, AutoCAD creates a text file. You can choose to export the file in either comma-delimited or tab-delimited format. If you have Microsoft Excel or Access installed, you can also export the attribute data in a format compatible with these programs.

Performing the Extraction

In the past, extracting the attribute data from a drawing was an error-prone task requiring the creation of a template file. This template file had to contain a series of codes that described the data that you wanted to extract. AutoCAD has a greatly improved system for attribute data extraction in the form of the Data Extraction Wizard. The following exercises will walk you through a sample extraction.

> #### EXTRACTING DATA IN AUTOCAD 2018 LT
>
> The AutoCAD LT® software doesn't offer the Data Extraction Wizard. Instead, you see the more simplified Attribute Extraction dialog box, which offers the file-format options (comma- or space-delimited or DXF output), the output filename, and template file options. For AutoCAD LT, the template file is used as an option to filter the attributes.

USING THE DATA EXTRACTION WIZARD

In this first exercise, you'll explore the Data Extraction Wizard. You can use the 12c-plan.dwg sample file if you haven't done the tutorials from the beginning of the chapter.

1. Go back to the Plan.dwg file, and click Data Extraction in the Insert tab's Linking & Extraction panel. On the Begin page (see Figure 12.14), you can choose to start an extraction from scratch or use an existing data-extraction setup that you've created from previous extractions.

FIGURE 12.14
Starting the Data
Extraction Wizard

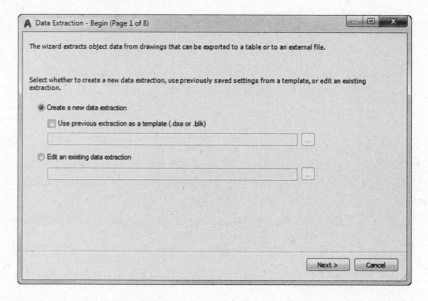

2. Click Next to open the Save Data Extraction As dialog box. This dialog box lets you save the data-extraction settings that you're about to set up in a file with the .dxe filename extension. Enter a name, pick a location for your file, and then click Save. The Define Data Source page opens (see Figure 12.15).

FIGURE 12.15
Defining a data
source

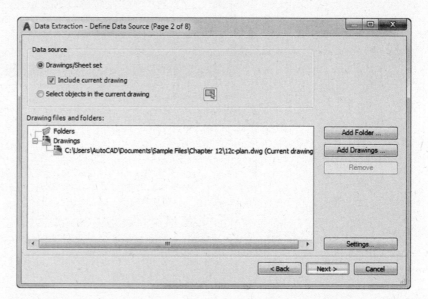

3. Click Settings to view other options. These options (see Figure 12.16) let you further refine the content of your extraction.

FIGURE 12.16
Additional settings

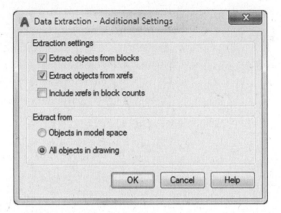

4. Click Cancel to close the Additional Settings dialog box, and then click Next to open the Select Objects page (see Figure 12.17).

FIGURE 12.17
The Select Objects
page

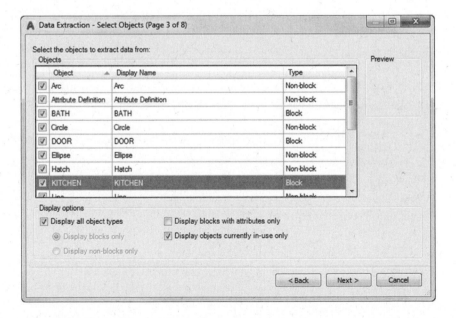

Take a moment to study the Select Objects page. It's the heart of the extraction process. Here you select the blocks that contain attributes as well as the specific attributes that you want to extract. The list shows all the object types in the drawing. You'll pare down this list to show only the blocks with attributes.

SELECTING WHAT TO EXTRACT

Let's continue by selecting specific information for the extraction:

1. Click the Display All Object Types option in the Display Options group to turn it off, and make sure that the Display Blocks Only radio button is selected.

2. Select the Display Blocks With Attributes Only option.

3. In the Objects list, remove the check mark next to all but the S-DOOR item. If you have a lot of blocks listed, you can select groups of names from the list by clicking the item at the top of the list and then Shift+clicking the item at the bottom. (Click any check box in a selected item to remove the check marks.) You can also Ctrl+click in the list to select multiple, nonconsecutive items.

4. Click Next to open the Select Properties page (see Figure 12.18), which displays a list of the different types of data available for extraction.

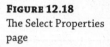

FIGURE 12.18
The Select Properties page

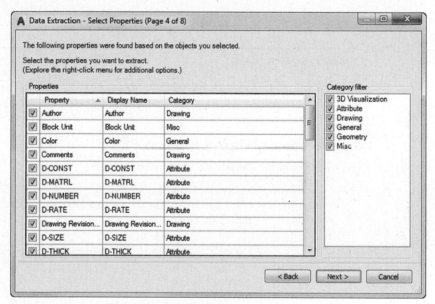

5. In the Category Filter group list on the right, deselect all of the options except Attribute. Now you see only the attribute data listed in the Properties panel.

6. Make sure that each item in the Properties panel is selected. A check mark should appear by each item.

7. Click Next. The Refine Data page appears (see Figure 12.19). Here you can continue to filter out data. For example, you can deselect the Show Count Column and Show Name Column options because they may be unnecessary for your purpose. You can also get a preview of your extracted data by clicking the Full Preview button.

FIGURE 12.19
The Refine Data page

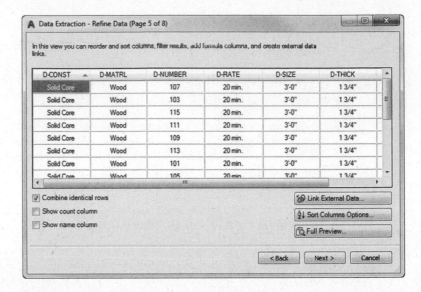

If you want to sort your data by column, you can do so by clicking the column title. To change the order of the columns, click and drag the column titles horizontally.

SAVING THE ATTRIBUTE DATA TO A FILE

Now let's complete the extraction process:

1. Click Next. The Choose Output page appears (see Figure 12.20). This window lets you determine whether to convert the data into a table in the drawing, extract the data as an external data file, or do both.

FIGURE 12.20
Decide how to convert
your attribute data.

2. Select the Output Data To External File option. The box just below the option becomes available for input (see Figure 12.21). You can type a location for the external file, or you can click the Browse button to browse to a location.

FIGURE 12.21
Enter the location to which you'll extract the data.

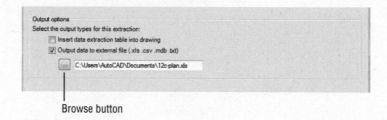

Browse button

3. You have the option to extract an XLS, CSV, MDB, or TXT file. You can select the type of file to use when you click the Browse button to show where you want the file to go. The Browse button opens a Save As dialog box where you can select the type of file to save from the File Of Type drop-down list. The default filename is the current drawing filename with an `.xls` extension. Click Save to go to the next step.

4. Click Next to open the Finish screen (see Figure 12.22). It gives you a brief message explaining what to do next.

FIGURE 12.22
Completing the wizard

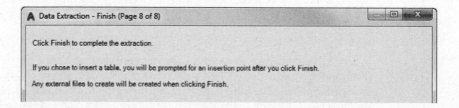

5. Click Finish. A file with the current drawing name and the `.xls` filename extension is created. By default, the file is placed in the `Documents` folder unless you specify a different location in step 3.

You now have a file called `Plan.xls` (`12c-plan.xls` if you used the sample file) that contains the data you saw earlier in the Full Preview window of the Data Extraction Wizard. You can open this file with Microsoft Excel.

Extracting Attribute Data to an AutoCAD Table

You may have noticed the option to extract the attribute data to an AutoCAD table in the Choose Output screen of the Data Extraction Wizard. This option lets you convert the attribute data directly into a table in the current drawing. Besides making it easy to create parts lists or other types of tables in your drawing, you get the added benefit of having tables update automatically whenever attribute data changes.

If you turn on this option and click Next, you'll see the Table Style screen (see Figure 12.23) instead of the Finish screen.

FIGURE 12.23
Styling your table

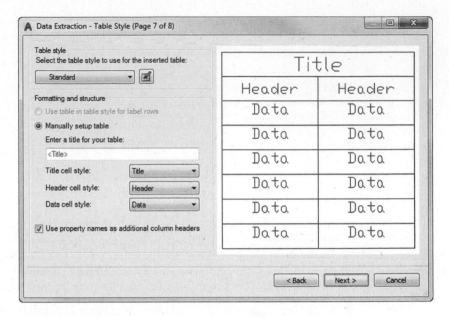

From here, you can follow these steps:

1. Select a table style for the extracted data, enter a title, and click Next. The Finish screen opens.

2. Click Finish. You're prompted to select a point. Click in the drawing to place the table.

The table may appear at a small size depending on the scale of your drawing. Zoom in to the location where you clicked, and you'll see the table (see Figure 12.24). If you link your exported spreadsheet using the Link External Data option in the Refine Data page (Figure 12.19), you will see the Data Link icon in the lower-right corner of the AutoCAD window.

FIGURE 12.24
The table and the Data Link icon

Quantity	D-CONST	D-MATRL	D-NUMBER	D-RATE	D-SIZE	D-THICK	D-TYPE	Name
1	Solid Core	Wood	103	20 min.	3'-0"	1 3/4"	B	S-DOOR
1	Solid Core	Wood	111	20 min.	3'-0"	1 3/4"	B	S-DOOR
1	Solid Core	Wood	108	20 min.	3'-0"	1 3/4"	B	S-DOOR
1	Solid Core	Wood	107	20 min.	3'-0"	1 3/4"	B	S-DOOR
1	Solid Core	Wood	115	20 min.	3'-0"	1 3/4"	B	S-DOOR
1	Solid Core	Wood	102	20 min.	3'-0"	1 3/4"	B	S-DOOR
1	Solid Core	Wood	101	20 min.	3'-0"	1 3/4"	B	S-DOOR
1	Solid Core	Wood	105	20 min.	3'-0"	1 3/4"	B	S-DOOR
1	Solid Core	Wood	113	20 min.	3'-0"	1 3/4"	B	S-DOOR
1	Solid Core	Wood	109	20 min.	3'-0"	1 3/4"	B	S-DOOR
1	Solid Core	Wood	112	20 min.	3'-0"	1 3/4"	B	S-DOOR
1	Solid Core	Wood	116	20 min.	3'-0"	1 3/4"	B	S-DOOR
1	Solid Core	Wood	106	20 min.	3'-0"	1 3/4"	B	S-DOOR
1	Solid Core	Wood	104	20 min.	3'-0"	1 3/4"	B	S-DOOR
1	Solid Core	Wood	110	20 min.	3'-0"	1 3/4"	B	S-DOOR
1	Solid Core	Wood	114	20 min.	3'-0"	1 3/4"	B	S-DOOR

With the table in place, you can make changes to the attribute data. When you're ready to update the table, select the table, right-click, and select Update Table Data Links from the context menu. The table will be updated to reflect the latest attribute values.

The Bottom Line

Create attributes.   Attributes are a great tool for storing data with drawn objects. You can include as little or as much data as you like in an AutoCAD block.

Master It   What is the name of the object that you must include in a block to store data?

Edit attributes.   The data that you include in a block is easily changed. You may have several copies of a block, each of which must contain its own unique set of data.

Master It   What is the simplest way to gain access to a block's attribute data?

Extract and export attribute information.   Attribute data can be extracted in a number of ways so that you can keep track of the data in a drawing.

Master It   How do you start the data-extraction process?

Chapter 13

Copying Existing Drawings from Other Sources

This chapter discusses ways to import existing drawings into the AutoCAD® 2018 software through tracing, scaling, and scanning. At times, you'll want to turn an existing drawing into an AutoCAD drawing file. The original drawing may be hand drawn, or it might be a PDF from another source. You may be modifying a design that someone else created or converting your library of older, hand-drafted drawings for AutoCAD use. Perhaps you want to convert a hand-drawn sketch into a formal drawing. In addition to importing drawings, you'll learn how to incorporate drawings in Portable Document Format (PDF) into your AutoCAD work.

In this chapter, you will learn to

◆ Convert paper drawings into AutoCAD files

◆ Import a raster image

◆ Work with a raster image

◆ Work with PDF files

◆ Use a geolocation map

Methods for Converting Paper Drawings to AutoCAD Files

Tracing with a special piece of hardware known as a digitizing tablet used to be the only way to enter a hand-drafted drawing into AutoCAD. However, a traced drawing usually requires some cleanup and reorganization.

Scaling a drawing is the method of taking measurements directly from a paper drawing using an architect's or engineer's scale. It is the most flexible method because you don't need special peripherals to do it and, generally, you're faced with fewer cleanups afterward. Scaling also facilitates the most accurate input of orthogonal lines because you can read dimensions directly from the drawing and enter them into AutoCAD. The main drawback with scaling is that if the hand-drafted drawing does not contain written dimensions, it will be difficult to produce an accurate copy. In addition, you must constantly look at the hand-drafted drawing and measure distances with a scale, and irregular curves are difficult to scale accurately.

Programs are available that automatically convert an image file into an AutoCAD drawing file consisting of lines and arcs. These programs may offer some help, but they require some editing and checking for errors.

Scanning, much like tracing, is best used for drawings that are difficult to scale, such as complex topographical maps containing a large number of contours or nontechnical line art, such as letterhead and logos.

The simplest method for converting paper drawings, and the method we show you in this chapter, is to scan your drawings as image files to be used as a background in AutoCAD. You can import your image files into AutoCAD and then trace directly over them. This technique allows you to see the original drawing in the AutoCAD window, removing the need to refer constantly to documents in other programs.

Importing a Raster Image

If you have a scanner and you'd like to use it to import drawings and other images into AutoCAD, you can take advantage of the program's ability to import raster images. There are many reasons you may want to import a scanned image. In architectural plans, a vicinity map is frequently used to show the location of a project. With the permission of its creator, you can scan a map into AutoCAD and incorporate it into a cover sheet. That cover sheet can also contain other images, such as photographs of the site, computer renderings and elevations of the project, and company logos. In architectural projects, scans of older drawings can be used as backgrounds for renovation work. This can be especially useful for historical buildings where the building's owner wishes to keep the original architectural detail.

Another reason for importing a scanned image is to use the image as a reference over which to trace. You can trace a drawing with a good deal of accuracy by using a scanned image. A scanner can be a cost-effective tool for tracing a wide variety of graphic material, or you can use your smartphone camera to photograph a drawing. In this section, you'll learn how you can import an image as a background for tracing.

1. Using the acad.dwt (acadiso.dwt) template, create a new file called Rastertrace.dwg and switch off the background grid.

2. Click the External References tool on the Insert tab's Reference panel (see Figure 13.1) to open the External References palette, which lets you import a full range of raster image files.

FIGURE 13.1
The External References palette allows you to import raster images.

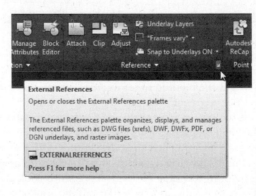

You can also type **XR**↵. This palette should look familiar from Chapter 7, "Mastering Viewing Tools, Hatches, and External References." It's the same palette that you used to manage external references. Just like external references (Xrefs), raster images are loaded when the current file is open but they aren't stored as part of the current file when it is saved. This helps keep file sizes down, but it also means that you need to keep track of inserted raster files. You must make sure that they're kept together with the AutoCAD files in which they're inserted. For example, you might want to keep image files in the same folder as the drawing file to which they're attached.

AutoCAD has a utility called eTransmit that collects AutoCAD files and their related support files, such as raster images, external references, and fonts, into any folder or drive that you specify. See Chapter 25, "Managing and Sharing Your Drawings," for details.

Another similarity between Xrefs and imported raster images is that you can clip a raster image so that only a portion of the image is displayed in your drawing. Portions of a raster file that are clipped aren't stored in memory, so your system won't get bogged down even if the raster file is huge.

The following exercises gives you step-by-step instructions for importing a raster file. It also lets you see how scanned resolution translates into an image in AutoCAD. This is important if you're interested in scanning drawings for the purpose of tracing over them.

First, you need to set up your drawing for scale and size. If you are using Imperial units, set up the Rastertrace.dwg file as an architectural drawing with a 1/4" = 1' scale on an 8-1/2" × 11" sheet of paper. Metric users should set up their drawing at a 1:50 scale on an A4 Size sheet. Here are the steps:

1. If you use Imperial units, set the Limits settings to 0,0 for the lower-left corner and 528,408 for the upper-right corner. The Limits settings for metric users should be 0,0 for the lower-left corner and 1480,1050 for the upper-right corner.

2. Make sure that the drawing units type is set to Architectural and the insertion scale is set to inches. Metric users should set up their drawing at a 1:50 scale on an A4 size sheet and set the insertion scale to centimeters.

Now you're ready to import the raster file. Do the following:

1. Choose Zoom All from the Zoom flyout on the Navigation bar or type **Z**↵**A**↵ to make sure that the entire area of the drawing limits is displayed on the screen. Ensure that the grid is switched off.

2. Draw a line across the screen from coordinates 0,20' to 64',20'. Metric users should draw the line from 0,600 to 1820,600. Remember that if Dynamic Input is turned on (it's on by default), you need to use the # sign in front of the second coordinate to indicate absolute coordinates. You'll use this line in a later exercise.

3. Click the line that you just drew, and then select Red from the Object Color drop-down list in the Home tab's Properties panel. This helps make the line more visible. If you have the Quick Properties feature turned on, you can select the color from the Quick Properties panel.

4. If you haven't done so already, click the External References tool in the title bar of the Insert tab's Reference panel to open the External References palette.

5. On the External References palette's menu bar, click the arrowhead next to the Attach DWG tool and then choose Attach Image from the flyout.

In the Select Reference File dialog box, locate and select the raster1.jpg project file. You can see a preview of the file on the right side of the dialog box.

6. Click Open to open the Attach Image dialog box (see Figure 13.2).

FIGURE 13.2
The Attach Image
dialog box

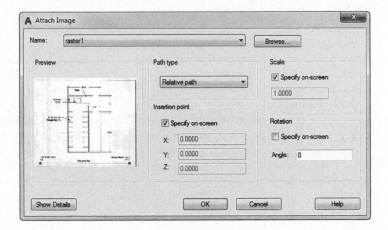

7. Uncheck the Specify On-Screen option in the Insertion Point group to accept the 0,0,0 coordinates.

8. Click OK, and then, at the Specify scale factor <1>: prompt, use the cursor to scale the image so that it fills about half of the screen, as shown in Figure 13.3. The raster1.jpg filename appears in the External References palette.

FIGURE 13.3
Manually scaling
the raster image

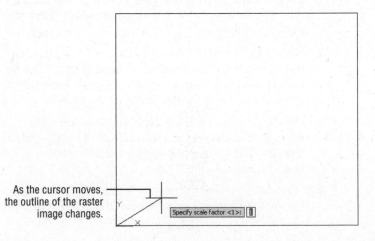

As the cursor moves, the outline of the raster image changes.

Working with a Raster Image

Once you've imported a raster image, you can begin to work with it in a variety of ways. You can resize the image to suit your needs and even adjust its size to a particular scale. Raster images can be made to overlap AutoCAD objects, or you can have raster images appear in the background. There are also rudimentary controls for brightness, contrast, and transparency. In the following sections, you'll continue to use the image that you attached to your drawing to explore some of these options.

 Real World Scenario

TIPS FOR IMPORTING RASTER IMAGES

When you scan a document into your computer, you get a raster image file. Unlike AutoCAD files, *raster image files* are made up of a matrix of colored pixels that form a picture, which is why raster images are also sometimes called *bitmaps. Vector files*, like those produced by AutoCAD, are made up of instructions to draw lines, arcs, curves, and circles. The two formats, raster and vector, are so different that it's difficult to convert one format to the other accurately. It's easier to trace a raster file in AutoCAD than it is to try to use a computer program to make the conversion for you.

But even tracing a raster image file can be difficult if the image is of poor quality. Having worked with scanned images in AutoCAD for a variety of projects, we've discovered that you can make your work a lot easier by following a few simple rules:

◆ Scan in your drawing using a grayscale or color scanner, or convert your black-and-white scanned image to grayscale using your image-editing software. This will give you more control over the appearance of the image once it's in AutoCAD.

◆ Use an image-editing program, such as Adobe Photoshop or your scanner software, to clean up unwanted gray or spotted areas in the file before importing it into AutoCAD.

◆ If your scanner software or image-editing program has a "de-speckle" or "de-spot" feature, use it. It can help clean up your image and ultimately reduce the raster image's file size.

◆ Scan at a reasonable resolution. Scanning at 150 dpi to 200 dpi may be more than adequate.

◆ If you plan to make heavy use of raster imports, upgrade your computer to the fastest processor and install as much memory as you can afford.

The raster import commands can incorporate paper maps or plans into 3D AutoCAD drawings for presentations. We know of one architectural firm that produces impressive presentations with little effort by combining 2D scanned images with 3D massing models for urban design studies. (A *massing model* shows only the rough outline of buildings without giving too much detail, thus showing the general scale of a project without being too fussy.)

Scaling a Raster Image

The raster1.jpg file was scanned as a grayscale image at 100 dpi. This shows that you can get a reasonable amount of detail at a fairly low scan resolution.

Now suppose that you want to trace over this image to start an AutoCAD drawing. The first thing that you should do is scale the image to the appropriate size. You can scale an image file to full size. Try the following steps to see how you can begin the process:

1. Choose Zoom Extents from the Zoom flyout on the Navigation bar, or type **Z↵E↵**. You may also want to pan the view or move the Xref palette to get a clear view of the drawing.

2. Turn on Polar Tracking or Ortho mode, and then click Scale on the Home tab's Modify panel.

3. Click the edge of the raster image to select it.

4. Press ↵ to finish your selection.

5. At the Specify base point: prompt, click the X in the lower-left corner of the image.

6. At the Specify scale factor or [Copy/Reference]: prompt, enter **R↵** to use the Reference option.

7. At the Specify reference length <0′ -1″>: prompt, type **@↵**. This tells AutoCAD that you want to use the last point selected as one end of the reference length. After you enter the @ symbol, you'll see a rubber-banding line emanating from the X.

8. At the Specify second point: prompt, click the X at the lower-right corner of the image.

9. At the Specify new length or [Points] <0′ -1″ >: prompt, enter **44′↵**. Metric users should enter **1341↵**. The image enlarges. Remember that this reference line is 44′, or 1341 cm, in length.

The image is now scaled properly for the plan it portrays. You can proceed to trace over the image. You can also place the image on its own layer and turn it off from time to time to check your trace work. Even if you don't trace the scanned floor plan line for line, you can read the dimensions of the plan from your computer monitor instead of having to go back and forth between measuring the paper image and drawing the plan on the computer.

Controlling Object Visibility and Overlap with Raster Images

With the introduction of raster image support, AutoCAD inherited a problem that's fairly common to programs that use such images: Raster images obscure other objects that were placed previously. The image you imported in the previous exercise, for example, obscures the line you drew when you first opened the file. In most cases, this overlap isn't a problem. However, in some situations, you'll want AutoCAD vector objects to overlap an imported raster image. An example is a civil-engineering drawing showing an AutoCAD drawing of a new road superimposed over an aerial view of the location for the road.

Paint and page-layout programs usually offer a "to front/to back" tool to control the overlap of objects and images. AutoCAD offers the Draworder command. Here's how it works:

1. Click Zoom Extents on the Navigation bar or type **Z↵E↵** to get an overall view of the image.

2. Choose the Bring Above Objects tool from the Draworder flyout on the Home tab's expanded Modify panel.

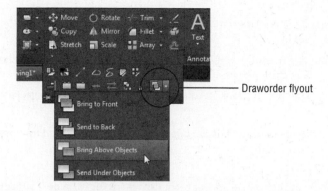

Draworder flyout

3. At the Select objects: prompt, select the horizontal line that you drew when you first opened the file.

4. If there are other objects in the drawing that you want to "bring above objects," you can select them as well. Press ↵ to finish your selection.

5. At the Select reference objects: prompt, click the edge of the raster image of the utility room and then press ↵.

The drawing regenerates, and the entire line appears, no longer obscured by the raster image.

MASKING AN AREA OF AN IMAGE

You can mask out areas of an imported raster image by creating a solid hatch area and using the Draworder command to place the solid hatch on top of the raster image. Such masks can be helpful as backgrounds for text that must be placed over a raster image. You can also use the Wipeout command (select Wipeout on the Home tab's expanded Draw panel) to mask areas of a drawing.

The Draworder tool that you just used has nine options in the Draworder flyout on the Home tab's Modify panel:

Bring To Front Places an object or a set of objects at the top of the draw order for the entire drawing. The effect is that the objects are completely visible.

Send To Back Places an object or a set of objects at the bottom of the draw order for the entire drawing. The effect is that other objects in the drawing may obscure those objects.

Bring Above Objects Places an object or a set of objects above another object in the draw order. This has the effect of making the first set of objects appear above the second selected object.

Send Under Objects Places an object or a set of objects below another object in the draw order. This has the effect of making the first set of objects appear underneath the second selected object.

Bring Text To Front   Automatically places all text in a drawing in front of all objects.

Bring Dimensions To Front   Automatically places all dimensions in a drawing in front of all objects.

Bring Leaders To Front   Automatically places all dimension leaders in a drawing in front of all objects.

Bring All Annotations To Front   Automatically places all annotation objects in a drawing, including dimensions, in front of all objects.

Send Hatches To Back   Automatically sends all hatch patterns in a drawing behind other objects.

You can also use the **DR** keyboard shortcut to issue the Draworder command. If you do this, you see these prompts:

```
Select objects:
Enter object ordering option [Above objects/Under objects/Front/Back]<Back>:
```

You must then select the option by typing the capitalized letter of the option.

Although this section discussed the Draworder tools in relation to raster images, they can also be invaluable in controlling visibility of line work in conjunction with hatch patterns and solid fills. See Chapter 7 for a detailed discussion of the Draworder tools and hatch patterns.

Adjusting Brightness, Contrast, and Fade

AutoCAD offers a tool that enables you to adjust the brightness, contrast, and fade of a raster image. Try making some adjustments to the raster image of the utility room in the following exercise:

1. Click the edge of the raster image. The Image tab appears in the Ribbon (see Figure 13.4).

FIGURE 13.4
The Image tab appears when you select a raster image.

2. In the Adjust panel of the Image tab, click and drag the Fade slider to the right so that it's near the middle of the slider scale, or enter **50** in the Fade box to the right of the slider. The sample image fades to the AutoCAD background color as you move the slider.

3. Press the Esc key to unselect the raster image. The Image tab closes.

4. Save the file as Rasterimport.dwg.

You can adjust the brightness and contrast by using the other two sliders in the Adjust panel of the Image tab.

By using the Image tab in conjunction with image clipping, you can create special effects. Figure 13.5 shows an aerial view of downtown San Francisco with labels. This view consists of two copies of the same raster image. One copy serves as a background, which was lightened using the method demonstrated in the previous exercise. The second copy is the darker area of the image with a roughly triangular clip boundary applied. You might use this technique to bring focus to a particular area of a drawing that you're preparing for a presentation.

FIGURE 13.5
Two copies of the same image can be combined to emphasize a portion of the drawing.

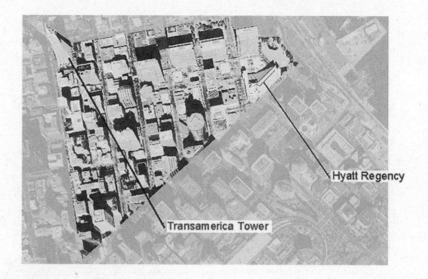

If the draw order of objects is incorrect after you open a file or perform a Pan or Zoom, issue a Regen to recover the correct draw-order view.

In addition to the tools in the Adjust panel, there are several tools in the Image tab that can be used to modify raster images. Table 13.1 gives you a rundown of their function.

TABLE 13.1:   The tools on the Image tab

TOOL	FUNCTION
Brightness	Adjusts the brightness of an image.
Contrast	Adjusts the contrast of an image.
Fade	Adjusts the fade value of an image.
Create Clipping Boundary	Allows you to create a clipping boundary. This tools works just like the Clip tool.
Remove Clipping	Removes a clipping boundary.
Show Image	Toggles an image on and off.
Background Transparency	Toggles the transparency of an image on and off.
External References	Opens the External References palette.

Clipping a Raster Image

In Chapter 7, you saw how you could clip an external reference object so that only a portion of it appears in the drawing. You can clip imported raster images in the same way. Just as with Xrefs, you can create a closed outline of the area that you want to clip, or you can specify a simple rectangular area.

IMAGES AND THE EXTERNAL REFERENCES PALETTE

The External References palette that you saw in Chapter 7 helps you manage your imported image files. It's especially helpful when you have a large number of images in your drawing. You can control imported images in a way similar to how you control Xrefs; you can temporarily unload images (to help speed up the editing of AutoCAD objects) and reload, detach, and relocate raster image files. See Chapter 7 for a detailed description of these options.

In the following exercise, you'll try the Clip command to control the display of the raster image.

1. Select the Clip tool from the Insert tab's Reference panel, or type **Clip**⏎.

2. At the `Select object to clip:` prompt, click the edge of the raster image.

3. At the `Enter image clipping option [ON/OFF/Delete/New boundary]<New>:` prompt, press ⏎ to create a new boundary.

4. At the `[Select polyline/Polygonal/Rectangular/Invert clip] <Rectangular>:` prompt, enter **P**⏎ or click Polygonal in the command-line interface to draw a polygonal boundary.

5. Select the points shown in the top image in Figure 13.6 and then press ⏎. The raster image is clipped to the boundary that you created, as shown in the second image in Figure 13.6.

As the prompt in step 3 indicates, you can turn the clipping off or on, or you can delete an existing clipping boundary through the Clip Image option.

After you clip a raster image, you can adjust the clipping boundary by using its grips:

1. Click the boundary edge of the raster image to expose its grips.

2. Click a grip in the upper-right corner, as shown in the bottom image in Figure 13.6.

3. Drag the grip up and to the right, and then click a point. The image adjusts to the new boundary.

4. You can save the `Rasterimport.dwg` file for future reference and exit the file.

FIGURE 13.6

Adjusting the boundary
of a clipped image

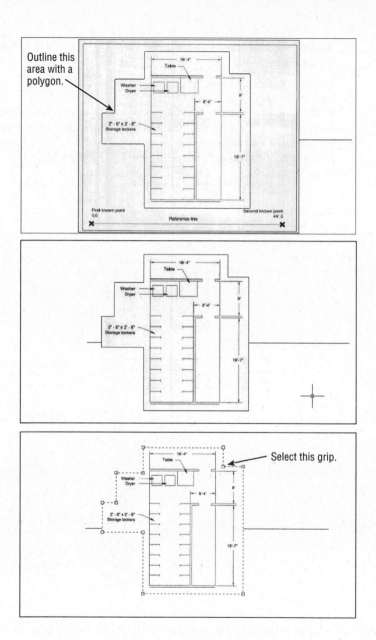

In addition to hiding portions of a raster image that are unimportant to you, clipping an image file reduces the amount of RAM the raster image uses during your editing session. AutoCAD loads only the visible portion of the image into RAM and ignores the rest.

Turning Off the Frame, Adjusting Overall Quality, and Controlling Transparency

You can make three other adjustments to your raster image: frame visibility, image quality, and image transparency.

By default, a raster image displays an outline, or a *frame*. In many instances, this frame can detract from your drawing. You can turn off image frames globally by typing **Imageframe**⏎**0** ⏎. This sets the Imageframe setting to 0, which turns off the frame visibility. If it's set to 1, the frame is made visible. You can also set it to 2, which leaves the frame visible but doesn't plot it (see Figure 13.7).

FIGURE 13.7
A raster image with the frame on (top) and off (bottom)

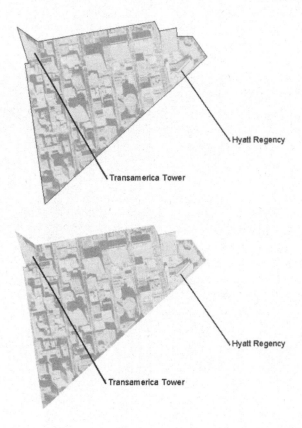

Frames can also be controlled through the Frame flyout on the Insert tab's Reference panel. If you turn off a raster image's frame, you can't click the image to select it for editing, although you can still select an image using the All, Previous, or Last selection option (see Chapter 2, "Creating Your First Drawing," for more on selection options). To make a raster image selectable with your mouse, turn on the image frame using the Display And Plot Frames or the Display But Don't Plot Frames option.

If your drawing doesn't require the highest-quality image, you can set the image quality to Draft mode. You may use Draft mode when you're tracing an image or when the image is already of a high quality. To set the image quality, enter **Imagequality**↵ and then enter **H** for High mode (high quality) or **D** for Draft mode. In Draft mode, your drawing will regenerate faster.

High mode softens the pixels of the raster image, giving the image a smoother appearance. Draft mode displays the image in a raw, pixelated state. If you look carefully at the regions between the motorcycle and the background in the second image in Figure 13.8, you'll see that the edges of the motorcycle appear a bit jagged. The top image in Figure 13.8 uses the High setting to soften the edges of the motorcycle. You may need to look closely to see the difference.

FIGURE 13.8
A close-up of a raster image with quality set to High (top) and Draft (bottom)

Finally, you can control the transparency of raster image files that allow transparent pixels. Some file formats, such as GIF (Global Interchange Format), allow you to set a color in the image to be transparent (usually the background color). Most image-editing programs support this format because it's a popular one used on web pages.

When you turn on the Transparency setting, objects normally obscured by the background of a raster image may show through. Select the raster image and then, in the Image tab's Options panel, select Background Transparency. You can also right-click and select Image ➤ Transparency and then select On or Off from the Dynamic Input menu. In addition, you can enter **Transparency**↵ and then select the raster image that you want to make transparent. Press ↵, and then enter **On** or **Off**, depending on whether you want the image to be transparent. Unlike the Frame and Quality options, Transparency works on individual objects rather than operating globally.

The Properties palette offers many of the same adjustments described in this section. You can use it for quick access to the Transparency setting and other raster image settings.

CAN'T GET TRANSPARENCY TO WORK?

The Transparency command does not work on all types of images. As mentioned, it works with GIF files that have the background removed. You can also use a bitonal image, meaning the image must have only two colors, typically black and white. A bitonal image is also referred to as a *bitmap* image in Photoshop. It cannot be grayscale or multicolor. PDF files that have been exported from AutoCAD may also work with the Transparency command.

You can put images that do not work with the Transparency command on a layer with transparency set to a value greater than 0. Transparency can also be set using the Transparency slider in the Home tab's Properties panel. To use the Transparency slider, select the object, such as an image or hatch pattern, and then adjust the slider to achieve the level of transparency that you want. You can start at 50 and adjust downward or upward.

Note that if you want your image to print or plot with the transparency in effect, you must select the Plot Transparency option in the Plot Or Page Setup dialog box.

Working with PDF Files

If you're using a computer as part of your daily work activity, you will encounter a PDF document. PDFs have become a part of everyday life, so it's no surprise that AutoCAD offers a fair amount of support for PDFs.

In the following sections, you'll learn how to import a PDF document into AutoCAD and how you can control various properties of the document, such as fading and the ability to snap to objects in the PDF.

Importing a PDF

To import a PDF, you use a method similar to the one you used earlier to import an image file. In fact, you could perform all of the steps in the exercise in the section "Importing a Raster Image" earlier in this chapter using a PDF file instead of the raster1.jpg file. You just need to know how to set up the Select Reference File dialog box to allow you to locate PDFs.

Try the following to see how to import a PDF:

1. Open a new file using the acad.dwt file as a template.

2. Use the Save As option in the Application menu, and save the drawing as PDFunderlay.dwg.

3. Click the Attach tool in the Insert tab's Reference panel or type **attach.⏎** to open the Select Reference File dialog box.

4. In the Files Of Type drop-down list at the bottom of the dialog box, select PDF Files (*.pdf).

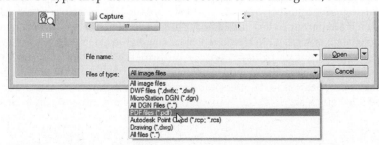

5. Locate and select the `SampleImport.pdf` file.

6. Click Open to open the Attach PDF Underlay dialog box (see Figure 13.9). Notice that you have an option to select a specific page of the PDF document if you are opening a multi-page PDF.

FIGURE 13.9
The Attach PDF
Underlay dialog box

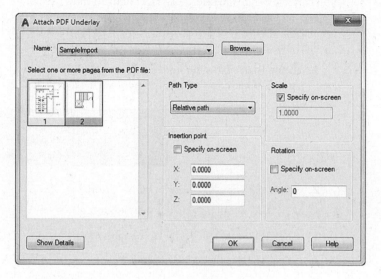

7. Click page 2 of the page preview on the left side of the dialog box.

8. Make sure the Specify On-Screen options are selected for Scale and Insertion Point.

9. Click OK and then, at the `Specify insertion point:` prompt, place the outline of the drawing so that it is roughly centered in the drawing area and click.

10. At the `Specify scale factor or [Unit] <1.0000>:` prompt, use the cursor to scale the image so that it fills the screen (see Figure 13.10). Page 2 of the `SampleImport.pdf` file appears in the drawing.

FIGURE 13.10
Manually scaling
the PDF image

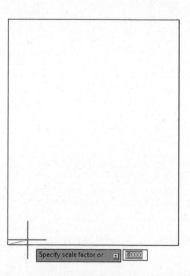

Scaling and Osnaps with PDFs

In an earlier exercise, you were able to scale an image file, though you had to use a reference line that was already in the image file to scale the drawing roughly to its proper size in AutoCAD. If you have a PDF that was created from an AutoCAD file or from another vector-based program, you can use osnaps to select exact locations in the PDF.

Try the following exercise to see how you can use osnaps to select geometry in the PDF. You'll scale the drawing so that the width of the stairs conforms to the known distance for that area.

First make sure the Snap To Underlays feature is turned on:

1. In the Insert tab's Reference panel, click the Snap To Underlays tool. Depending on your AutoCAD window width, you may see the icon only and not the "Snap To Underlays" label.

2. Select the Snap To Underlays ON option.

Now you are ready to scale the PDF drawing:

1. Click the Scale tool in the Home tab's Modify panel or type **SC**↵.

2. Select the attached PDF file and press ↵.

3. At the Specify base point: prompt, turn on the osnaps and select the left endpoint of the horizontal line near the top of the drawing, as shown in Figure 13.11.

FIGURE 13.11
Selecting the first end-
point of the line for the
Scale command

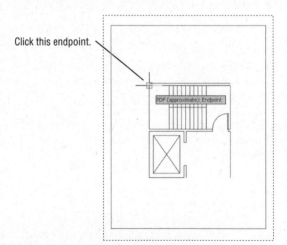

Click this endpoint.

4. At the Specify scale factor or [Copy/Reference]: prompt, type **R**↵ to use the Reference option.

5. At the Specify Reference length <1.0000>: prompt, click the same endpoint again or type **@**↵.

6. At the Specify second point: prompt, click the endpoint of the line shown in Figure 13.12.

FIGURE 13.12

Selecting the second endpoint of the line for the Scale command

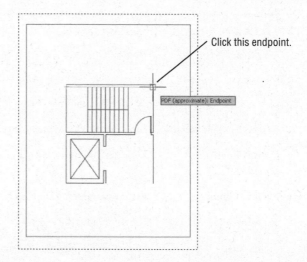

Click this endpoint.

PDF (approximate): Endpoint

7. At the Specify new length or [Points] <1.0000>: prompt, enter **196**, which is the inch equivalent of 16'-4".

8. In the Navigation bar, choose the Zoom Extents option from the Zoom flyout to center the drawing in the drawing area.

In this exercise, you were able to use object snaps directly on the imported PDF drawing. You may have noticed that a tool tip appeared with the message "PDF (approximate): Endpoint." The PDF drawing is not an exact representation of the original drawing, so the tool tip reminds you that even though you are using an osnap to select a location in the drawing, it is not an exact location as it would be in an AutoCAD file.

Controlling the PDF Display

You can take advantage of a number of other features of a PDF file. Just as with a typical Xref or image file, you can fade the PDF so that it appears as a background image. You can also use the Clip feature that you saw earlier in this chapter to clip the PDF to a specific area.

You can gain access to these and other PDF display features through the PDF Underlay Ribbon tab. This tab appears automatically whenever you select an attached PDF drawing. Click the PDF drawing of the lobby, and you'll see the PDF Underlay tab appear in the Ribbon (see Figure 13.13).

FIGURE 13.13

The panels on the PDF Underlay Ribbon tab

Table 13.2 describes the tools in the PDF Underlay Ribbon tab. The tools are fairly self-explanatory. For example, the tools in the Adjust panel let you control the fade and contrast of the PDF drawing. The Display In Monochrome option displays a color PDF in monochrome.

TABLE 13.2:   The PDF Underlay tab tools

OPTION	USE
Contrast	Adjusts the contrast setting for the PDF
Fade	Adjusts the amount of fade applied to the PDF
Display In Monochrome	Displays the PDF in monochrome
Create Clipping Boundary	Adds a clipping boundary to the PDF
Remove Clipping	Removes a clipping boundary
Show Underlay	Shows or hides the PDF
Enable Snap	Enables or disables the PDF snap feature
External References	Opens the External References palette
Edit Layers	Opens the Underlay Layers dialog box, allowing you to control layer visibility
Import As Objects	Converts an attached vector PDF into AutoCAD drawing objects

One option that you'll want to take a closer look at is the Edit Layers tool in the PDF Layers panel. If the source PDF is a drawing that contains layers, you can control the visibility of those layers using this tool. With an imported PDF selected, click the Edit Layers tool to open the Underlay Layers dialog box (see Figure 13.14).

FIGURE 13.14
The Underlay
Layers dialog box

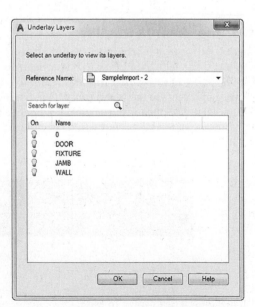

You can turn the visibility of a layer on or off by clicking the light bulb icon to the left of it in the list. For example, if you turn off the WALL layer in the Underlay Layers dialog box for the SampleImport example, the PDF drawing will change so that the walls will not be shown (see Figure 13.15).

FIGURE 13.15
The imported PDF with the WALL layer turned off

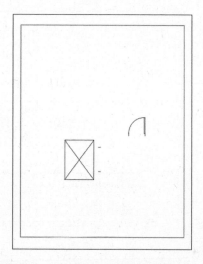

ADDING LAYERS TO YOUR PDF

If you want to create a PDF with layers, you can do so by printing a drawing to a PDF file using the AutoCAD DWG To PDF.pc3 Printer/Plotter option. You can find this option in the Name drop-down list in the Page Setup Or Plot dialog box. (See Chapter 8, "Introducing Printing, Plotting, and Layouts," for more on the Name drop-down list.) You don't have to do anything special. If your drawing contains layers, the DWG to PDF.pc3 plotter will include them in the PDF. Adobe Acrobat 6.0 and later will also include layers when used from AutoCAD.

Importing a PDF as an AutoCAD Drawing

PDFs can contain both raster and vector data. If you have a PDF that is a line drawing or 3D model, there is a good chance that it is stored in a vector format. PDFs containing vector information and text can be imported into AutoCAD as an AutoCAD drawing. For example, a PDF floor plan produced from AutoCAD can be imported back into AutoCAD and then edited as a normal AutoCAD drawing, as the following exercise will show:

1. Click the Open icon in the Quick Access toolbar, and open the PDFimport.dwg file from the samples folder. This is just a blank file with the units set to Architectural.

2. Open the Application menu by clicking the AutoCAD icon in the upper-left corner of the AutoCAD window, and then select Import ➤ PDF. The cursor will change to a pickbox. At the Select underlay or [File] <File>: prompt, press ↵.

3. In the Import file dialog box, browse to the Chapter 13 sample files and open the PDFvector.pdf file. The Import PDF dialog box appears (see Figure 13.16). Here you have a number of options that give you control over how the file is imported. For this exercise, you'll use the default settings.

FIGURE 13.16
The Import PDF
dialog box

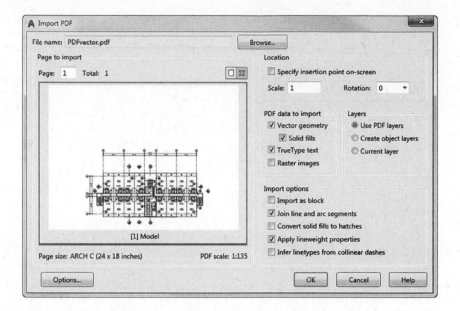

4. Click OK. The PDF is imported into the current file as an AutoCAD drawing.

5. Click any object, and you'll notice that individual objects are selectable.

6. Click a room label. You'll notice that the text has been converted to lines.

7. Zoom into the left side of the drawing to enlarge the C and D grid lines.

8. Click the Measure tool in the Home tab's Utilities panel, and then select the endpoints of the grid lines between grids C and D. Notice that measurement is the same as the dimensioned distance.

This exercise demonstrates a few features of the Import PDF feature. In step 6, you discovered that the room label was imported as lines. For drawings that contain TrueType fonts, you have the option to import text in the original font. This will enable you to edit the text using the AutoCAD text editing tools. In step 4, you saw that the drawings imported to scale. The distance between grid lines C and D measured the same as the dimensioned distance.

The PDFvector.dwg file was created using the AutoCAD PDF (High Quality Print) .pc3 printer option. In addition, it was plotted from model space. Had it been printed from a layout, measurements taken in the drawing would reflect the print size and not a full, 1-to-1 scale drawing. For example, measuring the distance between grid lines C and D would have returned a distance in inches as if measured from a scale paper drawing.

Be aware that PDF plots created from model space will lose some accuracy, even though they will import to a 1-to-1 scale. In addition, PDF drawings from other vector programs may not import to scale, in which case you can use the Scale option in the Import PDF dialog box to adjust the scale of the imported drawing. Or you can just scale the drawing after it is imported using the methods described earlier in this chapter.

Let's take a look at the options in the Import PDF dialog box shown in Figure 13.16. These options enable you to control how the PDF is imported. You can set whether raster data is imported into the drawing or, if the PDF contains layers, how the layers are translated. You can also control how types of geometry are converted. For example, in the Import Options section, you can set the PDF to be imported as a block or convert solid fills in the PDF to hatches. The options are fairly self-explanatory, but a few may need a bit more explanation.

If the PDF file that you want to import contains multiple pages, you can select a page using the Page option just above and to the left of the preview image. You can also get a matrix view of the pages by selecting the thumbnail toggle above and to the right of the preview. The Options button in the lower-left of the dialog box opens the Options dialog box to the File tab, where you can set the location for the storage of any raster images that are imported. (See Appendix B for more on the Files tab of the Options dialog box.)

CONVERT A PDF UNDERLAY INTO AUTOCAD OBJECTS

If you already have a vector PDF inserted as an underlay into your drawing, you can convert part or all of the underlay into AutoCAD objects by using the Import As Objects tool found in the PDF Underlay tab (Figure 13.13) or by using the Select Underlay option in the previous exercise. For example, you can click the PDF underlay you inserted in the PDFunderlay.dwg file exercise and then click the Import As Objects tool in the PDF Underlay tab. You are prompted to select an area to import. Once it's selected, you have the option to keep the PDF underlay, detach it, or unload it. Once you've selected your option, the selected portion of the PDF is converted to AutoCAD objects, which you can edit using the usual editing tools.

Reconstructing Imported AutoCAD SHX Fonts

The PDF file format does not support AutoCAD's SHX fonts such as Simplex and Txt. When you export an AutoCAD file to a PDF, TrueType fonts are maintained as fonts but AutoCAD SHX fonts are converted to drawing geometry such as lines and polylines, so when you import a PDF that was created from an AutoCAD drawing, SHX fonts will be imported as lines and polylines.

Fortunately, AutoCAD offers the Recognize SHX Text tool that can recognize imported SHX fonts and convert them back to AutoCAD text (see Figure 13.17). To use this tool, go to the Import panel in the Insert tab and select Recognize SHX Text. You can also enter **PDFSHXTEXT**↵. Next, select the geometry you want to convert back to AutoCAD text. Try to avoid including non-text geometry in your selection. Once you've selected the geometry to convert, press ↵. When AutoCAD is finished with the conversion, you see a dialog box telling you how many text objects were created and how many fonts were used.

FIGURE 13.17
The Recognize
SHX Text tool and
the Recognition
Settings tool

AutoCAD also offers the PDF Text Recognition Settings dialog box, which enables you to determine the font that AutoCAD uses for the conversion (see Figure 13.18). This dialog box can be opened by using the Recognition Settings tool in the Insert tab's Import panel (see Figure 13.17) or by selecting the Settings command option in the Recognize SHX Text tool.

FIGURE 13.18
The PDF Text
Recognition
Settings dialog box

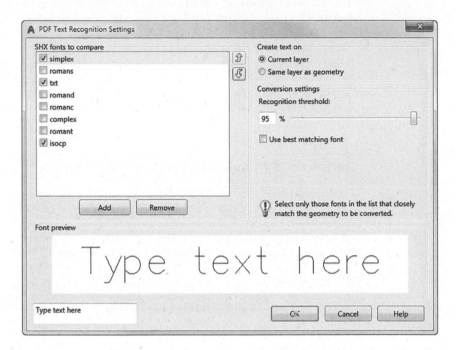

The PDF Text Recognition Settings dialog box contains a list that is populated with the most commonly used AutoCAD fonts. You can use the Add button to add other SHX fonts to the list, including custom and third-party fonts.

Coordinating Geographic Locations

Architects and engineers use geolocation and mapping tools to help place their projects on their chosen sites. Usually, a program like Google Earth or another mapping program is used to get an idea of the site conditions. Street views from Google Maps can help designers get a better idea of how their buildings will appear from a street level.

Geolocation tools can help the designer coordinate information between the different disciplines involved in a project. Designers can place their projects over an aerial view of a site and coordinate the orientation and location of key features of their design.

The Geographic Location feature in AutoCAD allows you to place an accurately scaled map or aerial view in your drawing. You can then draw your designs directly on the map or import an existing AutoCAD design. Unlike an imported image, the Geographic Location map will always remain in the background so you don't have to be concerned about an overlapping image. You can also easily switch between a map view and an aerial view as the need arises.

START AN AUTODESK® 360 ACCOUNT TO USE GEOGRAPHIC LOCATION

Before you start to work with the Geographic Location feature, you will need to create an Autodesk 360 account and be signed in. Click the Sign In drop-down list in the InfoCenter, and select Sign In To Autodesk 360. A browser appears that takes you to the Autodesk 360 website where you can sign up for a free account. If you already have an account, just sign in.

Let's take a look at how the Geographic Location feature works:

1. In a new file, select the Insert Ribbon tab, and in the Location panel, click Set Location, and select From Map.

2. You will see a message asking "Do you want to use Online Map Data?" Click Yes.

3. The Geographic Location dialog box appears (see Figure 13.19). Here, you can enter an address, a location name, or the latitude and longitude of a site.

FIGURE 13.19

The Geographic Location dialog box

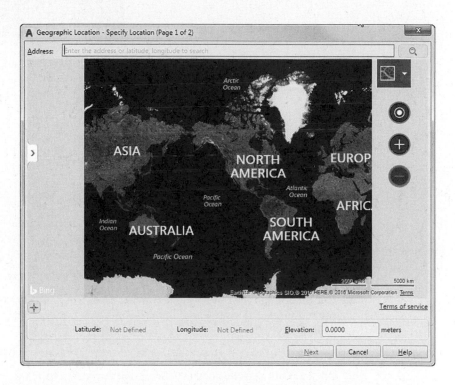

4. Enter a location name or address in the text box at the top of the dialog box, and click the magnifying glass icon. For this exercise, enter **Fort Mason, San Francisco**. The dialog box changes to show an aerial view map of Fort Mason. In the left side, you see a list keyed to numbered locations on the map (see Figure 13.20). If there are multiple locations that contain the name you entered in this step, you will see them labeled with numbers.

FIGURE 13.20
An aerial view of your selected location appears in the dialog box.

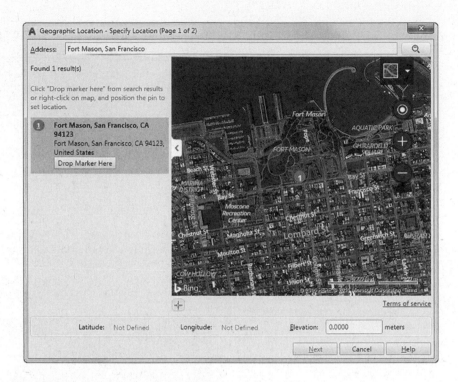

5. Click the Drop Marker Here button just under Fort Mason, San Francisco, CA 94123. A red marker appears in the map.

6. Click the Next button at the bottom of the dialog box.

7. At the next dialog box, you are asked to select a coordinate system. Select NSRS11.SFO-CS13F, which is at the top of the list, and then select Next. The dialog box closes, and you see the prompt

   ```
   Select a point for the location <0.0000,0.0000.0.0000>::
   ```

8. Click a point at the center of the drawing area. The point that you select corresponds to the red marker that appeared in the Geographic Location dialog box. You see the next prompt:

   ```
   Specify the north direction angle or [First point] <90>:
   ```

9. Click a point directly above the first point that you selected to indicate a north direction pointing up. An aerial view of the northern tip of San Francisco appears (see Figure 13.21).

10. Once the aerial view appears in the drawing, you can zoom in and out using the standard AutoCAD view tools. Use the wheel of your mouse to zoom in to get a closer look at Fort Mason.

FIGURE 13.21
The drawing area
with the Geographic
Location aerial view

You may notice that the Geolocation Ribbon tab appears with a set of options (see Figure 13.22). These options allow you to modify your geolocation view. For example, the Map Aerial flyout lets you switch to a map view and back again.

FIGURE 13.22
The Geolocation
Ribbon tab panels

Try it in the following exercise:

1. In the Online Map panel of the Geolocation tab, click the Map Aerial flyout and select Map Road. The view changes to show a graphic representation of the roads.

2. In the Online Map panel of the Geolocation tab, click the Map Road flyout and select Map Aerial. The view changes back to the aerial view.

Making Adjustments to the Map

As you can see from the previous steps, you can easily switch between an aerial view and a map view. You also have the option to show a combined aerial and map view using the Map Hybrid option or to turn the geolocation background off entirely using the Map Off option.

OPTIONS ON THE LOCATION PANEL

Besides controlling the geolocation background image, the Geolocation Ribbon tab lets you make other adjustments to your background. Here is a rundown of the tools and features that you'll find in the Location panel:

Edit Location   Offers two options: From Map and From File. If you select From Map, the Geographic Location dialog box opens, enabling you to enter new location data. The From File option lets you find a location using a KML or KMZ file. KML files are used with Google Earth to enable location, tagging, and placement of 3D models on a Google Earth map. KMZ files are archive files similar to zip files, and they contain KML files and any support files needed for the KML file.

Reorient Marker   Lets you reposition the original marker location and reset the north orientation. You are asked to select a point for the location of the address or latitude-longitude position, and then you are asked for the north orientation.

Remove Location   Lets you remove the geolocation map from the drawing. When you click this tool, you are asked if you want to remove the location data and the assigned coordinate system from the current drawing.

OPTIONS ON THE TOOLS PANEL

The Tools panel in the Geolocation tab offers tools that let you mark locations in the geolocation background. You've already seen what the Map Aerial and Map Road options do. The following list describes the other tools in this panel:

My Location   Lets you find your location on the aerial view or map. This feature is available only if your computer is equipped with a GPS or other feature that is able to provide your location data.

Mark Position   Lets you place a marker in the aerial or map view. The following options are available in the flyout: The Lat-Long option lets you specify the latitude and longitude for the marker location. The My Location option is similar to the Locate Me tool, and it places a marker at your current location. The Point option enables you to point to a location to place a marker. Once you click a location, you are prompted to enter a text description for the location. AutoCAD opens the Text Editor Ribbon tab, giving you the ability to format your text description.

OPTIONS ON THE ONLINE MAP PANEL

The Online Map panel in the Geolocation tab gives you control over the map's appearance. It also lets you capture a portion of the map:

Map Aerial   Lets you select from a number of display options. You can choose to display a map (see Figure 13.23) or a combined map and aerial view. You can also turn the map off completely.

FIGURE 13.23
The Map Road view

Capture Area   Lets you place a selection rectangle over a portion of the displayed map. You can then copy the selected area to the Clipboard. You can also capture the entire map that is in the display. Once you place a selection rectangle, the Map Image Ribbon tab appears, enabling you to adjust brightness, contrast, and fade of the selected area. You can also control the quality of the image. Note that you can select the type of image that you want from the Map flyout to the far left of the ribbon. You have the choice of Map Aerial, Map Road, and Map Hybrid.

The captured map area is stored with the drawing and is not dependent on an Internet connection. It can also be moved, rotated, or resized in a manner similar to an imported raster image. The captured area will also appear in the Layout viewports.

Finding Measurements and Distances

In the first Geolocation exercise, you may have noticed the Drawing Unit option in the Geographic Location dialog box. By default, this option is set to inches, but you can set it to feet, meters, miles, or some other unit of measure. By accepting the default inches for the Drawing Unit option, any measurements you take on the map will return distances using inches as the drawing unit. If the unit style of your drawing is set to Architectural, distances will be displayed in feet and inches—inches are the base drawing unit. Try the following exercise to see how distances are displayed:

1. Type **Units**↵ to open the Drawing Units dialog box.

2. Select Architectural from the Type drop-down list, and then click OK.

3. Choose Map Road from the Map Aerial flyout in the Map Tools Ribbon panel.

4. Zoom into the map view so that it looks similar to Figure 13.23.

5. Choose Measure from the Home tab's Utilities panel.

6. Measure the distance from Laguna Street to Van Ness Avenue. The Measure tool reports a distance of 2446′, give or take a few feet.

In this exercise, the distance reported by the Measure tool is in feet. Had you not changed drawing unit in steps 1 and 2, the distance reported by the Measure tool would have been 29,043 units, which is the distance in inches.

You can use other methods to find measurements in your map. For example, you could get a rough estimate of the size of an existing building by drawing a closed polyline around the building outline (see Figure 13.24). Select the polyline and hover over a grip to view the dimensions of the outline closest to the grip.

FIGURE 13.24
Dimensions from a building outline

The Bottom Line

Convert paper drawings into AutoCAD files. AutoCAD gives you some great tools that let you convert your paper drawings into AutoCAD files. Several options are available. Depending on your needs, you'll find at least one solution that will allow you to convert your drawings quickly.

> **Master It** Describe the different methods available in AutoCAD for converting paper drawings into CAD files.

Import a raster image. You can use bitmap raster images as backgrounds for your CAD drawings or as underlay drawings that you can trace over.

> **Master It** Import a raster image of your choice, and use the AutoCAD drawing tools to trace over your image.

Work with a raster image. Once imported, raster images can be adjusted for size, brightness, contrast, and transparency.

> **Master It** Import a raster image of your choice, and fade the image so that it appears to blend into the background with less contrast.

Work with PDF files. AutoCAD allows you to import and control the display of PDF files. This is significant since the PDF file format is so prevalent in the business world.

> **Master It** In a PDF that includes layers, how do you gain access to the layer settings?

Use a geolocation map. You can include a correctly scaled background aerial view or road map of a site in your drawing to help you better coordinate your design with site conditions.

> **Master It** Name three types of information that you can use to find a site in the Geographic Location dialog box.

Chapter 14

Advanced Editing and Organizing

Because you may not know all of a project's requirements when it begins, you usually base the first draft of a design on anticipated needs. As the plan goes forward, you adjust for new requirements as they arise. As more people enter the project, additional design restrictions come into play, and the design is further modified. This process continues throughout the project, from the first draft to the end product.

In this chapter, you'll gain experience with tools that will help you edit your drawings more efficiently. You'll take a closer look at Xrefs and how they may be used to help streamline changes in a drawing project. You'll also be introduced to tools and techniques that you can use to minimize duplication of work, such as the Quick Select tool and the QuickCalc feature. The AutoCAD® 2018 software can be a powerful timesaving tool if used properly. This chapter examines ways to harness that power.

In this chapter, you will learn to

- ◆ Use external references (Xrefs)
- ◆ Manage layers
- ◆ Use advanced tools: Filter and Quick Select
- ◆ Use the QuickCalc calculator

Using External References

Chapter 7, "Mastering Viewing Tools, Hatches, and External References," mentioned that careful use of blocks, external references (Xrefs), and layers can help improve your productivity. In the following sections, you'll see firsthand how to use these features to help reduce design errors and speed up delivery of an accurate set of drawings. You do so by controlling layers in conjunction with blocks and Xrefs to create a common drawing database for several drawings. You can also use AutoCAD DWF and Acrobat PDF files as Xrefs. See Chapter 13, "Copying Existing Drawings from Other Sources," for more on PDF files and Chapter 25, "Managing and Sharing Your Drawings," for more on DWF files.

Later, you'll start to use Xrefs to create different floor plans for the building that you worked on earlier in this book. To save you some time, we've created a second one-bedroom unit plan called Unit2 that you'll use in these exercises (see Figure 14.1). You can find this new unit plan in the Chapter 14 folder of sample files at this book's web page, www.sybex.com/go/masteringautocad2018.

FIGURE 14.1

The one-bedroom unit

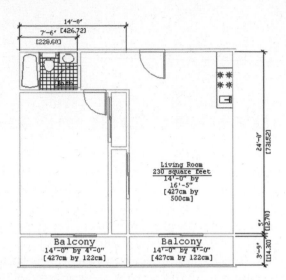

Preparing Existing Drawings for External Referencing

Chapter 7 discussed how you can use Xrefs to assemble one floor of the apartment. In this section, you'll explore the creation and use of Xrefs to build multiple floors, each containing slightly different sets of drawing information. By doing so, you'll learn how Xrefs enable you to use a single file in multiple drawings to save time and reduce redundancy. You'll see that by sharing common data in multiple files, you can reduce your work and keep the drawing information consistent.

You'll start by creating the files that you'll use later as Xrefs:

1. Open the 14a-plan.dwg or 14a-plan-metric file (see Figure 14.2). Select Zoom All from the Navigation bar to center the drawing.

FIGURE 14.2

The overall plan

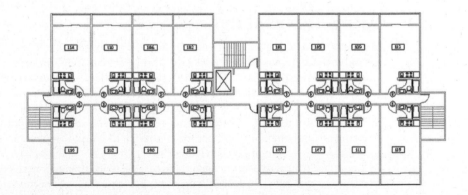

2. Turn off the Ceiling and Flr-pat layers to get a clear, uncluttered view of the individual unit plans.

3. Use the Wblock command (enter **W**⏎ at the Command prompt), and write the eight units in the corners of your plan to a file called **Floor1.dwg** in your My Documents folder (see Figure 14.3). When you select objects for the Wblock, be sure to include the S-DOOR door reference symbols and apartment number symbols for those units. Use 0,0 for the Wblock insertion base point. Also make sure that the Delete From Drawing check box is selected in the Write Block dialog box before you click OK.

FIGURE 14.3
Units to be exported to the Floor1.dwg file

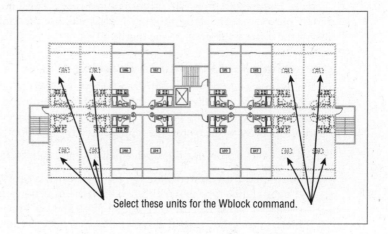

Select these units for the Wblock command.

4. Using Figure 14.4 as a guide, insert the Unit2.dwg file into the corners where the other eight units were previously. Metric users should use Unit2-metric.dwg.

FIGURE 14.4
Insertion information for Unit2 metric coordinates is shown in brackets.

Insert Unit2 at coordinate 31'-5",104'-6" [957,3184]; x-scale factor = 1; y-scale factor = -1 (minus one).

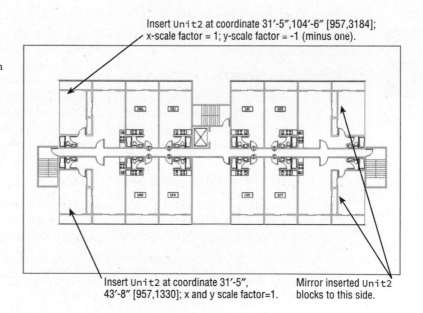

Insert Unit2 at coordinate 31'-5", 43'-8" [957,1330]; x and y scale factor=1.

Mirror inserted Unit2 blocks to this side.

5. After you've accurately placed the corner units, use the Wblock command to write these corner units to a file called **Floor2.dwg**. Again, use the 0,0 coordinate as the insertion base point for the Wblock, and make sure that the Delete From Drawing check box is selected.

6. Choose Save As from the Application menu to turn the remaining set of unit plans into a file called **Common.dwg**.

You've just created three files: Floor1.dwg, Floor2.dwg, and Common.dwg. Each file contains unique information about the building. Next, you'll use the Xref command to recombine these files for the different floor plans in your building.

Assembling Xrefs to Build a Drawing

You'll now create composite files for each floor using Xrefs of only the files needed for the individual floors. You'll use the Attach option of the Xref command to insert all the files that you exported from the Plan.dwg file.

Follow these steps to create a file representing the first floor:

1. Close the Common.dwg file, open a new file, and call it Xref-1.dwg.

2. For Imperial measurement users, use the Drawing Units dialog box (**Units**↵) to set the drawing units type to Architectural and the insertion scale to Inches. Use the Limits command to set the lower-left corner at 0,0 and the upper-right corner at 2112,1632. Metric users should set the drawing units type to Decimal and the insertion scale to Centimeters. Set the lower-left corner limits to 0,0 and the upper-right corner limits to 5940 cm × 4200 cm. For both measurement systems, select All from the Zoom flyout on the View tab's Navigate panel or type **Z**↵**A**↵ so that your drawing area is adjusted to the window.

3. Set the Ltscale value to 192. Metric users should set it to 200.

4. Click Attach in the Insert tab's Reference panel or type **XA**↵ to open the Select Reference File dialog box.

5. Locate and select the Common.dwg file.

6. In the Attach External Reference dialog box, make sure that the Specify On-Screen check box in the Insertion Point group isn't selected. Then make sure that the X, Y, and Z values in the Insertion Point group are all 0 (see Figure 14.5). Because the insertion points of all the files are the same (0,0), they will fit together perfectly when they're inserted into the new files.

7. Click OK. The Common.dwg file appears in the drawing.

The drawing may appear faded. This is because AutoCAD has a feature that allows you to fade an Xref so that it is easily distinguished from other objects in your current drawing. You can quickly change the reference fade setting by doing the following:

1. In the Insert tab's expanded Reference panel, locate the Xref Fading slider.

2. Click and drag the Xref Fading slider all the way to the left, or you can click in the Xref Fading slider value box to the right and enter 0↵.

FIGURE 14.5
The Attach External
Reference dialog box

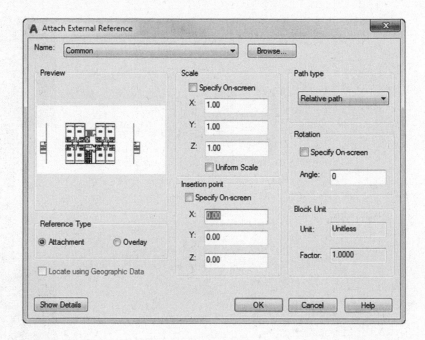

Your Xref should now appear solid. Remember the Xref Fading slider; you may find that you'll need it frequently when working with Xrefs.

Now continue to add some reference files:

1. Click Attach from the Reference panel, and then locate, select, and insert the Floor1.dwg or Floor1-metric.dwg file.

2. Repeat step 1 to insert the Col-grid.dwg or Col-grid-metric.dwg file from the Chapter 14 sample files folder as an Xref. You now have the plan for the first floor.

3. Save this file.

Next, use the current file to create another file representing a different floor:

1. Choose Save As from the Application menu, and save this file as **Xref-2.dwg**.

2. Click the External References tool in the Insert tab's Reference panel title bar, or type **XR**↵.

3. In the External References palette, select Floor1 in the list of Xrefs. Notice that as you hover over the Floor1 name, a description of the file appears with a thumbnail view (see Figure 14.6). This can help you quickly identify Xref files in the list. If you click an Xref name, the Xref will be highlighted in the drawing.

FIGURE 14.6
Highlight Floor1 in the
list of Xrefs.

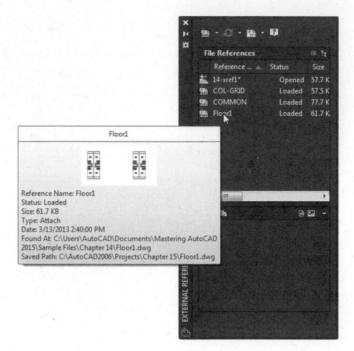

4. Right-click and select Detach from the context menu.

5. Right-click in the blank portion of the list in the External References palette, and select Attach DWG from the context menu.

6. Locate and select Floor2.dwg.

7. In the Attach External Reference dialog box, make sure that the X, Y, and Z values in the Insertion Point group are all set to 0.

8. Click OK. The Floor2 drawing appears in place of Floor1. Turn off the Notes layer to see the plan clearly.

Now when you need to make changes to Xref-1.dwg or Xref-2.dwg, you can edit their individual Xref files. The next time you open Xref-1.dwg or Xref-2.dwg, the updated Xrefs will automatically appear in their most recent forms.

Xrefs don't need to be permanent. As you saw in the previous exercise, you can attach and detach them easily at any time. This means that if you need to get information from another file—to see how well an elevator core aligns, for example—you can temporarily attach the other file as an Xref to check alignments quickly and then detach it when you're finished.

Think of these composite files as final plot files that are used only for plotting and reviewing. You can then edit the smaller, more manageable Xref files. Figure 14.7 illustrates the relationship of these files.

FIGURE 14.7
A diagram of Xref file relationships

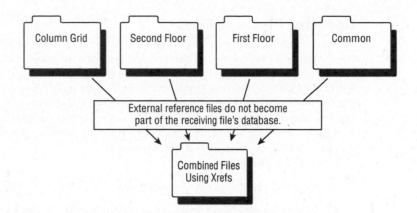

The combinations of Xrefs are limited only by your imagination.

KEEPING TRACK OF XREF LOCATIONS

Because Xref files don't become part of the file into which they're referenced, you must take care to keep them in a location where AutoCAD can find them when the referencing file is opened. This can be a minor annoyance when you need to send files to others outside your office. To help keep track of Xrefs, choose Publish eTransmit from the Application menu. See Chapter 25 for details.

LOCATING XREF FILES

If you move an Xref file after you insert it into a drawing, AutoCAD may not be able to find it later when you attempt to open the drawing. If this happens, you can click the Browse button of the Saved Path option at the bottom of the External References palette to tell AutoCAD the new location of the Xref file. The Browse button appears at the far right of the Saved Path text box when you click in the text box.

If you know that you'll be keeping your project files in one place, you can use the Projectname system variable in conjunction with the Options dialog box to direct AutoCAD to look in a specific location for Xref files. Here's what to do:

1. Choose Options from the Application menu or type **OP**↵.

2. Click the Files tab, and then locate and select the Project Files Search Path option.

3. Click Add and either enter a name for your project or accept the default name of Project1.

4. Click Browse and locate and select the folder where you plan to keep your Xref files.

5. Close the Options dialog box, and then enter **Projectname**↵ at the command-line interface. Enter the project name you used in step 3.

6. Save your file so that it remembers this setting.

Updating Blocks in Xrefs

Several advantages are associated with using Xref files. Because the Xrefs don't become part of the drawing file's database, the referencing files remain small. Also, because Xref files are easily updated, work can be split up among several people in a workgroup environment or on a network. For example, for your hypothetical apartment building project, one person can be editing the Common.dwg file while another works on Floor1.dwg and so on. The next time the composite Xref-1.dwg or Xref-2.dwg file is opened, it automatically reflects any new changes made in the Xref files. If the Xref is updated while you still have the receiving file open, you see a balloon message telling you that an Xref requires a reload.

Let's see how to set this up:

1. Save and close the Xref-2.dwg file, and then open the Common.dwg file.

2. In Windows Explorer, make a copy of the 14b-unit.dwg file and rename the copy to **Unit.dwg**. Metric users should make a copy of the 14b-unit-metric.dwg file and rename it **Unit.dwg**.

3. Click Insert in the Home or Insert tab's Block panel, and then click More Options. You can also type **Insert↵**.

4. In the Insert dialog box, make sure the Specify On-Screen option is selected in the Insert group.

5. Click the Browse button and then locate and select Unit.dwg. You may also use the method described in the sidebar "Substituting Blocks" in Chapter 7 to insert 14b-unit.dwg or 14b-unit-metric.dwg.

6. At the Insertion point: prompt, press the Esc key. You see the new unit plan in place of the old one (see Figure 14.8).

FIGURE 14.8
The Common.dwg file with the revised unit plan

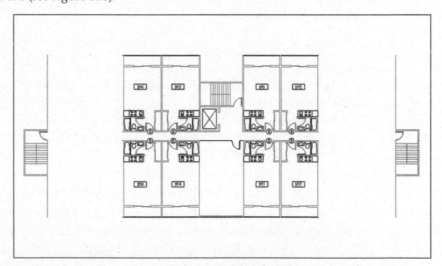

7. If the Notes layer is on, use the layer drop-down list to turn it off.

8. Click the Insert tool in the Block panel again, and replace the empty room across the hall from the lobby with the utility room (utility.dwg or utility-metric.dwg) from the Chapter 14 sample files (see Figure 14.9). You may want to make some adjustments to the utility room so that it aligns with the plan.

FIGURE 14.9
The utility room
inserted

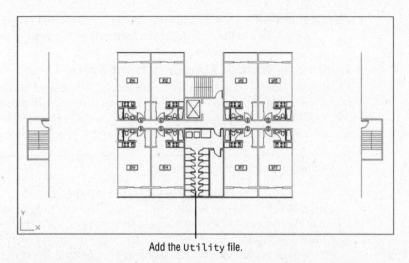

Add the Utility file.

9. Save the Common.dwg file.

10. Open the Xref-1.dwg file, right-click Common in the External References palette, and select Reload from the context menu. You can also right-click the Manage Xrefs icon in the lower-right corner of the AutoCAD window and select Reload DWG Xrefs. You see the utility room and the typical units in their new form. Your drawing should look like the top image in Figure 14.10.

FIGURE 14.10
The Xref-1.dwg and
Xref-2.dwg files with
the units updated

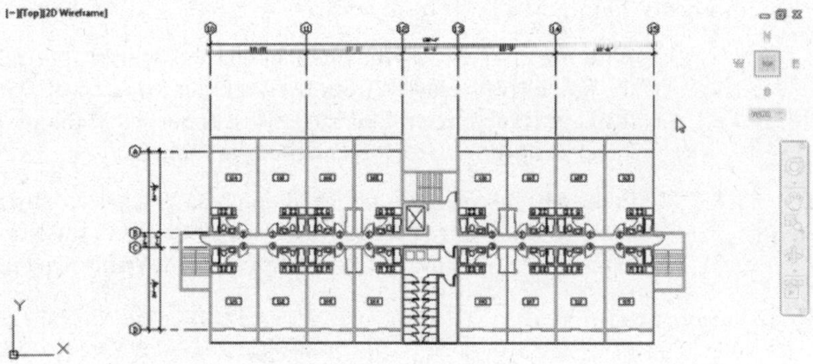

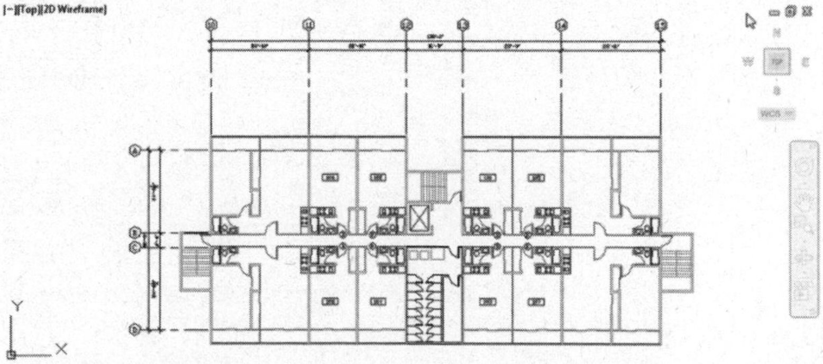

11. Open Xref-2.dwg. You see that the utility room and typical units are updated in this file as well. (See the bottom image in Figure 14.10.)

Importing Named Elements from Xrefs

Chapter 5, "Keeping Track of Layers and Blocks," discussed how layers, blocks, linetypes, and text styles—called *named elements*—are imported along with a file that is inserted into another file. Xref files don't import named elements. You can, however, review their names and use a special command to import the ones that you want to use in the current file.

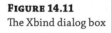

> ### SAVING XREF LAYER SETTINGS
>
> You can set the Visretain system variable to 1 to force AutoCAD to remember layer settings of Xref files. Another choice is to turn on the Retain Changes To Xref Layers option in the Open And Save tab of the Options dialog box. You can also use the Layer States Manager in the Layer Properties Manager dialog box to save layer settings for later recall. The Layer States Manager is described in detail in the section "Saving and Recalling Layer Settings" later in this chapter.

AutoCAD renames named elements from Xref files by giving them the prefix of the filename from which they come. For example, the Wall layer in the Floor1.dwg file is called Floor1|WALL in the Xref-1.dwg file; the Toilet block is called Floor1|TOILET. You can't draw on the layer Floor1|WALL, nor can you insert Floor1|TOILET, but you can view Xref layers in the Layer Properties Manager dialog box, and you can view Xref blocks by using the Insert dialog box.

Next, you'll look at how AutoCAD identifies layers and blocks in Xref files, and you'll get a chance to import a layer from an Xref:

1. With the Xref-1.dwg file open, open the Layer Properties Manager palette. Notice that the names of the layers from the Xref files are all prefixed with the filename and the vertical bar (|) character. Exit the Layer Properties Manager palette. You can also open the Layer drop-down list to view the layer names.

2. Enter **XB**↵ to open the Xbind dialog box. You see a listing of the current Xrefs. Each item shows a plus sign to the left. This list box follows the Microsoft Windows format for expandable lists, much like the tree view in Windows File Explorer (see Figure 14.11).

FIGURE 14.11
The Xbind dialog box

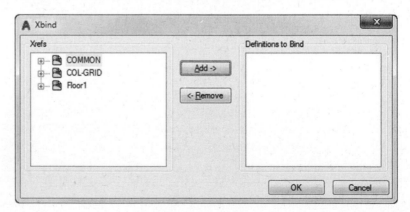

3. Click the plus sign next to the Floor1 Xref item. The list expands to show the types of elements available to bind (see Figure 14.12).

FIGURE 14.12
The expanded Floor1 list

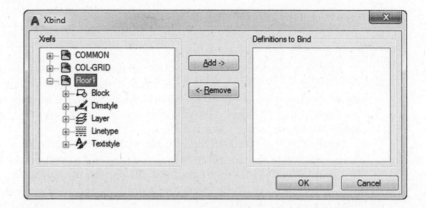

4. Click the plus sign next to the Layer item. The list expands further to show the layers available for binding (see Figure 14.13).

FIGURE 14.13
The expanded Layer list

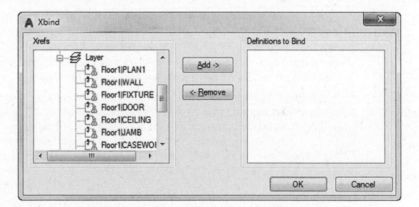

5. Locate Floor1|WALL in the list, click it, and then click the Add button. Floor1|WALL is added to the list to the right, Definitions To Bind.

6. Click OK to bind the Floor1|WALL layer.

7. Open the Layer Properties Manager palette.

8. Scroll down the list, and look for the Floor1|WALL layer. You won't find it. In its place is a layer called Floor1$0$WALL.

9. Close the current file without saving it so that you will have an unaltered file if you want to practice these exercises again. You may also use Save As to save it under a different name from the original file.

IMPORT DRAWING COMPONENTS WITH DESIGNCENTER

The AutoCAD DesignCenter™ lets you import settings and other drawing components from any drawing, not just Xref drawings. You'll learn more about the DesignCenter in Chapter 25.

As you can see, when you use Xbind to import a named item, such as the Floor1|WALL layer, the vertical bar (|) is replaced by two dollar signs surrounding a number, which is usually 0. (If for some reason the imported layer name Floor1$0$WALL already exists, the 0 in that name is changed to 1, as in Floor1$1$WALL.) Other named items are renamed in the same way, using the 0 replacement for the vertical bar.

You can also use the Xbind dialog box to bind multiple layers as well as other items from Xrefs attached to the current drawing. You can bind an entire Xref to a drawing, converting it to a simple block. By doing so, you have the opportunity to maintain unique layer names of the Xref being bound or to merge the Xref's similarly named layers with those of the current file. See Chapter 7 for details.

NESTING XREFS AND USING OVERLAYS

Xrefs can be nested. For example, if the Common.dwg file created in this chapter used the Unit.dwg file as an Xref rather than as an inserted block, you would still get the same result in the Xref-1.dwg file. That is, you would see the entire floor plan, including the unit plans, when you opened Xref-1.dwg. In this situation, Unit.dwg would be nested in the Common.dwg file, which is in turn externally referenced in the Xref-1.dwg file.

Although nested Xrefs can be helpful, take care in using Xrefs this way. For example, you might create an Xref by using the Common.dwg file in the Floor1.dwg file as a means of referencing walls and other features of the Common.dwg file. You might also reference the Common.dwg file into the Floor2.dwg file for the same reason. After you did so, however, you'd have three versions of the Common plan in the Xref-1.dwg file because each Xref would have Common.dwg attached to it. And because AutoCAD would dutifully load Common.dwg three times, Xref-1.dwg would occupy substantial computer memory, slowing your computer when you edited the Xref-1.dwg file.

To avoid this problem, use the Overlay option in the Attach External Reference dialog box. An overlaid Xref can't be nested. For example, if you use the Overlay option when inserting the Common.dwg file into the Floor1.dwg and Floor2.dwg files, the nested Common.dwg files are ignored when you open the Xref-1.dwg file, thereby eliminating the redundant occurrence of Common.dwg. In another example, if you use the Overlay option to import the Unit.dwg file into the Common.dwg file and then attach the Common.dwg into Xref-1.dwg as an Xref, you don't see the Unit.dwg file in Xref-1.dwg. The nested Unit.dwg drawing is ignored.

If you have used the Attach option to insert an Xref and want to change it to Overlay, you can do so in the External References palette. Click the External References icon in the Insert tab's Reference panel's title bar, and then in the External References palette, right-click the name of the Xref that you want to change and select Xref Type Overlay. Use the same steps to convert an Overlay Xref into an Attached Xref, but use Xref Type Attach after you right-click the Xref name.

Controlling the Xref Search Path

One problem AutoCAD users encountered in the past was lost or broken links to an Xref. This occurs when an Xref file is moved from its original location or when you receive a set of drawings that includes Xrefs. The Xref links are broken because AutoCAD doesn't know where to look.

When you insert an Xref, the Attach External Reference dialog box opens, offering you options for insertion point, scale, and rotation. This dialog box also provides the Path Type option, which enables you to select a method for locating Xrefs. You can choose from three path type options:

No Path Perhaps the most flexible option, No Path tells AutoCAD to use its own search criteria to find Xrefs. When this option is selected, AutoCAD first looks in the folder that contains the host drawing; then it looks in the project search path defined in the Files tab of the Options dialog box. (See Appendix B, "Installing and Setting Up AutoCAD," for more on the Options dialog box.) Finally, AutoCAD looks in the Support File Search Path option, also defined in the Files tab of the Options dialog box. If you plan to send your files to a client or a consultant, you may want to use this option.

Relative Path (default) Lets you specify a file location relative to the location of the current or host drawing. For example, if the host drawing is in a folder called C:\mycadfiles and the Xrefs are in a folder called C:\mycadfiles\xrefs, you can specify .\xrefs for the location of the Xref file. This option is useful when you know that you'll maintain the folder structure of the host and Xref files when moving or exchanging these files. Note that because this is a relative path, this option is valid only for files that reside on the same local hard disk. Unlike in previous versions of AutoCAD, the Relative Path option can be used with new unnamed files.

Full Path Lets you specify the exact filename and path for an Xref, including the disk drive or network location. Use this option when you want AutoCAD to look in a specific location for the Xref.

You can change the path type using two features in the External References palette. First, select the Xref or Xrefs that you want to change; then right-click and select Change Path Type in the context menu. You can also click the Change Path tool in the External References palette toolbar.

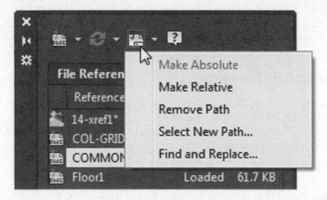

You will see five options. The first three are Make Absolute, Make Relative, and Remove Path. You'll notice that one option is grayed out. The grayed-out option is the current setting for the selected Xref. Select the option that you desire for the selected Xref.

You'll also notice two additional options in the Change Path tool: Select New Path and Find and Replace. The Select New Path option lets you select a new path for a missing Xref. If there are other missing xrefs from the same location, AutoCAD gives you the option to update all missing xrefs with the new path.

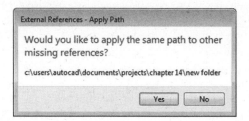

The Find and Replace option finds all of the selected Xrefs from a path you identify and replaces the path with a new one.

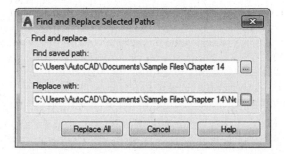

IF YOU PREFER THE OLD DEFAULT PATH FOR XREFS

In previous versions of AutoCAD, the default Xref path type was Full Path. If you prefer to stick with the previous default, you can use the Refpathtype system variable. Enter **Refpathtype↵** at the command prompt, then enter **0** for no path, **1** for relative path, or **2** for full path.

Managing Layers

In a survey of AutoCAD users, Autodesk discovered that one of the most frequently used features in AutoCAD is the Layer command. You'll find that you turn layers on and off to display and edit the many levels of information contained in your AutoCAD files. As your files become more complex, controlling layer visibility becomes more difficult. Fortunately, AutoCAD offers the Layer States Manager to make your work a little easier.

Saving and Recalling Layer Settings

The Layer States Manager lets you save layer settings. This can be crucial when you're editing a file that serves multiple uses, such as a floor plan and reflected ceiling plan. You can, for example, turn layers on and off to set up the drawing for a reflected ceiling plan view and then save the layer settings. Later, when you need to modify the ceiling information, you can recall the layer settings to view the ceiling data.

The following steps show you how the Layer States Manager works:

1. In AutoCAD, open the 14b-unit.dwg file. Click the Layer Properties tool in the Home tab's Layers panel to open the Layer Properties Manager, and turn on all the layers except Notes and Flr-pat. Your drawing should look similar to the top image in Figure 14.14.

FIGURE 14.14
The view of the 14b-unit.dwg file before and after changing layer settings

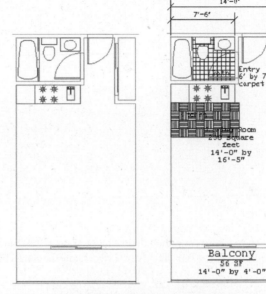

2. Click the Unsaved Layer State drop-down list in the Home tab's expanded Layers panel.

3. Click Manage Layer States to open the resizable Layer States Manager dialog box. Take a moment to look at the options in this dialog box. This is where you can specify which layer settings you want to be saved with this layer state (see Figure 14.15). If your list of Layer States is larger than can be displayed, you can enlarge the dialog box to view more of the list.

FIGURE 14.15
The Layer States
Manager dialog box

4. You're ready to save the current layer state. Click the New button in the Layer States Manager dialog box. The New Layer State To Save dialog box opens (see Figure 14.16).

FIGURE 14.16
The New Layer State To
Save dialog box

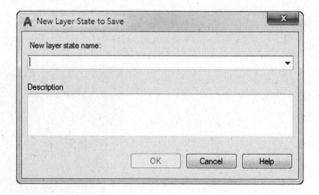

5. Enter **blank floor plan** in the New Layer State Name box. Note that you can also enter a brief description of your layer state. Click OK to return to the Layer States Manager dialog box.

6. Click the More Restore Options button (see Figure 14.17) in the lower-right corner of the Layer States Manager dialog box to expand the list of options.

FIGURE 14.17
The More Restore
Options button

7. Make sure the On/Off check box is selected, and then click Close. Several other options are available, but you can leave them as they are.

8. Back in the Layer Properties Manager dialog box, turn on the Flr-pat and Notes layers and turn off the Ceiling layer.

Your drawing looks like the bottom image in Figure 14.14.

You've just saved a layer state and then changed the layer settings to something different from the saved state. The following steps demonstrate how you can restore the saved layer state:

1. In the Home tab's expanded Layers panel, click the Unsaved Layer State drop-down list and hover over Blank Floor Plan. Notice that you see a preview of the layer state as you hover over the name. Go ahead and select Blank Floor Plan. Your drawing reverts to the previous view with the Notes and Flr-pat layers turned off and the Ceiling layer turned on.

2. This brings you to the end of the Layer States Manager exercise. Save the file and close it.

The layer states are saved with the file so that you can retrieve them at a later date. As you can see in the Layer States Manager dialog box, you have a few other options, as shown in Table 14.1.

TABLE 14.1:   Layer States Manager dialog box options

OPTION	PURPOSE
New	Creates a new layer state.
Update	Updates the selected layer state after edits.
Edit	Lets you edit the layer settings for the selected layer state.
Rename	Renames a selected layer state.
Delete	Deletes a layer state from the list.
Import	Imports a set of layer states that have been exported using the Export option of this dialog box.
Export	Saves a set of layer states as a file. By default, the file is given the name of the current layer state with the .las filename extension. You can import the layer-state file into other files.
Layer Properties To Restore (in the expanded dialog box)	Lets you select the layer properties to be controlled by the Layer States Manager.

In addition to saving layer states by name, you can quickly revert to a previous layer setting by clicking the Previous tool on the Home tab's expanded Layers panel. This tool enables you to revert to the previous layer settings without affecting other settings in AutoCAD. Note that Previous mode doesn't restore renamed or deleted layers, nor does it remove new layers.

After you become familiar with these layer-state tools, you'll find yourself using them frequently in your editing sessions.

Other Tools for Managing Layers

A number of tools are available that help you quickly set up layers as you work. In the following sections, you'll learn about some of the other tools that you've seen in the Layers panel. All the tools discussed in these sections have keyboard command equivalents. Check the tool tip for the keyboard command name when you select one of these tools from the Layers panel.

USING LAYER WALK TO EXPLORE LAYERS

When you work with a file that was produced by someone else, you usually have to spend some time becoming familiar with the way layers are set up in it. This process can be tedious, but the Layer Walk tool can help.

As the name implies, the Layer Walk tool lets you "walk through" the layers of a file, visually isolating each layer as you select its name from a list. You can use Layer Walk to select the layers that you want to be visible, or you can turn layers on and off to explore a drawing without affecting the current layer settings. To open the LayerWalk dialog box, do the following:

1. Click the Layer Walk tool on the expanded Layers panel, or enter **Laywalk**↵.

2. The LayerWalk dialog box appears (see Figure 14.18). You can click and drag the bottom edge of the dialog box to expand the list so that you can see all of the layers in the drawing.

FIGURE 14.18
The LayerWalk dialog box

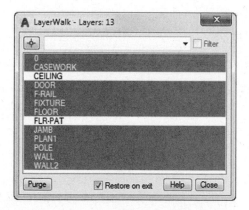

When you first open the LayerWalk dialog box, you see the current visible layers selected. Layers that are off aren't selected. Click a single layer, and AutoCAD displays just that layer. With a single layer selected, you can "walk" through the layers by pressing the down and up arrow keys.

You can use this dialog box to set up layer settings visually by Ctrl+clicking layer names to make them visible. Turn off Restore On Exit to maintain the layer settings that you set up in the LayerWalk dialog box, or turn it on if you want the drawing to revert to the layer settings that were in place before you opened the LayerWalk dialog box. Right-click the list of layers to display a set of other options that let you save the layer state and invert the selection.

CHANGING THE LAYER ASSIGNMENT OF OBJECTS

In addition to the Layer Walk tool, the Layers panel includes two tools that change the layer assignments of objects: the Match Layer tool and the Change To Current Layer tool on the expanded Layers panel.

The Match Layer tool is similar to the Match Properties tool, but it's streamlined to operate only on layer assignments. After clicking this tool in the Layers panel, select the object or objects that you want to change, press ↵, and then select an object whose layer you want to match.

The Change To Current Layer tool on the expanded Layers panel changes an object's layer assignment to the current layer.

CONTROLLING THE DISPLAY OF XREF OBJECTS

In AutoCAD 2018, you can control the display of Xref objects that are not set to ByLayer. A new system variable called Xrefoverride can be set to a value of 1 to cause non-ByLayer Xref objects to behave as if they are set to ByLayer. See the sidebar "Assigning Colors, Linetypes, and Linetype Scales to Individual Objects" in Chapter 5 for more on the ByLayer setting.

CONTROLLING LAYER SETTINGS THROUGH OBJECTS

The remaining Layer tools let you make layer settings by selecting objects in the drawing. These tools are easy to use: click a tool, and then select an object.

The following list describes each tool:

Layer Isolate/Layer Unisolate   Layer Isolate turns off all the layers except for the layer of the selected object. Layer Unisolate restores the layer settings to the way the drawing was set before you used Layer Isolate.

Freeze   Freezes the layer of the selected object.

Off   Turns off the layer of the selected object.

Lock/Unlock   Locks the layer of the selected object. A locked layer is visible but can't be edited.

Layer Walk   Lets you dynamically change layer visibility.

Copy Objects To New Layer   Copies an object or a set of objects to a different layer.

Make Object's Layer Current   Enables you to set the current layer by selecting an object that is on the desired layer.

Turn All Layers On   Turns all layers on.

Thaw All Layers   Thaws all layers.

VP Freeze In All Viewports Except Current   Enables you to freeze layers in all but the current viewport by selecting objects that are on the layers to be frozen.

Merge   Combines several layers into one layer. First select objects whose layers you want to merge, press ↵, and then select an object whose layer you want to merge with.

Delete   Deletes all objects on a layer and then deletes the layer.

MERGING MULTIPLE LAYERS INTO ONE LAYER

If you find that you have several layers that you want to merge into one layer, you can use the Merge option in the Layer Manager. You can merge a single layer or a set of layers into an existing layer, other than one that has been selected. If the layer you want to use for the merge does not exist, create it first. Then, in the Layer Manager, select the layer or layers that you want to merge, right-click, and select the Merge Selected Layer(s) To option. The Merge To Layer dialog box appears (see Figure 14.19). You can select the layer name from the list. The merged layers are automatically purged from the drawing.

FIGURE 14.19
The Merge To Layer
dialog box

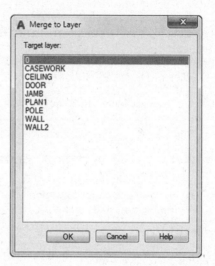

Using Advanced Tools: Filter and Quick Select

Two other tools are extremely useful in your day-to-day work with AutoCAD: selection filters and Quick Select. We've saved the discussion of these tools until this part of the chapter because you don't need them until you've become accustomed to the way AutoCAD works. Chances are that you've already experimented with some of the AutoCAD menu options not yet discussed in the exercise. Many of the drop-down menu options and their functions are self-explanatory. Selection filters and QuickCalc (the latter is discussed later in this chapter) don't appear in any of the menus and require further explanation.

Let's start with selection filters. AutoCAD includes two selection-filtering tools: The *Quick Select tool* offers a quick way to locate objects based on their properties. The *Filter tool* lets you select objects based on a more complex set of criteria.

Filtering Selections

Suppose that you need to isolate just the walls of your drawing in a separate file. One way to do this is to turn off all the layers except the Wall layer. You can then use the Wblock command and select the remaining walls, using a window to write the wall information to a file. Filters can simplify this operation by enabling you to select groups of objects based on their properties.

Follow these steps to select objects based on their layer assignment:

1. Open the `Unit.dwg` file.

2. Type **W**↵ to start the Wblock command. Then, in the Write Block dialog box, click the Browse button to the right of the File Name And Path text box.

3. Browse to a location for the file, and name the file **Unitwall**. Click the Save button.

4. Back at the Write Block dialog box, make sure that the Objects and Retain radio buttons are selected, and then click the Select Objects button in the Objects group. The dialog box closes so that you can select objects.

5. At the `Select Objects:` prompt, type **'Filter**↵ to open the Object Selection Filters dialog box (see Figure 14.20).

FIGURE 14.20
The Object Selection
Filters dialog box

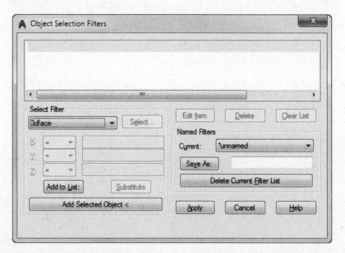

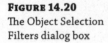

GETTING NOTIFICATION OF NEW LAYERS

AutoCAD can notify you when new layers are added to Xrefs in a drawing or to the current drawing itself. Such new layers are called *unreconciled* layers. This feature can be helpful when you are working with others and need to stay informed about the condition of a drawing. By default, the notification comes in two forms. When new layers are added, a warning icon appears in the right side of the status bar. If you attempt to plot a drawing that contains new layers, the following message appears: "Unreconciled new layers exist in the drawing." The warning will not prevent you from doing anything. It is just intended as a way to notify you of changes. In addition, the unreconciled layers are grouped into a layer property filter called Unreconciled New Layers, which can be viewed in the Layer Properties Manager.

continues

continued

To "reconcile" unreconciled layers, open the Layer Properties Manager, select the unreconciled layers, and right-click and select Reconcile Layers from the context menu.

New layer notification is turned on by default, and it is controlled by the Layerevalctl system variable. Type **Layerevalctl⏎1⏎** to turn it on and **Layerevalctl⏎0⏎** to turn it off.

You can also set how you are notified of new layers through the Layereval and Layernotify system variables. Layereval controls when the Unreconciled New Layer filter displays new layers and can be set to 0, 1, or 2. The setting 0 turns Layereval off, 1 sets it to detect new layers in Xrefs, and 2 sets it to detect new layers in Xrefs and the current drawing. Layernotify determines how you are notified of new layers. The setting 0 means no notification; 1 means notify when you start a plot; 2 when the drawing is open; 4 when Xrefs are loaded, reloaded, or attached; 8 when you are restoring a layer state; 16 when you are saving a file; and 32 when you are inserting a drawing.

6. Open the drop-down list in the Select Filter group.

7. Scroll down the list, and find and highlight the Layer option.

8. Click the Select button next to the drop-down list to display a list of layers. Highlight Wall, and click OK.

9. Click the Add To List button toward the bottom of the Select Filter group to add Layer = Wall to the list box.

10. Click Apply to close the Object Selection Filters dialog box.

11. Type **ALL⏎** to select everything in the drawing. Only the objects assigned to the Wall layer are selected. You see a message in the Command window indicating how many objects were found.

12. Press ⏎. You see the message "Exiting Filtered selection Resuming WBLOCK command – Select objects: 20 found."

13. Press ⏎ again to complete the selection, and then click OK to complete the Wblock command. All of the walls are written to a file called Unitwall.

In this exercise, you filtered out a layer by using the Filter command. After you designate a filter, you then select the group of objects through which you want AutoCAD to filter. AutoCAD finds the objects that match the filter requirements and passes those objects to the current command.

As you've seen from the previous exercise, you can choose from many options in this utility. Let's take a closer look.

WORKING WITH THE OBJECT SELECTION FILTERS DIALOG BOX

To use the Object Selection Filters dialog box, first select the criterion for filtering from the drop-down list. If the criterion that you select is a named item (layer, linetype, color, or block), you can then click the Select button to choose specific items from a list. If there is only one choice, the Select button is dimmed.

After you've determined what to filter, you must add it to the list by clicking the Add To List button. The filter criterion then appears in the list box at the top of the Object Selection Filters dialog box, and you can apply that criterion to your current command or to a later command.

AutoCAD remembers your filter settings, so if you need to reselect a filtered selection set, you don't have to redefine your filter criteria.

SAVING FILTER CRITERIA

If you prefer, you can preselect filter criteria. Then, at any Select objects: prompt, you can type **'Filter.⏎**, highlight the appropriate filter criteria in the list box, and click Apply. The specifications in the Object Selection Filters dialog box remain in place for the duration of the current editing session.

You can also save a set of criteria by entering a name in the text box next to the Save As button and then clicking the button. The criteria list data is saved in a file called Filter.nfl in the C:\Users\User Name\AppData\Roaming\Autodesk\AutoCAD 2018\22.0\enu\Support folder. You can access the criteria list at any time by opening the Current drop-down list and choosing its name.

FILTERING OBJECTS BY LOCATION

Notice the X, Y, and Z drop-down lists just below the main Select Filter drop-down list in the Object Selection Filters dialog box. These lists become accessible when you select a criterion that describes a geometric property or a coordinate (such as an arc's radius or center point). You can use these lists to define filter selections even more specifically using greater than (>), less than (<), equal to or greater than (>=), equal to or less than (<=), equal to (=), or not equal to (!=) (called *relational operators*).

For example, suppose that you want to grab all the circles whose radii are greater than 4.0 units. To do this, choose Circle Radius from the Select Filter drop-down list. Then, in the X list, select >. Enter **4.0** in the text box to the right of the X list, and click Add To List. The items

```
Circle Radius > 4.0000
Object = Circle
```

are added to the list box at the top of the dialog box. You used the > operator to indicate a circle radius greater than 4.0 units.

CREATING COMPLEX SELECTION SETS

At times, you'll want to create a specific filter list. For instance, say that you need to filter out all the Door blocks on the layer Floor2 *and* all arcs with a radius equal to 1. To do this, you use the *grouping operators* found at the bottom of the Select Filter drop-down list. You'll need to build a list as follows:

```
** Begin OR
** Begin AND
Block Name = Door
Object = Block
Layer = Floor2
** End AND
** Begin AND
Object = Arc
Arc Radius = 1.0000
** End AND
** End OR
```

Notice that the Begin and End operators are balanced—that is, for every Begin OR or Begin AND, there is an End OR or End AND.

This list may look simple, but it can get confusing. If criteria are bounded by the AND grouping operators, objects must fulfill *both* criteria before they're selected. If criteria are bounded by the OR grouping operators, objects fulfilling *either* criterion will be selected. If you add the wrong option accidentally, select it from the list and click the Delete button. If you need to insert an option in the middle of the list, select the item that comes after the item you want to insert, and then select and add the item.

Here are the steps to build the previous list:

1. In the Select Filter drop-down list, choose **Begin OR, and then click Add To List. Do the same for **Begin AND.

2. Click Block Name in the Select Filter drop-down list, click the Select button, and select Door from the list that appears. Click Add To List.

3. For the layer, click Layer in the Select Filter drop-down list. Click Select, choose the layer name, and click Add To List.

4. In the Select Filter drop-down list, choose **End AND, and then click Add To List. Do the same for **Begin AND.

5. Select Arc from the Select Filter drop-down list, and click Add To List.

6. Select Arc Radius from the Select Filter list, and enter **1.0** in the text box next to the X drop-down list. Be sure that the equal sign (=) shows in the X drop-down list, and then click Add To List.

7. Choose **End AND, and click Add To List. Do the same for **End OR.

If you make an error in any step, highlight the item, select an item to replace it, and click the Substitute button instead of the Add To List button. If you need only to change a value, click the Edit Item button near the center of the dialog box.

QUICK ACCESS TO YOUR FAVORITE COMMANDS

As IT managers, we've discovered that AutoCAD users are possessive of their keyboard and tool shortcuts, and they are usually the first custom item that a new employee will install. You can collect your favorite commands into a single toolbar or Ribbon panel by using the AutoCAD customization feature. This way, you can have ready access to your most frequently used commands. Chapter 24, "Customizing Toolbars, Menus, Linetypes, and Hatch Patterns," gives you all the information you need to create your own custom toolbars and Ribbon panels.

Using Quick Select

The Filter command offers a lot of power in isolating specific types of objects, but in many situations you may not need such an elaborate tool. The Quick Select dialog box can filter your selection based on the object properties, which are the more common filter criteria. To access the Quick Select dialog box, click Quick Select in the Home tab's Utilities panel, or right-click the drawing area when no command is active and choose Quick Select from the context menu.

Quick Select is offered as an option in a few other dialog boxes as well. Try using the Wblock command again, this time using the Quick Select option offered in its dialog box:

1. With the Unit.dwg file open, type **W**↵ to start the Wblock command. Then, in the Write Block dialog box, enter **Unitwall2** in the File Name And Path text box.

2. Make sure that the Objects radio button is selected at the top of the dialog box and the Delete From Drawing option is selected from the Objects group.

3. Click the Quick Select tool to the right of the Select Objects button in the Objects group to open the Quick Select dialog box (see Figure 14.21).

FIGURE 14.21
The Quick Select dialog box

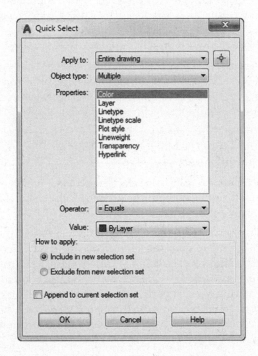

4. Select Layer from the Properties list.

5. Select Wall from the Value drop-down list near the bottom of the dialog box.

6. Click the Select Objects button in the upper-right corner of the dialog box. The dialog boxes close so that you can select objects.

7. Select the entire drawing by using a window; press ↵ to finish your selection. Both dialog boxes return.

8. Click OK, and then click OK in the Write Block dialog box. The walls disappear, indicating that they have been written to a file.

9. Click the Undo button to undo the deletion.

The Qselect command selects objects based on their properties, as shown in the Properties list box. You can apply the selection criteria based on the entire drawing, or you can use the Select Objects button in the upper-right corner of the dialog box to isolate a set of objects to which you want to apply the selection criteria.

In the previous exercise, you used Quick Select from within another dialog box. As mentioned earlier, you can also use Quick Select by clicking Quick Select in the Home tab's Utilities panel or by right-clicking the drawing area when no command is active and choosing Quick Select from the context menu. Quick Select then uses the Noun/Verb selection method: You select objects using Quick Select first, and then you apply editing commands to the selected objects.

If you want to use Quick Select with a command that doesn't allow the Noun/Verb selection method, you can select objects by using Quick Select, start the command that you want to use, and then use the Previous Selection option.

Here is a description of the Quick Select dialog box options:

Apply To   Lets you determine the set of objects to which you want to apply the Quick Select filters. The default is the entire drawing, but you can use the Select Objects button to select a set of objects. If you select a set of objects before issuing the Quick Select command, you also see the Current Selection option in the Apply To drop-down list.

Object Type   Lets you limit the filter to specific types of objects such as lines, arcs, circles, and so on. The Multiple option lets you filter your selection from all of the objects in the drawing regardless of type.

Properties   Lets you select the property of the object type that you want to filter, after you select an object type. The Properties list changes to reflect the properties that are available to be filtered.

Operator   Offers a set of criteria to apply to the property that you select in the Properties list to make your selection. You can select objects that are equal to or not equal to the criteria that you select in the Object Type and Properties lists. Depending on the property that you select, you also may have the option to select objects that are greater than or less than a given property value. For example, you can select all lines whose x-coordinate is less than 5 by choosing Line from the Object Type drop-down list and Start X from the Properties list. You then select < Less Than from the Operator drop-down list and enter **5** in the Value box.

Value   Displays the values of the property that you select in the Properties list. For example, if you select Layer from the Properties list, the Value option lists all of the available layers.

How To Apply   Lets you specify whether to include or exclude the filtered objects in a new selection set.

Append To Current Selection Set   Lets you append the filtered objects to an existing selection set or create an entirely new selection set.

SELECT SIMILAR OBJECTS OR ISOLATE OBJECT FOR EASIER EDITING

Certification
Objective

A few features in the context menu can help speed up object selection. If you select an object and right-click, you'll see the Select Similar option.

Just as the name implies, it will select all objects in the drawing that are similar to the one currently selected. For example, if you select a hatch pattern, right-click, and then click Select Similar, all of the hatch patterns in the drawing will be selected. Click a line, right-click, and then click Select Similar, and all of the lines that are on the selected line's layer will be selected. You can also use the Selectsimilar command to do the same thing.

You can control how the Select Similar feature behaves by entering **Selectsimilar˽SE˽**. This opens the Select Similar Settings dialog box, which lets you set the basis for the similar selection such as layer, color, or linetype, to name a few.

Another handy right-click option is Isolate. If you have a set of objects and you right-click and select Isolate ➤ Isolate Objects, all but the selected objects will be made invisible. Or you can right-click and select Isolate ➤ Hide Objects to hide the selected objects. To bring back the objects that were made invisible, right-click and select Isolate ➤ End Object Isolation.

Using the QuickCalc Calculator

You may have noticed a calculator icon in some of the options in the Properties palette or in the context menu. This is the QuickCalc tool. If you click it, you'll see the QuickCalc calculator, shown in Figure 14.22. At first glance, it looks like a typical calculator. It has the standard math functions as well as the scientific functions that are available when you click the More button. If your view of QuickCalc doesn't look like Figure 14.22, click the More/Less button and then expand the Number Pad or Scientific section by clicking the arrow in the title bar. You'll also see a section for converting units, which comes in handy when you want to find the metric equivalent of an Imperial measurement.

FIGURE 14.22
QuickCalc and its parts

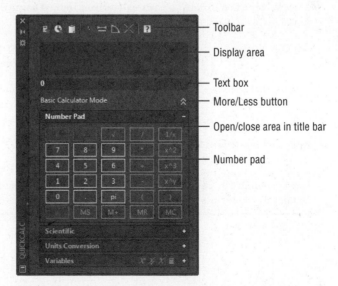

At the bottom is a section for variables. This area lets you store custom formulas and values to which you want to refer frequently.

Near the top is the display area. This is where QuickCalc keeps a running record of your calculation results. It also allows you to recall both the results and formulas that you've used. Just below the display area is the text box. As you type, or as you click the keys of QuickCalc, your input appears in this box. Pressing Enter displays the resulting value both in the text box and in the display area.

Above the display area is a set of tools. These tools let you obtain other types of data from the drawing, such as the coordinate of a point or the intersection of two lines (see Figure 14.23).

FIGURE 14.23
The QuickCalc tools

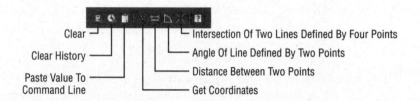

Clear
Clear History
Paste Value To Command Line
Intersection Of Two Lines Defined By Four Points
Angle Of Line Defined By Two Points
Distance Between Two Points
Get Coordinates

The function of these tools will become clearer as you become familiar with QuickCalc. Table 14.2 describes each tool. Next, you'll get a chance to try out QuickCalc on some typical AutoCAD tasks.

TABLE 14.2:   QuickCalc tools

TOOL	PURPOSE
Clear	Clears the value from the text box.
Clear History	Clears the display area.
Paste Value To Command Line	Pastes data from the text box to the command line.
Get Coordinates	Temporarily closes QuickCalc and prompts you to pick a point or points. Coordinates of the point or the angle value are placed in the input area.
Distance Between Two Points	Temporarily closes QuickCalc and prompts you to enter a point. Select two points; the distance between the points is placed in the input area of QuickCalc.
Angle Of Line Defined By Two Points	Returns the angle of two points.
Intersection Of Two Lines Defined By Four Points	Returns the coordinate of the intersection of four points.

Adding Foot and Inch Lengths and Finding the Sum of Angles

Although QuickCalc may look simple, it provides a powerful aid in your work in AutoCAD. Besides offering the typical calculator functions, QuickCalc lets you quickly add and subtract angle values, feet-and-inches lengths, and much more. You can paste the results from calculations into the command line so that you can easily include results as part of command-line responses.

To get a full appreciation of what QuickCalc can do for you, try the following exercises.

Imagine that you have a renovation project for which someone has taken dimensions in the field. You may be asked to draw a section of wall for which the overall dimension isn't given but portions of the wall are dimensioned in a sketch, as shown in Figure 14.24.

FIGURE 14.24
A sketch of measurements taken from an existing building

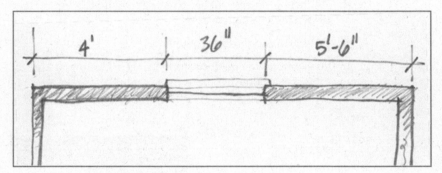

You can use QuickCalc to add a series of feet-and-inches dimensions:

1. Open the QuickCalc.dwg sample file, which contains some lines with which you can work. It's set up to use architectural units.

2. Right-click, and select the QuickCalc tool from the context menu.

3. Double-click in the QuickCalc text box, and then enter **4'+36+5'6**. As you type, your entry appears in the text box (see Figure 14.25).

FIGURE 14.25
The QuickCalc text box

4. Press ↵. The sum of the lengths, 12'-6", appears in the text box and in the display area.

Notice that you only had to enter the foot (') sign. QuickCalc assumes that a value is in inches unless you specify otherwise. You can also enter distances in the more traditional way using dashes and zeros, as in 4'-0" or 5'-6". QuickCalc ignores the dashes.

Now, suppose that you want to use your newfound length to draw a line. You can quickly add the results from the text box to the command line, as shown in the following exercise:

1. Click the Line tool, and then click a point in the left portion of the drawing area.

2. In the QuickCalc toolbar, click the Paste Value To Command Line tool. Notice that the value in the text box appears in the command line.

3. Make sure the Polar Tracking mode is turned on in the status bar.

4. While pointing the rubber-banding line directly to the right, press ↵. A horizontal line is drawn to the length of 12'-6".

5. Press ↵ to end the Line command.

In this example, you used the Paste Value To Command Line tool in the QuickCalc toolbar. If you want to use a value that has scrolled up in the display area, you can select that value, right-click, and choose Paste To Command Line (see Figure 14.26).

FIGURE 14.26
The Paste To Command Line option in the context menu

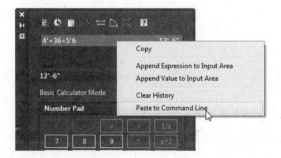

This approach is especially useful when you've used QuickCalc to add several strings of dimensions and you need to recall them individually from the display area. In addition to adding feet and inches, you can perform other math functions, such as dividing a length by 2 or multiplying a length. If the input value is in feet and inches, the resulting value is returned in feet and inches. For example, if you divide 25' by 6, the result is 4'-2".

Another useful QuickCalc tool is Angle Of Line Defined By Two Points, which allows you to obtain the angle defined by two points:

1. In QuickCalc, click the Angle Of Line Defined By Two Points tool. QuickCalc temporarily closes to allow you to select points.

2. With osnaps turned on, select the endpoints of the lower line, starting with the bottom endpoint, as shown in Figure 14.27.

FIGURE 14.27
Select these endpoints using the Angle Of Line Defined By Two Points option.

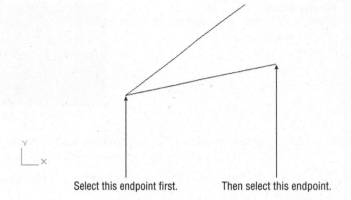

Select this endpoint first.   Then select this endpoint.

3. Back in QuickCalc, click the plus button in the number pad or enter **+**. Then click the Angle Of Line Defined By Two Points tool again.

4. Select the endpoints of the upper line, starting with the bottom end of the line.

5. Back in QuickCalc, you see the angle value of the second line added to the text box. Click the equal button in the QuickCalc number pad to get the total angle value.

Here you added the angle of two lines, but you could just as easily have subtracted one angle from another or multiplied the value of a single angle. This can be useful if you need to find a fraction or a multiple of an angle. For example, you might need to find one-quarter of the angle described by a line, or you might want to find the angle that bisects two lines. You can do so by adding the value of two angles, as described in the exercise, and then dividing by 2 using the number pad or by including /2 in the text box. Once you've obtained a value, you can paste it into the command line while specifying angles for drawing input.

Converting Units with QuickCalc

In addition to performing math functions on distances and angles, you can do some basic unit conversions. QuickCalc performs length, area, volume, and angle conversions in its Units Conversion group. Try the following exercise to learn how to convert a length from centimeters to feet and inches. In the process, you'll also learn how you can move a value from the Units Conversion area to the QuickCalc text box.

Suppose that you have a paper drawing that was done in metric and you need to turn it into an AutoCAD drawing in feet and inches. Here's an example of how you can convert centimeters to feet and inches:

1. In QuickCalc, expand the Units Conversion section by clicking the plus sign to the right of the Units Conversion title bar (see Figure 14.28).

FIGURE 14.28
The expanded Units
Conversion section

2. Make sure that Length appears for the Units Type option. If not, click in the box to the right of the Units Type option and select Length from the drop-down list that appears.

3. Select Centimeters from the Convert From drop-down list.

4. Select Feet from the Convert To drop-down list.

5. In the Value To Convert box, enter **450**↵ for 450 cm. The equivalent value in feet appears in the Converted Value box.

6. Click the Converted Value option, and you also see the QuickCalc icon to the far right. Click this icon to display the value in the text box at the top of QuickCalc.

The value is in feet and decimal feet. You can convert the value to feet and inches by doing the following:

1. Edit the value in the text box to read as follows: 14' +(**.7637795*12**).

2. Press ↵. The value converts to a feet-and-inches value of 14'-9-3/16".

One limitation to the unit-conversion feature is that it won't take feet-and-inches input when converting from feet. For example, if you want to convert 12'-4" to centimeters, you have to enter 12.333. In other words, you have to convert the inches to decimal feet. Because the Unit Conversion area is part of QuickCalc, this just means an extra step. You can quickly calculate the decimal feet equivalent of feet and inch values and then transfer them to the Units Conversion area.

Try the following to see how this works:

1. Click the Clear button in the QuickCalc toolbar (it looks like a calculator with a small red X next to it), and then double-click in the QuickCalc text box.

2. Enter **12 + (4 / 12)**↵ in QuickCalc's text box. The first 12 is the 12 feet. The 4 / 12 is for the 4 inches converted to decimal feet. Once you press ↵, the value of 12.3333333 appears.

3. Right-click in the QuickCalc text box, ignore the context menu, and then click in the Value To Convert box in the Units Conversion panel. The 12.3333333 value is pasted into the text box.

4. Select Feet from the Convert From drop-down list, and select Centimeters from the Convert To drop-down list. The centimeter equivalent of 12.3333333 feet appears in the Converted Value box.

Here you saw how values from the text box automatically transfer to the Units Conversion area. You can also cut and paste values from other sources into either the main calculator text box or the Units Conversion box.

Using QuickCalc to Find Points

You've seen how QuickCalc will let you add values of distances and angles and how it can perform unit conversions. You can also use it to calculate coordinate locations. To work with coordinates, you need to use a few special functions built into QuickCalc that let you select points and manipulate their value.

AutoCAD offers the Midpoint Between Two Points osnap, which enables you to select a point midway between two other points without drawing a temporary line. The AutoCAD Cal keyboard shortcut offers another way to accomplish this. In the following steps, you'll use QuickCalc to perform the same function as an example of how you can acquire point data and manipulate it to derive other coordinate locations:

1. Click the Clear button on the QuickCalc toolbar; then double-click in the QuickCalc text box.

2. In the QuickCalc text box, enter **(end + end)/2**↵. QuickCalc closes temporarily to allow you to select points.

3. Select the endpoints of the two lines, as shown in Figure 14.29.

FIGURE 14.29
The endpoints of the
two lines

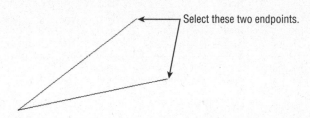

Select these two endpoints.

QuickCalc returns and displays the coordinates of a point exactly between the two endpoints that you selected in step 3.

In step 2, you used the *end* function that is built into QuickCalc. As you saw, the end function lets you select the endpoint of an object (as you did in step 3). The end + end in the formula tells QuickCalc to add the two coordinates that you selected in step 3. The /2 in the formula divides the sum of the coordinates to find their average, which happens to be the midpoint between the two points.

If you were to perform this calculation using pencil and paper, you would add the x-, y-, and z-coordinate values of each point separately and then divide each coordinate by 2. Finally, you would combine the resulting x-, y-, and z-coordinates back into a single point location.

Using Osnap Modes in QuickCalc Expressions

In the previous exercise, you used osnap modes as part of arithmetic formulas (or *expressions*, as they're called in AutoCAD). QuickCalc treats osnap modes as temporary placeholders for point coordinates until you pick the points.

The expression

```
(end ǀ end)/2
```

finds the average of two values. In this case, the values are coordinates, so the average is the midpoint between the two coordinates. You can take this one step further and find the centroid of a triangle by using this expression:

```
(end + end + end)/3
```

Note that you enter only the first three letters of the osnap mode in calculator expressions. Table 14.3 shows what to enter in an expression for osnap modes.

TABLE 14.3: The geometry calculator's osnap modes

CALCULATOR OSNAP	MEANING
End	Endpoint
Ins	Insert
Int	Intersection
Mid	Midpoint
Cen	Center
Nea	Nearest
Nod	Node
Qua	Quadrant
Per	Perpendicular
Tan	Tangent
Rad	Radius of object
Cur	Cursor pick

The table includes two items that aren't really osnap modes, although they work similarly when they're used in an expression. The first is Rad. When you include Rad in an expression, you get the following prompt:

```
Select circle, arc or polyline segment for RAD function:
```

You can then select an arc, a polyline arc segment, or a circle to obtain a radius for the expression.

The other item, Cur, prompts you for a point. Instead of looking for specific geometry on an object, it just locates a point. You could have used Cur in the previous exercise in place of the End modes to create a more general-purpose midpoint locator, as in the following formula:

```
(cur + cur)/2
```

PASTING TO THE COMMAND LINE

Now that you have the coordinate for the midpoint, try the next exercise to apply that coordinate to a command. In this example, you'll use the coordinate found in step 3 as the starting point for a line:

1. Click the Line tool on the Draw panel.

2. In QuickCalc, right-click the (end + end)/2 listing in the display area, and then select Paste To Command Line (see Figure 14.30).

FIGURE 14.30
Select Paste To Command Line.

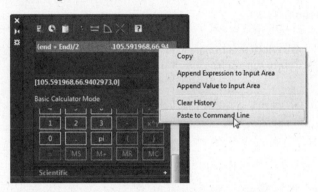

3. The coordinate value from the display area is pasted into the command line at the Line command's Specify first point: prompt. Press ↵ to accept the input from QuickCalc. You see a rubber-banding line beginning at a point midway between the two endpoints of the lines that you selected in the previous exercise (see Figure 14.31).

FIGURE 14.31
Starting a line between two endpoints

The line starts midway between the two endpoints.

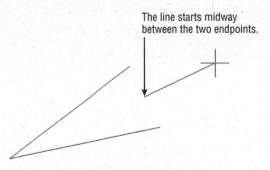

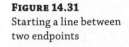

4. Click another point to place the line in the drawing, and then press ↵ to exit the Line command.

Finding Fractional Distances between Two Points

Another ability AutoCAD users commonly need is to find a location that is a fractional distance along a line. For example, users frequently need to find a point that is one-third the distance from the endpoint of a line. Here's how that can be accomplished using QuickCalc:

1. If the QuickCalc text box is not clear, click the Clear tool in the QuickCalc toolbar.

2. Enter **plt (end, end, 0.333)**↵ in the QuickCalc text box. QuickCalc closes temporarily to allow you to select points.

3. Click the endpoints of the line shown in Figure 14.32, starting with the lower-left endpoint. QuickCalc returns with the coordinates of a point that is 33.33 percent of the length of the line from the first endpoint that you selected.

FIGURE 14.32

Select these points to find a point that is one-third the distance from an endpoint.

Click the endpoints of this line.

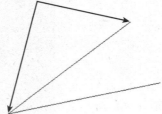

4. Click the Line tool.

5. Click in the QuickCalc display area on the last entry, right-click, and choose Paste To Command Line.

6. Press ↵ and you see a line start at a point that is one-third the distance from the endpoint (see Figure 14.33).

FIGURE 14.33

A line starting at a point that is one-third the distance from the endpoint

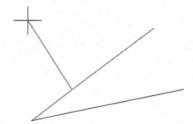

7. Press Esc to exit the Line command. You don't need to draw the line because this exercise is intended to show you only how the formula in step 2 works.

In step 2, you used a formula that contained the plt function. This function finds a point that is a particular percentage between two points. You specify the two points first, using the now familiar end function, and then you specify the percentage between the two endpoints as a decimal value. The (end, end, 0.333) indicates the two endpoints that you selected in step 3 and the percentage as a decimal value of 0.333.

In the formulas you've seen so far, you've used the end function to select endpoints. If you prefer to select your own osnaps during the point-selection process, you can use the cur function. Cur lets you use any osnap you want when selecting points. In the first example, you could use (cur + cur)/2 instead of (end + end)/2.

The plt function is just one of several special functions that you can use with QuickCalc. Table 14.4 lists other functions that you can use to find points in your drawing and gather other data. In the table, 2D points are represented as pt1, pt2, and so on. Three-dimensional points, or points describing a plane, are indicated by ptp1, ptp3, and so on. The center of an arc or a circle is indicated with *apex* for a 2D location and *apex1* and *apex2* for a 3D axis.

TABLE 14.4:   Functions in QuickCalc and the formats for their use

FUNCTION AND FORMAT	DESCRIPTION
Getvar(*system variable name*)	Gets the value of a system variable
Vec(*pt1,pt2*)	Returns the vector described by the distance between the two points
Vec1(*pt1,pt2*)	Returns the vector described by 1 unit length
Abs(*vector*)	Returns the absolute value of the length of a vector
Cur(no arguments required)	Gets a point
@(no arguments required)	Returns the last point
w2u(*point*) and u2w(*point*)	Converts world coordinates to current user coordinates (w2u) or user coordinates to world
Pld(*pt1,pt2,distance*)	Returns the point on a line at a specified distance
Plt(*pt1,pt2,percent*)	Returns the point on a line at a percentage (decimal) of the line length
Rot(*pt1,apex,angle*) or Rot(*pt1,apex1,apex2,angle*)	Returns the rotation angle of a point (pt1) about an apex
Ill(*pt1,pt2,pt3,pt4*)	Returns the intersection between two lines
Ilp(*pt1,pt2,ptp1,ptp2,ptp3*)	Returns the intersection between a line and a plane; five points required
Dist(*pt1,pt2*)	Returns the distance between two points
Dpl(*point,pt1,pt2*)	Returns the shortest distance between a point and a line
Dpp(*point,ptp1,ptp2,ptp3*)	Returns the shortest distance between a point and a plane
Rad (no arguments required)	Returns a radius
Ang(*vector* or *pt1,pt2* or *apex,pt1,pt2* or *apex1,pt1,pt2,apex2*)	Returns an angle; can use up to four parameters when working in 3D
Nor(*vector* or *pt1,pt2* or *ptp1,ptp2,ptp3*)	Finds the normal of a vector or plane

Using QuickCalc While in the Middle of a Command

In all the previous examples, you've used QuickCalc as a stand-alone calculator. You've also seen how you can insert a calculation into the command line while a command is in progress. A third way to work with QuickCalc is to open it while in the middle of a command.

In a previous exercise, you used the (end + end)/2 formula to find the midpoint between two points, and then you inserted the resulting value into the Line command. Suppose that you start the Line command before you open QuickCalc. Try the following to see how you can use QuickCalc once a command has been initiated:

1. Close QuickCalc.

2. Start the Line command.

3. Enter '**qc**↵ to open QuickCalc.

4. In the QuickCalc text box, type **(end + end)/2** but don't press ↵. Instead, click the Apply button at the bottom of the QuickCalc window.

5. Select the endpoints of two lines. A line starts at the midpoint between the two points.

6. Click another point to draw the line, and then press ↵ to end the Line command.

In this exercise, you saw that an Apply option appears at the bottom of the QuickCalc window along with Close and Help buttons. These buttons aren't present when you open QuickCalc with no command active. The Apply button executes the formula and then immediately returns the resulting value to the command. Using QuickCalc in this way eliminates a few steps.

You may have also noticed that QuickCalc appeared with a light background instead of a dark one. This can serve as a reminder that you are using QuickCalc in the middle of another command. You will also see "Active Command:" followed by the current active command name.

FINDING A POINT RELATIVE TO ANOTHER POINT

Now, suppose that you want to start a line at a relative distance from another line. The following steps describe how to use the calculator to start a line from a point that is 2.5" in the x-axis and 5.0" in the y-axis from the endpoint of another line:

1. Make sure that QuickCalc is closed, start the Line command, and select a point.

2. Right-click, select the QuickCalc tool, and type **end + [2.5,5.0]** in the text box.

3. Click the Apply button at the bottom of the QuickCalc window.

4. Click the endpoint of the line that you just drew. The new line connects to a point that is at a distance of 2.5 in the x-axis and 5.0 in the y-axis from the endpoint that you selected.

In this example, you used the Endpoint osnap mode to indicate a point of reference. This is added to Cartesian coordinates in square brackets, describing the distance and direction from the reference point. You could enter any coordinate value within the square brackets. You also could enter a polar coordinate in place of the Cartesian coordinate, as in the following: **end + [5.59<63]**.

You can replace the *end* in the expression with the at sign (@) to continue from the last point that you selected. Also, it's not necessary to include every coordinate in the square brackets. For example, to indicate a displacement in only one axis, you can leave out a value for the other two coordinates while leaving in the commas, as in the following examples:

```
[4,5] = [4,5,0]
[,1] = [0,1,0]
[,,2] = [0,0,2]
```

COMBINING COORDINATES AND EXPRESSIONS

In the previous two examples, you saw that you can use an expression or enter coordinates. But what if you want to combine an expression within a coordinate? For example, in the beginning of this section, you added feet and inches and then transferred the result to the command line. In that example, you had to switch back and forth between QuickCalc and the command line to create the response for the Command prompt. If you prefer, you can create an expression that supplies the entire command input. Here are the steps to do this:

1. Close QuickCalc, and then start the Line command.

2. Enter **'qc**↵ to open QuickCalc.

3. Enter the following in the text box:

   End + [(4'+36+5'6)<45]

4. Click Apply.

5. In the drawing area, click the endpoint of a line. AutoCAD draws a line that begins at 12'-6" and at a 45° angle to the endpoint that you select.

In this exercise, you used the expression (4'+36+5'6) right in the middle of a coordinate value. As described earlier, the coordinate is within square brackets. By using this method, you can calculate measurements and apply them to commands more easily. The trick is to become familiar with the syntax QuickCalc requires so that you can write these expressions without errors.

Storing Expressions and Values

The ability to create expressions to manipulate coordinates can be useful, but you may find it difficult to remember an expression once you've created it. Fortunately, QuickCalc offers the Variables section, which allows you to store frequently used expressions and values. The Variables section has its set of tools in its title bar (see Figure 14.34).

These tools let you add items to the list, edit items, or delete items from the list. A fourth option lets you send a variable to the main calculator text box. You can also right-click in the Variables section list box and select the same options from a context menu. In addition, the context menu lets you create a new category and rename an existing one.

The Variables section also contains a list of currently stored variables. Some sample variables are shown in the list. If you hover over a variable, you see a description of that variable's function in a tool tip by the cursor.

To use an existing variable, select it from the list and click the Return Variable To Input Area button; it looks like a calculator. To add a variable to the list, click the New Variable button, which opens the Variable Definition dialog box (see Figure 14.35).

FIGURE 14.34
The Variables group

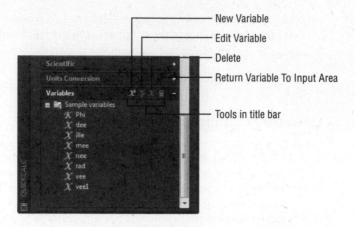

FIGURE 14.35
The Variable Definition
dialog box

This dialog box lets you enter the properties of the variable and choose the type. In the Variable Properties group, you enter the name of the variable in the Name text box. In the Group With drop-down list, you select a category under which your formula will appear in the Variables list. You can also create a new category. The Value Or Expression box is where you put your formula; it can also be a single value, such as a number or a coordinate. At the bottom is a space to enter a description for the variable. This description will appear in the Variables group's detail box at the bottom of QuickCalc.

At the top, in the Variable Type group, you see two options: Constant and Function. If you choose Function, your variable will behave as it normally does when you enter it in the text box. If you choose Constant and your variable is a formula, your variable will be executed when you close the Variable Definition dialog box. The resulting value will become the value for the variable.

To edit an existing variable, highlight it in the Variables group list, and then click the Edit Variable button to open the Variable Definition dialog box.

Guidelines for Working with QuickCalc

You may notice some patterns in the way expressions are formatted for the calculator. Here are some guidelines to remember:

◆ Coordinates are enclosed in square brackets.

◆ Nested or grouped expressions are enclosed in parentheses.

◆ Operators are placed between values, as in simple math equations.

◆ Object snaps can be used in place of coordinate values.

Table 14.5 lists the operators and functions available in QuickCalc. You may want to experiment with these functions on your own. You can enter many of these operators using the keys on the numeric keypad or in the scientific group.

TABLE 14.5:   The QuickCalc functions

OPERATOR/ FUNCTION	WHAT IT DOES	EXAMPLE
+ or –	Adds or subtracts numbers or vectors	$2 – 1 = 1 [a,b,c] + [x,y,z] = [a+x, b+y, c+z]$
* or /	Multiplies or divides numbers or vectors	$2 * 4.2 = 8.4 a*[x,y,z] = [a*x, a*y, a*z]$
^	Returns the exponent of a number	$3^2 = 9$
Sin	Returns the sine of an angle	$\sin(45) = 0.707107$
Cos	Returns the cosine of an angle	$\cos(30) = 0.866025$
Tang	Returns the tangent of an angle	$\tan(30) = 0.57735$
Asin	Returns the arcsine of a real number	$\text{asin}(0.707107) = 45.0$
Acos	Returns the arccosine of a real number	$\text{acos}(0.866025) = 30.0$
Atan	Returns the arctangent of a real number	$\text{atan}(0.57735) = 30.0$
Ln	Returns the natural log	$\ln(2) = 0.693147$
Log	Returns the base-10 log	$\log(2) = 0.30103$
Exp	Returns the natural exponent	$\exp(2) = 7.38906$

TABLE 14.5:   The QuickCalc functions   *(CONTINUED)*

OPERATOR/ FUNCTION	WHAT IT DOES	EXAMPLE
Exp10	Returns the base-10 exponent	exp10 (2) = 100
Sqr	Squares a number	sqr (9) = 81.0
Abs	Returns the absolute value	abs (−3.4) = 3.4
Round	Rounds to the nearest integer	round (3.6) = 4
Trunc	Drops the decimal portion of a real number	trunc (3.6) = 3
r2d	Converts radians to degrees	r2d (1.5708) = 90.0002
d2r	Converts degrees to radians	d2r (90) = 1.5708
Pi	Provides the constant pi	3.14159

QuickCalc is capable of much more than the typical uses you've seen here. A description of its full capabilities extends beyond the scope of this book. However, the processes described in these sections will be helpful as you use AutoCAD. If you want to know more about QuickCalc, consult the AutoCAD Help User Documentation (enter **QuickCalc** in the InfoCenter text box).

SINGLING OUT PROXIMATE OBJECTS

You'll sometimes need to select an object that overlaps or is very close to another object. Often in this situation, you end up selecting the wrong object. To select the exact object that you want, you can use the Selection Cycling tool and the Draworder command.

Selection cycling lets you cycle through objects that overlap until you select the one that you want. To use this feature, hover over the overlapping objects so that one of them is highlighted; then hold down the Shift key and press the spacebar. With each press of the spacebar, a different overlapping object will be highlighted. When the object that you want to select is highlighted, click it.

Another way to gain access to an overlapped object is to use the Draworder command. You can select the overlapping object and then choose Send To Back from the Draworder flyout in the Home tab's expanded Modify panel.

One reason that you would want to select an overlapping object is simply to delete a redundant line. AutoCAD offers the Delete Duplicate Object tool, which can be found in the Home tab's expanded Modify panel.

This tool is designed to help you easily remove overlapping objects that are not easily seen. To use it, click the Delete Duplicate Object tool or type **Overkill**↵. At the Select objects: prompt, select the objects that are overlapping. A selection window can be used to select an area. Press ↵ and the Delete Duplicate Objects dialog box appears.

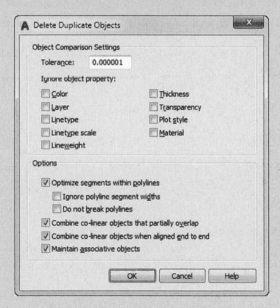

This dialog box gives you control over the criteria that AutoCAD uses to determine whether an object should be deleted. Make any changes necessary to the dialog box, and then click OK to remove duplicate overlapping objects.

The Bottom Line

Use external references (Xrefs).   You've seen how you can use Xrefs to quickly build variations of a floor plan that contain repetitive elements. This isn't necessarily the only way to use Xrefs, but the basic idea of how to use Xrefs is presented in the early exercises.

Master It Try putting together another floor plan that contains nothing but the Unit2 plan.

Manage layers. Once you start to edit complex drawings, you'll find that you'll want to save the On/Off or Freeze/Thaw layer states so that you can access parts of a drawing more easily. The Layer States Manager lets you save as many layer conditions as you may need in the course of a project.

Master It What part of the Layer States Manager dialog box lets you control the layer properties that are affected by a saved layer state?

Use advanced tools: Filter and Quick Select. The Filter and Quick Select tools are great for isolating objects in a crowded drawing. You can select objects by their color or layer assignment. You can select all instances of a specific block.

Master It True or false: The Quick Select tool lets you select a set of objects to limit your selections.

Use the QuickCalc calculator. The QuickCalc calculator offers many standard calculator tools plus a few that you may not see in other calculators.

Master It Name a few of the more unusual features offered by the QuickCalc calculator.

Chapter 15

Laying Out Your Printer Output

Your set of drawings for the studio apartment building would probably include a larger-scale, more detailed drawing of the typical unit plan. You already have the beginnings of this drawing in the form of the Unit.dwg file.

As you've seen, the notes and dimensions that you entered into the Unit.dwg file can be turned off or frozen in the Plan.dwg file so that they don't interfere with the graphics of the drawing. The Unit.dwg file can be part of another drawing file that contains more detailed information about the typical unit plan at a larger scale. To this new drawing, you can add notes, symbols, and dimensions. Whenever the Unit.dwg file is altered, you update its occurrence in the large-scale drawing of the typical unit as well as in the Plan.dwg file. The units are thus quickly updated, and good coordination is ensured among all the drawings for your project.

Now suppose that you want to combine drawings that have different scales in the same drawing file—for example, the overall plan of one floor plus an enlarged view of one typical unit. You can do so using the layout views and a feature called paper space.

In this chapter, you will learn to

◆ Understand model space and paper space

◆ Work with paper space viewports

◆ Create odd-shaped viewports

◆ Understand lineweights, linetypes, and dimensions in paper space

Understanding Model Space and Paper Space

Certification
Objective

So far, you've explored ways to get around in your drawing while using a single view. This single-view representation of your AutoCAD® drawing is called *Model Space* display mode. You can also set up multiple views of your drawing by using what are called *floating viewports*. You create floating viewports in layout views in what is called *Paper Space* mode.

To get a clear understanding of the Model Space and Paper Space modes, imagine that your drawing is a full-sized replica or model of the object that you're drawing. Your computer screen is your window into a "room" where this model is being constructed, and the keyboard and mouse are your means of access to this room. You can control your window's position in relation to the object through the use of Pan, Zoom, View, and other display-related commands. You can also construct or modify the model by using drawing and editing commands. Think of this room as your model space.

You've been working on your drawings by looking through a single window into model space. Now, suppose that you can step back and add windows with different views looking into your model space; the effect is like having several video cameras in your model space room, each connected to a different monitor. You can view all your windows at once on your computer screen or enlarge a single window to fill the entire screen. Furthermore, you can control the shape of your windows and easily switch from one window to another. This is what paper space is like.

Paper space lets you create and display multiple views of model space. Each view window, called a *viewport*, acts like an individual virtual screen. One viewport can have an overall view of your drawing while another can be a close-up. You can also control layer visibility individually for each viewport and display different versions of the same area of your drawing. You can move, copy, and stretch viewports and even overlap them. You can set up another type of viewport, called the *tiled viewport*, in model space. Chapter 21, "Using Advanced 3D Features," discusses this type of viewport.

One of the more powerful features of paper space is the ability to plot several views of the same drawing on one sheet of paper. You can also include graphic objects such as borders and notes that appear only in paper space. In this function, paper space acts much like a page-layout program such as QuarkXPress or Adobe InDesign. You can paste up different views of your drawing and then add borders, title blocks, general notes, and other types of graphic and textual data. Figure 15.1 shows the Plan drawing set up in Paper Space mode to display several views.

FIGURE 15.1
Different views of the same drawing in paper space

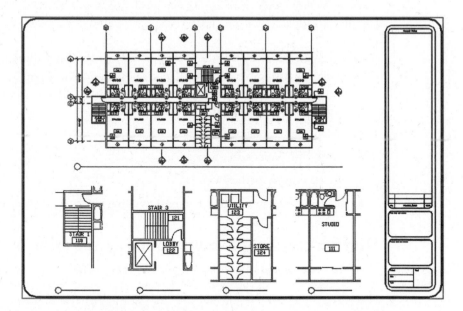

Switching from Model Space to Paper Space

Certification Objective

You can get to paper space by clicking any of the Layout tabs below the drawing area. You can also use the layout previews in the drawing tab.

> **DON'T SEE THE LAYOUT TABS?**
>
> If your version of AutoCAD does not show the Layout and Model tabs, you can turn them on by doing the following: Right-click in the drawing area, and select Options from the context menu. In the Options dialog box, select the Display tab and then, in the Layout Elements panel, turn on the Display Layout and Model tabs option. Click OK when you are finished.

Let's start with the basics of switching between model and paper space:

1. Open the Xref-1 file that you saved from the previous chapter, and make sure that your display shows the entire drawing. You can also use 15-xref1.dwg or 15-xref1-metric.dwg.

2. Click the Layout1 tab in the lower-left corner of the drawing area. You see your drawing appear in a kind of page preview view (see Figure 15.2).

FIGURE 15.2
Your drawing in a page preview view

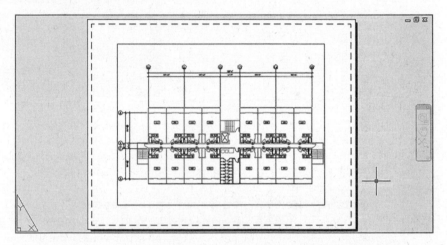

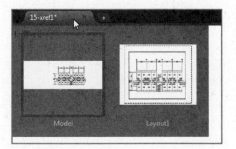

3. Click the Model tab in the lower-left corner of the drawing area to return to model space.

This brief exercise shows you how quickly you can shift between model space and paper space by using the Model and Layout1 tabs:

1. Hover over the Drawing tab, and you'll see preview images of the model and paper space layouts (see Figure 15.3). The current layout is highlighted with a blue border.

FIGURE 15.3
The Drawing tab's model and paper space preview

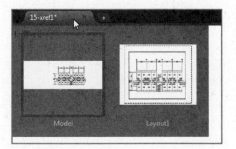

2. Point to Layout1 preview image; the drawing area will temporarily display a full view of the layout.

3. Click in the Layout1 image to confirm your selection of the layout view.

4. Hover over the drawing tab again, but this time move the cursor to the preview panel to the left labeled Model.

5. Click the Model image to go back to the Model Space view.

Note that when you hover over a preview image, the Plot and Publish icons appear in the top corners of the image (see Figure 15.4).

FIGURE 15.4
The Plot and Publish icons

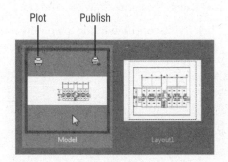

If you prefer, you can use keyboard shortcuts to switch between model and paper space. Press Ctrl+PgDn to go from model space to paper space. Press Ctrl+PgUp to go from paper space to model space. If there are several paper space layout tabs, Ctrl+PgDn opens the next layout tab to the right and Ctrl+PgUp opens the next layout tab to the left.

Setting the Size of a Paper Space Layout

We mentioned that paper space is like a page-layout program, and you saw how a paper space layout looks like a print preview. You can set up your layout for a specific set of printer settings, including the paper size and printer.

Let's continue with our look at paper space by seeing how you can set up a paper space layout for your printer:

1. Click the Layout1 tab.

2. Right-click the Layout1 tab, and choose Page Setup Manager to open the resizable Page Setup Manager dialog box. Notice that the name of the current layout is shown in the list of current page setups (see Figure 15.5).

3. Click the Modify button to open the Page Setup dialog box.

4. Select the Letter paper-size option from the Paper Size drop-down list. Metric users should select A4 (210 mm x 297 mm). The paper size that you select here determines the shape and margin of the paper space layout area.

5. Select a printer from the Printer/Plotter Name drop-down list.

6. Click OK to close the Page Setup dialog box, and then click Close to close the Page Setup Manager.

FIGURE 15.5
The Page Setup
Manager

AutoCAD bases the paper space layout on the paper size and printer that you specify in steps 4 and 5. The area shown in paper space reflects the area of the paper size that you selected in step 4, and the printer determines the paper margin, shown by a dashed line. If for some reason you need to change the paper size, repeat steps 2 through 5. You can also store the way you've set up your paper space layout using the Page Setup Manager that you saw in step 2. See Chapter 8, "Introducing Printing, Plotting, and Layouts," for more on this feature.

Creating New Paper Space Viewports

As you saw in Chapter 8, the different look of the layout view tells you that you're in paper space. You also learned that a viewport is automatically created when you first open a layout view. The layout viewport displays an overall view of your drawing to no particular scale.

In this section, you'll work with multiple viewports in paper space instead of just the default single viewport that you get when you open the layout view.

This first exercise shows you how to create three new viewports at once:

1. Click the viewport's outline to select it. The viewport is the solid rectangle surrounding your drawing, just inside the dashed rectangle.

2. Click the Erase tool in the Home tab's Modify panel to erase the viewport. Your drawing disappears. Don't panic; remember that the viewport is like a window to model space. The objects in model space are still there.

3. Click the Named tool in the Layout tab's Layout Viewports panel to open the Viewports dialog box. You can also type **Vports**.↵.

4. Click the New Viewports tab. This tab contains a set of predefined viewport layouts (see Figure 15.6). You'll learn more about the Viewports dialog box and its options in Chapter 21.

FIGURE 15.6
The Viewports dialog
box

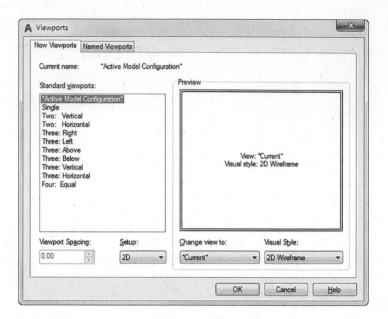

5. Click the Three: Above option in the Standard Viewports list box. The box to the right shows a sample view of the Three: Above layout that you selected.

6. Click OK. The `Specify first corner or [Fit] <Fit>:` prompt appears.

7. Press ↵ to accept the default Fit option. The Fit option fits the viewport layout to the maximum area allowed in your paper space view. Three rectangles appear in the formation, as shown in Figure 15.7. Each of these is a viewport to your model space. The viewport at the top fills the whole width of the drawing area; the bottom half of the screen is divided into two viewports.

FIGURE 15.7
The newly created
viewports

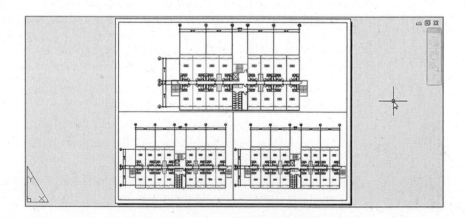

When you create new viewports, AutoCAD automatically fills them with the extents of your model space drawing. You can specify an exact scale for each viewport, as you'll see later.

Notice that the dashed line representing your paper margin has disappeared. That's because the viewports are pushed to the margin limits, thereby covering the dashed line.

You could have kept the original viewport that appeared when you first opened the Layout1 view and then added two new viewports. Completely replacing the single viewport is a bit simpler because the Viewports dialog box fits the viewports into the allowed space for you.

After you've set up a paper space layout, it remains part of the drawing. You may prefer to use model space for doing most of your drawing and then use paper space layouts for setting up views for printing. Changes that you make to your drawing in model space will automatically appear in your paper space layout viewports.

Reaching Inside Viewports

Now, suppose that you need access to the objects in the viewports in order to adjust their display and to edit your drawing. First you'll need to open the Navigate panel in the Layout ribbon tab to enable you to zoom in and out of your view:

1. Click the View tab.

2. Right-click in a blank area of the ribbon and select Show Panels ➤ Navigate. The Navigate panel appears. You'll use this panel in the following exercise.

Next, to see how to work inside a viewport, try these steps:

1. Double-click inside a viewport. This gives you control over model space even though you're in paper space. (You can also enter **MS**↵ as a keyboard shortcut to enter Model Space mode.)

   The first thing that you notice is that the UCS icon changes back to its L-shaped form.

2. Move your cursor over each viewport. In one of the viewports, the cursor appears as the AutoCAD crosshair cursor, whereas in the other viewports it appears as an arrow pointer. The viewport that shows the AutoCAD cursor is the active one; you can pan, zoom, and edit objects in the active viewport.

3. Click in the lower-left viewport to activate it.

4. Click Window from the Zoom flyout on the View tab's Navigate 2D panel, and place a window selection around the elevator area.

5. Click the lower-right viewport, and choose Zoom Window from the Zoom flyout on the Navigation bar to enlarge your view of a typical unit. You can also use the Pan and Zoom Realtime tools. If you don't see the UCS icon, it has been turned off. Type **UCSicon**↵**On.**↵ to turn it on. See Chapter 21 for more on the UCS icon.

You can move from viewport to viewport even while you're in the middle of most commands. For example, you can issue the Line command, pick the start point in one viewport, go to a different viewport to pick the next point, and so on. To activate a different viewport, you click inside the viewport (see Figure 15.8).

FIGURE 15.8
The three viewports, each with a different view of the plan

Model Space UCS icon

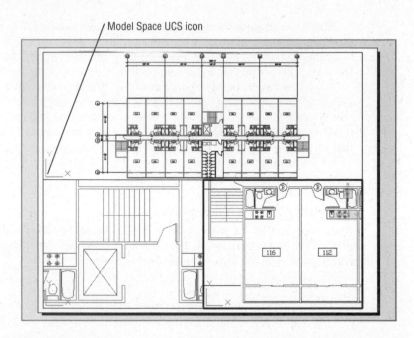

SWITCHING BETWEEN VIEWPORTS

We've found that users will have a need to overlap viewports from time to time. When they do this, they are often at a loss over how to switch between the overlapping viewports, especially when one is completely surrounded by another or when they are exactly the same size and in the same position. In this situation, you can move between viewports by pressing Ctrl+R repeatedly until you get to the viewport that you want.

You've seen how you can zoom into a viewport view, but what happens when you use the Zoom command while in paper space? Try the following exercise to find out:

1. Double-click an area outside the viewports to get out of Floating model space.

2. Select Zoom Realtime from the Zoom flyout in the Navigation bar and then zoom into the paper space view. The entire view enlarges, including the views in the viewports.

3. Click All from the Zoom flyout or press the Escape key and enter **Z↵A↵** to return to the overall view of paper space.

This brief exercise showed that you can use the Zoom tool in paper space just as you would in model space. All of the display-related commands are available, including the Pan command.

Working with Paper Space Viewports

Paper space is intended as a page-layout or composition tool. You can manipulate viewports' sizes, scale their views independently of one another, and even set layering and linetype scales independently.

Let's try manipulating the shape and location of viewports by using the Home tab's Modify panel options:

1. Make sure that Object Snap is turned off in the status bar.

2. Make sure that you're in a layout view. Then click the bottom edge of the lower-left viewport to expose its grips (see the top image in Figure 15.9).

FIGURE 15.9

Stretching, erasing, and moving viewports

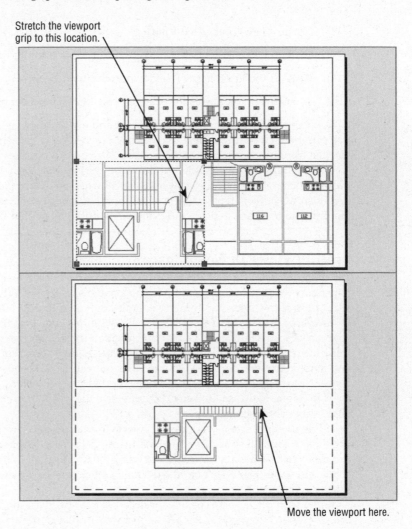

Stretch the viewport grip to this location.

Move the viewport here.

3. Click the upper-right grip, and drag it to the location shown in the top image in Figure 15.9.

4. Press the Esc key, and erase the lower-right viewport by selecting it and clicking Erase in the Home tab's Modify panel or by pressing the Delete key.

5. Move the lower-left viewport so that it's centered in the bottom half of the window, as shown in the bottom image in Figure 15.9.

In this exercise, you clicked the viewport edge to select it for editing. If while in paper space you attempt to click the image in the viewport, you won't select anything. Later, you'll see that you can use the osnap modes to snap to parts of the drawing image in a viewport.

Because viewports are recognized as AutoCAD objects, you can manipulate them by using all of the editing commands, just as you would manipulate any other object. In the previous exercise, you moved, stretched, and erased viewports. Next, you'll see how layers affect viewports:

1. Create a new layer called **Vport**.

2. Using the Properties palette, assign the viewports to the Vport layer.

3. Turn off the Vport layer. The viewport outlines disappear.

4. After reviewing the results of step 3, turn the Vport layer back on.

You can assign a layer, a color, a linetype, and even a lineweight to a viewport's outline. If you put the viewport on a layer that has been turned off or frozen, that outline becomes invisible, just like any other object on such a layer. Or you can put the viewport on a nonprinting layer so that the outline will be visible while you're editing. Making a viewport's outlines invisible or putting them on a nonprinting layer is helpful when you want to compose a final sheet for printing. Even when turned off, the active viewport has a heavy outline around it when you switch to Floating model space, and all of the viewports still display their views.

Scaling Views in Paper Space

Paper space has its own unit of measure. You've already seen how you're required to specify a paper size when opening a layout view to a paper space view. When you first enter paper space, regardless of the area your drawing occupies in model space, you're given limits that are set by the paper size that you specify in the Page Setup dialog box. If you keep in mind that paper space is like a paste-up area that is dependent on the printer that you configured for AutoCAD, this difference of scale becomes easier to comprehend. Just as you might paste up photographs and maps representing several square miles onto an 11" × 17" board, so too you can use paper space to paste up views of scale drawings representing city blocks or houses on an 8-1/2" × 11" sheet of paper. However, in AutoCAD, you have the freedom to change the scale and size of the objects that you're pasting up.

While in paper space, you can edit objects in a model space viewport, but to do so you must use Floating model space. To get to Floating model space, double-click inside a viewport. You can then click inside any viewport and edit in that viewport. In this mode, objects that were created in paper space can't be edited. Double-click outside a viewport to go back to the paper space environment.

If you want to be able to print your drawing at a specific scale, you must indicate a scale for each viewport. Viewport scales are set in a way similar to the annotation scale in the Model tab. Let's see how to put together a sheet in paper space and still maintain accuracy of scale:

1. Make sure that you're in paper space. You can tell by the shape and location of the UCS icon. If it looks like a triangle in the lower-left corner of the layout view, then you are in paper space.

2. Click the topmost viewport's outline to select it.

3. In the lower-right portion of the AutoCAD window, click the Viewport Scale drop-down list and select 1/32″ = 1′-0″. Metric users should click Custom and add a custom scale of 1:400. Then select the 1:400 scale from the Viewport Scale drop-down list. Notice how the view in the upper viewport changes.

4. Press the Esc key twice to clear the selection of the viewport.

5. Click the lower viewport border.

6. Click the Viewport Scale drop-down list again, and select 3/16″ = 1′-0″ from the list. Metric users should click Custom and add a custom scale of 1:80 and then select the 1:80 scale from the Viewport Scale drop-down list. The view in the viewport changes to reflect the new scale (see Figure 15.10).

FIGURE 15.10
Paper space viewport views scaled to 1/32″ = 1′-0″ and 3/16″ = 1′-0″ (1:400 and 1:80 for metric users)

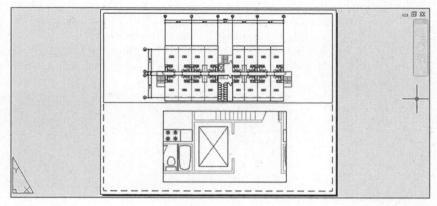

It's easy to adjust the width, height, and location of the viewports so that they display only the parts of the unit you want to see. While in paper space, use the Stretch, Move, Scale, or Rotate command to edit any viewport border, or use the viewport's grips to edit its size and shape. The view in the viewport remains at the same scale and location while the viewport changes in size. You can move and stretch viewports with no effect on the size and location of the objects in the view. When you rotate the viewport, the view inside the viewport will also rotate.

If you need to overlay one drawing on top of another, you can overlap viewports. Use the osnap overrides to select geometry in each viewport, even while in paper space. This lets you align one viewport on top of another at exact locations.

You can also add a title block in paper space at a 1:1 scale to frame your viewports and then plot this drawing from paper space at a scale of 1:1. Your plot appears just as it does in paper space at the appropriate scale. Paper space displays a dashed line to show you where the non-printable areas occur near the edge of the paper.

While you're working in paper space, pay close attention to whether you're in paper space or Floating model space. It's easy to pan or zoom in a Floating model space viewport accidentally when you intend to pan or zoom your paper space view. This can cause you to lose your viewport scaling or alignment with other parts of the drawing.

It's a good idea to save viewport views in case you happen to change a viewport view accidentally. You can do this by using the following procedure: Double-click inside a viewport whose view you want to save. Select View Manager from the View tab's Views panel, and then, in the View Manager, click the New button (see "Saving Views" in Chapter 7, "Mastering Viewing Tools, Hatches, and External References," for a description of the View Manager dialog box).

Another way to prevent your viewport view from being accidentally altered is to turn on View Lock. To do this, while in paper space click a viewport's outline. Right-click to open the context menu, and then choose Display Locked ➤ Yes. After the view is locked, you can't pan or zoom within a viewport. This setting is also available in the viewport's Properties palette and in the status bar to the left of the Viewport Scale tool when a viewport is selected or when you are in Floating model space.

Setting Layers in Individual Viewports

Another unique feature of paper space viewports is their ability to freeze layers independently. You can, for example, display the usual plan information in the overall view of a floor but show only the walls in the enlarged view of one unit.

You control viewport layer visibility through the Layer Properties Manager. You may have noticed that there are three sun icons for each layer listing.

To see all the layer options, you may need to widen the Layer Properties Manager to view all of the columns. To do so, click and drag the right border of the dialog box to the right.

You're already familiar with the sun icon farthest to the left. This is the Freeze/Thaw icon that controls the freezing and thawing of layers globally. Several columns to the right of that icon are two sun icons with transparent rectangles. These icons control the freezing and thawing of layers in individual viewports. Of this pair, the one on the left controls newly created viewports and the one on the right controls settings for existing viewports.

This exercise shows you firsthand how the sun icon for existing viewports works:

1. Double-click inside a viewport to go to Floating model space.

2. Activate the lower viewport.

3. Open the Layer Properties Manager.

4. Locate the COMMON|WALL layer, and then click its name to help you see the layer clearly.

5. Click the column labeled VP Freeze for the selected layer (see Figure 15.11). You may need to widen the Layer Properties Manager to do this; the column title may show only V until you widen the column. The VP Freeze column is the seventh column from the right side of the dialog box. Click the icon, which looks like a transparent rectangle behind a sun. The sun changes to a snowflake, telling you that the layer is now frozen for the current viewport.

FIGURE 15.11
Select the VP Freeze option for the COMMON|WALL layer.

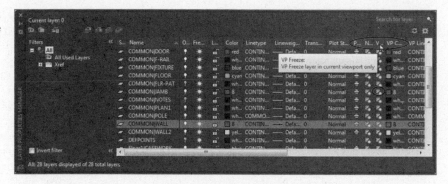

The Wall layer of the Common Xref becomes invisible in the current viewport. However, the walls remain visible in the other viewport (see Figure 15.12).

FIGURE 15.12
The drawing with the COMMON|WALL layer turned off in the active viewport

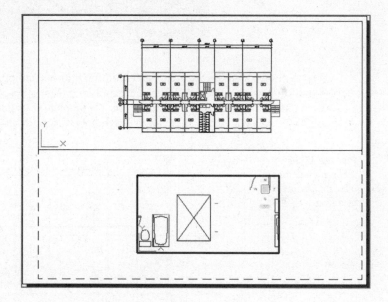

6. After reviewing the effects of the VP Freeze setting, go back to the Layer Properties Manager and thaw the COMMON|WALL layer by clicking its VP Freeze icon again so that it turns back into a sun.

7. Take a moment to study the drawing, and then save the Xref-1.dwg file.

You may have noticed another, identical sun icon next to the one that you used in the previous exercise. This icon controls layer visibility in any new viewports that you create next rather than in existing viewports.

If you prefer, you can use the layer drop-down list in the Layers panel to freeze layers in individual viewports. Double-click in the viewport that you want to modify, select the layer from the list, and then click the same sun icon with the small rectangle behind it.

In addition to setting the visibility of layers, you can set the other layer properties—such as color, linetype, and lineweight—for each viewport. First, make sure that you're in Floating model space for the viewport whose layers you want to set up, and then open the Layer Properties Manager. You can set the properties for the current viewport using the VP Freeze, VP Color, VP Linetype, VP Lineweight, VP Transparency, and VP Plot Style settings for each layer (see Figure 15.13).

FIGURE 15.13
The VP Freeze, VP Color, VP Linetype, VP Lineweight, VP Transparency, and VP Plot Style columns in the Layer Properties Manager

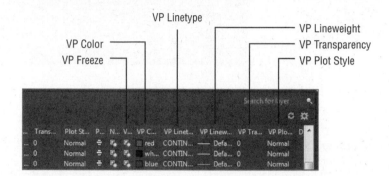

This section concludes the apartment building tutorial. Although you haven't drawn the complete building, you've learned all the commands and techniques that you need to do so. Figure 15.14 shows you a completed plan of the first floor. To complete your floor plans and get some practice using AutoCAD, you may want to add the symbols shown in this figure to your Plan.dwg file.

FIGURE 15.14
A completed floor of the apartment building

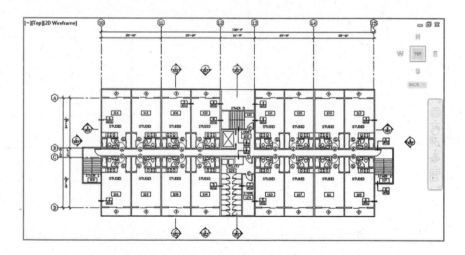

Because buildings like this one often have the same plans for several floors, the plan for the second floor can also represent the third floor. Combined with the first floor, this gives you a three-level apartment building. This project might also have a ground-level garage, which would be a separate file. You can use the Col-grid.dwg or Col-grid-metric.dwg file in the garage file as a reference for dimensions. The other symbols can be blocks stored as files that you can retrieve in other files.

> ### MASKING OUT PARTS OF A DRAWING
>
> Chapter 7 described a method for using the AutoCAD Draworder feature to hide floor patterns under equipment or furniture in a floor layout. You can use a similar method to hide irregularly shaped areas in a paper space viewport. This is desirable for plotting site plans, civil plans, or floor plans that require portions of the drawing to be masked out. You may also want to mask part of a plan that is overlapped by another to expose dimension or text data.

Creating and Using Multiple Paper Space Layouts

Certification Objective

You're not limited to just one or two paper space layouts. You can have as many as you want, with each layout set up for a different sheet size containing different views of your drawing. You can use this feature to set up multiple drawing sheets based on a single AutoCAD drawing file. For example, suppose that a client requires full sets of plans in both 1/8″ = 1′ scale and 1/16″ = 1′ scale. You can set up two Layout tabs, each with a different sheet size and viewport scale.

You can also set up different paper space layouts for the various types of drawings. A single drawing can contain the data for mechanical layout, equipment and furnishings, floor plans, and reflected ceiling plans. Although a project can require a file for each floor plan, a single file with multiple layout views can serve the same purpose in AutoCAD 2018.

To create new layout views, do the following:

1. Click the New Layout tab from the layout tabs in the lower-left corner of the drawing area (see Figure 15.15). A new preview panel appears, labeled Layout2.

FIGURE 15.15
The New Layout tab

2. Click the new Layout2 tab. The new layout appears with a single default viewport.

You've just seen how you can create a new layout using the New Layout tab. You can also right-click any layout tab to open a context menu that offers a New Layout option (see Figure 15.16).

FIGURE 15.16
The New Layout context menu option

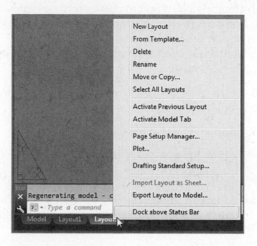

The Layout tab context menu also includes the From Template option and the Move Or Copy option. The From Template option lets you create a paper space layout based on an AutoCAD template file. AutoCAD provides several standard layouts that include title blocks based on common sheet sizes. The Move Or Copy option lets you move or copy an existing tab. For example, to move a layout tab to the far right, right-click the tab you want to move and then select the Move Or Copy option to open the resizable Move Or Copy dialog box (see Figure 15.17). Select (Move To End) and click OK. The selected layout tab will move to the right end of the tabs.

FIGURE 15.17
The layout tab's Move Or Copy dialog box

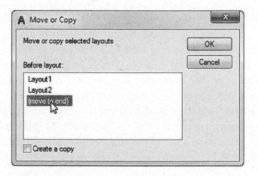

Finally, if you want to delete or rename a layout, right-click the layout tab that you want to edit. You can then select Delete or Rename from the context menu that appears. If you select Delete, you'll see a warning message telling you that AutoCAD will permanently delete the layout you have chosen to delete. Click OK to confirm your deletion.

Creating Odd-Shaped Viewports

In many situations, a rectangular viewport doesn't provide a view appropriate for what you want to accomplish. For example, you might want to isolate part of a floor plan that is L shaped or circular. You can create viewports for virtually any shape you need. You can grip-edit a typical rectangular viewport to change its shape into a trapezoid or other irregular four-sided polygon. You can also use the Clip tool to create more complex viewport shapes, as the following exercise demonstrates.

Follow these steps to set up a layout view that shows only the lower apartment units and the elevators and stairs:

1. Click the Clip tool in the Layout tab's Layout Viewports panel. You can also type **Vpclip↵**.

2. At the Select viewport to clip: prompt, click the viewport border.

3. At the Select clipping object or [Polygonal] <Polygonal>: prompt, press ↵.

4. Turn off Object Snap, and draw the outline shown in the top portion of Figure 15.18.

5. After you finish selecting points, press ↵. The viewport changes to conform to the new shape as shown in the bottom portion of Figure 15.18.

FIGURE 15.18

Drawing a polygon outline for a viewport

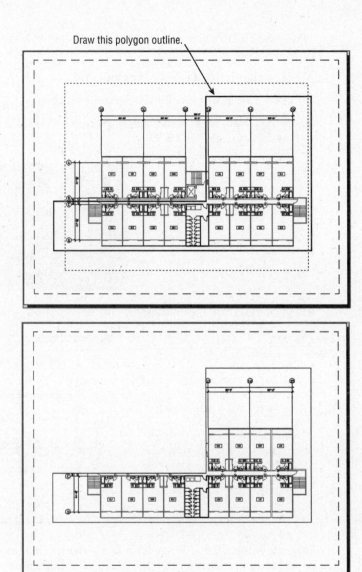

Draw this polygon outline.

6. Click the viewport border to expose its grips.

7. Click a grip, and move it to a new location. The viewport view conforms to the new shape.

The new viewport shape gives you more flexibility in isolating portions of a drawing. This can be especially useful if you have a large project that is divided into smaller sheets. You can set up several layout views, each displaying a different portion of the plan.

What if you want a viewport that isn't rectilinear? This exercise shows you how to create a circular viewport:

1. Erase the viewport that you just modified.

2. Draw a circle that roughly fills the paper space area.

3. In the Layout tab's Layout Viewports panel, choose Object from the Viewport flyout. You can also type **-VPORTS↵O↵**.

4. Click the circle. The plan appears inside the circle, as shown in Figure 15.19.

FIGURE 15.19
A circular viewport

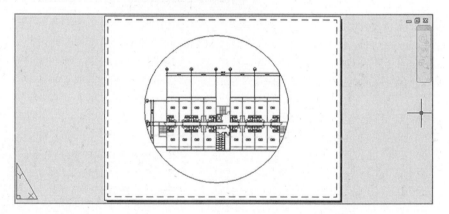

To simplify this exercise, you were asked to draw a circle as the basis for a new viewport. However, you aren't limited to circles; you can use a closed polyline or spline of any shape. (See Chapter 18, "Drawing Curves," for a detailed discussion of polylines and splines.) You can also use the Polygon tool on the Home tab's Draw panel to create a shape and then turn it into a viewport.

If you look carefully at the series of prompts for the previous exercise, you'll notice that the Layout Viewports Object tool invokes a command-line version of the Vports command (-vports), which offers some options that the standard Vports command doesn't. The following options are available with the command-line version of Vports:

```
_-VPORTS
Specify corner of viewport or
[ON/OFF/Fit/Shadeplot/Lock/Object/Polygonal/Restore/LAyer/2/3/4]<Fit>:
```

You used two of the options—Polygonal and Object—in the two previous exercises.

Understanding Lineweights, Linetypes, and Dimensions in Paper Space

The behavior of several AutoCAD features depends on whether you're in paper space or model space. The most visible of these features are lineweights, linetypes, and dimensions. In the following sections, you'll take a closer look at these features and see how to use them in conjunction with paper space.

Controlling and Viewing Lineweights in Paper Space

Lineweights can greatly improve the readability of technical drawings. You can make important features stand out with bold lineweights while keeping the noise of smaller details from overpowering a drawing. In architectural floor plans, walls are traditionally drawn with heavier lines so that the outline of a plan can be easily read. Other features exist in a drawing for reference only, so they're drawn in a lighter weight than normal.

If you look at Bonus Chapter 5, "Understanding Plot Styles," available at www.omura.com/chapters, you will see how to control lineweights in AutoCAD by using plot style tables. You can apply either a named plot style table or a color plot style table to a drawing. If you already have a library of AutoCAD drawings, you may want to use color plot style tables for backward compatibility. AutoCAD also enables you to assign lineweights directly to layers or objects and to view the results of your lineweight settings in paper space.

Here's an exercise that demonstrates how to set lineweights directly:

1. Open the Layer Properties Manager.

2. Right-click the Layer list, and choose Select All.

3. Click the Lineweight column (not the column header) to open the Lineweight dialog box (see Figure 15.20).

FIGURE 15.20
The Lineweight dialog box

4. Select 0.13 mm from the list, and click OK. You've just assigned the 0.13 mm lineweight to all layers.

5. Right-click the Layer list again, and choose Clear All.

6. Click the COMMON|WALL layer, and Ctrl+click the Floor1|WALL layer to select these two layers.

7. Click the Lineweight column for either of the two selected layers to open the Lineweight dialog box again.

8. Select 0.40 mm from the dialog box, and click OK. You've just assigned the 0.40 mm lineweight to the two selected layers.

9. Click Close in the Layer Properties Manager.

Although you set the lineweights for the layers in the drawing, you need to make a few more changes to the file settings before they're visible in paper space:

1. Type **LW**↵ to open the Lineweight Settings dialog box (see Figure 15.21).

FIGURE 15.21
The Lineweight
Settings dialog box

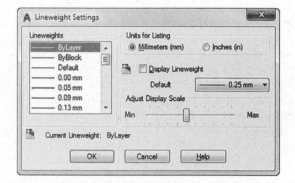

2. Select the Display Lineweight check box, and then click OK.

3. Make sure that you're in paper space, and then zoom into the drawing. The lines representing the walls are now thicker, as shown in Figure 15.22.

FIGURE 15.22
An enlarged view of the
plan with lineweights
displayed

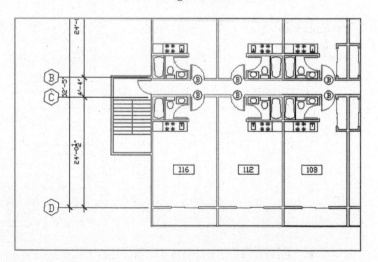

4. After reviewing the results of this exercise, close the file. You may save it for future reference.

With the ability to display lineweights in paper space, you have better control over your output. Instead of using a trial-and-error method to print your drawing and then checking your printout to see whether the lineweights are correct, you can see the lineweights on your screen.

This exercise showed you how to set lineweights so that they appear in paper space as they will when you plot your drawing. If you normally plot your drawings in black, you can go one step further and set all your layer colors to black to see how your plots will look. But you'll need to save your layer settings so that you can restore the layers to their original colors. Another way to view your drawing in black and white without affecting your layer settings is to use the color plot style table described in Bonus Chapter 5.

LINEWEIGHT DISPLAY SHORTCUT

When lineweight display is turned on, you see lineweights in model space as well as in paper space. Lineweights can be distracting while you work on your drawing in model space, but you can quickly turn them off by entering **Lwdisplay.⏎Off.⏎** at the command line. Entering **Lwdisplay.⏎On.⏎** turns the lineweight display back on. If you find that you need to do this often, you can add the LineWeight tool to the status bar. This tool will turn lineweight display on and off with a click of your mouse. You can add this tool to the status bar by clicking the Customization tool in the lower-right corner of the AutoCAD window and selecting LineWeight.

The Lineweight Settings Dialog Box

The Lineweight Settings dialog box includes a few other settings that you didn't use in the previous exercise. Here is a description of those settings:

Units For Listing   You can choose between millimeters and inches for the unit of measure for lineweights. The default is millimeters.

Adjust Display Scale   This setting lets you control just how thick lineweights appear in the drawing. Move the slider to the right for thicker lines and to the left for thinner lines. This setting affects only the display on your monitor. As you move the slider, you can see a sample of the results in the Lineweights list box just to the left of the slider. You may have to scroll down the list box to view the effects.

Default Drop-Down List   This drop-down list lets you select the default lineweight that you see in the Layer Properties Manager. You may want to lower the default lineweight to 0.005" (0.13 mm) as a matter of course because most printers these days can print lines that size and even smaller.

Linetype Scales and Paper Space

As you've seen in previous exercises, you must carefully control drawing scales when creating viewports. Fortunately, this is easily done through the Properties palette. Although paper space offers the flexibility of combining images of different scale in one display, it also adds to the complexity of your task in controlling that display. Your drawing's linetype scale in particular needs careful attention.

In Chapter 5, "Keeping Track of Layers and Blocks," you saw that you had to set the linetype scale to the scale factor of the drawing in order to make the linetype visible. If you intend to plot that same drawing from paper space, you have to set the linetype scale back to 1 to get the linetypes to appear correctly. This is because AutoCAD faithfully scales linetypes to the current unit system. Remember that paper space units are different from model space units. When you scale a model space image down to fit in the smaller paper space area, the linetypes remain scaled to the increased linetype scale settings. In the Chapter 5 example, linetypes are scaled up by a factor of 24. This causes noncontinuous lines to appear as continuous in paper space because you see only a small portion of a greatly enlarged noncontinuous linetype.

The Psltscale system variable enables you to determine how linetype scales are applied to paper space views. You can set Psltscale so that the linetypes appear the same regardless of whether you view them directly in model space or through a viewport in paper space. By default, this system variable is set to 1. This causes AutoCAD to scale all the linetypes uniformly across all the viewports in paper space. You can set Psltscale to 0 to force the viewports to display linetypes exactly as they appear in model space. Psltscale is not a global setting. You must set it for each layout view that you create; otherwise, the default value of 1 will be used.

You can also control this setting in the Linetype Manager dialog box (type **LT**↵). When you click the Show Details button, you see a setting called Use Paper Space Units For Scaling in the lower-left corner. When this check box is selected, Psltscale is set to 1. When it isn't selected, Psltscale is set to 0.

Dimensioning in Paper Space Layouts

At times, you may find it more convenient to add dimensions to your drawing in paper space rather than directly on your objects in model space. This can be useful if you have a small project with several viewports in a layout and you want to keep dimensions aligned between viewports. You have two basic options when dimensioning model space objects in paper space. The Associative Dimensioning feature can make quick work of dimensions for layout views containing drawings of differing scales. Alternatively, if you prefer not to use Associative Dimensioning, you can adjust settings for individual dimension styles.

USING ASSOCIATIVE DIMENSIONING IN PAPER SPACE

Perhaps the simplest way to dimension in paper space is to use the Associative Dimensioning feature. With this feature turned on, you can dimension model space objects while in a paper space layout. Furthermore, paper space dimensions of model space objects are automatically updated if the model space object is edited.

Try the following exercise to see how Associative Dimensioning works:

1. Click New from the Quick Access toolbar, and use the acad.dwt template to create a new blank file. Metric users should use the acadiso.dwt template.

2. Draw a rectangle 12 units wide by 4 units high. If you're using a metric file, make the rectangle 480 units wide by 160 units high.

3. Select the Layout1 tab.

4. Right-click the Layout1 tab, and select Page Setup Manager.

5. In the Page Setup Manager, click Modify. Then, in the Page Setup dialog box, select a printer from the Printer/Plotter group's Name drop-down list.

6. Choose the Letter paper size in the Paper Size section. Metric users can pick ISO A4 (297.00 × 210.00 mm).

7. Click OK, and then close the Page Setup Manager.

8. Right-click in the drawing area, and choose Options from the context menu.

9. In the Options dialog box, click the User Preferences tab and make sure that the Make New Dimensions Associative option in the Associative Dimensioning group is turned on (shows a check mark). Click OK to exit the dialog box.

Next, you'll use the rectangle you drew in model space to test the Associative Dimensioning feature in the Layout1 view:

1. Click Linear from the Annotate tab's Dimensions panel. Using the Endpoint osnap, dimension the bottom edge of the rectangle that you drew in model space. The dimension shows 12.0000 (480 for metric drawings), the actual size of the rectangle.

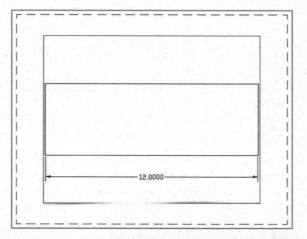

2. Double-click inside the viewport, and use the Zoom Realtime tool to zoom out a bit so that the rectangle appears smaller in the viewport. Do not use the scroll wheel of your mouse to do this (see the next section, "Updating Associative Dimensions"). After you exit the Zoom Realtime tool, the dimension follows the new view of the rectangle.

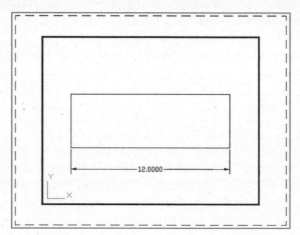

3. While you're in Floating model space, click the rectangle and then click the grip in the lower-left corner and drag it upward and to the right.

4. Click again to place the corner of the rectangle in a new location. The dimension changes to conform to the new shape.

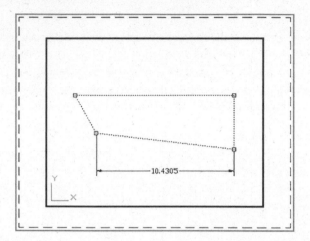

5. Close the rectangle file without saving it. You won't need it in the future.

You've just seen how you can dimension an object in model space while in paper space. You can dimension model space Xrefs in paper space in much the same way. The only difference is that changes to the Xref file don't automatically update dimensions made in paper space. You need to employ the Dimregen command to refresh paper space dimensions of Xref objects.

UPDATING ASSOCIATIVE DIMENSIONS

If you use a wheel mouse to pan and zoom in a Floating model space viewport, you may need to use the Dimregen command to refresh an associative dimension. To do so, type **Dimregen**↵ at the command line. You can also use Dimregen to refresh dimensions from drawings that have been edited in earlier versions of AutoCAD or, as mentioned already, to refresh dimensions of objects contained in external references.

PAPER SPACE DIMENSIONING WITHOUT ASSOCIATIVE DIMENSIONING

In some situations, you may not want to use Associative Dimensioning, although you still want to dimension model space objects in paper space. For example, you might be in an office that has different versions of AutoCAD, or you might be sharing your drawings with other offices that aren't using AutoCAD 2018, and the use of Associative Dimensioning creates confusion.

To dimension model space objects in paper space without Associative Dimensioning, you need to have AutoCAD adjust the dimension text to the scale of the viewport from which you're dimensioning. You can have AutoCAD scale dimension values in paper space so that they correspond to a viewport zoom-scale factor. The following steps show you how this setting is made:

1. Open the Dimension Style Manager by clicking the Dimension Style tool in the Home tab's expanded Annotation panel.

2. Select the dimension style that you want to edit and click Modify.

3. Click the Primary Units tab.

4. In the Measurement Scale group, enter the scale factor of the viewport that you intend to dimension in the Scale Factor text box. For example, if the viewport is scaled to a 1/2″ = 1′-0″ scale, enter **24**.

5. Click the Apply To Layout Dimensions Only check box.

6. Click OK, and then click Close in the Dimension Style Manager. You're ready to dimension in paper space without associative dimensions.

Remember that you can snap to objects in a floating viewport so that you can add dimensions as you normally would in model space. If you're dimensioning objects in viewports of different scales, you need to set up multiple dimension styles, one for each viewport scale.

Other Uses for Paper Space

The exercises in the preceding sections should give you a sense of how you work in paper space and layout views. We've given examples that reflect common uses of paper space. Remember that paper space is like a page-layout portion of AutoCAD—separate yet connected to model space through viewports.

You needn't limit your applications to floor plans. You can take advantage of paper space with interior and exterior elevations, 3D models, and detail sheets. When used in conjunction with the raster-import capabilities in AutoCAD, paper space can be a powerful tool for creating large-format presentations.

EXPORTING LAYOUT VIEWS TO MODEL SPACE

You may encounter a situation where you want to export a layout view as a model space drawing. You can do so by following these steps:

1. At the bottom of the drawing area, click the Layout tab of the layout you want to export.

2. Right-click the tab, and select Export Layout To Model from the context menu. The Export Layout To Model Space Drawing dialog box appears. This is a typical Save dialog box that allows you to select the location and name for your exported layout.

3. Select a folder location, enter a name for your exported layout, and then click Save. Once the file is saved, a dialog box will ask if you want to open the newly created file.

Your layout view will be saved as a separate drawing file with the layout appearing in the model space of that file. It will also be in the same scale as the original layout view instead of in full scale. Other drawing elements such as layers, blocks, linetypes, and styles will also be exported, although they may be scaled down to fit the drawing.

The Bottom Line

Understand model space and paper space. AutoCAD offers two viewing modes for viewing and printing your drawings. Model space is where you do most of your work; it's the view that you see when you create a new file. Layouts, also called paper space, are views that let you arrange the layout of your drawing, similar to the way that you would in a page-layout program.

Master It   What are three ways of moving from model space to paper space?

Work with paper space viewports.   While in paper space, you can create views in your drawing using viewports. You can have several viewports, each showing a different part of your drawing.

Master It   Name some of the ways that you can enlarge a view in a viewport.

Create odd-shaped viewports.   Most of the time, you'll probably use rectangular viewports, but you have the option to create a viewport of any shape.

Master It   Describe the process for creating a circular viewport.

Understand lineweights, linetypes, and dimensions in paper space.   You can get an accurate view of how your drawing will look on paper by making a few adjustments to AutoCAD. Your layout view will reflect how your drawing will look when plotted.

Master It   Name the two dialog boxes that you must use to display lineweights in a layout view.

Chapter 16

Making "Smart" Drawings with Parametric Tools

Don't let the term *parametric drawing* scare you. *Parametric* is a word from mathematics, and in the context of AutoCAD® drawings, it means that you can define relationships between different objects in a drawing. For example, you can set up a pair of individual lines to stay parallel or set up two concentric circles to maintain an exact distance between the circles no matter how they may be edited.

Parametric drawing is also called *constraint-based modeling*, and you'll see the word *constraint* used in the AutoCAD Ribbon to describe sets of tools. The term *constraint* is a bit more descriptive of the tools that you'll use to create parametric drawings because when you use them, you are applying a constraint on the objects in your drawing.

This chapter shows you how the parametric drawing tools work and how you can apply them to your needs.

In this chapter, you will learn to

◆ Use parametric drawing tools

◆ Connect objects with geometric constraints

◆ Control sizes with dimensional constraints

◆ Use formulas to control dimensions

◆ Put constraints to use

Why Use Parametric Drawing Tools?

If you're not familiar with parametric drawing, you may be wondering what purpose it serves. With careful application of the parametric tools, you can create a drawing that you can quickly modify with just a change of a dimension or two instead of editing the lines that make up the drawing. Figure 16.1 shows a drawing that was set up so that the arcs and circles increase in size to an exact proportion when the overall length dimension is increased. This approach can save a lot of time if you're designing several parts that are similar with only a few dimensional changes.

You can also mimic the behavior of a mechanical assembly to test your ideas. The parametric drawing tools let you create linkages between objects so that if one moves, the others maintain their connection like a link in a chain. For example, you can create 3D AutoCAD models of a crankshaft and piston assembly of a car motor (see Figure 16.2) or the parallel arms of a Luxo lamp. If you move one part of the model, the other parts move in a way consistent with a real motor or lamp.

FIGURE 16.1
The d1 dimension in the top image was edited to change the drawing to look like the one in the lower half.

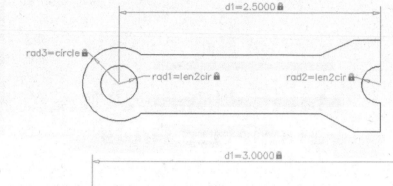

FIGURE 16.2
Move one part of the drawing and the other parts follow.

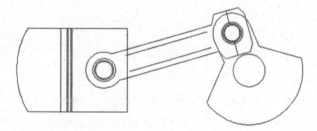

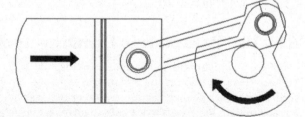

Connecting Objects with Geometric Constraints

You'll start your exploration of parametric drawing by adding geometric constraints to an existing drawing and testing the behavior of the drawing with the constraints in place. Geometric constraints let you assign constrained behaviors to objects to limit their range of motion.

Limiting motion to improve editing efficiency may seem counterintuitive, but once you've seen these tools in action, you'll see their benefits.

Using AutoConstrain to Add Constraints Automatically

Start by opening a sample drawing and adding a few geometric constraints. The sample drawing is composed of two parallel lines connected by two arcs, as shown in Figure 16.3. These are just lines and arcs and are not polylines.

FIGURE 16.3
The `Parametric01`
`.dwg` file containing
simple lines and arcs

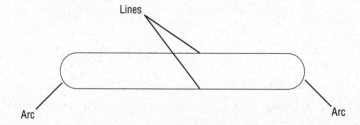

Here are the steps:

1. Open the `Parametric01.dwg` file from the sample files for this chapter (see Figure 16.3).

2. Select the Parametric tab, and click the AutoConstrain tool in the Geometric panel, or type **Autoconstrain**.

3. Use a selection window to select all the objects in the drawing, and press ↵.

You've just used the AutoConstrain command to add geometric constraints to all the objects in the drawing. You can see a set of icons that indicate the constraints that have been applied to the objects (see Figure 16.4). The AutoConstrain command makes a "best guess" at applying constraints.

FIGURE 16.4
The drawing with
geometric constraints
added

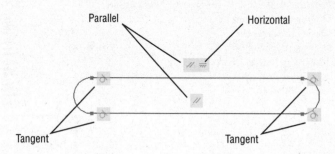

Notice that the constraint icons in the drawing match those you see in the Geometric panel. If you hover your mouse pointer over an icon, you'll see a tool tip that shows the name of the constraint.

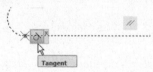

The Tangent constraints that you see at the ends of the lines keep the arcs and the lines tangent to each other whenever the arcs are edited. The Parallel constraint keeps the two lines parallel, and the Horizontal constraint keeps the lines horizontal.

There is one constraint that doesn't show an icon, but you see a clue to its existence by the small blue squares where the arcs join the lines:

1. Place your cursor on one of the blue squares. A new icon appears below the tangent icon along with a description of the arc. The arc description may hide the new icon, so look carefully or move the cursor away and try again. The new icon appears immediately, whereas the arc description takes a second to appear.

2. Hover your cursor over the icon that has just appeared. You see the icon appear for the Coincident constraint.

The Coincident constraint makes sure that the endpoints of the lines and arcs stay connected, as you'll see in the next few exercises.

Editing a Drawing Containing Constraints

Now try editing the drawing to see how these constraints work:

1. Click the arc on the left side of the drawing (see the top of Figure 16.5).

2. Click the grip at the bottom of the arc and move it downward to increase the radius of the arc. The objects move in unison to maintain their geometric constraints (see the bottom of Figure 16.5).

FIGURE 16.5
Moving the endpoint of one arc causes the other parts of the drawing to follow because of their geometric constraints.

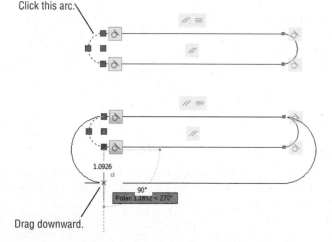

3. Click again to accept the change in the arc radius.

4. Click the Undo tool in the Quick Access toolbar to undo your change.

In this exercise, you saw how the Tangent, Parallel, Horizontal, and Coincident constraints worked to keep the objects together while you changed the size of one object. Next, you'll see what happens if you remove a constraint.

Removing a Constraint

The AutoConstrain tool applied quite a few geometric constraints to the drawing. Suppose that you want to remove a constraint to allow for more flexibility in the drawing. In the next exercise, you'll remove the Parallel constraint and then try editing the drawing to see the results:

1. Click the Parallel constraint icon that is just above the lower line.

2. Right-click and select Delete. Notice that the Parallel icon disappears from both the top and bottom line.

3. Click the line at the bottom of the drawing.

4. Click the grip at the left end of the line, drag it downward, and then click. This time, the left end of the line moves downward. The lines are no longer parallel, but they remain tangent to both arcs and their endpoints remain connected (see Figure 16.6).

FIGURE 16.6
Editing the arc with the Parallel constraint removed

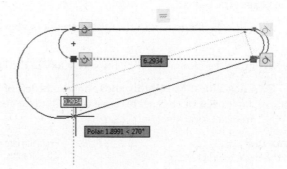

Notice that the top line remains horizontal as you edit the arc. The top line still has the Horizontal constraint. Next try removing the Horizontal constraint:

1. Click the Undo tool in the Quick Access toolbar to return to the previous shape.

2. Right-click the Horizontal constraint icon above the top line and select Delete.

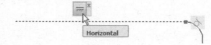

3. Select the arc on the left side again as you did earlier.

4. Hover over the bottom grip of the arc, and select Stretch from the multifunction grip menu.

5. Move the grip downward. This time both the lines change their orientation, as shown in Figure 16.7.

FIGURE 16.7
Without the Horizontal constraint, both lines change as the arc is edited.

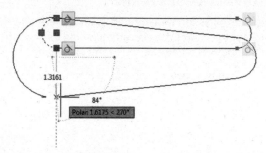

Notice that lines and arcs remain connected and tangent to each other. This is because the Coincident and Tangent constraints are still in effect.

ADDING A CONSTRAINT

You've seen how the AutoConstrain tool applies a set of constraints to a set of objects. You can also add constraints "manually" to fine-tune the way that objects behave. In the next exercise, you'll add a circle to the drawing and then add a few specific constraints that you'll select from the Geometric panel:

1. Click the Undo tool in the Quick Access toolbar to change the drawing back to its original shape.

2. From the Home tab, click the Circle tool in the Draw panel.

3. Click a location roughly above and to the left of the drawing, as shown in Figure 16.8. You don't need to be exact because you will use a geometric constraint to move the circle into an exact location.

FIGURE 16.8
Place the circle roughly in the location shown here.

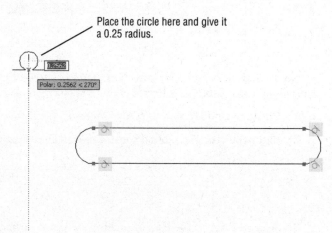

Place the circle here and give it a 0.25 radius.

4. Type **0.25**↵ for the radius of the circle.

5. Select the Parametric tab, and click the Concentric tool in the Geometric panel.

6. Click the arc at the left side of the drawing, and then click the circle that you just added. The circle moves to a location that is concentric to the arc, as shown in Figure 16.9.

FIGURE 16.9
The circle is concentric to the arc on the left side.

In this exercise, you used the geometric constraint as an editing tool to move an object into an exact location. The Concentric constraint will also keep the circle inside the arc no matter where the arc moves.

THE ORDER MAKES A DIFFERENCE

When you add constraints, sometimes the order in which you add them makes an important difference. In the Concentric constraint example, you selected the arc first and then the circle. Had you selected the circle first, the arcs and lines would have moved to the circle. Instead, as you saw in the exercise, the circle moved to the inside of the arc.

Using Other Geometric Constraints

You've seen how several of the geometric constraints work. For the most part, each constraint is fairly easy to understand. The Tangent constraint keeps objects tangent to each other. The Coincident constraint keeps the location of objects together, such as endpoints or midpoints of lines and arcs. The Parallel constraint keeps objects parallel.

You have many more geometric constraints at your disposal. Table 16.1 gives you a concise listing of the constraints and their purposes. Note that, with the exception of Fix and Symmetric, all of the constraints affect pairs of objects.

TABLE 16.1:   The geometric constraints

NAME	USE
Coincident	Keeps point locations of two objects together, such as the endpoints or midpoints of lines. Allowable points vary between objects, and they are indicated by a red circle marked with an X while points are being selected.
Collinear	Keeps lines collinear. The lines need not be connected.
Concentric	Keeps circles and arcs concentric.
Fix	Fixes a point on an object to a location in the drawing.

TABLE 16.1: The geometric constraints *(CONTINUED)*

NAME	USE
Parallel	Keeps lines parallel.
Perpendicular	Keeps lines or polyline segments perpendicular.
Horizontal	Keeps lines horizontal.
Vertical	Keeps lines vertical.
Tangent	Keeps curves, or a line and curve, tangent to each other.
Smooth	Maintains a smooth transition between splines and other objects. The first object selected must be a spline. You can think of this constraint as a tangent constraint for splines.
Symmetric	Maintains symmetry between two curves about an axis that is determined by a line. Before using this constraint, draw a line that you will use for the axis of symmetry. You can also use the Fix, Horizontal, or Vertical constraint to fix the axis to a location or orientation.
Equal	Keeps the length of lines or polylines equal, or the radius of arcs and circles equal.

The behavior of the geometric constraints might sound simple, but you may find that they can act in unexpected ways. Within the limited space of this book, we can't give exercise examples for every geometric constraint, so we encourage you to experiment with them on your own. And have some fun with them!

Using Constraints in the Drawing Process

Earlier you saw how the Concentric constraint allowed you to move a circle into a concentric location to an arc. You can use other geometric constraints in a similar way. For example, you can move a line into a collinear position with another line using the Collinear constraint. Or you can move a line into an orientation that's tangent to a pair of arcs or circles, as shown in Figure 16.10. The top image shows the separate line and circles, and the bottom image shows the objects after applying the Tangent constraint. Note that although the line is tangent to the two circles, its length and orientation do not change.

Controlling Sizes with Dimensional Constraints

At the heart of the AutoCAD parametric tools are the dimensional constraints. These constraints allow you to set and adjust the dimension of an assembly of parts, thereby giving you an easy way to adjust the size and even the shape of a set of objects.

For example, suppose that you have a set of parts that you are drafting, each of which is just slightly different in one dimension or another. You can add geometric constraints and then add dimensional constraints, which will let you easily modify your part just by changing the value of a dimension. To see how this works, try the following exercises.

FIGURE 16.10
You can connect two circles so that they are tangent to a line by using the Tangent constraint.

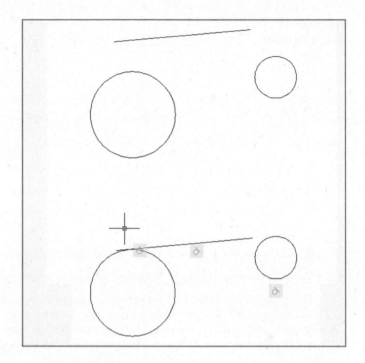

Adding a Dimensional Constraint

In this first dimensional constraint exercise, you'll add a horizontal dimension to the drawing that you've been working on already. The drawing already has some geometric constraints with which you are familiar, so you can see how the dimensional constraints interact with the geometric constraints.

Start by adding a dimensional constraint between the two arcs:

1. In the Parametric tab, click the Aligned tool in the Dimensional panel.

2. Shift+right-click, and select the Center osnap option from the context menu.

3. Place the cursor on the arc on the left side of the drawing so that the Center osnap marker appears for the arc (see Figure 16.11) and click to select the center. Notice that the arc is highlighted as you select the center.

FIGURE 16.11
Use the Center osnap to select the center of the arc.

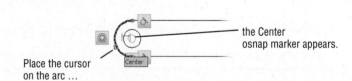

the Center osnap marker appears.

Place the cursor on the arc …

4. Shift+right-click, and select the Center osnap option as you did in step 2.

5. Click the arc on the right side of the drawing (see Figure 16.12).

FIGURE 16.12
Adding the dimensional constraint

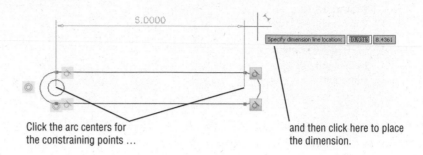

Click the arc centers for the constraining points …

and then click here to place the dimension.

6. Click a location above the drawing, as shown in Figure 16.12.

7. At the `Dimension text =` prompt, press ↵ to accept the current value.

The dimensional constraint appears above the drawing and shows a value of d1=6.0000. The d1 is the name for that particular dimensional constraint. Each dimensional constraint is assigned a unique name, which is useful later when you want to make changes. You can select from a number of dimensional constraints in the Parametric tab's Dimensional panel. Table 16.2 gives you a list of the dimensional constraint options.

TABLE 16.2: The dimensional constraints

NAME	USE
Linear	Constrains the distance along the x- or y-axis between two points
Horizontal	Constrains the distance along the x-axis between two points
Vertical	Constrains the distance along the y-axis between two points
Aligned	Constrains the distance between two points in any direction
Radius	Constrains the radius of a circle or arc
Diameter	Constrains the diameter of a circle or arc
Angular	Constrains the angle between two line segments
Convert	Converts a dimension into a dimensional constraint

Now let's see how you can use the dimensional constraint that you just added.

Editing a Dimensional Constraint

A dimensional constraint is linked to objects in your drawing so that when you modify a dimension value, the objects to which the constraint is linked change. To see how this works, try editing the part by changing the dimension:

1. Double-click the dimension value of the dimensional constraint (see Figure 16.13).

2. Type **4.5**↵. The part shortens to the dimension that you entered. Press ↵ to clear the command.

FIGURE 16.13
Double-click the
dimension value.

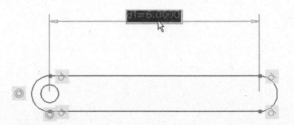

OSNAPS ARE FORCED OFF

In an earlier exercise, you had to select the Center osnap from the Osnap menu. When placing dimensional constraints, you'll need to use the Osnap menu to select Center osnaps. Running osnaps are automatically turned off when you use the dimensional constraint tools. This is because the dimensional constraint tools use their own method of finding locations on objects.

Next, add a dimension to the arc on the left side:

1. Click the Aligned tool from the Dimensional panel.

2. Select the top endpoint of the arc on the left side (top of Figure 16.14). Do this by first hovering over the arc near the endpoint. When you see the endpoint marker, click the mouse. If the constraint icons are in the way, you can zoom in to the drawing to see the marker.

3. Select the bottom endpoint of the arc in the same way.

4. Click a point to the left of the arc to place the dimension (bottom of Figure 16.14).

5. At the Dimension text = prompt, press ↵ to accept the current value.

Notice that the new dimensional constraint has been given the name d2. Now try changing the size of the arc using the dimensional constraint:

1. Double-click the dimension value of the d2 dimensional constraint (see Figure 16.15).

2. Enter **2**↵. The part adjusts to the new dimension.

FIGURE 16.14
Adding a dimensional
constraint to the arc

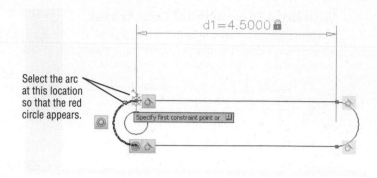

Select the arc
at this location
so that the red
circle appears.

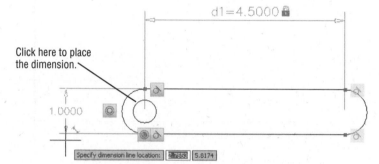

Click here to place
the dimension.

FIGURE 16.15
Adjusting the arc
dimension

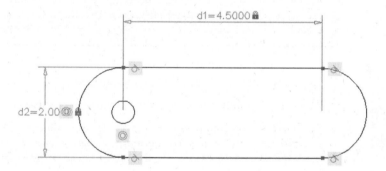

As you can see from this example, you can control the dimensions of your drawing by changing the dimensional constraint's value. This is a much faster way of making accurate changes to your drawing. Imagine what you would have to do to make these same changes if you didn't have the geometric and dimensional constraints available.

Using Formulas to Control and Link Dimensions

In the previous exercise, you saw how the dimensional constraint attached to the arc affected the drawing. But in that example, the circle on the left end of the drawing remained unaffected by the change in the arc size. Now suppose that you want that circle to adjust its size in relation to the size of the arc. To do this, you can employ the Parameters Manager and include a formula that manages the size of the circle.

In the following exercise, you'll add a dimensional constraint to the circle and then apply a formula to that constraint so that the circle will always be one-half the diameter of the arc, no matter how the arc is modified.

Start by adding a Diameter constraint to the circle:

1. Click the Undo tool in the Quick Access toolbar to change the drawing back to its previous shape.

2. Click the Diameter tool in the Dimensional panel.

3. Click the circle to select it.

4. Click a location inside the drawing to place the constraint, as shown in Figure 16.16.

5. Press ⏎ to accept the constraint value.

FIGURE 16.16
Adding a Diameter
constraint to the circle

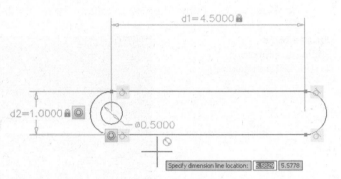

The Diameter constraint that you just added is given the name *dia1*. It controls only the diameter of the circle; you could change the value of that constraint, but it would affect only the circle.

Adding a Formula Parameter

Now let's add a formula that will "connect" the value of the circle diameter to the diameter of the arc:

1. Click the Parameters Manager tool in the Manage panel. The Parameters Manager appears (see Figure 16.17). Notice that the Parameters Manager gives a list of all the dimensional constraints that exist in the drawing.

FIGURE 16.17
The Parameters
Manager

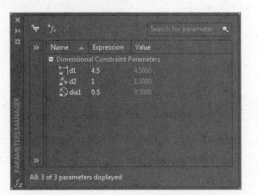

2. Click the Creates A New User Parameter tool at the top of the Parameters Manager. A new category appears in the list called User Parameters, and you see a user1 parameter appear.

3. Double-click in the Expression column for the user1 parameter (see Figure 16.18).

FIGURE 16.18
Adding an expression
to the user1 parameter

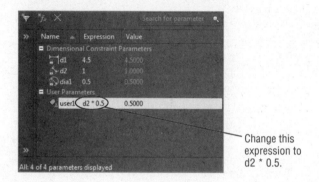

Change this
expression to
d2 * 0.5.

4. With the user1 expression value highlighted, type **d2 * 0.5**↵. You will see your entry replace the expression value (see Figure 16.18). This expression is saying, "Give the user1 variable the value of half the d2 constraint." Remember that the d2 constraint is the one given to the arc.

5. Now double-click the Expression column for the dia1 parameter (see Figure 16.19). This is the parameter for the circle's diameter.

FIGURE 16.19
Applying the user1
parameter to the dia1
parameter

Change the
expression for
the dia1 parameter
to user1.

6. Type **user1↵** to change the dia1 expression from 0.5 to user1. This tells AutoCAD to use the expression in the user1 parameter in place of the fixed 0.5 diameter value.

You've set up your circle to follow any changes to the width of the part. Now any changes to the d2 dimensional constraint will affect the circle.

Testing the Formula

Try the following to see the parameters in action:

1. In the Parameters Manager, double-click the Expression column for the d2 parameter.

2. Change the value from 1 to 2 and observe the effect on the part (see Figure 16.20).

FIGURE 16.20
Change the d2 parameter and the part changes in size, including the circle.

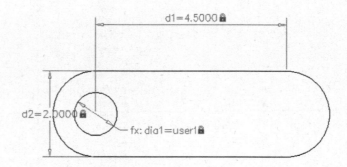

The part changes in width, and the circle also enlarges to maintain its proportion to the width of the part. Here you see that you can apply a formula to a constraint so that it is "linked" to another constraint's value. In this case, you set the circle's diameter to follow the width constraint of the part.

In addition, you can adjust the constraint value from the Parameters Manager. You could also have changed the width of the part as before by double-clicking the dimensional constraint for the arc.

Using Other Formulas

In the previous exercise, you used a simple formula that multiplied a parameter, d2, by a fixed value. You used the asterisk to indicate multiplication. You could have used the minus sign in the formula if, for example, you wanted the circle to be an exact distance from the arc. Instead of d2 * 0.5, you could use d2 – 0.125, which would keep the circle 0.125 from the overall width of the part.

You can also choose from a fairly large list of formulas. If you double-click an expression in the Parameters Manager and then right-click, you can select Expressions from the context menu that appears. You can then select from a list of expressions for your parameter (see Figure 16.21).

FIGURE 16.21
The expressions offered
from the Parameters
Manager

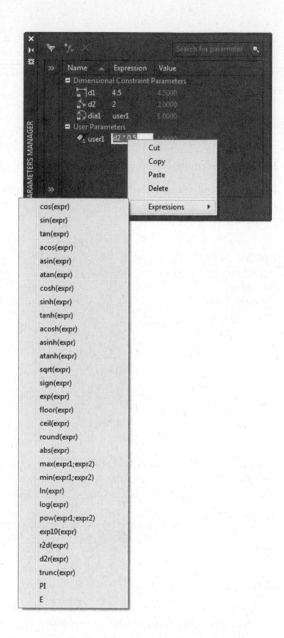

As you can see from the list, you have quite a few expressions from which to choose. We won't try to describe each expression, but you should recognize most of them from your high school math class.

ORGANIZING PARAMETERS

If you find that you have a lot of parameters in the Parameters Manager, you can organize them using groups and filters. In the Parameters Manager, click the double arrowhead in the bar to the left of the parameter list.

The bar expands to display the Filters list. Click the funnel-shaped tool in the upper-left corner of the Parameters Manager to create a new group filter. Click and drag parameters from the parameters list to the group filter name to add parameters to your group filter.

Editing the Constraint Options

AutoCAD offers a number of controls that you can apply to the constraints feature. Like most other controls, these are accessible through a settings dialog box that is opened from the Ribbon panel title bar. If you click the Constraint Settings tool on the Geometric panel title bar, the Constraint Settings dialog box opens (see Figure 16.22).

You can see that the Constraint Settings dialog box offers three tabs across the top: Geometric, Dimensional, and AutoConstrain. The settings in the Geometric tab let you control the display of the constraint bars, which are the constraint icons that you see in the drawing when you add constraints. You can also control the transparency of the constraint bars using the slider near the bottom of the dialog box.

Like the Geometric tab, the Dimensional tab (see Figure 16.23) gives you control over the display of dimensional constraints. You can control the format of the text shown in the dimension and whether dynamic constraints are displayed.

Finally, the AutoConstrain tab (see Figure 16.24) gives you control over the behavior of the AutoConstrain command. You can control the priority of the constraints applied to a set of objects as well as which geometric constraints are allowed.

At this point, you can close the `Parametaric01.dwg` file without saving it so that you can come back to it later for practice.

FIGURE 16.22
The Constraint
Settings dialog
box showing the
Geometric tab

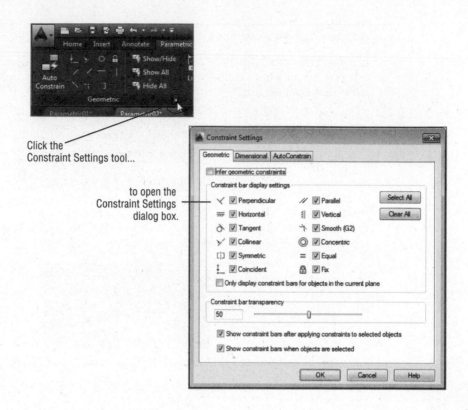

Click the
Constraint Settings tool...

to open the
Constraint Settings
dialog box.

FIGURE 16.23
The Dimensional tab of
the Constraint Settings
dialog box

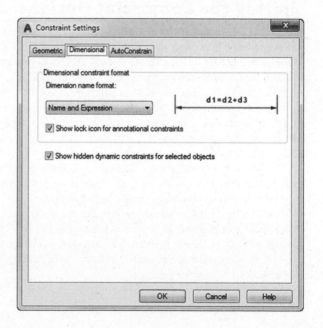

FIGURE 16.24
The AutoConstrain
tab of the Constraint
Settings dialog box

FIGURE 16.24
The AutoConstrain
tab of the Constraint
Settings dialog box

Putting Constraints to Use

So far, you've seen some simple applications of the parametric tools available in AutoCAD. Although the parametric tools may seem simple, you can build some fairly elaborate parametric models using the geometric and dimensional constraints you've learned about here.

Besides having a drawing of a part that adjusts itself to changes in dimensional constraints, you can create assemblies that will allow you to study linkages and motion. For example, you can create a model of a piston and crankshaft from a gas engine and have the piston and crankshaft move together.

In the next exercise, you'll look at a drawing that has been established to show just how constraints can be set up to mimic the way a mechanical part behaves:

1. Open the `piston.dwg` file from the sample drawings.

2. Click the arc in the right side of the drawing (see Figure 16.25).

FIGURE 16.25
The piston drawing in
motion

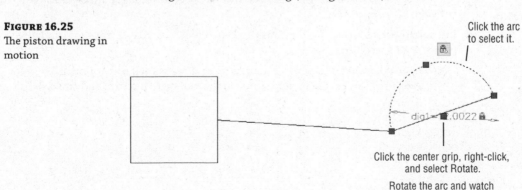

Click the arc
to select it.

Click the center grip, right-click,
and select Rotate.

Rotate the arc and watch
how the drawing changes.

3. Click the center grip of the arc, and then right-click and select Rotate.

4. Move the cursor to rotate the arc. Notice that the "piston" that is connected to the arc with a fixed-length line follows the motion of the arc just as a piston would follow the motion of a crankshaft in a gas engine.

As you can see from this example, you can model a mechanical behavior using constraints. The piston in this drawing is a simple rectangle that has been constrained in both its height and width. A Horizontal constraint has also been applied so that it can move only in a horizontal direction. The line connecting the piston to the arc is constrained in its length. The Coincident constraint connects it to the piston at one end and the arc at the other end. The arc itself, representing the crankshaft, uses a Diameter constraint, and a Fix constraint is used at its center to keep its center fixed in one location. The net result is that when you rotate the arc, each part moves in unison.

The Bottom Line

Use parametric drawing tools.   Parametric drawing tools enable you to create an assembly of objects that are linked to each other based on geometric or dimensional properties. With the parametric drawing tools, you can create a drawing that automatically adjusts the size of all its components when you change a single dimension.

Master It   Name two examples given in the beginning of the chapter of a mechanical assembly that can be shown using parametric drawing tools.

Connect objects with geometric constraints.   You can link objects together so that they maintain a particular orientation to each other.

Master It   Name at least six of the geometric constraints available in AutoCAD.

Control sizes with dimensional constraints.   Dimensional constraints, in conjunction with geometric constraints, let you apply dimensions to an assembly of objects to control the size of the assembly.

Master It   Name at least four dimensional constraints.

Use formulas to control dimensions.   Dimensional constraints allow you to link dimensions of objects so that if one dimension changes, another dimension follows.

Master It   What example was used to show how formulas could be used with dimensional constraints?

Put constraints to use.   Constraints can be used in a variety of ways to simulate the behavior of real objects.

Master It   Name at least three geometric or dimensional constraints used in the piston.dwg sample file to help simulate the motion of a piston and crankshaft.

Chapter 17

Using Dynamic Blocks

Blocks are a great way to create and store ready-made symbols. They can be a real time-saver, especially when you have assemblies that you use often. Earlier in this book you learned how to create a basic, no-frills block. When you understand the basics of block creation, you can begin to work with *dynamic blocks*.

Dynamic blocks have properties that you can modify using grips. For example, you can create a dynamic block of a door and then easily grip-edit its size and orientation. Or you can use a single block to represent several versions of a similar object. You can have a single block of a bed that can be modified to show a double, queen-sized, or king-sized shape.

In this chapter, you'll explore the use of dynamic blocks through a series of exercises. Each exercise will show you a different way to use dynamic blocks. This will help you become familiar with the methods involved in creating dynamic blocks. You'll start by looking at the Block Editor, which in itself makes editing blocks much easier. Then you'll be introduced to the tools used to create dynamic blocks.

In this chapter, you will learn to

- ◆ Work with the Block Editor
- ◆ Create a dynamic block
- ◆ Add Scale and Stretch actions to a parameter
- ◆ Add more than one parameter for multiple grip functions
- ◆ Create multiple shapes in one block
- ◆ Rotate objects in unison
- ◆ Fill in a space automatically with objects

Exploring the Block Editor

Before you start to add dynamic block features to blocks, you'll want to get familiar with the Block Editor. The Block Editor offers an easy way to make changes to existing blocks, and as you'll see a bit later, it's also the tool that you'll use to give your blocks some additional capabilities.

Opening the Block Editor

As an introduction to the Block Editor, you'll make changes to the now familiar unit plan from earlier tutorials. Start by editing the Kitchen block in the unit:

1. Open the Unit.dwg file that you saved from earlier exercises, and freeze the Notes layer. If you have been working in metric or did not create the file earlier, you can also use the 17-unit.dwg file.

2. Double-click the kitchenette in the plan to open the Edit Block Definition dialog box (see Figure 17.1). Notice that all the blocks in the drawing are listed in the dialog box and that the Kitchen block is highlighted. You also see a preview of the block in the preview group.

FIGURE 17.1
The Edit Block
Definition dialog box

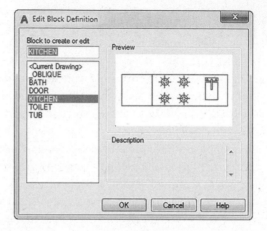

3. With the KITCHEN block name selected, click OK. You see an enlarged view of the kitchenette in the drawing area with a light gray background (see Figure 17.2).

FIGURE 17.2
The Block
Editor and its
components

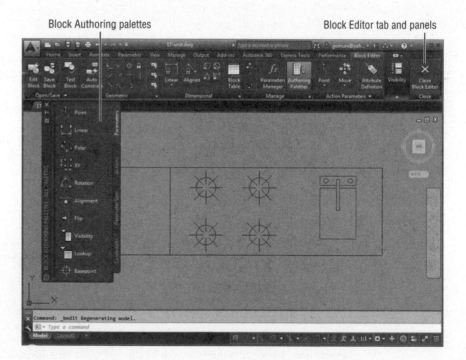

Block Authoring palettes

Block Editor tab and panels

The gray background tells you that you're in the Block Editor. You'll also see the Block Editor tab along the top of the drawing area and the Block Authoring palettes, as shown in Figure 17.2.

Take a moment to look over the panels and tools on the Block Editor tab. This tab offers several housekeeping tools that let you open and save blocks and exit the Block Editor. You can point to each tool in the tab's panels to see its description. Figure 17.3 shows the Block Editor tab and tools.

FIGURE 17.3
The Block Editor tab

Both the Block Editor tab and the Block Authoring palettes offer tools for adding dynamic block features that you'll explore later in this chapter. You may notice that the Block Editor tab contains the geometric and dimensional constraint panels that you learned about in Chapter 16, "Making 'Smart' Drawings with Parametric Tools." Let's continue our look at the basic features of the Block Editor.

Editing a Block and Creating New Blocks

Certification Objective

The Block Editor lets you edit a block using all of the standard Autodesk® AutoCAD® editing tools. In the following exercise, you'll modify the kitchen sink and save your changes to the drawing:

1. Delete the rectangle that represents the sink in the Kitchen block.

2. Click Close Block Editor on the Block Editor tab's Close panel (see the right side of Figure 17.3).

3. A message appears asking if you want to save your changes to the Kitchen block. Click Save The Changes To KITCHEN. Your view returns to the standard AutoCAD drawing area, and you can see the changes that you made to the kitchen, as shown in Figure 17.4.

FIGURE 17.4
The unit plan with the edited Kitchen block

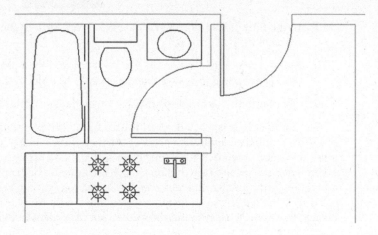

As you can see, editing blocks with the Block Editor is straightforward. In this example, you deleted part of the block, but you can perform any type of drawing or editing to modify the block. The Block Editor tab also offers other block-saving options in its panels. You can save the block as you work by clicking the Save Block Definition button. If you need to create a variation on the block that you're currently editing, you can click the Save Block As tool on the Block Editor's expanded Open/Save panel to create a new block or overwrite an existing one with the drawing that is currently in the Block Editor.

If you want to edit a different block after editing the current one, you can click the Save Block tool on the Block Editor's Open/Save panel to save your current block and then click the Edit Block tool.

This tool opens the Edit Block Definition dialog box that you saw earlier. You can then select another block to edit or create a new block by entering a name for your block in the Block To Create Or Edit box.

Creating a Dynamic Block

Certification Objective

Now that you've seen how the Block Editor works, you can begin to explore the creation of dynamic blocks. As an introduction, you'll create a rectangle that you'll use to replace the sink in the kitchen. You'll add a dynamic block feature that will allow you to adjust the width of the sink using grips. In addition, you'll add a control that limits the size to one-unit increments.

Start by creating a block from scratch using the Block Editor:

1. Click the Block Editor tool in the Home tab's Block panel.

2. In the Edit Block Definition dialog box, enter **Sink** in the Block To Create Or Edit box and then click OK.

3. Make sure that you are on the Fixture layer, and then use the Rectangle tool on the Home tab's Draw panel to draw a rectangle that is 12 units in the x-axis and 15 units in the y-axis.

4. Zoom into the rectangle so that your view looks similar to Figure 17.5.

You could save this block now, and you'd have a simple, static block. Next, you'll add a couple of features called *parameters* and *actions*. As their names imply, parameters define the parameters, or limits, of what the dynamic block will do, and actions describe the particular action taken when the grips of the dynamic block are edited. For example, in the next section, you'll add a Linear parameter that tells AutoCAD that you want to restrain the grip-editing to a linear direction. You'll also add a Stretch action that tells AutoCAD that you want the grip-edit to behave like a Stretch command that pulls a set of vertices in one direction or another.

FIGURE 17.5
The rectangle for
the Sink block

FIGURE 17.5
The rectangle for
the Sink block

Adding a Parameter

The first parameter that you'll add establishes the base point for the block. This will let you determine the point used when inserting the block in your drawing:

1. In the Block Authoring palettes, select the Parameters tab.

2. Click the Basepoint tool, Shift+right-click, select the Endpoint osnap, and then click the lower-left corner of the rectangle. This is how you determine the base point, or insertion point, of a block while using the Block Editor.

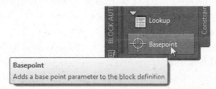

Next, you'll add a parameter that will determine the type of editing that you want to add to the block. In this case, you want to be able to grip-edit the width of the block. For that you'll use the Linear Parameter tool:

1. Click the Linear tool on the Parameters tab of the Block Authoring palettes, or expand the Parameter tool (Point) on the Block Editor tab's Action Parameters panel and click Linear.

2. At the prompt

   ```
   Specify start point or [Name/Label
   /Chain/Description/Base/Palette/Value set]:
   ```

   Shift+right-click and select the Midpoint osnap; then select the left side of the rectangle.

3. Shift+right-click again, select Midpoint from the Osnap menu, and select the right side of the rectangle.

4. At the Specify label location: prompt, the parameter name appears with the parameter label at the cursor. Click below the rectangle to place the label, as shown in Figure 17.6.

FIGURE 17.6
Placing the Linear
parameter

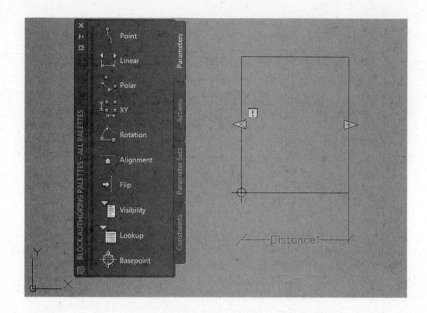

The parameter that you just added lets you modify the block in a linear fashion. In this case, it will allow you to change the width of the rectangle. As you'll see, the locations of the parameter's arrows later become the grip locations for the dynamic block.

But just adding the parameter doesn't make the block dynamic. You need to include an action before a parameter can be used. You may have noticed the warning symbol in the parameter that you just added. It tells you that you need to take some further steps to make the parameter useful.

Adding an Action

Next, you'll add a Stretch action that will enable you to use the Linear parameter that you just added. The Stretch action will let you stretch the block horizontally by using grips. As you add the action, notice that it's similar to the Stretch command. The only difference is that you don't stretch the object; you only specify the vertices to stretch and the object you want to stretch.

Follow these steps:

1. Turn off osnaps and then click the Actions tab in the Block Authoring palettes and select Stretch.

2. At the Select parameter: prompt, click the Distance1 parameter you just created.

3. At the `Specify parameter point to associate with action or enter [sTart point/Second point] <Start>:` prompt, point to the left-pointing arrow. You see a circle with an X through it showing the location of a parameter point.

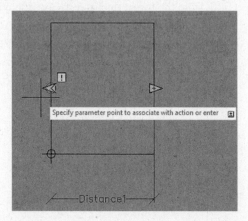

4. Click the circle with the X.

5. At the `Specify first corner of stretch frame or [CPolygon]:` prompt, place a selection window around the entire left side of the rectangle. This selects the portion of the rectangle that is to be stretched when you grip-edit the block.

6. At the `Specify objects to stretch Select Object:` prompt, select the rectangle and the base point you added earlier and then press ↵ to complete your selection.

You've just added an action to the Linear parameter that you added earlier. You'll see an action icon appear below and to the right of the Distance1 linear parameter. The icon looks like the Stretch tool in the Actions tab to help you identify the action. If you hover over the icon, the parts affected by the action are highlighted.

Notice that the warning symbol is still showing. You need to add another action to the right side of the parameter because the parameter expects that you'll want to be able to grip-edit both sides:

1. Repeat the previous set of steps, but instead of clicking the left circle with the X as you did in step 4 of the preceding exercise, click the right arrow.

2. Place a window selection around the right side of the rectangle (as you did around the left side in step 5 in the preceding exercise).

3. At the `Specify objects to stretch:` prompt, select the rectangle again.

A second action icon appears next to the first one to the lower right of the Distance1 linear parameter. This time the warning symbol disappears, telling you that you've completed the steps that you need for the parameter. You're ready to save the block and try it out:

1. Click Close Block Editor on the Block Editor tab's Close panel.

2. At the message asking if you want to save changes to the Sink block, click Save The Changes To Sink.

Next, insert the sink to see how it works:

1. Click the Insert tool in the Home tab's Block panel.

2. Select Sink from the Insert flyout, scrolling down if you can't see it at first. The sink appears at the cursor.

3. Place the block at the location shown in Figure 17.7.

FIGURE 17.7
The Sink block in place

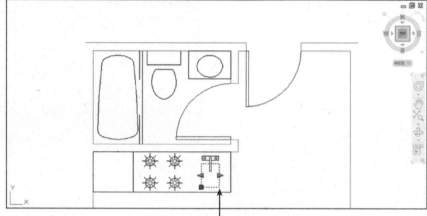

Place the block in this location.

4. Click the newly inserted sink. You see two arrows at the vertical midpoints of the block.

5. Turn on Ortho mode, and click and drag the arrow on the right side of the block. The width of the block follows the arrow as you drag it. You also see the dimension of the sink as you drag the arrow.

6. Enter 15⏎. The width of the block changes to 15 inches from the original 12.

Although you entered a value in step 6 to change the width of the sink, you could have clicked the mouse to change the width visually. The rectangle is still a block. You didn't have to explode it to change its width. If you hover the cursor over the dynamic block grip, you see the block's width dimension.

Adding an Increment Value

You can grip-edit your dynamic Sink block to modify its width, and as you saw in the previous exercise, you can enter a specific value for the width as well. But suppose that you'd like to limit grip movement so that the sink changes in only 1″ steps. You can set parameters to have an increment value so that grip edits are limited to a specific distance.

The following steps show how you can set up the Linear parameter of the Sink block so that the sink width can be grip-edited to 1″ increments:

1. Double-click the Sink block. Then, in the Edit Block Definition dialog box, make sure that Sink is selected and click OK. You may need to zoom into the sink.

2. Click the Linear parameter's Distance1 label, right-click, and choose Properties.

3. In the Properties palette, scroll down to the Value Set group and click the Dist Type listing. The Dist Type option changes to a drop-down list.

4. Expand the list and select Increment.

5. Click in the Dist Increment text box just below the Dist Type options, and enter **1** for an increment distance of 1 inch.

6. Close the Properties palette, and then click Close Block Editor on the Block Editor tab's Close panel.

7. Save the changes.

8. Click the Sink block to expose its grips.

9. Click and drag the right arrow grip to the right. As soon as you click the grip, you'll see a set of increment marks appear indicating the increment steps for the grip. As you move the grip, the sink width jumps to the increment marks, which are 1″ apart, as shown in Figure 17.8.

10. Set the width of the sink back to 12″.

FIGURE 17.8
Grip-editing the Sink block with the Linear parameter's increment value set to 1

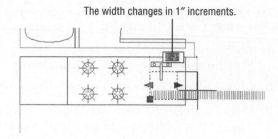

The width changes in 1″ increments.

In addition to an increment distance, you can set a range of movement for the Linear parameter. You may have noticed the minimum and maximum text boxes in the Properties palette in steps 3 through 5. You can enter values for these settings that define the range of movement allowed for the grip edits.

UNDERSTANDING THE CYCLING OPTION

You can turn on the Cycling option in the Misc group of the Properties palette of any parameter grip. Cycling allows you to use the parameter grip as an insertion point. With this option turned on, you can press the Ctrl key to cycle between the standard insertion point and the cycle-enabled grip of a parameter while inserting the block.

The sink exercise is a simple demonstration of how you can create and use dynamic blocks. But as you can see from the Block Authoring palettes, you can add many other parameters and actions to a block.

Editing Parameters and Actions

In the previous exercises, you inserted parameters and actions using the default settings. These settings give you default names and labels for the parameters and actions, but you can always change them later. To change the label that appears for a parameter, double-click the label. The label will then appear in a rectangular box showing you that you can change its text.

If you want to include additional objects for an action, click the action icon to select it and then right-click and select Action Selection Set ➤ Modify Selection Set. You can also choose Action Selection Set ➤ New Selection Set if you want to change the object of the action.

Keeping an Object Centered

Now suppose that you want to add a drain to the sink, but to make things a little more complicated, you want to make sure that the drain remains centered if the sink is widened or made narrower. You can alter the way the Linear parameter behaves so that both sides of the sink move symmetrically. Here's how it works:

1. Double-click the Sink block to open the Edit Block Definition dialog box. Make sure that Sink is selected and click OK. Make sure that you are on the Fixture layer.

2. Add a 3″ diameter circle in the center of the rectangle. This circle will represent the drain (see Figure 17.9). You can use the Geometric Center Osnap to locate the center of the rectangle representing the Sink.

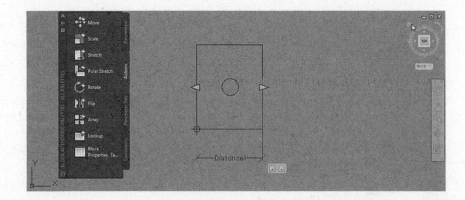

3. Select the Distance1 linear parameter, and then right-click and select Properties.

4. In the Properties palette, scroll down to the bottom and look for the Base Location setting under the Misc section.

5. Click the Base Location option, and then select Midpoint from the drop-down list that appears to the right.

6. Close the Properties palette.

7. Click Close Block Editor in the Close panel, and save the Sink block changes.

Now try grip-editing the block to see how the Stretch action affects the sink drain:

1. Click the sink to select it.

2. Click and drag the right arrow grip to the right. The drain stays centered in the sink while the two sides expand outward.

In this exercise, you changed the Base Location option for the Linear parameter, which causes the block to behave differently when you edit its grips. You can also employ a completely different method to achieve similar results. The Geometric and Dimensional panels of the Block Editor tab offer a set of tools that work in a way that's similar to how the parameters and actions with which you've worked already function. You will learn how these tools work next.

Using Constraints in Dynamic Blocks

In the sink example, you added two Stretch actions to a Linear parameter. This enabled the block to be stretched in both the left and right directions. The actions and parameters offer one way of creating dynamic blocks, but you can also use the geometric and dimensional constraints to which you were introduced in the previous chapter.

In this section, you'll turn a simple door block into a dynamic block that will allow you to resize the door to any opening. In the process, you'll learn how to apply geometric and dimensional constraints to create a dynamic block.

At first, you may think that all you need to do to resize a door is to change the scale. But when you scale the door, all of its features, including the door width, are scaled proportionally. To be very accurate, you only want to stretch the door width and scale the door swing, leaving the door thickness at the same dimension. This can be accomplished by adding two aligned dimensional constraints and a few geometric constraints to the door.

Start by opening the Door block in the Block Editor and adding the geometric constraints to the door:

1. Press Esc to clear any current selections, and then click the Block Editor tool in the Home tab's Block panel.

2. In the Edit Block Definition dialog box, select DOOR and then click OK.

3. Click the AutoConstrain tool in the Block Editor tab's Geometric panel, and then select the rectangle representing the door, as shown in Figure 17.10. To select the door using a window, click above and to the left of the door, and then click below and to the right.

FIGURE 17.10
Select the rectangle representing the door.

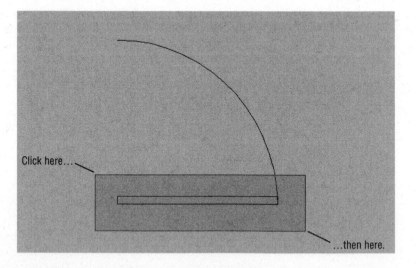

4. Press ↵ when the door has been selected. You'll see the geometric constraint icons appear around the door.

The geometric constraints will make sure that the door maintains its rectangular shape when you apply changes to the door through the dynamic block feature. The constraints used are Parallel, Perpendicular, Coincident, and Horizontal. Note that the Coincident constraint will not show an icon unless you hover over one of the corners of the rectangle.

You'll need to add a constraint to keep the arc connected to the rectangle:

1. Click the Coincident tool in the Geometric panel.

2. Place the cursor near the right end of the bottom horizontal line of the rectangle.

3. When you see the red circle and X marker, click.

4. Place the cursor near the lower end of the arc where it meets the rectangle. When you select this end, make sure that the arc is highlighted, indicating that the arc will be selected. You may need to zoom in to the location to ensure that you are selecting the correct point.

5. When you see the red circle and X marker, click the mouse.

The Coincident constraint that you just added will keep the arc and rectangle connected at the bottom-right corner of the rectangle.

Next, add a dimensional constraint. Most likely, you'll need to scale the door based only on the door opening, so place a dimensional constraint between the door hinge and the end of the door swing arc:

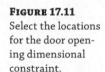

1. Click the Aligned tool in the Block Editor tab's Dimensional panel.

2. At the `Specify first constraint point or [Object/Point & line/2Lines] <Object>:` prompt, point to the line at the bottom of the drawing near the left endpoint, as shown in Figure 17.11.

FIGURE 17.11
Select the locations for the door opening dimensional constraint.

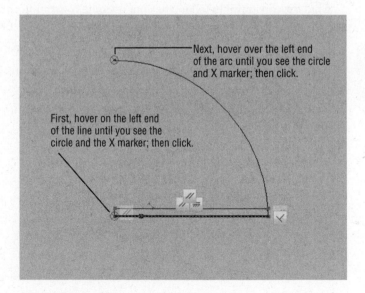

3. When you see the red circle with the X appear at the left endpoint of the line, click.

4. At the Specify second constraint point: prompt, place the cursor on the top end of the arc so that you see the circle and X marker again at the left end of the arc, as indicated in Figure 17.11, and click.

5. At the Specify dimension line location: prompt, place the dimension to the left of the arc (see Figure 17.12).

6. With the dimension highlighted, press ↵. Your drawing will look similar to Figure 17.12.

FIGURE 17.12
The aligned dimensional constraint applied to the door opening

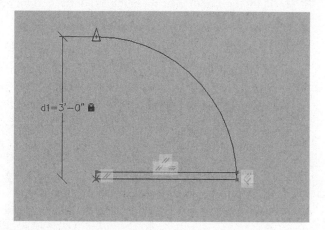

Notice that the constraint you just added is named d1. This will be an important feature in the next two constraints that you add.

Next, add another dimensional constraint to the width of the door rectangle. This time, you want the constraint to follow the door opening constraint, so instead of accepting the default value for the dimension, you'll enter the name of the first dimensional constraint:

Aligned

1. Click the Aligned tool again from the Dimensional panel.

2. Select the left end of the bottom horizontal line again, as you did in the previous exercise (see Figure 17.13).

FIGURE 17.13
The door with the opening and door constraints added

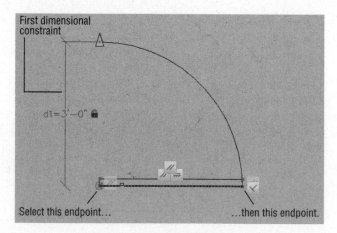

3. Select the right end of the bottom horizontal line, as shown in Figure 17.13.

4. Place the dimension line below the door roughly the same distance away from the door as the first dimensional constraint.

5. With the newly placed dimension highlighted, enter **d1**↵. This will cause the door rectangle to follow the dimension of the d1 door opening dimensional constraint.

Finally, add the dimensional constraint for the arc:

1. Click the Radius tool in the Block Editor tab's Dimensional panel.

2. Click anywhere on the arc.

3. Position the Radius dimensional constraint anywhere toward the outside of the arc.

4. With the radius dimension highlighted, enter **d1**↵. This will cause the arc to follow the dimension of the door opening dimensional constraint.

5. You now have all of the constraints in place and are ready to try out your dynamic block (see Figure 17.14). Click Close Block Editor in the Close panel to save the block and return to the drawing.

FIGURE 17.14
The door with all the constraints added

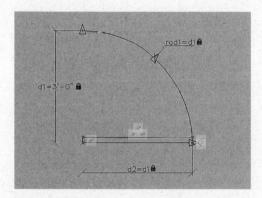

Now try out your new dynamic block by adjusting the door size:

1. Pan your view so that you can see the entry door clearly, as shown in Figure 17.15.

FIGURE 17.15
The Door block with its grips exposed

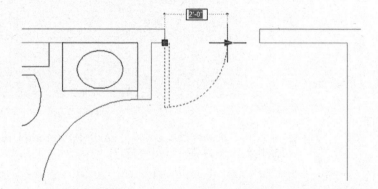

2. Click the door to select it. The added aligned constraint arrow appears as a grip on the right end of the Door block.

3. Click the arrow grip. The length dimension becomes available for your input, and as you move the mouse, the door changes in size. Note that the thickness of the door doesn't change as you alter its width.

4. Enter 24↵ to change the door width to 24".

Notice that, although you were able to enter a door dimension directly to the block, you didn't change the door thickness when the door size changed. Only the door swing and width changed to accommodate the new door size. This is most apparent if you scale the door to a small size such as 6" or 12".

Adding a List of Predefined Options

Earlier, you saw how you can add an increment value set to make a dynamic block stay in a set range of sizes. You can also set up a dynamic block to offer a range of sizes in a pop-up list. To do so, you need to employ the Block Table feature.

In the following exercise, you'll add a selectable list to the Door block to allow the door size to be selected from a list. Start by adding the block table that will allow you to define a set of predefined door dimensions:

1. Double-click the door to open the Edit Block Definition dialog box and then click OK.

2. In the Block Editor tab's Dimensional panel, click the Block Table tool.

3. At the `Specify parameter location or [Palette]:` prompt, place the block table in the location shown in Figure 17.16.

FIGURE 17.16
Placing the block table

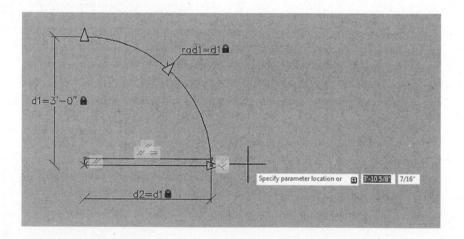

4. At the `Enter number of grips [0/1] <1>:` prompt, press ↵. The Block Properties Table dialog box appears (see Figure 17.17).